Sunset

ALL-TIME
FAVORITE RECIPES

By the Editors of Sunset Books and Sunset Magazine

Sunset Publishing Corporation • *Menlo Park, California*

OUR READERS' FAVORITES

A t *Sunset*, we've been collecting wonderful recipes for over 60 years. This volume presents the cream of the crop: more than 500 reader-selected favorites, old and new. In *All-Time Favorite Recipes*, you'll find not only rich, traditional choices like barbecued spareribs and chocolate chip cookies, but also some of the leaner, fresher dishes made popular in recent years. And each one is tried and true. • Throughout this book, we've included numerous special features. Some focus on perennially popular dishes—ice cream, chilis, and sourdough bread, for example—while others offer advice on culinary techniques. Page 97, for example, lists a number of suggestions for "lightening up" your cooking. In each chapter, you'll also notice text boxes highlighting *Sunset* history, culinary lore, popular Western ingredients, and more. • For their help in the final selection of recipes, we thank Bernadette Hart, Reader Service Coordinator, *Sunset* Magazine, and Rita Burgelman, *Sunset* Hospitality Manager. • We thank Rebecca LaBrum for editing the manuscript. We acknowledge with appreciation the editorial assistance of Carrie Sanders and Kevin Freeland. • For our recipes, we provide a nutritional analysis (see page 5) prepared by Hill Nutrition Associates, Inc., of Florida.

Research & Text
Lisa Chaney

Contributing Editors
Annabel Post
Tori Ritchie

Coordinating Editor
Cornelia Fogle

Design
Susan Sempere

Illustrations
Dick Cole

Senior Editor (Food and Entertaining)
Sunset Magazine
Jerry Anne Di Vecchio

Cover
A dozen cloves of cooked garlic add sweet, mild flavor to Garlic Chicken & New Potatoes (page 98). Design by Image Network, Inc. Photography by Barbara Thompson. Photo and food styling by Pouké.

Back Cover Photographers
(Left to right): Top row: Red Pepper Dip, Kevin Sanchez; San Francisco-style Cioppino, Tom Wyatt. Middle row: Chicken & Capellini Soup, Nikolay Zurek; Asparagus with Tomatillos, Tom Wyatt. Bottom row: California Shrimp Salad, Nikolay Zurek; Garden Vegetable Fettuccine, Kevin Sanchez.

Editorial Director, Sunset Books: Kenneth Winchester

Second printing August 1994

CONTENTS

OUR ALL-TIME FAVORITES

*F*rom warmly fragrant fresh-baked bread to satisfying, hearty winter stews, favorite recipes rank among life's unforgettable pleasures. These are the dishes that children ask for on birthdays, the never-fail supper standbys for busy work weeks, and the impressive introductions to company dinners or holiday feasts. • For over 60 years, Sunset has reported on trends in Western cooking. We've printed thousands of recipes—some created here at home, others taken from countries around the world. Our pages have provided a forum both for new ingredients and techniques and for the time-honored specialties that remain popular year after year.

Time-tested Recipes

Recently we asked our readers to select their all-time *Sunset* favorites, old and new—any recipe published from 1929 to the present was eligible for nomination. Replies came in by the hundreds, including votes for over 1,000 recipes. Of these, more than 500 appear in this volume, along with features on entertaining, cooking methods, and some of our classic regional specialties. *Sunset* printed similar cook books in 1949, 1969, and 1982—and in *All-Time Favorite Recipes,* we present yet another comprehensive recipe collection, covering everything from appetizers to desserts,

from simple family fare to elegant choices for entertaining.

For each recipe, we offer a complete nutritional analysis. If your favorites are higher in fat and calories than you'd like, you may want to use the nutritional information to help keep your diet on track. You might also consult our "Lightening-up Tips" (page 97) for ways to slim down your selections.

For history buffs, we've included some of the culinary lore and legend surrounding a few ever-popular dishes. And you'll notice that certain recipes are flagged as "Western Classics." These are long-time favor-ites created here in the West, often showcasing our native ingredients.

Reader Participation

From our earliest issues, we've encouraged reader contributions and suggestions. Our monthly recipe exchanges, "Kitchen Cabinet" and "Chefs of the West," help us keep up with trends in food and entertaining, letting us know what Westerners are cooking at home. Close attention to our readers' interests plays a big part in the signature *Sunset* style—a style that treasures tradition, but also explores all the ingredients and attitudes popular with today's home cook.

Comfort Food

Many of *Sunset*'s best-loved dishes are undeniably the rich "comfort foods" of earlier years. In the following pages, you'll find dozens of such favorites, among them beef Stroganoff, chicken Kiev, hamburger soup, potato salad, tomato-meat lasagne, chocolate chip cookies, and apple crisp. Neither Western in origin nor "modern" in appeal, these classics are prized for both their wonderful flavor and their nostalgic, old-time charm.

Dining al Fresco

We like to cook and eat outdoors. Dining al fresco suits the informal Western style—and because our climate is so mild, patio barbecues and picnic meals are pleasant in almost any season. We've become experts in grilling just about everything: meats, fish, poultry, fresh produce, even crisp-crusted pizza. You'll learn how to use an outdoor grill as a portable burner, keeping spaghetti and sauces warm for a casual backyard pasta party.

Picnics are featured in our pages nearly every year. In 1946, *Sunset* came up with the "tailgate picnic," an idea that has since caught on all over the country. Sandwiches are among our most popular picnic choices, of course, and on pages 47–49, you'll find suggestions for both hot and cold varieties.

Fresh Ingredients

Western cooks are blessed with a wealth of fresh ingredients, from wonderful fruits and vegetables to top-quality poultry and shellfish. And we've always made a point of introducing our readers to locally available foods. In 1929, we ran features on both avocados and artichokes; more recently, we've highlighted market newcomers like pummelos, Asian pears, tropical fruits, and organic lettuces, as well as an increasing selection of locally produced cheeses and Pacific seafood. Dishes made with everything from mangoes and lemon grass to Northwest salmon have joined our list of cherished favorites.

For those who might not have ready access to well-stocked markets, we're careful to suggest more widely available alternatives to fresh foods.

Western Style Evolves

The international influence on Western cooking distinguishes many *Sunset* recipes. Early ethnic specialties included Mexican and Italian fare such as guacamole, enchiladas, and lasagne. In recent years, we've expanded our regional cuisine to embrace the foods and culinary techniques of Latin America, Southeast Asia, the Orient, and the Pacific islands. Guided by *Sunset* articles, our readers have learned to use all kinds of new ingredients and methods, bringing the flavors of various foreign cuisines to their everyday meals.

About Our Nutritional Data

•

For our recipes, we provide a nutritional analysis stating calorie count; percentage of calories from fat; grams of protein, carbohydrates, total fat, and saturated fat; and milligrams of cholesterol and sodium. Generally, the analysis applies to a single serving, based on the number of servings given for each recipe and the amount of each ingredient. If a range is given for the number of servings and/or the amount of an ingredient, the analysis is based on an average of the figures given.

The nutritional analysis does not include optional ingredients or those for which no specific amount is stated. If an ingredient is listed with a substitution, the information was calculated using the first choice.

A P P E T I Z E R S

In the last 50 years, few aspects of our culture have changed more dramatically than the way we entertain. Early Sunset menus featured elegant hors d'oeuvres that were passed to guests before dressy sit-down dinners or luncheons. But entertaining has since become far more relaxed. Today's parties are rarely as formal as yesterday's, nor are they as time-consuming to arrange. In the pages of Sunset, the "walk-around" party came into vogue, boosting the popularity of dips, tortas, and other simple "eat-out-of-hand" specialties. Our recipes also mirrored the West's ethnic diversity, including ideas from Mexico, France, and Southeast Asia. ● In this chapter, you'll find a bit of everything—from Super Nachos and Soy-Chili Chicken Wings to Dried Tomato Torta and Zucchini Madeleines. Hot or cold, simple or more elaborate, all have become often-requested favorites.

Melted Brie in a Crust

Readers like this recipe. It looks impressive and tastes wonderful, and it's a cinch to prepare. You just fit a round of Brie into a hollowed-out loaf of French bread, then bake. Delicious!

- 1 **round or oval loaf (about 1 lb.) day-old French bread**
- ⅓ **cup olive oil; or ⅓ cup butter or margarine, melted**
- 2 **cloves garlic, minced or pressed**
- 1 **to 1½ pounds Brie, Camembert, or St. André cheese**

With a serrated knife, cut straight down through top of bread to leave a shell about ½ inch thick on all sides; do not cut through bottom crust. Slide your fingers down into cuts and pull center of loaf free in a single piece, leaving a ½-inch-thick base in shell. Around rim of shell, make cuts 1½ inches deep and 1½ inches apart. Cut bread from center of loaf into ½-inch-thick slices; set aside.

In a small bowl, combine oil and garlic. Brush inside of shell with about 3 tablespoons of the oil; brush bread slices with remaining oil. Place cheese in bread shell, trimming to fit. You may leave rind on cheese or trim it off.

Place filled shell and bread slices in a single layer in a 10- by 15-inch rimmed baking pan. Bake in a 350° oven until bread slices are toasted (about 10 minutes). Remove slices to a rack to cool. Continue to bake filled shell until cut edges of bread are golden and cheese is melted (about 10 more minutes).

Place filled shell on a board; surround with toasted bread slices to dip into melted cheese. When all bread slices have been eaten, snap off crisp pieces from edge of shell for dippers. Makes about 40 servings.

Per serving: 96 calories (57 percent from fat), 4 g protein, 6 g carbohydrates, 6 g total fat (0.3 g saturated fat), 15 mg cholesterol, 155 mg sodium

Red Radish Cheese Spread

Nippy red radishes, horseradish, and green onions add a pleasantly peppery accent to smooth cream cheese. Rye crispbread and crunchy fresh vegetables balance the strong flavors nicely.

- 1 **large package (8 oz.) Neufchâtel or light cream cheese, at room temperature**
- ½ **cup (¼ lb.) butter or margarine, at room temperature**
- 1 **tablespoon prepared horseradish**
- 1 **teaspoon Worcestershire**
- 1½ **cups finely chopped red radishes**
- ¼ **cup thinly sliced green onions** **Salt or celery salt** **Thin rye crispbread and crisp raw vegetables**

In a bowl, beat Neufchâtel cheese, butter, horseradish, and Worcestershire with an electric mixer until smoothly blended. Stir in radishes and onions until well distributed. Season mixture to taste with salt. If made ahead, cover and refrigerate for up to 4 hours; bring to room temperature before serving. Serve with crispbread and vegetables. Makes about 2½ cups.

Per tablespoon: 36 calories (89 percent from fat), 0.6 g protein, 0.4 g carbohydrates, 4 g total fat (2 g saturated fat), 11 mg cholesterol, 49 mg sodium

Dilled Shrimp Spread

Use a fish-shaped mold or other attractive dish for this elegant shrimp spread.

- 1 **envelope (1 tablespoon) unflavored gelatin**
- 3 **tablespoons cold water**
- 1 **can (about 10¾ oz.) condensed cream of mushroom soup**
- 2 **small packages (3 oz. *each*) cream cheese, cut into chunks**
- ½ **cup *each* mayonnaise, sour cream, chopped parsley, and chopped celery**
- ¼ **cup thinly sliced green onions**
- 2 **tablespoons lemon juice**
- ¼ **to ½ teaspoon liquid hot pepper seasoning**
- ¼ **teaspoon dry dill weed**
- ½ **pound small cooked shrimp** **Toasted baguette slices or crisp raw vegetables**

In a bowl, combine gelatin and water; let stand for 5 minutes to soften.

Place soup in a 2-quart pan over medium heat. Add gelatin mixture and cook, stirring, until gelatin is dissolved. Add cream cheese and stir until melted; remove from heat and let cool.

Add mayonnaise, sour cream, parsley, celery, onions, lemon juice, hot pepper seasoning, dill weed, and shrimp to cooled gelatin mixture; stir until blended. Spoon into a 6-cup mold. Cover and refrigerate until firm (at least 4 hours) or for up to 2 days.

To serve, dip mold in warm water up to rim for a few seconds; lift mold from water and invert a platter over it. Holding mold and platter together, invert both. Gently shake mold to loosen shrimp spread, then lift off mold. Serve with bread. Makes 8 to 10 servings.

Per serving: 247 calories (79 percent from fat), 9 g protein, 5 g carbohydrates, 22 g total fat (8 g saturated fat), 83 mg cholesterol, 477 mg sodium

Creamy Crab Dip

Serve this flavorful spread with crackers, or stuff it into artichokes or avocado halves for an impressive first course.

- 1 **large package (8 oz.) cream cheese, at room temperature**
- 2 **tablespoons** *each* **dry white wine and lemon juice**
- 1 **clove garlic, minced or pressed**
- 1 **teaspoon Dijon mustard**
- ½ **teaspoon Worcestershire**
- ¼ **cup thinly sliced green onions**
- ½ **pound crabmeat**
  Salt and pepper
  Assorted crackers

In a large bowl, beat cream cheese, wine, lemon juice, garlic, mustard, and Worcestershire with an electric mixer until smoothly blended. Stir in onions and crab. Season to taste with salt and pepper. If made ahead, cover and refrigerate until next day. Serve with crackers. Makes about 2 cups.

Per tablespoon: 33 calories (72 percent from fat), 2 g protein, 0.4 g carbohydrates, 3 g total fat (2 g saturated fat), 15 mg cholesterol, 47 mg sodium

Fresh Mushroom Pâté

To vary the taste and texture of this traditional recipe, use different varieties of fresh mushrooms. Regular mushrooms lend a milder flavor, shiitakes a richer, earthier one.

- ¼ **cup butter or margarine**
- ⅓ **pound regular or shiitake mushrooms (or a combination), coarsely chopped**
- ⅓ **cup finely chopped onion**
- 1 **tablespoon dry sherry or chicken broth**
- 1 **small package (3 oz.) cream cheese, at room temperature**
- ¼ **cup minced parsley**
  Toasted baguette slices, crackers, or crisp raw vegetables

Melt butter in a wide frying pan over medium heat. Add mushrooms and onion; cook, stirring often, until mushrooms are browned (about 15 minutes). Stir in sherry.

In a small bowl, beat cream cheese and parsley until blended. Stir in mushroom mixture. If made ahead, cover and refrigerate for up to 3 days; bring to room temperature before serving. Serve with bread. Makes about 1 cup.

Per tablespoon: 49 calories (86 percent from fat), 0.7 g protein, 1 g carbohydrates, 5 g total fat (3 g saturated fat), 14 mg cholesterol, 46 mg sodium

Shrimp Cheese Stack

Tiny, tender shrimp and spicy chili sauce add variety to seasoned cream cheese. Spread the combination on crisp crackers.

- 2 **large packages (8 oz.** *each***) cream cheese, at room temperature**
- 2 **tablespoons Worcestershire**
- ¼ **teaspoon grated lemon peel**
- 1 **tablespoon lemon juice**
- ½ **cup thinly sliced green onions**
- ⅛ **teaspoon liquid hot pepper seasoning**
- 1 **bottle (about 12 oz.) tomato-based chili sauce**
- 1 **tablespoon prepared horseradish**
- ¾ **pound small cooked shrimp**
  Assorted crackers

In a large bowl, beat cream cheese, Worcestershire, lemon peel, lemon juice, onions, and hot pepper seasoning with an electric mixer until smoothly blended. Spoon mixture into

a wide, shallow serving dish and smooth top. (At this point, you may cover and refrigerate until next day.)

Just before serving, stir together chili sauce and horseradish in a small bowl; spread over cheese layer. Top with shrimp. Serve with crackers. Makes 12 to 16 servings.

Per serving: 166 calories (62 percent from fat), 8 g protein, 8 g carbohydrates, 12 g total fat (7 g saturated fat), 83 mg cholesterol, 502 mg sodium

Marinated Cheese

Cheeses marinated in oil and herbs make a simple, satisfying appetizer— and when packed in attractive glass containers, they're lovely gifts. To vary the flavor, you might include a different selection of fresh seasonal herbs or use a flavored olive oil. (You'll find oils accented with garlic, hot chiles, and other seasonings in many well-stocked supermarkets.)

- 8 **ounces feta cheese or unripened goat cheese (such as Montrachet); or 3 slightly soft whole breakfast cheeses (about 3 oz. each)**
  About 5 fresh or dry marjoram, rosemary, oregano, or thyme sprigs (each about 3 inches long); or 2 tablespoons total of the dry herbs, crushed
- 3 **cloves garlic, peeled**
- 5 **or 6 Niçoise olives, salt-cured olives, or Spanish-style green olives**
  About ½ cup olive oil
  Toasted baguette slices or assorted crackers

If using feta cheese, cut into large chunks; if using goat cheese, cut into 1½-inch-thick slices. If using breakfast cheeses, leave whole.

Fit cheese compactly into a small (about 1½-cup) jar or crock. Add herbs, garlic, and olives. Fill jar with oil to cover cheese; cover jar and refrigerate for at least 5 days or up to

6 weeks (oil congeals, but liquefies at room temperature).

To serve, bring to room temperature. Serve with bread. Makes 6 to 8 servings.

Per serving: 229 calories (88 percent from fat), 5 g protein, 2 g carbohydrates, 23 g total fat (7 g saturated fat), 29 mg cholesterol, 388 mg sodium

Layered Cheese Torta with Pesto

Layers of aromatic pesto and delicate, buttery cheese have made this simple, yet dramatic appetizer a *Sunset* favorite since it first appeared in our pages in 1983. Like the traditional cheese tortas of Italy, it should be served with crisp toasts or fresh seasonal vegetables.

> **Easy Pesto (recipe follows)**
> 2 **large packages (8 oz. *each*) cream cheese or Neufchâtel cheese, at room temperature**
> 1½ **cups (¾ lb.) unsalted butter (do not use margarine), at room temperature**
> **Basil sprigs**
> **Toasted baguette slices or crisp raw vegetables**

Prepare Easy Pesto and set aside. In a large bowl, beat cream cheese and butter with an electric mixer until smoothly blended.

You will need a 5- to 6-cup straight-sided plain mold such as a tall brioche or charlotte pan (or use a loaf pan). Line mold with a double thickness of cheesecloth (large enough to hang over sides of mold) which has been moistened with water and wrung dry.

With a rubber spatula, spread a sixth of the cheese mixture in mold. Cover with a fifth of the pesto, spreading it evenly to sides of mold. Repeat to use remaining cheese and pesto, finishing with cheese.

Fold ends of cloth over mold; press down lightly with your hands to compact. Refrigerate until torta feels firm when pressed (1 to 1½ hours); unfold cloth from top, invert torta onto a serving dish, and gently pull off cloth. (If torta is chilled in its mold for over 1½ hours, cloth will act as a wick and cause pesto color to bleed onto cheese.) If made ahead, cover and refrigerate for up to 5 days.

To serve, garnish torta with basil sprigs. Serve with bread. Makes 16 servings.

Easy Pesto. In a blender or food processor, combine 2½ cups lightly packed **fresh basil leaves,** 1 cup (about 4 oz.) grated **Parmesan or Romano cheese,** and ⅓ cup **olive oil.** Whirl to form a paste. Stir in ¼ cup **pine nuts;** season to taste with **salt** and **pepper.**

Per serving: 342 calories (89 percent from fat), 6 g protein, 3 g carbohydrates, 35 g total fat (19 g saturated fat), 83 mg cholesterol, 219 mg sodium

Dried Tomato Torta

We like dried tomatoes for their versatility and tart, pungent flavor. They're sold both loose (like dried fruit) and packed in oil; this torta, created in 1988, uses the oil-packed variety. Serve the rich spread with toasted sliced French bread or pita triangles.

> 1 **large package (8 oz.) cream cheese or Neufchâtel cheese, at room temperature**
> 1 **cup (½ lb.) unsalted butter (do not use margarine), at room temperature**
> 1 **cup (about 4 oz.) grated Parmesan cheese**
> ½ **cup dried tomatoes packed in oil, drained (reserve oil)**
> **About 2 cups lightly packed fresh basil leaves**
> **Toasted baguette slices or pita bread wedges**

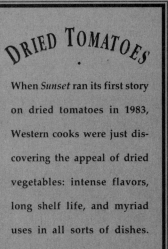

DRIED TOMATOES

When *Sunset* ran its first story on dried tomatoes in 1983, Western cooks were just discovering the appeal of dried vegetables: intense flavors, long shelf life, and myriad uses in all sorts of dishes. Since dried tomatoes weren't commonly available in Western markets, we told readers how to dry tomatoes (and other vegetables) at home in an oven or dehydrator.

In a large bowl, beat cream cheese, butter, and Parmesan cheese with an electric mixer until smoothly blended; set aside.

Cut 4 of the tomatoes into thin strips; cover and refrigerate. In a blender or food processor, whirl remaining tomatoes, 2 tablespoons of the reserved oil from tomatoes, and ½ cup of the cheese mixture until puréed. Add purée to remaining cheese mixture and beat until creamy. Cover and refrigerate until firm enough to shape (about 20 minutes); then mound on a platter. If made ahead, cover and refrigerate for up to 3 days.

To serve, arrange basil leaves and reserved tomato strips around torta. Spread torta on bread; for extra flavor, top cheese with a basil leaf and a tomato strip. Makes 12 to 16 servings.

Per serving: 232 calories (84 percent from fat), 5 g protein, 4 g carbohydrates, 22 g total fat (13 g saturated fat), 60 mg cholesterol, 205 mg sodium

Guacamole, *caponata, bagna cauda*—the names of *Sunset*'s most popular dips reveal how thoroughly the international influence has shaped Western cuisine. Dips in particular seem to have counterparts in every nation: the custom of sharing food from a communal dish is one that's enjoyed all over the world.

The recipes we offer here may not be new, but you can easily give them a fresh look by updating the accompaniments. Crisp leaves of baby romaine serve as scoops for heartier dips; toasted pita triangles, bagel chips, and crunchy Stretch Breadsticks (page 188) are excellent choices too. Out-of-the-ordinary vegetables such as yellow cherry tomatoes, baby bok choy, jicama, or wild mushrooms can give a simple herb dip an exotic air. We suggest dippers for each of the following seven recipes, but feel free to change our selections to suit your taste.

Bagna Cauda

- 1 cup (½ lb.) butter or margarine
- ½ cup olive oil
- 5 large cloves garlic, minced or pressed
- 2 tablespoons lemon juice
- 1½ teaspoons pepper
- 2 cans (about 2 oz. *each*) flat anchovy fillets
  Crisp raw vegetables, cut into bite-size chunks
  Thinly sliced crusty French bread

In a 3- to 4-cup heatproof container or chafing dish, combine butter, oil, garlic, lemon juice, and pepper. Heat over medium heat, stirring, until butter is melted. Drain oil from anchovies into

butter mixture; finely chop anchovies and stir in.

To serve, dip vegetables into sauce; hold a slice of bread under each bite to catch any drips as you eat. Keep sauce warm over a candle or low alcohol flame, or reheat periodically. Sauce may brown slightly, but don't let it burn. Makes about 2 cups.

Per tablespoon: 88 calories (94 percent from fat), 0.9 g protein, 0.3 g carbohydrates, 9 g total fat (4 g saturated fat), 17 mg cholesterol, 162 mg sodium

Caponata

- ½ cup olive oil
- 2 cups finely chopped celery
- 1 medium-size eggplant (about 1 lb.), unpeeled, cut into ½-inch cubes
- 1 large onion, finely chopped
- ⅓ cup wine vinegar
- 1 teaspoon sugar
- 2 large tomatoes, peeled and finely chopped
- 1 cup water
- 1 tablespoon capers, drained
- ¼ cup sliced pimento-stuffed green olives
- 1 can (about 2¼ oz.) sliced ripe olives, drained
- 2 tablespoons minced parsley
  Salt
  Toasted baguette slices or assorted crackers

Heat oil in a wide frying pan over medium heat. Add celery and cook,

stirring often, until tender to bite (about 7 minutes). With a slotted spoon, lift from pan; set aside.

Add eggplant to pan. Cook over medium heat, stirring often, until lightly browned and tender to bite (about 10 minutes). Add onion and cook, stirring often, until soft (about 5 minutes). Lift eggplant and onion from pan with slotted spoon; set aside.

Add vinegar, sugar, tomatoes, and water to pan. Cook over medium heat, stirring constantly, for 5 minutes. Return celery, eggplant, and onion to pan, then stir in capers, green and ripe olives, and parsley. Simmer, uncovered, for about 20 minutes. Season to taste with salt. Remove from heat and let cool. If made ahead, cover and refrigerate for up to 2 days; bring to room temperature before serving. Serve with bread. Makes about 3 cups.

Per tablespoon: 29 calories (75 percent from fat), 0.2 g protein, 2 g carbohydrates, 3 g total fat (0.3 g saturated fat), 0 mg cholesterol, 39 mg sodium

Hot Artichoke Cheese Dip

- 1 can (about 8½ oz.) water-packed artichoke hearts, drained and chopped
- 1 jar (about 6 oz.) marinated artichoke hearts, drained and chopped
- 1 small can (about 4 oz.) diced green chiles
- ⅓ cup mayonnaise
- 1½ to 2 cups (6 to 8 oz.) shredded Cheddar cheese
  Tortilla chips, crackers, or crusty French bread slices

Spread canned and marinated artichokes in a well-greased shallow 2-quart baking pan (or 7- by 11-inch baking pan). Scatter chiles on top, then carefully spread mayonnaise over all.

...per... 80 calories (76 percent from fat),
1 g protein, 0.9 g carbohydrates, 3 g total fat (1 g
saturated fat), 6 mg cholesterol, 82 mg sodium

Green Goddess Dip

1 **clove garlic, minced or pressed**
¼ **cup** *each* **coarsely chopped parsley, sliced green onions, and coarsely chopped watercress**
1 **teaspoon** *each* **dry tarragon and anchovy paste**
2 **teaspoons lemon juice**
½ **cup** *each* **mayonnaise and sour cream**
  Onion salt
  Crisp raw vegetables or assorted crackers

In a blender or food processor, combine garlic, parsley, onions, watercress, tarragon, anchovy paste, and lemon juice; whirl until smoothly puréed. Stir in mayonnaise and sour cream until well blended. Season to taste with onion salt. Serve with vegetables. Makes about 1½ cups.

Per tablespoon: 45 calories (93 percent from fat),
0.3 g protein, 0.5 g carbohydrates, 5 g total fat (1
g saturated fat), 5 mg cholesterol, 37 mg sodium

Aïoli

7 **or 8 large cloves garlic, minced or pressed**
1 **egg**
  Yolk of 1 hard-cooked egg
1 **tablespoon lemon juice**
1 **cup olive oil**
  Salt
  Crisp raw vegetables

[In] a blender or food processor, combine [gar]lic, egg, hard-cooked egg yolk, and [lem]on juice; whirl until blended. With [mo]tor running, gradually add oil in a [thi]n, steady stream, whirling until [blen]ded. Season to taste with salt.

If made ahead, cover and refrigerate until next day. Bring to room temperature before serving. Serve with vegetables. Makes about 1½ cups.

Per tablespoon: 87 calories (96 percent from fat),
0.4 g protein, 0.4 g carbohydrates, 9 g total fat (1
g saturated fat), 18 mg cholesterol, 3 mg sodium

Red Pepper Dip

3 **tablespoons olive oil**
3 **large onions, thinly sliced**
2 **jars (about 7 oz.** *each***) roasted red peppers, drained**
2 **teaspoons fresh thyme leaves or 1 teaspoon dry thyme**
2 **tablespoons tomato paste**
½ **cup** *each* **grated Parmesan cheese and ricotta cheese**
  Thyme sprigs (optional)
  Crisp raw vegetables, toasted baguette slices, or potato chips

Heat oil in a wide frying pan over medium-low heat. Add onions and cook until very soft and golden (about 30 minutes); stir occasionally at first, then more often as onions begin to turn golden. Onions should not show signs of browning during the first 15 minutes; if they do, reduce heat.

Add peppers, thyme leaves, and tomato paste to onions; cook, stirring often, for 5 more minutes. Let mixture cool slightly.

In a blender or food processor, whirl pepper mixture, Parmesan cheese, and ricotta cheese until puréed. Transfer to a serving bowl. If made ahead, cover and refrigerate until next day. Serve cold or at room temperature; garnish with thyme sprigs, if desired. Serve with vegetables. Makes about 4 cups.

Per tablespoon: 17 calories (58 percent from fat),
0.6 g protein, 1 g carbohydrates, 1 g total fat (0.3
g saturated fat), 1 mg cholesterol, 18 mg sodium

Easy Guacamole

2 **large ripe avocados**
2 **to 3 tablespoons lemon or lime juice**
1 **clove garlic, minced or pressed**
1 **to 2 tablespoons chopped cilantro**
2 **to 4 tablespoons canned diced green chiles**
1 **medium-size tomato, peeled, seeded, and chopped**
  Minced fresh jalapeño or serrano chiles (optional)
  Salt
  Tortilla chips or crisp raw vegetables

Pit avocados and scoop pulp into a medium-size bowl; mash coarsely with a fork. Stir in lemon juice, garlic, cilantro, green chiles, and tomato. Add jalapeño chiles to taste, if desired. Season to taste with salt. Serve with tortilla chips. Makes about 1⅔ cups.

Per tablespoon: 33 calories (75 percent from fat),
0.4 g protein, 2 g carbohydrates, 3 g total fat (0.5
g saturated fat), 0 mg cholesterol, 9 mg sodium

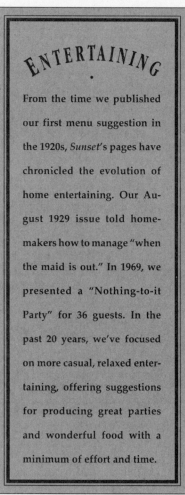
Olive-filled Cheese Balls

These hot tidbits have been reader favorites for over 30 years. To make each bite-size treat, just wrap an olive in a layer of flaky Cheddar pastry.

1   cup (about 4 oz.) shredded sharp Cheddar cheese
2   tablespoons butter or margarine, at room temperature
½   cup all-purpose flour
     Dash of ground red pepper (cayenne)
25   medium-size pitted ripe or pimento-stuffed green olives, drained well

In a small bowl, beat cheese and butter until well blended. Stir in flour and

red pepper. Wrap 1 to 2 teaspoons of dough around each olive, covering completely. Place 1 inch apart on a baking sheet. Bake in a 400° oven until pastry is crisp but not browned (12 to 15 minutes). Makes 25 appetizers.

Per appetizer: 40 calories (64 percent from fat), 1 g protein, 2 g carbohydrates, 3 g total fat (2 g saturated fat), 7 mg cholesterol, 71 mg sodium

Zucchini Madeleines

For a savory twist on the traditional shell-shaped cakes of France, try these unusual, cheese-laced bites.

1   pound zucchini, shredded
2   teaspoons salt
6   tablespoons olive oil
1   medium-size onion, chopped
5   eggs
2   tablespoons milk
1½   cups (about 6 oz.) grated Parmesan cheese
1   clove garlic, minced or pressed
2   tablespoons chopped fresh basil or 1 teaspoon dry basil
¼   teaspoon pepper
1   cup all-purpose flour
1   tablespoon baking powder

In a colander, mix zucchini with salt. Let stand until zucchini is limp and liquid has drained from it (about 30 minutes). Rinse and drain zucchini well, squeezing out as much water as possible.

While zucchini is draining, heat 2 tablespoons of the oil in a wide frying pan over medium-high heat. Add onion and cook, stirring often, until soft (about 4 minutes). Remove pan from heat.

In a large bowl, beat eggs, milk, remaining ¼ cup oil, cheese, garlic, basil, and pepper with a wire whisk until blended. Add zucchini and onion and mix well. Add flour and baking powder; stir just until evenly moistened.

Spoon batter into greased, floured madeleine pans (1½- or 2-tablespoon size) or tiny (about 1½-inch) muffin pans, filling to rims. Bake in a 400° oven until puffed and lightly browned (about 15 minutes for 1½-tablespoon madeleines, about 18 minutes for 2-tablespoon madeleines, about 20 minutes for muffins). Let cool for 5 minutes; invert pans to remove madeleines. Serve hot or cooled.

If made ahead, let cool completely, then wrap airtight; refrigerate until next day or freeze for longer storage (thaw before reheating). To reheat, place madeleines in a single layer on baking sheets and heat, uncovered, in a 350° oven until warm (about 5 minutes). Makes about 3 dozen appetizers.

Per appetizer: 70 calories (60 percent from fat), 3 g protein, 4 g carbohydrates, 5 g total fat (1 g saturated fat), 33 mg cholesterol, 258 mg sodium

Happy Hour Mushrooms

A reader from Sacramento, California, sent this recipe to us in 1967. Warm and fragrant, the succulent mushrooms rarely last longer than the first few minutes of any happy hour!

20   medium-size mushrooms (about 1 lb. *total*)
¾   cup (¼ lb. plus ¼ cup) butter or margarine, at room temperature
2   cloves garlic, minced or pressed
6   tablespoons shredded jack cheese
¼   cup dry white or red wine
2   teaspoons soy sauce
⅔   cup fine cracker crumbs

Remove and discard stems from mushrooms. Melt ¼ cup of the butter; brush over mushroom caps, coating thoroughly. In a medium-size bowl, combine remaining ½ cup butter, garlic, and cheese; stir until well blended. Stir in wine, soy sauce, and crumbs.

Place mushrooms, cavity side up, on a large rimmed baking sheet. Evenly mound filling in each mushroom, pressing it in lightly. Broil about 6 inches below heat until bubbly and lightly browned (about 3 minutes). Serve warm. Makes 20 appetizers.

Per appetizer: 86 calories (82 percent from fat), 1 g protein, 3 g carbohydrates, 8 g total fat (4 g saturated fat), 20 mg cholesterol, 143 mg sodium

Roasted Potatoes with Asiago Cheese

Asiago, a hard Italian cheese with a rich, nutty flavor, is a winning complement for robust roasted potatoes.

16 **tiny red thin-skinned potatoes** (*each* 1½ to 2 inches in diameter), scrubbed
½ **cup grated Asiago or Parmesan cheese**
½ **cup mayonnaise**
2 **tablespoons thinly sliced green onion**
About 1 teaspoon paprika

Pierce each potato in several places with a fork. Place potatoes in a baking pan and bake in a 375° oven until tender throughout when pierced (about 1 hour). Let cool; if baked ahead, cover and refrigerate until next day.

In a small bowl, mix cheese, mayonnaise, and onion. Cut each potato in half. Scoop a small (about ½-inch-deep) cavity in each potato half. Set halves, cut side up, in a 10- by 15-inch rimmed baking pan (if needed, trim a sliver off rounded sides of potato halves so they rest steadily). Spoon cheese mixture equally into each potato half. Dust liberally with paprika. Bake potatoes in a 350° oven until heated through (about 15 minutes). Serve hot. Makes 32 appetizers.

Per appetizer: 55 calories (53 percent from fat), 1 g protein, 5 g carbohydrates, 3 g total fat (0.7 g saturated fat), 3 mg cholesterol, 50 mg sodium

Artichoke Nibbles

Flavorful marinated artichoke hearts and nippy cheese in a light, spicy custard make this recipe a favorite with *Sunset* readers and editors.

2 **jars (about 6 oz. *each*) marinated artichoke hearts**
1 **small onion, finely chopped**
1 **clove garlic, minced or pressed**
4 **eggs**
¼ **cup fine dry bread crumbs**
¼ **teaspoon salt**
⅛ **teaspoon *each* pepper, dry oregano, and liquid hot pepper seasoning**
2 **cups (about 8 oz.) shredded sharp Cheddar cheese**
2 **tablespoons minced parsley**

Drain marinade from one jar of artichokes into a small frying pan. Drain remaining jar; reserve marinade for other uses. Chop all artichokes; set aside. Heat marinade in pan over medium heat. Add onion and garlic; cook, stirring often, until onion is soft (about 5 minutes).

In a bowl, beat eggs to blend. Stir in crumbs, salt, pepper, oregano, hot pepper seasoning, cheese, parsley, artichokes, and onion mixture. Pour into a greased 7- by 11-inch baking pan and spread out evenly.

Bake in a 325° oven until center of custard feels set when lightly touched (about 30 minutes). Let cool slightly in pan, then cut into 1-inch squares. Serve warm or at room temperature,

or cover and refrigerate to serve cold. To reheat, bake, uncovered, in a 325° oven until heated through (10 to 12 minutes). Makes about 6½ dozen appetizers.

Per appetizer: 22 calories (66 percent from fat), 1 g protein, 0.7 g carbohydrates, 2 g total fat (0.7 g saturated fat), 14 mg cholesterol, 54 mg sodium

Hot Ham & Cheese Pastry Squares

You can bake the pastry for these savory hot appetizer squares ahead of time, then add the toppings just before serving.

All-purpose Pastry (page 61) or purchased pastry shell for a single-crust 9-inch pie, unbaked
1 **egg yolk**
½ **cup *each* sour cream and shredded Cheddar cheese**
1 **tablespoon toasted instant minced onion**
¼ **teaspoon caraway seeds**
¼ **pound thinly sliced cooked ham**
1 **large tomato, thinly sliced**

Prepare All-purpose Pastry as directed; roll out on an 18-inch-long piece of wax paper to make a 9- by 12-inch rectangle. Using paper as a support, invert pastry onto a 12- by 15-inch baking sheet. Peel off paper. Prick pastry all over with a fork. Bake in a 350° oven until golden (about 10 minutes); let cool.

In a small bowl, stir together egg yolk, sour cream, cheese, onion, and caraway seeds until well blended. Cover pastry crust with ham, then tomato; spread with cheese mixture.

Broil 3 to 4 inches below heat just until topping begins to brown (about 3 minutes). Cut into 12 squares; serve warm. Makes 1 dozen appetizers.

Per appetizer: 169 calories (59 percent from fat), 6 g protein, 11 g carbohydrates, 11 g total fat (6 g saturated fat), 66 mg cholesterol, 242 mg sodium

Super Nachos

Ground beef, spicy sausage, beans, and chiles "beef up" the traditional nacho base of melted cheese and tortilla chips.

- ½ pound *each* lean ground beef and chorizo, casings removed; or use 1 pound lean ground beef and omit chorizo
- 1 large onion, chopped
  Salt
  Liquid hot pepper seasoning
- 1 or 2 cans (about 1 lb. *each*) refried beans
- 1 small can (about 4 oz.) diced green chiles
- 2 to 3 cups (8 to 12 oz.) shredded jack or mild Cheddar cheese
- ¾ cup purchased green or red taco sauce
  Crisp-fried Tortilla Pieces (recipe follows) or about 8 cups purchased tortilla chips
  Garnishes (suggestions follow)

Crumble beef and sausage into a wide frying pan. Add onion and cook over medium-high heat, stirring often, until meat is lightly browned. Discard fat; season meat mixture to taste with salt and hot pepper seasoning.

Spread beans in a large, shallow baking pan. Top evenly with meat mixture. Sprinkle with chiles, cover evenly with cheese, and drizzle with taco sauce. (At this point, you may cover and refrigerate until next day.)

Prepare Crisp-fried Tortilla Pieces.

Bake bean-meat mixture, uncovered, in a 400° oven until heated through (20 to 25 minutes). Remove pan from oven. Immediately add garnishes: mound avocado dip and sour cream in center, then add green onions, olives, pickled pepper, and cilantro sprigs as desired. Tuck Crisp-fried Tortilla Pieces around edges of bean mixture and serve at once. If desired, keep pan hot on a warming tray. Makes 12 to 16 servings.

Crisp-fried Tortilla Pieces. Stack 12 **corn tortillas;** cut stack into 6 equal wedges. In a deep 2- to 3-quart pan, heat about ½ inch of **salad oil** over medium-high heat to 350° to 375°F on a deep-frying thermometer. Add one stack of tortilla wedges and stir to separate. Cook until crisp (1 to 1½ minutes); lift from oil with a slotted spoon and drain on paper towels. Repeat to cook remaining wedges. If desired, sprinkle lightly with **salt.** If made ahead, let cool; then store airtight until next day.

Garnishes. Have ready 1 can (about 8 oz.) **frozen avocado dip,** thawed (or 1 medium-size ripe avocado, pitted, peeled, coarsely mashed, and mixed with 1 tablespoon lemon juice); 1 cup **sour cream;** about ¼ cup thinly sliced **green onions;** about 1 cup **pitted ripe olives;** 1 **mild red pickled pepper;** and **cilantro or parsley sprigs.**

Per serving: 282 calories (51 percent from fat), 14 g protein, 20 g carbohydrates, 16 g total fat (2 g saturated fat), 37 mg cholesterol, 544 mg sodium

Mexican Chile-Cheese Logs

These savory little pinwheels feature pork sausage and ground turkey swirled around a succulent filling of Cheddar cheese, green chiles, and ripe olives. The spicy bites are delicious eaten plain; you might also let guests make their own open-faced "sandwiches" by topping tortilla chips with a meat round, an avocado slice, and a cherry tomato half.

- 2 eggs
- 2 slices firm-textured white bread, torn into small pieces
- 1 beef bouillon cube dissolved in 1 tablespoon hot water
- ½ cup purchased red taco sauce
- 2 tablespoons instant minced onion
- 1½ teaspoons *each* dry oregano and chili powder
- 1 teaspoon salt
- ½ teaspoon ground cumin
- 2½ cups (about 10 oz.) shredded sharp Cheddar cheese
- 2 cloves garlic, minced or pressed
- 1¼ pounds bulk pork sausage
- 1 pound ground turkey
- 2 small cans (about 4 oz. *each*) whole green chiles, drained and split
- 1 can (about 4 oz.) sliced or wedged ripe olives, drained
- ¾ teaspoon cumin seeds
  Tortilla chips (optional)
  Avocado slices and cherry tomato halves (optional)

In a large bowl, beat eggs until blended. Add bread, bouillon mixture, ¼ cup of the taco sauce, and onion; let stand for 5 minutes. With your hands or a spoon, mix in oregano, chili powder, salt, ground cumin, 1 cup of the cheese, garlic, sausage, and turkey until well blended.

Turn meat mixture out onto a 12- by 20-inch piece of foil and shape into a 10- by 18-inch rectangle. Cut through meat and foil to make three 6- by 10-inch rectangles.

Flatten chiles and arrange a third of them down center of each rectangle. Sprinkle each rectangle with a third each of the olives and cumin seeds and ½ cup of the remaining cheese.

Starting from a long side, lift meat off foil and tightly roll each rectangle into a log; firmly pinch together at seam and ends to seal in cheese. Using foil to help lift, place logs in a greased 10- by 15-inch rimmed baking pan; remove foil. Brush tops of logs with remaining ¼ cup taco sauce.

Bake in a 350° oven until meat feels firm to the touch (about 45 minutes). Let cool; then wrap in foil. Refrigerate for at least 8 hours or up to 3 days; or freeze for up to 2 months (thaw before serving).

To serve, thinly slice cold logs. If desired, serve with tortilla chips, avocado slices, and cherry tomatoes. Makes about 9 dozen appetizers.

Per appetizer: 39 calories (71 percent from fat), 2 g protein, 0.7 g carbohydrates, 3 g total fat (1 g saturated fat), 12 mg cholesterol, 116 mg sodium

Fila Cheese Onion Rolls

The flaky, nearly transparent dough used to make these cheese- and onion-stuffed pastries is a common Mid-eastern ingredient that's sold in the refrigerator or freezer case of most supermarkets. The spelling varies; in addition to "fila," you'll see "filo," "fillo," and "phyllo."

½ **cup (¼ lb.) butter or margarine**

3 **large onions, thinly sliced crosswise**

2 **small packages (3 oz. *each*) cream cheese, at room temperature**

1½ **cups (about 6 oz.) shredded Gruyère, Samsoe, or Swiss cheese**

½ **teaspoon caraway seeds (optional)**

9 **to 12 sheets fila dough (¼ to ⅓ lb. *total*), thawed if frozen**

Melt 3 tablespoons of the butter in a wide frying pan over medium-low heat. Add onions and cook until very soft and golden (about 30 minutes); stir occasionally at first, then more often as onions begin to turn golden. Onions should not show signs of browning during the first 15 minutes; if they do, reduce heat. Remove onions from heat and let cool slightly. Add cream cheese, Gruyère cheese, and

caraway seeds (if desired); stir until combined.

Melt remaining 5 tablespoons butter. Stack 3 or 4 sheets of fila, brushing a few strokes of butter over each sheet. Spoon a third of the cheese-onion mixture in an even band along widest edge of top fila sheet; roll to enclose. Brush surface of roll with butter. Cut roll in half; place halves, seam side down, a few inches apart on a buttered baking sheet. Repeat with remaining fila sheets and filling. (At this point, you may cover and refrigerate until next day.)

Cut rolls on baking sheets into 1-inch pieces (leave them in place on sheets). Bake in a 400° oven until well browned (about 12 minutes; about 17 minutes if refrigerated). Serve warm. Makes about 5 dozen pieces.

Per piece: 45 calories (68 percent from fat), 1 g protein, 2 g carbohydrates, 3 g total fat (2 g saturated fat), 10 mg cholesterol, 43 mg sodium

Soy-Chili Chicken Wings

Sunset's food editors discovered these spicy-hot chicken wings during a trip through China in 1987.

2 **pounds chicken wing drumettes**

2 **tablespoons salad oil**

¼ **cup soy sauce**

2 **tablespoons rice wine or dry sherry**

2 **tablespoons sugar**

1 **teaspoon chili oil or 2 small dried hot red chiles**

4 **quarter-size slices fresh ginger**

2 **cloves garlic, peeled**

2 **green onions**

1 **cup water**

Rinse chicken and pat dry. Heat salad oil in a wide frying pan over high heat. Add chicken, a portion at a time (do not crowd pan); cook, turning as needed, until browned on all sides.

Return all chicken to pan, then add soy sauce, wine, sugar, chili oil, ginger, garlic, whole onions, and water. Bring to a boil. Then reduce heat, cover, and simmer until meat near bone is no longer pink; cut to test (about 20 minutes). Uncover and boil, turning chicken often, until sauce is thick enough to coat wings (10 minutes). If made ahead, let cool; cover and refrigerate until next day. Serve warm or at room temperature; to reheat, place chicken in a single layer on baking sheets and heat in a 350° oven until warm. Makes 8 servings.

Per serving: 179 calories (54 percent from fat), 15 g protein, 5 g carbohydrates, 11 g total fat (2 g saturated fat), 62 mg cholesterol, 579 mg sodium

Hasty Hots

Among the simplest of our recipes, this ever-popular appetizer dates from *Sunset*'s earliest years.

- **4 green onions, very thinly sliced**
- **½ cup grated Parmesan cheese**
- **6 to 8 tablespoons mayonnaise**
- **24 slices cocktail-size rye bread or 24 baguette slices**

In a small bowl, stir together onions, cheese, and 6 tablespoons of the mayonnaise until well blended. If needed, add more mayonnaise to give mixture a firm spreading consistency. Place bread in single layer on a baking sheet; broil 4 to 6 inches below heat until golden brown. Turn slices over and spread with cheese mixture. Return to oven and broil until bubbly and lightly browned (about 3 minutes). Makes 2 dozen appetizers.

Per appetizer: 54 calories (61 percent from fat), 1 g protein, 4 g carbohydrates, 4 g total fat (0.9 g saturated fat), 4 mg cholesterol, 93 mg sodium

Cocktail Walnuts

Crisp walnuts seasoned with soy and ginger are tasty alongside your favorite beverage. Try the same recipe with pecans, almonds, or any other variety of nut.

- **2 tablespoons butter or margarine, melted**
- **2 teaspoons soy sauce**
- **½ teaspoon *each* ground ginger and salt**
- **¼ teaspoon garlic powder**
- **2 cups (about ½ lb.) walnut halves**

In a 9- by 13-inch baking pan, combine butter, soy sauce, ginger, salt, and garlic powder; mix well. Add walnuts and stir to coat; then spread out in a single layer. Bake in a 250° oven until crisp (about 45 minutes), stirring occasionally. Let cool, then store airtight for up to 1 month. Makes 2 cups.

Per ¼ cup: 209 calories (83 percent from fat), 4 g protein, 5 g carbohydrates, 20 g total fat (3 g saturated fat), 8 mg cholesterol, 255 mg sodium

Dry-roasted Potato Chips

Long baking in a low oven produces chips just as crisp as the familiar deep-fried kind. Try them with your choice of dips; we offer a variety on pages 10 and 11.

- **1 pound white thin-skinned potatoes, scrubbed**
- **2 quarts water**
  Vegetable oil cooking spray
  Salt

Using a food slicer (mandolin) or food processor, cut potatoes into very thin slices. In a 3- to 4-quart pan, bring water to a boil. Add a third of the potatoes; cook until slightly translucent (about 1½ minutes). Lift out with a slotted spoon; drain on paper towels. Repeat to cook and drain remaining potato slices.

Place wire racks on large baking sheets (you'll need about 4 sheets to bake chips all at once). Lightly coat racks with cooking spray.

Arrange potato slices on racks in a single layer. Season to taste with salt. Bake in a 200° oven until chips are crisp (2 to 2½ hours). Serve hot or at room temperature. If made ahead, let cool; store airtight for up to 1 week. Makes about 4 cups.

Per ½ cup: 48 calories (7 percent from fat), 1 g protein, 10 g carbohydrates, 0.4 g total fat (0 g saturated fat), 0 mg cholesterol, 4 mg sodium

Nacho Popcorn

For the diet-conscious snacker, plain popcorn is a perfect choice: it's good-tasting, high in fiber, and lower in fat than traditional favorites like peanuts and chips. Every now and then, though, you'll want to dress up your popcorn—as in this recipe. When you're in the mood for a splurge, top the puffy kernels with chiles, olives, and cheese for a nacho-style treat.

- **¼ cup butter or margarine**
- **1 fresh or canned jalapeño chile, seeded and minced**
- **2 teaspoons chili powder**
- **½ teaspoon ground cumin**
- **3 quarts air- or oil-popped popcorn (about ½ cup popcorn kernels)**
- **2 cups (about 8 oz.) finely shredded Cheddar cheese**
- **¼ cup sliced ripe olives**
  Salt

Melt butter in a wide frying pan over medium heat. Add chile, chili powder, and cumin; cook, stirring, until chile is soft (about 5 minutes).

Spread popcorn in a 12- by 17-inch roasting pan. Pour butter mixture over top; mix well. Sprinkle with cheese and olives; season to taste with salt. Bake in a 300° oven, stirring every 5 minutes, until cheese is melted (about 15 minutes). Pour into a shallow bowl and serve hot. Makes about 3 quarts.

Per cup: 146 calories (65 percent from fat), 6 g protein, 7 g carbohydrates, 11 g total fat (6 g saturated fat), 30 mg cholesterol, 185 mg sodium

BEVERAGES

The choice of a beverage, like that of a party hat, is subject to whim and fancy. And just as much as the rest of the menu, the drinks you serve help set the mood of the meal. These classic recipes, some of them more than a few decades old, incorporate ingredients and ideas from all over the world, from Scandinavia to the tropics.

Chilled Citrus Sangría

2 bottles (about 750 ml. *each*) dry red wine

4 cups fresh orange juice

1 cup *each* fresh lime juice and fresh lemon juice

½ cup sugar, or to taste

4 cups sparkling water or club soda, chilled

Orange slices

Crushed ice or ice cubes

In a large bowl, stir together wine, orange juice, lime juice, lemon juice, and sugar. Cover and refrigerate until cold.

Just before serving, stir in sparkling water and garnish with orange slices. Ladle into ice-filled glasses. Makes about 4 quarts.

Per cup: 127 calories (2 percent from fat), 0.7 g protein, 17 g carbohydrates, 0.1 g total fat (0 g saturated fat), 0 mg cholesterol, 18 mg sodium

Lemon Grass Lemonade

Lemon Grass Syrup (recipe follows)

5 cups water

6 tablespoons lemon juice

Crushed ice or ice cubes

Prepare Lemon Grass Syrup; pour into a 2-quart pitcher and stir in water and lemon juice. Cover and refrigerate until next day. To serve, pour into ice-filled glasses. Makes about 6 cups.

Lemon Grass Syrup. Cut off leafy tops and peel tough outer layers from 3 stalks **fresh lemon grass.** Trim off and discard discolored or dry parts of root ends; cut stalks into 2-inch lengths and crush lightly with a mallet (or thinly slice stalks crosswise).

In a 1- to 1½-quart pan, combine lemon grass and 1 cup *each* **sugar** and **water.** Bring to a boil over high heat; reduce heat and simmer, uncovered, until syrup is reduced to 1 cup (about 30 minutes). Let cool. If made ahead, cover and refrigerate for up to 2 weeks. Discard lemon grass before using syrup.

Per cup: 132 calories (0.3 percent from fat), 0.1 g protein, 34 g carbohydrates, 0 g total fat (0 g saturated fat), 0 mg cholesterol, 4 mg sodium

Ginger Punch

1 small pineapple (3 to 3½ lbs.), peeled, halved, cored, and cut into 1-inch chunks; or 4 cups pineapple juice

4 cups water

¼ pound fresh ginger, scrubbed and cut into 1-inch chunks

½ cup lemon juice

¾ cup sugar, or to taste

Crushed ice or ice cubes

Whirl pineapple chunks, a portion at a time, in a blender or food processor with 2 cups of the water until puréed. Pour purée through a fine strainer into a large bowl, squeezing and pressing pulp to remove juice; discard pulp. (If using pineapple juice, simply mix it with 2 cups water in a large bowl.)

Place ginger in blender or food processor with remaining 2 cups water; whirl until puréed. Then pour purée through strainer into pineapple juice, squeezing liquid from pulp; discard pulp. Stir in lemon juice and sugar. Pour into a pitcher, cover, and refrigerate un-

til cold. To serve, stir well and pour into ice-filled glasses. Makes about 2 quarts.

Per cup: 154 calories (1 percent from fat), 0.7 g protein, 39 g carbohydrates, 0.2 g total fat (0 g saturated fat), 0 mg cholesterol, 6 mg sodium

Hot Cranberry Glögg

4 cups cranberry-apple juice cocktail

2 cups dry red wine

¾ cup *each* sugar and water

1 cinnamon stick (3 to 4 inches long)

3 whole cardamom pods, lightly crushed

4 whole cloves

Thin orange slice

½ cup *each* raisins and whole blanched almonds

In a large glass or stainless steel bowl, combine juice cocktail, wine, sugar, water, cinnamon stick, cardamom, and cloves. (At this point, you may cover and refrigerate for up to 2 days.)

To serve, pour punch into a 3- to 4-quart pan; warm over medium heat just until heated through. Float orange slice on top. Keep warm over a candle or on a warming tray, if desired. Ladle into cups or mugs, adding raisins and almonds to individual servings. Makes about 2 quarts.

Per cup: 278 calories (17 percent from fat), 2 g protein, 50 g carbohydrates, 5 g total fat (0.5 g saturated fat), 0 mg cholesterol, 8 mg sodium

Nonalcoholic Cranberry Glögg

Follow directions for **Hot Cranberry Glögg**, but omit wine, sugar, and water. Increase cranberry-apple juice cocktail to 6 cups. Makes about 7 cups.

Per cup: 233 calories (20 percent from fat), 3 g protein, 46 g carbohydrates, 5 g total fat (0.5 g saturated fat), 0 mg cholesterol, 7 mg sodium

SOUPS

Soup probably had its start as the simplest of suppers: odds and ends of vegetables, meats, and grains, heated in a single pot to make a nourishing meal. Inventive Western cooks, blessed with a treasure house of fresh regional ingredients, became expert in combining diverse flavors in both hearty one-pot dinners and lighter, more elegant first-course fare. • In this chapter, vegetable soups showcase a wealth of Western produce. Fresh Pacific seafood, poultry, and beef lend flavor and substance to simple chowders and stews. Chilled soups celebrate a summer harvest of ripe fruits and vegetables. • Though many of these recipes redefine the classics to incorporate seasonal or ethnic ingredients, most maintain the tradition and simplicity that have made soup the quintessential comfort food.

Chilled Avocado Soup

Tender avocados lend buttery texture and mild, faintly nutlike flavor to this summertime soup. For best results, use fully ripe avocados; to speed the ripening process, you can try storing the fruit in a paper bag at room temperature.

- 1 tablespoon salad oil
- 1 clove garlic, minced or pressed
- ½ cup chopped onion
- 3 large ripe avocados
- ¼ cup lemon juice
- 3 tablespoons dry sherry
- 3 chicken bouillon cubes dissolved in 2½ cups hot water
- ¾ teaspoon liquid hot pepper seasoning
- 2 tablespoons chopped cilantro
- 2 cups milk
  Salt

Heat oil in a small pan over medium heat. Add garlic and onion; cook, stirring often, until onion is soft (about 5 minutes). Remove from heat.

Halve and pit 2 of the avocados; scoop pulp into a blender or food processor. Add lemon juice, onion mixture, and sherry; whirl until puréed. Add bouillon and hot pepper seasoning; whirl until smoothly puréed. Pour purée into a large serving bowl. Stir in cilantro and milk. Season to taste with salt. Cover and refrigerate until cold.

To serve, pit and peel remaining avocado; cut into thin slices. Ladle soup into mugs or bowls; top with avocado slices. Makes 6 servings.

Per serving: 295 calories (71 percent from fat), 6 g protein, 16 g carbohydrates, 24 g total fat (5 g saturated fat), 12 mg cholesterol, 625 mg sodium

Vichyssoise

Through the years, *Sunset* has printed many variations of vichyssoise, but this recipe is our favorite. The delicately flavored potato-and-leek soup is traditionally served cold, but it's just as delicious hot.

- 4 medium-size leeks
- ¼ cup butter or margarine
- 1 large onion, thinly sliced
- 3 large russet potatoes, peeled and diced
- 4 cups chicken broth
- 1 cup whipping cream
  About 1 cup milk
  Salt and white pepper
  Snipped chives or thinly sliced green onion tops

Cut off and discard root ends from leeks. Trim tops, leaving about 3 inches of green leaves. Discard coarse outer leaves. Split leeks in half lengthwise and rinse well; then thinly slice crosswise.

Melt butter in a deep 3-quart pan over low heat. Add leeks and onion; cook, stirring often, until onion is very soft but not browned (about 25 minutes). Add potatoes and broth. Bring to a boil over high heat; then reduce heat, cover, and simmer until potatoes are tender when pierced (about 20 minutes).

In a blender or food processor, whirl soup, a portion at a time, until puréed. Pour into a large serving bowl. Stir in cream and 1 cup of the milk; if necessary, add more milk for a thinner consistency. Season to taste with salt and white pepper. Cover and refrigerate until cold. To serve, ladle soup into bowls and sprinkle with chives. Makes 8 servings.

Per serving: 245 calories (61 percent from fat), 5 g protein, 19 g carbohydrates, 17 g total fat (10 g saturated fat), 53 mg cholesterol, 587 mg sodium

Tomato Gazpacho with Avocado

So simple that it first appeared in an article on cooking for kids, this gazpacho has an easy elegance that has made it an enduring favorite among children and adults alike. To keep your gazpacho icy cold, serve it in chilled bowls.

- ½ medium-size cucumber
- ½ medium-size mild red or white onion
- ½ medium-size avocado, pitted and peeled
- ½ teaspoon dry oregano
- 3 tablespoons olive oil or salad oil
- 2 tablespoons wine vinegar
- 4 cups tomato juice
  Ice cubes
- 2 limes, cut into wedges

Peel cucumber, if desired. Cut a few thin slices from cucumber and onion; reserve for garnish. Finely chop remaining cucumber and onion; slice or chop avocado. Combine cucumber, onion, avocado, oregano, oil, and vinegar in a serving bowl. Stir in tomato juice. Top with reserved cucumber and onion slices; then cover and refrigerate until cold.

To serve, place 2 or 3 ice cubes in each individual bowl; ladle soup into bowls over ice. Serve with lime wedges. Makes 6 servings.

Per serving: 123 calories (64 percent from fat), 2 g protein, 10 g carbohydrates, 9 g total fat (1 g saturated fat), 0 mg cholesterol, 592 mg sodium

White Spanish Gazpacho

In the 1960s, when Westerners were just discovering versatile cold soups, we introduced this fresh-tasting cucumber gazpacho as an innovative opener for a summer menu. For a dramatic presentation, serve the soup nestled in bowls of shaved ice.

- 3 **medium-size cucumbers, peeled and cut into chunks**
- 1 **small clove garlic, peeled**
- 3 **cups chicken broth**
- 3 **cups sour cream**
- 3 **tablespoons white wine vinegar or distilled white vinegar, or to taste**
- 2 **teaspoons salt, or to taste**
  Condiments (suggestions follow)

In a food processor or blender, whirl cucumbers and garlic with a little of the broth until puréed. Add 1 cup of the sour cream; whirl until blended. Transfer to a large serving bowl. Whisk in remaining 2 cups sour cream, then remaining broth, until blended. Stir in vinegar and salt. Cover and refrigerate until cold.

To serve, ladle soup into wide, shallow bowls; offer condiments to add to taste. Makes 8 servings.

Condiments. Arrange in separate dishes: 4 medium-size **tomatoes,** peeled and chopped; ½ cup *each* chopped **parsley** and sliced **green onions;** and ¾ cup **salted roasted whole almonds.**

Per serving: 315 calories (75 percent from fat), 8 g protein, 13 g carbohydrates, 27 g total fat (12 g saturated fat), 38 mg cholesterol, 1,093 mg sodium

Winter Tomato Soup

Based on canned stewed tomatoes, this easy-to-prepare classic offers comforting warmth on cold days. The soup gets its delightful gusto from smoky bacon drippings, white wine, and a dash of curry powder.

- 2 **tablespoons bacon drippings, butter, or margarine**
- ½ **cup chopped celery**
- 1 **can (about 14½ oz.) stewed tomatoes**
- 1 **can (about 10½ oz.) condensed consommé**
- ½ **cup dry white wine**
- 1 **tablespoon instant minced onion or 3 tablespoons thinly sliced green onions**
- 1 **tablespoon lemon juice**
- 1 **tablespoon cornstarch blended with ½ cup cold water**
  Dash of curry powder
  Purchased cheese-flavored croutons (optional)

Heat bacon drippings in a wide frying pan over medium-low heat. Add celery; cook, stirring often, until soft (about 5 minutes). Add tomatoes, consommé, wine, onion, lemon juice, cornstarch mixture, and curry powder; stir until blended. Bring to a boil over high heat; then reduce heat, cover, and simmer for 15 to 20 minutes, stirring occasionally.

To serve, ladle soup into bowls; garnish with croutons, if desired. Makes 6 servings.

Per serving: 83 calories (43 percent from fat), 3 g protein, 8 g carbohydrates, 4 g total fat (1 g saturated fat), 3 mg cholesterol, 464 mg sodium

Mushroom Velvet Soup

Named for its velvet-smooth texture, this soup can be ladled into shallow bowls for an elegant first course or offered in mugs for sipping.

- ¼ **cup butter or margarine**
- ½ **pound mushrooms, sliced**
- 1 **medium-size onion, coarsely chopped**
- ⅔ **cup finely chopped parsley**
- 1 **tablespoon all-purpose flour**
- 1 **can (about 14½ oz.) beef broth**
- 1 **cup sour cream**

Melt butter in a wide frying pan over medium-high heat. Add mushrooms, onion, and parsley; cook, stirring, until mushrooms are soft and liquid has evaporated (about 5 minutes). Stir in flour and cook, stirring, for 1 minute; then stir in broth. Bring to a boil over high heat, stirring constantly.

In a blender or food processor, whirl half the soup with ½ cup of the sour cream until smooth. Repeat to purée remaining soup with remaining ½ cup sour cream. If made ahead, let cool; then cover and refrigerate until next day.

To serve, return soup to pan and cook, stirring, until heated through; do not boil. Ladle into bowls or mugs. Makes 4 to 6 servings.

Per serving: 213 calories (79 percent from fat), 4 g protein, 8 g carbohydrates, 19 g total fat (12 g saturated fat), 45 mg cholesterol, 423 mg sodium

Chicken Lemon Soup

This soup is a heartier rendition of the Greek specialty *avgolemono*, a light soup featuring lemon juice and beaten eggs in a rich chicken broth. Be sure to use low heat once you combine the ingredients, since high heat will curdle the eggs.

- 4 cups chicken broth
- 3 tablespoons quick-cooking rice
- 4 eggs
- ¼ cup lemon juice
- 1 cup shredded cooked chicken; or 1 can (about 5 oz.) boneless chunk chicken, drained and shredded
- 1 lemon, thinly sliced

In a medium-size pan, bring broth to a boil over high heat. Add rice; remove pan from heat, cover, and let stand for 5 minutes.

In a bowl, beat eggs until light and foamy; beat in lemon juice. Gradually add some of the hot broth to egg mixture, beating constantly. Then return all egg mixture to broth in pan and stir in chicken. Stir over low heat until soup is thickened.

To serve, ladle soup into cups or small bowls; garnish with lemon slices. Makes 4 to 6 servings.

Per serving: 154 calories (41 percent from fat), 16 g protein, 7 g carbohydrates, 7 g total fat (2 g saturated fat), 195 mg cholesterol, 868 mg sodium

WESTERN CLASSIC
Mini-pumpkin Soup

Here's an ideal first course for a formal autumn dinner. Hollowed-out tiny pumpkins make whimsical bowls for a creamy pumpkin purée. At the table, you lift the tops from the little "tureens" to reveal the soup inside. (To keep soup hot, rinse shells with boiling water before you fill them.)

- 6 mini-pumpkins (¾ to 1 lb. *each*)
- 2 tablespoons butter or margarine
- 1 large onion, sliced
- 1 large jar (about 4 oz.) diced pimentos, drained
- ¼ teaspoon pepper
- 1¾ cups chicken broth
- 1 cup milk
- Ground nutmeg

Cut a lid about 3 inches in diameter from the top of each pumpkin. Trim undersides of lids to make them about ½ inch thick; reserve pumpkin flesh. Scrape out and discard seeds and strings from pumpkins. With a short, sharp knife, hollow out pumpkins to leave ½-inch-thick shells. Cut up any large pieces of pumpkin flesh. Set aside tops, shells, and flesh.

Melt butter in a 3- to 4-quart pan over medium-high heat. Add onion and cook, stirring often, until soft (about 4 minutes). Add pimentos, pepper, broth, and pumpkin flesh. Bring to a boil over high heat; then reduce heat, cover, and simmer until pumpkin is very tender when pierced (about 15 minutes).

In a blender or food processor, whirl pumpkin mixture until smoothly puréed. Return to pan and stir in milk. Heat soup over medium-high heat, stirring constantly, until steaming.

To serve, fill pumpkin shells with boiling water; then drain well and

place on individual plates. Ladle soup into shells. Sprinkle soup with nutmeg; then cover each shell with a lid. Makes 6 servings.

Per serving: 135 calories (36 percent from fat), 5 g protein, 19 g carbohydrates, 6 g total fat (3 g saturated fat), 16 mg cholesterol, 352 mg sodium

Cambria Corn Chowder

A native of Cambria, California, sent us this recipe in 1978. Serve the savory soup as a first course, or add spicy Italian sausages and offer it as an entrée.

- 3 slices bacon
- 1 large onion, chopped
- 3 mild Italian sausages, thinly sliced (optional)
- 1 large russet potato, peeled and diced
- 1 cup water
- 2 cans (about 17 oz. *each*) cream-style corn
- ⅓ cup canned diced green chiles
- 1 small jar (about 2 oz.) sliced pimentos, drained
- 2 cups milk or half-and-half
- Garlic salt and pepper

Cook bacon in a 4-quart pan over medium heat until crisp. Lift out, drain, crumble, and set aside. Discard all but 2 tablespoons of the drippings. Add onion and sausages (if desired) to pan; cook, stirring often, until onion is soft (about 5 minutes). Stir in potato and water. Bring to a boil over high heat; then reduce heat, cover, and simmer until potato is tender when pierced (about 15 minutes). Stir in corn, chiles, pimentos, and milk. Season to taste with garlic salt and pepper. Heat until steaming; do not boil.

To serve, ladle soup into bowls and garnish with bacon. Makes 6 to 8 servings.

Per serving: 219 calories (28 percent from fat), 6 g protein, 36 g carbohydrates, 7 g total fat (3 g saturated fat), 15 mg cholesterol, 532 mg sodium

Spring Garden Soup

Abundant with fresh spring vegetables, this soup is often included in our readers' lists of favorites: it's pretty to look at, simple to prepare, and tastes delicious. For an easy light supper, serve it with crusty French bread and assorted cheeses.

¼ cup butter or margarine

2 cups diced carrots

1 large can (about 49½ oz.) chicken broth

2 cups (about ¾ lb.) thinly sliced asparagus

½ cup thinly sliced green onions

1 to 2 cups shelled green peas or 1 package (about 10 oz.) frozen peas, thawed

¼ cup minced parsley
Salt and pepper

Melt butter in a deep 5-quart pan over medium-low heat. Add carrots and cook, stirring often, until tender-crisp to bite (5 to 7 minutes). Add broth and bring to a boil over high heat. Add asparagus, onions, and peas. Reduce heat to medium-low, cover, and simmer until asparagus is tender to bite (about 5 minutes). Stir in parsley. Season to taste with salt and pepper.

To serve, ladle soup into bowls or mugs. Makes 8 to 10 servings.

Per serving: 106 calories (51 percent from fat), 5 g protein, 9 g carbohydrates, 6 g total fat (3 g saturated fat), 14 mg cholesterol, 742 mg sodium

Curried Carrot-Peanut Soup

Pungent curry and creamy peanut butter lend Indian and Southeast Asian accents to this savory vegetable soup. To provide a fresh-tasting foil for the rich, nutty flavors, you stir in broccoli flowerets at the end of the cooking time.

1 pound carrots, chopped

6 cups chicken broth

½ cup finely chopped onion

¼ cup creamy peanut butter

1 clove garlic, minced or pressed

2 tablespoons curry powder

¼ cup rice

2 cups (about 6 oz.) small broccoli flowerets

In a 4- to 5-quart pan, combine carrots and 3 cups of the broth. Bring to a boil over high heat; then reduce heat to medium, cover, and boil gently until carrots are very tender to bite (25 to 30 minutes). Drain carrots, reserving broth.

In a blender or food processor, whirl carrots until smoothly puréed. Return purée to pan; add reserved cooking broth and stir until blended. Stir in remaining 3 cups broth, onion, peanut butter, garlic, curry powder, and rice. Bring to a boil over high heat; reduce heat, cover, and simmer, stirring occasionally, until rice is tender to bite (30 to 40 minutes). Add broccoli; cook just until tender when pierced (about 5 minutes). To serve, ladle soup into bowls. Makes 6 servings.

Per serving: 172 calories (37 percent from fat), 9 g protein, 20 g carbohydrates, 7 g total fat (0.9 g saturated fat), 0 mg cholesterol, 1,072 mg sodium

French Onion Soup

A crusty topping of melted cheese and broth-soaked French bread cloaks a wine-accented soup that gets its rich sweetness from caramelized onions.

Dry-toasted French Bread (recipe follows)

2 tablespoons butter or margarine

1 tablespoon olive oil or salad oil

6 large yellow onions (about 3 lbs. *total*), thinly sliced

1 tablespoon all-purpose flour

3 cans (about 14½ oz. *each*) beef broth

1 cup water

⅓ cup dry red wine
Salt and pepper

1 cup (about 4 oz.) shredded Swiss cheese

¼ cup grated Parmesan cheese

Prepare Dry-toasted French Bread; set aside.

Melt butter in oil in a 4-quart pan over medium-low heat. Add onions and cook, stirring occasionally, until very soft and caramel-colored but not browned (30 to 40 minutes). Stir in flour and cook, stirring, until lightly browned (about 2 minutes). Pour in about 1 cup of the broth, stirring to blend. Add remaining broth, water, and wine. Bring to a boil over high heat; then reduce heat, cover, and simmer for 30 minutes. Season to taste with salt and pepper.

Place six 1½- to 2-cup ovenproof soup bowls on a baking sheet; ladle hot soup into bowls. Float a piece of Dry-toasted French Bread on top of each serving; sprinkle equally with Swiss and Parmesan cheeses. Heat in a 425° oven for 10 minutes; then broil 4 to 6 inches below heat until cheese is lightly browned (about 2 minutes). Makes 6 servings.

Dry-toasted French Bread. Trim six ½-inch-thick slices **French bread** to fit inside 1½- to 2-cup ovenproof soup bowls. Place bread on an oven rack. Bake in a 325° oven until lightly toasted (20 to 25 minutes). Spread each slice with **butter** or margarine.

Per serving: 337 calories (47 percent from fat), 13 g protein, 32 g carbohydrates, 18 g total fat (9 g saturated fat), 41 mg cholesterol, 1,048 mg sodium

Tomato Soup with Fresh Basil

Based on a favorite from the Côte d'Azur, this fresh tomato soup is accented with pungent basil. A tablespoon of tiny pasta gives the broth texture and body; choose orzo or riso, or try another shape.

- 3 tablespoons butter or margarine
- 1 large onion, sliced
- 1 large carrot, shredded
- 4 large tomatoes (about 2 lbs. *total*), peeled, seeded, and coarsely chopped
- ¼ cup lightly packed fresh basil leaves
- ¾ teaspoon sugar
- ⅛ teaspoon white pepper
- 1 can (about 14½ oz.) chicken broth
- 1 tablespoon tiny soup pasta, such as orzo or riso
  Salt

Melt butter in a 3- to 4-quart pan over medium heat. Add onion and carrot; cook, stirring often, until onion is soft (about 5 minutes). Stir in tomatoes, basil, sugar, and white pepper. Bring to a boil over high heat, stirring constantly; then reduce heat, cover, and simmer for 10 minutes. In a blender or food processor, whirl soup, a portion at a time, until puréed; return to pan and set aside.

In a small pan, bring broth to a boil over high heat. Add soup pasta; reduce heat to medium and cook just until pasta is tender to bite (about 7 minutes). Stir broth mixture into tomato purée and heat, stirring occasionally, until steaming. Season to taste with salt. To serve, ladle soup into bowls. Makes 6 servings.

Per serving: 117 calories (48 percent from fat), 3 g protein, 13 g carbohydrates, 7 g total fat (4 g saturated fat), 16 mg cholesterol, 376 mg sodium

Baked Split Pea Soup

Lamb shank adds meaty flavor and extra protein to this simple classic from the 1960s. Despite the long cooking time, the soup is quite brothy—don't expect it to be as thick as traditional split pea soup.

- 1 cup dried split peas
- 2 quarts water
- 1 lamb shank (about 1½ lbs.)
- 1 carrot, diced
- 1 onion, sliced
- 1 stalk celery, sliced
- ⅛ teaspoon dry thyme
- ½ dry bay leaf, crumbled
  Salt and pepper

Rinse and sort through peas, discarding any debris. Drain peas; place in a 4- to 5-quart ovenproof pan or casserole. Add water, lamb, carrot, onion, celery, thyme, and bay leaf. Cover and bake in a 300° oven until meat is tender when pierced (3 to 4 hours).

Lift meat from soup; cover pan and return to a low oven to keep warm. Let meat cool briefly. Discard bone and fat; tear meat into bite-size pieces. Return meat to soup and season to taste with salt and pepper. To serve, ladle soup into bowls. Makes 6 servings.

Per serving: 323 calories (36 percent from fat), 26 g protein, 26 g carbohydrates, 13 g total fat (5 g saturated fat), 61 mg cholesterol, 68 mg sodium

Mediterranean Pasta Soup

Tangy lemon peel, thyme, and Italian sausage flavor this variation of classic minestrone. Garnish the hearty cold-weather soup with chunks of fresh tomato and, if you like, shredded Swiss cheese.

- ¼ pound mild Italian sausages, casings removed
- 1 small onion, diced
- 2 cloves garlic, minced or pressed
- 1½ teaspoons dry thyme
- ¼ teaspoon pepper
- ½ cup dried small white beans
- 3 quarts chicken broth
- 1 teaspoon grated lemon peel
- 2 small carrots, diced
- 2 stalks celery, diced
- 1 cup dry small pasta shells
- 1 medium-size tomato, cut into ½-inch cubes
  Shredded Swiss cheese (optional)

Crumble sausage into a 4- to 5-quart pan. Cook over medium-high heat, stirring often, until lightly browned. Add onion, garlic, thyme, and pepper; cook, stirring often, until onion is light golden (about 6 minutes).

Rinse and sort through beans, discarding any debris; drain. Add beans, broth, and lemon peel to pan. Bring to a boil over high heat; then reduce heat, cover, and simmer until beans are tender to bite (about 2 hours).

Add carrots, celery, and pasta to broth mixture. Bring to a boil over high heat; then reduce heat, cover, and simmer until vegetables and pasta are tender to bite (about 15 minutes).

To serve, ladle soup into bowls. Top with tomato and, if desired, sprinkle with cheese. Makes 6 to 8 servings.

Per serving: 216 calories (33 percent from fat), 13 g protein, 24 g carbohydrates, 8 g total fat (2 g saturated fat), 12 mg cholesterol, 1,830 mg sodium

Creamed Barley-Prosciutto Soup

Tiny grains of pearl barley, plumped in the fragrant broth, lend a chewy texture to this simple soup. Thin strips of prosciutto and green peas add touches of bright color—and pleasant flavors, too.

- ¼ **cup butter or margarine**
- ¼ **cup finely chopped shallots**
- 1 **cup pearl barley**
- 1 **large can (about 49½ oz.) chicken broth**
- ¼ **pound prosciutto or other dry-cured ham, cut into thin strips**
- ¼ **teaspoon pepper**
- 1 **cup half-and-half or whipping cream**
- 1 **package (about 10 oz.) frozen tiny peas, thawed**
   Ground nutmeg
   Grated Parmesan cheese

Melt butter in a 5- to 6-quart pan over medium heat. Add shallots and cook, stirring often, until soft (about 3 minutes). Add barley; cook, stirring, until light golden. Stir in broth, prosciutto, and pepper. Bring to a boil over high heat; then reduce heat, cover, and simmer until barley is tender to bite (about 30 minutes). Add half-and-half and peas; cook, stirring occasionally, just until heated through.

To serve, ladle soup into bowls and sprinkle with nutmeg; offer cheese to add to taste. Makes 6 to 8 servings.

Per serving: 287 calories (42 percent from fat), 12 g protein, 30 g carbohydrates, 14 g total fat (7 g saturated fat), 40 mg cholesterol, 1,365 mg sodium

Minestrone Genovese

The cooking of Genoa, on Italy's northern Mediterranean coast, is distinguished by its liberal use of fresh basil. In this classic minestrone, the fragrant herb is used in a pesto sauce that's both stirred into the soup and spooned into individual servings.

   Classic Pesto (page 53)
- 2 **large leeks**
- 3 **quarts chicken broth**
- 2 **large carrots, cut into ½-inch chunks**
- 3 **large stalks celery, thinly sliced**
- 2 **cans (about 15 oz. *each*) cannellini (white kidney beans), drained and rinsed**
- 2 **cups (about 8 oz.) dry elbow macaroni**
- 1 **pound yellow crookneck squash or yellow zucchini, cut into ½-inch chunks**
- 1 **large red bell pepper, seeded and cut into ½-inch pieces**
- 1 **package (about 1 lb.) frozen tiny peas, thawed**
   Salt and pepper

Prepare Classic Pesto; set aside.

Cut off and discard root ends of leeks. Trim tops, leaving about 3 inches of green leaves. Discard coarse outer leaves. Split leeks in half lengthwise and rinse well; then thinly slice crosswise.

In an 8- to 10-quart pan, combine leeks, broth, carrots, and celery. Bring to a boil over high heat; then reduce heat, cover, and simmer for 10 minutes. Add beans, macaroni, squash, and bell pepper.

Return to a boil; then reduce heat, cover, and simmer until macaroni is just tender to bite (about 10 minutes). Add peas; bring to a boil over high heat. Stir ½ cup of the pesto into soup. If made ahead, let cool; then cover and refrigerate until next day. Serve cold or at room temperature, or reheat to serve hot.

To serve, ladle soup into bowls. Offer remaining Classic Pesto, salt, and pepper to add to taste. Makes 10 to 12 servings.

Per serving: 272 calories (23 percent from fat), 15 g protein, 38 g carbohydrates, 7 g total fat (1 g saturated fat), 4 mg cholesterol, 1,348 mg sodium

WESTERN CLASSIC
Garden Fresh Vegetable Soup

Rich beef broth, beans, tomatoes, and shredded greens make a savory base for this hearty soup; you add color and variety with a seasonal selection

MINESTRA

In Italy, *minestra* is the word most often applied to a soup of medium thickness, frequently containing meat and vegetables. *Minestrina* means "little soup"—one based on a thin broth. *Minestrone* refers to a thick vegetable soup, usually including pasta and sometimes peas or beans. It's generally hearty enough to serve as a main course.

of fresh vegetables. With or without meat, the dish is filling enough for a full meal.

½ **pound lean ground beef (optional)**

4 **slices bacon, chopped (optional)**

3 **tablespoons butter or margarine (if not using meat)**

1 **large onion, chopped**

2 **cloves garlic, minced or pressed**

6 **cups prepared vegetables, such as diced or sliced carrots; chopped or sliced celery; cut green beans; diced new potatoes; peas; corn kernels; and sliced zucchini or crookneck squash**

2 **quarts beef broth**

1 **can (about 15 oz.) red kidney beans, drained and rinsed**

½ **teaspoon *each* dry basil, dry oregano, and dry rosemary**

1 **can (about 8 oz.) tomato sauce**

2 **large tomatoes, seeded and chopped**

⅔ **cup dry elbow macaroni (or dry spaghetti, broken into pieces)**

2 **cups shredded cabbage, spinach, or chard**

Salt and pepper

Grated Parmesan cheese

If using beef and bacon, crumble beef into a deep 5- to 6-quart pan; add bacon. Cook over medium heat, stirring often, until fat is rendered—3 to 5 minutes. (If not using meat, melt butter in pan over medium heat.) Add onion, garlic, and prepared vegetables to pan; cook, stirring often, until beef loses its pink color and onion is soft (about 5 minutes).

Discard fat from pan. Add broth, kidney beans, basil, oregano, and rosemary. Bring to a simmer; cover and simmer for about 30 minutes.

Add tomato sauce, tomatoes, and macaroni to pan. Return to a simmer; cover and simmer until macaroni is tender to bite—10 to 15 minutes. (At this point, you may let cool, then cover and refrigerate until next day; reheat before continuing.)

Stir cabbage into soup; cover and simmer just until wilted (about 5 minutes). Season to taste with salt and pepper. To serve, ladle soup into bowls; offer cheese to add to taste. Makes 8 servings.

Per serving: 224 calories (25 percent from fat), 10 g protein, 34 g carbohydrates, 6 g total fat (3 g saturated fat), 12 mg cholesterol, 1,139 mg sodium

Sour Cream Spinach Soup with Corned Beef Brisket

The first version of our enduringly popular puréed spinach soup was published in July 1955. It's still as tasty as ever—and with blenders and food processors in today's kitchens, it's also exceptionally easy to make. This version starts with boiled beef brisket; the brisket broth makes the soup base, while the sliced meat can be used in sandwiches to round out a classic meal. (For a shortcut, purchase the brisket cooked and use canned chicken broth to make the soup.)

4 **pounds corned beef brisket (preferably center-cut)**

1 **dry bay leaf**

1 **cinnamon stick (3 to 4 inches long)**

1 **small dried hot red chile**

½ **teaspoon *each* whole coriander, whole allspice, and mustard seeds**

1 **large onion, sliced**

2 **packages (about 10 oz. *each*) frozen chopped spinach**

2 **cups sour cream or plain yogurt; or 1 cup *each* sour cream and plain yogurt**

Rinse corned beef well under cold running water, then place meat in a 6- to 8-quart pan. Cover with 2 quarts water and bring to a boil; drain and cover with 2 more quarts water. Bring

to a boil over high heat; then reduce heat so liquid simmers. Add bay leaf, cinnamon stick, chile, coriander, allspice, mustard seeds, and onion. Cover and simmer until meat is very tender when pierced (about 4 hours). Skim and discard fat from broth.

Dip out 4 cups of the broth and pour through a fine wire strainer set over a bowl; discard residue. Taste broth. If it's too salty, discard it; instead, use 2 cans (about 14½ oz. *each*) chicken broth. Keep brisket hot; or let cool, then cover and refrigerate.

Combine the 4 cups broth with spinach in a 3- to 4-quart pan. Bring to a boil, breaking spinach apart as quickly as possible. Whirl spinach mixture, a portion at a time, in a blender or food processor until puréed. While blending, add sour cream to one portion of the spinach mixture.

Return all soup to pan; stir well. Reheat, if needed; do not boil. Or cover and refrigerate to serve cold. Strain remaining brisket broth; stir into chilled soup as desired for a thinner consistency, or use in other soups. Slice brisket to use in sandwiches. Makes 6 to 8 servings.

Per serving of soup: 184 calories (67 percent from fat), 5 g protein, 10 g carbohydrates, 15 g total fat (9 g saturated fat), 29 mg cholesterol, 550 mg sodium

Per serving of meat: 213 calories (70 percent from fat), 15 g protein, 0.4 g carbohydrates, 16 g total fat (5 g saturated fat), 83 mg cholesterol, 964 mg sodium

Eggplant Supper Soup

A favorite among *Sunset* staff and readers since 1967, this soup serves up a full meal in a single bowl. The diced eggplant soaks up the broth like a sponge, absorbing the rich flavors of beef, spices, and vegetables.

2 tablespoons butter or margarine

2 tablespoons olive oil or salad oil

1 medium-size onion, chopped

1 pound lean ground beef

1 medium-size eggplant (about 1 lb.), unpeeled, diced

1 clove garlic, minced or pressed

½ cup *each* chopped carrot and sliced celery

1 large can (about 28 oz.) tomatoes

2 cans (about 14½ oz. *each*) beef broth

1 teaspoon sugar

½ teaspoon *each* pepper and ground nutmeg

½ cup dry salad macaroni

2 tablespoons minced parsley
   Salt
   Grated Parmesan cheese

Melt butter in oil in a deep 4- to 5-quart pan over medium heat. Add onion and cook, stirring often, until soft (about 5 minutes). Crumble in beef and cook, stirring often, until lightly browned. Stir in eggplant, garlic, carrot, and celery. Cut up tomatoes; stir in tomatoes and their liquid, broth, sugar, pepper, and nutmeg. Bring to a boil over high heat; then reduce heat, cover, and simmer for about 30 minutes. Add macaroni and parsley; simmer, uncovered, until macaroni is tender to bite (about 10 minutes). Season to taste with salt.

To serve, ladle soup into bowls; offer cheese to add to taste. Makes 6 to 8 servings.

Per serving: 329 calories (59 percent from fat), 16 g protein, 19 g carbohydrates, 22 g total fat (8 g saturated fat), 58 mg cholesterol, 706 mg sodium

Meatball Minestrone

Light-textured beef-and-spinach meatballs are the flavor starter for this busy-day minestrone. Whimsical bow-shaped or corkscrew pasta cooks right in the broth.

   Spinach Meatballs (recipe follows)

1 tablespoon salad oil

1 large onion, chopped

7 cups beef broth

1 can (about 14½ oz.) stewed tomatoes

1 can (about 15 oz.) red kidney beans

½ teaspoon *each* dry oregano and dry basil

1 cup *each* sliced carrots and sliced celery

1 cup dry pasta bow ties or pasta twists

Prepare Spinach Meatballs. Heat oil in a 4- to 5-quart pan over medium heat. Add meatballs and cook, turning as needed, until browned on all sides. Remove from pan and set aside.

Add onion to pan and cook, stirring often, until soft (about 5 minutes). Stir in broth, tomatoes, beans and their liquid, oregano, and basil. Bring to a boil over high heat; then reduce heat, cover, and simmer for 10 minutes. Add carrots and celery. Cover and simmer for 10 more minutes.

Stir in pasta; cover and simmer until tender to bite (about 10 minutes). Skim and discard fat from soup. Add Spinach Meatballs and heat until soup is steaming and meatballs are heated through. To serve, ladle soup into bowls. Makes 6 servings.

Spinach Meatballs. In a large bowl, thoroughly mix 1 package (about 10 oz.) **frozen chopped spinach,** thawed and squeezed dry; 1½ pounds **lean ground beef;** ⅓ cup **fine dry bread crumbs;** 1 **egg;** ½ teaspoon **salt;** and ¼ teaspoon **pepper.** Shape mixture into 1-inch balls.

Per serving: 519 calories (50 percent from fat), 32 g protein, 34 g carbohydrates, 29 g total fat (10 g saturated fat), 121 mg cholesterol, 1,755 mg sodium

Hamburger Soup

This hearty stew has a permanent place in the ranks of time-honored *Sunset* favorites. Vegetables, macaroni, split peas, and 2 pounds of ground beef combine in a filling one-pot meal for eight.

2 tablespoons olive oil or salad oil

2 pounds lean ground beef

¼ teaspoon *each* pepper, dry oregano, and dry basil

⅛ teaspoon seasoned salt

1 envelope (1 to 1½ oz.) onion soup mix
   About 6 cups water

1 can (about 8 oz.) tomato sauce

1 tablespoon soy sauce

1 cup sliced celery

¼ cup coarsely chopped celery leaves

1 cup sliced carrots

⅓ cup dried split peas

1 cup dry elbow macaroni
   Salt
   Grated Parmesan cheese

Heat oil in a deep 4- to 5-quart pan over medium-high heat. Crumble in beef and cook, stirring often, until browned. Add pepper, oregano, basil, seasoned salt, and onion soup mix. Stir in 6 cups of the water, tomato sauce, and soy sauce. Bring to a boil; then reduce heat, cover, and simmer for about 15 minutes. Add celery, celery leaves, carrots, and peas; cover and simmer for 30 more minutes. Add macaroni, cover, and simmer until tender to bite (10 to 15 minutes); add more water, if needed. Season to taste with salt.

To serve, ladle soup into bowls; offer cheese to add to taste. Makes 8 servings.

Per serving: 440 calories (57 percent from fat), 25 g protein, 22 g carbohydrates, 27 g total fat (10 g saturated fat), 85 mg cholesterol, 795 mg sodium

Italian Sausage Soup

Serve this chunky sausage soup with crisp breadsticks, a big green salad, and a carafe of red wine.

1½ **pounds mild Italian sausages, cut into ½-inch-thick slices**

2 **cloves garlic, minced or pressed**

2 **large onions, chopped**

1 **large can (about 28 oz.) Italian-seasoned tomatoes**

3 **cans (about 14½ oz. *each*) beef broth**

1½ **cups dry red wine or water**

½ **teaspoon dry basil**

3 **tablespoons chopped parsley**

1 **medium-size green bell pepper, seeded and chopped**

2 **medium-size zucchini, cut into ½-inch-thick slices**

3 **cups (about 5 oz.) dry pasta bow ties**

Grated Parmesan cheese

Cook sausage slices in a deep 5-quart pan over medium-high heat, stirring often, until lightly browned. Lift out sausage with a slotted spoon and set aside. Discard all but 3 tablespoons of the fat from pan. Add garlic and onions to pan; cook over medium heat, stirring often, until onions are soft (about 5 minutes).

Cut up tomatoes; then add tomatoes and their liquid to pan. Add sausage slices, broth, wine, and basil; stir to combine. Bring to a boil; then reduce heat, cover, and simmer for 20 minutes. Stir in parsley, bell pepper, zucchini, and pasta. Cover and simmer, stirring occasionally, until pasta and zucchini are tender to bite (10 to 15 minutes). Skim and discard fat from soup.

To serve, ladle soup into bowls; offer cheese to add to taste. Makes 6 servings.

Per serving: 505 calories (50 percent from fat), 24 g protein, 39 g carbohydrates, 28 g total fat (9 g saturated fat), 69 mg cholesterol, 2,020 mg sodium

Kraut & Rib Soup

Reminiscent of the tart, earthy-flavored dishes of Eastern Europe, this peasant-style soup is a great choice for supper on cold days. Long, slow cooking is the key to success with the recipe, so be sure to get started well ahead of serving time.

3 **to 3½ pounds country-style pork spareribs, trimmed of fat**

3 **tablespoons white wine vinegar**

2 **tablespoons salad oil**

1 **large onion, thinly sliced**

1 **teaspoon caraway seeds**

2 **dry bay leaves**

1 **large jar (about 27 oz.) sauerkraut, drained and rinsed**

½ **pound cabbage, shredded**

½ **cup pearl barley**

1 **can (about 14½ oz.) tomatoes**

2 **quarts beef broth**

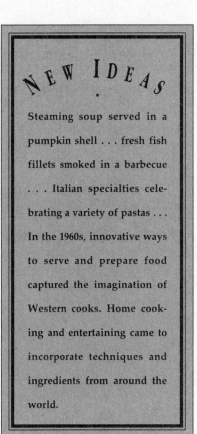

Cook ribs in a deep 6- to 8-quart pan over medium-high heat, turning as needed, until browned on all sides (about 25 minutes). Remove ribs from pan; set aside.

Add vinegar to pan and stir to scrape browned bits free. Add oil, onion, caraway seeds, and bay leaves. Cook, stirring, until onion is translucent (about 3 minutes). Stir in sauerkraut, cabbage, and barley. Cut up tomatoes; stir tomatoes and their liquid into cabbage mixture.

Return ribs to pan. Pour in broth. Bring to a boil over high heat; then reduce heat, cover, and simmer until meat pulls easily from bones (2½ to 3 hours). Skim and discard fat from soup. If made ahead, let cool; then cover and refrigerate for up to 3 days. Reheat before serving. To serve, ladle soup into bowls. Makes 6 servings.

Per serving: 515 calories (62 percent from fat), 24 g protein, 25 g carbohydrates, 36 g total fat (11 g saturated fat), 84 mg cholesterol, 1,566 mg sodium

Chicken & Capellini Soup

Delicate in flavor yet satisfyingly sturdy, this comforting soup was developed in *Sunset*'s test kitchens during the 1980s.

- 4 skinless, boneless chicken breast halves (about 1½ lbs. *total*)
- 2 tablespoons butter or margarine
- ¼ cup finely chopped shallots
- 1 clove garlic, minced or pressed
- ¼ teaspoon dry thyme
- ⅛ teaspoon white pepper
- 1 can (about 14½ oz.) chicken broth
- 1½ cups water
- ½ cup dry white wine
- 1 medium-size carrot, thinly sliced
- 2 ounces dry capellini (angel hair pasta), broken in half
- 2 cups shredded Swiss chard
- 1 medium-size tomato, seeded and chopped
  Salt
  Grated Parmesan cheese

Rinse chicken, pat dry, and cut into bite-size pieces. Set aside.

Melt butter in a deep 3- to 4-quart pan over medium heat. Add shallots and cook, stirring often, until soft (about 3 minutes). Stir in garlic, thyme, white pepper, and chicken. Cook, stirring often, until chicken is no longer pink (about 3 minutes). Add broth, water, wine, and carrot. Bring to a boil over high heat; then reduce heat, cover, and boil gently until carrot is tender to bite (about 5 minutes).

Add capellini. Bring to a boil over high heat; boil, stirring often, until pasta is barely tender to bite (4 to 5 minutes). Add chard and tomato; cover, remove from heat, and let stand just until tomato is heated through (about 2 minutes). Season soup to taste with salt.

To serve, ladle soup into bowls; offer cheese to add to taste. Makes 4 servings.

Per serving: 349 calories (25 percent from fat), 44 g protein, 17 g carbohydrates, 9 g total fat (4 g saturated fat), 114 mg cholesterol, 667 mg sodium

Tortellini & Chicken Soup

Succulent cheese-filled tortellini and chunks of tender chicken add heartiness to this homey favorite. It's a good choice for a lowfat lunch.

- 1 pound skinless, boneless chicken breasts
- 4½ quarts or 3 large cans (about 49½ oz. *each*) chicken broth
- 1 package (about 9 oz.) fresh cheese-filled spinach tortellini
- 1 pound spinach, rinsed well, stems removed, and leaves coarsely chopped
- ½ pound mushrooms, sliced
- 1 medium-size red bell pepper, seeded and diced
- 1 cup cooked rice
- 2 teaspoons dry tarragon
  Grated Parmesan cheese (optional)

Rinse chicken, pat dry, and cut into ½-inch chunks. Set aside.

Pour broth into an 8- to 10-quart pan; cover and bring to a boil over high heat. Add tortellini; reduce heat to medium and boil gently, uncovered, just until tortellini are tender to bite (about 6 minutes). Add chicken, spinach, mushrooms, bell pepper, rice, and tarragon; return to a boil over high heat. Reduce heat, cover, and simmer until chicken is no longer pink in center; cut to test (about 2 minutes).

To serve, ladle soup into bowls; offer cheese to add to taste, if desired. Makes 10 to 12 servings.

Per serving: 197 calories (19 percent from fat), 20 g protein, 20 g carbohydrates, 4 g total fat (0.2 g saturated fat), 37 mg cholesterol, 1,773 mg sodium

Turkey Soup

The soup of choice for post-holiday turkey adventures, this light poultry-vegetable stock makes savory use of the bird's remains. The bones contribute rich flavor; the meat adds substance and texture. Stir in a generous helping of sweet napa cabbage and serve the soup on its own as a luncheon dish. Or, if you prefer, omit the cabbage and use the broth as a base for a variety of homemade soups.

- 1 roasted turkey carcass with some meat attached
- 2½ quarts water
- 1 medium-size onion, sliced
- 1 medium-size carrot, sliced
- 5 cups finely shredded napa cabbage
  Salt and pepper
  Chopped parsley

Strip turkey carcass of any large pieces of meat; dice enough meat to make 2 cups and set aside.

In a 5- to 6-quart pan, combine turkey carcass, water, onion, and carrot. Bring to a boil over high heat; then reduce heat, cover, and simmer for 2 hours. Let cool slightly, then pour through a fine wire strainer set over a bowl. Remove any remaining meat from bones; stir into broth along with diced turkey meat. Discard vegetables and bones.

Return broth mixture to pan. Skim and discard any fat from broth; then bring to a boil over high heat. Add cabbage; reduce heat, cover, and simmer until cabbage is tender to bite (about 10 minutes). Season to taste with salt and pepper.

To serve, ladle soup into bowls; garnish with parsley. Makes 8 servings.

Per serving: 100 calories (30 percent from fat), 13 g protein, 4 g carbohydrates, 3 g total fat (0.9 g saturated fat), 27 mg cholesterol, 85 mg sodium

Few culinary disputes have raged as hotly as the debate over the origin of Western chili. Some say the fiery brew was invented by enterprising cowboys, bent on disguising the tough, unaged beef of the Southwestern cattle trail with a passel of the region's chile peppers. But others believe the Aztecs created the first authentic chili centuries earlier, during the time of the Spanish conquistadores.

In fact, regional dishes of chiles, beans, and herbs were known to the Incas, Aztecs, and Mayas long before the days of Columbus or the conquistadores. But it was the cattle drovers and trail hands moving through small Texas towns in the early 1800s who did the most to popularize the modern-day dish. Even Frank and Jesse James are known to have slugged down a few bowls of "red" before saddling up for their now-legendary bank heists and train robberies.

Sunset has published numerous chili recipes, many of them contributed by readers from across the West. Here, we present two of our favorites: a red beef chili and a meatless green dish made with bell peppers, tomatillos, and two kinds of chiles.

Green, Green Pepper Chili

3   tablespoons olive oil or salad oil
4   large onions (about 2 lbs. *total*), sliced
2   cloves garlic, minced or pressed
4   large green bell peppers (about 2 lbs. *total*), halved and seeded
2   large cans (about 7 oz. *each*) whole green chiles, drained and split
1   tablespoon dry oregano

2   cans (about 13 oz. *each*) tomatillos
6   cups chicken broth
4   fresh jalapeño chiles (*each* about 3 inches long), seeded and minced
½   cup chopped cilantro
    Shredded jalapeño jack cheese
    Sour cream or plain yogurt
    Cilantro sprigs

Heat oil in 6- to 8-quart pan over medium-low heat. Add onions and garlic and cook until onions are very soft and golden (about 30 minutes); stir occasionally at first, then more often as onions begin to turn golden. Onions should not show signs of browning during the first 15 minutes; if they do, reduce heat. Meanwhile, thinly slice bell peppers and green chiles crosswise.

When onions are golden, stir in bell peppers, green chiles, oregano, tomatillos and their liquid, broth, and jalapeño chiles. Bring to a boil over high heat; reduce heat, cover, and simmer until bell peppers are very tender to bite (about 15 minutes). If made ahead, let cool; cover and refrigerate for up to 2 days. Reheat before serving.

Just before serving, stir in chopped cilantro. To serve, ladle into bowls; offer cheese, sour cream, and cilantro sprigs to add to taste. Makes 8 servings.

Per serving: 172 calories (33 percent from fat), 6 g protein, 25 g carbohydrates, 7 g total fat (0.8 g saturated fat), 0 mg cholesterol, 1,136 mg sodium

Not-just-any-chili Chili

2   pounds lean ground beef
1   large onion, coarsely chopped
1   large can (about 28 oz.) tomatoes
1   can (about 15 oz.) tomato purée
2   cans (about 15 oz. *each*) red kidney beans, drained and rinsed
3   tablespoons *each* Worcestershire and aromatic bitters
1   can (about 12 oz.) beer
3   cloves garlic, minced or pressed
1   beef bouillon cube
1   teaspoon crushed red pepper flakes
2   dry bay leaves
1   tablespoon chili powder
1   teaspoon *each* ground coriander, ground cumin, dry thyme, dry oregano, and dry basil
    Shredded Cheddar cheese
    Sour cream
    Sliced green onions

Crumble beef into a deep 5- to 6-quart pan. Cook over medium heat, stirring often, until browned. Add chopped onion and cook, stirring often, until soft (about 5 minutes). Coarsely chop tomatoes; then stir in tomatoes and their liquid, tomato purée, beans, Worcestershire, bitters, beer, garlic, bouillon cube, red pepper flakes, bay leaves, chili powder, coriander, cumin, thyme, oregano, and basil.

Bring to a boil; then reduce heat and simmer, uncovered, stirring occasionally, until chili is thick and flavors are well blended (about 2 hours). Skim and discard fat from chili. To serve, ladle chili into bowls. Offer cheese, sour cream, and green onions to add to taste. Makes 6 to 8 servings.

Per serving: 444 calories (40 percent from fat), 32 g protein, 32 g carbohydrates, 19 g total fat (7 g saturated fat), 79 mg cholesterol, 859 mg sodium

Spiced Lentil & Barley Soup

Two standard soup ingredients—tiny lentils and hearty barley—meet in a chunky, salsa-spiced soup that's ideal for a cold-weather supper. Shredded chicken breast and morsels of sausage make this one-dish meal especially satisfying.

2   **chicken breast halves (about 1 lb.** *total***)**

½   **pound Italian sausages, casings removed**

1   **medium-size onion, chopped**

3   **cloves garlic, minced or pressed**

⅓   **cup pearl barley**

2   **quarts chicken broth**

½   **cup minced parsley**

1   **cup lentils**

1   **can (about 15 oz.) garbanzo beans, drained and rinsed**

1   **jar (about 12 oz.) chile salsa**

1   **pound spinach, rinsed well, stems removed, and leaves coarsely chopped**

Rinse chicken, pat dry, and set aside.

Crumble sausage into a 5- to 6-quart pan. Cook over medium heat, stirring often, until browned. Remove meat from pan with a slotted spoon; set aside. Add onion, garlic, and barley to fat in pan. Cook, stirring often, until onion is soft and barley is toasted (about 5 minutes). Add broth, parsley, chicken, and lentils. Bring to a boil over high heat. Then reduce heat, cover, and simmer until meat in thickest part of chicken is no longer pink; cut to test (about 30 minutes).

Remove chicken from pan and let cool briefly. Discard skin and bones; shred meat and return to pan. Add sausage, beans, and salsa. Bring to a simmer; stir in spinach. To serve, ladle soup into bowls. Makes 6 servings.

Per serving: 554 calories (33 percent from fat), 38 g protein, 57 g carbohydrates, 20 g total fat (6 g saturated fat), 61 mg cholesterol, 2,511 mg sodium

WESTERN CLASSIC
Browny's Clam Chowder

This chowder was a specialty of Browny's Seafood Broiler in Richmond Beach, just north of Seattle. The restaurant is no longer in business—but you can still enjoy the soup any time.

6   **slices bacon, chopped**

2   **medium-size carrots, thinly sliced**

2   **stalks celery, thinly sliced**

1   **small onion, chopped**

½   **small green bell pepper, seeded and chopped**

1   **clove garlic, minced or pressed**

1½   **pounds red thin-skinned potatoes, scrubbed and diced**

2   **bottles (about 8 oz.** *each***) clam juice**

8   **cans (about 6½ oz.** *each***) chopped clams**

1   **dry bay leaf**

½   **teaspoon liquid hot pepper seasoning**

¼   **teaspoon pepper**

1½   **teaspoons Worcestershire**

¾   **teaspoon dry thyme**

4   **cups half-and-half**
    Salt

Cook bacon in an 8- to 10-quart pan over medium heat until crisp, stirring often. Lift out with a slotted spoon, drain, and set aside. Discard all but 2 tablespoons of the drippings from pan. Add carrots, celery, onion, bell pepper, and garlic to pan; cook, stirring often, until vegetables are lightly browned (about 10 minutes).

Add potatoes and clam juice to pan. Bring to a boil over high heat; then reduce heat, cover, and simmer until potatoes are tender when pierced (about 15 minutes). Stir in clams and their liquid, bay leaf, hot pepper seasoning, pepper, Worcestershire, thyme, half-and-half, and bacon. Season to taste with salt. Heat until steaming, then ladle into bowls. Makes 8 to 10 servings.

Per serving: 386 calories (43 percent from fat), 29 g protein, 26 g carbohydrates, 18 g total fat (9 g saturated fat), 102 mg cholesterol, 371 mg sodium

Western Shellfish Bourride

Despite its name, this knife-and-fork soup is actually more akin to the tomato-based Italian-style *cioppino* than to the seafood *bourride* of southern France. The Western accent comes from meaty Dungeness crab and small Pacific oysters.

  Vegetable Clam Stock (recipe follows)

¼   **cup butter or margarine**

¾   **pound mushrooms, sliced**

1   **small jar (about 2 oz.) sliced pimentos, drained**

24   **to 36 small hard-shell clams, scrubbed; or 2 medium-size live or cooked Dungeness crabs (1½ to 2 lbs.** *each***), cracked; or some of each**

2   **pounds halibut or lingcod steaks or fillets**

1   **pound medium-size raw shrimp, shelled and deveined**

1   **jar (about 10 oz.) small Pacific oysters, drained**

  Buttered toasted French bread slices

  Grated Parmesan cheese

Prepare Vegetable Clam Stock. Bring to a simmer over medium-low heat.

Melt butter in a wide frying pan over medium heat; add mushrooms and cook, stirring occasionally, until soft (about 5 minutes). Add mushrooms, pimentos, and uncooked crab (if used) to simmering Vegetable Clam Stock; simmer, uncovered, for 5 minutes. Add clams (if used); simmer for 10 more minutes. Meanwhile, remove any skin and bones from fish; rinse fish, pat dry, and cut into pieces about 2 inches square. Add to stock; simmer for 2 more minutes. Add shrimp, oysters, and cooked crab (if used). Simmer until shrimp are opaque in center; cut to test (about 3 minutes).

To serve, ladle soup into shallow bowls. Serve with bread and cheese. Makes 8 to 10 servings.

Vegetable Clam Stock. Heat ¼ cup **olive oil** in a deep 8-quart pan over medium heat. Add 1 cup chopped **onion;** cook, stirring often, until golden (about 7 minutes). Add 5 cloves **garlic** (minced or pressed) and ⅓ cup minced **carrot;** cook, stirring often, until lightly browned. Coarsely chop tomatoes from 2 large cans (about 28 oz. *each*) **tomatoes;** stir in tomatoes and their liquid, 3 bottles (about 8 oz. *each*) **clam juice,** 1½ cups **dry white wine,** 2 **dry bay leaves,** ⅛ teaspoon crushed **fennel seeds,** ¼ cup chopped **parsley,** ½ teaspoon *each* **salt** and **pepper,** ¼ teaspoon **dry thyme,** and ¼ teaspoon **saffron threads,** if desired. Bring to a boil; then reduce heat, cover, and simmer for 15 minutes. If made ahead, let cool; then cover and refrigerate for up to 2 days.

Per serving: 402 calories (38 percent from fat), 42 g protein, 16 g carbohydrates, 16 g total fat (5 g saturated fat), 142 mg cholesterol, 817 mg sodium

Peach & Plum Soup

Here's a light soup you can serve as either first course or dessert. Stir tart yogurt into the fruit purée and you have a refreshing starter for a warm-weather meal; add whipping cream or sour cream, and you've created a smooth, velvety, and sophisticated ending for a special dinner.

¾ **pound peaches or nectarines**
¾ **pound red-skinned plums**
1 **cup *each* water and dry white wine**
1 **cinnamon stick (about 2 inches long)**
1½ **tablespoons lemon juice**
⅓ **to ½ cup granulated sugar**
1 **tablespoon cornstarch blended with 1 tablespoon cold water**
¼ **cup orange- or peach-flavored liqueur (optional)**
1 **cup whipping cream, sour cream, or plain yogurt**
Powdered sugar (optional)

Peel and pit peaches and plums; then cut fruit into chunks and place in a 3- to 4-quart pan. Add water, wine, cinnamon stick, and lemon juice. Bring to a boil over high heat; then reduce heat, cover, and simmer until fruit mashes easily (about 15 minutes). Remove from heat; remove and discard cinnamon stick.

In a food processor or blender, whirl fruit mixture, a portion at a time, until smooth. Return to pan and stir in granulated sugar. Then stir in cornstarch mixture; cook over high heat, stirring, until mixture is thickened (about 5 minutes). Remove from heat and let cool slightly. Skim off and discard any foam. Add liqueur (if desired) and ½ cup of the whipping cream. (If using sour cream or yogurt, beat ½ cup with a wire whisk until smooth; then whisk into soup until smoothly blended.) Cover soup and refrigerate until cold.

Beat remaining ½ cup whipping cream just until it holds soft peaks; sweeten with powdered sugar, if desired. (Or sweeten remaining ½ cup sour cream or yogurt to taste with powdered sugar.) To serve, ladle soup into bowls; pass sweetened cream at the table to spoon into individual servings. Makes 4 servings.

Per serving: 377 calories (48 percent from fat), 2 g protein, 43 g carbohydrates, 19 g total fat (12 g saturated fat), 66 mg cholesterol, 25 mg sodium

Apricot Soup

Follow directions for **Peach & Plum Soup,** but omit peaches and plums; instead, use 1½ pounds **apricots,** pitted but not peeled. Substitute **apricot- or almond-flavored liqueur** for orange-flavored liqueur. Increase granulated sugar to ¾ to 1 cup. Makes 4 servings.

Per serving: 470 calories (38 percent from fat), 4 g protein, 66 g carbohydrates, 19 g total fat (12 g saturated fat), 66 mg cholesterol, 27 mg sodium

Cherry Soup

Follow directions for **Peach & Plum Soup,** but omit peaches and plums; instead, use 1½ pounds **Bing cherries,** pitted. Substitute **kirsch** for orange-flavored liqueur. Reduce granulated sugar to ¼ to ⅓ cup. Makes 4 servings.

Per serving: 390 calories (49 percent from fat), 3 g protein, 44 g carbohydrates, 20 g total fat (12 g saturated fat), 66 mg cholesterol, 25 mg sodium

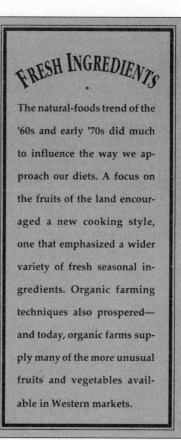

FRESH INGREDIENTS

The natural-foods trend of the '60s and early '70s did much to influence the way we approach our diets. A focus on the fruits of the land encouraged a new cooking style, one that emphasized a wider variety of fresh seasonal ingredients. Organic farming techniques also prospered—and today, organic farms supply many of the more unusual fruits and vegetables available in Western markets.

*F*resh! That's the first word that comes to mind in describing Western cuisine. And nowhere is freshness more apparent than in our salads, creative dishes that show off seasonal produce at its best • Through the years, we've tracked the fresh trend, introducing many lesser-known fruits and vegetables to our readers and offering ideas for using them—often in salads. We've also paid special attention to the classics that helped put western America on the culinary map, among them Cobb and Caesar salads (both included in this chapter). • The following pages highlight the abundance and ethnic influence that have become synonymous with Western cooking. From satisfying entrées to colorful side-dish compositions of vegetables and greens, we offer over 30 traditional and contemporary favorites.

Caesar Salad

Caesar Salad is said to have been created in 1924 by Caesar Cardini, an Italian chef and restaurant owner. Countless variations of the classic dish are served today—but this one, made with the traditional coddled-egg dressing, is a close adaptation of the original. (You may prefer to use our egg-safe recipe; for more on egg safety, see page 56.)

1 **small clove garlic, minced or pressed**

⅓ cup **olive oil or salad oil**

1 cup **purchased or homemade croutons**

1 **large head romaine lettuce, broken into bite-size pieces, rinsed, and crisped (you should have about 3 quarts)**

1 **egg**
   About 2 tablespoons **lemon juice**

3 or 4 **canned anchovy fillets, drained and chopped**

¼ cup **grated Parmesan cheese**
   Salt and pepper

In a small bowl, combine garlic and oil; if time permits, let mixture stand for several hours. Heat 2 tablespoons of the garlic-flavored oil in a wide frying pan over medium heat; add croutons and cook, stirring often, until browned. Set aside.

Place lettuce in a serving bowl. Pour remaining garlic oil over lettuce and toss until leaves are thoroughly coated.

Bring a small pan of water to a boil over high heat. Add egg and boil for 1 minute; remove and break into salad. Drizzle lemon juice over all and toss to coat evenly. Add anchovies, cheese, and croutons; toss gently. Season to taste with salt and pepper. Makes 6 servings.

Per serving: 197 calories (67 percent from fat), 6 g protein, 10 g carbohydrates, 15 g total fat (3 g saturated fat), 39 mg cholesterol, 268 mg sodium

Egg-safe Caesar Salad

Start by preparing this egg-safe dressing: mix 1 **egg white** with 2 tablespoons **lemon juice.** Cover airtight and refrigerate for at least 48 hours or up to 4 days (upon longer standing, egg begins to solidify). In a blender or food processor, whirl egg white with 2 tablespoons **lemon juice,** ½ cup **olive oil** or salad oil, 2 teaspoons **Worcestershire,** and ⅛ teaspoon **freshly ground pepper.** Finely chop 6 to 8 drained **canned anchovy fillets** and add to dressing.

To make salad, prepare croutons and lettuce as directed for **Caesar Salad,** but do not pour remaining garlic oil over lettuce (reserve it for other uses). Place croutons, lettuce, and ¼ cup grated **Parmesan cheese** in a large bowl; pour in dressing and toss to mix. Season to taste with **salt** and **pepper.** Makes 6 servings.

Per serving: 249 calories (73 percent from fat), 7 g protein, 10 g carbohydrates, 20 g total fat (3 g saturated fat), 5 mg cholesterol, 372 mg sodium

Spinach Salad with Pine Nut Dressing

Tossed with toasted pine nuts and a hint of lemon, fresh spinach takes on a Mediterranean flavor.

⅔ cup **pine nuts or slivered almonds**

7 tablespoons **olive oil or salad oil**

2½ tablespoons **wine vinegar**

⅛ teaspoon **ground nutmeg**

½ teaspoon *each* grated **lemon peel and dry tarragon**

1½ pounds **spinach, rinsed well, stems removed**
   Salt

Spread pine nuts in a shallow baking pan and toast in a 350° oven, stirring occasionally, until lightly browned (5 to 8 minutes). Let cool.

In a bowl, combine pine nuts, oil, vinegar, nutmeg, lemon peel, and tarragon. Cover and let stand at room temperature for at least 30 minutes or until next day.

To serve, select large leaves from spinach and use to line 8 salad plates. Cut remaining leaves into thin slivers; mound on plates. Stir dressing to blend, then drizzle over salads. Season to taste with salt. Makes 8 servings.

Per serving: 181 calories (82 percent from fat), 5 g protein, 4 g carbohydrates, 18 g total fat (3 g saturated fat), 0 mg cholesterol, 50 mg sodium

Cucumbers in Sour Cream

Easy to prepare and deliciously simple, this unassuming salad is a long-time favorite. It's a natural partner for fish; try it alongside Salmon Fillet with Mustard Glaze (page 117).

3 **large cucumbers, peeled and cut into ⅛-inch-thick slices**

1 teaspoon **salt**

1 cup **sour cream**

⅓ cup **mayonnaise**

1 tablespoon **tarragon wine vinegar**

2 **green onions, thinly sliced**

1 tablespoon **finely minced parsley**

1 **clove garlic, minced or pressed**

1 teaspoon **Worcestershire**

In a bowl, stir together cucumbers and salt. Let stand for 15 minutes; drain well on paper towels.

In another bowl, stir together sour cream, mayonnaise, and vinegar. Stir in onions, parsley, garlic, and Worcestershire. Add cucumbers and stir to coat. Cover and refrigerate for at least 2 hours. Serve cold. Makes 6 to 8 servings.

Per serving: 165 calories (81 percent from fat), 2 g protein, 6 g carbohydrates, 15 g total fat (6 g saturated fat), 21 mg cholesterol, 407 mg sodium

Spinach Salad with Bacon & Apples

For this traditional salad, choose spinach with crisp, dark green leaves.

- 6 slices bacon
- ⅓ cup sliced almonds
- ¼ cup olive oil or salad oil
- 3 tablespoons tarragon wine vinegar or white wine vinegar
- ⅛ teaspoon salt
- 1 teaspoon sugar
- ½ teaspoon dry mustard
  Dash of pepper
- 1½ pounds spinach, rinsed well, stems removed, and leaves torn into bite-size pieces
- 1 large red-skinned apple, cored and diced
- 3 tablespoons sliced green onions

Cook bacon in a wide frying pan over medium heat until crisp; lift out, drain, crumble, and set aside. Discard all but 1 tablespoon of the drippings from pan. Add almonds to pan and cook, stirring, until lightly browned (3 to 4 minutes). Lift from pan, drain, and set aside.

In a small bowl, whisk together oil, vinegar, salt, sugar, mustard, and pepper. In a large bowl, combine spinach, apple, onions, bacon, and almonds. Pour dressing over salad and toss gently. Makes 6 to 8 servings.

Per serving: 174 calories (71 percent from fat), 5 g protein, 8 g carbohydrates, 15 g total fat (3 g saturated fat), 6 mg cholesterol, 192 mg sodium

Spinach-Cauliflower Toss

Because this salad doesn't wilt readily, it's a good choice for a buffet dinner or potluck. Lightly toasted pine nuts or almonds add a nutty crunch to the pretty combination of cauliflowerets and spinach.

- ½ cup pine nuts or slivered almonds
- ½ pound spinach, rinsed well, stems removed, and leaves torn into bite-size pieces
- ½ medium-size head cauliflower, broken into flowerets, then cut into ¼-inch-thick slices
- 1 large avocado
- 1 tablespoon lemon juice
- ⅓ cup salad oil or olive oil
- 3 tablespoons white wine vinegar
- 1 large clove garlic, minced or pressed
- ½ teaspoon *each* salt, dry mustard, and dry basil
- ¼ teaspoon pepper
  Dash of ground nutmeg

Spread pine nuts in a shallow baking pan and toast in a 350° oven, stirring occasionally, until lightly browned (5 to 8 minutes). Let cool.

Place spinach and cauliflower in a serving bowl. Pit, peel, and slice avocado; sprinkle with lemon juice to coat. Add avocado to vegetables.

In a small bowl, whisk together oil, vinegar, garlic, salt, mustard, basil, pepper, and nutmeg. Pour dressing over vegetables. Add pine nuts and mix gently to coat. Makes 6 servings.

Per serving: 254 calories (80 percent from fat), 5 g protein, 8 g carbohydrates, 25 g total fat (3 g saturated fat), 0 mg cholesterol, 215 mg sodium

Cucumber Sunomono

Rice vinegar gives this cool Asian salad the most authentic flavor, but you can also use white wine vinegar. Avoid red wine and cider vinegars, since they'll tint the pale cucumbers.

- 2 large cucumbers
- ⅓ cup unseasoned rice vinegar or 3 tablespoons white wine vinegar
- 4 teaspoons sugar
- 1 teaspoon salt
- 2 quarter-size slices fresh ginger, finely chopped or slivered

Peel cucumbers, if desired; then cut in half lengthwise and remove any seeds. Cut cucumber halves crosswise into very thin slices.

In a small serving bowl, combine cucumbers with vinegar, sugar, salt, and ginger. Cover and refrigerate for at least 1 hour or until next day. Makes 6 servings.

Per serving: 22 calories (3 percent from fat), 0.4 g protein, 5 g carbohydrates, 0.1 g total fat (0 g saturated fat), 0 mg cholesterol, 371 mg sodium

Dilled Green Pea Salad

Plain green peas are an ideal foil for tart fresh dill in this classic from the 1960s. Serve the salad on lettuce-lined plates, garnished with wedges of hard-cooked egg.

- 2 packages (about 10 oz. *each*) frozen peas
- 3 tablespoons salad oil
- 1 to 2 tablespoons lemon juice
- ¾ teaspoon dry dill weed
- ¼ teaspoon dry basil
- 1 clove garlic, peeled
  Salt and pepper
- 1 cup thinly sliced celery
- 6 large butter lettuce leaves, rinsed and crisped
- 3 hard-cooked eggs, quartered (optional)

Cook peas according to package directions; drain, reserving ⅓ cup of the cooking water. In a large bowl, combine peas, the reserved ⅓ cup cooking water, oil, lemon juice, dill weed, basil, and garlic. Season to taste with salt and pepper. Cover and refrigerate for 1 hour. Discard garlic. Add celery and toss lightly.

To serve, place a lettuce leaf on each of 6 salad plates; top equally with pea mixture. Garnish each serving with 2 wedges of hard-cooked egg, if desired. Makes 6 servings.

Per serving: 139 calories (45 percent from fat), 5 g protein, 14 g carbohydrates, 7 g total fat (0.9 g saturated fat), 0 mg cholesterol, 125 mg sodium

Lemon-Mint Pea & Pastina Salad

This light salad was introduced in 1988 as part of a portable May Day picnic. If you plan to transport it, just pack it in a container and omit the lettuce.

- 1 **cup orzo, riso, or other tiny pasta shapes**
- 1 **package (about 1 lb.) frozen tiny peas, thawed**
- 1 **cup chopped celery**
- ½ **cup *each* thinly sliced green onions and chopped fresh mint**
- ½ **cup salad oil or olive oil**
- ¼ **cup lemon juice**
- 2 **teaspoons grated lemon peel**
  Salt and pepper
  Romaine lettuce leaves, rinsed and crisped
  Mint sprigs

In a large pan, cook pasta in about 3 quarts of boiling salted water just until

barely tender to bite (about 5 minutes); or cook according to package directions. Drain, rinse with cold water, and drain again.

In a large bowl, combine pasta, peas, celery, onions, and chopped mint. (At this point, you may cover and refrigerate until next day.) In a small bowl, whisk together oil, lemon juice, and lemon peel. Add to pea mixture; stir to mix well. Season to taste with salt and pepper. If made ahead, cover and refrigerate for up to 2 hours.

To serve, line 8 salad plates with lettuce leaves. Top equally with pea mixture; garnish with mint sprigs. Makes 8 servings.

Per serving: 270 calories (47 percent from fat), 7 g protein, 29 g carbohydrates, 14 g total fat (2 g saturated fat), 0 mg cholesterol, 94 mg sodium

Asparagus & Prosciutto Salad

A lovely first course for a springtime menu, this fresh-tasting salad appeared in our pages in 1990. The garlicky mustard dressing, speckled with slivers of salt-cured prosciutto, is an unusual complement to tender asparagus spears. You might serve the dish with grilled chicken or steak.

- **Prosciutto Dressing (recipe follows)**
- 2 **pounds asparagus**
- 1 **lemon, cut into 8 wedges**

Prepare Prosciutto Dressing; set aside.

Snap off and discard tough ends of asparagus; peel stalks, if desired. In a wide frying pan, bring 1 inch of water to a boil over high heat. Add asparagus; cover and cook until tender-crisp to bite (about 4 minutes). Drain, immerse in ice water until cool, and drain again. (At this point, you may cover and refrigerate until next day.)

To serve, divide asparagus among

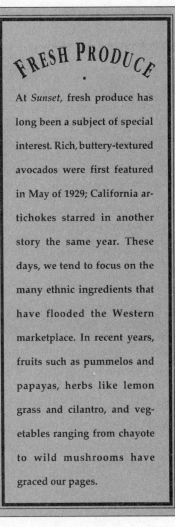

8 salad plates. Spoon Prosciutto Dressing over asparagus; serve with lemon wedges. Makes 8 servings.

Prosciutto Dressing. Cut ¼ pound thinly sliced **prosciutto** into fine slivers. Place in a wide frying pan and add 1 tablespoon **olive oil** and 2 cloves **garlic,** minced or pressed. Cook over medium heat, stirring often, until prosciutto and garlic are golden (8 to 10 minutes). Remove from heat and stir in 3 tablespoons *each* **olive oil** and **lemon juice** and 2 teaspoons **Dijon mustard.** If made ahead, pour into a small jar, cover, and let stand until next day. Stir before using.

Per serving: 116 calories (65 percent from fat), 7 g protein, 4 g carbohydrates, 9 g total fat (1 g saturated fat), 12 mg cholesterol, 303 mg sodium

Broccoli–Cheddar Cheese Salad

This room-temperature salad works equally well as a first course or a light luncheon entrée. Serve it with crusty French bread and a bowl of soup for a satisfying meal.

- **2 tablespoons pine nuts**
- **¾ pound broccoli**
  Chive Dressing (recipe follows)
- **4 ounces Cheddar cheese, cut into matchstick-size pieces**
- **¼ pound medium-size mushrooms, thinly sliced**

Spread pine nuts in a shallow baking pan and toast in a 350° oven, stirring occasionally, until lightly browned (5 to 8 minutes). Let cool.

Trim and discard ends of broccoli stalks. Cut flowerets from stalks; peel stalks and cut crosswise into thin slices. Arrange broccoli on a rack in a pan over 1 inch of boiling water; cover and steam until tender-crisp to bite (about 5 minutes). Drain, immerse in ice water until cool, and drain again. Prepare Chive Dressing.

Gently mix broccoli, cheese, mushrooms, and dressing in a serving bowl, coating vegetables well. Sprinkle with pine nuts. Makes 4 servings.

Chive Dressing. In a small bowl, whisk together ¼ cup **olive oil** or salad oil, 3 tablespoons **lemon juice**, 2 tablespoons snipped **chives** or thinly sliced green onion, ¼ teaspoon *each* **garlic salt** and **dry mustard,** and ⅛ teaspoon **white pepper.**

Per serving: 291 calories (75 percent from fat), 11 g protein, 8 g carbohydrates, 26 g total fat (8 g saturated fat), 30 mg cholesterol, 316 mg sodium

Roasted Potato & Carrot Salad

Roasted vegetable salads are a new favorite among *Sunset* editors. Withering heat intensifies the natural sweetness of many vegetables; here, we use carrots and potatoes. You can roast the vegetables a day ahead, then cover and chill them. But for best flavor, bring them to room temperature before dressing and serving.

- **2 pounds thin-skinned potatoes, scrubbed and cut into 1-inch chunks**
- **2 tablespoons olive oil**
- **8 large carrots (about 2 lbs. *total*), peeled and cut into 1-inch chunks**
  Citrus Dressing (recipe follows)
  Basil sprigs
  Salt and pepper

Combine potatoes with 1 tablespoon of the oil in a 10- by 15-inch rimmed baking pan. Combine carrots and remaining 1 tablespoon oil in another 10- by 15-inch rimmed baking pan.

Bake potatoes and carrots in a 475° oven, turning occasionally, until richly browned (35 to 45 minutes; if you bake both vegetables at once in the same oven, switch positions of pans halfway through baking). Let roasted vegetables cool until warm.

Prepare Citrus Dressing. In a shallow serving bowl, combine potatoes, carrots, and dressing; toss gently. Garnish with basil sprigs. Season to taste with salt and pepper. Makes 6 to 8 servings.

Citrus Dressing. In a small bowl, whisk together 2 teaspoons **grated orange peel;** ½ cup **orange juice;** 2 tablespoons **white wine vinegar** or distilled white vinegar; 2 tablespoons chopped **fresh basil;** 1 tablespoon **honey;** 2 teaspoons **Dijon mustard;** 1 teaspoon **ground cumin;** 2 cloves **garlic,** minced or pressed; and 1 **fresh jalapeño chile,** seeded and minced.

Per serving: 213 calories (18 percent from fat), 4 g protein, 41 g carbohydrates, 4 g total fat (0.6 g saturated fat), 0 mg cholesterol, 95 mg sodium

WESTERN CLASSIC
Tomato & Avocado Salad with Mogul Dressing

An Indian restaurant in San Francisco gave us this recipe over 25 years ago. Chinese five-spice—a blend of cinnamon, cloves, fennel, star anise, and Sichuan peppercorns—gives the dressing its unique flavor. If you can't find five-spice, you can substitute a mix of four different spices; see below.

- **Mogul Dressing (recipe follows)**
- **2 large tomatoes**
- **2 avocados**
  Romaine lettuce leaves, rinsed and crisped, and cucumber slices (optional)

SALAD BARS

Salad bars are now popular in restaurants of all kinds, including even some fast-food chains, but the idea is really nothing new. In a 1940 issue of *Sunset,* one chef described how he served salads: each element was presented separately, allowing guests to assemble their own servings to taste. Encouraging guests to participate in cooking and serving is still a *Sunset* trademark.

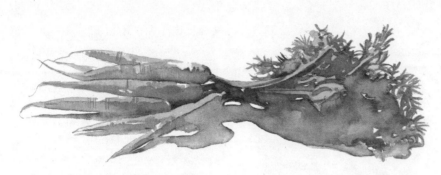

Prepare Mogul Dressing. Pour into a serving container, cover, and refrigerate for at least 2 hours.

Peel and thinly slice tomatoes; pit, peel, and slice avocados. Arrange tomato and avocado slices on a platter. Stir dressing to blend, then drizzle half of it over vegetables. Garnish with lettuce and cucumber, if desired. Offer remaining dressing to add to individual servings. Makes 4 to 6 servings.

Mogul Dressing. In a small bowl, whisk together ½ cup **salad oil;** 2 tablespoons **tarragon wine vinegar;** 1 teaspoon **dry basil;** 1 teaspoon **Chinese five-spice** (or ⅛ teaspoon *each* ground cloves, anise seeds, ground cinnamon, and ground ginger); ½ teaspoon **lemon juice;** 1 small clove **garlic,** minced or pressed; and ⅛ teaspoon *each* **dry mustard** and **pepper.** Season to taste with **salt.**

Per serving: 338 calories (87 percent from fat), 2 g protein, 10 g carbohydrates, 34 g total fat (5 g saturated fat), 0 mg cholesterol, 14 mg sodium

Thai Pummelo & Shrimp Salad

The pummelo is a large winter citrus fruit common in Asia. It's round or pear-shaped, with smooth yellow skin and pink or white flesh that varies in texture and moistness. The flavor is similar to that of grapefruit, but sweeter, with no bitterness. (The thick skin and pith are bitter, though, so be sure to remove them as you would for grapefruit.)

Tart-Hot Dressing (recipe follows)
3 tablespoons sweetened shredded or flaked coconut
1 tablespoon salad oil
2 large cloves garlic, peeled and thinly sliced
1 large pummelo (about 2½ lbs.)
⅓ pound small cooked shrimp
¼ cup thinly sliced shallots
Butter or green leaf lettuce leaves, rinsed and crisped
¼ cup salted peanuts, chopped
Cilantro sprigs

Prepare Tart-Hot Dressing; set aside.

Toast coconut in a small frying pan over low heat, stirring often, until golden (5 to 8 minutes). Pour out of pan and set aside. Add oil and garlic to pan. Stir over medium heat just until garlic is golden brown and crisp (2 to 3 minutes); set aside.

Peel pummelo and remove pith and membranes. Separate segments, then gently pull segments apart to separate the tiny juice sacs (firm, dry-textured fruit segments separate easily; if fruit does not do this readily, leave segments whole). In a bowl, gently mix shredded pummelo (do not mix in whole segments; set aside), shrimp, shallots, and dressing.

To serve, line 4 salad or dinner plates with lettuce. Spoon equal portions of shredded pummelo salad onto lettuce. (If using whole segments, arrange equal portions of segments on lettuce; spoon shrimp mixture over fruit.) Garnish salads equally with coconut, garlic, peanuts, and cilantro sprigs. Makes 4 servings.

Tart-Hot Dressing. In a small bowl, whisk together 2 tablespoons **lime juice,** 2 tablespoons **fish sauce** (*nuoc mam* or *nam pla*) or soy sauce, 1 tablespoon minced **fresh ginger,** 1 teaspoon **sugar,** and ½ to ¾ teaspoon **crushed red pepper flakes.**

Per serving: 243 calories (37 percent from fat), 13 g protein, 27 g carbohydrates, 10 g total fat (2 g saturated fat), 73 mg cholesterol, 172 mg sodium

Papaya, Orange & Avocado Salad

A nippy chili-onion dressing lends subtle spice to this pretty orange-and-green fruit salad.

Chili Dressing (recipe follows)
3 medium-size oranges
2 ripe avocados
1 papaya, peeled, seeded, and cut into chunks

Prepare Chili Dressing; set aside.

Holding fruit over a bowl to catch juice, use a sharp knife to cut peel and all white membrane from oranges; thinly slice fruit crosswise and drop into bowl. Pit, peel, and dice avocados. Add avocados and papaya to bowl. Pour dressing over fruit and toss gently. Cover and refrigerate for several hours.

Lift fruit from bowl with a slotted spoon and arrange on a platter. Pour dressing remaining in bowl into a serving container; offer dressing to pour over individual servings. Makes 4 servings.

Chili Dressing. In a small bowl, whisk together ¼ cup *each* **salad oil** and **lemon juice,** 1 tablespoon thinly sliced **green onion,** ½ teaspoon **chili powder,** and ¼ teaspoon **pepper.** Season to taste with **salt.**

Per serving of salad: 369 calories (67 percent from fat), 3 g protein, 29 g carbohydrates, 29 g total fat (4 g saturated fat), 0 mg cholesterol, 19 mg sodium

Merida Salad

This light, tart citrus salad, from the town of Merida on the Yucatán peninsula, is a delightful complement to spicy main dishes.

- **2 large oranges**
- **2 tangerines**
- **2 large pink grapefruit**
- **2 large green-skinned apples**
- **¼ cup lime juice**
  Salt
- **½ cup cilantro leaves**

Holding fruit over a bowl to catch juice, use a sharp knife to cut peel and all white membrane from oranges, tangerines, and grapefruit; then cut segments free. Core and thinly slice apples. Arrange fruit in a shallow serving dish and sprinkle with lime juice and any accumulated citrus juices. Season to taste with salt; garnish with cilantro. Makes 8 servings.

Per serving: 83 calories (4 percent from fat), 1 g protein, 21 g carbohydrates, 0.4 g total fat (0 g saturated fat), 0 mg cholesterol, 2 mg sodium

Cilantro Slaw

Minced cilantro and a tart citrus dressing give this slaw its special flavor. Serve it with grilled fish or chicken for a refreshing addition to a summer barbecue; or use it in tacos in place of lettuce.

- **Lime & Garlic Dressing (recipe follows)**
- **1 small head green cabbage, finely shredded**
- **1 small onion, minced**
- **2 to 4 tablespoons minced cilantro**
- **1 thin-skinned (English or Armenian) cucumber, peeled and seeded**
- **Salt and pepper**

Prepare Lime & Garlic Dressing.

In a large bowl, combine cabbage,

onion, and cilantro. Cut cucumber into 3-inch-long sticks. (At this point, you may cover and refrigerate cabbage mixture and cucumber separately until next day.)

Pour dressing over cabbage mixture; toss gently to coat. Season to taste with salt and pepper. Transfer to a large serving bowl or platter. Garnish with cucumber. Makes 6 to 8 servings.

Lime & Garlic Dressing. In a small bowl, whisk together ½ cup **salad oil**, ⅓ cup **lime juice**, and 2 cloves **garlic,** minced or pressed. If made ahead, cover and refrigerate for up to 2 days; stir before using.

Per serving: 165 calories (83 percent from fat), 1 g protein, 6 g carbohydrates, 16 g total fat (2 g saturated fat), 0 mg cholesterol, 16 mg sodium

Zucchini-Apple Slaw

Sure to become a summertime favorite, this crisp slaw is made with coarsely shredded zucchini in place of the traditional cabbage. The crunch comes from sliced green onions and chunks of apple.

- **½ cup mayonnaise**
- **3 tablespoons cider vinegar**
- **1 tablespoon sugar**
- **1 teaspoon caraway seeds**
- **4 cups coarsely shredded zucchini**
- **¼ cup thinly sliced green onions**
- **2 or 3 medium-size tart red- or green-skinned apples**
- **Salt and pepper**

In a small bowl, stir together mayonnaise, vinegar, sugar, and caraway seeds.

In a large bowl, combine zucchini and onions. Core apples; peel, if desired. Cut into ½-inch chunks (you should have about 3 cups). Add apples to zucchini mixture; pour dressing over salad and mix lightly to coat. Season to taste with salt and pepper. Cover and refrigerate for at least 2 hours or up to 4 hours.

To serve, transfer salad to a serving bowl with a slotted spoon. Makes 6 servings.

Per serving: 189 calories (67 percent from fat), 1 g protein, 15 g carbohydrates, 15 g total fat (2 g saturated fat), 11 mg cholesterol, 108 mg sodium

WESTERN CLASSIC

Autumn Slaw

Dotted with diced red bell pepper and green onion slices, this delectable salad is a tasty choice for a buffet or potluck supper at any time of year. You can make the salad well in advance; the sweet-tart dressing helps keep the vegetables crisp.

- **1 medium-size head green cabbage, finely shredded**
- **1 teaspoon salt**
- **1¼ cups *each* sugar and water**
- **1 cup white wine vinegar**
- **3 cups thinly sliced celery**
- **1 large red or green bell pepper, seeded and chopped**
- **½ cup thinly sliced green onions**
- **1 teaspoon *each* celery seeds and mustard seeds**

Place cabbage in a colander, sprinkle with salt, and let drain for 2 hours.

Meanwhile, in a small pan, combine sugar, water, and vinegar. Bring to a boil over high heat, stirring until sugar is dissolved; boil for 2 minutes. Remove from heat; let cool to room temperature.

In a large bowl, combine cabbage, vinegar mixture, celery, bell pepper, onions, celery seeds, and mustard seeds; mix until moistened. Cover and refrigerate for at least 24 hours or up to 1 week.

To serve, transfer salad to a serving bowl with a slotted spoon. Makes 8 to 10 servings.

Per serving: 149 calories (2 percent from fat), 2 g protein, 37 g carbohydrates, 0.4 g total fat (0 g saturated fat), 0 mg cholesterol, 299 mg sodium

Olive-Pecan Chicken Slaw

Tender chunks of chicken, butter-toasted pecans, and crunchy apple add up to an ideal light supper or lunch.

2	teaspoons butter or margarine
½	cup pecans
	Mustard Cream Dressing (recipe follows)
2	cups shredded cabbage
1½	cups cubed cooked chicken breast
1	medium-size Red Delicious apple, cored and diced
1	small jar (about 2 oz.) diced pimentos, drained
1	can (about 2¼ oz.) sliced ripe olives, drained
¼	cup thinly sliced celery
	Salt

Melt butter in a wide frying pan over medium heat. Add pecans and cook, stirring often, until nuts turn a darker brown (about 7 minutes). Drain on paper towels.

Prepare Mustard Cream Dressing. Add cabbage, chicken, apple, pimentos, olives, and celery to dressing; toss to coat evenly. Sprinkle pecans over salad; season to taste with salt. Makes 6 servings.

Mustard Cream Dressing. In a serving bowl, stir together ½ cup **mayonnaise,** 2 tablespoons **lemon juice,** 1 teaspoon **Dijon mustard** or regular prepared mustard, ½ teaspoon **sugar,** and ¼ teaspoon **pepper.**

Per serving: 299 calories (72 percent from fat), 12 g protein, 9 g carbohydrates, 24 g total fat (4 g saturated fat), 44 mg cholesterol, 272 mg sodium

Marinated Bean Salad

An excellent source of protein, beans are a nutritious addition to any light meal. Here, they show up in a make-ahead salad that packs well for a picnic or casual summer buffet. To let the flavors meld, prepare the salad a day before serving.

1	can (about 15 oz.) red kidney beans
1	can (about 8 oz.) cut green beans; or 1 cup cut fresh green beans, cooked
1	can (about 15 oz.) garbanzo beans
1	can (about 15 oz.) black-eyed peas
2½	cups chopped celery
1	cup finely minced parsley
1	bunch green onions, thinly sliced
1	small jar (about 3 oz.) pimento-stuffed green olives, drained and halved
1	can (about 4 oz.) chopped ripe olives, drained
½	cup olive oil or salad oil
½	cup red wine vinegar

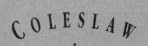

COLESLAW

The name comes from the Dutch *koolsla* ("cabbage salad")—and coleslaw is traditionally a mixture of shredded cabbage plus mayonnaise, vinaigrette, or another simple dressing. *Sunset* has featured dozens of slaws, often embellishing the traditional base with nuts, fruit, or meat. Like many of our favorite picnic salads, slaws often taste best if made a few hours before serving.

2	tablespoons firmly packed brown sugar
1	clove garlic, pressed
	Salt and pepper
	Romaine lettuce leaves, rinsed and crisped

Empty kidney beans, green beans, garbanzo beans, and peas into a large colander. Rinse with water; drain. Transfer to a large bowl and stir in celery, parsley, onions, green olives, and ripe olives.

In a small bowl, whisk together oil, vinegar, sugar, and garlic. Pour over bean mixture. Mix lightly and season to taste with salt and pepper. Cover and refrigerate until next day.

To serve, toss mixture well and arrange in a serving bowl lined with lettuce leaves. Makes about 8 servings.

Per serving: 295 calories (53 percent from fat), 8 g protein, 27 g carbohydrates, 18 g total fat (2 g saturated fat), 0 mg cholesterol, 744 mg sodium

Black Bean, Corn & Pepper Salad

This spirited Mexican-style salad was developed as an accompaniment for grilled London broil in a Father's Day menu. Fresh jalapeños lend a fiery kick to a cool combination of black beans, sweet corn kernels, and red bell pepper.

- 2 cans (about 15 oz. *each*) black beans or cannellini (white kidney beans), drained and rinsed
- 1½ cups cooked fresh corn kernels; or 1 package (about 10 oz.) frozen corn kernels, thawed
- 1 large red bell pepper, seeded and diced
- 2 small fresh jalapeño chiles, seeded and minced
- ½ cup firmly packed chopped cilantro
- ¼ cup lime juice
- 2 tablespoons salad oil
  Salt and pepper
  Lettuce leaves, rinsed and crisped

In a large bowl, mix beans, corn, bell pepper, chiles, cilantro, lime juice, and oil. Season to taste with salt and pepper. Cover and refrigerate for at least 1 hour or until next day.

To serve, transfer bean mixture to a salad bowl lined with lettuce leaves. Serve cold or at room temperature. Makes 6 servings.

Per serving: 193 calories (26 percent from fat), 9 g protein, 28 g carbohydrates, 6 g total fat (0.7 g saturated fat), 0 mg cholesterol, 186 mg sodium

Cannery Row Potato Salad

A restaurant on Monterey's Cannery Row created this salad many years ago. Ripe olives, green onions, and pimentos add festive, colorful accents to tender potatoes in a creamy dressing.

- 3½ pounds medium-size red thin-skinned potatoes, scrubbed
- ½ cup olive oil or salad oil
- 3 cloves garlic, minced or pressed
- ¼ cup sweet pickle relish
- ½ cup mayonnaise
- 1 can (about 2¼ oz.) sliced ripe olives, drained
- ½ cup *each* thinly sliced celery and green onions
  Salt and pepper
- 1 small jar (about 2 oz.) sliced pimentos, drained
  Chopped parsley

Cook potatoes in boiling water until tender throughout when pierced (about 20 minutes). Drain and let cool briefly; cut into ½-inch cubes and place in a large bowl. Add oil and garlic; mix lightly until potatoes are well coated. Let stand until cool.

Add pickle relish, mayonnaise, olives, celery, and onions to potatoes. Mix lightly until combined. Season to taste with salt and pepper. Cover and refrigerate for at least 3 hours or until next day.

Just before serving, garnish salad with pimentos and parsley. Makes 8 to 10 servings.

Per serving: 360 calories (56 percent from fat), 4 g protein, 36 g carbohydrates, 23 g total fat (3 g saturated fat), 7 mg cholesterol, 201 mg sodium

Danish Potato Salad

Sliced red radishes, slivers of green onion, and chopped hard-cooked eggs bring flair to a classic Scandinavian-style potato salad.

- 1 clove garlic, peeled and halved
- 2 tablespoons olive oil or salad oil
- ¼ cup tarragon wine vinegar
- 1 teaspoon *each* salt and sugar
- ½ teaspoon dry dill weed or 1½ teaspoons chopped fresh dill
- 1 pound new potatoes, peeled
- 3 hard-cooked eggs
- 2 green onions, sliced
- 3 large radishes, sliced
- ⅓ cup mayonnaise
  Chopped parsley or dill sprigs

In a large bowl, combine garlic and oil. Let stand for 10 minutes; discard garlic. Stir in vinegar, salt, sugar, and dill weed. Set aside.

Cook potatoes in boiling water until tender throughout when pierced (about 15 minutes). Drain and let cool briefly; then cut into ½-inch cubes. Add to dressing and toss to coat. Cover and refrigerate for at least 1 hour or until next day.

Just before serving, chop 2 of the eggs. Add chopped eggs, onions, radishes, and mayonnaise to potatoes; mix gently. Cut remaining egg into wedges; garnish salad with egg wedges and sprinkle with parsley. Makes 4 to 6 servings.

Per serving: 274 calories (66 percent from fat), 6 g protein, 18 g carbohydrates, 20 g total fat (3 g saturated fat), 136 mg cholesterol, 569 mg sodium

Wild Rice Salad

A relatively new California crop, wild rice is grown in significant amounts in the Sacramento Valley. The cultivated grain tends to be larger than truly "wild" wild rice, but it's no less flavorful. Accented with a simple vinaigrette, it makes a savory salad or a nice accompaniment for poultry and game birds.

1½ cups wild rice

3 cups chicken broth

⅓ cup salad oil or olive oil

2 tablespoons raspberry or wine vinegar

2 tablespoons minced shallots or onion

2 teaspoons Dijon mustard

¼ teaspoon pepper

Rinse rice with water; drain. In a 2- to 3-quart pan, combine rice and broth; bring to a boil over high heat. Reduce heat to low, cover, and simmer, stirring occasionally, until rice is tender to bite and almost all liquid has been absorbed (about 50 minutes). Remove from heat and let cool.

In a small bowl, whisk together oil, vinegar, shallots, mustard, and pepper. Stir into cooled rice. If made ahead, cover and let stand at room temperature for up to 4 hours or refrigerate for up to 2 days. Bring to room temperature before serving. Makes 8 servings.

Per serving: 201 calories (43 percent from fat), 6 g protein, 24 g carbohydrates, 10 g total fat (1 g saturated fat), 0 mg cholesterol, 411 mg sodium

Quick Artichoke Pasta Salad

Bottled marinated artichoke hearts add tasty pep to this vegetable-laden macaroni salad. The dish keeps well, making it a good choice for a picnic or casual buffet.

1 cup dry salad macaroni or other medium-size pasta

1 jar (about 6 oz.) marinated artichoke hearts

¼ pound small mushrooms

1 cup cherry tomatoes, cut into halves

1 cup medium-size pitted ripe olives

1 tablespoon chopped parsley

½ teaspoon dry basil
Salt and pepper

In a large pan, cook macaroni in about 1½ quarts of boiling salted water until tender to bite (about 7 minutes); or cook according to package directions. Drain macaroni well, rinse with cold water, and drain again. Transfer to a large bowl.

Drain liquid from artichokes over macaroni. Cut artichokes into halves or thirds. Add artichokes, mushrooms, cherry tomatoes, olives, parsley, and basil to macaroni. Toss gently. Season to taste with salt and pepper. Cover and refrigerate for at least 4 hours or until next day before serving. Makes 6 servings.

Per serving: 132 calories (32 percent from fat), 4 g protein, 19 g carbohydrates, 5 g total fat (0.7 g saturated fat), 0 mg cholesterol, 346 mg sodium

Niçoise Salad

If you see the word "Niçoise" in the name of a recipe, you know the dish is prepared in the style of Nice, France—and that means it probably includes tomatoes, olives, and anchovies. The classic Niçoise salad contains those ingredients, as well as sliced potatoes, tender green beans, tuna, and hard-cooked eggs.

¾ cup olive oil or salad oil

¼ cup red wine vinegar

2 tablespoons thinly sliced green onion or snipped chives

2 tablespoons finely chopped parsley
Salt and pepper

4 large thin-skinned potatoes (about 2 lbs. *total*), scrubbed

1½ pounds green beans, ends and strings removed

2 large tomatoes, cut into wedges

2 or 3 hard-cooked eggs, quartered

½ cup Niçoise olives or pitted ripe olives

1 tablespoon drained capers (optional)
Butter lettuce leaves, rinsed and crisped

1 can (about 6⅛ oz.) water-packed solid-pack tuna

10 to 12 canned anchovy fillets, drained

In a small bowl, whisk together oil, vinegar, onion, and parsley. Season to taste with salt and pepper, then cover and set aside.

Cook potatoes in boiling water until tender throughout when pierced (about 25 minutes). Drain, immerse in ice water until cool, and drain again. Peel and slice potatoes; place in a bowl and pour just enough dressing over slices to coat them. Mix gently, cover, and refrigerate for at least 2 hours.

Cut beans into 1½-inch lengths and cook in boiling water until tender-crisp to bite (about 7 minutes). Drain, immerse in ice water until cool, and drain again.

On a rimmed platter, arrange potatoes, beans, tomatoes, and eggs in separate mounds. Garnish with olives and capers, if desired. (At this point, you may cover and refrigerate for up to 6 hours.)

Just before serving, arrange lettuce leaves around edge of platter. Drain tuna (without removing it from can); then invert can on top of salad. Carefully lift off can. Garnish salad with anchovies; pour remaining dressing over all ingredients. Makes 4 servings.

Per serving: 752 calories (56 percent from fat), 27 g protein, 57 g carbohydrates, 48 g total fat (7 g saturated fat), 156 mg cholesterol, 770 mg sodium

Basil & Scallop Pasta Salad

This green-and-white combination of seafood, broccoli, pasta, and fresh basil is perfect for a light entrée or an elegant first course. Use either bay scallops or sea scallops.

- 8 ounces dry pasta twists or medium-size shells
- 4 cups (about ¾ lb.) broccoli flowerets, cut into 1-inch pieces
- 1 pound scallops, cut into ¼-inch-thick slices if large
- ¼ cup *each* lemon juice and white wine vinegar
- ½ cup *each* olive oil and salad oil
- 1 teaspoon *each* dry mustard and sugar
- 1 clove garlic, minced or pressed
- 1 cup finely chopped fresh basil
  Salt and pepper

In a large pan, cook pasta in about 2½ quarts of boiling salted water until tender to bite (about 8 minutes); or cook according to package directions. Drain, rinse with cold water, and drain again.

In a wide frying pan, bring ¼ inch of water to a boil over medium-high heat. Add broccoli, cover, and cook until tender-crisp to bite (about 2 minutes). Drain, immerse in ice water until cool, and drain again. Set aside. Add another ¼ inch of water to pan; bring to a boil, then add scallops.

Cover and cook until scallops are opaque in center; cut to test (about 3 minutes). Drain.

In a large bowl, combine pasta, broccoli, and scallops. In a small bowl, whisk together lemon juice, vinegar, olive oil, salad oil, mustard, sugar, garlic, and basil. Pour dressing over broccoli mixture; mix gently. Season to taste with salt and pepper. Cover and refrigerate for at least 2 hours or until next day before serving. Makes 4 to 6 servings.

Per serving: 670 calories (60 percent from fat), 24 g protein, 44 g carbohydrates, 45 g total fat (6 g saturated fat), 30 mg cholesterol, 168 mg sodium

California Shrimp Salad

A lemony onion vinaigrette complements avocado and poached shrimp in this tasty summer salad.

- 2 pounds medium-size raw shrimp
  Green Onion Dressing (recipe follows)
- 1 large avocado
- 1 large head iceberg lettuce, shredded

Bring a 4- to 5-quart pan of water to a boil over high heat. Add shrimp. Reduce heat and simmer, uncovered, until shrimp are just opaque in center; cut to test (4 to 5 minutes). Drain shrimp; then shell and devein.

Prepare Green Onion Dressing. Pit, peel, and cube avocado. Combine shrimp and avocado in a serving bowl. Pour dressing over avocado and shrimp; mix to coat well. Cover and refrigerate for 1 to 2 hours.

Arrange lettuce on a platter. With a slotted spoon, lift shrimp mixture from bowl (reserve dressing) and mound on lettuce. Offer reserved dressing to spoon over individual servings. Makes 6 to 8 servings.

Green Onion Dressing. In a small bowl, whisk together ¼ cup **olive oil** or salad oil, ¼ cup **white wine vinegar,** 2 tablespoons **lemon juice,** ½ teaspoon **garlic salt,** ⅛ teaspoon **seasoned pepper,** and ½ cup thinly sliced **green onions.**

Per serving: 259 calories (52 percent from fat), 23 g protein, 8 g carbohydrates, 15 g total fat (2 g saturated fat), 160 mg cholesterol, 301 mg sodium

Full-meal Salad

In 1954, we created the Full-meal Salad to exemplify a true "Western salad," one combining diverse ingredients with creative flair. Tender baby lima beans marinated in well-seasoned French dressing make an interesting vegetable base for this inventive salad.

- 1 package (about 10 oz.) frozen baby lima beans, cooked and drained
- 1 clove garlic, minced or pressed
- ½ cup purchased French dressing or Spicy French Dressing (page 45)
- 1 teaspoon dry mustard
- ¼ teaspoon paprika
- ½ teaspoon Italian herb seasoning; or ⅛ teaspoon *each* dry basil, dry marjoram, dry oregano, and dry thyme
  Salt
- 3 green onions, sliced
- 4 radishes, sliced
- 1 to 1½ cups julienne strips of cooked ham
- 2 ounces Cheddar cheese, cut into matchstick-size pieces
  Iceberg lettuce leaves, rinsed and crisped
  Mayonnaise (optional)

In a bowl, combine beans, garlic, French dressing, mustard, paprika, and herb seasoning; toss to coat beans. Season to taste with salt. Cover and refrigerate until cold.

Just before serving, add onions, radishes, ham, and cheese to bean mixture; toss gently. Spoon salad into a lettuce-lined serving bowl; top with a dollop of mayonnaise, if desired. Makes 4 servings.

Per serving: 374 calories (53 percent from fat), 20 g protein, 25 g carbohydrates, 22 g total fat (7 g saturated fat), 41 mg cholesterol, 1,233 mg sodium

WESTERN CLASSIC

Cobb Salad

The original Cobb Salad was made famous by Hollywood's Brown Derby Restaurant in the 1930s, but the recipe didn't appear in our pages until 1958. If you like, you can substitute turkey, shrimp, or crabmeat for the chicken.

- 1 medium-size head iceberg lettuce, shredded
- 6 tablespoons white wine vinegar
- ⅛ teaspoon *each* garlic powder and freshly ground pepper
- 3 tablespoons snipped chives
- ½ cup salad oil or olive oil
  Salt
- 1 large tomato, seeded and chopped
- 1½ cups diced cooked chicken
- 1 large avocado, pitted, peeled, diced, and tossed with 1 tablespoon lemon juice
- 1 pound sliced bacon, crisply cooked, drained, and crumbled
- 2 hard-cooked eggs, chopped
- 3 ounces blue-veined cheese, finely crumbled
  Watercress sprigs (optional)

Spread lettuce in a large, wide salad bowl. In a small bowl, whisk together vinegar, garlic powder, pepper, chives, and oil; season to taste with salt. Pour dressing over lettuce and toss to mix, then spread out in an even layer in bowl. On top of lettuce, place tomato, chicken, avocado, bacon, and eggs, arranging each ingredient in a separate wedge-shaped section. Place cheese in center. Garnish with watercress sprigs, if desired. Toss salad at the table. Makes 4 servings.

Per serving: 774 calories (75 percent from fat), 36 g protein, 13 g carbohydrates, 66 g total fat (16 g saturated fat), 196 mg cholesterol, 901 mg sodium

WESTERN CLASSIC

Overnight Layered Chicken Salad

The idea of an overnight layered salad was still new when we published this recipe in the mid-'70s. Favored by *Sunset* editors for its simplicity and creamy curry-flavored dressing, the salad has become a make-ahead classic. For the prettiest presentation, layer the ingredients in a clear glass serving bowl.

- 6 cups shredded iceberg lettuce
- ¼ pound (about 1⅔ cups) bean sprouts
- 1 can (about 8 oz.) water chestnuts, drained and sliced
- ½ cup thinly sliced green onions
- 1 medium-size cucumber, thinly sliced
- 4 cups 2- to 3-inch-long strips of cooked chicken
- 2 packages (about 6 oz. *each*) frozen Chinese pea pods, thawed
- 2 cups mayonnaise
- 2 teaspoons curry powder
- 1 tablespoon sugar
- ½ teaspoon ground ginger
- ½ cup Spanish peanuts
- 12 to 18 cherry tomatoes, cut into halves

Spread lettuce evenly in a wide glass serving bowl. Top with bean sprouts, water chestnuts, onions, cucumber, and chicken, arranging ingredients in layers. Pat pea pods dry and arrange evenly over chicken.

In a small bowl, stir together mayonnaise, curry powder, sugar, and ginger. Spread mayonnaise mixture over pea pods. Cover and refrigerate for several hours or until next day.

Garnish salad with peanuts and cherry tomato halves. To serve, lift out portions with a spoon and fork, scooping to bottom of bowl to include all layers. Makes 10 to 12 servings.

Per serving: 468 calories (74 percent from fat), 19 g protein, 12 g carbohydrates, 39 g total fat (6 g saturated fat), 69 mg cholesterol, 281 mg sodium

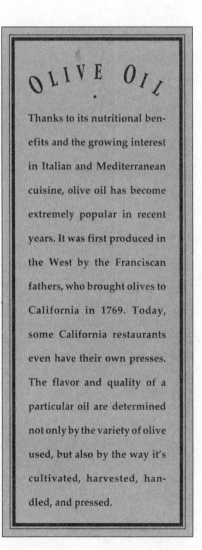

OLIVE OIL

Thanks to its nutritional benefits and the growing interest in Italian and Mediterranean cuisine, olive oil has become extremely popular in recent years. It was first produced in the West by the Franciscan fathers, who brought olives to California in 1769. Today, some California restaurants even have their own presses. The flavor and quality of a particular oil are determined not only by the variety of olive used, but also by the way it's cultivated, harvested, handled, and pressed.

Chinese Chicken Salad

Westerners were just discovering Chinese-style chicken salad when we featured this traditional recipe in 1970. Through the years, we've published many simpler variations but still count the original version our favorite. The bean threads, gossamer and translucent in their dried form, become opaque when fried.

- **2 chicken breast halves (about 1 lb. *total*) and 2 chicken thighs (about ¾ lb. *total*)**
- **¼ cup all-purpose flour**
- **½ teaspoon Chinese five-spice; or ⅛ teaspoon *each* ground cloves, anise seeds, ground cinnamon, and ground ginger**
- **½ teaspoon salt**
- **Dash of pepper**
- **3 ounces bean threads**
- **Salad oil**
- **Soy Dressing (recipe follows)**
- **½ cup sesame seeds**
- **4 cups finely shredded iceberg lettuce**
- **3 green onions, thinly sliced**
- **1 large bunch cilantro, rinsed, stemmed, and chopped**
- **1 cup coarsely chopped salted peanuts**

Rinse chicken; pat dry. In a shallow dish, mix flour, five-spice, salt, and pepper. Coat chicken in flour mixture and shake off excess. Set chicken aside.

Break bean threads into small sections. In a wok or deep pan, heat 1½ inches of oil to 375°F on a deep-frying thermometer. Drop a handful of bean threads into oil. As bean threads puff and expand, push them down into oil with a wire skimmer or slotted spoon; then turn over entire mass. When bean threads stop crackling (about 30 seconds), lift them out with skimmer and drain on paper towels. Skim and discard any bits of bean threads from oil. Repeat to fry remaining bean threads. Let cool.

If necessary, bring oil temperature back to 375°F. Add chicken. Cook, turning after 5 or 6 minutes, until meat near bone is no longer pink; cut to test (about 10 minutes for breasts, 12 minutes for thighs). Drain on paper towels; let cool briefly. Meanwhile, prepare Soy Dressing.

Cut chicken meat and skin from bones, then cut into bite-size pieces. (At this point, you may hold prepared ingredients until next day. Package bean threads airtight and store at room temperature; cover chicken and dressing and refrigerate separately.)

Toast sesame seeds in a wide frying pan over medium heat, stirring often, until golden (2 to 3 minutes). Let cool.

Arrange lettuce in a large serving bowl; top with chicken, onions, and cilantro. Sprinkle with sesame seeds and peanuts. Stir dressing, then drizzle over salad and toss. Add bean threads, lightly crushing some of them with your hands; toss lightly. Serve immediately (noodles soften quickly with standing). Makes 4 servings.

Soy Dressing. In a small bowl, whisk together ¾ teaspoon **dry mustard,** 1 teaspoon *each* **sugar** and **grated lemon peel,** 1 tablespoon *each* **soy sauce** and **lemon juice,** and ¼ cup **salad oil.**

Per serving: 923 calories (63 percent from fat), 44 g protein, 42 g carbohydrates, 67 g total fat (11 g saturated fat), 93 mg cholesterol, 932 mg sodium

Taco Salad

For a whole-meal salad that's reminiscent of a tostada, spoon a hot, chili-seasoned topping of ground beef and red beans over a crisp base of shredded lettuce.

- **About ¾ cup Easy Guacamole (page 11)**
- **1 pound lean ground beef**
- **1 medium-size onion, finely chopped**
- **1 can (about 15 oz.) red kidney beans, drained and rinsed**
- **1½ teaspoons chili powder**
- **½ teaspoon ground cumin**
- **½ cup catsup or tomato sauce**
- **1 medium-size avocado**
- **1 medium-size head iceberg lettuce, shredded**
- **1 cup (about 4 oz.) shredded Cheddar or jack cheese**
- **2 medium-size tomatoes, cut into wedges**
- **3 hard-cooked eggs, cut into wedges**
- **Tortilla chips**
- **Garnishes: Sour cream, red onion rings, sliced ripe olives, sliced green onions, green peperoncini (optional), and lime wedges (optional)**

Prepare Easy Guacamole; refrigerate.

Crumble beef into a wide frying pan. Add onion and cook over medium-high heat, stirring often, until meat is no longer pink and onion is soft. Discard fat from pan. Stir in beans, chili powder, cumin, and catsup; simmer over low heat for about 5 minutes.

Pit, peel, and slice avocado. Arrange lettuce on 4 individual plates. Layer hot beef mixture, cheese, guacamole, tomatoes, eggs, and avocado on lettuce. Surround with tortilla chips. Top with garnishes. Makes 4 servings.

Per serving: 731 calories (57 percent from fat), 42 g protein, 40 g carbohydrates, 47 g total fat (16 g saturated fat), 258 mg cholesterol, 832 mg sodium

Homemade dressings add flavor and richness to even the simplest combinations of fresh ingredients. And by making a few quick changes in the traditional recipes, you can streamline many of your old favorites.

Try Spicy French Dressing or Orange-Basil Vinaigrette as a light complement to fresh greens or seasonal fruits. You'll enjoy our lightened-up creamy dressings, too. Green goddess, Thousand Island, and blue cheese dressings are as flavorful and smooth as the originals, but we cut the fat by using lowfat buttermilk and reduced-calorie mayonnaise.

Spicy French Dressing

- ½ cup *each* sugar and cider vinegar
- 1 tablespoon all-purpose flour
- 1 teaspoon *each* salt and Worcestershire
- 1 medium-size onion, finely chopped
- 1 clove garlic, minced or pressed
- 2 tablespoons salad oil or olive oil
- ⅓ cup catsup
- 1 teaspoon celery seeds

In a small pan, stir together sugar, vinegar, and flour. Cook over medium heat, stirring, until bubbly (about 5 minutes). In a blender or food processor, combine vinegar mixture, salt, Worcestershire, onion, and garlic; whirl until smooth. With blender on lowest speed, gradually pour in oil. Transfer dressing to a bowl and stir in catsup and celery seeds. If made ahead, cover and refrigerate for up to 1 month. Makes about 2 cups.

Per tablespoon: 25 calories (30 percent from fat), 0.1 g protein, 4 g carbohydrates, 0.9 g total fat (0.1 g saturated fat), 0 mg cholesterol, 100 mg sodium

Thousand Island Dressing

- 1 cup reduced-calorie or regular mayonnaise
- ¼ cup tomato-based chili sauce
- 2 teaspoons minced onion
- 1 tablespoon *each* minced green bell pepper and pimento
- 2 tablespoons sweet pickle relish
- 1 hard-cooked egg, finely chopped
  Salt and pepper
  Milk or half-and-half (optional)

In a small bowl, stir together mayonnaise, chili sauce, onion, bell pepper, pimento, pickle relish, and egg. Season to taste with salt and pepper. If desired, thin with a little milk. If made ahead, cover and refrigerate for up to 1 week. Makes about 1¾ cups.

Per tablespoon: 30 calories (74 percent from fat), 0.4 g protein, 2 g carbohydrates, 2 g total fat (0.6 g saturated fat), 10 mg cholesterol, 89 mg sodium

Creamy Blue Cheese Dressing

- ¾ cup lowfat buttermilk
- 2 tablespoons *each* chopped parsley, plain nonfat yogurt, white wine vinegar, and crumbled blue-veined cheese
- 1 teaspoon salad oil or olive oil
- 1 tablespoon minced shallot
  White pepper

In a blender or food processor, combine buttermilk, parsley, yogurt, vinegar, cheese, oil, and shallot; whirl until smooth. Season to taste with white pepper. If made ahead, cover and refrigerate for up to 1 week. Makes about 1 cup.

Per tablespoon: 13 calories (49 percent from fat), 0.7 g protein, 0.9 g carbohydrates, 0.7 g total fat (0.3 g saturated fat), 1 mg cholesterol, 28 mg sodium

Orange-Basil Vinaigrette

- 1 cup orange juice
- 2 teaspoons cornstarch
- ⅓ cup white wine vinegar
- 2 teaspoons *each* Dijon mustard and dry basil
- 2 teaspoons olive oil

In a small pan, combine orange juice and cornstarch; stir until cornstarch is dissolved. Bring to a boil over medium heat; boil, stirring, for 30 seconds. Pour into a small bowl and refrigerate until cold. Then whisk in vinegar, mustard, basil, and oil until blended. If made ahead, cover and refrigerate until next day. Makes about 1 cup.

Per tablespoon: 15 calories (36 percent from fat), 0.1 g protein, 2 g carbohydrates, 0.6 g total fat (0.1 g saturated fat), 0 mg cholesterol, 19 mg sodium

Green Goddess Buttermilk Dressing

- ⅓ cup lowfat buttermilk
- ¼ cup *each* sliced green onions, coarsely chopped parsley, and coarsely chopped watercress
- ½ teaspoon dry tarragon
- 2 teaspoons lemon juice
- ½ teaspoon anchovy paste
- ½ cup reduced-calorie or regular mayonnaise
  Salt and pepper

In a blender or food processor, combine buttermilk, onions, parsley, watercress, tarragon, lemon juice, and anchovy paste; whirl until herbs are finely chopped. Add mayonnaise; whirl just until blended. Season to taste with salt and pepper. If made ahead, cover and refrigerate for up to 10 days. Makes about 1 cup.

Per tablespoon: 24 calories (78 percent from fat), 0.3 g protein, 1 g carbohydrates, 2 g total fat (0.5 g saturated fat), 3 mg cholesterol, 54 mg sodium

SANDWICHES & PIZZA

•

When does Sunset suggest serving sandwiches or pizza? Any time you want a simple meal—for a quick lunch, a light supper, a sunny patio picnic, or a late-night snack. Through the years, we've supplied the Western cook with a variety of ideas for transforming what was once considered mere finger food into satisfying, flavorful fare worthy of main-dish status. • This chapter showcases some of our best traditional sandwiches, such as the timeless Reuben and Monte Cristo, along with contemporary classics like Italian focaccia. We also offer suggestions for serving familiar favorites in new ways. Try a hero-style sandwich loaf baked to a golden crisp, lean burgers served in pita pockets, even pizza cooked on the barbecue.

Giant Baked Hero Sandwich

Originally published as the star player in a Super Bowl supper menu, this meat- and cheese-filled loaf rises to yeasty perfection as it bakes. You slice the golden brown bread to reveal mounds of melted fontina cheese, tender ham, and spicy salami, all accented with roasted red peppers and grilled onion.

    Garlic Oil (recipe follows)
    Grilled Onion (recipe follows)
  2 loaves (about 1 lb. *each*) frozen
    white bread dough, thawed
    and kneaded together
  ½ pound *each* thinly sliced dry
    salami and cooked ham
  ¼ pound thinly sliced dry coppa
    (optional)
  8 ounces thinly sliced fontina or
    jack cheese
  1 jar (about 7 oz.) roasted red
    peppers, drained

Prepare Garlic Oil and Grilled Onion; set aside.

On a lightly floured board, roll dough out to a 12- by 18-inch rectangle. Brush surface of rectangle evenly with 2 tablespoons of the Garlic Oil. Cover half the dough lengthwise with overlapping layers of salami, ham, coppa (if desired), cheese, Grilled Onion, and peppers. Lift plain half of dough and fold over filling (if dough sticks to board, loosen it gently with a spatula). Press edges of dough firmly together to seal.

Using 2 wide spatulas, transfer loaf to an oiled 12- by 17-inch baking sheet; tuck ends of dough under to fit on sheet. Brush loaf with remaining Garlic Oil. Let rise in a warm place until puffy (about 20 minutes). Bake in a 400° oven until richly browned (15 to 20 minutes). Let loaf cool slightly before serving.

To serve, cut loaf in half lengthwise; then cut crosswise into 3-inch-wide slices. Makes 6 to 8 servings.

Garlic Oil. In a small bowl, combine 3 tablespoons **olive oil**; 2 cloves **garlic,** minced or pressed; and ½ teaspoon *each* **dry basil, dry oregano,** and **dry thyme.**

Grilled Onion. In a wide frying pan, combine 1 tablespoon **olive oil,** 2 tablespoons **balsamic or red wine vinegar,** and 1 large **onion,** sliced. Cook over medium-high heat, stirring often, until onion begins to brown (8 to 10 minutes). Remove from heat.

Per serving: 757 calories (46 percent from fat), 34 g protein, 68 g carbohydrates, 38 g total fat (14 g saturated fat), 89 mg cholesterol, 1,979 mg sodium

Curried Tuna-Apple Sandwiches

Spicy and sweet flavors mingle temptingly in these out-of-the-ordinary tuna sandwiches. To make them, you combine the traditional canned tuna and mayonnaise with raisins, chopped apple, crisp celery, and green onion, then serve the mixture open-faced on raisin bread.

  ¼ cup mayonnaise
  ½ teaspoon curry powder
  ¼ teaspoon garlic salt
    Dash of ground red pepper
    (cayenne)
  1 tablespoon lemon juice
  1 can (about 6⅛ oz.) water-packed
    chunk-style tuna, drained and
    flaked
  ¾ cup chopped apple
  ½ cup finely chopped celery
  ¼ cup raisins
  2 tablespoons thinly sliced
    green onion
  4 slices raisin bread or whole
    wheat bread, lightly toasted
    and buttered
    Alfalfa sprouts (optional)

In a bowl, stir together mayonnaise, curry powder, garlic salt, red pepper, and lemon juice. Add tuna, apple, celery, raisins, and onion; stir until blended.

Spread an equal portion of tuna mixture over each slice of bread. Top with alfalfa sprouts, if desired. Makes 4 servings.

Per serving: 265 calories (41 percent from fat), 14 g protein, 25 g carbohydrates, 12 g total fat (2 g saturated fat), 24 mg cholesterol, 446 mg sodium

Chicken Supper Sandwiches

Served hot from the oven and teamed with your favorite soup or salad, these easy-to-make sandwiches are perfect for a light supper.

  4 slices bacon, *each* cut in half
    crosswise
  1½ cups sliced cooked chicken or
    turkey breast
  2 English muffins, split, toasted,
    and buttered
  4 slices mild red onion
  1 large tomato, peeled and cut
    into 4 thick slices
  ½ cup shredded Cheddar cheese

Partially cook bacon in a wide frying pan over medium heat to remove most of fat (bacon should still be limp). Lift out and drain on paper towels.

Arrange chicken over muffin halves. Top chicken on each muffin half with an onion slice, a tomato slice, and 2 tablespoons of the cheese. Then arrange 2 bacon pieces atop each half.

Place muffin halves in a rimmed baking pan. Broil about 6 inches below heat until cheese is bubbly and bacon is crisp (3 to 5 minutes). Serve sandwiches open-faced; eat with knife and fork. Makes 2 servings.

Per serving: 634 calories (50 percent from fat), 46 g protein, 32 g carbohydrates, 35 g total fat (14 g saturated fat), 144 mg cholesterol, 742 mg sodium

Chile Relleno Sandwiches

When this recipe was developed in 1963, an oven-baked version of *chiles rellenos* was a popular dinner casserole. This succulent batter-fried sandwich, topped with tangy tomato sauce, is a simple variation on the Mexican favorite. It's best eaten with a knife and fork.

Zesty Tomato Sauce (optional; recipe follows)
10   slices French bread
5   slices jack or mild Cheddar cheese (about 4 oz. *total*)
1   small can (about 4 oz.) whole green chiles
3   eggs
¼   cup milk or half-and-half
¼   teaspoon salt
⅓   cup butter or margarine

Prepare Zesty Tomato Sauce, if desired; keep hot.

Top each of 5 slices of bread with a slice of cheese. Split each chile down one side; gently remove any seeds, then rinse and drain. Lay chiles equally over cheese, then top each sandwich with another slice of bread.

In a shallow bowl, beat together eggs, milk, and salt. Melt butter in a wide frying pan over medium heat. Quickly dip both sides of each sandwich into egg mixture. Add sandwiches to pan, a few at a time (do not crowd pan); cook, turning once, until bread is lightly browned and cheese is melted. Serve plain or with Zesty Tomato Sauce. Makes 5 servings.

Zesty Tomato Sauce. In a small pan, combine 1 can (about 8 oz.) **tomato sauce,** 1 teaspoon **instant minced onion,** and 1 tablespoon **lemon juice.** Season to taste with **salt.** Heat just until boiling. Makes about 1 cup.

Per sandwich: 387 calories (56 percent from fat), 14 g protein, 28 g carbohydrates, 24 g total fat (9 g saturated fat), 182 mg cholesterol, 840 mg sodium

Per tablespoon of Zesty Tomato Sauce: 5 calories (3 percent from fat), 0.2 g protein, 1 g carbohydrates, 0 g total fat (0 g saturated fat), 0 mg cholesterol, 86 mg sodium

Monte Cristo Sandwiches

The classic Monte Cristo is a crisp batter-fried version of the traditional ham and cheese sandwich.

12   slices white bread
About ⅓ cup mayonnaise
12   thin slices natural Swiss cheese (about 1 oz. *each*)
6   thin slices *each* baked ham and roast turkey (about ¾ lb. *total*)
3   eggs
¼   cup milk or half-and-half
¼   teaspoon salt
⅓   cup butter or margarine

Spread one side of each slice of bread with a thin coating of mayonnaise. Assemble 6 sandwiches, using 2 slices of cheese and 1 slice each of ham and turkey in each sandwich. Trim crusts and filling with a sharp knife, making edges of sandwiches even.

In a shallow bowl, beat together eggs, milk, and salt. Melt butter in a wide frying pan over medium heat. Quickly dip both sides of each sandwich into egg mixture. Add sandwiches to pan, a few at a time (do not crowd pan); cook, turning once, until lightly browned on both sides. Transfer sandwiches to a baking sheet. Bake in a 400° oven just until cheese is melted (3 to 5 minutes). Makes 6 servings.

Per serving: 648 calories (60 percent from fat), 35 g protein, 29 g carbohydrates, 43 g total fat (20 g saturated fat), 223 mg cholesterol, 1,467 mg sodium

Reuben Sandwiches

The origin of this delectable corned beef, cheese, and sauerkraut sandwich is still in dispute. According to one theory, the delicacy was created for a local starlet by Arthur Reuben, who owned New York's once-famous but now defunct Reuben's Delicatessen. But a second camp attributes the delicacy to a wholesale grocer named Reuben Kay, said to have come up with the idea during a poker game in Omaha in 1955.

¼   cup mayonnaise
1   tablespoon tomato-based chili sauce
8   slices dark Russian or sourdough rye bread (from an oval-shaped loaf)
½   pound thinly sliced cooked corned beef
8   ounces thinly sliced Swiss cheese
1   cup sauerkraut, drained
Butter or margarine, at room temperature

In a small bowl, stir together mayonnaise and chili sauce. Spread about 2 teaspoons of the mixture over one side of each slice of bread.

To assemble each sandwich, place a fourth of the corned beef on one slice of bread and a fourth of the cheese on another; cover corned beef with ¼ cup of the sauerkraut. Close sandwiches and spread outside surfaces with butter.

Place sandwiches, a few at a time, in a wide frying pan (do not crowd pan); cook over medium-high heat, turning once, until cheese is melted and sandwiches are heated through. Before serving, cut each sandwich diagonally into halves or thirds. Makes 4 servings.

Per serving: 624 calories (57 percent from fat), 32 g protein, 35 g carbohydrates, 39 g total fat (16 g saturated fat), 116 mg cholesterol, 1,491 mg sodium

WESTERN CLASSIC

Chile- & Cheese-stuffed Burgers

Devotion to the all-American all-meat hamburger may waver in favor of this mildly spicy stuffed variation. What appears to be an ordinary beef patty contains a surprise filling of pickled jalapeño chiles and Cheddar cheese.

1½ **pounds lean ground beef**
  3 **ounces Cheddar cheese, cut into matchstick-size pieces**
  2 **to 3 tablespoons minced pickled jalapeño chiles**
    Pepper and garlic salt

  4 **round sourdough French rolls (*each* about 4 inches in diameter) or hamburger buns, split**
    Mayonnaise
    Green leaf lettuce leaves, rinsed and crisped
    Sliced tomatoes

Divide beef into 8 equal portions; shape each portion into a ¼-inch-thick patty. Top 4 of the patties with equal amounts of the cheese and chiles; cover with remaining patties and press edges together to seal. Sprinkle both sides of each patty lightly with pepper and garlic salt.

Place patties on a lightly greased grill 4 to 6 inches above a solid bed of hot coals. Cook, turning once, until well browned on both sides and done to your liking; cut to test (10 to 12 minutes for medium-rare). When you turn patties over, place rolls, cut side down, around outside of grill to toast. Serve patties on rolls. Offer mayonnaise, lettuce, and tomatoes to add to taste. Makes 4 servings.

Per serving: 571 calories (50 percent from fat), 40 g protein, 30 g carbohydrates, 31 g total fat (14 g saturated fat), 127 mg cholesterol, 648 mg sodium

Lamb Pocket Burgers

This savory Mideastern-inspired dish is simple to prepare: you just slip curry-spiced lamb patties into halved rounds of pita bread. Serve with sliced cucumbers, chutney, and tart yogurt.

  1 **pound lean ground lamb**
  1 **small onion, chopped**
  ¼ **cup fine dry bread crumbs**
  ⅓ **cup finely chopped dried apricots**
  1 **egg**
  2 **teaspoons curry powder**
  3 **pita breads (*each* about 7 inches in diameter), cut into halves**
    Chopped Major Grey's chutney
    Plain yogurt
    Sliced cucumbers

In a bowl, combine lamb, onion, crumbs, apricots, egg, and curry powder. Mix well; shape into 6 oblong patties, each 3 to 4 inches long. If you want to heat pita bread halves, stack them and wrap in heavy-duty foil.

Place lamb patties on a lightly greased grill 4 to 6 inches above a solid bed of hot coals. Cook, turning once, until well browned on outside but still pink in center; cut to test (8 to 10 minutes). Also heat foil-wrapped bread at side of grill (not directly above coals) until warm, turning several times.

To serve, place each patty in a pita bread half. Offer chutney, yogurt, and cucumbers to add to taste. Makes 6 servings.

Per serving: 287 calories (38 percent from fat), 18 g protein, 27 g carbohydrates, 12 g total fat (5 g saturated fat), 86 mg cholesterol, 254 mg sodium

Focaccia Milano

Thicker and softer than traditional pizza, Italian *focaccia* often features baked vegetables atop its springy mattress of olive oil–anointed dough. Here, we offer a selection of four toppings: eggplant, tomato, onion, and tangy green olive. If you want to get a head start, make the dough ahead and let it rise slowly overnight in the refrigerator. Or save even more time and use purchased frozen bread dough.

    Focaccia Dough (recipe follows); or 2 loaves (about 1 lb. *each*) frozen white bread dough, thawed and kneaded together
  2 **tablespoons olive oil**
    Vegetable Topping (choices and directions follow)
    Salt and pepper

Prepare Focaccia Dough. Coat bottom of a 10- by 15-inch rimmed baking pan with 1 tablespoon of the oil.

(Continued on next page)

Punch dough down and knead briefly on a lightly floured board. Roll dough out to a rectangle about ½ inch thick. Lift dough into pan; pat firmly out to pan edges. (If dough is too elastic, let rest for about 5 minutes, then continue.) Cover dough lightly and let rise in a warm place until almost doubled (about 45 minutes). While dough is rising, prepare Vegetable Topping of your choice.

Brush remaining 1 tablespoon oil lightly over dough. With your fingers, gently press dough down all over, forming dimples in surface. Also gently push dough to fit into corners of baking pan. Evenly cover dough with topping; sprinkle lightly with salt and pepper.

Bake focaccia in a 400° oven until well browned on edges and bottom (30 to 40 minutes). If topping is browned before bread is done, cover loosely with foil for last 10 to 15 minutes of baking.

Serve hot, warm, or cool; to serve, cut into pieces. If made ahead, cover and let stand at room temperature for up to 8 hours. To reheat, cover loosely with foil and heat in a 350° oven until warm to the touch (10 to 15 minutes). Makes 12 servings.

Focaccia Dough. In a large bowl, combine 1 package **active dry yeast** and 1½ cups **warm water** (about 110°F); let stand until yeast is softened (about 5 minutes). Stir in ½ teaspoon **salt** and 2 tablespoons **olive oil.** Then add 2½ cups **all-purpose flour;** stir to blend. Beat with a dough hook of an electric mixer on medium speed until dough is glossy and elastic (3 to 5 minutes). Stir in 1⅓ cups more **all-purpose flour.**

To knead by hand, scrape dough onto a lightly floured board and knead until smooth and springy (about 10 minutes), adding more flour as needed to prevent sticking. Place dough in a greased bowl; turn over to grease top.

To knead with a dough hook, beat dough on medium speed until it pulls from sides of bowl and is springy (5 to 7 minutes); if dough is sticky, add more flour, 1 tablespoon at a time.

Cover bowl of dough kneaded by either method with plastic wrap; let dough rise in a warm place until doubled—about 45 minutes. (Or let rise in refrigerator until next day.)

Vegetable Topping. Choose one of the following.

Eggplant. Seed and coarsely chop 1 large **red bell pepper.** Cut 2 medium-size unpeeled **eggplants** (about 1 lb. *each*) into ¾-inch cubes. Place vegetables in a 10- by 15-inch rimmed baking pan. Mix in 3 tablespoons **olive oil;** spread vegetables out in an even layer. Bake in a 450° oven, stirring once, until eggplant is lightly browned and beginning to soften (about 25 minutes).

Over dimpled dough, sprinkle 2 cups (about 8 oz.) shredded **mozzarella cheese.** Distribute eggplant mixture over cheese. After baking, sprinkle focaccia with 2 tablespoons chopped **Italian parsley.**

Per serving: 301 calories (37 percent from fat), 9 g protein, 39 g carbohydrates, 12 g total fat (4 g saturated fat), 15 mg cholesterol, 167 mg sodium

Tomato. Coat a 10- by 15-inch rimmed baking pan with 1 tablespoon **olive**

oil. Cut 2 pounds large **pear-shaped (Roma-type) tomatoes** lengthwise into ½-inch-thick slices. Lay slices in baking pan in a single layer, overlapping slightly if necessary. Drizzle 2 tablespoons **olive oil** over tomatoes. Bake in a 450° oven until tomatoes look dry and pan juices have evaporated (about 25 minutes). Gently loosen tomatoes from pan with a wide spatula.

Evenly space tomatoes over dimpled dough. Sprinkle with 1 teaspoon *each* **dry basil** and **dry oregano.**

Per serving: 233 calories (33 percent from fat), 5 g protein, 34 g carbohydrates, 9 g total fat (1 g saturated fat), 0 mg cholesterol, 99 mg sodium

Onion. Cut 3 medium-size **onions** in half lengthwise, then slice ¼ inch thick and place in a 10- by 15-inch rimmed baking pan. Mix in 2 tablespoons **olive oil.** Bake in a 450° oven, stirring occasionally, until onions are soft but not browned (about 20 minutes). Stir in ¼ cup **golden raisins** and 1 tablespoon chopped, drained **canned anchovy fillets.** Scatter over dimpled dough.

Per serving: 235 calories (28 percent from fat), 5 g protein, 37 g carbohydrates, 7 g total fat (1 g saturated fat), 0.8 mg cholesterol, 149 mg sodium

Olive. Cut 20 to 25 **large pitted green olives** (at least 1 inch long) in half lengthwise. Press olive halves, cut sides down, in even rows into dimpled dough, spacing about 1 inch apart. Sprinkle with 1 teaspoon **dry thyme.**

Per serving: 201 calories (29 percent from fat), 5 g protein, 31 g carbohydrates, 6 g total fat (0.8 g saturated fat), 0 mg cholesterol, 390 mg sodium

Italian Sausage Pizza

If you enjoy sausage pizza, this delicious traditional recipe is sure to become one of your favorites. Shredded cheese, slices of green pepper, spicy tomato sauce, and lots of Italian sausage all stack up on a soft and yeasty crust.

1 package active dry yeast
1 cup warm water (about 110°F)
½ teaspoon salt
2 teaspoons olive oil
  About 3 cups all-purpose flour
  Tomato Sauce (recipe follows)
1 pound mild Italian sausages, casings removed
  Olive oil or salad oil
½ green bell pepper, seeded and cut into thin strips
3 cups (about 12 oz.) shredded mozzarella cheese

In a large bowl, combine yeast and warm water; let stand until yeast is softened (about 5 minutes). Stir in salt and the 2 teaspoons oil. Gradually mix in 3 cups of the flour to form a soft dough. Turn dough out onto a floured board and knead until smooth and elastic (about 5 minutes), adding more flour as needed to prevent sticking. Place dough in a greased bowl and turn over to grease top; cover and let rise in a warm place until doubled (about 1 hour).

Meanwhile, prepare Tomato Sauce and set aside. Crumble sausage into a wide frying pan; cook over medium heat, stirring often, until browned. Remove sausage from pan with a slotted spoon, drain well, and set aside.

Punch dough down and knead on a lightly floured board to shape into a smooth ball. Divide dough in half. Roll each half out about ¾ inch thick, then gently pull and stretch to make an oval 12 to 14 inches long and 8 to 10 inches wide.

Place each crust on a greased baking sheet and brush generously with oil. Spread Tomato Sauce over crusts; top equally with sausage, bell pepper, and cheese. Bake pizzas on lowest rack of a 500° oven until crust is browned (12 to 15 minutes). Cut pizzas into wedges to serve. Makes 2 pizzas (4 to 6 servings *each*).

Tomato Sauce. Drain liquid from 3 cans (about 14½ oz. *each*) **tomatoes** into a 4-quart pan. Cut up tomatoes and add to pan; then add 1 can (about 6 oz.) **tomato paste**; 1 clove **garlic,** minced or pressed; 1 teaspoon **dry basil;** and ½ teaspoon *each* **dry rosemary** and **dry oregano**. Bring to a boil over medium-high heat; boil, uncovered, stirring occasionally, until sauce is thickened and reduced to about 2 cups. Remove from heat.

Per serving: 414 calories (44 percent from fat), 19 g protein, 39 g carbohydrates, 20 g total fat (8 g saturated fat), 52 mg cholesterol, 879 mg sodium

Whole Wheat Zucchini Pizza

Use a chewy whole wheat crust as your canvas—then create a colorful topping with a selection of fresh seasonal ingredients. A spicy tomato sauce enhances all the flavors.

1 package active dry yeast
1½ cups warm water (about 110°F)
2 tablespoons salad oil or olive oil
1 teaspoon *each* salt, sugar, dry basil, and dry oregano
¼ cup wheat germ
  About 1½ cups all-purpose flour
1½ cups whole wheat flour
  Tomato Sauce (recipe follows)
2 medium-size zucchini, thinly sliced
½ green or red bell pepper, seeded and thinly sliced
4 green onions, thinly sliced
1 can (about 2¼ oz.) sliced ripe olives, drained
1 can (about 14 oz.) water-packed artichoke hearts, drained and quartered
3 cups (about 12 oz.) shredded jack cheese
¼ cup grated Parmesan cheese

In a large bowl, combine yeast and warm water; let stand until yeast is softened (about 5 minutes). Add oil, salt, sugar, basil, oregano, wheat germ, and 1½ cups of the all-purpose flour.

Beat with a dough hook of a heavy-duty electric mixer until smooth—about 3 minutes. (Or beat with a heavy spoon until smooth.) Then beat in whole wheat flour until dough holds together.

Turn dough out onto a board lightly floured with all-purpose flour and knead until smooth and elastic (about 5 minutes). Place dough in a greased bowl and turn over to grease top. Cover and let rise in a warm place until doubled (about 45 minutes). Meanwhile, prepare Tomato Sauce.

Punch dough down and divide in half. On a lightly floured board, roll out each half to a 14-inch circle. Transfer each circle to a greased 14-inch pizza pan; gently push dough out to edges of pan. Partially bake crusts, one at a time, on next-to-lowest rack of a 450° oven until bottom of crust starts to brown (about 7 minutes). During baking, watch carefully and prick any bubbles that form. Remove from oven.

To assemble pizzas, spread Tomato Sauce over crusts; top equally with zucchini, bell pepper, onions, olives, and artichokes. Sprinkle evenly with jack cheese and Parmesan cheese.

Bake in a 450° oven until cheese is melted (12 to 15 minutes). Cut pizzas into wedges to serve. Makes 2 pizzas (6 servings *each*).

Tomato Sauce. Heat 2 tablespoons **olive oil** or salad oil in a wide frying pan over medium heat. Add 1 large **onion,** chopped; cook, stirring often, until soft (about 5 minutes). Stir in 1 can (about 15 oz.) **tomato sauce,** 1 can (about 6 oz.) **tomato paste,** ½ cup **dry red wine,** and 1 teaspoon *each* **dry oregano** and **dry basil**. Bring to a simmer; then simmer, uncovered, for 10 minutes. Season to taste with **salt**. Remove from heat.

Per serving: 332 calories (41 percent from fat), 14 g protein, 35 g carbohydrates, 15 g total fat (1 g saturated fat), 26 mg cholesterol, 753 mg sodium

Pizza on the Barbecue

One of *Sunset*'s most popular grilling innovations is barbecue-cooked pizza—it has the same crisp crust and smoky flavor as pizzas baked in a traditional Italian wood-burning oven. We offer two toppings, one with Italian sausage and the other with marinated artichoke hearts and roasted red peppers.

- 1 **can or jar (about 1 lb.) marinara sauce**
- 2 **cups hickory or mesquite wood chips**
- 1 **pound mild Italian sausages, casings removed**
  Olive oil
- 1 **tablespoon cornmeal**
- 1 **loaf (about 1 lb.) frozen white bread dough, thawed**
- 2 **cups (about 8 oz.) shredded mozzarella cheese**
- 1 **cup (about 4 oz.) shredded jack cheese**
- ½ **small onion, thinly sliced crosswise**
- ½ **medium-size red bell pepper, seeded and thinly sliced crosswise**
- ¼ **to ⅓ cup calamata or Niçoise olives (optional)**
- 1 **cup lightly packed fresh basil leaves**

Pour marinara sauce into a 5- to 6-quart pan. Bring to a boil over medium-high heat; boil, stirring often, until reduced to about ¾ cup. Set aside.

Soak wood chips in warm water to cover for at least 30 minutes or up to 4 hours.

Crumble sausages into a wide frying pan; then cook over medium-high heat, stirring often, until well browned. Remove from pan with a slotted spoon, drain well, and set aside.

On the fire grate of a barbecue with a lid, ignite charcoal briquets— 50 briquets for a 22- to 24-inch round barbecue, 75 briquets for an 18- by 32-inch rectangular barbecue. When coals are covered with gray ash (after 30 to 40 minutes), push them out in a ring or rectangle just slightly larger than your pizza pan. (If you plan to cook more than one pizza, at this time add 10 briquets to a round barbecue, 20 briquets to a rectangular one; space briquets evenly.) Set grill in place 4 to 6 inches above coals. Cover barbecue, open vents, and heat until temperature in barbecue is 400° to 450° (about 15 minutes). To test temperature, set an oven thermometer in center of grill, not over coals; or refer to thermostat on barbecue, which should read hot.

Meanwhile, oil a 14-inch pizza pan or a 10- by 15-inch rimmed baking pan. Sprinkle with cornmeal. Roll out dough on a lightly floured board. For pizza pan, roll out dough to a 15- to 16-inch round; for rectangular pan, roll out to an 11- by 16-inch rectangle. Lift dough into pan and pat firmly out to pan edges.

Spread reduced marinara sauce over dough to within about 1 inch of edges. Mix mozzarella and jack cheeses; scatter over sauce. Top cheese with sausage, onion, bell pepper, and olives (if desired). Let stand until barbecue is ready.

Drain wood chips and sprinkle over coals. Place pizza on grill within (not over) rim of coals; cover barbecue. Cook with vents open until crust is well browned on bottom (lift with a wide spatula to check) and cheese is melted (about 15 minutes; check crust after 10 minutes). Remove from barbecue and top with basil; cut into wedges to serve. Makes 6 servings.

Per serving: 637 calories (50 percent from fat), 31 g protein, 50 g carbohydrates, 35 g total fat (11 g saturated fat), 93 mg cholesterol, 1,595 mg sodium

Artichoke & Roasted Pepper Pizza

Follow directions for **Pizza on the Barbecue,** but omit sausage, onion, and bell pepper; olives are optional. For toppings, use 1 jar (about 6 oz.) **marinated artichoke hearts,** drained; ⅓ cup crumbled crisp-cooked **bacon;** and 1 jar (about 7 oz.) **roasted red peppers,** drained. Cook as directed. Makes 6 servings.

Per serving: 514 calories (45 percent from fat), 22 g protein, 50 g carbohydrates, 26 g total fat (8 g saturated fat), 55 mg cholesterol, 1,334 mg sodium

---

BARBECUED PIZZA

To barbecue pizza, simply stoke the barbecue with a measured number of charcoal briquets. When the coals are hot, spread them out and cover the barbecue, allowing the heat to build. Then sprinkle the coals with soaked wood chips and let the pizza bake to a nice golden brown in the swirling smoke.

Up-to-date sauces get a lively boost from a variety of herbs, spices, and seasonal vegetables. Ranging from mild and creamy to spicy and chunky, the choices on this page bring savory flavors—and delicious contrasts in texture—to all kinds of dishes.

Classic Pesto

- 2 cups lightly packed fresh basil leaves
- 1 cup (about 4 oz.) grated Parmesan cheese
- ¼ cup olive oil
- 2 tablespoons pine nuts
- 1 or 2 cloves garlic

In a food processor or blender, combine basil, cheese, oil, pine nuts, and garlic; whirl until puréed. If made ahead, cover and refrigerate until next day. Bring to room temperature before using. Makes about 1 cup.

Per tablespoon: 75 calories (70 percent from fat), 4 g protein, 2 g carbohydrates, 6 g total fat (2 g saturated fat), 6 mg cholesterol, 133 mg sodium

Bellins' Garden Marinara Sauce

- ¼ cup olive oil
- 3 large onions, coarsely chopped
- 3 or 4 cloves garlic, minced or pressed
- 6 pounds ripe tomatoes, peeled and chopped; or 4 large cans (about 28 oz. *each*) tomatoes, drained and chopped
- 1 cup lightly packed fresh basil leaves, chopped
- ½ to 1 tablespoon sugar
  Salt and pepper

Heat oil in a wide frying pan over medium heat. Add onions and garlic; cook, stirring often, until onions are golden brown (about 20 minutes). Add

tomatoes and basil. Cook over medium heat, uncovered, stirring occasionally to prevent sticking, until sauce is reduced to about 2 quarts (45 to 60 minutes). Add sugar and season to taste with salt and pepper. If made ahead, let cool; then cover and refrigerate for up to 1 week or freeze for up to 6 months. Reheat to boiling before serving. Makes about 2 quarts.

Per ½ cup: 85 calories (38 percent from fat), 2 g protein, 12 g carbohydrates, 4 g total fat (0.5 g saturated fat), 0 mg cholesterol, 16 mg sodium

Homemade Mayonnaise

- 1 large egg or 3 egg yolks
- 1 teaspoon Dijon mustard
- 1 tablespoon white wine vinegar or lemon juice
- 1 cup salad oil or olive oil
  Salt (optional)

In a blender or food processor, combine egg, mustard, and vinegar. Whirl until well blended (3 to 5 seconds). With motor running, add oil in a slow, steady stream, whirling until mixture is smoothly blended. Season to taste with salt, if desired. If made ahead, cover and refrigerate for up to 2 weeks. Makes about 1½ cups.

Per tablespoon: 84 calories (98 percent from fat), 0.3 g protein, 0.1 g carbohydrates, 9 g total fat (1 g saturated fat), 9 mg cholesterol, 9 mg sodium

Egg-safe Mayonnaise

Mix 1 egg white with 2 tablespoons lemon juice. Cover airtight and refrigerate for at least 48 hours or up to 4

days (upon longer standing, egg begins to solidify). In a blender or food processor, whirl acidified egg white with 2 tablespoons water and 2 teaspoons Dijon mustard. With motor running, add 1 cup salad oil or olive oil in a slow, steady stream, whirling until mixture is smoothly blended. Season to taste with lemon juice and salt; whirl until blended. If made ahead, cover and refrigerate for up to 4 days. Makes about 1¼ cups.

Per tablespoon: 98 calories (99 percent from fat), 0.2 g protein, 0.2 g carbohydrates, 11 g total fat (1 g saturated fat), 0 mg cholesterol, 18 mg sodium

Green Mayonnaise

In a small bowl, combine 8 watercress sprigs, 6 to 10 spinach leaves, and 5 parsley sprigs; cover with boiling water and let stand for about 5 minutes. Drain, rinse with cold water, and drain again, pressing out excess moisture. Transfer greens to a blender or food processor. Add 2 teaspoons lemon juice; whirl until greens are finely minced. Then follow directions for Homemade Mayonnaise or Egg-safe Mayonnaise, adding egg, mustard, and vinegar to blender with minced greens. Makes about 1½ cups.

Per tablespoon: 84 calories (98 percent from fat), 0.3 g protein, 0.1 g carbohydrates, 9 g total fat (1 g saturated fat), 9 mg cholesterol, 10 mg sodium

Chipotle Chile Mayonnaise

Prepare Homemade Mayonnaise or Egg-safe Mayonnaise. Then add 3 canned chipotle chiles in adobo sauce, minced, and 1 tablespoon sauce from chiles to mayonnaise in blender. Whirl until chiles are finely minced. Makes about 1½ cups.

Per tablespoon: 89 calories (94 percent from fat), 0.3 g protein, 1 g carbohydrates, 9 g total fat (1 g saturated fat), 9 mg cholesterol, 46 mg sodium

EGGS & CHEESE

*F*ew ingredients complement each other as perfectly as eggs and cheese, so it's no wonder that this simple combination is favored the world over as a base for both savory and sweeter dishes. • This chapter presents a collection of long-time favorites—most featuring both eggs and cheese, some starring just one of the pair. We've included traditional Swiss fondue, classic deviled eggs, a pair of quiches, and a variety of international specialties. From France comes the light and airy soufflé. Italy gives us savory frittata and crusty, golden brown torta rustica. Mexico offers spicy enchiladas and chiles rellenos. All in all, you'll find more than 20 great ideas for breakfast, brunch, lunch, or supper.

Mexican Quiche

In 1980, we offered this crustless Mexican-spiced interpretation of the classic French quiche. Chunks of chorizo sausage, mild green chiles, and whole kernels of corn give the tender jack-cheese custard a south-of-the-border flair.

> About 1 pound chorizo sausages, casings removed
>
> 2 medium-size onions, chopped
>
> 1 teaspoon salt
>
> ⅛ teaspoon pepper
>
> ¼ cup diced fresh mild green chiles or canned diced green chiles
>
> 10 eggs
>
> 2 cups milk or half-and-half
>
> 1 can (about 2¼ oz.) sliced ripe olives, drained
>
> 1 can (about 8¾ oz.) whole-kernel corn, drained
>
> 3 cups (about 12 oz.) shredded jack cheese
>
> Avocado and tomato slices
>
> Cilantro sprigs

Crumble chorizo into a wide frying pan and cook over medium-high heat, stirring often, until browned. Add onions and cook, stirring often, until soft (about 4 minutes). Discard fat. Stir in salt, pepper, and chiles. Remove from heat.

In a large bowl, beat eggs and milk until blended. Stir in chorizo mixture, olives, corn, and cheese. Evenly spread mixture in a greased 10- by 15-inch rimmed baking pan.

Bake in a 375° oven until a knife inserted in center comes out clean (25 to 30 minutes). Let stand for 10 minutes before serving. To serve, cut into squares and garnish with avocado, tomato, and cilantro sprigs. Makes 6 to 8 servings.

Per serving: 549 calories (62 percent from fat), 33 g protein, 19 g carbohydrates, 38 g total fat (8 g saturated fat), 395 mg cholesterol, 1,093 mg sodium

Spanish Tortilla

In Spain, this pepper-studded egg-and-potato dish is called a *tortilla*. It's often served at room temperature, as a snack with sherry—or as a light supper, accompanied by fresh fruit or salad.

> 3 tablespoons olive oil
>
> 1 small onion, finely chopped
>
> 2 cloves garlic, minced or pressed (optional)
>
> 2 medium-size thin-skinned potatoes, scrubbed and cut into ¼-inch cubes
>
> 1 can (about 6 oz.) pitted ripe olives, drained
>
> 1 jar (about 7 oz.) roasted red peppers or pimentos, drained; or 1 large can (about 7 oz.) diced green chiles
>
> 9 eggs
>
> Sour cream (optional)

Heat 1 tablespoon of the oil in a wide nonstick frying pan over medium heat. Add onion and garlic (if desired); cook, stirring often, just until onion is soft (about 5 minutes). Add remaining 2 tablespoons oil, then potatoes; turn with a wide spatula to coat potatoes evenly with oil. Cook over medium-high heat, turning often, until potatoes are golden and tender to bite (about 15 minutes). Coarsely chop olives and peppers; stir into potato mixture.

In a large bowl, beat eggs until blended. Reduce heat under potatoes to low; add eggs. Cover and cook until eggs are set about 1 inch around pan edges but still look liquid in center (about 8 minutes). Uncover; tilt pan and, with a spatula, slightly lift edges of tortilla to let any uncooked egg flow underneath. Cover and cook until eggs are set but tortilla is still moist on top (5 to 10 minutes).

Ease spatula down sides and beneath tortilla to loosen it from pan. Invert a flat plate or rimless baking sheet (wider than pan) over pan. Protecting your hands, hold plate and pan together; invert both, then lift off pan. With a spatula, slide tortilla from plate back into pan, cooked side up. Cook, uncovered, until eggs are set on bottom; lift with spatula to test (about 1 minute).

Slide tortilla onto a platter. Serve hot, warm, or at room temperature. To serve, cut into wedges. Offer sour cream to add to taste, if desired. Makes 4 to 6 servings.

Per serving: 318 calories (59 percent from fat), 14 g protein, 19 g carbohydrates, 21 g total fat (4 g saturated fat), 383 mg cholesterol, 422 mg sodium

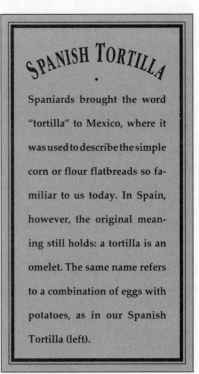

SPANISH TORTILLA

Spaniards brought the word "tortilla" to Mexico, where it was used to describe the simple corn or flour flatbreads so familiar to us today. In Spain, however, the original meaning still holds: a tortilla is an omelet. The same name refers to a combination of eggs with potatoes, as in our Spanish Tortilla (left).

Make-ahead Layered Mushrooms & Eggs

Eighteen eggs, mushrooms, cheese, and a hearty splash of sherry meet in this crowd-pleasing casserole. Because it can be prepared a day ahead, it's an excellent timesaver for a party or potluck menu.

- 1 can (about 10¾ oz.) condensed cream of mushroom soup
- 3 tablespoons dry sherry or milk
- 1½ cups (about 6 oz.) *each* shredded sharp Cheddar cheese and shredded jack cheese
- 18 eggs
- 2 tablespoons milk
- 1 teaspoon parsley flakes
- ½ teaspoon dry dill weed
- ⅛ teaspoon pepper
- ¼ cup butter or margarine
- ¼ pound mushrooms, sliced
- ¼ cup sliced green onions
  Paprika

In a small pan, combine soup and sherry. Cook over medium heat, stirring occasionally, until mixture is smooth and heated through. Remove from heat and set aside. In a small bowl, lightly mix Cheddar and jack cheeses; set aside. In a large bowl, beat eggs with milk, parsley, dill weed, and pepper until blended; set aside.

Melt butter in a wide frying pan over medium-low heat. Add mushrooms and onions; cook, stirring often, until onions are soft (about 7 minutes). Add egg mixture and cook, gently lifting cooked portion to let uncooked egg flow underneath, until eggs are set but still moist on top.

Spoon half the egg mixture into a 7- by 11-inch baking dish and cover with half the soup mixture; sprinkle evenly with half the cheese. Repeat layers; sprinkle top with paprika. (At this point, you may let cool, then cover and refrigerate until next day.)

Bake, uncovered, in a 300° oven until bubbly and heated through (30 to 35 minutes; about 1 hour if refrigerated). Let stand for 10 minutes before serving. To serve, cut into squares. Makes 8 to 10 servings.

Per serving: 384 calories (70 percent from fat), 23 g protein, 6 g carbohydrates, 30 g total fat (11 g saturated fat), 476 mg cholesterol, 674 mg sodium

Creamy Eggs & Sweet Onions

The French call this fragrant egg dish *oeufs à la tripe*—but that doesn't mean the sauce is made with tripe! The name refers to the sautéed onions, which look something like tripe. Serve the creamy entrée for brunch or supper, with toasted baguette slices or English muffins.

- 2½ pounds onions
- ¼ cup butter or margarine
- ½ cup all-purpose flour
- 4 cups hot milk
- 12 hard-cooked eggs, cut crosswise into ½-inch-thick slices
  Salt and pepper

Cut onions in half lengthwise, then thinly slice crosswise. Melt butter in a deep 5- to 6-quart pan over medium heat. Add onions and cook, stirring often, until soft but not browned (about 20 minutes). Stir in flour and cook, stirring, for 1 minute (do not brown). Gradually stir in milk and cook over medium heat, stirring constantly, until sauce boils and thickens.

Reserve 8 to 10 perfect egg slices; stir remaining egg slices into onion mixture and season to taste with salt and pepper. To serve, spoon into a warm serving dish and garnish with reserved egg slices. Makes 8 to 10 servings.

Per serving: 288 calories (50 percent from fat), 14 g protein, 22 g carbohydrates, 16 g total fat (8 g saturated fat), 312 mg cholesterol, 192 mg sodium

Curried Eggs with Shrimp Sauce

Blanketed with a creamy sauce of shrimp and cheese, curry-seasoned deviled eggs are just right for a rich, hearty supper dish.

    8   hard-cooked eggs
    1   teaspoon salt
    ½   teaspoon *each* curry powder and
        paprika
    ¼   teaspoon dry mustard
    1½ tablespoons lemon juice
        Dash of Worcestershire
    2   to 3 tablespoons sour cream
    2   tablespoons butter or margarine
    2   tablespoons all-purpose flour
    2   cups milk
    1   cup (about 4 oz.) shredded
        sharp Cheddar cheese
    1   teaspoon Worcestershire
        Salt and pepper
    2   cups small cooked shrimp
        or 2 cans (about 5 oz. *each*)
        shrimp, drained

Cut eggs in half lengthwise and remove yolks. Place yolks in a bowl and add the 1 teaspoon salt, curry powder, paprika, mustard, lemon juice, and a dash of Worcestershire; mash with a fork until blended. Add sour cream; blend until smooth. Fill egg halves with yolk mixture and press halves together to make 8 whole eggs. Place eggs in a greased 8- or 9-inch baking dish; set aside.

Melt butter in a small pan over medium heat. Stir in flour and cook, stirring, for 1 minute (do not brown). Remove from heat and gradually stir in milk. Then return to heat and cook, stirring constantly, until sauce boils and thickens. Stir in cheese and the 1 teaspoon Worcestershire; stir until cheese is melted. Season to taste with salt and pepper. Add shrimp; stir until combined. Pour sauce over eggs. Bake in a 350° oven until bubbly and heated through (about 20 minutes). Makes 4 to 6 servings.

Per serving: 391 calories (60 percent from fat), 29 g protein, 9 g carbohydrates, 26 g total fat (13 g saturated fat), 481 mg cholesterol, 893 mg sodium

Viennese Eggs

First featured in *Sunset* in 1969, these deviled eggs have become a classic. For an elegant presentation, use a pastry bag with a rosette tip to pipe the yolk mixture into the whites.

    9   hard-cooked eggs
    ½   cup sour cream
        Salt
        Thin lime slices, cut into
        quarters
        About 1½ tablespoons black
        caviar

Cut eggs in half lengthwise and remove yolks, being careful not to tear whites. Place yolks in a bowl and mash to a smooth paste with a fork. Blend in sour cream and season to taste with salt. Spoon yolk mixture into whites (or force through a pastry bag fitted with a large rosette tip). Top each egg half with a quarter-slice of lime and about ¼ teaspoon of the caviar. If made ahead, cover loosely with plastic wrap, being careful not to let wrap touch eggs, and refrigerate until next day. Makes 1½ dozen deviled-egg halves.

Per egg half: 56 calories (68 percent from fat), 4 g protein, 0.8 g carbohydrates, 4 g total fat (2 g saturated fat), 117 mg cholesterol, 54 mg sodium

Baked Artichoke Frittata

The traditional Italian *frittata* is a thick, flat omelet, often laden with a variety of seasonal vegetables. Some frittatas are flipped in the pan to cook both sides, but this variation is made Florentine style—it's baked to a light golden brown.

    1   package (about 9 oz.) frozen
        artichoke hearts, cooked and
        drained
    6   eggs
    ½   cup half-and-half
    ¼   teaspoon salt
    ⅛   teaspoon *each* pepper and
        ground nutmeg
    1   cup (about 4 oz.) shredded
        fontina or jack cheese
    ½   cup grated Parmesan cheese

Spread artichokes evenly in a well-greased shallow 1½- to 2-quart baking pan (round or oval). In a bowl, beat eggs with half-and-half, salt, pepper, and nutmeg. Stir in fontina cheese. Pour egg mixture over artichokes.

Bake in a 350° oven until edges are lightly browned and center feels firm when lightly pressed (about 30 minutes). Sprinkle evenly with Parmesan cheese; return to oven and continue to bake until puffy and lightly browned (5 to 8 more minutes). Serve at once. Makes 4 servings.

Per serving: 348 calories (64 percent from fat), 23 g protein, 8 g carbohydrates, 25 g total fat (13 g saturated fat), 376 mg cholesterol, 704 mg sodium

Torta Rustica

Easy to pack and delicious served at any temperature, this traditional Northern Italian specialty is a perfect choice for a no-fuss picnic. Our recipe lets you exercise some creativity—you can take your pick from three fillings and two different shapes.

>   **Torta Filling (choices and recipes follow)**
> 1 **package (about 1 lb.) hot yeast roll mix, plus water, butter or margarine, and egg as specified on package**
> 1 **egg, lightly beaten**

Prepare Torta Filling; set aside.

Prepare hot yeast roll mix according to package directions; knead briefly on lightly floured board. Cut off a third of the dough; set aside. Roll out remaining portion to a 13-inch round; fit over bottom and up sides of a greased 9-inch spring-form pan. Cover evenly with filling.

Shape reserved dough as a lattice or wedges. *For lattice,* roll dough out to a 9-inch square and cut into strips about 1 inch wide. Weave strips over filling in a lattice pattern, tucking ends of dough down around filling at pan rim. *For wedges,* roll dough out to a 9-inch round; cut into 8 wedges. Arrange wedges side by side on filling, with tips meeting in center.

Lightly cover torta and let rise in a warm place until puffy (30 to 40 minutes). Uncover; brush top with egg.

Bake on lowest rack of a 350° oven until richly browned (35 to 40 minutes). Let cool in pan on a rack for about 5 minutes, then remove pan rim. Serve warm or at room temperature. If made ahead, let cool; then cover and refrigerate until next day. To reheat, wrap cold torta in foil and bake in a 350° oven for 40 minutes (it takes as long to reheat as to bake).

To serve, cut torta into wedges. Makes 6 to 8 servings.

Torta Filling. Choose one of the following.

Spinach & ricotta. In a bowl, combine 2 packages (about 10 oz. *each*) **frozen chopped spinach,** thawed and squeezed dry; 1 cup **ricotta cheese;** ½ cup grated **Parmesan cheese;** 1 **egg yolk;** ½ teaspoon **garlic salt;** and ⅛ teaspoon **pepper.** Stir until blended.

Per serving: 364 calories (32 percent from fat), 15 g protein, 47 g carbohydrates, 13 g total fat (7 g saturated fat), 122 mg cholesterol, 748 mg sodium

Tuna & cheese. Thinly slice 1 small **onion** and separate into rings. Heat 1 tablespoon **olive oil** in a small frying pan over medium heat. Add onion and ¼ cup finely chopped **green or red bell pepper;** cook, stirring, until onion is lightly browned (about 10 minutes). Remove from heat and add 1 can (about 6⅛ oz.) **chunk-style tuna,** drained and chopped, and ¼ teaspoon **dry oregano;** stir until blended. Season to taste with **salt.** Distribute filling over dough as directed; cover with 1 cup (about 4 oz.) shredded **fontina or jack cheese.**

Per serving: 398 calories (33 percent from fat), 19 g protein, 47 g carbohydrates, 15 g total fat (6 g saturated fat), 93 mg cholesterol, 682 mg sodium

Sausage & tomato. Remove casings from ¾ pound **mild Italian sausages.** Crumble meat into a wide frying pan and cook over medium heat, stirring often, until browned; remove from heat. Discard fat. Stir in ¼ cup finely

chopped **parsley** and 2 tablespoons grated **Parmesan cheese.** Distribute filling over dough as directed, then top with ½ cup well-drained **canned sliced tomatoes** and 1 cup (about 4 oz.) shredded **mozzarella cheese.**

Per serving: 436 calories (39 percent from fat), 19 g protein, 47 g carbohydrates, 19 g total fat (8 g saturated fat), 111 mg cholesterol, 914 mg sodium

Roasted Cheese-stuffed Chiles

Preparing this recipe could hardly be quicker—just stuff cheese into seeded fresh chiles and bake. The result? Tender, smoky-flavored chiles oozing with melted cheese. Delicious! For added flavor, top this first-course or side-dish treat with tomato sauce or salsa and guacamole.

>   **Easy Guacamole (page 11) or purchased guacamole (optional)**
> 4 **fresh red or green California (Anaheim) chiles (about ½ lb. total)**
> ½ **cup *each* shredded Cheddar cheese and shredded mozzarella cheese**
>   **Tomato sauce or salsa (optional)**

Prepare Easy Guacamole, if desired. Refrigerate.

Leave stems on chiles. Slit each chile lengthwise; remove any seeds or pith. Lightly mix Cheddar and mozzarella cheeses; fill chiles equally with cheese.

Place chiles, side by side and slit side up, in a 9-inch-square baking pan. Bake in a 400° oven until chiles are soft and lightly tinged with brown (about 25 minutes). To serve, offer chiles on a small platter or individual plates; top with tomato sauce and guacamole, if desired. Makes 4 servings.

Per serving: 114 calories (60 percent from fat), 7 g protein, 4 g carbohydrates, 8 g total fat (5 g saturated fat), 26 mg cholesterol, 144 mg sodium

This delicious puffed pancake originated at Manca's, a family-run Seattle restaurant popular during the first half of this century. Victor Manca baked the batter for a big German pancake in miniature size; the results were christened "Dutch babies" by his children. Manca's recipe remains a family secret, but enterprising cooks have come up with numerous variations similar to the original.

Our recipe for a giant-size Dutch baby has been a favorite since it first appeared in *Sunset* decades ago. The rich batter puffs dramatically in the oven. For the most impressive rise, use a large, shallow pan (such as an ovenproof frying pan, baking dish, or paella pan) and be sure to adjust the amounts of ingredients to match the size of your pan. Serve the pancake with your choice of toppings, for brunch or as a homey dessert.

Dutch Baby Pancakes

Select pan of the appropriate size (see below). Place **butter** in pan and set in a 425° oven. While butter is melting, place **eggs** in a blender or food processor and whirl at high speed for 1 minute. With motor running, gradually pour in **milk,** then slowly add **flour;** continue whirling for 30 seconds. (Or, in a bowl, beat eggs until blended; gradually beat in milk, then flour.)

Remove pan from oven and pour in batter. Return pan to oven and bake until pancake is well browned and puffy (20 to 25 minutes, depending on pan size).

Dust pancake with **ground nutmeg,** if desired. To serve, cut into wedges; serve at once with any of the following toppings. Makes 3 to 6 servings.

Toppings. Choose one of the following; or create your own topping.

Cherries Jubilee. Prepare **Cherries Jubilee** (page 218). Spoon hot sauce over pancake.

Powdered sugar classic. Have a shaker or bowl of **powdered sugar** and thick wedges of **lemon** at the table. Sprinkle sugar on hot pancake; then squeeze lemon juice over all.

Fruit. Use your favorite **fresh fruit** (cored and sliced, if necessary) or canned fruit. Top pancake with fruit; drizzle with **honey** or dust with **powdered sugar.**

Hot fruit. Cook **apple or pear slices** in melted **butter** or margarine over medium heat until tender; spoon over pancake and offer with **sour cream** or plain yogurt. Or heat **banana or papaya slices** in melted **butter** or margarine over medium heat; spoon over pancake and serve with **lime wedges**.

Canned pie filling. Combine 1 can (about 21 oz.) **cherry or apple pie filling** with **lemon juice** and **ground cinnamon** to taste. Serve cold or warm over pancake; top with **plain yogurt.**

Syrups. Offer **maple syrup,** honey, or any favorite fruit sauce or topping.

Per serving (without topping): 302 calories (48 percent from fat), 12 g protein, 27 g carbohydrates, 16 g total fat (8 g saturated fat), 244 mg cholesterol, 181 mg sodium

Cinnamon Apple Dutch Baby

Melt 2 tablespoons **butter** or margarine in 2- to 3-quart baking pan over medium heat. Stir in 2 teaspoons **ground cinnamon** and 3 tablespoons **sugar.** Add 2 medium-size **tart apples** (such as Gravenstein or Granny Smith), peeled, cored, and sliced; cook, stirring, until apples begin to soften (about 5 minutes). Spray inside edge of pan with **vegetable oil cooking spray.** Place pan in a 425° oven for 5 minutes.

Then follow directions for 2- to 3-quart **Dutch Baby Pancake,** but omit butter. Instead, pour batter into pan with apples. Bake until pancake is well browned and puffy (15 to 20 minutes). To serve, dust with **powdered sugar;** cut into wedges. Makes 6 servings.

Per serving: 232 calories (44 percent from fat), 6 g protein, 27 g carbohydrates, 12 g total fat (6 g saturated fat), 131 mg cholesterol, 125 mg sodium

Pan Size	Butter or Margarine	Eggs	Milk & All-purpose Flour
2–3 qt.	2 tablespoons	3	¾ cup *each*
3–4 qt.	3 tablespoons	4	1 cup *each*
4–4½ qt.	¼ cup	5	1¼ cups *each*
4½–5 qt.	¼ cup	6	1½ cups *each*

Chile-Egg Puff

Similar to a creamy frittata, this simple egg dish may be served as either an appetizer or a brunch entrée. For appetizer-size servings, simply bake the egg mixture in mini-muffin pans rather than a square pan.

  5 **eggs**
  1 **cup cottage cheese**
  ¼ **cup butter or margarine, melted and cooled**
  ¼ **cup all-purpose flour**
  ½ **teaspoon** *each* **baking powder and salt**
  2 **cups (about 8 oz.) shredded jack cheese**
  1 **small can (about 4 oz.) diced green chiles**

In a large bowl, beat eggs with an electric mixer until thick and lemon-colored. Stir in cottage cheese, butter, flour, baking powder, and salt. Then add cheese and chiles; stir just until combined.

If serving chile puff as a main dish, pour egg mixture into a greased 8-inch-square baking pan. Bake in a 350° oven until edges are lightly browned and center feels firm when lightly pressed (about 35 minutes). If serving as an appetizer, spoon egg mixture into tiny (about 1-inch) muffin pans, using about 1½ tablespoons egg mixture per pan; bake in a 350° oven until firm (15 to 18 minutes). Makes 6 to 8 main-dish servings or about 40 appetizers.

Per main-dish serving: 288 calories (68 percent from fat), 17 g protein, 6 g carbohydrates, 22 g total fat (6 g saturated fat), 204 mg cholesterol, 703 mg sodium

WESTERN CLASSIC
Chiles Rellenos

Chiles rellenos ("stuffed chiles") are a long-time favorite of *Sunset* readers. To make this version of the popular Mexican dish, you fill canned chiles with sticks of jack cheese, then cloak them with a golden, puffy egg coating.

     Easy Tomato Sauce (recipe follows); or 2 cups purchased red chile sauce, heated
  2 **small cans (about 4 oz.** *each***) whole green chiles, drained**
  8 **ounces jack cheese**
     About ⅓ cup all-purpose flour
     Puffy Coating (recipe follows)
     Salad oil
     Shredded jack cheese or sliced green onions

Prepare Easy Tomato Sauce and keep warm.

Cut a slit down one side of each chile; gently remove any seeds and pith. Cut the 8 ounces of cheese into sticks about ½ inch wide, ½ inch thick, and 1 inch shorter than chiles; stuff chiles with cheese. Spread flour in a shallow dish. Coat each chile thoroughly with flour; gently shake off excess.

Prepare Puffy Coating. In a wide, deep frying pan, heat about 1½ inches of oil over medium heat. Gently dip stuffed chiles, a few at a time, into coating; place on a saucer and slide into hot oil (do not crowd pan). Cook, turning once, until chiles are golden brown on both sides (6 to 8 minutes). Lift out with a slotted spoon, drain on paper towels, and keep warm.

To serve, top chiles with Easy Tomato Sauce and sprinkle with shredded cheese. Makes 4 servings.

Easy Tomato Sauce. Melt 1 tablespoon **butter** or margarine in a small pan over medium-low heat. Add 3 tablespoons finely chopped **onion** and 1 clove **garlic,** minced or pressed; cook, stirring often, until onion is golden (about 10 minutes). Stir in 1 can (about 15 oz.) **tomato sauce,** ⅓ cup **water,** and ¼ teaspoon **dry oregano.** Season to taste with **salt.** Bring to a simmer; simmer, uncovered, for 15 minutes.

Puffy Coating. Separate 3 **eggs.** In a medium-size bowl, beat whites until they hold soft peaks. In a small bowl, beat yolks with 1 tablespoon **water,** 3 tablespoons **all-purpose flour,** and ¼ teaspoon **salt** until thick and creamy; fold into whites.

Per serving: 462 calories (59 percent from fat), 22 g protein, 25 g carbohydrates, 31 g total fat (4 g saturated fat), 217 mg cholesterol, 1,506 mg sodium

Crustless Bacon & Cheese Quiche

This crustless quiche combines smoky bacon and ham with Swiss cheese. To serve the quiche, just cut it into squares—small ones for appetizers, larger pieces for a light lunch entrée.

    1   pound sliced bacon, cut into
        1-inch pieces
    4   medium-size leeks
    10 eggs
    2   cups milk
    ½   teaspoon salt
    ⅛   teaspoon ground nutmeg
    3   cups (about 12 oz.) shredded
        Swiss cheese
    ¼   pound sliced cooked ham,
        cut into strips

Cook bacon in a wide frying pan over medium heat until crisp, stirring often. Lift out, drain, and set aside. Discard all but 2 tablespoons of the drippings.

Cut off and discard root ends of leeks. Trim tops, leaving about 3 inches of green leaves. Discard coarse outer leaves. Split leeks in half lengthwise and rinse well, then thinly slice crosswise and add to drippings in pan. Cook over medium heat, stirring often, until leeks are limp. Remove from heat.

In a large bowl, lightly beat eggs until blended. Stir in milk, salt, and nutmeg. Reserve ¼ cup *each* of the bacon and cheese. Add remaining bacon, remaining 2¾ cups cheese, leeks, and ham to egg mixture; stir until blended. Pour into a greased 2-quart baking dish and sprinkle with reserved cheese and bacon. Bake in a 350° oven until a knife inserted in center comes out clean (35 to 40 minutes). Let stand for 10 minutes before serving. Makes 6 to 8 servings.

Per serving: 509 calories (65 percent from fat), 35 g protein, 10 g carbohydrates, 36 g total fat (17 g saturated fat), 386 mg cholesterol, 964 mg sodium

Green Chile & Cheese Pie

California green chiles lend a mild piquancy to this simple pie. The creamy creation is easy to make—just mix the chiles with eggs and plenty of jack and Cheddar cheeses, then bake in a flaky pastry shell.

        All-purpose Pastry (recipe
        follows)
    1½ cups (about 6 oz.) shredded
        jack cheese
    1   cup (about 4 oz.) shredded
        mild Cheddar cheese
    1   small can (about 4 oz.) diced
        green chiles
    3   eggs
    1   cup milk or half-and-half
    ¼   teaspoon salt
    ⅛   teaspoon ground cumin
        (optional)

Prepare All-purpose Pastry. On a lightly floured board, roll out pastry; fit pastry into a 9- or 10-inch pie pan. Trim and flute edges; lightly prick bottom and sides of pie shell with a fork. Bake in a 400° oven just until pale golden (about 12 minutes); let cool slightly.

Sprinkle all the jack cheese and ½ cup of the Cheddar cheese over bottom of pie shell. Distribute chiles over cheese. In a bowl, beat eggs with milk, salt, and cumin (if desired); pour into pie shell. Sprinkle remaining ½ cup Cheddar cheese lightly over top.

Bake in a 325° oven until center of pie appears set when pan is gently shaken (about 40 minutes). Let stand for about 15 minutes before serving. Serve hot or cold; to serve, cut into wedges. Makes 6 servings.

All-purpose Pastry. In a food processor or a bowl, combine 1¼ cups **all-purpose flour** and 6 tablespoons cold **butter** or margarine, cut into chunks. Whirl (or cut with a pastry blender or 2 knives) until mixture resembles fine crumbs. Add 1 **egg** and whirl until pastry holds together—about 8 seconds. (Or mix with a fork until pastry holds together.) Shape into a ball.

Per serving: 458 calories (62 percent from fat), 20 g protein, 24 g carbohydrates, 31 g total fat (13 g saturated fat), 223 mg cholesterol, 654 mg sodium

Chive Oven Omelet

This elegant omelet rises just like a soufflé. Serve it hot from the oven, while it's still high and puffy.

    8   eggs, separated
    2   tablespoons all-purpose flour
    3   tablespoons milk
    2   teaspoons snipped chives
    ½   teaspoon *each* salt and onion
        salt
    ¼   teaspoon Worcestershire
        Dash of pepper

In a large bowl, beat egg yolks until blended. Beat in flour, milk, chives, salt, onion salt, Worcestershire, and pepper; set aside. In a clean medium-size bowl, beat egg whites with an electric mixer or a wire whisk until they hold distinct but moist peaks. Fold whites into yolk mixture. Spoon into a greased shallow 2-quart baking pan. Bake in a 400° oven until top of omelet is golden brown (13 to 15 minutes). Serve at once. Makes 6 servings.

Per serving: 126 calories (60 percent from fat), 9 g protein, 3 g carbohydrates, 8 g total fat (3 g saturated fat), 288 mg cholesterol, 421 mg sodium

At *Sunset*, breakfast food is fuel for the day. Substantial morning meals have been favored by our readers since our first breakfast feature ran in 1930. While early articles included hot cereals, baked fruit, and the classic ham and eggs, recent reader-recommended favorites offer more up-to-date adaptations of traditional breakfast fare.

Many of the following specialties first appeared in "Chefs of the West." Breakfast Scramble is modeled on the German *Bauernfrühstück* ("farmers' breakfast") of eggs scrambled with potatoes and leftover meat; Haitian French Toast takes on tropical appeal with a liberal shot of orange juice. The crisp cornmeal waffles gain interest from crunchy flecks of wheat germ and a warm honey topping. All six recipes offer a delicious way to begin the day.

Country Omelet

- **4 slices bacon**
- **⅓ cup walnut pieces**
- **1 small thin-skinned potato, peeled and cut into ¼-inch cubes**
- **¼ cup finely chopped onion**
- **2 tablespoons butter or margarine**
- **3 or 4 eggs, lightly beaten**
- **¼ cup diced Swiss cheese**
- **2 tablespoons shredded Swiss cheese**
- **1 tablespoon minced parsley**
  About ¼ cup sour cream (optional)
  Salt

Cook bacon in a wide frying pan over medium heat until crisp. Lift out, drain, crumble, and set aside.

Add walnuts to drippings in pan; cook over medium heat, stirring often, until lightly browned (1 to 2 minutes;

watch carefully, since nuts scorch easily). Lift out and set aside.

Discard all but 2 tablespoons of the drippings. Add potato and onion to pan, reduce heat to medium-low, and cook, stirring, until potato is soft but only lightly browned (about 10 minutes). Remove potato mixture from pan and keep warm.

Wipe pan clean, then melt butter over medium-low heat. Pour in eggs and cook, gently lifting cooked portion to let uncooked egg flow underneath, until eggs are set but still moist on top. Sprinkle evenly with bacon, potato mixture, diced and shredded cheeses, and parsley.

If desired, mound sour cream in center of omelet; garnish omelet with walnuts. Season to taste with salt. To serve, cut omelet into wedges. Makes 2 servings.

Per serving: 646 calories (76 percent from fat), 25 g protein, 15 g carbohydrates, 55 g total fat (20 g saturated fat), 442 mg cholesterol, 556 mg sodium

Haitian French Toast

- **1 long loaf (about 1 lb.) French bread**
- **1 cup orange juice**
- **½ cup whipping cream**
- **2 eggs**
- **1 teaspoon ground cinnamon**
- **¼ cup granulated sugar**
  Dash of ground nutmeg
- **3 tablespoons butter or margarine**
  Powdered sugar
  Maple syrup

Cut bread crosswise into 1½-inch-thick slices. Let stand, uncovered, for at least 4 hours or until next day.

In a 9- by 13-inch pan, whisk together orange juice, cream, eggs, cinnamon, granulated sugar, and nutmeg. Lay bread in pan; let soak, turning several times, until all liquid has been absorbed (3 to 5 minutes).

Melt butter in a wide frying pan over medium heat. Add soaked bread, a few slices at a time (do not crowd pan). Cook, turning as needed, until slices are richly browned on both sides.

To serve, dust toast liberally with powdered sugar. Offer syrup to add to taste. Makes 4 to 6 servings.

Per serving: 472 calories (36 percent from fat), 11 g protein, 64 g carbohydrates, 19 g total fat (10 g saturated fat), 130 mg cholesterol, 657 mg sodium

Breakfast Scramble

- **2 tablespoons butter or margarine**
- **1½ cups diced cooked red thin-skinned potatoes**
- **½ to 1 cup finely diced cooked chicken, beef, ham, or sausage**
- **2 tablespoons thinly sliced green onion**
- **¼ cup diced red bell pepper**
- **6 eggs**
- **2 tablespoons water**
- **⅛ teaspoon liquid hot pepper seasoning**
- **¼ teaspoon lemon pepper or black pepper**
- **¼ teaspoon dry dill weed**
  Salt
  Sour cream (optional)

Melt butter in a wide frying pan over medium-high heat. Add potatoes; cook, turning occasionally with a spatula, until lightly browned (about 5 minutes). Reduce heat to medium-low and scatter chicken, onion, and bell pepper over potatoes; cook for about 1 more minute.

Meanwhile, in a small bowl, beat eggs, water, hot pepper seasoning, lemon pepper, and dill weed until blended. Pour egg mixture over potato mixture. When edges begin to set, gently lift with spatula to let uncooked egg flow underneath; repeat until eggs are done to your liking. Season to taste with salt; top with sour cream, if desired. Makes 4 servings.

Per serving: 261 calories (53 percent from fat), 18 g protein, 12 g carbohydrates, 15 g total fat (6 g saturated fat), 358 mg cholesterol, 234 mg sodium

Cottage Cheese Pancakes

- 3 **eggs**
- 1 **cup small-curd cottage cheese**
- 2 **tablespoons salad oil**
- ¼ **cup all-purpose flour**
- ¼ **teaspoon salt**
  Maple syrup

In a small bowl, beat eggs with a wire whisk or an electric mixer until thick and lemon-colored. Press cottage cheese through a fine wire strainer into eggs. Add oil; stir until blended. Then stir in flour and salt.

Spoon 4-inch circles of batter onto a lightly greased hot griddle. Cook pancakes, turning once, until golden brown on both sides. Offer syrup to add to taste. Makes 2 to 4 servings.

Per serving: 305 calories (65 percent from fat), 16 g protein, 10 g carbohydrates, 22 g total fat (5 g saturated fat), 223 mg cholesterol, 527 mg sodium

Honey-topped Cornmeal Waffles

  Honey Topping (recipe follows)
- 2 **eggs, separated**
- 2 **cups buttermilk**
- 6 **tablespoons butter or margarine, melted**
- 1 **cup whole wheat flour or all-purpose flour**
- ¾ **cup cornmeal**
- 2 **teaspoons baking powder**
- 1 **teaspoon baking soda**
- ½ **teaspoon salt**
- 2 **tablespoons sugar**
- ¼ **cup wheat germ**

Prepare Honey Topping; keep warm.

In a medium-size bowl, beat egg yolks, buttermilk, and butter until blended. In a large bowl, mix flour, cornmeal, baking powder, baking soda, salt, sugar, and wheat germ. Add egg yolk mixture; stir to blend.

In a small bowl, beat egg whites with a wire whisk or an electric mixer until they hold distinct but moist peaks. Fold into batter just until blended.

Bake batter in a preheated waffle iron until golden brown. Serve with Honey Topping. Makes 6 servings.

Honey Topping. In a small pan, combine 1 cup **honey,** 6 tablespoons **butter** or margarine, and 4 teaspoons **lemon juice.** Stir over low heat until butter is melted. Makes about 1 cup.

Per serving of waffles: 325 calories (41 percent from fat), 10 g protein, 39 g carbohydrates, 15 g total fat (8 g saturated fat), 105 mg cholesterol, 781 mg sodium

Per tablespoon of Honey Topping: 103 calories (36 percent from fat), 0.1 g protein, 18 g carbohydrates, 4 g total fat (3 g saturated fat), 12 mg cholesterol, 45 mg sodium

Super-crisp Sourdough Waffles

- ¾ **cup sourdough starter (page 182), at room temperature**
- 1½ **cups warm water (about 110°F)**
- 1¾ **cups all-purpose flour**
- 2 **eggs, separated**
- ¼ **cup salad oil; or ¼ cup butter or margarine, melted**
- ¾ **teaspoon *each* salt and baking soda**
- 1½ **tablespoons sugar**
  Maple syrup or fruit preserves

In a medium-size bowl, combine starter with warm water and flour. Cover and let stand in a warm place until next day.

Add egg yolks and oil to sourdough mixture; stir until blended. In a small bowl, beat egg whites with a wire whisk or an electric mixer until they hold distinct but moist peaks. Stir salt, baking soda, and sugar into sourdough batter; then fold in egg whites just until blended.

Bake batter in a preheated waffle iron until well browned. Offer maple syrup or preserves to add to taste. Makes 4 servings.

Per serving: 456 calories (34 percent from fat), 12 g protein, 62 g carbohydrates, 17 g total fat (3 g saturated fat), 107 mg cholesterol, 703 mg sodium

Sour Cream Enchiladas

Sour cream is both filling and garnish for these rich enchiladas. They're prepared a bit differently than the traditional dish: two tortillas are overlapped and rolled together to make a single enchilada.

- **2   cups sour cream**
- **1   cup sliced green onions**
- **½   teaspoon ground cumin**
- **4   cups (about 1 lb.) shredded Longhorn cheese**
- **1   can (about 10 oz.) enchilada sauce**
     Salad oil
- **12   corn tortillas**
     Sour cream (optional)
     Sliced green onions (optional)

In a bowl, stir together the 2 cups sour cream, the 1 cup onions, cumin, and 1 cup of the cheese; set aside.

In a small frying pan, heat enchilada sauce over low heat; keep warm. In another small frying pan, heat ¼ inch of oil over medium heat; keep hot. Working with one tortilla at a time, heat each tortilla in oil until it blisters and becomes limp (this takes just a few seconds). Using tongs, lift tortilla from oil and dip it into heated sauce. Arrange tortillas 2 at a time in a 7- by 11-inch or 9-inch-square baking pan. Start by overlapping 2 tortillas at

one end of pan; allow part of one tortilla to extend over pan rim. Spread about 6 tablespoons of the sour cream filling down center of tortillas; fold the extending sections over filling to make one rolled enchilada.

Repeat to fill remaining tortillas, placing them side by side and completely covering pan bottom. Sprinkle remaining 3 cups cheese evenly over top. (At this point, you may cover and refrigerate for up to 4 hours.)

Bake, uncovered, in a 375° oven until cheese is melted (about 20 minutes; about 30 minutes if refrigerated). Garnish with sour cream and onions, if desired. Makes 6 servings.

Per serving: 725 calories (68 percent from fat), 25 g protein, 33 g carbohydrates, 56 g total fat (28 g saturated fat), 113 mg cholesterol, 1,047 mg sodium

Stacked Cheese Enchiladas

This quick, easy version of enchiladas comes from the state of Sonora in northern Mexico. Instead of rolling the tortillas, you stack them, layering cheese, onions, and sauce in between. To serve, just cut the stack into wedges.

- **1   cup purchased red chile sauce**
     Salad oil
- **10   corn tortillas**
- **1   cup (about 4 oz.) shredded sharp Cheddar cheese**
- **1   to 1½ cups sliced green onions**

In a small frying pan, heat chile sauce over low heat; keep warm. In another small frying pan, heat ¼ inch of oil over medium heat; keep hot.

Work with one tortilla at a time. Heat each tortilla in oil until it blisters and becomes limp (this takes just a few seconds). Using tongs, lift tortilla from oil and dip it into heated sauce, then place it in a round, shallow

baking pan and top with about 1½ tablespoons of the cheese, 1½ to 2½ tablespoons of the onions, and 1 tablespoon of the sauce. Repeat layers 9 more times, stacking tortillas one on top of the other. Pour remaining sauce over stack and top with any remaining cheese.

Bake in a 350° oven until heated through (15 to 20 minutes). To serve, cut into wedges. Makes 4 servings.

Per serving: 485 calories (51 percent from fat), 13 g protein, 49 g carbohydrates, 28 g total fat (8 g saturated fat), 30 mg cholesterol, 1,195 mg sodium

Swiss Fondue

Classic Swiss fondues, like this one from a 1960 *Sunset* cook book, are delicious but never foolproof. For the most reliable results, use imported Swiss cheese and keep the heat moderate—high heat will make the cheese stringy and oily, while low heat will make it too thick for dipping.

- **1   clove garlic, peeled and halved**
     About 2 cups dry white wine
- **4   cups (about 1 lb.) shredded Swiss, Emmenthaler, or Gruyère cheese**
- **1   tablespoon cornstarch**
- **3   tablespoons kirsch**
     Salt and pepper
     Dash of ground nutmeg
- **1   loaf (about 1 lb.) French bread, cut into bite-size pieces**

Rub garlic over bottom of a ceramic fondue pot or chafing dish; discard garlic. Add 2 cups of the wine and heat over low heat. Mix cheese with cornstarch. When bubbles rise to surface of wine, add a handful of the cheese-cornstarch mixture; stir constantly until cheese is melted. Continue to add cheese mixture in handfuls, stirring after each addition until cheese is completely melted. When cheese mixture is smooth and starts to bubble lightly, gradually pour

in kirsch, stirring constantly until blended. Season to taste with salt and pepper; stir in nutmeg. Keep warm over heat source (fondue should bubble slowly).

To serve, offer fondue forks or bamboo skewers to spear bread for dipping. If needed, pour a little warm wine into cheese to maintain correct consistency. Makes 8 servings.

Per serving: 410 calories (41 percent from fat), 21 g protein, 35 g carbohydrates,17 g total fat (10 g saturated fat), 52 mg cholesterol, 496 mg sodium

Creamy Parmesan Fondue

This quick fondue blends cream cheese with grated Parmesan for an easy variation on the traditional dish. Served with bite-size chunks of firm French bread, the rich dip doubles as a supper dish for four or a hot appetizer for more than a dozen.

> 2 large packages (about 8 oz. *each*) cream cheese or Neufchâtel cheese
>
> About 2 cups milk
>
> 2 small cloves garlic, minced or pressed
>
> 1½ cups (about 6 oz.) grated Parmesan cheese
>
> Salt
>
> White pepper or thinly sliced green onion
>
> About ½ pound French bread, cut into bite-size pieces

Place cream cheese in top pan of a double boiler set over simmering

water. As cheese melts, gradually add 2 cups of the milk, stirring until smooth. Add garlic and Parmesan cheese; stir until cheese is melted and mixture is thickened. Season to taste with salt; if needed, add more milk to thin to a good dipping consistency.

To serve, transfer fondue to a ceramic fondue pot or chafing dish and keep warm over heat source. Sprinkle with white pepper. Offer fondue forks or bamboo skewers to spear bread for dipping. Makes 4 servings.

Per serving: 821 calories (63 percent from fat), 35 g protein, 40 g carbohydrates, 58 g total fat (36 g saturated fat), 175 mg cholesterol, 1,533 mg sodium

Cheese Soufflé

Cheese soufflé is among the most impressive egg-based dishes in the French culinary repertoire. Soufflés will rise highest if you beat the egg whites until firm, but still moist and uncrumbly, before folding them into the yolk mixture.

> 3 tablespoons butter or margarine
>
> 3 tablespoons all-purpose flour
>
> 1 cup milk
>
> Dash of ground red pepper (cayenne)
>
> ¼ teaspoon dry mustard
>
> 1 cup (about 4 oz.) shredded Cheddar or Swiss cheese
>
> Salt
>
> 4 or 5 eggs, separated

Melt butter in a medium-size pan over medium heat. Stir in flour and cook, stirring, for 1 minute (do not brown). Remove from heat and gradually stir in milk; then add red pepper and mustard. Return to heat and cook, stirring constantly, until sauce boils and thickens. Add cheese; stir until melted. Season to taste with salt. Remove from heat and beat in egg yolks, one at a time.

In a small bowl, beat egg whites with an electric mixer or a wire whisk until they hold distinct but moist peaks. Stir about a fourth of the whites into cheese mixture, then carefully fold in remaining whites until blended.

Pour into a well-buttered 1½-quart soufflé dish or four to six 1-cup ramekins. Draw a circle on surface of soufflé batter about 1 inch from rim, using a spoon or the tip of a knife. Bake in a 375° oven until soufflé feels firm when lightly tapped and crack looks fairly dry (about 35 minutes for a 1½-quart soufflé dish; about 20 minutes for ramekins). Serve at once. Makes 4 to 6 servings.

Per serving: 280 calories (71 percent from fat), 13 g protein, 7 g carbohydrates, 22 g total fat (12 g saturated fat), 245 mg cholesterol, 307 mg sodium

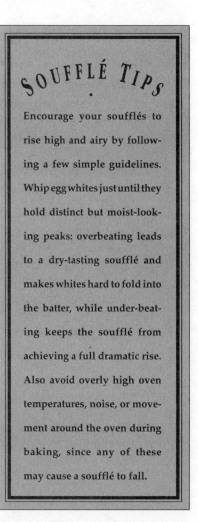

SOUFFLÉ TIPS

Encourage your soufflés to rise high and airy by following a few simple guidelines. Whip egg whites just until they hold distinct but moist-looking peaks: overbeating leads to a dry-tasting soufflé and makes whites hard to fold into the batter, while under-beating keeps the soufflé from achieving a full dramatic rise. Also avoid overly high oven temperatures, noise, or movement around the oven during baking, since any of these may cause a soufflé to fall.

MEATS

.

The Western cook has long enjoyed beef, lamb, pork, and veal in a wide range of cuts—some tender, some leaner and tougher. And at Sunset, we've come up with delicious recipes for all of them, always with an eye towards new cooking methods and fresh local ingredients. • *Grilling has always been popular with our readers, and barbecue specialties are well represented here. You'll find traditional lamb shish kebabs and grilled flank steak as well as more contemporary dishes, such as a butterflied beef roast studded with peppers and served with a mellow chile cream. Braising is another favored method, so it's no surprise that our readers and staff chose plenty of stews and pot roasts for this chapter.* • *And what about often-requested classics like meat loaf, tamale pie, veal scaloppine, and pork ribs? They're here, too, though we've updated some to give them a lighter, fresher look.*

Tostada for Two

Mildly spicy ground beef, kidney beans, shredded jack cheese, and fresh tomato top a bed of crisp lettuce for a saladlike version of tostadas. Though this recipe is proportioned for two, it can easily be doubled or tripled to make a family-size meal.

- ½ **pound lean ground beef**
- 1 **small onion, chopped**
- 1 **small can (about 8 oz.) red kidney beans, drained and rinsed**
- ¾ **teaspoon chili powder**
- ¼ **teaspoon ground cumin**
- 3 **tablespoons catsup**
  About 3 cups shredded iceberg lettuce
- ½ **cup shredded jack cheese**
- 1 **medium-size tomato, cut into wedges**
  Tortilla chips

Crumble beef into a medium-size frying pan. Add onion and cook over medium heat, stirring often, until meat has lost its pink color and onion is soft (about 5 minutes). Discard fat from pan. Add beans, chili powder, cumin, and catsup; cover and simmer gently for 5 minutes.

To serve, divide lettuce equally between 2 dinner plates. Spoon hot beef mixture over lettuce, then sprinkle with cheese and garnish with tomato wedges and tortilla chips. Serve at once; offer additional chips alongside. Makes 2 servings.

Per serving: 562 calories (53 percent from fat), 36 g protein, 30 g carbohydrates, 33 g total fat (10 g saturated fat), 110 mg cholesterol, 663 mg sodium

Picnic Salami

This homemade salami is wrapped in nylon net and slowly baked; as it cooks, the excess fat drains out, leaving easy-to-slice meat rolls. The nylon net you'll need is sold in most fabric stores. To find curing salt, check with butchers' equipment and supply stores or fish markets.

- 4 **pounds ground beef**
- ¼ **cup curing salt**
- 2 **tablespoons liquid smoke flavoring**
- 1½ **teaspoons garlic powder**
- 1½ **teaspoons ground pepper or 2 teaspoons whole black peppercorns**
- 4 **pieces large-weave nylon net (*each* 12 by 18 inches)**

In a large bowl, combine beef, salt, smoke flavoring, garlic powder, and pepper; mix until well blended. Cover and refrigerate for 24 hours.

Divide beef mixture into 4 equal portions. Shape each into a compact 8-inch log; place each log on a piece of nylon net. Roll up tightly and tie ends with string. Place logs on a rack in a broiler pan and bake in a 225° oven for 4 hours.

Remove net from rolls, then pat rolls well with paper towels to absorb excess fat. Let cool slightly, then wrap in foil and refrigerate for up to 3 weeks or freeze for up to 2 months. Makes about 3 pounds.

Per ¼ pound: 306 calories (67 percent from fat), 24 g protein, 0.4 g carbohydrates, 22 g total fat (9 g saturated fat), 92 mg cholesterol, 1,535 mg sodium

Herb Beef Salami

Follow directions for **Picnic Salami,** but omit liquid smoke flavoring and pepper and reduce garlic powder to 1 teaspoon. Add 3 tablespoons **dry red wine,** 2 tablespoons **mustard seeds,** 1 tablespoon *each* **dry basil** and **dry oregano,** 1 teaspoon **onion powder,** and ⅔ cup grated **Parmesan cheese;** stir until blended. Makes about 3 pounds.

Per ¼ pound: 337 calories (66 percent from fat), 27 g protein, 2 g carbohydrates, 24 g total fat (10 g saturated fat), 96 mg cholesterol, 1,619 mg sodium

Spicy Beef Salami

Follow directions for **Picnic Salami,** but omit liquid smoke flavoring and pepper and reduce garlic powder to 1 teaspoon. Add 3 tablespoons **dry white wine,** 2 tablespoons **chili powder,** 2 teaspoons **crushed red pepper flakes,** and 1 teaspoon **ground cumin;** stir until blended. Makes about 3 pounds.

Per ¼ pound: 311 calories (66 percent from fat), 25 g protein, 1 g carbohydrates, 22 g total fat (9 g saturated fat), 92 mg cholesterol, 1,548 mg sodium

Enchilada Pie

We still receive frequent requests for this enchilada casserole, which was already a favorite back in 1955.

- 1 **pound lean ground beef**
- 1 **onion, chopped**
- 1 **tablespoon chili powder**
- 1 **can (about 8 oz.) tomato sauce**
  Salt and pepper
- 6 **corn tortillas, spread with butter or margarine**
- 1 **can (about 4 oz.) chopped ripe olives, drained**
- 1½ **cups (about 6 oz.) shredded sharp Cheddar cheese**
- ½ **cup water**

Crumble beef into a wide frying pan. Add onion and cook over medium heat, stirring often, until meat is browned. Stir in chili powder and tomato sauce. Season to taste with salt and pepper. In a 2-quart round baking dish, alternate layers of buttered tortillas, meat sauce, olives, and cheese. Pour water over top.

Cover and bake in a 400° oven until cheese is melted and tortilla stack is hot in center (about 20 minutes). Makes 4 to 6 servings.

Per serving: 541 calories (63 percent from fat), 28 g protein, 23 g carbohydrates, 38 g total fat (18 g saturated fat), 116 mg cholesterol, 857 mg sodium

Navajo Tacos

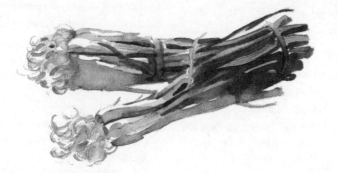

Puffy fried bread rounds filled with beans and beef are popular fare at rodeos, fairs, and fiestas throughout the West. If you don't mind a bit of a mess, eat these big sandwiches with your hands. Or use a knife and fork.

Fiesta Chili Beans (recipe follows)

Fry Bread (page 171)

1 or 2 large firm-ripe tomatoes

3 cups (about 12 oz.) shredded mild Cheddar cheese

4 cups finely shredded iceberg lettuce

1¼ cups thinly sliced green onions

1 cup purchased red or green chile salsa

1 cup sour cream (optional)

Prepare Fiesta Chili Beans; keep warm. Prepare Fry Bread; keep hot.

Cut a thin slice off the top and bottom of each tomato. Then cut tomatoes crosswise into ⅛-inch-thick slices. On each slice, make a cut from edge just to center; set aside.

To assemble each taco, lay a piece of hot Fry Bread, cupped side up, on a plate. Spoon Fiesta Chili Beans equally into each cup, then top with cheese, lettuce, and onions. Arrange 1 or 2 tomato slices on top of each taco as follows: hold each slice on opposite sides of center cut, then fold the flaps in opposite directions to form a base so slice stands upright. Set tomato slices on tacos.

Top tacos equally with salsa and, if desired, sour cream. Makes 6 servings.

Fiesta Chili Beans. Rinse and sort through 1 cup **dried Great Northern or pinto beans,** discarding any debris. Combine beans and 4 cups **water** in a 3- to 4-quart pan. Cover and bring to a rolling boil over high heat; boil for 10 minutes. Remove from heat and let stand for at least 1 hour or until next

day. Drain beans, discarding liquid. Set beans aside.

Rinse and dry pan. Heat 1 tablespoon **olive oil** or salad oil in pan over medium heat. Add 1 large **onion,** chopped; cook, stirring often, until onion is soft (about 5 minutes). Add onion to drained beans.

Crumble 1 pound **lean ground beef** or bulk pork sausage into pan and cook over high heat, stirring often, until well browned. Discard fat.

Add beans and onion to meat. Then stir in 3 cups **chicken broth;** 1 tablespoon **chili powder;** 2 cloves **garlic,** minced or pressed; and 2 teaspoons *each* **ground cumin, dry oregano,** and **dry basil.** Bring to a boil over high heat; then reduce heat, cover, and simmer until beans are tender to bite (1½ to 2 hours). For a thicker consistency, uncover and boil, stirring often, until liquid is reduced to desired thickness. If made ahead, let cool; then cover and refrigerate for up to 3 days. Reheat before serving.

Per serving: 874 calories (48 percent from fat), 44 g protein, 69 g carbohydrates, 47 g total fat (19 g saturated fat), 106 mg cholesterol, 1,600 mg sodium

Spoonbread Tamale Pie

When *Sunset* printed this recipe in 1966, tamale pies were already long-time favorites with Western cooks. In fact, Spoonbread Tamale Pie is much like Fiesta Tamale Pie, which became

popular in the '30s—but it substitutes lean ground beef for the combination of beef and pork used in the older recipe, and adds green bell pepper and cornmeal to the filling.

Cornmeal Topping (recipe follows)

¼ cup salad oil or olive oil

1½ pounds lean ground beef

1 large onion, chopped

1 small green bell pepper, seeded and chopped

1 clove garlic, minced or pressed

1 can (about 14½ oz.) tomatoes

1 can (about 12 oz.) whole-kernel corn

1 teaspoon salt

4 to 6 teaspoons chili powder

¼ teaspoon pepper

½ cup yellow cornmeal

1 cup water

1 cup pitted ripe olives

Prepare Cornmeal Topping; set aside.

Heat oil in wide frying pan over medium heat. Crumble in beef; then add onion, bell pepper, and garlic. Cook, stirring often, until onion is golden (about 10 minutes). Cut up tomatoes; stir in tomatoes and their liquid, corn, salt, chili powder, and pepper. Bring to a boil; then reduce heat, cover, and simmer for 5 minutes.

In a small bowl, mix cornmeal and water; stir into meat mixture and simmer, uncovered, stirring occasionally, for 10 more minutes. Stir in olives. Pour mixture into a 9- by 13-inch baking dish and spread with Cornmeal Topping. Bake in a 375°

oven until topping is golden brown (about 40 minutes). Makes 8 servings.

Cornmeal Topping. In a small pan, combine 1½ cups **milk**, ½ teaspoon **salt**, and 2 tablespoons **butter** or margarine. Bring mixture to a simmer over medium-low heat. Gradually add ½ cup **yellow cornmeal**; cook, stirring, until thickened. Remove from heat; stir in 1 cup (about 4 oz.) shredded **Cheddar cheese** and 2 **eggs**, beaten.

Per serving: 559 calories (60 percent from fat), 25 g protein, 31 g carbohydrates, 37 g total fat (14 g saturated fat), 146 mg cholesterol, 990 mg sodium

Mom's Magic Meat Loaf

Serve this heart-shaped meat loaf as a special surprise for mom on Mother's Day. Topped with tomato sauce, the savory treat is surrounded by a fluffy border of mashed potatoes.

- **1 cup fine dry bread crumbs**
- **½ cup grated Parmesan cheese**
- **1 tablespoon dry basil**
- **½ teaspoon pepper**
- **2 eggs**
- **2 cloves garlic, minced or pressed**
- **2 cans (about 8 oz. *each*) tomato sauce**
- **2 pounds lean ground beef**
- **3 pounds thin-skinned potatoes, peeled**
- **1 large can (about 12 oz.) evaporated skim milk**
- **Salt and pepper**

In a large bowl, combine crumbs, cheese, basil, the ½ teaspoon pepper, eggs, garlic, and 1 cup of the tomato sauce. Add beef and, using your hands or a spoon, mix until combined. In a shallow baking pan (about 10 inches in diameter), shape mixture into a 2-inch-thick heart or oval. Bake in a 400° oven for 45 minutes. Remove from oven; carefully drain fat from pan, then top loaf with remaining tomato sauce. Bake for 15 more minutes.

While loaf is baking, cook potatoes in boiling water until tender throughout when pierced (about 30 minutes). Drain potatoes and mash with a potato masher or an electric mixer until smooth; slowly beat in milk. Season to taste with salt and pepper. To serve, carefully transfer meat loaf to a serving dish. Spoon potatoes into a pastry bag fitted with a large star tip; pipe potatoes around meat loaf. (Or simply spoon potatoes around loaf.) Makes 8 servings.

Per serving: 538 calories (40 percent from fat), 33 g protein, 48 g carbohydrates, 23 g total fat (9 g saturated fat), 134 mg cholesterol, 698 mg sodium

WESTERN CLASSIC

Joe's Special

Joe's Special had already been a San Francisco favorite for over two generations when we printed this recipe in 1968. A hearty mixture of beef, onions, spinach, and eggs, it makes a satisfying meal at any time of day or night.

- **2 tablespoons olive oil or salad oil**
- **2 pounds lean ground beef**
- **2 medium-size onions, finely chopped**
- **2 cloves garlic, minced or pressed**
- **½ pound mushrooms, sliced (optional)**
- **1¼ teaspoons salt**
- **¼ teaspoon *each* ground nutmeg, pepper, and dry oregano**

- **1 package (about 10 oz.) frozen chopped spinach, thawed and squeezed dry; or ½ pound fresh spinach, rinsed, stems removed, and leaves chopped (about 4 cups)**
- **4 to 6 eggs, lightly beaten**

Heat oil in a wide frying pan over high heat. Crumble in beef and cook, stirring often, until browned. Add onions, garlic, and, if desired, mushrooms; reduce heat to medium and cook, stirring occasionally, until onions are soft (about 5 minutes). Stir in salt, nutmeg, pepper, oregano, and spinach; cook for about 5 more minutes. Add eggs. Reduce heat to low and cook, stirring constantly, just until eggs are softly set. Makes 6 servings.

Per serving: 537 calories (68 percent from fat), 34 g protein, 8 g carbohydrates, 40 g total fat (15 g saturated fat), 291 mg cholesterol, 651 mg sodium

JOE'S SPECIAL

The origin of this famous San Francisco specialty—a quick-cooking combination of ground beef, spinach, and eggs—is still in hot dispute. Some say it was created as an after-hours snack by dance-band musicians of the 1920s. Others insist it was devised by a San Francisco chef as a variation on the Italian frittata. A third theory attributes the dish to miners who frequented the city's riotous Barbary Coast district in the 1850s.

Flank Steak Barbecue

A simple marinade of soy sauce, honey, and ginger brings Asian appeal to barbecued flank steak.

- ¼ **cup soy sauce**
- 3 **tablespoons honey**
- 2 **tablespoons vinegar**
- 1½ **teaspoons garlic powder**
- 1½ **teaspoons ground ginger or 2 tablespoons minced fresh ginger**
- ¾ **cup salad oil or olive oil**
- 1 **green onion, thinly sliced**
- 1 **flank steak (about 1½ lbs.), trimmed of fat**

In a large bowl, stir together soy sauce, honey, vinegar, garlic powder, and ginger. Add oil and onion.

Place meat in a shallow dish and pour marinade over it. Cover and refrigerate, turning meat occasionally, for at least 4 hours or until next day.

Lift meat from marinade and drain briefly (reserve marinade). Then place meat on a grill 4 to 6 inches above a solid bed of medium-hot coals. Cook, turning once and basting occasionally with marinade, until done to your liking; cut to test (about 8 minutes for medium-rare). To serve, cut meat across the grain into thin slanting slices. Makes 4 servings.

Per serving: 585 calories (67 percent from fat), 36 g protein, 12 g carbohydrates, 44 g total fat (9 g saturated fat), 86 mg cholesterol, 890 mg sodium

INDIRECT GRILLING

For indirect grilling on the barbecue, ignite about 50 charcoal briquets in a barbecue with a lid. When the coals are covered with gray ash (after 30 to 40 minutes), push an equal number to opposite sides of the grate or arrange them around the grate's perimeter. Evenly distribute 5 or 6 more briquets on the coals, then set a foil drip pan on the grate between the coals. Place grill 4 to 6 inches above the coals. (If you'll be cooking for over 1 hour, add 5 or 6 more briquets to each side of coals every 30 minutes to maintain an even heat.)

Butterflied Beef Cross-rib with Cilantro-Jalapeño Cream

A fresh citrus marinade gives this butterflied beef roast its delicate tang. The presentation is especially pretty: you nestle thin slivers of red and yellow pepper into cuts in the roast before grilling, then serve the meat with a chile-herb sauce.

- 1 **boneless beef cross-rib roast (5 to 5½ lbs.), trimmed of fat**
- ½ **cup *each* orange juice and lime juice**
- 1½ **teaspoons ground cumin**
- ½ **cup minced cilantro**
  Cilantro-Jalapeño Cream (recipe follows)
- 1 ***each* large red and yellow bell pepper, seeded and thinly sliced lengthwise (or use 2 peppers of the same color)**
  Cilantro sprigs
  Salt and pepper

If beef is tied, snip off strings. With a sharp knife, make a lengthwise cut down center of meat, cutting about two-thirds of the way through. Pull cut open to spread out meat. Holding knife at about a 45-degree angle from center of meat, cut lengthwise about two-thirds of the way through the 2 thick sections. Pull cuts open and pat meat to make as evenly thick as possible. At even intervals, make 6 crosswise cuts, again cutting about two-thirds of the way through meat.

In a large bowl or 2-gallon heavy-duty plastic bag, combine orange juice, lime juice, cumin, and minced cilantro. Reserve ¼ cup of the marinade; add meat to the remaining marinade. Turn to coat; then cover (or seal bag) and refrigerate, turning meat (or bag) occasionally, for at least 2 hours or until next day. Also cover and refrigerate reserved marinade. Meanwhile, prepare Cilantro-Jalapeño Cream.

Lift meat from marinade and drain briefly; discard marinade. Lay meat flat, cut side up. Fit bell pepper strips into crosswise slashes, distributing evenly. Thread 3 long (at least 18-inch), sturdy metal skewers parallel to each other lengthwise through meat, securing peppers with skewers.

Prepare barbecue as directed in "Indirect Grilling" (at left). Set meat, pepper side up, on lightly greased grill above drip pan. Cover barbecue and adjust vents as needed to maintain an even heat. Cook meat, brushing occasionally with reserved marinade, until a meat thermometer inserted in thickest part registers 135° to 140°F for rare (40 to 45 minutes); do not turn meat over.

Transfer meat to a carving board and remove skewers. To serve, cut meat across the grain into slices. Garnish with cilantro sprigs. Offer Cilantro-Jalapeño Cream, salt, and pepper to season individual servings. Makes 12 to 16 servings.

Cilantro-Jalapeño Cream. In a bowl, stir together 1 cup minced **cilantro**; 1 cup **reduced-fat sour cream**, regular sour cream, or reduced-calorie mayonnaise; 2 **fresh jalapeño chiles**, seeded and minced; and 2 tablespoons **lime juice.** If made ahead, cover and refrigerate until next day. Makes 1⅓ cups.

Per serving of meat: 166 calories (48 percent from fat), 19 g protein, 3 g carbohydrates, 9 g total fat (3 g saturated fat), 54 mg cholesterol, 52 mg sodium

Per tablespoon of Cilantro-Jalapeño Cream: 20 calories (66 percent from fat), 0.8 g protein, 1 g carbohydrates, 2 g total fat (0.8 g saturated fat), 4 mg cholesterol, 0.5 mg sodium

WESTERN CLASSIC
Fajitas

Probably invented by Mexican ranch hands as a simple outdoor meal, *fajitas* are a great favorite throughout the West. Along the Mexican border, the word *fajitas* means "skirt steaks"—but elsewhere, it's become a catch-all term for burritos made with grilled beef of any cut, or even with chicken or fish.

- **3 pounds skirt steaks or flank steak, trimmed of fat**
- **½ cup lime juice**
- **⅓ cup salad oil or olive oil**
- **⅓ cup tequila or lime juice**
- **4 cloves garlic, minced or pressed**
- **1½ teaspoons ground cumin**
- **1 teaspoon dry oregano**
- **½ teaspoon pepper**
- **4 or 5 small onions (unpeeled), cut in half lengthwise**
  Salsa Fresca (recipe follows)
  Easy Guacamole (page 11) or purchased guacamole
- **3 cans (about 1 lb. *each*) refried beans**
  Sour cream
  Cilantro sprigs
- **16 to 20 flour tortillas (*each* about 8 inches in diameter)**

Cut steaks crosswise into about 12-inch lengths, then arrange in a 9- by 13-inch dish. In a small bowl, whisk together lime juice, oil, tequila, garlic, cumin, oregano, and pepper. Pour over meat; turn meat to coat. Place onion halves, cut side down, in marinade alongside meat. Cover and refrigerate for at least 4 hours or until next day, turning meat occasionally.

Prepare Salsa Fresca and Easy Guacamole; set aside. Heat beans in a large pan; keep warm.

Place onion halves on a lightly greased grill 4 to 6 inches above a solid bed of hot coals. Cook for about 7 minutes; turn over. Lift meat from marinade and drain briefly (reserve marinade); set meat on grill. Brush marinade generously over meat and onion halves. Continue to cook onion halves until soft and browned (5 to 9 more minutes). Cook meat, turning once, until done to your liking; cut to test (about 6 minutes for rare).

Transfer meat and onions to a carving board. Cut meat into thin slices (if using flank steak, cut across the grain into thin slanting slices). In individual serving dishes, arrange meat, onions, heated beans, Salsa Fresca, guacamole, sour cream, and cilantro sprigs.

Heat tortillas on grill as needed, turning often with tongs, just until softened (15 to 30 seconds). To make a burrito, place a few slices of meat down center of a tortilla; top with beans, a few pieces of onion from onion halves, Salsa Fresca, guacamole, sour cream, and cilantro sprigs. Fold to enclose filling; eat out of hand. Makes 8 to 10 servings.

Salsa Fresca. In a medium-size bowl, stir together 3 large ripe **tomatoes,** diced; ½ cup chopped **cilantro;** 1 small **onion,** chopped; 5 to 7 tablespoons seeded, minced **fresh hot chiles;** and 3 to 4 tablespoons **lime juice.** Season to taste with **salt.**

Per serving: 778 calories (34 percent from fat), 46 g protein, 78 g carbohydrates, 29 g total fat (8 g saturated fat), 75 mg cholesterol, 1,077 mg sodium

WESTERN CLASSIC
Flank Steak with Mustard-Caper Sauce

Dijon mustard and tiny capers meet in a piquant sauce for thinly sliced rare flank steak.

- **¼ cup butter or margarine**
- **1 tablespoon olive oil or salad oil**
- **1 flank steak (about 1½ lbs.), trimmed of fat**
- **3 tablespoons dry vermouth or dry white wine**
- **1 tablespoon Dijon mustard**
- **¼ teaspoon Worcestershire**
- **1½ tablespoons drained capers**
  Watercress sprigs (optional)

Melt 1 tablespoon of the butter in oil in a wide frying pan over medium-high heat. Add meat and cook, turning once, until well browned on both sides and done to your liking; cut to test (6 to 8 minutes for rare).

Transfer meat to a carving board and keep warm. Reduce heat under frying pan to low; add remaining 3 tablespoons butter, vermouth, mustard, Worcestershire, and capers. Stir to blend. To serve, cut meat across the grain into thin slanting slices. Arrange meat in a serving dish or on individual plates and top with sauce. Garnish with watercress sprigs, if desired. Makes 4 servings.

Per serving: 416 calories (63 percent from fat), 35 g protein, 2 g carbohydrates, 28 g total fat (13 g saturated fat), 116 mg cholesterol, 441 mg sodium

Singapore Satay

A spicy, mildly sweet peanut sauce is the flavorful secret to successful satay. This version of the popular Asian dish can be made with your choice of meat or poultry. It's adapted from a recipe that won raves from *Sunset* editors during a culinary tour of Singapore in the early '70s.

- **3 to 4 pounds lean boneless meat, such as beef sirloin or top round, lamb shoulder or leg, or chicken breast or thigh (use one kind or a combination)**
- **2 tablespoons curry powder**
- **½ cup olive oil or salad oil**
- **½ cup soy sauce**
- **4 cloves garlic, minced or pressed**
- **2 tablespoons sugar**
  Peanut Sauce (recipe follows); or 2½ cups purchased peanut sauce

Cut meat into ¾-inch cubes, keeping different kinds of meat separate.

In a small bowl, stir together curry powder, oil, soy sauce, garlic, and sugar. Place meat cubes in a large bowl; pour marinade over meat cubes. (Or, if you use more than one kind of meat, put each in a heavy-duty plastic bag, set bags together in a bowl, and pour marinade into each one.) Cover (or seal bags) and refrigerate for at least 4 hours or up to 2 days; stir meat or turn bags over occasionally.

If using bamboo skewers, soak them in water to cover for 30 minutes. Prepare Peanut Sauce; keep warm.

Thread meat on long, sturdy bamboo or metal skewers (use only one kind of meat on each skewer). Place skewers on a grill about 2 inches above a solid bed of medium-hot coals. Cook, turning frequently, until meat is browned (8 to 10 minutes). Offer skewers of meat alongside dishes of Peanut Sauce for dipping. Makes 8 to 10 servings.

Peanut Sauce. In a blender or food processor, whirl 1 cup **salted peanuts** until finely ground; remove from blender and set aside.

Add 1 large **onion** (cut into chunks), 2 cloves **garlic,** and 4 or 5 **small dried hot red chiles** to blender; whirl until smooth. Heat 2 tablespoons **salad oil** in a frying pan over medium heat. Add onion mixture, 2 teaspoons **ground coriander,** and 1 teaspoon **ground cumin;** cook, stirring occasionally, for 5 minutes.

Reduce heat to low and add ground peanuts. Then gradually stir in 1 can (about 12 oz.) **frozen unsweetened coconut milk** (thawed), 3 tablespoons firmly packed **brown sugar,** and 2 tablespoons *each* **lemon juice** and **soy sauce.** Bring sauce to a simmer; then continue to simmer (do not boil), uncovered, stirring occasionally, until sauce is thickened (about 15 minutes).

Serve sauce warm or at room temperature in wide, shallow rimmed dishes. If made ahead, let cool; then cover and refrigerate until next day. Reheat just until warm before serving. Makes about 2½ cups.

Per serving of meat: 325 calories (45 percent from fat), 41 g protein, 3 g carbohydrates, 16 g total fat (5 g saturated fat), 118 mg cholesterol, 545 mg sodium

Per tablespoon of Peanut Sauce: 52 calories (72 percent from fat), 1 g protein, 3 g carbohydrates, 4 g total fat (2 g saturated fat), 0 mg cholesterol, 83 mg sodium

Barbecued Skirt Steaks with Fresh Herbs

In a 1982 feature on fresh herbs, we suggested tucking sprigs of fresh rosemary, thyme, or tarragon into skewered skirt steaks before grilling. Heat from the barbecue releases the herbs' volatile oils, lending tantalizing aroma and flavor to the meat and meat juices.

- **1½ to 2 pounds skirt steaks or flank steak, trimmed of fat**
- **½ cup olive oil**
- **3 tablespoons red wine vinegar**
- **1 tablespoon Dijon mustard**
- **1 clove garlic, minced or pressed**
- **¼ teaspoon pepper**
- **25 to 30 fresh thyme, rosemary, or tarragon sprigs (*each* about 3 inches long)**

Cut steaks crosswise into about 12-inch lengths, then arrange in a 9- by 13-inch dish. In a small bowl, stir together oil, vinegar, mustard, garlic, and pepper until well blended. Pour marinade over meat; turn meat to coat on all sides. Cover and refrigerate for at least 4 hours or until next day, turning meat occasionally.

Soak herb sprigs in water to cover for about 30 minutes.

Lift meat from marinade and drain briefly (reserve marinade). Weave each piece of meat onto a long metal skewer, rippling meat very slightly and tucking an herb sprig between skewer and meat on both sides of meat.

Place skewers on a grill 4 to 6 inches above a solid bed of hot coals. Cook, turning often and basting with marinade, until meat is done to your liking; cut to test (about 6 minutes for rare). Makes 6 servings.

Per serving: 384 calories (72 percent from fat), 26 g protein, 1 g carbohydrates, 30 g total fat (8 g saturated fat), 66 mg cholesterol, 154 mg sodium

Richly seasoned basting sauces and marinades bring an appealing new dimension to any variety of meat, poultry, or seafood. Simply prepared in minutes, the savory choices on this page offer an easy way to enhance the flavor and texture of foods before (and during) grilling, broiling, or roasting.

For best results, marinate foods for at least an hour, then baste frequently during cooking.

Lemon-Soy Marinade

Poultry, Beef, Seafood, Pork

- ⅓ cup soy sauce
- ½ cup lemon juice
- 4 cloves garlic, minced or pressed
- 2 tablespoons minced fresh ginger

In a bowl, stir together soy sauce, lemon juice, garlic, and ginger. Makes about 1 cup.

Per ¼ cup: 26 calories (4 percent from fat), 2 g protein, 5 g carbohydrates, 0.1 g total fat (0 g saturated fat), 0 mg cholesterol, 1,365 mg sodium

Wine Marinade

Poultry, Beef, Lamb, Pork

- 1 large onion, coarsely chopped
- 1 clove garlic, peeled
- ½ teaspoon black pepper
  Dash of ground red pepper (cayenne)
- ¼ cup white wine vinegar
- ½ cup dry white wine
- 2 tablespoons olive oil
- ¾ teaspoon dry thyme
- ¼ teaspoon grated lemon peel
- 1 tablespoon lemon juice
- ½ teaspoon honey

In a blender or food processor, combine onion, garlic, black pepper, red pepper, vinegar, wine, oil, thyme, lemon peel, lemon juice, and honey. Whirl until mixture is smooth. Makes about 1¾ cups.

Per ¼ cup: 62 calories (66 percent from fat), 0.4 g protein, 4 g carbohydrates, 4 g total fat (0.5 g saturated fat), 0 mg cholesterol, 2 mg sodium

Teriyaki Sauce

Poultry, Beef, Lamb, Pork

- 2 tablespoons cornstarch
- ⅓ cup soy sauce
- ¼ cup sugar
- 1 clove garlic, minced or pressed
- 2 teaspoons minced fresh ginger
- ¼ cup dry white wine (optional)
- 2 cups beef broth (or 2¼ cups, if not using wine)

In a small pan, stir together cornstarch, soy sauce, sugar, garlic, and ginger. Stir in wine (if desired) and broth. Cook over medium heat, stirring, until thickened. Makes about 2½ cups.

Per ¼ cup: 36 calories (6 percent from fat), 1 g protein, 8 g carbohydrates, 0.2 g total fat (0 g saturated fat), 0 mg cholesterol, 729 mg sodium

Spicy Chili Sauce

Poultry, Beef, Seafood

- ¾ cup tomato-based chili sauce
- ½ cup chopped onion
- 3 tablespoons lemon juice
- 2 tablespoons olive oil or salad oil
- 2 teaspoons tarragon wine vinegar
- 1 clove garlic, minced or pressed
- 1 teaspoon firmly packed brown sugar
- ½ teaspoon liquid hot pepper seasoning
- ¼ teaspoon *each* dry mustard and salt

In a small pan, stir together chili sauce, onion, lemon juice, oil, vinegar, garlic, sugar, hot pepper seasoning, mustard, and salt. Bring mixture to a boil over high heat; then reduce heat and simmer, uncovered, for 5 minutes. Makes about 1¼ cups.

Per ¼ cup: 104 calories (46 percent from fat), 1 g protein, 13 g carbohydrates, 6 g total fat (0.7 g saturated fat), 0 mg cholesterol, 672 mg sodium

Savory Raisin Baste

Poultry, Pork

- ½ cup finely chopped raisins
- ¼ cup chopped onion
- 1 clove garlic, minced or pressed
- ½ cup catsup
- ½ cup beef broth or dry white wine
- 3 tablespoons olive oil
- 2 tablespoons wine vinegar
- 1 tablespoon firmly packed brown sugar
- 1 teaspoon prepared mustard
- ½ teaspoon salt
- ⅛ teaspoon dry dill weed
- 1 teaspoon liquid smoke flavoring (optional)

In a 1½- to 2-quart pan, combine raisins, onion, garlic, catsup, broth, oil, vinegar, sugar, mustard, salt, dill weed, and smoke flavoring (if desired). Bring to a boil over high heat; then reduce heat and simmer, uncovered, for 10 to 15 minutes. Makes about 1¾ cups.

Per ¼ cup: 113 calories (45 percent from fat), 0.9 g protein, 16 g carbohydrates, 6 g total fat (0.8 g saturated fat), 0 mg cholesterol, 431 mg sodium

Steak with Green Peppercorn Sauce

The tangy flavor of green peppercorns distinguishes the creamy sauce for this tender steak. You can buy the peppercorns canned (packed in salt water or vinegar) or dried; the recipe works well with either kind, though the canned type will be slightly softer.

1⅓ to 2 pounds tender boneless beef steak, cut 1 to 1½ inches thick

1 tablespoon butter or margarine

1 tablespoon olive oil or salad oil

6 tablespoons brandy, warmed

¼ to ½ cup minced shallots

1 to 2 tablespoons canned green peppercorns, rinsed and drained; or 1 to 2 tablespoons dried green peppercorns

¾ cup whipping cream or crème fraîche

1 tablespoon Dijon mustard

½ teaspoon dry tarragon

Salt and pepper

Trim fat from steak or score fat to prevent meat from curling as it cooks.

Melt butter in oil in a wide frying pan over medium-high heat. Add meat and cook, turning once, until well browned on both sides and done to your liking; cut to test (6 to 8 minutes for rare). Move pan into an open area, away from exhaust fans and flammable items. Add brandy and ignite; shake or tilt pan until flame dies. Transfer meat to a serving dish and keep warm.

Add shallots to pan; cook over high heat, stirring, until shallots are soft (2 to 3 minutes). Add peppercorns, cream, mustard, and tarragon. Bring to a boil; boil, stirring, until large, shiny bubbles form and sauce is slightly thickened (3 to 4 minutes). Stir in any accumulated meat juices from serving dish. Season sauce to taste with salt and pepper; pour over meat. Makes 4 to 6 servings.

Per serving: 461 calories (67 percent from fat), 31 g protein, 5 g carbohydrates, 32 g total fat (16 g saturated fat), 125 mg cholesterol, 236 mg sodium

Most-requested Liver

An Oregon restaurant chef shared this popular menu item in our "Kitchen Cabinet." To make the savory dish, you top lightly sautéed liver with chunks of tomato, onion, green pepper, and bacon, then bake.

6 slices bacon

1½ pounds baby beef liver, cut into serving-size pieces

All-purpose flour

1 large onion, sliced

1 green bell pepper, seeded and sliced

1 envelope (1 to 1½ oz.) onion soup mix

1 can (about 14½ oz.) stewed tomatoes

Seasoned salt and pepper

Hot cooked noodles (optional)

Cook bacon in a wide frying pan over medium heat until crisp. Lift out, drain, crumble, and set aside. Pour off and reserve drippings; return 2 tablespoons of the drippings to pan.

Dust liver with flour and shake off excess. Add liver to pan, a few pieces at a time (do not crowd pan). Cook over medium heat, turning as needed, until lightly browned on both sides; add more drippings to pan as needed to prevent sticking. Arrange liver in a 9- by 13-inch baking dish.

Add onion and bell pepper to frying pan; cook, stirring often, until onion is soft (about 5 minutes). Spoon vegetables evenly over liver, sprinkle with soup mix, and pour tomatoes over all. Sprinkle with bacon and season to taste with seasoned salt and pepper. Cover and bake in a 350° oven until heated through (about 25 minutes). Serve with noodles, if desired. Makes 6 servings.

Per serving: 290 calories (35 percent from fat), 27 g protein, 20 g carbohydrates, 11 g total fat (4 g saturated fat), 410 mg cholesterol, 884 mg sodium

WESTERN CLASSIC
Spicy Meat-filled Burritos

In 1973, we offered this burrito recipe as one way to make the most of leftover holiday roast. The spicy filling is delicious with any kind of meat.

- **Tomato & Chile Relish (recipe follows)**
- **Easy Guacamole (page 11) or purchased guacamole**
- **Spicy Meat Filling (recipe follows)**
- 18 to 24 **flour tortillas** (*each* about 8 inches in diameter)
- 1 **large can** (about 29 oz.) **refried beans**
- 3 cups (about 12 oz.) **shredded jack cheese**
- 1 cup **sour cream** (optional)

Prepare Tomato & Chile Relish and Easy Guacamole; cover and refrigerate until ready to serve.

Prepare Spicy Meat Filling. While filling is cooking, stack tortillas and wrap in foil. Heat in a 350° oven until warm and soft (about 15 minutes). Meanwhile, heat beans in a large pan.

Serve tortillas in a towel-lined basket. Alongside, arrange Tomato & Chile Relish, guacamole, Spicy Meat Filling, beans, cheese, and sour cream (if desired) in individual bowls. To assemble burritos, top tortillas with fillings and roll to enclose; eat out of hand. Makes 8 to 10 servings.

Tomato & Chile Relish. In a bowl, stir together 3 medium-size **tomatoes,** seeded and finely chopped; 1 cup thinly sliced **green onions;** 2 to 4 tablespoons **canned diced green chiles;** and ½ teaspoon *each* **ground coriander** and **salt.** Cover and refrigerate until ready to serve.

Spicy Meat Filling. Heat 2 tablespoons **olive oil** or salad oil in a wide frying pan over medium heat. Add l large **onion,** finely chopped, and 2 cloves **garlic,** minced or pressed. Cook, stirring often, until onion is soft (about 5 minutes).

Stir in 4 cups finely diced **cooked meat,** such as beef or pork roast, chicken, or turkey. Stir in 1 can (about 10 oz.) **red chile sauce,** ½ teaspoon each **ground cinnamon** and **ground**

cumin, and 2 to 4 tablespoons **canned diced green chiles.** Season to taste with **salt.** Bring to a boil; then reduce heat and simmer, uncovered, for about 5 minutes.

Per serving: 957 calories (37 percent from fat), 52 g protein, 98 g carbohydrates, 40 g total fat (7 g saturated fat), 107 mg cholesterol, 2,062 mg sodium

Beef Burgundy

This hearty French stew first appeared in our pages in 1964, as an easy entrée for a buffet dinner. Since it doesn't require much last-minute attention, it's the perfect selection for no-fuss entertaining.

- **Bouquet garni (directions follow)**
- ¼ cup **butter** or margarine
- 16 small white **boiling onions,** peeled
- 6 slices **bacon,** diced
- 4 pounds **boneless beef chuck,** trimmed of fat and cut into 1½-inch cubes
- ¼ cup **brandy** (optional), warmed
- 2 cups **burgundy** or other dry red wine
- 2 cloves **garlic,** peeled
- 2 cups small **mushrooms,** sliced
- 1½ cups **water**
- 6 tablespoons **all-purpose flour**
- ½ cup cold **water**
- **Salt and pepper**
- **Hot cooked white or wild rice (optional)**

Prepare bouquet garni; set aside.

Melt butter in a large, heavy pan over medium heat. Add onions and bacon; cook, stirring often, until onions are lightly browned (about 10 minutes). Lift out onions and bacon with a slotted spoon and set aside.

Add beef to pan, a portion at a time (do not crowd pan). Cook, turning as needed, until well browned on all sides. If using brandy, move pan into an open area, away from exhaust fans and flammable items. Add brandy to pan and ignite; shake or tilt pan until flame dies.

Return all meat to pan; add burgundy, garlic, mushrooms, the 1½ cups water, bouquet garni, onions, and bacon. Bring to a boil; then reduce heat, cover, and simmer until meat is tender when pierced (about 1½ hours). With a slotted spoon, transfer meat, mushrooms, and onions to a serving dish; keep warm.

Pour meat juices through a fine wire strainer set over a medium-size pan; discard residue in strainer. In a small bowl, mix flour and the ½ cup water to make a smooth paste. Stir flour mixture into meat juices; cook over medium heat, stirring constantly, until sauce is thick and smooth. Season to taste with salt and pepper.

Pour sauce over meat and vegetables. If made ahead, let cool; then cover and refrigerate until next day. To reheat, transfer to a baking dish; cover and bake in a 350° oven until bubbly and heated through (about 35 minutes). Serve over rice, if desired. Makes 8 servings.

Bouquet garni. Tie in a square of damp cheesecloth: 1 **carrot** (quartered), 1 **celery top,** 1 **dry bay leaf,** 1 or 2 **parsley sprigs,** and 1 **fresh thyme sprig** (or 1 teaspoon dry thyme).

Per serving: 482 calories (49 percent from fat), 51 g protein, 9 g carbohydrates, 26 g total fat (11 g saturated fat), 163 mg cholesterol, 335 mg sodium

Beef Stroganoff with Noodles

For this make-ahead classic, the beef mixture can easily be prepared in advance and refrigerated (or frozen). To serve, cook the noodles while you reheat the meat and sauce; stir sour cream into the sauce at the very last.

- **2** pounds round steak, cut 1 inch thick
- **3** tablespoons salad oil or olive oil
- **¼** cup dry red wine
- **½** pound small white boiling onions, peeled
- **½** pound mushrooms, sliced
- **1** clove garlic, minced or pressed
- **3** tablespoons all-purpose flour
- **1** can (about 10½ oz.) condensed consommé
- **¼** cup tomato paste
- Salt and pepper
- **1** dry bay leaf
- **8** ounces dry medium-wide noodles
- **½** cup sour cream
- **2** tablespoons chopped parsley

Cut steak across the grain into ¼-inch-thick slices. Heat 1½ tablespoons of the oil in a wide frying pan over medium-high heat. Add meat, a portion at a time (do not crowd pan); cook, turning as needed, until browned on all sides. Transfer to a 3-quart baking dish. Stir in wine.

Heat remaining 1½ tablespoons oil in pan. Add onions and cook over medium heat, stirring often, until golden (about 7 minutes). Add mushrooms and garlic; cook, stirring often, until mushrooms are limp. With a slotted spoon, transfer vegetables to baking dish.

Stir flour into drippings in pan; cook, stirring, until flour is golden. Remove from heat and gradually stir in consommé and tomato paste.

Season to taste with salt and pepper. Return to high heat and bring sauce to a boil, stirring; pour sauce over meat and vegetables. Add bay leaf, cover, and bake in a 350° oven until meat is tender to bite (about 1½ hours). If made ahead, let cool; then cover and refrigerate until next day (freeze for longer storage). Reheat before serving.

To serve, in a large pan, cook noodles in about 2½ quarts of boiling salted water until tender to bite (about 8 minutes); or cook according to package directions.

Drain noodles and spoon into center of a rimmed serving dish. Stir sour cream into hot meat mixture. Spoon meat mixture over noodles and sprinkle with parsley. Makes 6 servings.

Per serving: 613 calories (48 percent from fat), 41 g protein, 39 g carbohydrates, 32 g total fat (11 g saturated fat), 140 mg cholesterol, 449 mg sodium

Savory Swiss Steak

Lean round steak, tenderized by pounding with a meat mallet, gains lusty flavor from a hearty tomato-vegetable sauce in this recipe from 1960. You can simmer the meat on the range or, if you prefer, bake it in the oven.

- **½** cup all-purpose flour
- **1** tablespoon dry mustard
- **1½** pounds round steak, cut 1 inch thick
- **2** tablespoons salad oil or bacon drippings
- **1** can (about 14½ oz.) tomatoes
- **1** cup sliced onions
- **½** cup diced celery
- **2** or 3 carrots, diced
- **2** tablespoons Worcestershire
- **1** tablespoon firmly packed brown sugar
- Salt and pepper

Mix flour with mustard. Sprinkle flour mixture over steak and pound

it in with a cleated meat mallet. Cut pounded steak into serving-size pieces.

Heat oil in a wide, heavy frying pan over medium-high heat. Add meat and cook, turning once, until browned on both sides. If you are baking meat, transfer it to a shallow baking pan.

Cut up tomatoes; add tomatoes and their liquid, onions, celery, carrots, Worcestershire, and sugar to meat in baking pan or frying pan. Season to taste with salt and pepper. Cover and bake in a 350° oven (or bring to a boil, then reduce heat, cover, and simmer) until meat is tender when pierced (about 1½ hours). Makes 4 servings.

Per serving: 547 calories (49 percent from fat), 39 g protein, 30 g carbohydrates, 30 g total fat (9 g saturated fat), 107 mg cholesterol, 372 mg sodium

Green Chile & Beef Pie

To make this hearty treat, you envelop a spicy stew of tender beef chunks, diced green chiles, and corn in an easy cream cheese pastry. To save time, you can assemble the pie up to 2 days before baking.

- **Cream Cheese Pastry** (recipe follows); or purchased pastry shell for a single-crust 9-inch pie
- **Green Chile & Beef Filling** (recipe follows)
- **1** cup (about 4 oz.) shredded Cheddar cheese
- **1** egg, beaten

Prepare Cream Cheese Pastry; refrigerate. Prepare Green Chile & Beef Filling; pour into a 9-inch pie pan or dish. (At this point, you may cover and refrigerate until next day.)

Sprinkle beef filling with cheese. On a lightly floured board, roll pastry out to a 10-inch round. With a cookie cutter, cut 1 or 2 pieces from center of pastry; reserve cutouts. Lay pastry over filling; fold edges under and press firmly against pan to seal. Flute edges decoratively; top pie with cutouts. (At this point, you may cover and refrigerate for up to 2 days if filling is fresh, up to 1 day if filling was made a day ahead.)

Set pie in a 10- by 15-inch rimmed baking pan. Brush pastry and cutouts with egg. Bake on lowest rack of a 400° oven until pastry is well browned and filling is hot in center (40 to 55 minutes). If edges or cutouts darken excessively before center of crust is brown, drape edges and cover cutouts with foil.

Serve pie hot. Or, if made ahead, let cool; then cover and refrigerate until next day. To reheat pie, place it in a 350° oven and heat, uncovered, until filling is hot in center (30 to 40 minutes); lay foil over crust if it begins to darken. Makes 8 servings.

Cream Cheese Pastry. In a food processor (or a bowl), combine 1¼ cups **all-purpose flour;** ½ cup (¼ lb.) **butter** or margarine, cut into chunks; and ⅓ cup **Neufchâtel or cream cheese.** Whirl (or rub with your fingers) until mixture resembles coarse crumbs. Add 1 **egg;** whirl until pastry holds together (about 8 seconds; or mix with a fork). Shape into a ball. If made ahead, cover and refrigerate for up to 3 days.

Green Chile & Beef Filling. In a 4- to 5-quart pan, combine 2 pounds **skirt steaks** or boneless beef chuck, trimmed of fat and cut into 1-inch pieces; 1 large **onion,** coarsely chopped; 2 tablespoons *each* **soy sauce** and **water;** 2 cloves **garlic,** minced or pressed; and 1 teaspoon **dry oregano.** Bring to a boil; reduce heat, cover, and simmer for 30 minutes. Uncover; boil over high heat until liquid has evaporated. When meat sizzles, add ¼ cup **water** and stir to scrape browned bits free. When liquid has evaporated again, repeat procedure once, using ¼ cup more **water.** After liquid has evaporated, add 1 cup more **water.** Bring to a boil; reduce heat, cover, and simmer until meat is very tender when pierced (about 30 minutes). Stir in 1 package (about 10 oz.) **frozen corn kernels** and 1 large can (about 7 oz.) **diced green chiles.**

Mix 3 tablespoons **cornstarch** and ¾ cup **beef broth.** Add two-thirds of the cornstarch mixture to meat mixture; bring to a boil, stirring. Remove from heat and let cool; stir in remaining cornstarch mixture.

Per serving: 543 calories (54 percent from fat), 33 g protein, 30 g carbohydrates, 32 g total fat (17 g saturated fat), 165 mg cholesterol, 827 mg sodium

WESTERN CLASSIC

Oven-simmered Beef Brisket

Oven-simmered in wine and soy, this succulent brisket—from our "Kitchen Cabinet"—is a comfort-food favorite. Serve it hot from the oven or refrigerate the meat to slice for sandwiches.

2½ cups sweet vermouth or apple juice

½ cup soy sauce

¼ cup salad oil

2 dry bay leaves

1 clove garlic, minced or pressed

1 large onion, chopped

½ teaspoon ground ginger

¼ teaspoon pepper

1 beef brisket (about 4 lbs.), trimmed of fat

¼ cup cornstarch blended with ¼ cup cold water (if serving meat hot)

In a large baking pan, combine vermouth, soy sauce, oil, bay leaves, garlic, onion, ginger, and pepper; mix lightly. Add brisket; turn to coat. Cover and refrigerate, turning meat occasionally, until next day.

Leave meat in marinade and bake, covered, in a 350° oven until tender when pierced (about 3 hours). Transfer meat to a serving dish. Skim and discard fat from pan juices; discard bay leaves.

To serve brisket hot, stir cornstarch mixture into pan juices. Cook over medium heat, stirring constantly, until sauce is thickened; offer sauce to spoon over individual servings.

To serve brisket cold, omit cornstarch mixture. Return meat to pan juices and let cool; then cover and refrigerate until cold or for up to 2 days. Lift out meat and cut across the grain into thin slices. Makes 8 to 10 servings.

Per serving: 432 calories (45 percent from fat), 43 g protein, 15 g carbohydrates, 21 g total fat (6 g saturated fat), 125 mg cholesterol, 1,081 mg sodium

Black Bean Beef Fillet

High in protein and rich in flavor, juicy beef tenderloin is quick and easy to cook. Here, the meat is seasoned before roasting with a pungent blend of garlic, fresh ginger, and salted black beans.

1¾ pounds narrow end section beef tenderloin, trimmed of fat
2 tablespoons fermented salted black beans, rinsed and drained
1 clove garlic, peeled
1 tablespoon Oriental sesame oil
1 teaspoon minced fresh ginger

Fold and tie narrow end of beef under to form a compact, evenly shaped roast.

Combine beans, garlic, and oil in a blender or food processor; whirl until smooth. Stir in ginger. Smear bean mixture evenly over meat. (At this point, you may cover and refrigerate until next day.)

Place meat on a rack in a 9- by 13-inch baking pan. Bake in a 450° oven until a meat thermometer inserted in thickest part registers 135° to 140°F for rare (about 30 minutes). To serve, cut meat across the grain into thin slanting slices; discard string. Makes 6 servings.

Per serving: 246 calories (52 percent from fat), 28 g protein, 0.5 g carbohydrates, 14 g total fat (5 g saturated fat), 82 mg cholesterol, 206 mg sodium

Fillet of Beef in a Crust

When we featured this recipe in one of our 1965 issues, pastry-wrapped fillet of beef—also known as beef Wellington—was considered *the* entrée to offer at special-occasion dinners. You can roast the beef and make the pastry, duxelles, and wine sauce in advance; on serving day, you need only assemble and bake the dish.

Madeira Sauce (recipe follows), Dijon mustard, or prepared horseradish
1 beef tenderloin (about 4 lbs.), trimmed of fat
1 tablespoon butter or margarine, at room temperature
  Salt and pepper
  Rich Pastry (recipe follows)
  Traditional Duxelles (recipe follows)
1 egg
1 tablespoon water
  Watercress or parsley sprigs

Prepare Madeira Sauce; set aside.

Tie beef every 1½ inches with cotton string to form a compact, evenly shaped roast; place in a shallow baking pan and rub with butter. Sprinkle with salt and pepper. Bake in a 425° oven for 30 minutes; remove from oven and let cool. (At this point, you may cover and refrigerate until next day.) Prepare pastry and duxelles.

Measure length of meat and its diameter at widest section. On a floured cloth, roll pastry into a neat rectangle a little more than 5 inches longer than meat and wide enough to enclose it. Trim uneven edges of pastry with a knife; save scraps. Spread duxelles over pastry to within 1 inch of edges; press duxelles lightly but firmly with your hand to make a compact layer.

Remove strings from cooled meat; center meat on duxelles. Gently lift (do not pull) pastry up over length of meat. Overlap pastry edges, compactly encasing meat; press edges firmly together to seal. Fold in ends of

pastry and seal. If too much pastry is accumulating at ends as you seal them, pinch out some of it, so that layer of pastry at ends has the same thickness as pastry wrapped around meat. Gently lift roll and place, seam side down, on an ungreased baking sheet. Roll out scraps of pastry on a floured cloth or board; cut out decorative shapes and arrange on pastry-wrapped meat. (At this point, you may cover and refrigerate for up to 6 hours.)

In a small bowl, beat together egg and water; brush over pastry. Bake pastry-wrapped meat in a 400° oven until richly browned (35 to 40 minutes). Slip a spatula under pastry to loosen it from pan; then carefully slide pastry-wrapped meat onto a platter and garnish with watercress sprigs.

To serve, cut into 1-inch-thick slices (pastry will break if you try to cut thin slices). Offer Madeira Sauce alongside. Makes 8 to 10 servings.

Madeira Sauce. In a wide frying pan, combine 3 slices **bacon,** chopped; 2 medium-size **carrots,** minced; 1 small **onion,** minced; and ¼ cup minced **parsley.** Stir over medium-high heat until vegetables are slightly soft and lightly browned. Warm ¼ cup **Madeira** in a small pan over low heat. Move pan into an open area, away from exhaust fans and flammable items; ignite Madeira and pour over vegetables, then shake or tilt frying pan until flame dies. Set vegetables aside.

In a deep 1½-quart pan, combine 2 cans (about 14½ oz. *each*) or 3½ cups **beef broth** and 3 **marrow-filled beef bones** (*each* about 3 inches long). Bring to a boil; then reduce heat and simmer, uncovered, for 15 minutes. Lift bones from broth. With a long, slender knife, ease marrow from bones; cut into chunks and set aside. Discard bones. Boil broth over high heat until reduced to 2 cups.

Stir 2 tablespoons **all-purpose flour** into vegetables, then gradually stir in reduced broth. Add 1 **dry bay leaf** and ½ teaspoon **dry thyme.** Bring to a boil, stirring constantly. (At this point, you may let sauce cool, then cover and refrigerate sauce and marrow separately until next day. Reheat before continuing.) Gently mix marrow into hot sauce and add more **Madeira** to taste, if desired. Keep warm.

Rich Pastry. In a large bowl, mix 4 cups **all-purpose flour** and 1 teaspoon **salt.** Using a pastry blender or 2 knives, cut in 1½ cups (¾ lb.) **butter** or margarine until mixture resembles coarse crumbs. Stir in 6 tablespoons **water,** adding 1 tablespoon of water at a time and mixing lightly; stir until pastry holds together. Shape into a ball. If made ahead, cover and refrigerate for up to 4 days; bring to room temperature before using.

Traditional Duxelles. Melt ¼ cup **butter** or margarine in a wide frying pan over medium-high heat. Add 1½ pounds **mushrooms,** finely chopped; cook, stirring often, until all liquid has evaporated and mushrooms are just beginning to brown. Add ¼ cup **Madeira,** ½ cup chopped **shallots** or sliced green onions, and ½ cup chopped **parsley.** Bring to a boil; boil, stirring often, until liquid has evaporated. Let cool. If made ahead, cover and refrigerate until next day.

Per serving: 972 calories (56 percent from fat), 53 g protein, 54 g carbohydrates, 60 g total fat (31 g saturated fat), 253 mg cholesterol, 1,114 mg sodium

One Rib for Two

To make a rib roast and baked potatoes for two, place one potato on either side of the frozen roast—then bake. The potatoes hold the meat upright, allowing the high oven heat to sear the surface and trap the juices inside.

- 1 **rib (about 2½ lbs.) of a standing rib roast, trimmed of fat**
- 1 **tablespoon salad oil or olive oil**
- 1 **small clove garlic, pressed**
- 2 **large russet potatoes, scrubbed**

Wrap meat airtight and freeze until solid. Combine oil and garlic; rub evenly over frozen meat. Stand meat, rib bone down, in a rimmed baking pan. Pierce each potato in several places with a fork; then place potatoes like bookends on either side of meat.

Bake in a 400° oven until potatoes are soft when pressed and meat is done to your liking; cut to test (about 1 hour and 25 minutes for medium-rare). To serve, cut meat parallel to the bone into 2 slices. Makes 2 servings.

Per serving: 833 calories (43 percent from fat), 74 g protein, 41 g carbohydrates, 39 g total fat (14 g saturated fat), 205 mg cholesterol, 202 mg sodium

Forgotten Short Ribs

As they slowly bake, these meaty short ribs absorb delicious flavor from a sweet, smoky sauce. They're messy to eat, so be sure to have plenty of napkins at the table!

- 1½ **teaspoons salt**
- ½ **teaspoon pepper**
- 3 **to 4 pounds beef short ribs**
- 1 **can (about 8 oz.) tomato sauce**
- 2 **tablespoons *each* molasses and cider vinegar**
- 1 **teaspoon liquid smoke flavoring**
- 1 **tablespoon instant minced onion**

Sprinkle salt and pepper on all sides of ribs, then transfer ribs to a deep 3-quart pan or baking dish. Set aside.

In a small pan, combine tomato sauce, molasses, vinegar, smoke flavoring, and onion. Bring to a boil over high heat; then reduce heat and simmer, uncovered, for 5 minutes. Pour sauce over ribs. Cover; bake in a 275° oven until meat is very tender when pierced (3 to 4 hours). Skim and discard fat from sauce before serving. If made ahead, let cool; then cover and refrigerate until next day. Lift off and discard any solidified fat before reheating. Makes 4 to 6 servings.

Per serving: 786 calories (77 percent from fat), 35 g protein, 10 g carbohydrates, 67 g total fat (28 g saturated fat), 149 mg cholesterol, 1,014 mg sodium

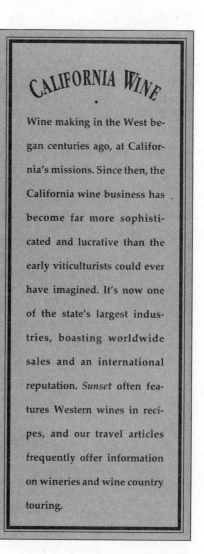

CALIFORNIA WINE

Wine making in the West began centuries ago, at California's missions. Since then, the California wine business has become far more sophisticated and lucrative than the early viticulturists could ever have imagined. It's now one of the state's largest industries, boasting worldwide sales and an international reputation. *Sunset* often features Western wines in recipes, and our travel articles frequently offer information on wineries and wine country touring.

Braised Veal Shanks

Long, slow cooking tenderizes tougher cuts of meat like these veal shanks. A richly seasoned lemon-and-herb sauce is a superb complement to the fork-tender meat.

- **6 veal shanks,** *each* **about 6 inches long (about 6 lbs.** *total***)**
- **4 cups beef broth**
- **1 lemon (unpeeled), chopped (discard seeds)**
- **1 teaspoon dry marjoram**
- **1 dry bay leaf**
- **½ teaspoon whole black peppercorns**
- **¼ teaspoon coriander seeds**
- **2 tablespoons balsamic or red wine vinegar**
- **1 tablespoon cornstarch blended with 2 tablespoons cold water**
  Salt

Lay veal shanks in a single layer in a close-fitting pan (about 9 by 13 inches). Bake in a 400° oven until browned (about 35 minutes). Then turn shanks over; add broth, lemon, marjoram, bay leaf, peppercorns, and coriander seeds to pan. Cover and continue to bake until meat is tender enough to pull easily from bones (about 1½ more hours).

Lift shanks from pan and arrange in a single layer in a serving dish; keep warm. Pour broth from pan through a fine wire strainer set over a wide frying pan; discard residue.

Skim and discard fat from broth. Add vinegar to broth and bring to a boil over high heat; boil, stirring occasionally, until reduced to 1½ to 2 cups (8 to 12 minutes). Stir in cornstarch mixture and bring to a boil, stirring constantly. Season to taste with salt. Offer sauce to spoon over individual servings. Makes 6 servings.

Per serving: 376 calories (25 percent from fat), 65 g protein, 4 g carbohydrates, 10 g total fat (4 g saturated fat), 234 mg cholesterol, 740 mg sodium

Veal Scaloppine with Marsala

Through the years, *Sunset* has come up with numerous ways to prepare tender veal scallops. This variation, sauced with Marsala and mushrooms, is one of our all-time favorites.

- **¼ cup butter or margarine**
- **½ pound mushrooms, thinly sliced**
- **1½ tablespoons lemon juice**
- **1½ pounds boneless veal cutlets, cut about ⅓ inch thick**
- **¼ cup all-purpose flour**
- **1 teaspoon salt**
- **¼ teaspoon pepper**
- **¾ cup Marsala or dry sherry**
- **1 teaspoon instant beef bouillon; or 1 beef bouillon cube, crumbled**
- **1 tablespoon minced parsley**

Melt 2 tablespoons of the butter in a wide frying pan over medium heat. Add mushrooms and lemon juice; cook, stirring often, just until mushrooms are soft. Remove from heat and keep warm.

Place veal between 2 sheets of plastic wrap or wax paper; pound with a flat-surfaced mallet until about ⅛ inch thick. Then cut into strips about 1 inch wide. In a shallow pan, mix flour, salt, and pepper; dust meat with flour mixture and shake off excess.

Melt remaining 2 tablespoons butter in frying pan over medium-high

heat. Add meat, a portion at a time (do not crowd pan). Cook, turning as needed, until browned on both sides. Transfer meat to a platter and keep warm. Add Marsala and bouillon to pan; stir to scrape browned bits free. Cook over high heat, stirring constantly, until sauce is smooth and thick. To serve, arrange mushrooms on platter with meat; spoon sauce over meat and sprinkle with parsley. Makes 4 to 6 servings.

Per serving: 319 calories (39 percent from fat), 31 g protein, 12 g carbohydrates, 12 g total fat (6 g saturated fat), 131 mg cholesterol, 796 mg sodium

Veal Piccata

Classic veal *piccata* is renowned for its delightful balance of flavors and textures. A pleasantly rich sauce, accented with tart lemon, cloaks the firm, tender cutlets.

- **1½ pounds boneless veal cutlets, cut about ⅓ inch thick**
- **3 tablespoons all-purpose flour**
- **1 teaspoon salt**
- **½ teaspoon pepper**
- **¼ cup butter or margarine**
- **⅔ cup dry white wine**
- **2 teaspoons grated lemon peel**
  Lemon slices

Place veal between 2 sheets of plastic wrap or wax paper; pound with a flat-surfaced mallet until about ¼ inch thick. Then cut meat into strips about 1½ inches wide and 3 inches long. In a shallow pan, mix flour, salt, and pepper. Dust meat with flour mixture and shake off excess.

Melt 2 tablespoons of the butter in a wide frying pan over medium-high heat. Add meat, a portion at a time (do not crowd pan). Cook, turning as needed, until browned on both sides; add 1 more tablespoon butter to pan as needed to prevent sticking. Transfer meat to a platter and keep warm. Add wine to pan; bring to a boil, stirring to scrape browned bits free. Stir in lemon peel and remaining 1 tablespoon butter; heat, stirring, until butter is melted. Spoon sauce over meat and garnish with lemon slices. Makes 4 to 6 servings.

Per serving: 267 calories (44 percent from fat), 30 g protein, 4 g carbohydrates, 12 g total fat (6 g saturated fat), 131 mg cholesterol, 623 mg sodium

Pork Tenderloins with Onion-Apple Cream

As these pork tenderloins bake, you brush them with a creamy sherry baste. The same sauce enriches the slow-cooked apple and onion slices that accompany the meat.

> **Sherry Baste (recipe follows)**
> 2 **pork tenderloins (about 1½ lbs. *total*), trimmed of fat**
> 2 **tablespoons butter or margarine**
> 1 **large onion, thinly sliced**
> 1 **large Golden Delicious apple, peeled, cored, and thinly sliced**
> **Parsley sprigs**

Prepare Sherry Baste. Fold and tie narrow end of each pork tenderloin under to give meat an even thickness. Place meat on a rack in a baking pan; brush with Sherry Baste. Bake in a 425° oven until a meat thermometer inserted in thickest part of meat registers 150° to 155°F (20 to 25 minutes); baste often during cooking.

Meanwhile, melt butter in a wide frying pan over medium heat. Add onion and apple and cook, stirring often, until onion is soft and golden (about 20 minutes).

When meat is done, add remaining Sherry Baste to apple mixture and bring to a boil; transfer to a small serving bowl. To serve, cut meat across the grain into thin slanting slices; discard string. Garnish meat with parsley

sprigs. Offer apple mixture to spoon over individual servings. Makes 4 to 6 servings.

Sherry Baste. In a small bowl, stir together ⅔ cup **whipping cream,** ¼ cup **cream sherry,** 2 teaspoons **Dijon mustard,** 1 teaspoon **prepared horseradish,** and ½ teaspoon **salt.**

Per serving: 372 calories (50 percent from fat), 32 g protein, 12 g carbohydrates, 20 g total fat (11 g saturated fat), 148 mg cholesterol, 412 mg sodium

Spicy Pork Tenderloins

This lowfat, low-calorie favorite gets its kick from mustard and chili powder. Honey adds sweetness and gives the tender pork a delicate glaze.

> 2 **pork tenderloins (about 1½ lbs. *total*), trimmed of fat**
> ¼ **cup *each* honey and prepared mustard**
> ¼ **teaspoon *each* salt and chili powder**

Fold and tie narrow end of each pork tenderloin under to give meat an even thickness.

In a large bowl, stir together honey, mustard, salt, and chili powder. Add meat and turn to coat. Cover and refrigerate, turning meat occasionally, for at least 4 hours or until next day.

Prepare barbecue as directed in "Indirect Grilling" (page 70). Set meat on grill above drip pan. Cover barbe-

cue and adjust vents as needed to maintain an even heat. Cook until a meat thermometer inserted in thickest part of meat registers 150° to 155°F (18 to 22 minutes). To serve, cut meat across the grain into thin slanting slices; discard string. Makes 4 to 6 servings.

Per serving: 241 calories (22 percent from fat), 32 g protein, 15 g carbohydrates, 6 g total fat (2 g saturated fat), 100 mg cholesterol, 339 mg sodium

Swedish-cured Barbecued Pork Loin

To cure pork loin the Swedish way, rub the meat with sugar and salt, then let it marinate for several days. Add cumin seeds and cardamom for a bit of extra flavor, if you like.

> 1 **boned, rolled, and tied pork loin (3½ to 4 lbs.)**
> 3 **tablespoons sugar**
> 2 **tablespoons salt**
> 1 **teaspoon cumin seeds (optional)**
> ½ **teaspoon ground cardamom (optional)**

Place pork in a close-fitting glass dish. Mix sugar, salt, and, if desired, cumin seeds and cardamom; rub onto meat. Cover and refrigerate for 24 to 36 hours. Discard juices; rinse meat well under cool running water, rubbing to release salt. Pat dry.

Prepare barbecue as directed in "Indirect Grilling" (page 70). Set meat on lightly greased grill above drip pan. Cover barbecue and adjust vents as needed to maintain an even heat. Cook until a meat thermometer inserted in thickest part of meat registers 150° to 155°F (about 1 hour). To serve, cut meat into thin slices; discard strings. Makes 8 to 10 servings.

Per serving: 423 calories (64 percent from fat), 36 g protein, 1 g carbohydrates, 29 g total fat (11 g saturated fat), 129 mg cholesterol, 459 mg sodium

Chili Pork Steaks

Serve these spicy marinated pork shoulder steaks with toppings of guacamole, mild chile salsa, and cool sour cream.

 4 pork shoulder steaks (about 6 oz. *each*), cut ½ inch thick
 1½ tablespoons chili powder
 1 teaspoon *each* dry oregano and garlic salt
 ¼ teaspoon ground cumin
 3 tablespoons wine vinegar
 3 tablespoons salad oil
   Green Chile Salsa (recipe follows)
 ¾ cup Easy Guacamole (page 11) or purchased guacamole
   Sour cream

Trim and discard fat from pork steaks. In a small bowl, combine chili powder, oregano, garlic salt, cumin, vinegar, and 1 tablespoon of the oil. Rub mixture on both sides of each steak. Cover and refrigerate for at least 2 hours or until next day.

Meanwhile, prepare Green Chile Salsa and Easy Guacamole; cover and refrigerate.

Heat remaining 2 tablespoons oil in a wide frying pan over medium-high heat. Add steaks and cook, turning once, until meat is no longer pink in thickest part; cut to test (about 10 minutes).

Place salsa, guacamole, and sour cream in individual bowls; offer alongside steaks to add to taste. Makes 4 servings.

Green Chile Salsa. In a bowl, stir together 1 large **tomato,** chopped; 1 small **onion,** chopped; 1 small can (about 4 oz.) **diced green chiles;** and 1 tablespoon **white wine vinegar** or distilled white vinegar.

Per serving: 489 calories (60 percent from fat), 35 g protein, 14 g carbohydrates, 33 g total fat (7 g saturated fat), 114 mg cholesterol, 824 mg sodium

Sherried Pork Chops & Pears

Cinnamon, brown sugar, and sherry lend sweet appeal to this cold-weather casserole of juicy winter pears and pork chops.

 6 to 8 center-cut pork chops (*each* about ¾ inch thick)
   Salt
 3 or 4 firm-ripe Anjou pears
 2 tablespoons lemon juice
 ¼ cup firmly packed brown sugar
 ½ teaspoon ground cinnamon
 ¼ cup dry sherry
 1 tablespoon butter or margarine
 ½ teaspoon cornstarch blended with ½ teaspoon cold water

Trim fat from pork chops. Place a little of the fat in a wide frying pan; cook over medium heat, stirring, until pan is lightly greased. Add chops to pan, a few at a time (do not crowd pan); cook, turning as needed, until browned on all sides. Season chops to taste with salt and arrange on one side of a shallow baking pan.

Cut pears into halves lengthwise; remove cores and stems. Place pear halves, cut side up, beside chops; sprinkle meat and fruit with lemon juice. Mix sugar and cinnamon and distribute over meat and fruit; then pour sherry over all. Put a dot of butter in hollow of each pear half. Cover and bake in a 350° oven for 20 minutes. Uncover and continue to bake until meat is no longer pink in center; cut to test (about 20 more minutes).

Spoon or siphon out pan juices and transfer to a small pan. Blend in cornstarch mixture; bring to a boil, stirring constantly. Transfer sauce to a small serving dish. Arrange chops and pear halves on a platter; offer sauce to spoon over individual servings. Makes 6 to 8 servings.

Per serving: 367 calories (37 percent from fat), 34 g protein, 22 g carbohydrates, 15 g total fat (6 g saturated fat), 102 mg cholesterol, 121 mg sodium

Sweet & Spicy Baby Back Ribs

Like Finger-lickin' Spareribs (facing page), these succulent baby back ribs first appeared in "Chefs of the West." The secret to the recipe's success? An uncommonly good basting sauce that combines over a dozen ingredients for a flavor that's sweet, sour, and spicy all at once.

 2 tablespoons butter or margarine
 1 medium-size onion, chopped
 ½ cup *each* water, catsup, and tomato-based chili sauce
 ¼ cup cider vinegar
 2 tablespoons lemon juice
 ½ cup firmly packed brown sugar
 2 tablespoons Worcestershire
 ½ cup dark molasses
 2 teaspoons dry mustard
 ½ teaspoon *each* pepper and paprika
 2 teaspoons liquid smoke flavoring
 3 to 4 pounds pork baby back ribs, trimmed of fat

Melt butter in a wide frying pan over medium heat. Add onion and cook, stirring often, until soft (about 5 minutes). Stir in water, catsup, chili sauce, vinegar, lemon juice, sugar, Worcestershire, molasses, mustard, pepper, paprika, and smoke flavoring. Bring to a boil over high heat; then reduce heat and simmer, uncovered, until reduced to about 2¼ cups (about 30 minutes). Remove from heat.

In a 6- to 8-quart pan, combine ribs with enough water to cover. Bring to a boil over high heat; then reduce heat to medium, cover, and boil gently for 5 minutes.

Drain ribs and arrange in a large baking pan (at least 12 by 14 inches). Brush ribs generously with sauce. Cover and bake in a 400° oven for 15 minutes. Uncover, baste generously again, and continue to bake, uncovered, basting every 15 minutes, until meat is very tender when pierced and all sauce has been used (about 1 more hour). To serve, cut ribs apart. Makes 4 servings.

Per serving: 955 calories (50 percent from fat), 48 g protein, 73 g carbohydrates, 53 g total fat (22 g saturated fat), 203 mg cholesterol, 1,148 mg sodium

Baby Back Ribs Baked with Sauerkraut

Well-seasoned sauerkraut and soft red cabbage make a savory bed for baby back ribs. Be sure you start preparing this dish a few hours before serving time—long, slow cooking is the key to perfect tenderness.

1   large jar (about 27 oz.) sauerkraut, drained and rinsed
4   cups shredded red cabbage
2   tablespoons plus 1 teaspoon paprika
4   cloves garlic, minced or pressed
1   can (about 14½ oz.) stewed tomatoes
3   pounds pork baby back ribs, trimmed of fat
½   teaspoon pepper
⅓   cup fine dry bread crumbs

Combine sauerkraut, cabbage, 1 tablespoon of the paprika, garlic, and tomatoes in a 10- by 15-inch rimmed baking pan; spread out in an even

layer. Arrange ribs on sauerkraut mixture, curved side up; sprinkle with pepper and 2 teaspoons of the remaining paprika. Cover pan tightly with foil. Bake in a 375° oven for 1½ hours.

Mix remaining 2 teaspoons paprika with crumbs. Uncover pan, turn ribs over, and sprinkle with paprika mixture; continue to bake, uncovered, until meat is very tender when pierced and crumbs are brown (about 20 more minutes).

To serve, cut ribs apart and arrange in a serving bowl with sauerkraut mixture. Makes 4 servings.

Per serving: 719 calories (64 percent from fat), 41 g protein, 25 g carbohydrates, 51 g total fat (20 g saturated fat), 165 mg cholesterol, 937 mg sodium

WESTERN CLASSIC
Finger-lickin' Spareribs

A reader from Oregon's Ponderosa pine country sent this hearty rib recipe to us in 1963. Originally featured in "Chefs of the West," it's a wonderful choice for a casual meal.

6   pounds country-style spareribs, trimmed of fat
½   cup *each* dry sherry and water
1   teaspoon salt
⅛   teaspoon pepper
¼   lemon, thinly sliced
½   cup finely chopped onion
1   teaspoon *each* chili powder and celery seeds
¼   cup *each* vinegar and Worcestershire
1   cup catsup
½   cup firmly packed brown sugar
2   cups water

In a large pan, cook spareribs over medium-high heat, turning often, until browned on all sides. Add sherry and the ½ cup water. Bring to a boil; then reduce heat, cover, and simmer for 1 hour. Meanwhile, in a medium-size pan, combine salt, pepper, lemon,

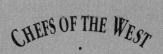

CHEFS OF THE WEST
•

"Chefs of the West," started as a recipe exchange "by men... for men," has been a popular *Sunset* feature since 1940. In the column's early years, many men had just begun to discover the pleasures of the kitchen. The recipes they sent in tended to be simple ones, with a focus on campfire cooking and barbecuing. Over time, though, our readers' submissions have grown more sophisticated. Today's *Sunset* "chefs"—both male and female—now develop dishes calling for a variety of international ingredients and new cooking methods.

onion, chili powder, celery seeds, vinegar, Worcestershire, catsup, sugar, and the 2 cups water. Bring to a boil; then reduce heat and simmer, uncovered, stirring occasionally, for 1 hour. Remove from heat.

Let spareribs cool in cooking liquid for 30 minutes; then drain ribs and arrange in a large, shallow baking pan. Pour sauce over spareribs and bake in a 300° oven until meat is very tender when pierced (about 1 hour). Makes 6 servings.

Per serving: 759 calories (64 percent from fat), 34 g protein, 34 g carbohydrates, 54 g total fat (19 g saturated fat), 156 mg cholesterol, 1,069 mg sodium

Tamales

Traditional Mexican tamales, prepared with a variety of fillings, have been popular at *Sunset* for over 30 years. In this version, tender masa dough surrounds succulent *carnitas*—shredded pork flavored with chiles and onions.

> Masa Dough (recipe follows)
> Tomatillo Salsa (recipe follows)
> Carnitas (recipe follows)
> 1 package (about ½ lb.) dried corn husks

Prepare Masa Dough and Tomatillo Salsa; refrigerate. Prepare Carnitas.

Sort through corn husks, discarding silk and other extraneous material. Place husks in a large baking pan, cover with warm water, and let stand until pliable (at least 20 minutes) or until next day. When ready to use, drain and pat dry.

For each tamale, select a wide, pliable husk. Lay husk flat, with tip pointing away from you. Evenly spread 2 tablespoons Masa Dough down center of husk, forming a rectangle adjacent with one side of husk, an inch from opposite side, an inch from bottom, and 3 inches from tip. If husk is not wide enough, use some of the dough to paste another husk onto back of first.

Spoon 2 rounded tablespoons Carnitas in center of dough. To enclose meat, fold husk so dough edges meet, wrapping plain part of husk around outside of tamale. Fold bottom end of husk over body of tamale; then fold in tip. Place, seam side down, on a tray; cover with damp paper towels until all tamales have been prepared.

To steam, place a rack in a 12- to 14-quart pan and pour in boiling water to a depth of 1 inch. (Water should not reach tamales; if rack is too low, rest it on 2 small empty cans.)

Stack tamales in steamer, arranging loosely so steam can circulate. Bring water to a boil; cover pan and adjust heat to keep water at a steady boil. Cook, adding boiling water as needed to maintain water level, until dough is firm and does not stick to husk; open a tamale from center of pan to test (about 1 hour).

Serve tamales hot or keep warm in steamer over low heat for up to an hour. To serve, peel off husks. Offer Tomatillo Salsa to add to individual servings. Makes 40 to 50 tamales (about 15 servings).

Masa Dough. In a medium-size bowl, beat 1⅓ cups (⅔ lb.) **lard,** butter, margarine, or solid vegetable shortening with an electric mixer (use paddle attachment if you have one) until fluffy. Blend in 4 cups **dehydrated masa flour** (corn tortilla flour); 2 teaspoons **salt** (optional); and 2⅔ cups **warm water,** chicken broth, or beef broth. Continue to beat until dough holds together well. If made ahead, let cool; then cover and refrigerate for up to 3 days. Bring to room temperature before using.

Tomatillo Salsa. Remove husks from 1¼ pounds **tomatillos.** Rinse tomatillos and arrange in a single layer on a baking sheet; bake in a 500° oven until slightly singed (about 15 minutes). Let cool. In a blender or food processor, whirl tomatillos with ⅓ cup chopped **cilantro** and 1 **small fresh hot chile** (such as jalapeño or serrano). Stir in ¾ cup **chicken broth** and ⅓ cup **lime**

juice; season to taste with **salt,** if desired. If made ahead, cover and refrigerate for up to 2 days.

Carnitas. In a 5- to 6-quart pan, combine 1 **bone-in pork shoulder or butt roast** (4 to 5 lbs.); 4 cups **chicken broth;** 1 large **onion,** quartered; 1 tablespoon *each* **coriander seeds** and **cumin seeds;** 1 teaspoon **dry oregano;** 2 **dry bay leaves;** and 3 **canned chipotle chiles in adobo sauce** (optional). Add enough **water** to cover meat. Bring to a boil; then reduce heat, cover, and simmer until meat is tender enough to pull apart easily (3 to 4 hours).

Lift meat from pan (reserve broth for other uses, if desired). Place meat in a large baking pan and bake in a 450° oven until sizzling and browned (about 20 minutes). Let meat cool slightly; then shred with 2 forks, discarding bones and fat.

Per serving: 487 calories (60 percent from fat), 22 g protein, 26 g carbohydrates, 32 g total fat (12 g saturated fat), 87 mg cholesterol, 191 mg sodium

Chinese Barbecued Pork

This Chinese favorite is often cut into small, thin slices and served as an appetizer. Our main-course variation of the dish is baked, not barbecued, and coated with a sticky honey-ginger marinade before cooking.

> ¼ cup soy sauce
> 2 tablespoons *each* honey, sugar, and dry sherry
> 1 teaspoon salt
> 1 teaspoon Chinese five-spice; or ¼ teaspoon *each* ground cloves, anise seeds, ground cinnamon, and ground ginger
> 3 quarter-size slices fresh ginger, crushed
> 3 pounds lean boneless pork (shoulder or butt), trimmed of fat and cut into 1-inch-thick slices

In a small pan, stir together soy sauce, honey, sugar, sherry, salt, five-spice, and ginger. Heat for 1 minute, stirring constantly, to dissolve sugar; let cool.

Place pork in a large heavy-duty plastic bag. Pour in cooled marinade; then seal bag and refrigerate, turning occasionally, for at least 4 hours or until next day.

Remove meat slices from marinade and place on a rack set over a foil-lined baking pan; reserve marinade. Bake in a 350° oven for 30 minutes. Turn slices over and continue to bake, brushing occasionally with marinade, until meat is no longer pink in center; cut to test (about 45 more minutes). Serve hot or cold; to serve, cut across the grain into thin slices. Makes 6 to 8 servings.

Per serving: 396 calories (45 percent from fat), 42 g protein, 10 g carbohydrates, 19 g total fat (7 g saturated fat), 133 mg cholesterol, 1,004 mg sodium

Twice-cooked Pork

The pork in this spicy Sichuan dish really is cooked twice—first simmered, then stir-fried. Hot and sweet bean sauces add a distinctive flavor, but if you can't find them, you may use dried chiles and hoisin sauce with equally delicious results.

1　**pound lean boneless pork (shoulder or butt), in one piece**
1　**tablespoon dry sherry**
1　**quarter-size slice fresh ginger, crushed**
3　**green onions**
2　**teaspoons hot bean sauce; or 2 small dried hot red chiles, crumbled**
4　**teaspoons sweet bean sauce or hoisin sauce**
1　**tablespoon soy sauce**
1　**teaspoon sugar**
2　**small green bell peppers or 1 *each* small green and red bell pepper**

3　**tablespoons salad oil**
½　**teaspoon salt**
2　**cloves garlic, minced or pressed**
1　**teaspoon minced fresh ginger**

In a 2-quart pan, combine pork, sherry, and ginger slice. Cut one of the onions in half crosswise and add to pan; then add just enough water to cover meat. Bring to a simmer; then cover and simmer until meat is tender when pierced (about 45 minutes).

Lift meat from cooking liquid; discard liquid and refrigerate meat until cold. Then cut meat into 1½-inch-square pieces about ⅛ inch thick; trim and discard fat.

In a bowl, stir together hot bean sauce, sweet bean sauce, soy sauce, and sugar. Seed bell peppers and cut into 1-inch squares; cut remaining 2 onions into 1-inch lengths.

Place a wok or wide frying pan over high heat. When pan is hot, add 2 tablespoons of the oil. When oil is hot, add bell peppers and cook, stirring, for 1½ minutes; add a few drops of water if pan appears dry. Sprinkle peppers with salt and stir once, then remove them from pan. Add remaining 1 tablespoon oil to pan. When oil begins to heat, add garlic and minced ginger and stir once; then add meat and cook, stirring, for 1 minute. Add bean sauce mixture and toss until meat is coated with sauce. Return peppers to pan, add onions, and cook, stirring, until heated through (about 30 seconds). Makes 4 servings.

Per serving: 329 calories (64 percent from fat), 23 g protein, 7 g carbohydrates, 23 g total fat (6 g saturated fat), 82 mg cholesterol, 768 mg sodium

Oven-braised Sausages with Grapes & Polenta

This classic Italian dish pairs wonderfully with a salad of fresh, crisp garden greens. Try combining the pan juices with a dash of vinegar for a flavorful dressing.

4　**cups seedless green grapes (about 1½ lbs.)**
1　**tablespoon minced fresh rosemary or 1½ teaspoons dry rosemary**
8　**mild Italian sausages (about 2 lbs. *total*)**
6　**cups chicken broth**
1½　**cups polenta or yellow cornmeal**
　　Rosemary sprigs (optional)

Spread grapes in an 11- by 17-inch roasting pan and cover tightly with foil. Bake in upper third of a 400° oven until grapes feel soft when pressed (about 25 minutes). Uncover pan and stir in minced rosemary. Pierce each sausage several times with a fork and arrange sausages in a single layer on top of grapes. Bake, uncovered, until sausages are lightly browned (about 20 minutes).

Mix broth and polenta in a shallow 3- to 4-quart baking pan. Place in lower third of oven. Turn sausages and stir grapes; continue to bake until sausages are well browned, juice from grapes has caramelized, and polenta has absorbed all broth but is still soft (about 50 more minutes). During baking, occasionally turn sausages and stir grapes and polenta.

To serve, spread polenta in a thick layer on a large platter. With a slotted spoon, lift sausages and grapes from pan and place on polenta. Garnish with rosemary sprigs, if desired. Makes 8 servings.

Per serving: 569 calories (59 percent from fat), 21 g protein, 37 g carbohydrates, 38 g total fat (13 g saturated fat), 86 mg cholesterol, 1,572 mg sodium

Chorizo

This spicy Mexican sausage is often used as a filling for tacos, tamales, or enchiladas. To cook, just crumble and brown the amount you need; or shape the mixture into patties or links.

  5 or 6 dried New Mexico or
     California (Anaheim) chiles
  ½ cup red wine vinegar
  ½ medium-size onion, quartered
  2¼ pounds ground pork
  4 cloves garlic, minced or pressed
  1½ teaspoons salt
  2½ teaspoons dry oregano
  ½ teaspoon *each* ground cumin
     and ground red pepper
     (cayenne)

Place chiles in a small bowl, add vinegar, and let chiles soak until soft (about 3 hours). Remove stems and seeds; then whirl chiles with vinegar and onion in a blender or food processor until smoothly puréed.

In a large bowl, combine chile purée, pork, garlic, salt, oregano, cumin, and red pepper; mix well. Cover and refrigerate for at least 2 hours or until next day.

To cook, crumble pork mixture into a frying pan. Cook over medium-high heat, stirring often, until browned; discard fat. Or shape mixture into patties or links and cook over medium-high heat, turning as needed, until no longer pink in center; cut to test (about 10 minutes). Makes about 2¼ pounds.

Per ¼ pound: 269 calories (59 percent from fat), 21 g protein, 7 g carbohydrates, 18 g total fat (6 g saturated fat), 73 mg cholesterol, 426 mg sodium

Greek Shish Kebab

In this popular Mideastern dish, tender chunks of marinated lamb are skewered and grilled with crisp red onion, bright bell pepper, and mushrooms.

  ⅓ cup olive oil or salad oil
  3 tablespoons lemon juice
  1 large onion, finely chopped
  2 dry bay leaves
  2 teaspoons dry oregano
  ½ teaspoon pepper
  2 pounds lean boneless lamb
     (leg or shoulder), trimmed of
     fat and cut into 1½-inch cubes
  1 large mild red onion, cut into
     1-inch pieces
  1 large green or red bell pepper,
     seeded and cut into 1½-inch
     squares
  ½ pound mushrooms

In a large bowl, stir together oil, lemon juice, chopped onion, bay leaves, oregano, and pepper. Add lamb; stir to coat. Cover and refrigerate for at least 4 hours or until next day, stirring several times.

Lift meat from marinade and drain briefly. Add red onion, bell pepper, and mushrooms to marinade; turn to coat, then lift out (reserve marinade). On 6 sturdy metal skewers, thread meat cubes alternately with vegetables.

Place skewers on a lightly greased grill 4 to 6 inches above a solid bed of medium-hot coals. Cook, turning and basting frequently with marinade, until meat and vegetables are well browned but meat is still pink in center; cut to test (12 to 15 minutes). Makes 6 servings.

Per serving: 370 calories (51 percent from fat), 34 g protein, 11 g carbohydrates, 21 g total fat (5 g saturated fat), 101 mg cholesterol, 86 mg sodium

Crusted Lamb with Mint Pesto

In a fresh approach to pesto sauce, mint and parsley replace the traditional basil. Pat the pesto over a butterflied leg of lamb, then grill the meat; the thick, creamy coating cooks to a crusty finish in the barbecue.

  2 cups lightly packed fresh
     mint leaves
  ½ cup lightly packed chopped
     parsley
  3 large cloves garlic, peeled
     and halved
  ¼ cup olive oil
  ⅓ cup Neufchâtel or cream
     cheese
  ¼ cup pine nuts or walnut
     pieces
  1½ tablespoons lemon juice
  ⅛ teaspoon pepper
  1 leg of lamb (6 to 7 lbs.),
     trimmed of fat, boned, and
     butterflied

In a food processor or blender, combine mint, parsley, 2 cloves of the garlic, oil, cheese, pine nuts, lemon juice, and pepper. Whirl to make a coarse paste, scraping down sides of container often.

Cut remaining garlic clove into thin slivers. Cut small slashes in surface of lamb and insert garlic slivers. Spread boned side of meat with about two-thirds of the mint pesto. Roll meat to enclose filling; tie snugly every 1½ inches with cotton string. Spread remaining mint pesto over meat.

Prepare barbecue as directed in "Indirect Grilling" (page 70). Set meat on lightly greased grill above drip pan. Cover barbecue and adjust vents as needed to maintain an even heat. Cook until a meat thermometer inserted in thickest part of meat registers 135° to 140°F for rare (about 1¼ hours). To serve, cut meat across the grain into thin slices; discard strings. Makes 8 to 10 servings.

Per serving: 402 calories (51 percent from fat), 47 g protein, 2 g carbohydrates, 22 g total fat (7 g saturated fat), 146 mg cholesterol, 142 mg sodium

Springtime Lamb Stew

Much like the traditional French *navarin printanier*, this hearty stew marries meaty chunks of lamb with tender spring vegetables. The rich flavor and deep amber color come from browning the meat before adding the vegetables to the cooking pot.

- **3 pounds boneless lamb stew meat (neck or shoulder), trimmed of fat and cut into 1- to 2-inch chunks**
- **2 tablespoons soy sauce**
- **½ cup Madeira or port**
- **4 teaspoons mustard seeds**
- **1 teaspoon fresh thyme leaves or ½ teaspoon dry thyme**
- **¼ teaspoon whole black peppercorns**
- **2 dry bay leaves**
- **1½ cups chicken broth**
- **1 cup dry red or white wine**
- **1½ to 2 pounds small red or white thin-skinned potatoes, scrubbed and cut into halves**
- **8 to 12 small carrots**
- **3 to 6 small turnips, peeled and cut into halves**
- **12 to 18 small white boiling onions, peeled**
- **¾ pound green beans (ends and strings removed), cut into halves**
- **1 cup whipping cream**
- **1 tablespoon Dijon mustard Watercress sprigs**

In a 5- to 6-quart pan, combine lamb and soy sauce. Bring to a boil over medium heat; then reduce heat, cover, and simmer for 30 minutes. Uncover and boil over high heat until juices have evaporated; then continue to cook, stirring often, until meat is well browned. Add Madeira to pan and stir to scrape browned bits free. Add mustard seeds, thyme, peppercorns, bay leaves, broth, and wine.

Arrange potatoes, carrots, turnips, and onions on meat. Bring to a boil; reduce heat, cover, and simmer until meat and vegetables are tender when pierced (about 1 hour).

After about 50 minutes, cook beans in boiling water until tender to bite (about 7 minutes). Drain.

With a slotted spoon, lift vegetables and meat from broth and mound separately on a wide, shallow platter; discard bay leaves. Arrange beans alongside other vegetables. Keep warm.

Add cream and mustard to cooking juices in pan. Bring to a boil over high heat; boil, stirring occasionally, until sauce is golden, slightly thickened, and reduced to 1¾ cups (8 to 10 minutes). Transfer to a small serving dish.

To serve, garnish meat and vegetables with watercress sprigs. Offer sauce to spoon over individual servings. Makes about 8 servings.

Per serving: 503 calories (39 percent from fat), 39 g protein, 37 g carbohydrates, 22 g total fat (10 g saturated fat), 146 mg cholesterol, 698 mg sodium

Mustard-coated Roast Leg of Lamb

Garlic and rosemary are classic seasonings for roast lamb. For satisfying Sunday dinner fare, serve with Best-ever Garlicky Potatoes (page 147) or Mustard-glazed Carrots (page 140).

- **3 cloves garlic, peeled**
- **½ cup Dijon mustard**
- **1 tablespoon soy sauce**
- **½ teaspoon ground ginger**
- **1 teaspoon dry rosemary**
- **¼ cup olive oil or salad oil**
- **1 leg of lamb (5 to 6 lbs.), trimmed of fat**

Mince or press 1 clove of the garlic; place in a small bowl and stir in mustard, soy sauce, ginger, rosemary, and oil. Set aside.

Place lamb on a rack in a baking pan. Cut remaining 2 cloves garlic into slivers. Cut small slashes in surface of meat and insert garlic slivers. Brush meat with mustard mixture, coating completely. Let stand at room temperature for 1 hour.

Roast in a 325° oven until a meat thermometer inserted in thickest part of meat (not touching bone) registers 135° to 140°F for rare (about 1½ hours). Transfer meat to a platter; keep warm. Skim and discard fat from pan juices; reheat juices and pour into a small serving dish.

To carve, grasp narrow end of leg (protect your hand with a pot holder) and slice meat, cutting parallel to bone. Offer juices to spoon over individual servings. Makes 6 to 8 servings.

Per serving: 420 calories, 49 g protein, 3 g carbohydrates, 22 g total fat (6 g saturated fat), 152 mg cholesterol, 778 mg sodium

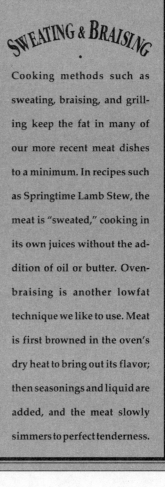

SWEATING & BRAISING

Cooking methods such as sweating, braising, and grilling keep the fat in many of our more recent meat dishes to a minimum. In recipes such as Springtime Lamb Stew, the meat is "sweated," cooking in its own juices without the addition of oil or butter. Oven-braising is another lowfat technique we like to use. Meat is first browned in the oven's dry heat to bring out its flavor; then seasonings and liquid are added, and the meat slowly simmers to perfect tenderness.

The West's growing ethnic diversity and our readers' more sophisticated palates inspired a heightened interest in Asian cooking in the late '50s and early '60s. *Sunset* featured wok cooking for the first time in 1961, introducing stir-fry technique nearly a decade later. In the years since then, stir-fry recipes have often appeared in our pages.

Stir-fries are appealing on several counts. Rapid cooking over high heat seals in moisture and flavor and limits the amount of oil needed to prevent sticking. Cooking takes only a few minutes—and because all the ingredients go into the same pan, cleanup is minimal. We offer five stir-fry favorites here; for others, see Cashew Chicken (page 92), Ginger Shrimp (page 129), and Snow Peas with Shrimp (page 126).

Since stir-frying goes so quickly, assemble all of the ingredients you'll need before heating your wok or frying pan.

Slivered Chicken & Walnuts

Cooking Sauce (recipe follows)
1 tablespoon soy sauce
1 teaspoon cornstarch
1 pound skinless, boneless chicken breasts, cut into thin strips
3 tablespoons salad oil
½ cup walnut halves
1 medium-size green bell pepper, seeded and cut into 1-inch squares
½ teaspoon finely minced fresh ginger or ⅛ teaspoon ground ginger

Prepare Cooking Sauce; set aside. In a medium-size bowl, stir together soy sauce and cornstarch. Add chicken and stir to coat; set aside.

Place a wok or wide frying pan over medium-high heat. When pan is hot, add oil. When oil is hot, add walnuts and cook, stirring, until browned; remove from pan with a slotted spoon and set aside. Add chicken to pan; cook, stirring, for 1½ minutes. Remove from pan with slotted spoon. Add bell pepper and ginger; cook, stirring, until pepper turns bright green. Return chicken to pan. Stir Cooking Sauce, add to pan, and cook, stirring, until sauce boils and thickens (about 1 minute). Add walnuts, stir once, and serve. Makes 4 servings.

Cooking Sauce. In a small bowl, stir together ½ teaspoon **cornstarch**, a dash of **liquid hot pepper seasoning**, ¾ teaspoon *each* **sugar** and **wine vinegar**, 1 teaspoon **dry sherry** or water, and 1 tablespoon **soy sauce**.

Per serving: 330 calories (57 percent from fat), 29 g protein, 7 g carbohydrates, 21 g total fat (2 g saturated fat), 66 mg cholesterol, 592 mg sodium

Kung Pao Chicken

---

1 tablespoon *each* dry sherry and cornstarch
½ teaspoon salt
⅛ teaspoon white pepper
1½ pounds skinless, boneless chicken breasts, cut into bite-size pieces
¼ cup salad oil
Cooking Sauce (recipe follows)
4 to 6 small dried hot red chiles
½ cup salted dry-roasted peanuts
1 teaspoon *each* minced garlic and minced fresh ginger
2 green onions, cut into 1½-inch lengths

In a large bowl, stir together sherry, cornstarch, salt, and white pepper.

Add chicken and stir to coat, then stir in 1 tablespoon of the oil and let stand for 15 minutes. Prepare Cooking Sauce and set aside.

Place a wok or wide frying pan over medium heat. When pan is hot, add 1 tablespoon of the oil. When oil is hot, add chiles and peanuts and cook, stirring, until chiles just begin to char. (If chiles become completely black, discard them; remove peanuts from pan and repeat with new chiles.) Remove from pan and set aside.

Heat remaining 2 tablespoons oil in pan over high heat. When oil is hot, add garlic and ginger; stir once. Then add chicken and cook, stirring, until opaque (about 3 minutes). Stir in chiles, peanuts, and onions. Stir Cooking Sauce, add to pan, and cook, stirring, until sauce boils and thickens. Makes 6 servings.

Cooking Sauce. In a small bowl, stir together 2 tablespoons **soy sauce,** 1 tablespoon *each* **white wine vinegar** and **dry sherry,** 3 tablespoons **chicken broth** or water, and 2 teaspoons *each* **sugar** and **cornstarch.**

Per serving: 307 calories (50 percent from fat), 30 g protein, 8 g carbohydrates, 17 g total fat (2 g saturated fat), 66 mg cholesterol, 731 mg sodium

Stir-fried Shrimp with Peking Sauce

Peking Stir-fry Sauce (recipe follows)
2 tablespoons salad oil
1 pound medium-size raw shrimp, shelled and deveined
1 large red onion, thinly sliced
2 cups (about 6 oz.) broccoli flowerets, broken into bite-size pieces
1 red bell pepper, seeded and cut into long, thin strips

1 **yellow or green bell pepper, seeded and cut into long, thin strips**

2 **to 4 tablespoons water**

2 **teaspoons cornstarch**

Prepare Peking Stir-fry Sauce and set aside.

Place a wok or wide frying pan over high heat. When pan is hot, add 1 tablespoon of the oil. When oil is hot, add shrimp and cook, stirring, just until opaque in center; cut to test (about 2 minutes). Remove shrimp from pan; set aside.

To pan, add remaining 1 tablespoon oil, onion, broccoli, bell peppers, and 1 tablespoon of the water. Cook, stirring, until broccoli is barely tender to bite (2 to 4 minutes), adding more water as needed.

Stir cornstarch into Peking Stir-fry Sauce. Add sauce to pan; cook, stirring, just until sauce boils and thickens. Add shrimp; stir just until heated through. Makes 4 servings.

Peking Stir-fry Sauce. In a small bowl, stir together 2 cloves **garlic,** minced or pressed; 2 tablespoons minced **fresh ginger** or 1½ teaspoons ground ginger; ½ cup **water;** ¼ cup **hoisin sauce;** 2 tablespoons **soy sauce;** 1 tablespoon **unseasoned rice vinegar;** and 2 teaspoons **sugar.**

Per serving: 248 calories (32 percent from fat), 22 g protein, 20 g carbohydrates, 9 g total fat (1 g saturated fat), 140 mg cholesterol, 1,178 mg sodium

Chile Beef Stir-fry on Mixed Greens

1 **pound lean boneless top sirloin steak (cut about 1 inch thick), trimmed of fat**

1 **fresh jalapeño or other small hot chile, seeded and minced**

2 **cloves garlic, minced or pressed**

½ **to ¾ teaspoon ground red pepper (cayenne)**

1 **tablespoon reduced-sodium soy sauce**

½ **teaspoon sugar**

⅓ **cup seasoned rice vinegar; or ⅓ cup white wine vinegar mixed with 2 tablespoons sugar**

1 **tablespoon salad oil**

2 **quarts bite-size pieces mixed greens (such as watercress, chicory, arugula, radicchio, butter lettuce, and leaf lettuce), rinsed and crisped**

Freshly ground black pepper

Cut steak across the grain into ⅛-inch-thick strips about 3 inches long. In a medium-size bowl, stir together chile, garlic, red pepper, soy sauce, and sugar. Add meat and turn to coat. Cover and refrigerate for at least 30 minutes or until next day.

Just before serving, stir together vinegar and 2 teaspoons of the oil in a large bowl. Add greens and turn to coat; arrange on individual plates and set aside.

Heat remaining 1 teaspoon oil in a wide nonstick frying pan over high heat. Add meat mixture and cook, stirring, until meat is browned (3 to 5 minutes). Spoon over greens and season to taste with black pepper. Makes 4 servings.

Per serving: 234 calories (34 percent from fat), 27 g protein, 12 g carbohydrates, 9 g total fat (2 g saturated fat), 69 mg cholesterol, 660 mg sodium

Yu-shiang Pork

1 **teaspoon cornstarch**

¼ **teaspoon salt**

Dash of white pepper

1 **tablespoon dry sherry**

3½ **tablespoons salad oil**

¾ **pound lean boneless pork (shoulder or butt), trimmed of fat and cut into matchstick-size pieces**

Sherry-Soy Sauce (recipe follows)

2 **cloves garlic, minced or pressed**

1 **teaspoon minced fresh ginger**

3 **or 4 small dried hot red chiles**

⅔ **cup sliced bamboo shoots, cut into matchstick-size pieces**

10 **green onions, cut into 2-inch lengths**

In a bowl, stir together cornstarch, salt, white pepper, sherry, and 1½ teaspoons of the oil. Add pork and stir to coat; let stand for 15 minutes. Prepare Sherry-Soy Sauce; set aside.

Heat a wok or wide frying pan over high heat. When pan is hot, add 2 tablespoons of the oil. When oil is hot, add garlic, ginger, and chiles; stir once. Add meat and cook, stirring, until lightly browned (about 4 minutes). Remove from pan.

Heat remaining 1 tablespoon oil in pan. Add bamboo shoots and onions; cook, stirring, for 1 minute. Return meat to pan. Stir Sherry-Soy Sauce, add to pan, and cook, stirring, until sauce boils and thickens. Makes 4 servings.

Sherry-Soy Sauce. In a small bowl, stir together 1 tablespoon *each* **sugar, vinegar,** and **dry sherry;** 2 tablespoons **soy sauce;** 3 tablespoons **chicken broth** or water; and 2 teaspoons **cornstarch.**

Per serving: 302 calories (56 percent from fat), 21 g protein, 12 g carbohydrates, 18 g total fat (4 g saturated fat), 54 mg cholesterol, 760 mg sodium

P O U L T R Y

*L*ow in fat, low in cost, and easy to prepare, poultry ranks among our favorite main-dish choices. Chicken and turkey offer a versatility and availability unparalleled by other meats—so it's not surprising to discover that the annual consumption of these two birds has risen by over 50 pounds per person in the last 30 years. • With the current focus on light dining, modern poultry recipes are often designed to be lean. But that doesn't mean that time-honored classics like chicken Kiev, pot pies, enchiladas, and creamy casseroles have been forgotten. On the contrary, they still top the list of Sunset's reader favorites! • In this chapter, you'll find both the rich, calorie-laden specialties of yester-year and the more streamlined selections so popular today.

Golden Chicken Cutlets

Triple-coated sautéed chicken breasts are juicy on the inside, delicately crunchy on the outside. A smooth reduction sauce, made from dry white wine and the pan juices, enhances the meat. Alongside, you might serve colorful Ratatouille (page 141).

- ⅓ **cup all-purpose flour**
- ½ **teaspoon salt**
- ⅛ **teaspoon** *each* **white pepper, ground nutmeg, and dry marjoram**
- 1 **egg**
- 1 **tablespoon water**
- ⅓ **cup fine dry bread crumbs**
- ¼ **cup grated Parmesan cheese**
- 6 **skinless, boneless chicken breast halves (about 2¼ lbs.** *total***)**
- ¼ **cup butter or margarine**
- 2 **tablespoons olive oil**
- ½ **cup dry white wine**
  Lemon wedges

Prepare 3 shallow dishes. In first dish, mix flour, salt, white pepper, nutmeg, and marjoram. In second dish, lightly beat egg with water. In third dish, mix crumbs and cheese. Set dishes aside.

Rinse chicken and pat dry. Place each breast half between 2 sheets of plastic wrap or wax paper; pound with a flat-surfaced mallet until about ¼ inch thick.

Working with one piece of chicken at a time, coat each piece lightly with flour mixture and shake off excess; then coat with egg and let excess drip off. Finally, coat with crumb mixture and shake off excess; secure remaining crumbs by pressing gently but firmly with your hand.

Melt butter in oil in a wide frying pan over medium-high heat. Add chicken, a few pieces at a time (do not crowd pan); cook, turning once, until golden brown on both sides (4 to 6 minutes). As chicken is cooked, transfer it to a serving dish and keep warm.

When all chicken has been cooked, add wine to frying pan and stir to scrape browned bits free. Bring sauce to a boil over high heat; boil, stirring, until sauce is slightly thickened. Pour sauce over chicken. Serve with lemon wedges. Makes 6 servings.

Per serving: 385 calories (41 percent from fat), 43 g protein, 10 g carbohydrates, 16 g total fat (7 g saturated fat), 157 mg cholesterol, 496 mg sodium

WESTERN CLASSIC
Steeped Chicken with Basil Dressing

Steeping involves bringing water to a boil, then turning off the heat, immersing food in the hot water, and letting it stand, undisturbed, until done. This method is perfect for cooking chicken breasts—the meat turns out exceptionally moist. Here, the chicken is served with fresh tomatoes and a fragrant basil dressing.

- 4 **chicken breast halves (about 2 lbs.** *total***)**
- 2 **thin slices** *each* **lemon and onion**
- 1 **quarter-size slice fresh ginger**
- 3 **parsley or thyme sprigs**
  Basil Dressing (recipe follows)
  Lettuce leaves
- 3 **large tomatoes, thinly sliced**
  Fresh basil or cilantro leaves

Rinse chicken and place in a 4- to 5-quart pan with a tight-fitting lid; pour in enough water to cover chicken by 1 to 2 inches. Lift out chicken; add lemon, onion, ginger, and parsley to water.

Cover pan and bring water to a boil over high heat. Remove from heat and quickly immerse chicken in water. Cover pan tightly and let stand for 18 minutes; do not uncover until this time is up. To check doneness, cut meat in thickest part; it should no longer look pink. If chicken is not done, return it to hot water, cover, and let steep for a few more minutes.

Drain chicken; immerse in ice water until cool, then drain again. Gently peel off skin and remove meat from bones, keeping chicken pieces whole. Discard skin and bones. (At this point, you may cover and refrigerate for up to 2 days.)

Prepare Basil Dressing. To serve, place lettuce at both ends of a platter; arrange tomato slices over lettuce. Cut chicken across the grain into ½-inch-thick slices; arrange in center of platter. Drizzle chicken and tomatoes with a little of the Basil Dressing. Garnish with basil leaves. Offer remaining dressing to spoon over individual servings. Makes 4 servings.

Basil Dressing. In a blender or food processor, combine 1 cup lightly packed **fresh basil leaves** (or 3 tablespoons dry basil and ¼ cup chopped parsley), 2 cloves **garlic**, ¼ cup **white wine vinegar**, ½ cup **olive oil** or salad oil, 2 tablespoons grated **Parmesan cheese**, and ⅛ teaspoon **pepper**. Whirl until puréed. Makes about 1 cup.

Per serving of chicken: 295 calories (20 percent from fat), 52 g protein, 6 g carbohydrates, 6 g total fat (2 g saturated fat), 139 mg cholesterol, 132 mg sodium

Per tablespoon of Basil Dressing: 66 calories (93 percent from fat), 0.4 g protein, 0.8 g carbohydrates, 7 g total fat (1 g saturated fat), 0.5 mg cholesterol, 12 mg sodium

Chicken Scaloppine

Pounded thin and quickly browned, boneless chicken breasts can taste much like the veal cutlets traditionally used for scaloppine.

- **6 skinless, boneless chicken breast halves (about 2¼ lbs. *total*)**
- **All-purpose flour**
- **Salt and pepper**
- **1 tablespoon salad oil or olive oil**
- **3 tablespoons butter or margarine**
- **½ pound mushrooms, sliced**
- **1 clove garlic, minced or pressed**
- **¼ teaspoon *each* salt, dry marjoram, and dry thyme**
- **1 tablespoon lemon juice**
- **1½ teaspoons cornstarch**
- **½ cup Marsala or chicken broth**
- **½ cup grated Parmesan cheese**
- **Lemon wedges**

Rinse chicken and pat dry. Place each breast half between 2 sheets of plastic wrap or wax paper; pound with a flat-surfaced mallet until about ¼ inch thick. Cut chicken into strips about 1 inch wide. Dust with flour and sprinkle with salt and pepper.

Heat oil in a wide frying pan over high heat. Add chicken, a portion at a time (do not crowd pan); cook, turning once, until browned on both sides. Transfer to a serving dish; keep warm.

Melt butter in frying pan over medium heat. Add mushrooms and garlic and cook, stirring often, until soft (about 5 minutes). Add salt, marjoram, thyme, and lemon juice. Combine cornstarch and Marsala and stir until smooth; stir into mushroom mixture. Cook, stirring to scrape browned bits free, until sauce boils and thickens. Pour sauce over chicken and sprinkle with cheese. Serve with lemon wedges. Makes 6 servings.

Per serving: 342 calories (35 percent from fat), 43 g protein, 7 g carbohydrates, 12 g total fat (6 g saturated fat), 120 mg cholesterol, 387 mg sodium

Cashew Chicken

Quick stir-frying intensifies the flavors of fresh vegetables and nuts in this colorful dish.

- **6 skinless, boneless chicken breast halves (about 2¼ lbs. *total*)**
- **¼ cup soy sauce**
- **2 tablespoons cornstarch**
- **½ teaspoon *each* sugar and salt**
- **¼ cup salad oil**
- **⅓ cup salted roasted cashews**
- **½ pound Chinese pea pods (also called snow or sugar peas), ends and strings removed; or 2 packages (about 6 oz. *each*) frozen Chinese pea pods, partially thawed**
- **½ pound mushrooms, sliced**
- **1 tablespoon instant chicken bouillon dissolved in 1 cup hot water; or 1 cup chicken broth**
- **2 cans (about 8 oz. *each*) bamboo shoots, drained and slivered**
- **4 green onions, cut into thin slanting slices**

Rinse chicken and pat dry. Cut each piece crosswise into ⅛-inch-thick slices; then cut slices into 1-inch squares. Set aside. In a small bowl, stir together soy sauce, cornstarch, sugar, and salt; set aside.

Place a wok or wide frying pan over medium-high heat. When pan is hot, add 1 tablespoon of the oil. When oil is hot, add cashews and cook, stirring, until lightly browned; remove with a slotted spoon and set aside.

Add remaining 3 tablespoons oil to pan. When oil is hot, add chicken and cook, stirring, until no longer pink. Add pea pods, mushrooms, and bouillon. Cover and simmer for 2 minutes.

Add bamboo shoots; then stir soy sauce mixture and add to pan. Cook, stirring, until sauce is thickened; then simmer, uncovered, for 1 minute. Add onions; stir until combined. Transfer to a large serving dish and sprinkle with cashews. Makes 6 to 8 servings.

Per serving: 316 calories (37 percent from fat), 38 g protein, 11 g carbohydrates, 13 g total fat (2 g saturated fat), 85 mg cholesterol, 1,298 mg sodium

Grilled Peanut Chicken

Smoldering wood chips impart a delicate smokiness to Asian-inspired chicken cooked on the grill.

- **2 cups hickory or other wood chips**
- **4 chicken breast halves (about 2 lbs. *total*)**
- **⅓ cup *each* creamy peanut butter and warm water**
- **2 tablespoons *each* soy sauce and Worcestershire**
- **¼ to ½ teaspoon ground red pepper (cayenne)**
- **2 tablespoons sliced green onion**
- **¼ cup finely shredded fresh basil**

Soak wood chips in warm water to cover for at least 30 minutes or for up to 4 hours.

Rinse chicken and pat dry. In a large bowl, stir together peanut butter, the ⅓ cup warm water, soy sauce, Worcestershire, and red pepper until blended. Add chicken; turn to coat.

Drain wood chips and scatter over a solid bed of medium-low coals in a barbecue with a lid. Set grill in place 4 to 6 inches above coals; lightly grease grill. Lift chicken from sauce and place on grill.

Cover barbecue and close vents about three-fourths of the way. Cook chicken, turning and basting every 5 minutes with sauce, until meat in thickest part is no longer pink; cut to test (25 to 30 minutes).

To serve, arrange chicken in a serving dish and sprinkle with onion and basil. Makes 4 servings.

Per serving: 384 calories (48 percent from fat), 44 g protein, 7 g carbohydrates, 20 g total fat (4 g saturated fat), 103 mg cholesterol, 785 mg sodium

WESTERN CLASSIC
Mexican-style Chicken Breasts

Festive vegetable garnishes and a crisp bed of shredded lettuce perfectly set off these Mexican-accented chicken breasts. Serve with Black Bean, Corn & Pepper Salad (page 40), and Bolillos (page 189) for a sensational summer meal.

- 2 **eggs**
- 1 **clove garlic, minced or pressed**
- ½ **cup purchased green chile salsa or taco sauce**
- 1 **cup fine dry bread crumbs**
- 2 **teaspoons *each* chili powder and ground cumin**
- ½ **teaspoon ground oregano**
- 6 **skinless, boneless chicken breast halves (about 2¼ lbs. *total*); or 12 chicken thighs (3 to 3½ lbs. *total*), skinned**
- 2 **tablespoons butter or margarine**
- 1 **large avocado**
- 4 **to 6 cups shredded iceberg lettuce**
- 12 **to 18 cherry tomatoes**
   Plain yogurt or sour cream
- 4 **green onions, thinly sliced**
   Lime wedges

In a shallow bowl, beat together eggs, garlic, and salsa. In another shallow bowl, mix crumbs, chili powder, cumin, and oregano.

Rinse chicken and pat dry. Working with one piece of chicken at a time, coat each piece with egg mixture, then with crumb mixture.

Melt butter in a 10- by 15-inch rimmed baking pan in a 375° oven. Add chicken and turn to coat with butter. Bake until meat in thickest part is no longer pink; cut to test (30 to 35 minutes for breasts, about 45 minutes for thighs).

Pit, peel, and slice avocado. Cover a platter with lettuce; arrange chicken on lettuce. Garnish with avocado, cherry tomatoes, and a dollop of yogurt; scatter onions over top. Serve with lime wedges. Makes 6 servings.

Per serving: 418 calories (33 percent from fat), 46 g protein, 24 g carbohydrates, 15 g total fat (5 g saturated fat), 180 mg cholesterol, 588 mg sodium

Creamy Baked Chicken Breasts

The star of a "step-saving, cost-saving" *Sunset* feature, this simple recipe is geared to save you time and effort. To prepare the chicken for baking, you'll need only about 5 minutes.

- 8 **chicken breast halves (about 4 lbs. *total*), skinned (and boned, if desired)**
- 8 **slices Swiss cheese (about 1 oz. *each*)**
- 1 **can (about 10¾ oz.) condensed cream of chicken soup**
- ¼ **cup dry white wine or water**
- 2 **cups seasoned stuffing mix**
- ⅓ **cup butter or margarine, melted**

Rinse chicken and pat dry. Arrange pieces, slightly apart, in a shallow baking dish; top each piece with a slice of cheese.

In a small bowl, stir together soup and wine; spoon evenly over chicken. Coarsely crush stuffing mix and sprinkle over chicken; then drizzle evenly with butter. Bake in a 350° oven until meat in thickest part is no longer pink; cut to test (45 to 55 minutes). Makes 8 servings.

Per serving: 440 calories (42 percent from fat), 45 g protein, 17 g carbohydrates, 20 g total fat (11 g saturated fat), 135 mg cholesterol, 800 mg sodium

Honeyed Chicken

Here's another delicious reader contribution from our "Kitchen Cabinet": chicken breasts basted with a sweet honey-mustard glaze. For a pretty presentation, accompany the chicken with Tomatoes Stuffed with Spinach (page 153) or Broccoli Soufflé Roll (page 140).

- 6 **skinless, boneless chicken breast halves (about 2¼ lbs. *total*)**
- 2 **tablespoons sesame seeds**
- 3 **tablespoons honey**
- ¼ **cup *each* dry sherry and Dijon mustard**
- 1 **tablespoon lemon juice**

Rinse chicken and pat dry. Then arrange pieces, slightly apart, in a 9- by 13-inch baking pan. Set aside.

Toast sesame seeds in a small frying pan over medium heat, stirring often, until golden (2 to 3 minutes). Transfer to a small bowl and add honey, sherry, mustard, and lemon juice; stir until blended. Drizzle honey mixture evenly over chicken. Bake in a 400° oven, basting several times with sauce, until meat in thickest part is no longer pink; cut to test (15 to 20 minutes). Makes 6 servings.

Per serving: 264 calories (16 percent from fat), 40 g protein, 12 g carbohydrates, 4 g total fat (0.8 g saturated fat), 99 mg cholesterol, 413 mg sodium

Sesame Chicken

Sesame seeds make a crusty, nutty-tasting coating for chicken soaked in a gingery soy marinade. Serve over hot rice or thin pasta strands.

- **6 skinless, boneless chicken breast halves (about 2¼ lbs. *total*)**
- **¼ cup soy sauce**
- **1 tablespoon *each* sugar and dry sherry**
- **1 tablespoon minced fresh ginger**
- **2 cloves garlic, minced or pressed**
- **1 egg**
- **¼ cup *each* all-purpose flour and sesame seeds**
- **2 tablespoons butter or margarine**
- **1 tablespoon salad oil**

Rinse chicken and pat dry. In a large bowl, combine soy sauce, sugar, sherry, ginger, and garlic; stir until sugar is dissolved. Add chicken and turn to coat. Cover and refrigerate for 1 to 2 hours.

Place a 10- by 15-inch rimmed baking pan in oven while it preheats to 500°. Meanwhile, remove chicken from refrigerator. Spoon 2 tablespoons of the marinade into a shallow bowl; add egg and beat lightly to blend. In another shallow bowl, mix flour and sesame seeds. Working with one piece of chicken at a time, lift each piece from remaining marinade and coat with egg mixture; let excess drip off. Then coat chicken with flour mixture; shake off excess.

Add butter and oil to baking pan, swirling pan to melt butter. Add chicken and turn to coat lightly with butter and oil. Bake for 7 minutes. Then turn pieces over and continue to bake until meat in thickest part is no longer pink; cut to test (3 to 5 more minutes). Makes 6 servings.

Per serving: 319 calories (35 percent from fat), 42 g protein, 8 g carbohydrates, 12 g total fat (4 g saturated fat), 136 mg cholesterol, 680 mg sodium

Chicken Jambalaya

Seasoned with plenty of red pepper, jambalaya is definitely not for timid tastes. This lowfat variation of the Cajun specialty combines cubed chicken and Canadian bacon with rice, tomatoes, onion, and bell peppers.

- **1½ pounds skinless, boneless chicken breasts**
- **1 tablespoon salad oil**
- **½ pound Canadian bacon, diced**
- **1 large onion, chopped**
- **3 cloves garlic, minced or pressed**
- **2 large green bell peppers, seeded and chopped**
- **1 cup chopped celery**
- **4 large tomatoes (about 2 lbs. *total*), chopped**
- **1 can (about 15 oz.) tomato sauce**
- **1 dry bay leaf, crumbled**
- **1 teaspoon dry thyme**
- **2 teaspoons white pepper**
- **1 teaspoon ground red pepper (cayenne)**
- **½ cup chopped parsley**
- **Salt (optional)**
- **1½ cups long-grain white rice**
- **3 cups chicken broth**

Rinse chicken, pat dry, and cut into bite-size pieces. Heat oil in a wide frying pan over medium-high heat. Add chicken and Canadian bacon; cook, stirring often, until browned on all sides. Transfer chicken and bacon to a 4- to 5-quart baking pan.

Add onion, garlic, bell peppers, and celery to frying pan. Cook over medium heat, stirring often, until

onion is soft (about 7 minutes). Add tomatoes, tomato sauce, bay leaf, thyme, white pepper, red pepper, and parsley. Cook, stirring occasionally, until sauce comes to a boil; boil gently for 5 minutes. Season to taste with salt, if desired.

Pour sauce over chicken; stir in rice and broth. Cover and bake in a 375° oven until rice is tender to bite (about 50 minutes). Makes 6 servings.

Per serving: 475 calories (15 percent from fat), 42 g protein, 58 g carbohydrates, 8 g total fat (2 g saturated fat), 85 mg cholesterol, 1,567 mg sodium

Easy Baked Chicken Kiev

Traditional chicken Kiev is deep-fried—but our favorite version of the dish is baked, making it lower in calories and easier to prepare than the original. It's a great make-ahead choice; you can assemble everything well in advance, then pop the pan in the oven 20 minutes before serving.

- **½ cup *each* fine dry bread crumbs and grated Parmesan cheese**
- **1½ teaspoons dry oregano**
- **½ teaspoon garlic salt**
- **¼ teaspoon pepper**
- **¼ cup butter or margarine, at room temperature**
- **1 tablespoon chopped parsley**
- **4 ounces jack cheese**
- **8 skinless, boneless chicken breast halves (about 3 lbs. *total*)**
- **5 tablespoons butter or margarine, melted**

In a shallow bowl, mix crumbs, Parmesan cheese, 1 teaspoon of the oregano, garlic salt, and pepper; set aside.

In a small bowl, mix the ¼ cup butter, parsley, and remaining ½ teaspoon oregano; set aside. Cut jack cheese into strips about ½ inch wide and 1½ inches long; set aside.

Rinse chicken and pat dry. Place each breast half between 2 sheets of plastic wrap or wax paper; pound with a flat-surfaced mallet until about ¼ inch thick.

Lay each chicken piece flat and spread with an eighth of the herb-butter mixture; place an eighth of the jack cheese strips crosswise at one end. Fold in sides so they overlap; then roll up chicken to enclose filling. Coat each chicken bundle with melted butter, then with crumb mixture. Arrange bundles, seam side down and slightly apart, in a shallow baking pan. Drizzle with any remaining butter. Cover and refrigerate for at least 4 hours or until next day.

Bake, uncovered, in a 400° oven until meat in center of bundles is no longer pink; cut gently to test (about 20 minutes). Makes 8 servings.

Per serving: 405 calories (48 percent from fat), 46 g protein, 5 g carbohydrates, 21 g total fat (10 g saturated fat), 150 mg cholesterol, 584 mg sodium

Meltdown Chicken Bundles

This Mexican-seasoned variation on chicken Kiev gets its zip from jalapeños, cumin, and chili. The tender chicken rolls are crisp and golden on the outside, creamy with melted cheese and chiles inside.

¼ **cup fine dry bread crumbs**

2 **tablespoons grated Parmesan cheese**

1 **teaspoon chili powder**

¼ **teaspoon *each* ground cumin and pepper**

4 **ounces jack cheese**

8 **skinless, boneless chicken breast halves (about 3 lbs. *total*)**

4 **pickled jalapeño chiles, seeded and cut lengthwise into ¼-inch-wide strips**

⅓ **cup butter or margarine, melted**
 Salt

In a shallow bowl, mix crumbs, Parmesan cheese, chili powder, cumin, and pepper; set aside.

Cut jack cheese into 8 equal strips; then set aside.

Rinse chicken and pat dry. Place each breast half between 2 sheets of plastic wrap or wax paper; pound with a flat-surfaced mallet until about ¼ inch thick.

Lay each chicken piece flat; place one strip of cheese and an eighth of the chiles crosswise at one end. Fold in sides so they overlap; then roll up chicken to enclose filling. Coat each chicken bundle with melted butter, then with crumb mixture. Arrange bundles, seam side down and slightly apart, in a shallow baking pan. Drizzle with any remaining butter. (At this point, you may cover and refrigerate until next day.)

Bake, uncovered, in a 425° oven until meat in center of bundles is no longer pink; cut gently to test (about 15 minutes). Season to taste with salt. Makes 8 servings.

Per serving: 329 calories (41 percent from fat), 44 g protein, 3 g carbohydrates, 15 g total fat (6 g saturated fat), 133 mg cholesterol, 429 mg sodium

Fila Chicken Packets

Enclosed in packets of paper-thin fila pastry, boneless chicken breasts steam to moist perfection. To keep the pastry from drying out, work with just two sheets at a time, keeping the rest tightly covered with plastic wrap until you're ready to use them.

6 **skinless, boneless chicken breast halves (about 2¼ lbs. *total*)**

¾ **cup *each* thinly sliced green onions and mayonnaise**

3 **tablespoons lemon juice**

¾ **teaspoon dry tarragon**

3 **cloves garlic, minced or pressed**

⅔ **cup (⅓ lb.) butter or margarine, melted**

12 **sheets fila dough (about ⅓ lb. *total*), thawed if frozen**
 Salt and pepper

2 **tablespoons grated Parmesan cheese**

Rinse chicken and pat dry; set aside. In a bowl, mix onions, mayonnaise, lemon juice, tarragon, and 2 cloves of the garlic; set aside. Combine remaining 1 clove garlic with butter.

To make each packet, place one sheet of fila on a flat surface and brush with about 2 teaspoons of the garlic butter. Put a second sheet on top and brush with 2 more teaspoons garlic butter. Sprinkle all sides of one chicken piece with salt and pepper, then spread one side with 1½ tablespoons of the mayonnaise mixture.

Place chicken, mayonnaise side down, in center of fila about 2 inches from one end. Spread chicken with 1½ more tablespoons mayonnaise mixture. Flip end of fila over chicken and roll once; then fold long sides over chicken and roll up completely.

Brush packets with remaining garlic butter and sprinkle with cheese. (At this point, you may arrange packets in a single layer in a container with a tight-fitting lid and freeze for up to 1 month. Thaw completely, covered, before baking.)

Arrange fila packets, seam side down and slightly apart, in a 10- by 15-inch rimmed baking pan. Bake in a 375° oven until golden brown (20 to 25 minutes). Makes 6 servings.

Per serving: 661 calories (62 percent from fat), 44 g protein, 20 g carbohydrates, 45 g total fat (17 g saturated fat), 172 mg cholesterol, 617 mg sodium

Broccoli- & Cheese-stuffed Chicken Breasts

Fresh color and flavor make this easy entrée a standout—and you can prepare it ahead, too. A day in advance, stuff tender chicken breasts with broccoli, onion, and Swiss cheese; then bake shortly before serving.

- 2 tablespoons butter or margarine
- 1 small onion, chopped
- 2 teaspoons dry tarragon
- ¾ pound broccoli
- 2 tablespoons water
- 1½ cups (about 6 oz.) shredded Swiss cheese
- 6 skinless, boneless chicken breast halves (about 2¼ lbs. *total*)
  Chive-Tarragon Sauce (recipe follows)

Melt butter in a wide frying pan over medium heat. Add onion and tarragon; cook, stirring often, until onion is soft (about 5 minutes).

Meanwhile, trim and discard ends of broccoli stalks. Cut flowerets from stalks; coarsely chop. Peel and chop stalks; add to flowerets. Add all broccoli and water to frying pan. Cover and cook, stirring occasionally, until broccoli is tender-crisp to bite (about 5 minutes). Remove from heat. Drain any liquid from pan; then stir in 1 cup of the cheese and let cool.

Rinse chicken and pat dry. Place each breast half between 2 sheets of plastic wrap or wax paper; pound with a flat-surfaced mallet until about ¼ inch thick. Lay each chicken piece

flat; mound a sixth of the broccoli mixture in center of each. Roll chicken around filling to enclose. Set chicken bundles, seam side down and slightly apart, in a greased 9- by 13-inch baking pan. Sprinkle with remaining ½ cup cheese. (At this point, you may cover and refrigerate until next day.)

Bake, uncovered, in a 450° oven until meat in center of bundles is no longer pink and filling is hot; cut to test (15 to 18 minutes). Meanwhile, prepare Chive-Tarragon Sauce and set aside.

When chicken is done, broil it 4 to 6 inches below heat just until cheese is browned (about 2 minutes). Offer sauce to spoon over individual servings. Makes 6 servings.

Chive-Tarragon Sauce. In a bowl, stir together ⅓ cup **seasoned rice vinegar** (or ⅓ cup white wine vinegar plus 2 tablespoons sugar), ½ teaspoon *each* **dry tarragon** and **sugar,** and 1 tablespoon snipped **fresh chives** or 1½ teaspoons dry chives.

Per serving: 359 calories (36 percent from fat), 49 g protein, 8 g carbohydrates, 14 g total fat (8 g saturated fat), 135 mg cholesterol, 495 mg sodium

Dijon Chicken with Panko Crust

The coarse dry bread crumbs known to the Japanese as *panko* give baked chicken breasts an especially crunchy coating. You can buy the crumbs in an Asian market or a well-stocked supermarket, but they're very easy to make at home.

- Dijon Sauce (recipe follows)
- ½ cup Homemade Panko (recipe follows) or purchased panko
- ¼ cup butter or margarine, melted
- ¼ cup Dijon mustard
- 2 cloves garlic, minced or pressed
- 2 tablespoons grated Parmesan cheese
- 1½ tablespoons minced parsley
- 8 skinless, boneless chicken breast halves (about 3 lbs. *total*)

Prepare Dijon Sauce; set aside. Prepare panko. In a large, shallow bowl, stir together butter, mustard, and garlic. In another shallow bowl, mix panko, cheese, and parsley.

Rinse chicken and pat dry. Working with one piece of chicken at a time, coat each piece with butter mixture; then dip rounded side in panko mixture. Arrange chicken pieces, crumb side up and slightly apart, in a 10- by 15-inch rimmed baking pan.

Bake in a 500° oven until crumbs are golden and meat in thickest part is no longer pink; cut to test (about 15 minutes). To serve, leave chicken pieces whole or cut them crosswise into thick slices. Offer Dijon Sauce to spoon over individual servings. Makes 8 servings.

Dijon Sauce. In a small bowl, stir together ½ cup **mayonnaise** and ¼ cup **Dijon mustard.** Makes ¾ cup.

Homemade Panko. Trim crusts from 2 slices **firm-textured white bread.** Cut bread into cubes; whirl in a food processor or blender until even, coarse crumbs form. Spread crumbs in a shallow baking pan. Bake in a 325° oven, stirring often, until dry and crisp, but not brown (8 to 10 minutes).

Per serving of chicken: 263 calories (32 percent from fat), 40 g protein, 3 g carbohydrates, 9 g total fat (4 g saturated fat), 115 mg cholesterol, 435 mg sodium

Per tablespoon of Dijon Sauce: 72 calories (94 percent from fat), 0.1 g protein, 1 g carbohydrates, 8 g total fat (1 g saturated fat), 5 mg cholesterol, 202 mg sodium

When it comes to favorite recipes, our readers and staff consider great flavor the most important quality—and that helps explain why the lists of best-loved dishes we receive include some of the creamiest, richest comfort foods in *Sunset*'s files. For daily meals, though, concerns with limiting fat, calories, and cholesterol seem to dominate the way we eat.

Fortunately, it's surprisingly easy to streamline everyday cooking. Just a few quick changes can lighten up many dishes, including the most sinful high-fat favorites. If you're interested in trimming fat from your diet, try using the techniques described here.

Oven-fry. Small pieces of food like meatballs, cut-up chicken or meat, and sliced vegetables (lightly brushed with oil) brown well in a very hot oven. Be sure to arrange food in a single layer, leaving enough space around the pieces to let moisture evaporate quickly. Set the oven between 400° and 500°, depending on the size and type of food.

Braise-deglaze. Recipes for soups, stews, sauces, and similar dishes often begin with chopped vegetables cooked in butter or oil to develop a flavor base. To streamline these recipes, replace the fat with enough liquid to cover the vegetables. Choose a liquid that will complement the finished dish—broth, wine, or just plain water.

Boil the vegetables and liquid over high or medium-high heat, uncovered, stirring occasionally, until the liquid evaporates and the vegetables begin to caramelize and stick to the pan. Add more liquid, 2 tablespoons at a time, stirring to scrape browned bits free, until the vegetables become limp and start to soak up the brown color. Then add the remaining ingredients to the vegetable mixture and continue to cook as the original recipe directs.

Fill in with water. You can give sauces a velvety quality without using much fat; just replace some or all of the butter, margarine, or oil with slightly thickened water or other liquid (as appropriate to the dish).

Popular thickeners include all-purpose flour, cornstarch, arrowroot, and potato starch. Flour can withstand the most heat without breaking down, but it makes an opaque sauce and requires several minutes of simmering to get rid of the starchy flavor. Cornstarch produces a clearer mixture that tastes cooked as soon as it boils; arrowroot and potato starch also make clear sauces that lose any starchy taste just before reaching a boil.

For each cup of liquid, use 1 tablespoon flour for a thin sauce, 2 tablespoons for a medium sauce, and 3 to 4 tablespoons for a thick sauce. If you use cornstarch, arrowroot, or potato starch, you'll need just half these amounts of starch for the same thickening effect.

Use more egg whites and fewer whole eggs and egg yolks. Egg whites serve the same function as yolks in many dishes, and omitting all or most of the yolks is an easy way to reduce calories, fat, and cholesterol. Consider that the white of one large egg has 18 calories and no fat or cholesterol, while the yolk has 70 calories, 6 grams of fat, and 300 milligrams of cholesterol.

Use lowfat & nonfat dairy foods. In most recipes, lowfat and nonfat dairy foods can be substituted for whole-milk products with only minimal loss of texture and body. The exception, in some cases, is whipping cream. Its high proportion of milkfat—30 to 36 percent—allows it to whip to a fine fluff. It can also be boiled, reduced, or mixed with acidic foods without curdling or separating (the higher the percentage of milkfat, the more stable the cream).

Percentages of fat in dairy products tend to vary, but in general, *skim (nonfat) milk* has less than .25 percent milkfat, *lowfat milk* 1 to 2 percent, and whole milk 3.25 percent. *Half-and-half* is 10 to 12 percent milkfat.

Sour cream (18 percent milkfat) now has a common reduced-fat alternative. Usually marketed as *light sour cream*, it has only 10 to 12 percent milkfat and is virtually always interchangeable with its heavier counterpart. Lowfat and/or nonfat versions of *yogurt* and *ricotta cheese* are also commonly available. You'll find reduced-fat *cream cheese*, too; look for Neufchâtel or "light" cream cheese.

Commercial *ice cream* must contain at least 10 percent milkfat and often has much, much more, but it does not always contain eggs; *ice milk* has 2 to 7 percent milkfat. There are a host of other ice cream–like products, including frozen yogurts, which are delicious alternatives to rich ice cream. Dressed up with a few quick finishing touches (see page 219), any of these reduced-fat frozen confections makes an impressive dessert.

Garlic Chicken & New Potatoes

With cooking, garlic loses its harshness and takes on such a sweet, mild flavor that you can use the aromatic cloves in quantity. Here, chicken legs and new potatoes simmer to tenderness, seasoned with a little rosemary— and a dozen cloves of garlic.

2 **whole chicken legs (about 1 lb.** **total)**

2 **tablespoons olive oil or salad** **oil**

4 **small thin-skinned potatoes,** **scrubbed and cut into halves**

12 **cloves garlic, peeled and** **slightly crushed**

½ **teaspoon dry rosemary**

2 **tablespoons water** **Salt and pepper**

Rinse chicken and pat dry. Heat oil in a wide frying pan over medium-high heat. Add chicken and potatoes and cook, turning as needed, until chicken is browned on all sides. Reduce heat to low and add garlic, rosemary, and water; cover and cook for 15 minutes.

Turn chicken and potatoes over. Continue to cook, covered, until meat near thighbone is no longer pink; cut to test (about 15 more minutes). Season to taste with salt and pepper. Makes 2 servings.

Per serving: 640 calories (48 percent from fat), 36 g protein, 47 g carbohydrates, 34 g total fat (7 g saturated fat), 138 mg cholesterol, 152 mg sodium

Chicken Cacciatore

In Italian-American culinary lingo, a dish described as *cacciatore* ("hunters'-style") is usually one that's prepared like this—simmered with mushrooms, onions, bell pepper, white wine, and tomatoes. You might serve the hearty entrée with hot spaghetti and a robust red wine.

4 **whole chicken legs (2 to 2½ lbs.** **total)**

2 **tablespoons butter or margarine**

1 **tablespoon olive oil**

½ **pound mushrooms, sliced**

1 **large onion, sliced**

2 **green bell peppers, seeded and** **finely chopped**

2 **cloves garlic, minced or pressed**

½ **cup dry white wine or chicken** **broth**

1 **can (about 15 oz.) tomato sauce**

¼ **teaspoon *each* dry marjoram,** **dry oregano, and dry thyme**

1 **teaspoon instant chicken** **bouillon**

2 **tablespoons minced parsley** **Salt**

Rinse chicken and pat dry.

Melt butter in oil in a wide frying pan over medium-high heat. Add chicken and cook, turning as needed, until browned on all sides. Remove from pan and set aside. Add mushrooms, onion, bell peppers, and garlic to pan and cook, stirring, until onion is soft (about 5 minutes). Stir in wine, tomato sauce, marjoram, oregano, thyme, bouillon, and parsley.

Return chicken to pan. Bring liquid to a boil over high heat. Then reduce heat, cover, and simmer until meat near thighbone is no longer pink; cut to test (about 30 minutes). If sauce is too thin, transfer chicken to a serving dish and keep warm. Bring sauce to a boil; boil, stirring, until slightly thickened. Season sauce to taste with salt; pour over chicken. Makes 4 servings.

Per serving: 512 calories (56 percent from fat), 38 g protein, 19 g carbohydrates, 32 g total fat (10 g saturated fat), 170 mg cholesterol, 1,096 mg sodium

Teriyaki Chicken Legs with Onions & Potatoes

Ginger, honey, and soy sauce glaze whole chicken legs in this barbecue favorite, first featured during the 1970s as part of a Memorial Day menu.

6 **whole chicken legs (about 3 lbs.** **total)**

⅔ **cup soy sauce**

⅓ **cup honey**

2 **teaspoons grated fresh ginger** **or ½ teaspoon ground ginger**

3 **tablespoons dry sherry**

½ **cup olive oil or salad oil**

1 **clove garlic, minced or pressed**

½ **cup thinly sliced green onions**

¼ **cup butter or margarine**

2 **large onions, thinly sliced**

4 **large thin-skinned potatoes** **(about 2 lbs. *total*), scrubbed,** **cooked, and thinly sliced**

Rinse chicken and pat dry. In a large bowl, stir together soy sauce, honey, ginger, sherry, oil, garlic, and green onions. Add chicken and turn to coat. Cover and refrigerate for at least 4 hours or until next day, turning often.

Lift chicken from marinade and drain briefly; reserve marinade. Arrange chicken on a grill 4 to 6 inches above a solid bed of low coals. Cook, turning several times, until meat near thighbone is no longer pink; cut to test (40 to 50 minutes). From about 15 minutes before chicken is done until about 5 minutes before it's done, baste frequently with marinade; do not baste during last 5 minutes of cooking.

As soon as chicken is arranged on grill, set a frying pan beside it. Melt butter in pan, add onion slices, and cook, uncovered, stirring occasionally, for 20 minutes. Add potatoes and cook, stirring occasionally, until potatoes are heated through and onions are soft—about 15 more minutes. (You may also cook onions and potatoes on the range. Melt butter in a wide frying pan over medium heat; add onions and cook, stirring often, until soft—about 5 minutes. Then add potatoes and cook, stirring often, until heated through—about 10 minutes. Keep vegetables warm until chicken is done.)

Serve potato-onion mixture alongside chicken. Makes 6 servings.

Per serving: 667 calories (50 percent from fat), 34 g protein, 49 g carbohydrates, 37 g total fat (11 g saturated fat), 124 mg cholesterol, 1,563 mg sodium

Green Tomatillo Chicken

Popular in Southwestern cuisine, tomatillos are now showing up in produce markets and supermarkets throughout the West. Cooking brings out their delightful lemon-herb flavor.

4 whole chicken legs (2 to 2½ lbs. *total*), skinned
2 tablespoons salad oil
1 pound tomatillos, husked and chopped; or 2 cans (about 13 oz. *each*) tomatillos, drained and coarsely chopped
1 large onion, chopped
2 fresh jalapeño chiles, seeded and chopped
1 clove garlic, minced or pressed
   Salt and pepper
½ cup cilantro leaves

Rinse chicken and pat dry.

Heat oil in a wide frying pan over medium-high heat. Add chicken and cook, turning as needed, until browned on all sides. Add tomatillos, onion, chiles, and garlic. Reduce heat, cover, and simmer until meat near thighbone is no longer pink; cut to test (about 30 minutes). With a slotted spoon, transfer chicken to a platter; keep warm.

Bring sauce to a boil over high heat; boil, stirring, until almost all liquid has

evaporated (6 to 8 minutes). Season sauce to taste with salt and pepper, then pour over chicken. Sprinkle with cilantro. Makes 4 servings.

Per serving: 288 calories (41 percent from fat), 32 g protein, 10 g carbohydrates, 13 g total fat (2 g saturated fat), 116 mg cholesterol, 128 mg sodium

Chicken Legs in Cassis

In Europe, fruit is a popular accent for meats and poultry. Here, black currants in three forms—vinegar, liqueur, and the tiny dried fruits—bring sweet-tart distinction to simmered chicken.

4 whole chicken legs (about 2 lbs. *total*)
   Salt, white pepper, and ground nutmeg
2 tablespoons butter or margarine
1 tablespoon salad oil
1 clove garlic, minced or pressed
2 tablespoons cassis vinegar or raspberry vinegar
2 teaspoons tomato paste
¼ cup dried currants
¾ cup chicken broth
¼ cup *each* dry white wine and crème de cassis (black currant liqueur)
1 tablespoon all-purpose flour

Rinse chicken, pat dry, and sprinkle with salt, white pepper, and nutmeg. Melt 1 tablespoon of the butter in oil in a wide frying pan over medium-high heat. Add chicken and cook, turning as needed, until browned on all sides. Stir in garlic, vinegar, and tomato paste; sprinkle chicken with currants.

Pour broth, wine, and crème de cassis into pan. Bring to a boil. Then reduce heat, cover, and simmer until meat near thighbone is no longer pink; cut to test (about 25 minutes). Meanwhile, smoothly mix remaining 1 tablespoon butter with flour; set aside.

Lift chicken from pan, reserving pan juices, and transfer to a serving

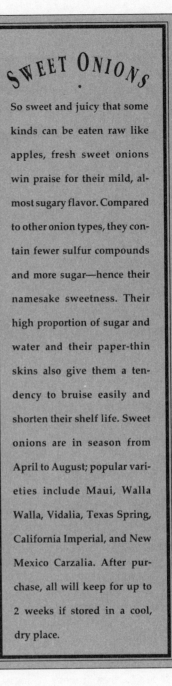

dish; keep warm. Bring juices in frying pan to a boil over high heat; boil, stirring often, until reduced by about a third. Stirring constantly with a whisk, blend in butter-flour mixture, a little at a time, until sauce is thickened and shiny. Pour sauce over chicken. Makes 4 servings.

Per serving: 496 calories (58 percent from fat), 31 g protein, 16 g carbohydrates, 30 g total fat (10 g saturated fat), 153 mg cholesterol, 398 mg sodium

Chutney-glazed Chicken Thighs

No fuss, no frills—just savory good-ness. Serve this tangy-sweet glazed chicken with Wild Rice with Golden Raisins (page 167) or Rice Pilaf with Fruit & Nuts (page 165).

    Vegetable oil cooking spray
  8 chicken thighs (about 2 lbs. *total*)
  ⅓ cup Major Grey's or other chutney, chopped

Spray a 12- by 15-inch baking pan with cooking spray. Rinse chicken and pat dry. Arrange chicken pieces, skin side up and slightly apart, in pan.

Bake in a 400° oven until meat near thighbone is no longer pink; cut to test (35 to 40 minutes). Brush chicken pieces evenly with chutney. Return to oven and bake just until glaze is set (about 5 more minutes). Makes 4 servings.

Per serving: 356 calories (48 percent from fat), 29 g protein, 16 g carbohydrates, 18 g total fat (5 g saturated fat), 109 mg cholesterol, 331 mg sodium

Broil-Bake Crispy Chicken

Chicken cooked by the "broil-bake" method is delightfully crisp and tender. Start by broiling chicken pieces on one side, then finish by baking them in a hot oven. To ensure moist-textured meat, bake the chicken on a rack set over a pan of boiling water.

  1 chicken (about 3½ lbs.), cut up; or 6 whole chicken legs (about 3 lbs. *total*); or 6 chicken breast halves (about 3 lbs. *total*)
    Seasoned salt and garlic powder
  ½ teaspoon dry thyme

Rinse chicken and pat dry. Lightly sprinkle both sides of each piece with

seasoned salt and garlic powder; then arrange, skin side down and slightly apart, on a rack in a shallow baking pan. Broil 4 to 6 inches below heat until chicken is lightly browned (about 10 minutes).

Remove pan from oven, adjust oven rack to center of oven, and reset oven to 500°. Turn chicken pieces over and sprinkle with thyme. Return pan to oven and pour boiling water into pan (beneath chicken) to a depth of ½ inch. Bake until chicken is browned and meat near thighbone (or meat in thickest part of breast) is no longer pink; cut to test (15 to 20 minutes). Makes 4 to 6 servings.

Per serving: 335 calories (53 percent from fat), 38 g protein, 0.1 g carbohydrates, 19 g total fat (5 g saturated fat), 123 mg cholesterol, 115 mg sodium

Curried Chicken with Papaya

The flavor of this moist chicken can almost make you believe you're on a tropical vacation. The meat is browned first to seal in juices, then cooked to tenderness in a creamy sauce scented with curry and ginger. Garnish the dish with thick slices of sweet ripe papaya.

  2½ pounds chicken drumsticks and thighs
  3 tablespoons all-purpose flour
  1 teaspoon salt
  ⅛ teaspoon pepper
  3 tablespoons salad oil
  1 large onion, chopped

  1 tablespoon curry powder
  ½ cup *each* water and whipping cream
  1 teaspoon instant chicken bouillon or 1 chicken bouillon cube
  2 tablespoons chopped candied ginger or ½ teaspoon ground ginger
    Hot cooked rice (optional)
  1 papaya, peeled, seeded, and thickly sliced
  2 tablespoons lime juice

Rinse chicken and pat dry. In a shal-low bowl, mix flour, salt, and pepper; coat chicken with flour mixture and shake off excess. Heat oil in a wide frying pan over medium-high heat. Add chicken, a few pieces at a time (do not crowd pan); cook, turning as needed, until browned on all sides. Set chicken aside. Add onion to pan and cook, stirring often, until soft (about 4 minutes). Stir in curry pow-der and cook, stirring, for about 1 min-ute. Gradually stir in water and cream; then stir in bouillon and ginger.

Return chicken to pan. Bring sauce to a boil over high heat. Then reduce heat, cover, and simmer until meat near thighbone is no longer pink; cut to test (about 40 minutes). To serve, spoon chicken over rice, if desired. Garnish with papaya, then sprinkle lime juice over all. Makes 4 servings.

Per serving: 649 calories (63 percent from fat), 40 g protein, 20 g carbohydrates, 45 g total fat (14 g saturated fat), 206 mg cholesterol, 971 mg sodium

WESTERN CLASSIC
Roast Chicken with Herbs

Roast chicken is a simple and delicious entrée that always finds favor with guests and family. Vegetable purées (see page 146) are a wonderful accom-paniment; try mixing them with the pan juices just before serving.

1 chicken (3 to 4 lbs.)

3 cloves garlic, peeled and halved

2 dry bay leaves

3 tablespoons butter or margarine, melted

¼ teaspoon ground sage

1 teaspoon Italian herb seasoning; or ¼ teaspoon *each* dry basil, dry marjoram, dry oregano, and dry thyme

Salt and pepper

Reserve chicken neck and giblets for other uses, if desired. Pull off and discard lumps of fat. Rinse chicken inside and out; pat dry.

Rub skin of chicken with 1 cut clove garlic; then put all garlic and bay leaves into body cavity. In a small bowl, stir together butter, sage, and herb seasoning; season to taste with salt and pepper. Spoon 1 tablespoon of the butter mixture into body cavity; then brush chicken with remaining butter mixture.

Place chicken, breast up, on a rack in a shallow baking pan. Roast in a 375° oven until a meat thermometer inserted in thickest part of thigh (not touching bone) registers 185°F or until meat near thighbone is no longer pink; cut to test (1 to 1½ hours). Baste chicken occasionally with pan drippings during the last 30 minutes of roasting time.

To serve, transfer chicken to a serving dish. Let stand for 10 minutes before carving. Makes 4 servings.

Per serving: 501 calories (60 percent from fat), 48 g protein, 1 g carbohydrates, 32 g total fat (12 g saturated fat), 177 mg cholesterol, 236 mg sodium

Five-spice Roast Chicken

Rubbed with a blend of soy and aromatic five-spice before roasting, this plump chicken has a thin, crisp skin. Serve the moist, tender bird with sauce made from the pan drippings.

1 chicken (4½ to 5 lbs.)

1 teaspoon salad oil

1½ teaspoons Chinese five-spice; or ½ teaspoon *each* ground cloves and anise seeds and ¼ teaspoon *each* ground cinnamon and ground ginger

3 tablespoons soy sauce

1 tablespoon *each* sugar and dry sherry

1 clove garlic, minced

3 tablespoons thinly sliced green onions

Reserve chicken neck and giblets for other uses, if desired. Pull off and discard lumps of fat. Rinse chicken inside and out; pat dry.

In a 2- to 3-cup pan, combine oil and five-spice. Cook over medium heat, stirring, until hot. Add soy sauce, sugar, sherry, and garlic. Place chicken, breast up, on a rack in a shallow baking pan; rub generously with five-spice mixture. Place remaining mixture in cavity of bird. Roast in a 375° oven until a meat thermometer inserted in thickest part of thigh (not touching bone) registers 185°F or until meat near thighbone is no longer pink; cut to test (1¼ to 1¾ hours).

Drain juices from chicken cavity into baking pan; transfer chicken to a serving dish. Place pan over medium heat and stir juices to scrape browned bits free. Pour juices into a small pitcher and skim off fat; then stir in onions. Offer juices to pour over individual servings. Makes 6 servings.

Per serving: 438 calories (54 percent from fat), 45 g protein, 4 g carbohydrates, 26 g total fat (7 g saturated fat), 141 mg cholesterol, 651 mg sodium

Chicken with Oranges

We first enjoyed this colorful chicken dish in a restaurant beside the Naranjo ("orange tree") River in east-central Mexico. Take a bite—and imagine that you, too, are dining on a bougainvillea-covered veranda where wild parrots flutter among mango, papaya, and orange trees.

1 chicken (about 4 lbs.), cut up

Salt and pepper

⅛ teaspoon *each* ground cinnamon and ground cloves

3 tablespoons salad oil

2 cloves garlic, peeled

1 medium-size onion, chopped

1 cup *each* orange juice and water

Pinch of saffron threads

2 tablespoons raisins

1 tablespoon drained capers

½ cup coarsely chopped blanched almonds

3 oranges, peeled and sliced crosswise

Rinse chicken, pat dry, and sprinkle with salt, pepper, cinnamon, and cloves. Heat oil in a wide frying pan over medium-high heat. Add chicken, a few pieces at a time (do not crowd pan); cook, turning as needed, until browned on all sides. Return all chicken to pan and add garlic and onion. Continue to cook, turning chicken occasionally, until chicken is well browned but not crusted.

Add orange juice, water, saffron, raisins, and capers to pan; bring liquid to a boil. Then reduce heat, cover, and simmer until meat near thighbone is no longer pink; cut to test (about 40 minutes).

About 5 minutes before chicken is done, remove garlic and stir in almonds. Garnish chicken with oranges. Makes 4 to 6 servings.

Per serving: 497 calories (60 percent from fat), 26 g protein, 25 g carbohydrates, 34 g total fat (7 g saturated fat), 87 mg cholesterol, 129 mg sodium

Chicken Sauté

Selected by readers for its make-ahead ease and delicious flavor, this decades-old recipe is a dinnertime standby in many families. You can brown the chicken pieces and make the sauce a day in advance.

- 1　**chicken (about 3½ lbs.), cut up**
  About ¼ cup all-purpose flour
- ¼　**cup olive oil or salad oil**
- 1　**clove garlic, minced or pressed**
- ½　**pound mushrooms, thinly sliced**
- 2　**tablespoons chopped parsley**
- 1　**cup dry white wine**
- ½　**teaspoon dry rosemary or dry marjoram (optional)**
  Salt and pepper

Rinse chicken, pat dry, and dust with flour. Heat oil in a wide frying pan over medium-high heat. Add chicken, a few pieces at a time (do not crowd pan); cook, turning as needed, until browned on all sides. Arrange chicken pieces, slightly apart, in a shallow baking pan. Add garlic and mushrooms to frying pan and cook, stirring often, until mushrooms are soft (about 5 minutes). Stir in parsley, wine, and rosemary (if desired); season to taste with salt and pepper. Pour sauce over chicken. (At this point, you may cover and refrigerate until next day.)

Bake, uncovered, in a 350° oven until meat near thighbone is no longer pink; cut to test (about 45 minutes). Baste frequently during baking. Makes 4 servings.

Per serving: 439 calories (68 percent from fat), 26 g protein, 9 g carbohydrates, 33 g total fat (7 g saturated fat), 95 mg cholesterol, 95 mg sodium

Lemon Chicken

The combination of poultry and citrus, popular for centuries in European cooking, is now a favorite throughout America as well. Here, chicken and fresh lemon pair up in a sweet-tart supper dish.

- 1　**chicken (about 3 lbs.), cut up**
- 2　**lemons**
- ⅓　**cup all-purpose flour**
- 1　**teaspoon salt**
- ½　**teaspoon paprika**
- ¼　**cup salad oil**
- 2　**tablespoons firmly packed brown sugar**
- 1　**cup chicken broth**
- 2　**mint sprigs**

Rinse chicken and pat dry. Grate peel (colored part only) from one lemon. Set peel aside; then cut lemon in half and squeeze halves over chicken, rubbing juice into each piece. In a shallow bowl, mix flour, salt, and paprika. Coat each chicken piece with flour mixture and shake off excess.

Heat oil in a wide frying pan over medium-high heat. Add chicken, a few pieces at a time (do not crowd pan); cook, turning as needed, until browned on all sides. Arrange chicken pieces, slightly apart, in a shallow baking pan. Sprinkle with grated lemon peel and sugar, then pour broth over chicken. Thinly slice remaining lemon; scatter lemon slices and mint sprigs over chicken.

Cover and bake in a 375° oven until meat near thighbone is no longer pink; cut to test (40 to 45 minutes). Discard mint before serving. Makes 4 servings.

Per serving: 552 calories (57 percent from fat), 43 g protein, 16 g carbohydrates, 34 g total fat (7 g saturated fat), 132 mg cholesterol, 922 mg sodium

Chicken with Sweet Onions

In this Moroccan-style recipe, mellow slow-cooked onions sweetened with brown sugar and cinnamon cloak pieces of tender chicken. At the table, offer lemon wedges to squeeze over the meat for a touch of tart flavor.

- 1　**chicken (3 to 3½ lbs.), cut up**
  Pepper and paprika
- ¼　**cup butter or margarine**
- 4　**or 5 large onions (2 to 2½ lbs. *total*), thinly sliced and separated into rings**
- 2　**tablespoons firmly packed brown sugar**
- ½　**teaspoon ground cinnamon**
  Salt
- ¼　**cup toasted slivered almonds**
  Lemon wedges

Rinse chicken, pat dry, and sprinkle with pepper and paprika. Arrange chicken pieces, skin side down, in a greased 10- by 15-inch rimmed baking pan. Bake in a 400° oven for 30 minutes. Turn pieces over and continue to bake until skin is browned and meat near thighbone is no longer pink; cut to test (15 to 20 more minutes).

While chicken is baking, melt butter in a wide frying pan over medium-low heat. Add onions and cook until very soft and golden (about 30 minutes); stir occasionally at first, then more often as onions begin to turn golden. Onions should not show signs of browning during the first 15 minutes; if they do, reduce heat. Sprinkle sugar and cinnamon over onions; stir until blended. Season to taste with salt.

Transfer chicken to a serving dish. Spoon onions over chicken and sprinkle with almonds. Serve with lemon wedges. Makes 4 servings.

Per serving: 663 calories (52 percent from fat), 49 g protein, 31 g carbohydrates, 38 g total fat (14 g saturated fat), 174 mg cholesterol, 261 mg sodium

Applejack Chicken

Apple juice spiked with brandy mimics the flavor of applejack in a light, creamy sauce for braised chicken.

- 1 **chicken (3 to 3½ lbs.), cut up**
  Salt and pepper
- 2 **tablespoons butter or margarine**
- 1 **medium-size onion, chopped**
- 1 **can (about 6 oz.) frozen apple juice concentrate, thawed**
- 1 **Newtown Pippin apple, peeled, cored, and diced**
- ¼ **pound mushrooms, sliced**
- ¼ **cup half-and-half**
- 1 **tablespoon cornstarch**
- 3 **tablespoons brandy or dry sherry**
  Chopped parsley

Rinse chicken, pat dry, and sprinkle lightly with salt and pepper. Melt butter in a wide frying pan over medium-high heat. Add chicken, a few pieces at a time (do not crowd pan); cook, turning as needed, until browned on all sides. Remove from pan.

Add onion to pan, reduce heat to medium, and cook, stirring often, until soft (about 5 minutes). Return chicken to pan; pour apple juice concentrate over chicken. Bring to a boil; then reduce heat, cover, and simmer for 20 minutes.

Add apple and mushrooms to pan, cover, and continue to simmer until meat near thighbone is no longer pink; cut to test (20 to 25 more minutes). With a slotted spoon, lift out chicken, vegetables, and apple; arrange on a platter and keep warm. In a small bowl, stir together half-and-half, cornstarch, and brandy. Stir cornstarch mixture into pan juices; cook, stirring, until sauce boils and thickens slightly. Pour sauce over chicken; sprinkle with parsley. Makes 4 servings.

Per serving: 491 calories (50 percent from fat), 24 g protein, 34 g carbohydrates, 26 g total fat (10 g saturated fat), 110 mg cholesterol, 163 mg sodium

Baked Chicken with Garlic Spaghetti

Thin strands of spaghetti, bold with sautéed garlic and marinara sauce, make a savory bed for baked chicken.

- 1 **chicken (about 3½ lbs.), cut up**
  Salt and pepper
- ½ **teaspoon *each* dry rosemary and dry thyme**
- 1 **can or jar (about 15 oz.) marinara sauce**
- ⅓ **cup butter or margarine**
- 3 **cloves garlic, minced or pressed**
- ½ **teaspoon *each* dry oregano and onion powder**
- 12 **ounces dry spaghetti, cooked and drained (keep hot)**

Rinse chicken, pat dry, and sprinkle with salt, pepper, rosemary, and thyme. Arrange chicken pieces, skin side down and slightly apart, in a greased shallow baking pan. Bake in a 375° oven for 20 minutes. Baste with ½ cup of the marinara sauce; bake for 10 more minutes. Turn chicken pieces over, baste with ½ cup more marinara sauce, and continue to bake until meat near thighbone is no longer pink; cut to test (20 to 30 more minutes).

When chicken is almost done, melt butter in a wide frying pan over medium heat. Add garlic; cook, stirring often, until soft (about 5 minutes). Add oregano, onion powder, and hot spaghetti; toss to mix well. Heat remaining marinara sauce and pour into a small serving dish.

To serve, pour spaghetti onto a rimmed platter and top with chicken. Offer sauce to spoon over individual servings. Makes 4 to 6 servings.

Per serving: 641 calories (44 percent from fat), 29 g protein, 60 g carbohydrates, 31 g total fat (12 g saturated fat), 109 mg cholesterol, 735 mg sodium

Barbecued Herb-Mustard Chicken

Simple herb-seasoned chicken is a never-fail supper favorite. For variety, try using different mustards in the marinade—Dijon, tarragon, green peppercorn, and German coarse-grained mustards are all possibilities.

- 1 **chicken (3 to 3½ lbs.), quartered**
- ½ **cup dry white wine**
- ⅔ **cup salad oil**
- ⅓ **cup wine vinegar**
- 2 **tablespoons minced onion**
- 1 **teaspoon Italian herb seasoning; or ¼ teaspoon *each* dry basil, dry marjoram, dry oregano, and dry thyme**
- 2 **cloves garlic, minced or pressed**
- ½ **teaspoon pepper**
- ¼ **cup spicy brown mustard**
  Salt

Rinse chicken and pat dry. In a large bowl, stir together wine, oil, vinegar, onion, herb seasoning, garlic, pepper, and mustard. Add chicken and turn to coat. Cover and refrigerate for at least 4 hours or until next day, turning occasionally.

Lift chicken from marinade and drain briefly; reserve marinade. Place chicken, skin side up, on a grill 4 to 6 inches above a solid bed of medium coals. Cook, turning and basting frequently with marinade, until meat near thighbone is no longer pink; cut to test (40 to 50 minutes). Season to taste with salt. Makes 4 servings.

Per serving: 565 calories (67 percent from fat), 45 g protein, 2 g carbohydrates, 41 g total fat (9 g saturated fat), 143 mg cholesterol, 216 mg sodium

Baked Chicken Paprika

Four simple seasonings—paprika, sugar, salt, and pepper—are all that's needed to enhance tender chicken pieces. For a delightful contrast in color and flavor, serve with Green Vegetable Medley (page 135) or Corn Casserole (page 141).

1 chicken (3 to 3½ lbs.), cut up
1 teaspoon paprika
¾ teaspoon salt
½ teaspoon sugar
⅛ teaspoon pepper

Rinse chicken and pat dry. Then arrange pieces, skin side down and slightly apart, in a lightly greased shallow baking pan. In a small dish, mix paprika, salt, sugar, and pepper; sprinkle over chicken.

Bake in a 400° oven for 35 minutes. Turn pieces over and continue to bake until meat near thighbone is no longer pink; cut to test (10 to 15 more minutes). Makes 4 servings.

Per serving: 392 calories (52 percent from fat), 44 g protein, 0.9 g carbohydrates, 22 g total fat (6 g saturated fat), 143 mg cholesterol, 545 mg sodium

Chicken & Artichoke Casserole

When *Sunset* celebrated its fiftieth anniversary with a special issue in 1979, this casserole was featured as an example of a classic "Kitchen Cabinet" recipe from the 1950s. We've tried many variations of the dish, but this one—which uses a bit less butter than the original—is our favorite.

1 chicken (3 to 3½ lbs.), cut up
 Salt, pepper, and paprika
¼ cup butter or margarine
1 can (about 14 oz.) water-packed artichoke hearts, drained and cut in half lengthwise
¼ pound mushrooms, sliced
2 tablespoons all-purpose flour
⅔ cup chicken broth
3 tablespoons dry sherry
¼ teaspoon dry rosemary

Rinse chicken, pat dry, and sprinkle lightly with salt, pepper, and paprika. Set aside.

Melt butter in a wide frying pan over medium heat. Add chicken, a few pieces at a time (do not crowd pan); cook, turning as needed, until browned on all sides. Arrange chicken pieces, slightly apart, in a shallow baking pan. Arrange artichokes between chicken pieces.

Discard all but 3 tablespoons of the drippings from frying pan. Add mushrooms and cook over medium heat, stirring often, until golden. Stir in flour; cook, stirring, for 1 minute (do not brown). Remove from heat; gradu-ally stir in broth, sherry, and rosemary. Then return to heat and cook, stirring constantly, until sauce boils and thickens. Pour sauce over chicken and artichokes. Cover and bake in a 375° oven until meat near thighbone is no longer pink; cut to test (about 40 minutes). Makes 4 servings.

Per serving: 647 calories (63 percent from fat), 48 g protein, 11 g carbohydrates, 44 g total fat (16 g saturated fat), 182 mg cholesterol, 451 mg sodium

Tarragon Chicken Casserole

You need only make this quick casserole once to commit the recipe to memory. Assembling the dish is extra-easy—you just arrange the chicken in a baking pan, top with onions, herbs, and canned soup, and bake.

1 chicken (2½ to 3 lbs.), cut up
1 or 2 medium-size onions, chopped
1½ teaspoons dry tarragon
¼ teaspoon poultry seasoning
 Salt and pepper
1 can (about 10¾ oz.) condensed cream of chicken soup
¼ cup milk
¼ cup sliced or slivered almonds (optional)

Rinse chicken and pat dry. Then place pieces, skin side up and slightly apart, in a shallow baking pan. Sprinkle with onions, tarragon, poultry seasoning, salt, and pepper. In a small bowl, stir together soup and milk until blended; spoon over chicken.

Bake in a 375° oven for 40 minutes; then sprinkle evenly with almonds, if desired. Continue to bake until meat near thighbone is no longer pink; cut to test (about 10 more minutes). Makes 4 servings.

Per serving: 435 calories (50 percent from fat), 41 g protein, 12 g carbohydrates, 24 g total fat (7 g saturated fat), 129 mg cholesterol, 721 mg sodium

Mexican Lasagne

Quick, easy, crowd-pleasing—all three words describe this Mexican-seasoned lasagne. To save you time and energy, the dish is made with canned soup and sauce; you can use deli-cooked meat, too, if you like.

- 2 tablespoons salad oil
- 1 large onion, chopped
- 2 cloves garlic, minced or pressed
- 1 red or green bell pepper, seeded and chopped
- 2 cans (about 10¾ oz. *each*) condensed tomato soup
- 1 can (about 10 oz.) enchilada sauce
- 1 tablespoon chili powder
- 1 teaspoon ground cumin
  Salt and pepper
  Fiesta Cheese Filling (recipe follows)
- 10 ounces dry lasagne noodles, cooked and drained
- 4 cups large pieces of cooked chicken or turkey
- 6 ounces *each* thinly sliced sharp Cheddar cheese and jack cheese

Heat oil in a wide frying pan over medium heat. Add onion, garlic, and bell pepper; cook, stirring often, until onion is soft (about 5 minutes). Add soup, enchilada sauce, chili powder, and cumin. Bring to a simmer; then simmer, stirring often, until thickened (about 10 minutes). Season to taste with salt and pepper.

Prepare Fiesta Cheese Filling.

Arrange half the noodles over bottom of a lightly greased shallow 3½- to 4-quart rectangular baking pan. Spread half the cheese filling over noodles; top with half the sauce. Scatter half the chicken over sauce; top with half the sliced cheeses. Repeat layers to use remaining noodles, cheese filling, sauce, chicken, and sliced cheeses. Cover with foil. (At this point, you may refrigerate until next day.)

Bake, covered, in a 375° oven until bubbly and heated through (about 35 minutes; about 50 minutes if refrigerated). Uncover and let stand for about 5 minutes before serving. Makes 10 to 12 servings.

Fiesta Cheese Filling. In a large bowl, stir together 2 cups **small-curd cottage cheese,** 2 **eggs,** ⅓ cup chopped **parsley,** and 3 to 4 tablespoons **canned diced green chiles.**

Per serving: 449 calories (40 percent from fat), 33 g protein, 34 g carbohydrates, 20 g total fat (6 g saturated fat), 119 mg cholesterol, 1,046 mg sodium

Tomatillo Chicken Enchiladas

A tart tomatillo sauce spiked with green chiles adds to the Southwestern appeal of these cheese- and chicken-filled enchiladas. For cool relief from the spicy heat, serve the enchiladas with frosty margaritas or tall glasses of lemonade.

- Tomatillo Sauce (recipe follows)
- 4 cups coarsely shredded cooked chicken or turkey
- 3 cups (about 12 oz.) shredded jack cheese
- 1 large can (about 7 oz.) diced green chiles
- 1½ teaspoons dry oregano
  Salt
  Salad oil
- 12 corn tortillas
- 1 to 1½ cups sour cream
- ½ cup chopped cilantro or cilantro sprigs
- 1 or 2 tomatillos, husked and thinly sliced; or 1 lime, thinly sliced

Prepare Tomatillo Sauce; set aside.

In a large bowl, stir together chicken, 2 cups of the cheese, chiles, and oregano. Season to taste with salt and set aside.

Heat ½ inch of oil in a small frying pan over medium heat; keep hot. Working with one tortilla at a time, heat each tortilla in oil until it blisters and becomes limp (this takes just a few seconds). Using tongs, lift tortilla from oil; drain on paper towels. Then spoon about ½ cup of the chicken mixture down center of tortilla and roll to enclose.

Set filled tortillas, seam side down, in a 10- by 15-inch rimmed baking pan; cover with foil. (At this point, you may refrigerate until next day.)

Bake enchiladas, covered, in a 350° oven until filling is hot in center (about 15 minutes; about 30 minutes if refrigerated). Uncover and sprinkle with remaining 1 cup cheese; continue to bake until cheese is melted (about 10 more minutes).

Meanwhile, reheat Tomatillo Sauce. To serve, spoon sauce into a large rimmed serving dish (or divide among 6 dinner plates). Set enchiladas on sauce. Spoon sour cream down center of enchiladas, sprinkle with cilantro, and garnish with tomatillo slices. Makes 6 servings.

Tomatillo Sauce. Heat ⅓ cup **salad oil** in a 3- to 4-quart pan over medium-high heat. Add 2 medium-size **onions,** chopped; cook, stirring often, until soft (about 4 minutes). Stir in 1 large can (about 7 oz.) **diced green chiles;** 2 cans (about 13 oz. *each*) **tomatillos,** drained; 1 cup **chicken broth;** 3 tablespoons **lime juice;** 2 teaspoons *each* **dry oregano** and **sugar;** and 1 teaspoon **ground cumin.** Bring to a boil; then reduce heat and simmer, stirring occasionally, for 25 minutes.

Spoon sauce into a blender or food processor; whirl until smooth. Season to taste with salt. If made ahead, cover and refrigerate until next day.

Per serving: 851 calories (58 percent from fat), 49 g protein, 42 g carbohydrates, 55 g total fat (11 g saturated fat), 154 mg cholesterol, 1,062 mg sodium

Chicken Tetrazzini

Luisa Tetrazzini, considered the greatest coloratura soprano of the turn-of-the-century era, was the toast of San Francisco. The chef of the Palace Hotel was so inspired by her lovely voice that he created a pasta dish in her honor. Though originally made with chicken, this creamy favorite often includes turkey or seafood today.

⅓ **cup butter or margarine**

5 **tablespoons all-purpose flour**

2½ **cups chicken broth**

1¼ **cups half-and-half**

½ **cup dry white wine**

¾ **cup grated Parmesan cheese**

¾ **pound mushrooms, sliced**

8 **ounces dry pasta strands such as spaghetti or tagliarini, cooked and drained**

3 **to 4 cups thinly sliced cooked chicken or turkey**
  Salt

Melt 2 tablespoons of the butter in a medium-size pan over medium heat. Add flour and cook, stirring, for 1 minute (do not brown). Remove from heat and gradually stir in broth, half-and-half, and wine. Then return to heat and cook, stirring constantly, for 3 minutes. Stir in ½ cup of the cheese. Measure out 1 cup of the sauce and set aside. Stir remaining ¼ cup cheese into remaining sauce. Remove from heat.

Melt remaining butter in a wide frying pan over medium heat. Add mushrooms and cook, stirring often, until lightly browned. Set aside a few mushroom slices; then add remaining mushrooms, pasta, and chicken to sauce in pan. Season mixture to taste with salt and pour into a large, shallow baking pan. Spoon reserved 1 cup sauce evenly over chicken mixture; then scatter reserved mushroom slices over top.

Bake in a 375° oven until bubbly and heated through (about 15 min-

utes). Then broil 4 to 5 inches below heat just until top is lightly browned. Makes 6 to 8 servings.

Per serving: 467 calories (44 percent from fat), 32 g protein, 33 g carbohydrates, 23 g total fat (12 g saturated fat), 108 mg cholesterol, 683 mg sodium

Chicken Yogurt Enchilada Bake

Yogurt stands in for the original sour cream in this updated version of a 1950s-style layered casserole.

¼ **cup butter or margarine**

¼ **cup all-purpose flour**

2 **cups chicken broth**

1 **cup plain yogurt**

1 **large can (about 7 oz.) diced green chiles**

12 **corn tortillas**

2 **cups bite-size pieces of cooked chicken**

1 **small onion, chopped**

2 **cups (about 8 oz.) shredded jack cheese**

¼ **cup thinly sliced green onions**

Melt butter in a 1½- to 2-quart pan over medium heat. Add flour and cook, stirring, for 1 minute (do not brown). Gradually stir in broth; bring sauce to a boil, stirring constantly until smooth. Remove from heat and stir in yogurt and chiles. Spread a third of the sauce evenly over bottom of a 9- by 13-inch baking pan.

Quickly dip tortillas in water. Drain briefly and cut into 1-inch strips. Scatter half the tortilla strips

over sauce, then cover evenly with chicken, chopped onion, two-thirds of the cheese, and half the remaining sauce. Top with remaining tortilla strips, remaining sauce, and remaining cheese. Cover and bake in a 400° oven until heated through (30 to 35 minutes); sprinkle with green onions. Makes 6 servings.

Per serving: 476 calories (48 percent from fat), 29 g protein, 34 g carbohydrates, 26 g total fat (7 g saturated fat), 100 mg cholesterol, 951 mg sodium

Chicken Pot Pie

Meat pie—a savory supper under a crust—is an old-fashioned dish now enjoying a revival in the West. Though the idea probably originated in England, the pot pie long ago became an American classic, one of this country's most cherished comfort foods.

Cream Cheese Pastry (page 77); or purchased pastry shell for a single-crust 9-inch pie, unbaked

1 **tablespoon butter or margarine**

1 **large onion, finely chopped**

1 **teaspoon dry thyme**

1 **dry bay leaf**

⅓ **cup water**

¾ **cup chicken broth**

3 **tablespoons cornstarch**

5 **cups cooked chicken thigh chunks (about 2 lbs. raw skinless, boneless chicken thighs)**

1½ **cups thinly sliced carrots**

1 **package (about 10 oz.) frozen tiny peas**

1 **cup plain nonfat yogurt**

1 **cup (about 4 oz.) shredded Cheddar cheese**

1 **egg, beaten**

Prepare Cream Cheese Pastry and refrigerate.

Melt butter in a 4- to 5-quart pan over medium heat. Add onion, thyme, and bay leaf; cook, stirring often, until onion is lightly browned (10 to 12 minutes). Add water and stir to scrape browned bits free; cook, stirring, until liquid has evaporated.

Mix broth with cornstarch. Add chicken, carrots, peas, yogurt, and two-thirds of the cornstarch mixture to pan; bring to a boil, stirring. Let cool. Stir in remaining cornstarch mixture. Pour chicken mixture into a 9-inch pie pan or dish. (At this point, you may cover and refrigerate until next day.)

Sprinkle chicken mixture with cheese. On a lightly floured board, roll out pastry to a 10-inch round. With a cookie cutter, cut 1 or 2 pieces from center of pastry; reserve cutouts. Lay pastry over filling; fold edges under and press firmly against pan to seal. Flute edges decoratively and top with cutouts. (At this point, you may cover and refrigerate for up to 2 days if filling is fresh, up to 1 day if filling was made a day ahead.)

Set pie in a 10- by 15-inch rimmed baking pan. Brush pastry and cutouts with egg. Bake on lowest rack of a 400° oven until pastry is well browned and filling is hot in center (40 to 55 minutes). If edges or cutouts darken excessively before center of crust is brown, drape edges and cover cutouts with foil.

Serve pie hot. Or, if made ahead, let cool; then cover and refrigerate until next day. To reheat pie, place it in a 350° oven; heat, uncovered, until filling is hot in center (30 to 40 minutes). Lay foil over crust if it begins to darken. Makes 8 servings.

Per serving: 494 calories (48 percent from fat), 35 g protein, 29 g carbohydrates, 26 g total fat (14 g saturated fat), 205 mg cholesterol, 541 mg sodium

Turkey Scaloppine with Peppers

For light cuisine at its best, try these turkey breast cutlets. The meat is pounded out thin, quickly sautéed, and topped with strips of red or yellow bell pepper for a splash of bright color.

- **1 pound boneless turkey breast, cut into ¼-inch-thick slices**
- **2 tablespoons butter or margarine**
- **3 medium-size red or yellow bell peppers, seeded and cut into ¼-inch-wide strips**
- **2 tablespoons all-purpose flour**
- **1 tablespoon salad oil**
- **⅓ cup shredded Swiss or fontina cheese**
  Pepper
  Lemon wedges

Rinse turkey and pat dry. Place each turkey slice between 2 sheets of plastic wrap or wax paper; pound with a flat-surfaced mallet until about ⅛ inch thick. (At this point, you may lay pounded slices slightly apart in single layers between pieces of wax paper or plastic wrap, then cover and refrigerate for up to 2 days.)

Melt 1 tablespoon of the butter in a wide frying pan over medium heat. Add bell peppers; cook, stirring often, until limp (10 to 12 minutes). Remove from pan with a slotted spoon.

Dust turkey slices with flour. Melt remaining 1 tablespoon butter in oil in frying pan over medium-high heat. Add turkey, a few pieces at a time (do not crowd pan); cook, turning once, until lightly browned on both sides (1½ to 2 minutes). As turkey is cooked, transfer it to an ovenproof serving dish, overlapping pieces slightly; keep warm.

When all turkey has been cooked, spoon bell peppers over top and sprinkle evenly with cheese. Bake in a 400° oven just until cheese is melted (3 to 5 minutes). Season to taste with pepper and serve with lemon wedges. Makes 4 servings.

Per serving: 271 calories (42 percent from fat), 32 g protein, 7 g carbohydrates, 13 g total fat (6 g saturated fat), 95 mg cholesterol, 140 mg sodium

Raspberry-glazed Turkey Tenderloins

A fruit glaze keeps lean turkey breast tenderloins moist during broiling. To balance the berry sweetness, you might serve a lightly dressed green salad alongside.

- **4 turkey breast tenderloins (about 2¼ lbs. *total*)**
- **½ cup seedless raspberry jam**
- **⅓ cup raspberry vinegar**
- **¼ cup Dijon mustard**
- **1 teaspoon grated orange peel**
- **½ teaspoon dry thyme**

Rinse turkey and pat dry; set aside.

In a 2- to 3-quart pan, whisk together jam, vinegar, mustard, orange peel, and thyme. Bring to a boil over high heat; then boil, stirring, until reduced by about a fourth. Reserve about ½ cup of the glaze; brush some of the remaining glaze over turkey.

Set turkey on a rack in a shallow baking pan. Broil about 4 inches below heat, turning and basting once with remaining glaze, until meat in thickest part is no longer pink; cut to test (8 to 10 minutes). To serve, cut across the grain into thin slices and arrange on dinner plates. Offer reserved ½ cup glaze to spoon over individual servings. Makes 4 to 6 servings.

Per serving: 331 calories (6 percent from fat), 50 g protein, 25 g carbohydrates, 2 g total fat (0.4 g saturated fat), 127 mg cholesterol, 464 mg sodium

Pot-roasted Turkey

Turkey continues to be one of the best buys at the meat counter, and dark-meat cuts are usually the most economical of parts. The legs and thighs are especially moist and flavorful when slowly pot-roasted, either in the oven or on the range.

- **4 pounds turkey thighs, drumsticks, or hindquarters**
- **1 tablespoon salad oil**
- **2 large onions, chopped**
- **2 cloves garlic, minced or pressed**
- **1 cup dry red wine or chicken broth**
- **1 can (about 10¾ oz.) condensed cream of mushroom soup**
- **1 teaspoon *each* dry basil, dry thyme, and ground sage**
- **1 tablespoon Dijon mustard**
- **8 *each* small whole carrots and small thin-skinned potatoes, scrubbed**
- **8 small white boiling onions, peeled**
- **3 tablespoons cornstarch blended with 3 tablespoons cold water**
- **Salt and pepper**

Rinse turkey and pat dry.

Heat oil in a wide frying pan over medium-high heat. Add turkey, a few pieces at a time (do not crowd pan); cook, turning as needed, until browned on all sides. With a slotted spoon or tongs, transfer turkey pieces to a 6- to 8-quart baking pan; set aside.

Add chopped onions and garlic to frying pan; cook, stirring often, until onions are soft (about 5 minutes). Then add wine, soup, basil, thyme, sage, and mustard. Bring to a boil, stirring often; pour over turkey. Cover and bake in a 325° oven (or simmer over medium-low heat) for 1 hour.

Add carrots, potatoes, and boiling onions to pan, pushing vegetables down into liquid. Cover and continue to bake (or simmer) until turkey and vegetables are tender when pierced (1 to 1½ more hours).

With a slotted spoon, transfer turkey and vegetables to a serving dish; cover and keep warm. Skim and discard fat from cooking liquid, then blend in cornstarch mixture. Cook, stirring, until sauce boils and thickens. Season to taste with salt and pepper.

Spoon a small amount of sauce over turkey. Offer remaining sauce to spoon over individual servings. Makes 8 servings.

Per serving: 418 calories (37 percent from fat), 38 g protein, 27 g carbohydrates, 17 g total fat (5 g saturated fat), 128 mg cholesterol, 524 mg sodium

Braised Turkey Legs

Braising is a good way to bring out the rich flavor of dark-meat turkey. Mashed Potato Casserole (page 147), a natural partner for saucy dishes, is a nice accompaniment to the meat and its herb-seasoned wine sauce.

- **4 turkey drumsticks (about 5 lbs. total)**
- **½ cup all-purpose flour**
- **1 teaspoon *each* salt and dry oregano**
- **½ teaspoon pepper**
- **¼ cup olive oil or salad oil**
- **2 large onions, chopped**
- **2 cloves garlic, minced or pressed**
- **1 cup chicken broth**
- **½ cup dry red wine**
- **1 dry bay leaf**
- **½ teaspoon *each* dry thyme and dry rosemary**

Rinse turkey and pat dry. In a shallow bowl, mix flour, salt, oregano, and pepper. Dust turkey with flour mixture; set remaining flour mixture aside.

Heat oil in a wide frying pan over medium heat. Add turkey, a few pieces at a time (do not crowd pan); cook, turning as needed, until browned on all sides. Transfer turkey to a 4- to 6-quart baking pan. Add onions and garlic to frying pan; cook, stirring often, until onions are soft (about 5 minutes). Add broth and wine, stirring to scrape browned bits free. Then add bay leaf, thyme, and rosemary.

Pour broth mixture over turkey, cover, and bake in a 350° oven until turkey is very tender when pierced (2 to 2½ hours).

Lift turkey from baking pan and arrange in a serving dish. Measure reserved flour mixture and blend with an equal amount of cold water; stir into pan juices. Cook, stirring, until sauce boils and thickens. Spoon some of the sauce over turkey; pour remainder into a small serving dish and offer to spoon over individual servings. Makes 4 servings.

Per serving: 801 calories (47 percent from fat), 78 g protein, 24 g carbohydrates, 40 g total fat (10 g saturated fat), 270 mg cholesterol, 1,084 mg sodium

WESTERN CLASSIC
Turkey Loco

Westerners sometimes choose to barbecue the Thanksgiving turkey, freeing the kitchen for other uses. To make turkey *loco,* you use a popular Mexican technique for barbecuing chicken—the bird is split and butterflied to cook more quickly. Lime juice adds tart flavor to the crisp, burnished skin.

1 **turkey (10 to 12 lbs.)**
   About 4 limes, cut into halves
   About 4 teaspoons dry oregano
   Salt and pepper

Reserve turkey neck and giblets for other uses, if desired. Using poultry shears or a sharp, heavy knife, cut through turkey down length of backbone. Pull turkey open and lay it on a flat surface, breast down; press to flatten (some ribs will crack). Pull off and discard lumps of fat. Rinse turkey and pat dry. (At this point, you may cover and refrigerate until next day.)

Prepare barbecue as directed in "Indirect Grilling" (page 70). Lay flattened bird, breast up, on grill above drip pan. Squeeze and rub 1 or 2 lime halves over turkey; sprinkle with oregano, then sprinkle lightly with salt and pepper. Cover barbecue and adjust vents as needed to maintain an even heat. Every 30 minutes, squeeze and rub 1 or 2 more lime halves over turkey and add 5 or 6 briquets to each side of coals to maintain a constant temperature. Cook turkey until a meat thermometer inserted in thickest part of breast (not touching bone) registers 170°F (1½ to 2 hours).

Transfer turkey to a platter. To carve, cut off wings and slice breast; cut off legs and slice meat from thighs. Makes 12 to 16 servings.

Per serving: 299 calories (26 percent from fat), 52 g protein, 1 g carbohydrates, 8 g total fat (3 g saturated fat), 135 mg cholesterol, 130 mg sodium

WESTERN CLASSIC

Turkey Enchiladas with Sour Cream

Enchiladas offer an ideal way to use Thanksgiving leftovers. Fill corn tortillas with a blend of shredded turkey, sour cream, and Cheddar; then top with chile-seasoned tomato sauce.

2 **tablespoons olive oil or salad oil**
2 **small cans (about 4 oz. *each*) diced green chiles**
1 **large clove garlic, minced**
1½ **pounds tomatoes, peeled and chopped**
2 **cups chopped onions**
½ **teaspoon dry oregano**
½ **cup water**
   Salt
3 **cups shredded cooked turkey**
2 **cups sour cream**
2 **cups (about 8 oz.) shredded Cheddar cheese**
⅓ **cup salad oil**
12 **corn tortillas**

Heat the 2 tablespoons oil in a wide frying pan over medium heat. Add chiles and garlic; cook, stirring, for 3 minutes. Add tomatoes, onions, oregano, and water. Bring to a simmer; then simmer, uncovered, stirring often, until thick (about 30 minutes). Remove from heat, season to taste with salt, and set aside.

In a medium-size bowl, stir together turkey, sour cream, and cheese. Season turkey mixture to taste with salt. Set aside.

In a small frying pan, heat the ⅓ cup oil over medium heat; keep hot. Working with one tortilla at a time, heat each tortilla in oil until it blisters and becomes limp (this takes just a few seconds). Using tongs, lift tortilla from oil; drain briefly on paper towels, then fill with a twelfth of the turkey mixture and roll to enclose. Arrange filled tortillas, side by side and seam side down, in a large, shallow baking pan. Pour tomato-chile sauce evenly over enchiladas and bake in a 350° oven until filling is hot in center (about 20 minutes). Makes 6 servings.

Per serving: 718 calories (58 percent from fat), 37 g protein, 39 g carbohydrates, 47 g total fat (21 g saturated fat), 127 mg cholesterol, 649 mg sodium

Grilled Game Hens with Jalapeño Jelly Glaze

Jalapeño jelly, available in most well-stocked supermarkets and specialty stores, makes a sticky, delicately spicy glaze for barbecued game hens. Halving the hens ensures quick, even cooking on the grill—and lets you make a light dinner for six from just three birds.

3 **Rock Cornish game hens (about 1½ lbs. *each*), thawed if frozen**
2 **tablespoons butter or margarine**
½ **cup jalapeño jelly**
1½ **tablespoons lime juice**

Reserve game hen necks and giblets for other uses, if desired. Using poultry shears or a sharp, heavy knife, cut each game hen in half through backbone and breastbone. Rinse hens and pat dry.

In a small pan, combine butter and jelly over medium-high heat; stir until melted. Remove from heat and stir in lime juice.

Place hen halves, skin side up, on a grill 4 to 6 inches above a solid bed of medium-hot coals. Cook, turning several times and basting with jelly mixture during last 15 minutes, until hens are browned and meat near thighbone is no longer pink; cut to test (30 to 40 minutes). Makes 6 servings.

Per serving: 461 calories (48 percent from fat), 41 g protein, 18 g carbohydrates, 24 g total fat (8 g saturated fat), 142 mg cholesterol, 167 mg sodium

Roast Duckling with Orange Sauce

Classic French *canard à l'orange* takes advantage of the delightful flavor compatibility of duck and citrus fruit. The caramel-colored sauce, scented with orange peel, is a rich complement to the dark, dense, full-flavored meat.

3 oranges
6½ cups water
1 duckling (4½ to 5 lbs.)
  Salt
1 onion, chopped
1 carrot, chopped
1 dry bay leaf
2 teaspoons instant chicken bouillon
¼ cup red wine vinegar
3 tablespoons sugar
½ cup port or Madeira
2 tablespoons cornstarch blended with ¼ cup cold water
1 tablespoon orange-flavored liqueur
  Pepper
1 tablespoon butter or margarine

Pare off thin outer layer of peel (colored part only) from oranges with a vegetable peeler, then cut peel into slivers about ¹⁄₁₆ inch wide and 1 inch long. In a small pan, bring 3 cups of the water to a boil; add slivered orange peel, cover, and simmer for 15 minutes. Drain peel and set aside.

Cut all remaining peel and white membrane from oranges. Cut between segments; lift segments free, cover, and refrigerate.

Remove duckling neck and giblets; reserve neck for other uses and set giblets aside. Pull off and discard lumps of fat from duckling; then rinse duckling inside and out and pat dry. Sprinkle inside and out with 1½ teaspoons salt. Sprinkle a third of the drained orange peel inside duckling. Tie legs and tail together. Place duckling breast down; with a long metal skewer, fasten neck skin to back, closing cavity securely. Tuck wingtips behind body. Prick skin all over at ½-inch intervals. Place duckling, breast down, on a rack in a shallow baking pan.

Roast duckling in a 375° oven for 30 minutes. Siphon or spoon out fat from pan; add ½ cup of the water, onion, and carrot to pan. Turn duckling breast up and continue to roast until legs move freely (about 1½ more hours). Transfer duckling to a serving dish and keep warm. Reserve pan drippings.

While duckling is roasting, combine giblets, ½ teaspoon salt, bay leaf, and remaining 3 cups water in a small pan. Bring to a boil; then reduce heat, cover, and simmer until giblets are tender when pierced (about 1½ hours). Remove giblets and bay leaf; boil broth, uncovered, over high heat until reduced to 2 cups. Remove from heat and add bouillon. In another small pan, combine vinegar and sugar. Simmer over medium-low heat until liquid turns a caramel color; then pour vinegar mixture into prepared duckling broth.

Skim and discard fat from roasting pan. Place pan over high heat and add port, stirring to scrape browned bits free. Pour port mixture through a fine wire strainer set over a bowl; discard vegetables. Add strained port mixture to duckling broth and bring to a boil. Stir in cornstarch mixture. Cook, stirring constantly, until sauce is thick and smooth. Stir in remaining orange peel and liqueur, then season sauce to taste with salt and pepper and blend in butter until melted. Pour sauce into a small serving dish.

Garnish duckling with orange segments. Offer sauce to spoon over individual servings. Makes 4 servings.

Per serving: 1,024 calories (65 percent from fat), 51 g protein, 35 g carbohydrates, 71 g total fat (25 g saturated fat), 275 mg cholesterol, 1,774 mg sodium

---

DELICIOUS DUCK

These days, a duck dinner only requires a trip to the meat market—you don't have to crouch for hours in a blind, the cold early-morning drizzle running down your neck, to bring home the main course! Ducks are fashionable fare today, and large, meaty farm-raised birds are available in variety. Once produced primarily in France, China, and New York, ducks are now bred in California and other Western states as well. The modern domestic birds are all descendants of either of two species—mallard or muscovy. In the United States, the most popular breed is the large, white-feathered Peking duck (also known as Long Island duck).

Roast Goose with Brandied Fruit Compote

Roast goose has been a holiday favorite for centuries. We like to serve the succulent bird with a spicy compote of poached dried fruit.

Brandied Fruit Compote (recipe follows)
1 **goose (9 to 11 lbs.)**
1 *each* **orange and lemon, thinly sliced**

Prepare Brandied Fruit Compote; after stirring in brandy, cover and refrigerate as directed.

Reserve goose neck and giblets for other uses, if desired. Pull off and discard lumps of fat. Rinse goose inside and out; pat dry. Place orange and lemon slices in body and neck cavities.

Place bird breast down and fasten neck skin to back with a long metal skewer, closing cavity securely. Then turn bird on its back. Tuck in tail, then fold skin over cavity; close with metal skewers. Prick skin all over at 1-inch intervals.

Place goose, breast down, on a rack in a large, shallow roasting pan. Roast in a 400° oven for 1 hour. Every 30 minutes, siphon or spoon out fat from pan.

After 1 hour, turn goose breast up. Reduce oven temperature to 325° and continue to roast until meat near thighbone is no longer pink; cut to test (1½ to 2 more hours). Continue to siphon or spoon out fat from pan every 30 minutes.

Reheat and thicken compote as directed. Spoon into a serving dish; let cool slightly. Offer compote to spoon over goose. Makes 8 servings.

Brandied Fruit Compote. In a 3-quart pan, combine 2 cups **water,** ½ cup **orange juice,** 3 tablespoons **honey,** 1 teaspoon **grated orange peel,** 5 whole **allspice,** ¼ teaspoon **ground ginger,** and 1 **cinnamon stick** (about 2 inches long). Stir in ½ cup **raisins;** 1 small **apple,** thinly sliced; and 2 cups **mixed dried fruit.** Bring to a boil over high heat; then reduce heat, cover, and simmer for 3 minutes. Remove from heat; stir in ½ cup **brandy** or orange juice. Let cool, then cover and refrigerate for at least 4 hours or until next day.

Stir together ½ cup of the fruit liquid and 1 tablespoon **cornstarch;** then stir into fruit. Cook over medium-high heat, stirring, until thickened. Makes 8 servings.

Per serving of goose: 816 calories (66 percent from fat), 67 g protein, 0.9 g carbohydrates, 58 g total fat (18 g saturated fat), 243 mg cholesterol, 187 mg sodium

Per serving of Brandied Fruit Compote: 200 calories (1 percent from fat), 1 g protein, 43 g carbohydrates, 0.3 g total fat (0 g saturated fat), 0 mg cholesterol, 9 mg sodium

Rabbit in Mustard Sauce

Rabbit lends itself admirably to rich and flavorful sauces. Here, serving-size pieces are browned in butter, flamed in brandy, and baked in a mustard cream sauce.

2 **rabbits (about 2½ lbs. *each*), cut up**
  Salt
  About ⅓ cup all-purpose flour
½ **cup (¼ lb.) butter or margarine**
3 **tablespoons brandy, warmed**
½ **cup thinly sliced green onions**
¼ **cup minced parsley**
1 **pound small whole mushrooms; or 1 pound large mushrooms, quartered**
2 **tablespoons Dijon mustard**
2 **cups whipping cream**
2 **tablespoons lemon juice**
3 **egg yolks, lightly beaten**
  Chopped parsley

Rinse rabbit and pat dry. Sprinkle rabbit pieces with salt, then dust with flour. Melt 5 to 6 tablespoons of the butter in a wide frying pan over medium-high heat. Add rabbit, a few pieces at a time (do not crowd pan); cook, turning as needed, until browned on all sides.

Transfer rabbit to a shallow 3½- to 4-quart baking pan. Move frying pan into an open area, away from exhaust fans and flammable items. Add brandy and ignite; shake or tilt pan until flame dies. Pour brandy mixture over rabbit in baking pan; set aside.

Melt remaining 2 to 3 tablespoons butter in frying pan over medium heat. Add onions, minced parsley, and mushrooms; cook, stirring often, until onions are soft (about 5 minutes). Stir in mustard, cream, and lemon juice and bring to a boil. Pour sauce over rabbit. Cover and bake in a 375° oven until rabbit is tender when pierced (45 to 55 minutes).

Drain cooking liquid into a wide frying pan and bring to a boil; boil for 1 minute. Beat some of the hot liquid into egg yolks, then return yolk mixture to pan. Cook, stirring constantly, until sauce is thickened; do not boil. Season to taste with salt. Transfer rabbit to a serving dish. Pour sauce over rabbit and sprinkle with chopped parsley. Makes 6 to 8 servings.

Per serving: 731 calories (64 percent from fat), 54 g protein, 11 g carbohydrates, 51 g total fat (26 g saturated fat), 343 mg cholesterol, 395 mg sodium

When deciding what to have for dinner, enterprising cooks want recipes that are low in fat, low in cost, and quick to prepare. Dishes made with skinless, boneless pieces of chicken or turkey usually meet all three demands—one reason why these poultry entrées are among the most popular main-course choices today.

Unlike most red meats, poultry doesn't have fat marbled through its flesh: most of the fat is in the skin or just beneath, where it's easily removed. A ¼-pound serving of skinned chicken or turkey breast has less than 2 grams of fat and under 130 calories.

When you're deciding how to cook skinless and boneless poultry, focus on techniques that make the most of its quick-cooking convenience and good, lean nutrition. We've experimented with a number of suitable methods, including microwaving, steeping, barbecuing, and stir-frying. Replacing ground chuck or sirloin with ground poultry is another way to lighten up rich recipes without sacrificing flavor.

Microwaving. The microwave is great for cooking poultry to use in salads, sandwiches, or other dishes calling for cooked meat. Follow the instructions below to microwave 1 pound of skinless, boneless chicken or turkey breast or chicken thighs. Rinse poultry pieces and pat dry, then cook in a 9-inch microwave-safe dish as directed below. Let all cuts of meat stand, covered, for 5 minutes after cooking time is complete.

Arrange *chicken or turkey breast* in a single layer in dish; pat turkey breast to give it an even thickness. Cover with microwave-safe plastic wrap and microwave on **HIGH (100%)**, turning once halfway through cooking time, for about 5 minutes for chicken breast halves, about 9 minutes for turkey breast. Meat should no longer be pink in center; cut to test.

Cut each *turkey tenderloin* in half lengthwise; cut away tendon in center. Fold thin ends under to make meat evenly thick. Cover with microwave-safe plastic wrap and microwave on **HIGH (100%)** for 8 minutes, giving dish a half-turn halfway through cooking time. Meat should no longer be pink in thickest part; cut to test.

Roll *chicken thighs* into compact shapes and arrange in dish. Cover with microwave-safe plastic wrap and microwave on **HIGH (100%)** for 7 minutes, turning pieces so center parts face outward halfway through cooking time. Meat should no longer be pink in thickest part; cut to test.

Steeping. Adapted from a classic Chinese cooking method, steeping involves bringing water to a boil, then turning off the heat, immersing food in the hot water, and letting it stand until done. It's a gentle, low-temperature technique that results in especially moist and tender meat. Lively seasonings distinguish the recipe below. Use the meat in a salad, as suggested; or try it in sandwiches.

Steeped Poultry with Chili & Anise

1 pound skinless, boneless chicken breasts, chicken thighs, or turkey breast

4 cups water

2 cups chicken broth

¼ cup *each* chili powder and firmly packed brown sugar

2 teaspoons dry oregano

1 star anise or 1 teaspoon anise seeds

3 tablespoons *each* olive oil and red wine vinegar

2 tablespoons *each* chopped cilantro and sliced green onion

12 to 16 large butter lettuce leaves, rinsed and crisped
Red pickled peppers

Rinse poultry and pat dry. *If using chicken breast halves or thighs,* cook as is. *If using a turkey breast piece,* cut across the grain into 1-inch-thick pieces. *If using turkey tenderloins,* place meat between 2 sheets of plastic wrap or wax paper; pound with a flat-surfaced mallet until ½ to ¾ inch thick.

In a 4- to 5-quart pan with a tight-fitting lid, combine water, broth, chili powder, sugar, oregano, and anise; bring to a boil. Remove pan from heat and quickly immerse poultry pieces, opened out flat, in water. Cover pan tightly and let stand for 15 minutes; do not uncover until this time is up. To check doneness, cut meat in thickest part; it should no longer look pink. If meat is not done, return it to hot water, cover, and let steep for a few more minutes.

Drain meat, reserving 2 cups of the steeping liquid. Boil reserved liquid over high heat until reduced to ⅓ cup; as liquid becomes concentrated, watch carefully to prevent scorching. Serve meat warm; or, to serve cold, cover meat and liquid and refrigerate separately for up to 2 days.

To serve, prepare a dressing by mixing reduced liquid with oil, vinegar, cilantro, and onion. Cut poultry pieces across the grain into thin slanting slices. Divide lettuce among 4 salad plates. Top with meat; spoon dressing over all. Garnish with peppers.

Per serving: 249 calories (44 percent from fat), 27 g protein, 7 g carbohydrates, 12 g total fat (2 g saturated fat), 66 mg cholesterol, 183 mg sodium

Barbecuing. The barbecue imparts a lightly smoky savor to poultry—with no added fat. For extra flavor, coat the meat with a baste or marinade (see page 73). You can grill poultry in a number of ways: thread cubes or strips on thin skewers; pound boneless breasts, grill quickly, and serve with a sprinkle of lemon juice, salt, and pepper; or barbecue ground turkey or chicken patties for a lighter rendition of the traditional hamburger.

In this recipe, skinless, boneless poultry breast is wrapped in prosciutto and romaine to help seal in moisture and add flavor.

Grilled Poultry in Romaine Wraps

Green Dressing (recipe follows)

4 skinless, boneless chicken breast halves (about 1½ lbs. *total*); or 1 pound skinless, boneless turkey breast, cut into 4 equal-size logs (*each* 1 to 1½ inches thick)

4 medium-size romaine lettuce leaves

4 thin slices prosciutto (about 2½ oz. *total*)

Salt and pepper

Prepare Green Dressing and set aside. Rinse poultry and pat dry.

In a wide frying pan, bring 1 inch of water to a boil. Add lettuce; cook for 1 minute. Lift out, immerse in cold water until cool, drain, and pat dry.

Wrap each chicken or turkey piece in one slice of prosciutto and one lettuce leaf. Place bundles on a grill 4 to 6 inches above a solid bed of medium-hot coals. Cook, turning occasionally, until meat in thickest part is no longer pink; cut to test (about 20 minutes for chicken, about 25 minutes for turkey).

Cut bundles across the grain into 1-inch-thick slices. Arrange slices, cut side up, on 4 dinner plates. Pour Green Dressing equally over poultry. Season to taste with salt and pepper. Makes 4 servings.

Green Dressing. In a blender or food processor, combine ⅓ cup **olive oil** or salad oil, ¼ cup **white wine vinegar,** 2 tablespoons minced **onion,** 1 tablespoon minced **parsley,** and 2 teaspoons *each* minced **fresh sage** and **fresh thyme** (or ¾ teaspoon *each* of the dry herbs). Makes ½ cup.

Per serving of poultry: 229 calories (19 percent from fat), 44 g protein, 0.2 g carbohydrates, 5 g total fat (1 g saturated fat), 113 mg cholesterol, 439 mg sodium

Per tablespoon of Green Dressing: 81 calories (97 percent from fat), 0 g protein, 0.6 g carbohydrates, 9 g total fat (1 g saturated fat), 0 mg cholesterol, 0.3 mg sodium

Stir-frying. Stir-frying—quickly cooking meat over high heat in a little oil—is one of the most popular ways to cook bite-size pieces of skinless, boneless poultry. Slivered Chicken & Walnuts (page 88), Kung Pao Chicken (page 88), and Cashew Chicken (page 92) are examples of our favorite poultry stir-fries.

Ground poultry. Ground turkey and chicken are now sold in most supermarkets; you can also have the meat ground for you at a butcher shop. Most ground poultry, though it consists primarily of dark meat, has under 15 percent fat—quite a low proportion, when you consider that ground beef can contain up to 30 percent fat. Ground chicken is milder tasting than turkey and usually slightly moister, but you can use the two interchangeably.

In this lowfat recipe, a savory turkey sauce is served over thin strands of spaghetti squash.

Ground Turkey Sauce with Spaghetti Squash

1 medium-size spaghetti squash (1½ to 2 lbs.)

1 pound ground turkey

1 large onion, finely chopped

2 cloves garlic, minced or pressed

6 ounces mushrooms, sliced

1 medium-size carrot, chopped

1 large can (about 15 oz.) and 1 small can (about 8 oz.) tomato sauce

1½ teaspoons dry oregano

1 teaspoon dry basil

½ teaspoon *each* sugar and salt

¼ teaspoon pepper

1 dry bay leaf

¼ cup grated Parmesan cheese

Pierce squash in several places with a fork. Place on a rimmed baking sheet. Bake in a 350° oven, turning after 45 minutes, until shell is tender when pierced (1¼ to 1½ hours).

About 45 minutes before squash is done, crumble turkey into a wide nonstick frying pan. Add onion, garlic, mushrooms, and carrot. Cook over medium heat, stirring often, until almost all liquid has evaporated. Stir in all tomato sauce, oregano, basil, sugar, salt, pepper, and bay leaf; cover and simmer for 30 minutes. Uncover and boil gently, stirring occasionally, until thickened.

To serve, cut squash in half; scrape out and discard seeds. Loosen squash strands and scoop them into a serving bowl, mounding strands around edge of bowl. Spoon turkey sauce into center. Offer cheese to add to taste. Makes 4 servings.

Per serving: 327 calories (30 percent from fat), 27 g protein, 32 g carbohydrates, 11 g total fat (3 g saturated fat), 87 mg cholesterol, 1,494 mg sodium

FISH & SHELLFISH

*A*t Sunset, we've always designed our fish and shellfish recipes with the Western cook in mind. In years past, that meant a focus on local varieties—salmon, river trout, Dungeness crab, and small Pacific oysters—in addition to a few long-time classics such as sole and shrimp. Today, however, we've expanded our repertoire to reflect the growing number of seafood choices in modern markets. We now offer readers ideas for serving orange roughy, fresh tuna, shark, swordfish, and other once lesser-known types. • In this chapter, you'll find both traditional favorites and more innovative selections: creamy casseroles from the 1940s and '60s meet the lighter recipes popularized in the '80s and early '90s. Cooking methods vary, too, from familiar pan-frying and oven-baking to steaming, stir-frying, and smoking in a covered barbecue. (For more information on fish-cooking techniques, see pages 118–119.)

Fish Fillets with Almond Butter

Golden fried fish topped with lemony almond butter is a simple entrée that both family and guests will enjoy. If you like, you can brown the fish ahead, then bake it later.

2 to 2½ pounds firm-textured white-fleshed fish fillets (*each* ¾ to 1 inch thick)

3 eggs

2 tablespoons grated Parmesan cheese

1 tablespoon chopped parsley

½ teaspoon salt

¼ teaspoon pepper
   About ½ cup all-purpose flour
   About 3 tablespoons olive oil

½ cup (¼ lb.) butter or margarine

¼ cup sliced almonds

3 tablespoons lemon juice

2 tablespoons dry white wine

Rinse fish, pat dry, and set aside. In a shallow bowl, beat eggs until well blended. Stir in cheese, parsley, salt, and pepper. Place flour in another shallow bowl.

Heat 2 tablespoons of the oil in a wide frying pan over medium heat. Working with one piece of fish at a time, coat fish in flour and shake off excess; then coat with egg mixture and let excess drip off.

Place fish in oil, a few pieces at a time (do not crowd pan). Cook, turning once, until golden brown on both sides and just opaque but still moist in center; cut to test (6 to 10 minutes). Add more oil to pan as needed to prevent sticking. As fish is cooked, transfer it to a platter and keep warm.

Melt butter in a clean frying pan over medium heat. Add almonds; stir until golden brown (about 3 minutes). Remove from heat; stir in lemon juice and wine. Spoon sauce over fish and serve. Makes 6 to 8 servings.

Note: To brown ahead and bake later, follow directions for **Fish Fillets with Almond Butter,** but when browning fish, increase heat to medium-high and cook fish just until browned on both sides (about 2 minutes). Arrange fish in an ovenproof serving dish; cover loosely and set aside at room temperature for up to 1 hour. To serve, bake, uncovered, in a 375° oven until just opaque but still moist in thickest part; cut to test (about 10 minutes). Prepare sauce as directed; spoon over fish.

Per serving: 404 calories (59 percent from fat), 32 g protein, 8 g carbohydrates, 26 g total fat (11 g saturated fat), 188 mg cholesterol, 445 mg sodium

---

WESTERN CLASSIC

Baked Trout with Wild Rice Stuffing

Small river trout become company fare when filled with a savory wild rice stuffing. Mustard-glazed Carrots (page 140) are excellent alongside.

1 tablespoon butter or margarine

½ cup chopped onion

2½ cups cooked wild rice

1 teaspoon grated lemon peel

½ teaspoon dry thyme

¼ teaspoon pepper

2 tablespoons dry sherry (optional)

1 tablespoon lemon juice
   Salt

6 cleaned whole trout (6 to 8 oz. *each*), boned

3 tablespoons butter or margarine, melted

1 can (about 14½ oz.) sliced tomatoes, drained

2 tablespoons chopped parsley

Melt the 1 tablespoon butter in a wide frying pan over medium heat. Add onion and cook, stirring often, until soft (about 5 minutes). Add rice, lemon peel, thyme, and pepper; cook, stirring, for 3 minutes. Remove from heat and stir in sherry (if desired) and lemon juice. Season to taste with salt.

Rinse fish; pat dry. Fill cavities with stuffing. Arrange fish in a single layer in a greased 12- by 15-inch baking pan. Brush fish with a little of the melted butter; set remaining butter aside.

Bake in a 400° oven until fish is just opaque but still moist in thickest part; cut to test (about 15 minutes). Meanwhile, in a small pan, combine tomatoes, remaining melted butter, and parsley; cook over medium heat, stirring, until heated through (about 5 minutes).

To serve, transfer each fish to a dinner plate; top with tomato mixture. Makes 6 servings.

Per serving: 331 calories (43 percent from fat), 28 g protein, 19 g carbohydrates, 16 g total fat (6 g saturated fat), 89 mg cholesterol, 254 mg sodium

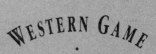

WESTERN GAME

The West's settlers found sustenance in the region's dense forests, bountiful rivers and ocean, and fertile soil. For these pioneers, fishing, hunting, and farming were a way of life. Many modern-day Westerners uphold this tradition, and *Sunset* responds to their interests with articles such as "From the Forest to the Frying Pan"—features that explore adventures in fishing, hunting, crabbing, and clamming.

Fish Fillets with Sherry-Mushroom Sauce

Any white fish works well in this recipe, but sea bass, lingcod, and rockfish are particularly good. If you enjoy spicier flavors, try adding a dash of red pepper flakes to the sauce.

1½ **pounds white-fleshed fish fillets (***each* **about ¾ inch thick), such as sea bass, lingcod, or rockfish**

2 **tablespoons olive oil, butter, or margarine**

¼ **pound mushrooms, thinly sliced**

1 **teaspoon cornstarch**

⅓ **cup water**

¼ **cup dry sherry**

1 **tablespoon soy sauce**

2 **cloves garlic, minced or pressed**

2 **teaspoons minced fresh ginger**

½ **cup sliced green onions**

Rinse fish, pat dry, and set aside.

Heat 1½ tablespoons of the oil in a wide frying pan over medium heat. Add mushrooms and cook, stirring often, until lightly browned (about 8 minutes); lift out with a slotted spoon and set aside.

Heat remaining 1½ teaspoons oil in pan over medium-high heat. Add fish, a few pieces at a time (do not crowd pan). Cover and cook, turning once, until just opaque but still moist in thickest part; cut to test (about 8 minutes). Transfer fish to a platter and keep warm.

In a small bowl, stir together cornstarch, water, sherry, soy sauce, garlic, and ginger. Pour cornstarch mixture into pan and stir to scrape browned bits free. Stir in mushrooms; bring to a boil, stirring. Stir in onions and pour sauce over fish. Makes 4 servings.

Per serving: 267 calories (38 percent from fat), 33 g protein, 6 g carbohydrates, 10 g total fat (2 g saturated fat), 70 mg cholesterol, 378 mg sodium

Grilled Fish Steaks with Mustard Sauce

Fish cooked over charcoal acquires a mellow smokiness—a flavor that's magnificently enhanced by robust toppings like the mustard sauce we suggest here. Choose firm-textured fish steaks; swordfish, halibut, sturgeon, and salmon are all good choices.

1½ **to 2 pounds firm-textured fish steaks (***each* **about 1 inch thick)**
   Olive oil or salad oil

¼ **cup *each* dry white wine and whipping cream**

1 **tablespoon Dijon mustard**

2 **tablespoons butter or margarine**
   Salt and pepper
   Chopped parsley

Rinse fish, pat dry, and brush lightly with oil. Place on a well-greased grill 4 to 6 inches above a solid bed of hot coals. Cook, turning once, until fish is just opaque but still moist in thickest part; cut to test (about 10 minutes). Transfer to a platter and keep warm.

In a wide frying pan, bring wine, cream, and mustard to a boil over high heat; boil, stirring occasionally, until reduced to ¼ cup. Remove from heat and whisk in butter; continue to whisk until sauce is thickened. Season sauce to taste with salt and pepper, spoon over fish, and sprinkle with parsley. Makes 4 to 6 servings.

Per serving: 289 calories (56 percent from fat), 30 g protein, 0.8 g carbohydrates, 17 g total fat (7 g saturated fat), 91 mg cholesterol, 249 mg sodium

Flounder & Crab Ramekins

Individual ramekins filled with a creamy-rich mixture of seafood and vegetables make an elegant entrée.

1 **to 1½ pounds flounder fillets (***each* **about ½ inch thick)**

1½ **cups water**

1 **dry bay leaf**

½ **lemon, thinly sliced**

¼ **teaspoon *each* salt and pepper**

¼ **cup butter or margarine**

1½ **cups thinly sliced celery**

½ **pound mushrooms, sliced**

1 **can (about 8 oz.) water chestnuts, drained and sliced**

1 **small green bell pepper, seeded and chopped**

5 **tablespoons all-purpose flour**

1½ **cups milk**

¼ **cup dry sherry (optional)**

1 **teaspoon dry savory**

2 **teaspoons Dijon mustard**

½ **teaspoon liquid hot pepper seasoning**

¼ **teaspoon pepper**

½ **pound crabmeat**
   Paprika
   Grated Parmesan cheese
   Chopped parsley

Rinse fish, pat dry, and cut into large pieces. In a wide frying pan, combine water, bay leaf, lemon, salt, and ¼ teaspoon pepper. Bring to a boil over high heat; then reduce heat, cover, and simmer for 5 minutes. Place fish in pan, cover, and simmer gently until just opaque but still moist in thickest part; cut to test (about 5 minutes). Lift out fish and drain on paper towels. If made ahead, let cool; then cover and refrigerate until next day. Break fish into bite-size pieces and set aside.

Discard poaching liquid from frying pan; then melt butter in pan over medium heat. Add celery, mushrooms, water chestnuts, and bell pepper; cook, stirring often, until mushrooms are soft (about 5 minutes). Stir in flour; cook, stirring, for 1 minute (do not brown). Remove from heat and gradually stir in milk. Then return to heat and cook, stirring constantly, until sauce boils and thickens. Add sherry (if desired), savory, mustard, hot pepper seasoning, and ¼ teaspoon pepper; stir until simmering. Remove from heat. Stir in fish and crab.

Spoon mixture into 6 greased 1- to 1½-cup ramekins or individual casseroles; sprinkle with paprika. (At this point, you may let cool, then cover and refrigerate until next day.)

Bake, uncovered, in a 350° oven until hot and bubbly (about 15 minutes; about 30 minutes if refrigerated). Sprinkle each serving with cheese and parsley. Makes 6 servings.

Per serving: 293 calories (37 percent from fat), 30 g protein, 17 g carbohydrates, 12 g total fat (6 g saturated fat), 112 mg cholesterol, 428 mg sodium

Grilled Soy-Lemon Halibut

True halibut—including both Pacific (Alaska or northern) and Atlantic varieties—is a firm-fleshed fish well suited to grilling. For a light entrée, soak thick steaks in a lemony teriyaki marinade, then cook quickly in a covered barbecue.

- 2 **pounds halibut, shark, or swordfish steaks (***each* ¾ **to 1 inch thick)**
- 2 **tablespoons butter or margarine, melted**
- 3 **tablespoons soy sauce**
- 2 **tablespoons lemon juice**
- 1 **tablespoon** *each* **sugar and Worcestershire**
- 1 **tablespoon minced fresh ginger or** ¾ **teaspoon ground ginger**
- 1 **clove garlic, minced or pressed**
- ⅛ **teaspoon pepper**
  Lemon wedges

Rinse fish and pat dry; cut into serving-size pieces, if necessary.

In a shallow dish, stir together butter, soy sauce, lemon juice, sugar, Worcestershire, ginger, garlic, and pepper. Add fish and turn to coat. Cover and refrigerate for 1 to 2 hours, turning occasionally.

Place fish on a lightly greased grill 4 to 6 inches above a solid bed of hot coals. Cover barbecue and adjust vents as needed to maintain an even heat. Cook, turning once, until fish is just opaque but still moist in thickest part; cut to test (8 to 10 minutes). Serve with lemon wedges. Makes 6 servings.

Per serving: 187 calories (33 percent from fat), 26 g protein, 4 g carbohydrates, 7 g total fat (3 g saturated fat), 50 mg cholesterol, 648 mg sodium

Orange Roughy Maître d'Hôtel

Thanks to its mild, unfishy flavor and firm, tender white flesh, orange roughy is a *Sunset* favorite. Simple enhancements like this one—a tart sauce of butter, lemon, and dill—are best for the delicate-tasting fillets.

- ⅓ **cup butter or margarine**
- ¼ **cup** *each* **lemon juice, chopped parsley, and snipped chives**
- 2 **teaspoons chopped fresh dill**
- ¼ **teaspoon ground red pepper (cayenne)**
- 2 **pounds orange roughy fillets (***each* ½ **to** ¾ **inch thick)**
  Salt

Melt butter in a small pan over medium heat. Stir in lemon juice, parsley, chives, dill, and red pepper; set aside.

Rinse fish, pat dry, and arrange in a single layer, overlapping slightly if necessary, in a 12- by 15-inch baking pan. Pour butter mixture over fish.

Bake in a 400° oven until fish is just opaque but still moist in thickest part; cut to test (8 to 10 minutes). Transfer

fish to a serving dish; keep warm. Bring juices in baking pan to a boil over high heat; boil, stirring occasionally, until reduced to about ½ cup. Drain any accumulated juices from fish into sauce; stir sauce and pour over fish. Season to taste with salt. Makes 6 servings.

Per serving: 284 calories (67 percent from fat), 22 g protein, 1 g carbohydrates, 21 g total fat (6 g saturated fat), 58 mg cholesterol, 202 mg sodium

Salmon Fillet with Mustard Glaze

A mustard glaze, lightly sweetened with honey, nicely complements rich-flavored broiled salmon.

- 1 **boned salmon fillet with skin (1½ to 2 lbs.)**
- 2 **tablespoons Dijon mustard**
- 1 **tablespoon** *each* **olive oil and honey**
- ¼ **teaspoon grated lemon peel**
- 1 **tablespoon lemon juice**
  Salt and pepper
  Parsley sprigs
  Lemon wedges

Set a sheet of heavy-duty foil in a 10- by 15-inch rimmed baking pan. Rinse fish and pat dry; then place, skin side down, on foil in pan. With scissors, cut through foil around fish; discard foil trimmings. In a small bowl, stir together mustard, oil, honey, lemon peel, and lemon juice. Brush fish with all of the mustard mixture.

Broil fish about 5 inches below heat until just opaque but still moist in thickest part; cut to test (9 to 12 minutes). Supporting fish with foil, transfer to a platter. Season to taste with salt and pepper. Garnish with parsley sprigs and serve with lemon wedges. Makes 4 to 6 servings.

Per serving: 270 calories (45 percent from fat), 32 g protein, 4 g carbohydrates, 13 g total fat (2 g saturated fat), 87 mg cholesterol, 251 mg sodium

To cook any fish perfectly, you'll need to master a few basic techniques—and then learn to match the method to the density, flavor, and fat content of the fish. Rich, firm-textured types take well to grilling and pan-frying, while lighter, soft-fleshed varieties are better suited to gentler procedures such as steaming and poaching.

Whatever technique you use, it's crucial that you know how to test for doneness. Seafood cooks quickly and, as a result, is easily overcooked, losing both moisture and flavor. Fish is done when the flesh has just turned from translucent to opaque, but still looks moist; to check, make a small cut in the center of the thickest part. Don't worry if the fish appears slightly undercooked when it's removed from the pan or oven, since it will continue to cook a bit longer from retained heat.

The recipes in this chapter employ a variety of cooking methods, among them grilling, broiling, steaming, and stir-frying. The techniques described on these two pages are special favorites as well—we've found them to be particularly versatile.

Oven-browning

Oven-browned fish is crisp on the outside, juicy inside. And since timing is less critical when you oven-cook, there's less chance of overcooking.

Medium-dense, flaky-fleshed fish are best for oven-browning. In this recipe, we use an easy crumb coating to give steaks, fillets, or small whole fish a crusty finish.

> 1 to 1½ pounds fish steaks or fillets (*each* ½ to 1 inch thick); or 4 cleaned small whole fish such as trout

> Cheese-Crumb Coating (recipe follows)
>
> 3 tablespoons butter or margarine, melted

Rinse fish; pat dry. Prepare Cheese-Crumb Coating.

Pour butter into a shallow dish. Coat fish in butter and let excess drip off; then coat thickly in Cheese-Crumb Coating. Place fish at least 1 inch apart in a foil-lined shallow baking pan.

Bake in a 425° oven until fish is just opaque but still moist in thickest part; cut to test (10 to 20 minutes). Makes 4 servings.

Cheese-Crumb Coating. Crumble 1 slice **firm-textured white bread** into a blender or food processor and whirl until soft crumbs form. In a shallow dish, mix crumbs with 1½ teaspoons grated **Parmesan cheese,** ¼ teaspoon **dry thyme,** and ½ teaspoon **paprika.**

Per serving: 234 calories (47 percent from fat), 27 g protein, 3 g carbohydrates, 12 g total fat (6 g saturated fat), 82 mg cholesterol, 227 mg sodium

Pan-frying

Pan-frying is a great way to cook almost any fillet, steak, or small whole fish.

For even browning, make sure the fish is dry before cooking, and select a pan that heats evenly. A light dusting of flour or a coating of crumbs or cornmeal also helps to ensure uniform browning, especially if you're using thin fillets that cook very quickly. Most thick, firm-fleshed fish, on the other hand, brown well without a coating—and may even overbrown if coated.

> 1 to 2 pounds fish steaks, fillets, or cleaned small whole fish
>
> Coating (optional; choices and recipes follow)

> ½ to 2 tablespoons salad oil
>
> ½ to 2 tablespoons butter or margarine
>
> Browned Butter Sauce (optional; recipe follows)
>
> Salt and pepper

Rinse fish, pat dry, and cut into serving-size pieces. If desired, prepare coating; working with one piece of fish at a time, coat fish as directed.

Heat 1½ teaspoons each of the oil and butter in a wide frying pan over medium heat. Add fish, a few pieces at a time (do not crowd pan). Cook, turning as needed, until browned on outside and just opaque but still moist in thickest part; cut to test. Allow 2 to 4 minutes for fish less than ½ inch thick; 4 to 8 minutes for fish ½ to ¾ inch thick; and 10 to 15 minutes for fish 1 to 1½ inches thick. Add more oil and butter to pan as needed to prevent sticking. If using Browned Butter Sauce, transfer fish to a platter and keep warm while preparing sauce.

Season fish to taste with salt and pepper; if using sauce, pour sauce over fish. Makes 4 to 6 servings.

Coating. Choose one of the following.

Flour coating. Coat fish in ½ cup **all-purpose flour** and shake off excess.

Light crumb coating. Pour ½ cup **milk** into a shallow dish. In another shallow dish, place ½ cup finely crushed **seasoned croutons** or cracker crumbs; or mix ¼ cup *each* all-purpose flour and yellow cornmeal. Coat fish in milk and let excess drip off; then coat in crumbs and shake off excess.

Heavy crumb coating. In a shallow dish, place ½ cup **all-purpose flour.** In a second shallow dish, beat 2 **eggs** with 2 tablespoons **milk.** In a third shallow dish, place 1 cup **crumbs** (choose from finely crushed seasoned croutons, cornmeal, fine dry bread crumbs, cracker crumbs, wheat germ, or a mixture of ⅓ cup fine dry bread crumbs and ⅔ cup finely ground almonds or walnuts). Coat fish in flour and shake off excess; then coat in egg mixture and let excess drip off. Finally, coat in crumbs and shake off excess. Arrange fish, slightly apart, on a baking sheet and refrigerate for 15 to 30 minutes before cooking.

Browned Butter Sauce. Place ¼ cup **butter** or margarine in a small frying pan. Heat over medium-high heat until butter foams and begins to brown. Remove from heat and stir in 2 tablespoons **lemon juice** and, if desired, 1 tablespoon finely chopped **parsley.**

Per serving without coating or sauce: 154 calories (31 percent from fat), 26 g protein, 0 g carbohydrates, 5 g total fat (0.8 g saturated fat), 65 mg cholesterol, 110 mg sodium

Pan-poaching

Any fish can be pan-poached with excellent results. Even thin fillets, which tend to fall apart quite easily, are well suited to this gentle cooking method. In this recipe, we steam fillets or steaks in a small amount of seasoned liquid; when the fish is done, you can reduce the liquid to make a light sauce.

- 1 **to 2 pounds fish fillets or steaks**
- 1½ **tablespoons butter or margarine**
- 3 **shallots or 3 green onions, finely chopped or sliced**
- 1 **clove garlic, minced or pressed**
- ½ **cup chicken broth; or ¼ cup *each* chicken broth and dry white wine**

Rinse fish, pat dry, and set aside.

Melt butter in a wide frying pan over medium heat. Add shallots and garlic; cook, stirring often, until soft (about 3 minutes). Add broth and bring to a boil. Arrange fish in a single layer in pan. Then reduce heat, cover, and simmer until fish is just opaque but still moist in thickest part; cut to test (3 to 4 minutes for fish ¼ to ⅓ inch thick; 4 to 6 minutes for fish ½ to ¾ inch thick).

With a wide spatula, lift out fish and arrange on a platter; keep warm. Bring pan juices to a boil; then boil until slightly thickened. Spoon sauce over fish. Makes 4 to 6 servings.

Per serving: 162 calories (30 percent from fat), 26 g protein, 1 g carbohydrates, 5 g total fat (3 g saturated fat), 75 mg cholesterol, 245 mg sodium

Cooking in Parchment

When wrapped and baked in parchment, fish steams in its own juices. In addition to sealing in moisture and flavor, the parchment packets make a lasting and elegant impression when brought to the table. Cut through the paper yourself; or let your guests slice the packages open, releasing the tempting aroma of deliciously seasoned seafood.

Despite its impressive looks, parchment-wrapped fish is easy to prepare. It's convenient, too—the packets can be assembled and stored in the refrigerator hours before you plan to cook. The recipe below is easily adjusted to suit your tastes; you might add your choice of cut-up vegetables or replace the dill and tangerine peel with a selection of fresh herbs, for example. (Since the packets bake for only 7 to 10 minutes, any vegetables you include should be parboiled.)

Look for parchment in well-stocked supermarkets, specialty food shops, or cookware stores.

- 3 **tablespoons *each* olive oil, white wine vinegar, and thinly sliced green onions**
- 1 **teaspoon chopped fresh dill or ½ teaspoon dry dill weed**
- 1 **teaspoon shredded tangerine or orange peel**
- 1½ **pounds fish fillets, *each* about 1 inch thick (choose fish with medium-dense, flaky flesh)**
- 3 **tablespoons butter or margarine, melted**
  Salt and pepper

In a small bowl, stir together oil, vinegar, onions, dill, and tangerine peel; set aside. Rinse fish, pat dry, and cut into 4 equal pieces.

Cut 4 parchment paper circles, each about 4 times the size of each piece of fish. Brush the center of one half of each circle with about 2 teaspoons of the butter. Set one piece of fish on buttered area of each paper; drizzle with a fourth of the oil mixture, then sprinkle with salt and pepper. To seal each packet, fold free half of parchment circle over fish, forming a semicircle. Beginning at one end, fold about ½ inch of the curved edge closed; continue sealing, making small folds along edge, until entire curve is sealed. (At this point, you may cover and refrigerate packets until next day.)

Place packets slightly apart, folded ends up, on baking sheets. Bake in a 500° oven until fish is just opaque but still moist in thickest part; cut a tiny slit through parchment into fish to test (7 to 10 minutes).

Immediately transfer packets to dinner plates. To serve, cut packets open with a sharp knife or scissors just enough to expose contents without letting juices run out. Makes 4 servings.

Per serving: 335 calories (61 percent from fat), 32 g protein, 0.9 g carbohydrates, 22 g total fat (8 g saturated fat), 93 mg cholesterol, 205 mg sodium

Peppered Salmon

Peppered and smoked salmon shares some of the characteristics of corned beef, but it's lighter in texture and flavor. In this recipe, you smoke the fish in a covered barbecue; to regulate the heat, simply use an oven thermometer to check the temperature periodically, then adjust the vents as needed.

1½ cups water
1 cup firmly packed brown sugar
⅓ cup salt
1 tablespoon minced fresh ginger
2 or 3 dry bay leaves
1 teaspoon crushed whole allspice
1 boned salmon fillet with skin (3 to 3½ lbs.), 1 to 1½ inches thick
About ½ cup apple or hickory wood chips

INDIAN SALMON

The Skokomish Indians, native to the Pacific Northwest, smoked whole salmon fillets beside beach bonfires in heavy alder-wood frames. The frames were driven into the sand 2 feet from the flames; then the fish was left to cook in the hot, aromatic smoke. *Sunset* first printed an eyewitness account of the Indians' method in 1933 and later presented many modern adaptations of the technique.

About ½ cup mixed whole peppercorns (pink, green, white, and black; for mildest flavor, use mainly pink and green peppercorns)
1 tablespoon honey
2 or 3 thin red onion slices
Dill sprigs
Condiments (suggestions follow)

In a small pan, combine the 1½ cups water, sugar, salt, ginger, bay leaves, and allspice. Bring to a boil, stirring until sugar is dissolved. Remove from heat and let cool slightly.

Rinse fish and pat dry; then place, skin side down, in a large, shallow dish. Pour sugar-salt mixture over fish. Cover and refrigerate for at least 4 hours or up to 24 hours, spooning marinade over fish occasionally.

Ignite 16 charcoal briquets in a barbecue with a lid.

While coals are heating, pour enough warm water over wood chips to cover; let soak for 30 minutes. Also pour enough hot water over peppercorns to make them float; let soak for at least 15 minutes.

Lift fish from marinade; rinse with cool water and pat dry (discard marinade). Set fish, skin side down, on a large sheet of heavy-duty foil. With scissors, cut through foil around fish; discard foil trimmings. Rub honey over fish; drain peppercorns and scatter evenly over fish, patting to set lightly in place.

When coals are dotted with gray ash (after 25 to 30 minutes), push half of them to each side of fire grate. Drain wood chips and scatter 2 tablespoons on each mound of coals. Set grill in place 4 to 6 inches above coals; lightly grease grill. Place fish on foil in center of grill (not above coals). Set an oven thermometer on center of fish.

Cover barbecue and close vents, leaving ¼-inch openings. After 30 minutes, add 3 briquets to each mound of

coals; repeat after every 30 minutes of cooking. Check thermometer often to maintain temperature at about 160°F. If temperature drops, open vents slightly; if temperature rises, close 1 or 2 of the vents. Add wood chips as needed to produce a faint, steady stream of smoke. (Moisture that accumulates on fish will evaporate.) Cook salmon until a meat thermometer inserted in thickest part registers 140°F (about 1½ hours).

Using foil and wide spatulas, slide fish onto a rimless baking sheet; then transfer fish to a platter. Serve warm or cool. Or, if made ahead, cover and refrigerate for up to 3 days and serve cold.

To serve, garnish fish with onion slices and dill sprigs. Cut fish across the grain into ¾-inch-thick slices; lift off skin. Offer condiments to add to taste. Makes 10 to 12 servings.

Condiments. Place in separate bowls: ¼ cup drained **capers,** 1 cup minced **red onion** mixed with 1 tablespoon **lime or lemon juice,** 1 cup **sour cream, thin toasts,** and **lime or lemon wedges.**

Per serving: 209 calories (36 percent from fat), 25 g protein, 7 g carbohydrates, 8 g total fat (1 g saturated fat), 70 mg cholesterol, 657 mg sodium

Gravlax Plus

Gravlax—fresh salmon cured with salt, sugar, and plenty of fresh dill—is a Swedish favorite. Serve the fish as an elegant appetizer; you might accompany it with thinly sliced Molasses Pumpernickel Bread (page 181).

1 boned salmon fillet with skin (about 2 lbs.)
¼ cup salad oil
⅓ cup *each* sugar and salt
1½ tablespoons whole white peppercorns, coarsely crushed
¼ cup cognac (optional)

1 **small red onion, thinly sliced**

2 **to 3 cups lightly packed dill sprigs**

Mustard Sauce (recipe follows) or sour cream

Lemon wedges

If using fresh salmon, freeze it for at least 1 week at 0°F before curing to destroy any dangerous parasites. If you buy frozen (or frozen and thawed) salmon, this step isn't necessary.

Rinse fish, pat dry, and rub with oil. Mix sugar, salt, and peppercorns; lightly rub some of the mixture all over fish. Choose a glass dish that's just big enough to hold fish (fish should almost fill dish). Place fish, skin side down, in dish. Pat remaining salt mixture over fish and pour cognac (if used) over top.

Place onion and 1 to 2 cups of the dill sprigs on fish. Cover dish tightly with plastic wrap. Refrigerate for 12 hours; baste fish with juices 3 or 4 times. Turn fish over, with onion and dill beneath it. Cover and refrigerate for 12 more hours; baste 3 or 4 times with juices. Meanwhile, prepare Mustard Sauce; cover and refrigerate.

After 24 hours, fish is ready to serve, though you may leave it in brine for another 24 hours. To keep for 2 additional days, remove fish from brine (it will grow increasingly salty otherwise), pat dry, enclose in a heavy-duty plastic bag, and refrigerate.

Place fish, skin side down, on a serving board; discard dill and onion. Garnish fish with remaining dill

sprigs. Cut fish into paper-thin slanting slices; lift off skin. Serve fish with lemon wedges and Mustard Sauce. Makes 10 to 12 servings.

Mustard Sauce. Mix ⅔ cup **Dijon mustard,** ½ cup **salad oil,** 1½ tablespoons **white wine vinegar,** and 1 tablespoon **sugar.** Just before serving, stir in ¼ cup chopped **fresh dill;** season to taste with **pepper.** Makes 1¼ cups.

Per serving of fish: 165 calories (48 percent from fat), 17 g protein, 4 g carbohydrates, 9 g total fat (1 g saturated fat), 45 mg cholesterol, 1,669 mg sodium

Per tablespoon of Mustard Sauce: 61 calories (88 percent from fat), 0 g protein, 2 g carbohydrates, 6 g total fat (0.7 g saturated fat), 0 mg cholesterol, 241 mg sodium

Salmon with Chive & Herb Sauce

Many of the recent contributions to our "Kitchen Cabinet" illustrate the trend towards simpler cooking that emphasizes fresh ingredients. In this recipe, thick salmon steaks poach in herb-seasoned chicken broth; when the fish is done, you use the broth as the base for a delicate sauce.

4 **salmon steaks (about 1½ lbs. *total*), *each* about 1 inch thick**

1 **cup chicken broth**

2 **teaspoons *each* minced fresh tarragon and fresh thyme; or ½ teaspoon *each* dry tarragon and dry thyme**

1 **clove garlic, minced or pressed**

1 **teaspoon cornstarch blended with 2 tablespoons cold water**

3 **tablespoons snipped chives**

Salt and pepper

Lemon wedges

Rinse fish, pat dry, and set aside.

In a wide frying pan, combine broth, tarragon, and thyme. Bring to a boil over high heat; gently lay fish in pan. Then reduce heat, cover, and simmer until fish is just opaque but still

moist in thickest part; cut to test (10 to 15 minutes). Lift fish to a platter and keep warm.

Add garlic to cooking liquid. Bring to a boil over high heat; boil, stirring occasionally, until reduced to ½ cup. Stir in cornstarch mixture; return to a boil, stirring. Stir in chives, then pour sauce over fish. Season to taste with salt and pepper. Serve with lemon wedges. Makes 4 servings.

Per serving: 225 calories (41 percent from fat), 31 g protein, 1 g carbohydrates, 10 g total fat (1 g saturated fat), 82 mg cholesterol, 313 mg sodium

Salmon Quiche

Because it starts with canned salmon and a purchased pastry shell, this creamy quiche is a snap to prepare.

3 **eggs**

1¼ **cups half-and-half**

2 **tablespoons minced parsley**

¼ **teaspoon *each* salt and onion powder**

1 **can (about 15½ oz.) salmon**

¾ **cup shredded mild Cheddar cheese**

Purchased pastry shell for a single-crust 9-inch pie

½ **cup sliced ripe olives**

In a medium-size bowl, beat eggs until blended. Beat in half-and-half, parsley, salt, and onion powder. Set aside. Drain salmon and separate into bite-size chunks. Lightly mix salmon and half the cheese; spoon into pastry shell. Scatter olives and remaining cheese over top. Carefully pour in egg mixture. Bake in a 425° oven for 10 minutes; reduce oven temperature to 350° and continue to bake until filling is set but still moist on top (about 25 more minutes). Let stand for a few minutes before serving. Makes 6 to 8 servings.

Per serving: 350 calories (61 percent from fat), 20 g protein, 14 g carbohydrates, 24 g total fat (9 g saturated fat), 140 mg cholesterol, 693 mg sodium

Canadian Salmon Pie

Shredded potato in the filling makes this double-crust salmon pie even heartier. For a pretty presentation, decorate the pie with pastry cutouts before baking.

Tender Pastry (recipe follows)
1   can (about 15½ oz.) salmon
2   tablespoons butter or margarine
1   medium-size onion, chopped
1   medium-size russet potato, cooked, peeled, and coarsely shredded
3   tablespoons milk
1½ tablespoons minced fresh dill or ½ teaspoon dry dill weed
¼   teaspoon freshly ground pepper
1   teaspoon milk

Prepare Tender Pastry; refrigerate. Drain salmon and separate into large chunks; set aside.

Melt butter in a medium-size frying pan over medium-high heat. Add onion and cook, stirring often, until soft and golden (about 6 minutes). Remove from heat; gently stir in potato, the 3 tablespoons milk, dill, pepper, and salmon (keep chunks large).

On a floured board, roll out half the pastry to an 11-inch round. Fit into a 9-inch pie pan. Fill with salmon mixture. Roll out remaining pastry to a 10-inch round. Cover pie with pastry; trim and flute edges. If desired, roll out pastry scraps and cut into decorative shapes; place cutouts on top of pie. Cut a few small slashes in top of pie. Gently brush pie with the 1 teaspoon milk.

Bake pie on lowest rack of a 425° oven until pastry is golden brown (30 to 35 minutes). If made ahead, let cool; then cover and refrigerate until next day. To reheat pie, place it in a 350° oven and heat, uncovered, until filling is hot in center (25 to 35 minutes). Makes 8 servings.

Tender Pastry. In a large bowl, mix 2 cups all-purpose flour, ¼ teaspoon salt, and 1 teaspoon sugar. Using a pastry blender or 2 knives, cut in ½ cup solid vegetable shortening and 3 tablespoons butter or margarine until mixture resembles coarse crumbs. Stir in 1 egg (lightly beaten), ½ teaspoon distilled white vinegar, and 1½ tablespoons cold water until pastry holds together.

Shape pastry into a ball, then divide in half; wrap each half in plastic wrap and refrigerate for at least 1 hour or up to 3 days.

Per serving: 394 calories (54 percent from fat), 15 g protein, 30 g carbohydrates, 24 g total fat (9 g saturated fat), 65 mg cholesterol, 377 mg sodium

Sole with Grapes

A delicate glaze of cream and a tumble of hot buttered grapes dress up thin sole fillets sautéed to a golden brown.

1½ pounds sole fillets
    Freshly grated nutmeg (optional)
    Salt (optional)
    All-purpose flour
2   tablespoons butter or margarine
2   tablespoons olive oil or salad oil
1   cup seedless green grapes
½   cup whipping cream

Rinse fish and pat dry; then cut into serving-size (about 3- by 5-inch) pieces. Sprinkle with nutmeg and salt, if desired. Coat fish with flour and shake off excess.

Melt 1 tablespoon of the butter in 1 tablespoon of the oil in a wide frying pan over medium heat. Add fish, a few pieces at a time (do not crowd pan). Cook, turning once, until lightly browned on both sides and just opaque but still moist in thickest part; cut to test (3 to 5 minutes). Add more butter and oil to pan as needed to prevent sticking. As fish is cooked, transfer it to a platter and keep warm.

When all fish has been cooked and removed from pan, add grapes and swirl over high heat just until warm and bright green. Pour over fish.

Add cream to pan and bring to a boil over high heat, stirring to scrape browned bits free; boil, stirring, until large, shiny bubbles form and cream is a light golden color. Pour cream evenly over fish and grapes. Makes 4 servings.

Per serving: 402 calories (54 percent from fat), 34 g protein, 12 g carbohydrates, 24 g total fat (11 g saturated fat), 130 mg cholesterol, 208 mg sodium

Sole Florentine

Spinach is the distinguishing ingredient of dishes prepared in the Florentine style. In this recipe, the greens are topped with loosely rolled and poached sole fillets cloaked in a thick, well-seasoned cream sauce.

4   small sole fillets (¾ to 1 lb. *total*)
1   bottle (about 8 oz.) clam juice
1   package (about 10 oz.) frozen chopped spinach, thawed and squeezed dry
¼   cup grated Parmesan cheese
2   tablespoons butter or margarine
2   tablespoons all-purpose flour
⅔   cup milk
⅛   teaspoon ground nutmeg
¼   teaspoon dry mustard
1   tablespoon *each* lemon juice and instant minced onion
    Chopped parsley

Rinse fish and pat dry. Loosely roll each fillet, beginning at one end; secure each roll with a wooden pick or skewer. In a medium-size pan, bring clam juice to a boil. Set fish in pan. Reduce heat, cover, and simmer until fish is opaque but still moist in thickest part; cut to test (about 2 minutes). Lift fish from pan and drain on paper towels. Bring clam juice to a boil; boil until reduced to about ½ cup. Pour into a cup and set aside.

Spread spinach evenly over bottom of a shallow 1-quart baking dish or 2 individual casseroles. Sprinkle with 1 tablespoon of the cheese. Remove picks from fish and arrange fish on spinach.

In pan used to cook fish, melt butter over medium-low heat. Stir in flour and cook, stirring, for 1 minute (do not brown). Remove from heat and gradually stir in milk and reduced clam juice. Then return to heat and cook, stirring constantly, until sauce boils and thickens. Stir in nutmeg, mustard, lemon juice, and onion. Spoon sauce over fish and spinach. Sprinkle with remaining 3 tablespoons cheese.

Bake in a 425° oven until bubbly and lightly browned (10 to 15 minutes). Sprinkle with parsley. Makes 2 servings.

Per serving: 442 calories (41 percent from fat), 48 g protein, 18 g carbohydrates, 20 g total fat (11 g saturated fat), 141 mg cholesterol, 861 mg sodium

Broiled Swordfish with Tomato-Olive Confetti

Today, cooks like recipes that focus on flavor and freshness. This delicious dish is a case in point: a bed of watercress sprigs is topped with hot broiled swordfish steaks and a bright tomato-olive salsa. Heat from the cooked fish wilts the cress and warms the tomatoes, intensifying all the flavors.

Tomato-Olive Confetti (recipe follows)
1½ **pounds swordfish steaks (***each* **about 1 inch thick)**
   About 1 tablespoon olive oil or salad oil
3 **cups lightly packed watercress sprigs, rinsed and crisped**
   Lime wedges (optional)

Prepare Tomato-Olive Confetti and set aside.

Rinse fish, pat dry, and cut into 4 equal pieces. Place fish on an oiled rack in a 12- by 14-inch broiler pan; brush fish with oil. Broil about 5 inches below heat for 5 minutes. Turn fish over, brush with oil again, and continue to broil until just opaque but still moist in thickest part; cut to test (5 to 6 more minutes).

Divide watercress sprigs equally among 4 dinner plates and place a piece of hot swordfish on each. Spoon Tomato-Olive Confetti evenly over fish. Serve with lime wedges, if desired. Makes 4 servings.

Tomato-Olive Confetti. In a small bowl, stir together 1 medium-size **tomato,** seeded and finely chopped; ½ cup sliced **pimento-stuffed green olives;** 2 tablespoons drained **capers;** 3 tablespoons *each* sliced **green onions** and **lime juice;** and 3 tablespoons **olive oil** or salad oil.

Per serving: 337 calories (59 percent from fat), 31 g protein, 3 g carbohydrates, 22 g total fat (4 g saturated fat), 59 mg cholesterol, 672 mg sodium

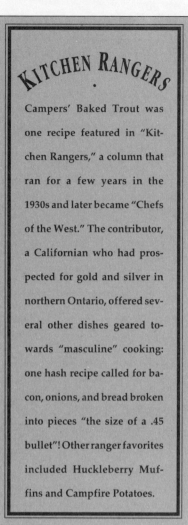
Seafood-Vegetable Tempura

What's the secret of the light, crisp coating that distinguishes the best tempura? To find out, *Sunset* food editors stowed away behind a Japanese restaurant's tempura bar. They learned that a cold, thin, lumpy batter creates the lacy crust so prized by connoisseurs. Serve tempura immediately after frying, since the fragile coating softens as it stands.

Tempura Dipping Sauce (recipe follows)
1 pound fish, such as salmon, sole, or lingcod (or a combination)

½ pound large raw shrimp, shelled and deveined
2 carrots, cut into ¼-inch-thick slanting slices; or 1 sweet potato, peeled and cut crosswise into ¼-inch-thick slices
1 green bell pepper, seeded and cut into ¼-inch-thick strips
12 mushrooms, cut in half lengthwise
1 zucchini, cut into ¼-inch-thick slanting slices; or ⅓ pound eggplant, cut in half lengthwise, then cut crosswise into ¼-inch-thick slices
Salad oil
Tempura Batter (recipe follows)

Prepare Tempura Dipping Sauce; pour into 4 individual serving bowls and set aside. Rinse fish, pat dry, and remove any skin and bones; then cut fish into 1½- by 3-inch pieces about ¼ inch thick. Arrange fish, shrimp, carrots, bell pepper, mushrooms, and zucchini on a tray near cooking pan.

In a wok or deep frying pan, heat 1½ to 2 inches of oil to 375°F on a deep-frying thermometer. While oil is heating, prepare Tempura Batter.

Working with one piece at a time, dip seafood and vegetables into batter, using chopsticks or tongs. Let excess batter drip off; then gently lower food into oil (you can cook several pieces at a time; do not crowd pan). Cook, turning occasionally, until coating is crisp and golden (2 to 3 minutes). Lift out, drain briefly on paper towels, and serve at once. Skim and discard bits of batter from oil frequently. Serve

with Tempura Dipping Sauce. Makes 4 servings.

Tempura Dipping Sauce. In a small pan, combine 1 bottle (about 8 oz.) **clam juice** and ¼ cup *each* **soy sauce** and **dry sherry.** Bring to a boil; then remove from heat and let cool. Offer about 3 tablespoons *each* shredded **daikon** (or regular radish), squeezed of excess liquid, and shredded **fresh ginger** to season sauce to taste.

Tempura Batter. In a small bowl, beat together 1 cup **ice-cold water,** 1 **egg,** and ¼ teaspoon *each* **baking soda** and **salt.** Add 1 cup **cake flour;** stir until blended (batter will be lumpy). Sprinkle ⅓ cup more **cake flour** over batter. With a fork, stir batter briefly (do not blend thoroughly); most of the ⅓ cup flour should be floating on top of the batter. Fill a large bowl half full of ice. Set bowl of batter in ice to keep batter cold while tempura cooks.

Per serving: 491 calories (38 percent from fat), 39 g protein, 35 g carbohydrates, 20 g total fat (3 g saturated fat), 173 mg cholesterol, 1,469 mg sodium

Grilled Tuna with Teriyaki Fruit Sauce

For tuna with tropical flair, top fillets or steaks with an exotic soy-ginger sauce and sliced fresh papaya. To keep the fish tender and moist, grill it very briefly over hot coals—just until lightly browned on the outside but still rare in the center.

¼ cup *each* soy sauce and sugar
⅓ cup sake or dry sherry
3 quarter-size slices fresh ginger or ¼ teaspoon ground ginger
1 pound tuna fillets or steaks (*each* ¾ to 1 inch thick), cut into 4 equal pieces
Olive oil or salad oil
1 papaya, peeled, seeded, and cut into 12 slices

2 teaspoons finely chopped candied or crystallized ginger

1 green bell pepper, seeded and cut into long, thin slivers

In a 2-quart pan, combine soy sauce, sugar, sake, and fresh ginger. Bring to a boil over high heat, stirring until sugar is dissolved; then boil until reduced to ⅓ cup. Discard ginger slices and keep sauce warm.

Rinse fish, pat dry, and brush lightly with oil. Place fish on a grill about 6 inches above a solid bed of hot coals. Cook, turning once, just until browned on outside but still pale pink in center; cut to test (3 to 4 minutes).

To serve, place each piece of fish on a dinner plate. Arrange 3 papaya slices atop each piece of fish; then top each serving equally with soy-ginger sauce and candied ginger. Garnish with bell pepper. Makes 4 servings.

Per serving: 336 calories (34 percent from fat), 28 g protein, 28 g carbohydrates, 12 g total fat (2 g saturated fat), 43 mg cholesterol, 1,079 mg sodium

Cantonese Crab Curry

Traditionally prepared in a wok, this savory curry is quick to cook—as long as you get all the ingredients ready before you begin. Serve with plenty of hot rice to soak up the sauce.

Cooking Sauce (recipe follows)

1 teaspoon *each* salt and sugar

4 teaspoons curry powder

¼ pound lean boneless pork, finely chopped or ground

1 medium-size cooked Dungeness crab (1½ to 2 lbs.), cleaned and cracked

3 tablespoons salad oil

1 large clove garlic, minced

1 medium-size onion, cut into wedges, layers separated

1 medium-size green bell pepper, seeded and cut into 1-inch squares

1 egg, lightly beaten
 Hot cooked rice

Prepare Cooking Sauce and set aside. Sprinkle salt, sugar, and curry powder over pork; mix well. Cut crab body into quarters; leave legs and claws whole.

Heat a wok or wide frying pan over high heat. When pan is hot, add oil. When oil begins to heat, add garlic and stir once. Then add pork and cook, stirring, until no longer pink (about 2 minutes). Stir in onion and bell pepper; cook, stirring, for 1 minute. Add crab and cook, stirring occasionally, until heated through (about 3 minutes). Stir Cooking Sauce, add to pan, and cook, stirring, until sauce boils and thickens. Add egg and stir just until egg begins to set (about 30 seconds). Serve curry over rice. Makes 4 servings.

Cooking Sauce. In a small bowl, stir together ¾ cup **chicken broth** and 1 tablespoon *each* **cornstarch, soy sauce,** and **dry sherry.**

Per serving: 249 calories (53 percent from fat), 18 g protein, 11 g carbohydrates, 15 g total fat (2 g saturated fat), 99 mg cholesterol, 1,170 mg sodium

WESTERN CLASSIC

Crab Casserole with Artichoke Hearts

Artichoke hearts, hard-cooked eggs, crab, and a creamy Cheddar sauce combine in this rich casserole, a *Sunset* favorite for over 30 years. Like many of our best casseroles, it can be assembled in advance, then baked before serving.

3 tablespoons butter or margarine

3 tablespoons all-purpose flour

1 cup milk

½ cup dry white wine or chicken broth

½ cup shredded medium-sharp Cheddar cheese or Swiss cheese

2 teaspoons Worcestershire

2 packages (about 9 oz. *each*) frozen artichoke hearts, thawed and drained

4 hard-cooked eggs, sliced

¾ pound crabmeat

2 tablespoons grated Parmesan cheese

Melt butter in a small pan over medium heat. Stir in flour and cook, stirring, for 1 minute (do not brown). Remove from heat and gradually stir in milk. Then return to heat and cook, stirring constantly, until sauce boils and thickens. Gradually stir in wine. Add Cheddar cheese and Worcestershire; cook, stirring, until cheese is melted.

Spoon a little of the sauce over bottom of a 1½-quart baking dish. Layer half the artichokes, half the eggs, and half the crab in dish; top with half the remaining sauce. Repeat layers, finishing with remaining sauce. Sprinkle with Parmesan cheese. (At this point, you may cover and refrigerate until next day.)

Bake, uncovered, in a 350° oven until casserole is hot in center (about 30 minutes; 40 to 45 minutes if refrigerated). Makes 4 to 6 servings.

Per serving: 351 calories (50 percent from fat), 27 g protein, 15 g carbohydrates, 19 g total fat (10 g saturated fat), 277 mg cholesterol, 513 mg sodium

Crab Vermouth

Delicate-tasting crab requires only the simplest of presentations. Here, the meat's mild, sweet flavor is enhanced by a well-seasoned broth accented with dry vermouth and garlic.

½   cup (¼ lb.) butter or margarine
2   tablespoons cornstarch (optional)
1   cup dry vermouth
1   can (about 14½ oz.) chicken broth
2   tablespoons *each* chopped parsley and minced or pressed garlic
1   tablespoon *each* soy sauce and lemon juice
1   teaspoon sugar
2   medium-size cooked Dungeness crabs (about 2 lbs. *each*), cleaned and cracked

Melt butter in a wide frying pan over medium heat. If you want a thicker sauce, remove pan from heat and stir in cornstarch. Return pan to heat; add ¾ cup of the vermouth, broth, parsley, garlic, soy sauce, lemon juice, and sugar. Bring to a boil over high heat; then reduce heat, cover, and simmer for 10 minutes. (At this point, you may let cool, then cover and refrigerate until next day. Reheat sauce before continuing.)

Add crabs to simmering sauce; cover and simmer until heated through (10 to 15 minutes). Stir in remaining ¼ cup vermouth. To serve, ladle sauce and crab into wide, shallow bowls. Makes 4 servings.

Per serving: 385 calories (68 percent from fat), 21 g protein, 5 g carbohydrates, 25 g total fat (14 g saturated fat), 126 mg cholesterol, 1,264 mg sodium

Snow Peas with Shrimp

Snow pea is just one name for the edible-pod pea used here; the tender vegetables are also known as Chinese pea pods, sugar peas, and mange-touts. Before cooking, be sure to break off the pod ends and remove the strings just as you would for fresh green beans.

½   teaspoon sugar
1   teaspoon soy sauce
1½ teaspoons cornstarch
1   tablespoon cold water
3   tablespoons peanut oil
½   teaspoon salt
14 large raw shrimp, shelled, deveined, and cut in half lengthwise
⅓   cup chicken broth
½   cup thinly sliced water chestnuts
1½ cups Chinese pea pods (also called snow or sugar peas), ends and strings removed
½   large onion, cut in half crosswise, then cut into thin wedges
2   small stalks celery, cut into ¼-inch-thick slanting slices

In a small bowl, stir together sugar, soy sauce, cornstarch, and water; set aside.

Heat oil in a wide frying pan or wok over high heat. When oil is hot, add salt and shrimp. Cook, stirring, until shrimp are opaque in center; cut to test (about 1 minute). Add broth, water chestnuts, pea pods, onion, and celery. Cover and cook, stirring once, for 1½ minutes. Stir soy sauce mixture and add to pan; cook, stirring, until sauce is slightly thickened (about 30 seconds). Makes 4 servings.

Per serving: 224 calories (47 percent from fat), 17 g protein, 13 g carbohydrates, 12 g total fat (2 g saturated fat), 105 mg cholesterol, 562 mg sodium

Hawaiian Shrimp Curry

You don't have to go to Hawaii to capture the flavor of the Islands—just reach for a can of coconut milk and some condiments. (If you can't find coconut milk, use an additional cup of cream or milk.)

⅓   cup butter or margarine
1   tablespoon curry powder
2   teaspoons ground ginger
½   teaspoon pepper
¼   cup finely minced onion
¼   cup water
7   tablespoons all-purpose flour
2   cups milk
1   cup unsweetened coconut milk
1½ tablespoons lemon juice
1½ pounds medium-size cooked shrimp, shelled and deveined
    Salt
    Hot cooked rice
    Curry Condiments (suggestions follow)

Melt butter in a large pan over low heat. Add curry powder, ginger, and pepper; cook, stirring constantly, until spices give off a nutty odor and darken slightly in color (do not let spices scorch).

Add onion and cook over medium heat, stirring often, until golden (about 10 minutes). Add water and simmer, uncovered, until liquid has evaporated and onion is very soft. Stir in flour and cook, stirring, for 1 minute (do not brown).

Remove pan from heat. Gradually stir in milk and coconut milk. (If you want a smooth sauce, pour mixture into a blender at this point and whirl until smooth.) Return pan to medium heat and cook, stirring often, until sauce boils and thickens.

Stir lemon juice and shrimp into sauce; season to taste with salt. Heat, stirring, just until shrimp are heated through. Serve with rice; offer condiments to add to taste. Makes 4 to 6 servings.

Curry Condiments. Arrange in separate small bowls: chopped **peanuts,** crumbled **crisp-cooked bacon, mango chutney** or chopped preserved ginger, chopped **green bell pepper** or onion (or a mixture of the two), **melon balls, papaya chunks,** diced **banana** (coated with **lemon juice**), and **toasted flaked coconut.**

Per serving: 396 calories (59 percent from fat), 24 g protein, 17 g carbohydrates, 26 g total fat (18 g saturated fat), 222 mg cholesterol, 381 mg sodium

Grilled Shrimp with Prosciutto & Basil

Prosciutto and fragrant fresh basil give these big grilled shrimp Italian appeal. Serve warm or cool, as a main dish or a substantial appetizer. (If you're serving the shrimp as an appetizer, offer them on skewers for easier eating.)

½ **cup dry white wine**
¼ **cup balsamic vinegar**
2 **tablespoons olive oil or salad oil**
2 **cloves garlic, minced or pressed**
16 **to 20 jumbo raw shrimp or prawns, shelled (except for tails) and deveined**
8 **to 10 thin slices prosciutto (about 7 oz. *total*)**
16 **to 20 large fresh basil leaves**

In a large bowl, whisk together wine, vinegar, oil, and garlic; spoon out and reserve 3 tablespoons of the mixture. Add shrimp to bowl and stir to coat; cover and refrigerate for at least 15 minutes or up to 4 hours. Meanwhile, if using bamboo skewers, soak about 14 skewers in water to cover for 30 minutes.

Cut each prosciutto slice in half lengthwise. Working with one shrimp at a time, lay a basil leaf against

shrimp; spiral a prosciutto half-slice around shrimp (not tail) and basil. Repeat to wrap all shrimp.

Thread a long metal or bamboo skewer through middle of 3 or 4 shrimp; run another skewer through shrimp parallel to first (to keep shrimp from spinning). Repeat to skewer remaining shrimp; discard marinade left in bowl.

Place skewered shrimp on a lightly greased grill 4 to 6 inches above a solid bed of hot coals. Cook, turning as needed to brown evenly, just until opaque in center; cut to test (6 to 8 minutes).

Push shrimp off skewers into a clean bowl; add reserved 3 tablespoons marinade and stir gently. Serve warm; or let cool, then cover and refrigerate to serve cold. (If serving shrimp as appetizers, thread them individually on clean bamboo skewers before serving.) Makes 4 servings.

Per serving: 301 calories (49 percent from fat), 33 g protein, 3 g carbohydrates, 15 g total fat (3 g saturated fat), 180 mg cholesterol, 1,056 mg sodium

Grilled Chiles Rellenos with Shrimp

To make a lighter version of *chiles rellenos*, stuff the chiles with shrimp and onions instead of cheese; then cook them on the grill rather than batter-frying them. Both cone-shaped poblano and slender, tapering California (Anaheim) chiles work well in this

recipe, but the broader poblanos are easier to fill and hold more.

Tomato Salsa (recipe follows)
8 **to 12 large fresh mild green chiles such as California (Anaheim), *each* 6 to 6½ inches long; or 8 to 12 fresh poblano chiles (*each* 3 to 5 inches long)**
1 **pound small cooked shrimp**
¾ **cup thinly sliced green onions Sour cream (optional)**

Prepare Tomato Salsa; refrigerate.

Using a barbecue with a lid, place chiles on lightly greased grill 4 to 6 inches above a solid bed of hot coals. Cook, uncovered, without turning, until chiles are blistered and slightly charred on one side (2 to 3 minutes). Remove from grill; peel off any blistered skin that comes off easily. Slit each chile lengthwise down cooked side. Scrape out seeds, but leave chiles whole.

In a medium-size bowl, mix shrimp and onions; fill chiles equally with shrimp mixture.

Place chiles, slit side up, on grill 4 to 6 inches above a solid bed of medium coals. Cover barbecue and adjust vents as needed to maintain an even heat. Cook until shrimp mixture is hot to the touch (5 to 7 minutes). Serve chiles with Tomato Salsa and, if desired, sour cream. Makes 4 main-dish servings.

Tomato Salsa. In a bowl, stir together 1 large **tomato,** coarsely chopped; ¼ cup chopped **onion;** 1 to 1½ tablespoons seeded, finely chopped **fresh or canned jalapeño chiles** or drained, seeded canned chipotle chiles in adobo sauce; 1 tablespoon *each* chopped **cilantro** and **white wine vinegar;** and 1 clove **garlic,** minced or pressed. Cover and refrigerate for at least 2 hours or until next day.

Per serving: 154 calories (9 percent from fat), 26 g protein, 9 g carbohydrates, 1 g total fat (0.3 g saturated fat), 221 mg cholesterol, 265 mg sodium

Two seafood stews—one from California, the other from Spain—provide a wonderful showcase for your favorite fish and shellfish.

San Francisco–style Cioppino

San Francisco is the birthplace of *cioppino*, but the exact origin of this Western classic is still unclear. Many attribute the dish to the Italian immigrants who worked on Meigg's Wharf, now known as Fisherman's Wharf, at the turn of the century.

Sunset has featured many variations of cioppino, each incorporating a different selection of Pacific seafood; this version uses shellfish alone.

- ¼ cup olive oil or salad oil
- 1 large onion, sliced
- 2 large cloves garlic, minced or pressed
- 1 green bell pepper, seeded and diced
- ⅓ cup chopped parsley
- 1 large can (about 28 oz.) tomatoes
- 1 can (about 15 oz.) tomato sauce
- 1 cup dry red or white wine
- 1 dry bay leaf
- 1 teaspoon dry basil
- ½ teaspoon dry oregano
- 12 small hard-shell clams in shell, scrubbed
- 1 pound large raw shrimp, shelled and deveined
- 2 medium-size cooked Dungeness crabs (1½ to 2 lbs. *each*), cleaned and cracked
- Salt and pepper

Heat oil in a 6- to 8-quart pan over medium heat. Add onion, garlic, bell pepper, and parsley; cook, stirring often, until onion is soft (about 5 minutes). Chop tomatoes; add tomatoes and their liquid, tomato sauce, wine, bay leaf, basil, and oregano to pan. Bring to a boil; then reduce heat, cover, and simmer for 20 minutes.

Add clams, shrimp, and crabs. Cover and simmer until clams pop open and shrimp are opaque in center; cut to test (about 20 minutes). Discard unopened clams. Season to taste with salt and pepper. Makes 6 servings.

Per serving: 294 calories (35 percent from fat), 30 g protein, 18 g carbohydrates, 11 g total fat (2 g saturated fat), 141 mg cholesterol, 944 mg sodium

Spicy Seafood Paella

Spain's famous *paella* originated in the Atlantic port of Valencia—but today, each region along the coast has its own version of the hearty stew. The basics are agreed on: olive oil, saffron, and rice. Beyond that, the cook's imagination and the resources at hand determine the final recipe.

Paella takes its name from the traditional cooking utensil, a round, flat two-handled iron pan. If you don't have a paella pan, a heavy casserole dish or wide frying pan will do just as well.

- ¼ cup olive oil
- 1 pound chorizo sausages, casings removed
- 1 green bell pepper, halved and seeded
- 1 medium-size red onion, chopped
- 4 large cloves garlic, minced or pressed
- ½ to 1 teaspoon crushed red pepper flakes
- 2½ cups long-grain rice
- 3 cups bottled clam juice
- ½ cup water
- 1 cup dry white wine
- ¼ teaspoon *each* saffron threads and black pepper
- 1 teaspoon salt
- ½ teaspoon dry basil
- 1 package (about 9 oz.) frozen artichoke hearts, thawed and drained
- 1½ pounds firm-textured white-fleshed fish fillets
- 12 small hard-shell clams in shell, scrubbed
- 1 pound medium-size raw shrimp, shelled and deveined
- 12 mussels in shell, scrubbed
- 1 pound cooked crab legs in shell, cracked
- 1 red bell pepper, seeded and cut into ¼-inch-wide strips

Heat oil in a 14-inch paella pan or 4-quart ovenproof pan over medium-high heat. Crumble chorizo into pan and cook, stirring often, until lightly browned. Coarsely chop half the green bell pepper; cut remaining half into ¼-inch-wide strips and set aside. Add chopped bell pepper, onion, garlic, and red pepper flakes to pan; cook, stirring often, until onion is soft (about 5 minutes). Stir in rice, clam juice, water, wine, saffron, black pepper, salt, basil, and artichokes. Bring mixture to a boil over high heat. Then remove from heat, cover, and bake in a 350° oven for 30 minutes, stirring twice. Meanwhile, rinse fish, pat dry, and cut into 1-inch pieces.

Stir rice mixture. Then stir in fish. Push clams, shrimp, and mussels into rice. Arrange crab on top. Cover and continue to bake until rice is tender to bite, clams pop open, and shrimp are opaque in center; cut to test (about 15 more minutes). Discard any unopened clams. Garnish paella with green and red bell pepper strips and serve at once. Makes 6 to 8 servings.

Per serving: 857 calories (40 percent from fat), 60 g protein, 62 g carbohydrates, 37 g total fat (11 g saturated fat), 205 mg cholesterol, 818 mg sodium

Shrimp Fajitas

Low in fat and high in protein, these simple-to-prepare fajitas provide a nutritious meal in a single package. To make the dish, you fill soft flour tortillas with a sauté of tender marinated shrimp, green bell peppers, and onions.

1 **pound medium-size raw shrimp, shelled and deveined**

1 **cup lightly packed chopped cilantro**

1 **clove garlic, minced or pressed**

⅓ **cup lime juice**

4 **to 6 flour tortillas (*each* about 8 inches in diameter)**

1 **tablespoon salad oil**

2 **large green bell peppers, seeded and thinly sliced**

1 **large onion, thinly sliced**

½ **cup plain nonfat yogurt or sour cream**

Purchased green tomatillo salsa

In a medium-size bowl, stir together shrimp, cilantro, garlic, and lime juice. Let stand at room temperature for 20 minutes.

Meanwhile, stack tortillas, wrap in foil, and heat in a 350° oven until warm and soft (about 15 minutes).

Heat oil in a wide nonstick frying pan over medium-high heat. Add bell peppers and onion; cook, stirring occasionally, until vegetables are soft (about 5 minutes). Lift out vegetables with a slotted spoon and keep warm. Add shrimp mixture to pan and cook over high heat, stirring often, just until shrimp are opaque in center; cut to test (about 3 minutes). Return vegetables to pan; stir to mix with shrimp.

Spoon shrimp mixture into tortillas, top with yogurt, and roll to enclose filling. Offer salsa to add to individual servings. Makes 4 to 6 servings.

Per serving: 262 calories (23 percent from fat), 20 g protein, 30 g carbohydrates, 7g total fat (1 g saturated fat), 112 mg cholesterol, 299 mg sodium

Scampi

Also known as langostinos and Dublin Bay prawns, *scampi* are small, lobsterlike crustaceans fished from the Adriatic Sea. Because true scampi are hard to find in the United States, we've substituted medium-size shrimp in this traditional Italian recipe. To make the delicious dish, you simply sauté the shellfish in butter with plenty of garlic and parsley.

¼ **cup butter or margarine**

1 **tablespoon thinly sliced green onion**

1 **tablespoon olive oil or salad oil**

4 **or 5 cloves garlic, minced or pressed**

2 **teaspoons lemon juice**

¼ **teaspoon salt**

About ¾ pound medium-size raw shrimp, shelled (except for tails) and deveined

¼ **teaspoon grated lemon peel**

2 **tablespoons minced parsley**

Dash of liquid hot pepper seasoning

Lemon wedges

Melt butter in a wide frying pan over medium heat. Stir in onion, oil, garlic, lemon juice, and salt; cook, stirring often, until bubbly. Add shrimp and cook, stirring occasionally, until opaque in center; cut to test (about 5 minutes). Stir in lemon peel, parsley, and hot pepper seasoning. Serve with lemon wedges. Makes 2 servings.

Per serving: 423 calories (69 percent from fat), 29 g protein, 4 g carbohydrates, 32 g total fat (16 g saturated fat), 273 mg cholesterol, 717 mg sodium

Ginger Shrimp

Ginger, prized for its spicy perfume and pungent flavor, is a popular seasoning in Asian cooking. Here, just 2 teaspoons of the grated fresh root add a lively acccent to a simple stir-fry of shrimp and vegetables.

¼ **cup white wine vinegar**

2 **tablespoons soy sauce**

5 **teaspoons sugar**

1 **teaspoon cornstarch**

3 **tablespoons salad oil**

2 **cloves garlic, minced or pressed**

2 **teaspoons grated fresh ginger**

1 **pound medium-size raw shrimp, shelled and deveined**

2 **stalks celery, cut into ½-inch-thick slanting slices**

1 **can (about 8 oz.) bamboo shoots, drained**

¼ **cup thinly sliced green onions**

1 **green onion, thinly sliced**

In a small bowl, stir together vinegar, soy sauce, sugar, and cornstarch. Set aside.

Heat 2 tablespoons of the oil in a wok or wide frying pan over medium-high heat. When oil is hot, add garlic and ginger and stir once. Then add shrimp and cook, stirring, just until opaque in center; cut to test (about 3 minutes). Remove shrimp mixture from pan and set aside.

Heat remaining 1 tablespoon oil in pan. Add celery, bamboo shoots, and the ¼ cup onions; cook, stirring, for 1 minute. Return shrimp to pan. Stir vinegar mixture and add to pan; then cook, stirring, until sauce boils and thickens (about 1 minute). Transfer shrimp mixture to a serving dish and sprinkle evenly with sliced onion. Makes 4 servings.

Per serving: 232 calories (46 percent from fat), 20 g protein, 11 g carbohydrates, 12 g total fat (2 g saturated fat), 140 mg cholesterol, 672 mg sodium

Fresh Oysters

The 18th-century satirist Jonathan Swift wrote, "He was a bold man that first ate an oyster." It's true that the shellfish is less than appealing in appearance, but its flavor and succulence—both before and after cooking—have made it a favorite for centuries.

In the West, popular oyster varieties include Pacific, Eastern, Olympia, and European flat. The types do differ in flavor, in part as a result of where each kind grows: oysters, being filter feeders, pick up varying flavors depending on the amount of salt and other nutrients in the water. In general, Pacific oysters have a distinct, full, briny taste, while Eastern (also known as Blue Point) oysters are milder. European flat oysters are mild, too, with slightly sweet and metallic overtones. Olympia oysters, native to the West Coast, are famed for their sweetness; they have a distinct metallic aftertaste.

WESTERN CLASSIC

Oven-fried Oysters

Oysters are prized for their creamy texture and delicate flavor. In this simple casserole, the shellfish are layered and topped with buttery, crunchy cracker crumbs. Serve with warm, crusty bread and a big green salad for an easy-to-make supper.

- **About 32 saltine crackers**
- **2 jars (about 10 oz. *each*) small Pacific oysters, drained**
- **¾ cup (¼ lb. plus ¼ cup) butter or margarine, melted**
- **Salt and pepper**

Crush enough crackers to make 1½ cups fine crumbs. Spread half the crumbs over bottom of a greased 9- by 13-inch baking dish.

In a small bowl, combine oysters and butter; stir to coat evenly. Lift oysters from bowl and arrange in a single layer over crumbs. Season to taste with salt and pepper. Top with remaining crumbs; then drizzle evenly with any butter left in bowl.

Bake on top rack of a 400° oven until crumbs are well browned (12 to 15 minutes). Serve at once. Makes 4 servings.

Per serving: 518 calories (70 percent from fat), 16 g protein, 23 g carbohydrates, 40 g total fat (23 g saturated fat), 171 mg cholesterol, 751 mg sodium

Oysters à la Osage

These rich baked oysters were the specialty of a ranch woman living in the Oklahoma hills during the early 1900s. Her son shared the recipe with *Sunset* in 1967. In his letter to us, he noted that the dish he enjoyed as a child used cream from the springhouse, homemade butter, crackers from a cracker barrel, nutmeg grated from the nut—and oysters obtained "someplace, somehow, somewhere."

Though we've updated the recipe, our modern version is still quite close to the original.

- **1 jar (about 10 oz.) small Pacific oysters**
- **⅛ teaspoon *each* freshly grated nutmeg and salt**
- **¼ teaspoon pepper**
- **6 slices bacon, crisply cooked, drained, and crumbled**
- **1 cup (about 4 oz.) shredded Swiss cheese**
- **1 cup whipping cream**
- **½ cup coarsely crushed saltine-type crackers with unsalted tops**
- **2 tablespoons butter or margarine**

Arrange oysters and their liquid in an even layer in a greased 9-inch-square baking dish. Sprinkle with nutmeg, salt, and pepper. Sprinkle bacon and cheese over oysters, then pour cream over all. Sprinkle cracker crumbs evenly over oyster mixture and dot with butter.

Bake in a 400° oven until crumbs are browned and oysters are hot (about 20 minutes). Makes 4 servings.

Per serving: 483 calories (73 percent from fat), 20 g protein, 13 g carbohydrates, 39 g total fat (22 g saturated fat), 155 mg cholesterol, 545 mg sodium

Coquilles St. Jacques in Butter

This classic French dish is prepared in a number of ways; some versions include a white sauce, while others feature a cheese topping. Our favorite variation is simpler and more traditional, adorning the scallops with nothing more than butter and parsley.

- 1½ **pounds sea scallops**
- 1½ **cups dry white wine; or ¾ cup** *each* **dry white wine and water**
- ⅓ **cup butter or margarine, melted**
- 2 **tablespoons chopped parsley Paprika**

Rinse and drain scallops, place in a wide frying pan, and add wine. Bring to a boil over high heat. Then reduce heat, cover, and simmer until scallops are opaque in center; cut to test (8 to 10 minutes). With a slotted spoon, lift out scallops; drain on paper towels. Let cool slightly, then cut into thick slices.

Arrange scallops in 4 scallop shells or individual casseroles. Spoon a fourth of the butter over top of each filled shell. Sprinkle 1½ teaspoons parsley over each; then sprinkle with paprika. Bake in a 350° oven until heated through (about 5 minutes). Makes 4 servings.

Per serving: 305 calories (53 percent from fat), 29 g protein, 4 g carbohydrates, 16 g total fat (10 g saturated fat), 97 mg cholesterol, 431 mg sodium

Scallop & Red Pepper Pasta

By pairing scallops with pasta, you can stretch a pound of this delectable but rather expensive seafood to feed four to six diners. Vary the amount of crushed red pepper to make the sauce as spicy as you like.

- 1 **lemon**
- 12 **ounces dry spaghetti**
- 1 **pound scallops**
- ¼ **cup butter or margarine**
- ¼ **cup olive oil**
- 3 **large red bell peppers, seeded and cut into thin slivers**
- 2 **cloves garlic, minced or pressed**
- ¼ **to ½ teaspoon crushed red pepper flakes**
- ¾ **cup chicken broth**
- ¼ **cup lemon juice**
- ¾ **cup finely chopped parsley Salt and pepper**

Using a zester, cut peel (colored part only) from lemon in fine shreds (or use a vegetable peeler to pare off colored part of peel, then cut peel into fine slivers). Set lemon peel aside. In a large pan, cook pasta in about 3 quarts of boiling salted water until tender to bite (8 to 10 minutes). Drain, rinse with cold water, and drain again; set aside. Rinse scallops and pat dry; if using sea scallops, cut into ¼-inch-thick slices. Set aside.

Melt butter in oil in a wide frying pan over medium-high heat. Add bell peppers, garlic, and red pepper flakes; cook, stirring, for 1 minute. Add broth and lemon juice to pan; bring to a boil. Add scallops, cover, and cook until opaque in center; cut to test (about 3 minutes). Remove from heat. Lift scallops and peppers from pan with a slotted spoon and set aside.

Add pasta to pan juices; lift and mix with 2 forks until pasta is hot. Pour pasta and sauce into a serving dish. Top with scallops and peppers; then sprinkle with parsley and lemon peel. Season to taste with salt and pepper. Before serving, mix lightly with a serving fork and spoon. Makes 4 to 6 servings.

Per serving: 538 calories (37 percent from fat), 25 g protein, 59 g carbohydrates, 22 g total fat (7 g saturated fat), 55 mg cholesterol, 400 mg sodium

Batter-fried Squid

Beer is the secret ingredient in this succulent batter-fried squid. It's traditional to serve the crisp, golden morsels with a squeeze of lemon and a sprinkling of malt vinegar and salt.

- 2 **pounds small whole squid, cleaned**
- 1 **cup all-purpose flour**
- ½ **teaspoon paprika**
- ¼ **teaspoon salt**
- ⅛ **teaspoon pepper**
- 1 **cup beer**
  Salad oil
  All-purpose flour
  Malt vinegar
  Salt
  Lemon wedges

Cut hoods of squid crosswise into ½-inch-thick rings. Rinse rings and tentacles; drain. In a medium-size bowl, mix the 1 cup flour, paprika, the ¼ teaspoon salt, and pepper. Add beer and stir until smooth.

In a deep pan, heat 1½ to 2 inches of oil to 400°F on a deep-frying thermometer. Dust squid with flour; shake off excess. Then dip squid, a few pieces at a time, into batter. Let excess batter drip off; then gently lower squid into oil (do not crowd pan). Cook, turning once, until golden (about 30 seconds). Lift out, drain on paper towels, and keep warm. Offer vinegar and salt to add to taste. Serve with lemon wedges. Makes 4 servings.

Per serving: 327 calories (28 percent from fat), 30 g protein, 25 g carbohydrates, 9 g total fat (2 g saturated fat), 413 mg cholesterol, 183 mg sodium

VEGETABLES

•

*T*he West is a treasure trove
of fresh garden vegetables. Whether simply prepared with a
sprinkling of herbs or combined with sauce in a savory
casserole, each season's jewels offer the cook myriad possibilities for delicious presentation. • The recipes in this chapter, many contributed by our readers, are the time-honored
favorites often reserved for potluck gatherings and special
family dinners. Rich, hearty choices such as Mashed Potato
Casserole, Ratatouille, and smoky Sweet & Sour Baked Beans
are among the most popular selections, but we've included a
number of lighter dishes as well. • And if you're looking for
vegetarian entrées, you'll find those, too—try Creamy Mushroom Enchiladas, Garbanzo Curry, or one of the other satisfying specialties in these pages.

Artichokes & Spinach au Gratin

Trimmed artichokes make perfect little nests for a simple spinach filling. Baked to a delicious golden brown, the tender cups are an elegant accompaniment for steaks or boneless chicken breasts.

> **Spinach Filling (recipe follows)**
> ½ **cup vinegar**
> 8 **large artichokes (*each* about 3½ inches in diameter)**
> 1 **tablespoon *each* dry thyme, coriander seeds, dry basil, and whole black peppercorns**
> ½ **teaspoon crushed red pepper flakes**
> 1 **cup (about 4 oz.) shredded Gruyère or Swiss cheese**

Prepare Spinach Filling and set aside.

In a large bowl, mix ¼ cup of the vinegar with about 4 cups water. Working with one artichoke at a time, cut off top two-thirds of each artichoke. Then cut off stems flush with bottoms; peel bottoms lightly to remove coarse fibers. Snap off coarse outer leaves, pulling them away from fleshy base until all coarse leaves have been removed. As artichokes are trimmed, drop them into vinegar water.

In a 4- to 5-quart pan, combine about 2 quarts water, remaining ¼ cup vinegar, thyme, coriander seeds, basil, peppercorns, and red pepper flakes. Bring to a boil over high heat. Drain artichokes and add to pan. Reduce heat, cover, and simmer until artichoke bottoms are tender when pierced (about 30 minutes). Let cool in cooking liquid; then drain, discarding liquid. Pull small leaves from each artichoke and scoop out fuzzy center with a spoon. Spoon Spinach Filling into each artichoke, mounding filling to use all of it.

Set artichokes in a 9- by 13-inch baking pan. (At this point, you may cover and refrigerate until next day.)

Sprinkle cheese evenly over artichokes and bake, uncovered, in a 350° oven until heated through (about 30 minutes; 40 to 45 minutes if refrigerated). Makes 8 servings.

Spinach Filling. Melt 5 tablespoons **butter** or margarine in a wide frying pan over medium-high heat. Add 1 large **onion,** minced; cook, stirring often, until lightly browned (about 7 minutes). Stir in 2 tablespoons **all-purpose flour** and cook, stirring, for 1 minute (do not brown). Remove from heat and gradually stir in 1 cup **chicken broth,** 6 tablespoons **half-and-half** or whipping cream, and ¼ teaspoon **ground nutmeg.** Return to heat and bring to a boil; boil, stirring, for about 1 minute. Add 2 packages (about 10 oz. *each*) **frozen chopped spinach,** thawed and squeezed dry; stir until blended. Remove from heat; season to taste with **salt** and **pepper.**

Per serving: 259 calories (44 percent from fat), 13 g protein, 26 g carbohydrates, 14 g total fat (8 g saturated fat), 39 mg cholesterol, 455 mg sodium

Asparagus Spears with Egg Dressing

Put leftover Easter eggs to delicious use with this creamy dressing, featured in our April 1981 "Kitchen Cabinet." Serve the dressing over asparagus or another favorite vegetable.

> 4 **hard-cooked eggs**
> ¼ **cup *each* chopped celery, chopped parsley, and mayonnaise**
> 1 **tablespoon *each* lemon juice and grated Parmesan cheese**
> 1 **teaspoon Dijon mustard**
> ¼ **teaspoon *each* celery salt and dry dill weed**
> 2 **pounds asparagus**

In a small bowl, chop eggs finely with a pastry blender or fork. Stir in celery, parsley, mayonnaise, lemon juice, cheese, mustard, celery salt, and dill weed. If made ahead, cover and refrigerate until next day.

Snap off and discard tough ends of asparagus; peel stalks, if desired. In a wide frying pan, bring 1 inch of water to a boil over high heat. Add asparagus; cover and cook just until barely tender when pierced (about 5 minutes). Drain and serve hot. Or, to serve cold, immerse in ice water until cool, then drain again.

To serve, arrange asparagus spears parallel on a platter and spoon egg dressing over top. Makes 6 servings.

Per serving: 142 calories (69 percent from fat), 7 g protein, 4 g carbohydrates, 11 g total fat (2 g saturated fat), 148 mg cholesterol, 200 mg sodium

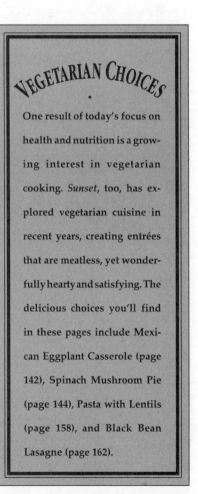

VEGETARIAN CHOICES

One result of today's focus on health and nutrition is a growing interest in vegetarian cooking. *Sunset,* too, has explored vegetarian cuisine in recent years, creating entrées that are meatless, yet wonderfully hearty and satisfying. The delicious choices you'll find in these pages include Mexican Eggplant Casserole (page 142), Spinach Mushroom Pie (page 144), Pasta with Lentils (page 158), and Black Bean Lasagne (page 162).

Asparagus with Orange-Butter Sauce

Fresh asparagus cloaked in a rich, citrusy butter sauce is a fitting accompaniment to an elegant meal. Strips of orange peel, tied into tiny knots, make a lovely garnish for the slender green spears.

2 pounds asparagus
½ cup (¼ lb.) butter or margarine
⅓ cup minced shallots
1¼ teaspoons Dijon mustard
1⅓ cups orange juice
   Strips of orange peel tied in knots; or orange slices (optional)

Snap off and discard tough ends of asparagus; peel stalks, if desired. In a wide frying pan, bring 1 inch of water to a boil over high heat. Add asparagus; cover and cook just until barely tender when pierced (about 5 minutes). Drain, transfer to a platter, and keep warm.

Melt 1 tablespoon of the butter in a small pan over medium heat. Add shallots and cook, stirring often, for 1 minute. Add mustard and orange juice. Bring to a boil over high heat; boil, stirring occasionally, until reduced to ⅔ cup. Reduce heat to low and add remaining 7 tablespoons butter all at once; cook, stirring constantly, until butter is melted and sauce is smooth. Spoon sauce over asparagus and garnish with orange peel, if desired. Makes 6 servings.

Per serving: 186 calories (72 percent from fat), 3 g protein, 11 g carbohydrates, 16 g total fat (10 g saturated fat), 41 mg cholesterol, 191 mg sodium

Asparagus Parmesan

Thinly sliced asparagus bakes until meltingly soft beneath an onion-cheese sauce lightly spiced with curry.

2½ pounds asparagus
¼ cup butter or margarine
2 to 3 tablespoons thinly sliced green onions
¼ teaspoon curry powder
½ teaspoon salt
⅓ cup all-purpose flour
2 cups milk; or 1⅔ cups milk plus ⅓ cup dry white wine
⅓ cup grated Parmesan cheese

Snap off and discard tough ends of asparagus; cut stalks into slanting slices. In a wide frying pan, bring 1 inch of water to a boil over high heat. Add asparagus; cover and cook just until tender-crisp to bite (about 3 minutes). Drain.

Melt butter in a medium-size pan over medium heat. Add onions, curry powder, and salt; cook, stirring often, until onions are soft (about 5 minutes). Stir in flour and cook, stirring, for 1 minute (do not brown). Remove from heat and gradually stir in milk. Then return to heat and cook, stirring constantly, until sauce boils and thickens. Stir in asparagus. Pour mixture into a shallow baking dish and sprinkle with cheese. Bake in a 400° oven until bubbly and heated through (15 to 20 minutes). Makes 6 to 8 servings.

Per serving: 159 calories (56 percent from fat), 7 g protein, 11 g carbohydrates, 10 g total fat (6 g saturated fat), 30 mg cholesterol, 330 mg sodium

Asparagus with Tomatillos

For a light and pretty springtime salad, top briefly cooked asparagus spears with a tart, simple tomato-tomatillo dressing.

1 pound asparagus
3 tablespoons olive oil
4 large tomatillos (*each* about 1½ inches in diameter), husked and finely diced
1 small pear-shaped (Roma-type) tomato, finely diced

¼ cup finely shredded Parmesan cheese
   Salt and pepper
   Lemon wedges

Snap off and discard tough ends of asparagus; peel stalks, if desired. In a wide frying pan, bring 1 inch of water to a boil over high heat. Add asparagus; cover and cook just until barely tender when pierced (about 5 minutes). Drain, immerse in ice water until cool, and drain again. Arrange asparagus spears equally on 4 salad plates (or arrange all asparagus on a platter).

In a bowl, mix oil, tomatillos, and tomato; spoon over asparagus. Sprinkle with cheese. Season to taste with salt and pepper; garnish with lemon wedges. Makes 4 servings.

Per serving: 152 calories (69 percent from fat), 5 g protein, 7 g carbohydrates, 12 g total fat (2 g saturated fat), 4 mg cholesterol, 97 mg sodium

Buttered Green Beans & Onions

Contrasting colors and complementary flavors make this combination of green beans and tiny onions a winner.

2 pounds green beans, cut into slanting slices; or 3 packages (about 9 oz. *each*) frozen cut green beans
2 tablespoons butter or margarine
1 tablespoon olive oil or salad oil
1 clove garlic, minced or pressed
¼ cup minced parsley
½ teaspoon salt
   Dash *each* of pepper and ground nutmeg
1 jar or can (about 1 lb.) small whole onions, drained

If using fresh beans, cook in boiling water until tender-crisp to bite (about 7 minutes). If using frozen beans, cook according to package directions until tender-crisp to bite. Drain beans, immerse in ice water until cool, and drain again.

Melt butter in oil in a wide frying pan over medium heat. Add garlic, parsley, salt, pepper, and nutmeg. Cook, stirring often, for 3 minutes. Add beans and onions. Cook, stirring occasionally, until heated through. Makes 8 to 10 servings.

Per serving: 78 calories (45 percent from fat), 2 g protein, 9 g carbohydrates, 4 g total fat (2 g saturated fat), 7 mg cholesterol, 341 mg sodium

Green Vegetable Medley

Peas, lima beans, and green beans combine in this cheese-topped casserole. If you like, you can put it together a day ahead, then pop it in the oven half an hour before serving.

- 1 **package (about 10 oz.) frozen baby lima beans**
- 1 **package (about 9 oz.) frozen cut green beans**
- 2 **tablespoons butter or margarine**
- ¼ **cup finely chopped onion**
- 1 **tablespoon all-purpose flour**
- ½ **cup *each* sour cream and mayonnaise**
- ½ **teaspoon dry basil**
- 1 **package (about 10 oz.) frozen peas, thawed**
  Salt and pepper
- ¾ **cup shredded sharp Cheddar cheese**

Following package directions, cook lima beans and green beans separately in boiling water just until tender-crisp to bite; do not overcook. Drain, immerse in ice water until cool, and drain again.

Melt butter in a wide frying pan over medium heat. Add onion and cook, stirring often, until soft (about 5 minutes). Stir in flour and cook, stirring, for 1 minute (do not brown). Remove from heat and add sour cream, mayonnaise, and basil; stir until blended. Stir in lima beans, green

beans, and peas. Season to taste with salt and pepper. Spoon into a 1½- to 2-quart baking dish and sprinkle with cheese. (At this point, you may cover and refrigerate until next day.)

Bake, uncovered, in a 325° oven until heated through (about 20 minutes; about 30 minutes if refrigerated). Makes 10 to 12 servings.

Per serving: 209 calories (63 percent from fat), 6 g protein, 13 g carbohydrates, 15 g total fat (5 g saturated fat), 24 mg cholesterol, 175 mg sodium

Green Beans with Herbs

The fresh green beans in this savory dish are accented by more than just herbs. Bell pepper, onion, and sliced tomato go into the pan as well.

- 2 **tablespoons olive oil or salad oil**
- 1 **small onion, thinly sliced**
- 1 **clove garlic, peeled and halved**
- 1 **large tomato, peeled and sliced**
- 1 **tablespoon *each* dry white wine, minced green bell pepper, minced parsley, and minced celery**
- ½ **teaspoon dry marjoram**
  Pinch of dry rosemary
- 1 **pound green beans, cut lengthwise into thin slivers**
  Salt and pepper

Heat oil in a medium-size frying pan over medium heat. Add onion and garlic; cook, stirring often, for 10 minutes. Add tomato, wine, bell pepper, parsley, celery, marjoram, and rosemary. Reduce heat to medium-low and simmer, uncovered, for 10 more

minutes. Meanwhile, cook beans in boiling water until tender-crisp to bite (about 7 minutes).

Drain beans; add to tomato mixture. Cover, and simmer for 5 minutes. Discard garlic. Season to taste with salt and pepper. Makes 4 servings.

Per serving: 118 calories (50 percent from fat), 3 g protein, 13 g carbohydrates, 7 g total fat (1 g saturated fat), 0 mg cholesterol, 13 mg sodium

Deviled Green Beans

The term "deviled" usually indicates a dish that's highly seasoned—and often hot and spicy. This recipe from the 1950s isn't particularly fiery, but it gets plenty of flavor from Cheddar cheese, mustard, and garlic.

- 1 **package (about 9 oz.) frozen cut green beans**
- 3 **tablespoons butter or margarine**
- 1 **medium-size onion, chopped**
- 1 **clove garlic, minced or pressed**
- ½ **green bell pepper, seeded and chopped**
- 2 **bottled pimentos, sliced or chopped**
- 2 **teaspoons prepared mustard**
- 1 **can (about 8 oz.) tomato sauce**
- 1 **cup (about 4 oz.) shredded Cheddar cheese**

Following package directions, cook beans in boiling water until tender-crisp to bite. Drain, immerse in ice water until cool, and drain again.

Melt butter in a medium-size frying pan over medium heat. Add onion, garlic, bell pepper, and pimentos; cook, stirring often, until onion is soft (about 5 minutes). Stir in beans, mustard, tomato sauce, and cheese. Spoon into a shallow 1-quart baking dish. Bake in a 350° oven until cheese is melted (about 25 minutes). Makes 4 servings.

Per serving: 256 calories (62 percent from fat), 10 g protein, 15 g carbohydrates, 18 g total fat (11 g saturated fat), 53 mg cholesterol, 646 mg sodium

Savory Beans & Tomatoes

A buttery, garlicky layer of crumbs and cheese tops fresh green beans, ripe tomatoes, and aromatic herbs in this crowd-size casserole.

2½ **pounds green or wax beans, ends and strings removed**

4 **large tomatoes (about 2 lbs. total)**

10 **tablespoons (¼ lb. plus 2 tablespoons) butter or margarine**

1 **large onion, chopped**

½ **pound mushrooms, sliced**

3 **cloves garlic, minced or pressed**

1½ **teaspoons each dry basil and dry oregano**
   Salt

1½ **cups soft bread crumbs**

⅓ **cup grated Parmesan cheese**

Cut beans into 2-inch pieces and arrange on a rack in a pan over 1 inch of boiling water; cover and steam until tender when pierced (8 to 12 minutes). Drain, immerse in ice water until cool, and drain again. Cut tomatoes into thin wedges; set aside.

Melt ¼ cup of the butter in a wide frying pan over medium-high heat. Add onion, mushrooms, and two-thirds of the garlic; cook, stirring often, until onion is soft and all liquid has evaporated (about 5 minutes). Stir in beans, tomatoes, and 1 teaspoon each of the basil and oregano. Season to taste with salt. Spoon into a shallow 3-quart baking dish.

Melt remaining 6 tablespoons butter in a small pan. Stir in remaining garlic, crumbs, cheese, and remaining ½ teaspoon each basil and oregano. (At this point, you may cover and refrigerate bean mixture and crumb topping separately for up to 2 days.)

Sprinkle crumb topping evenly over bean mixture. Bake, covered, in a 400° oven for 20 minutes (30 minutes if refrigerated); then uncover and continue to bake until heated through (about 5 more minutes). Makes 12 to 14 servings.

Per serving: 153 calories (56 percent from fat), 4 g protein, 14 g carbohydrates, 10 g total fat (6 g saturated fat), 26 mg cholesterol, 166 mg sodium

Sweet & Sour Baked Beans

For baked beans in a hurry, try this colorful casserole. Using canned beans keeps preparation and cooking time to a minimum.

½ **pound sliced bacon**

4 **large onions (about 2 lbs. total), thinly sliced**

1 **cup firmly packed brown sugar**

1½ **teaspoons dry mustard**

½ **cup cider vinegar**

2 **cans (about 15 oz. each) butter beans, drained and rinsed**

1 **can (about 15 oz.) green lima beans, drained and rinsed**

1 **can (about 15 oz.) red kidney beans, drained and rinsed**

1 **large can (about 28 oz.) New England–style baked beans**

In a wide frying pan, cook bacon over medium heat until crisp. Lift out, drain, crumble, and set aside. Discard all but ¼ cup of the drippings. Add onions to drippings and stir to coat. Stir in sugar, mustard, and vinegar. Cook over medium heat, stirring occasionally, until liquid is reduced by half (about 10 minutes).

In a 3- to 3½-quart baking pan, combine butter beans, lima beans, kidney beans, and baked beans. Add onion-vinegar mixture and all but 2 tablespoons of the bacon; stir gently until blended. (At this point, you may cover and refrigerate bean mixture and reserved bacon separately until next day.)

Bake, covered, in a 350° oven until bubbly and heated through (1¼ to 1½ hours). Sprinkle with reserved 2 tablespoons bacon before serving. Makes 10 to 12 servings.

Per serving: 349 calories (20 percent from fat), 13 g protein, 60 g carbohydrates, 8 g total fat (2 g saturated fat), 13 mg cholesterol, 676 mg sodium

Western Baked Beans

The special, mildly sweet flavor of this hearty dish depends on a combination of black-eyed peas and three kinds of dried beans—limas, white beans, and kidney beans—with plenty of brown sugar and molasses. Serve the beans with barbecued ribs or chicken; or try them as a supper entrée, with a salad and big squares of cornbread.

1 **cup each dried small white beans, lima beans, red kidney beans, and black-eyed peas**

2 **teaspoons salt**

½ **pound salt pork**

2 **small onions, chopped**

½ **teaspoon pepper**

1 **tablespoon each dry mustard and ground ginger**

½ **cup each firmly packed brown sugar and light molasses**

Rinse and sort through beans and peas, discarding any debris. Drain beans and peas, place in a large pan, and add water to cover by about 2 inches. Bring to a boil over high heat; then reduce heat, cover, and simmer for 2 minutes. Remove from heat and let stand for 1 hour. Add salt and bring to a boil over high heat; reduce heat, cover, and simmer for 15 minutes. Drain; reserve liquid.

Cut off a quarter of the salt pork and place it in a deep 5-quart baking pan. Cover with a 1-inch layer of beans, then a layer of onions. Continue to alternate layers to use remaining beans and onions, ending with a layer of beans. Score remaining piece of salt pork and press into beans until only rind shows.

In a small pan, combine reserved cooking liquid, pepper, mustard, ginger, sugar, and molasses. Bring to a boil; then pour over beans. Add more water if needed to cover beans. Cover and bake in a 250° oven until beans are very tender to bite (6 to 7 hours). Makes 10 to 12 servings.

Per serving: 472 calories (33 percent from fat), 17 g protein, 63 g carbohydrates, 18 g total fat (6 g saturated fat), 18 mg cholesterol, 712 mg sodium

Oaxacan Baked Black Beans

You'll need to plan ahead to make this dish from the coastal Mexican state of Oaxaca—the beans should bake for about 10 hours. If you prefer, you can use pinto beans in place of black ones.

2 **pounds dried black or pinto beans**
3 **quarts water**
2 **cloves garlic, minced or pressed**
1 **medium-size onion, chopped**
1½ **teaspoons cumin seeds**
   About 2 pounds lean ham hocks, trimmed of fat
   Salt
¼ **teaspoon pepper**

Rinse and sort through beans, discarding any debris. Drain beans and place in a deep 5-quart baking pan. Add water, garlic, onion, cumin seeds, ham hocks, 1 teaspoon salt, and pepper. Cover and bake in a 275° oven

until beans are very tender to bite (about 10 hours). Skim and discard fat from beans; season beans to taste with salt. Makes 10 to 12 servings.

Per serving: 327 calories (9 percent from fat), 22 g protein, 54 g carbohydrates, 3 g total fat (1 g saturated fat), 12 mg cholesterol, 277 mg sodium

WESTERN CLASSIC
Fiesta Frijoles

Simmered beans like these—rich with the smoky flavor of salt pork and bacon—are superb with grilled sausages, burgers, or steaks.

2 **pounds dried pink or red beans**
1 **pound salt pork, diced**
2 **cloves garlic, minced**
4 **slices bacon, chopped (or 2 to 3 tablespoons bacon drippings)**
1 **large onion, sliced**
2 **cans (about 14½ oz. *each*) tomatoes**
4 **or 5 small dried hot red chiles**
3 **tablespoons vinegar**
1 **tablespoon Worcestershire**
3 **tablespoons sugar**
1 **tablespoon finely chopped parsley**
2 **teaspoons chili powder**
2 **tablespoons grated Parmesan or Romano cheese**
   Salt

Rinse and sort through beans, discarding any debris. Soak beans overnight in enough water to cover by about 2 inches. (Or place beans in a large pan and add water to cover by about 2 inches. Bring to a boil over high heat; boil for 2 minutes. Remove from heat and let stand for 1 hour.)

After beans have soaked, add salt pork and garlic. Cook, uncovered, over medium-low heat until pork is tender when pierced (about 1 hour); add more water, if needed.

Meanwhile, cook bacon in a wide frying pan over medium heat until fat

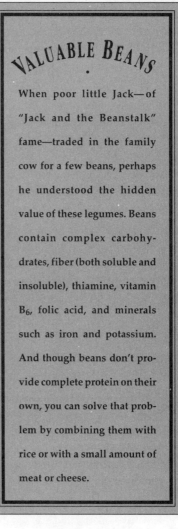

VALUABLE BEANS

When poor little Jack—of "Jack and the Beanstalk" fame—traded in the family cow for a few beans, perhaps he understood the hidden value of these legumes. Beans contain complex carbohydrates, fiber (both soluble and insoluble), thiamine, vitamin B₆, folic acid, and minerals such as iron and potassium. And though beans don't provide complete protein on their own, you can solve that problem by combining them with rice or with a small amount of meat or cheese.

is rendered (3 to 5 minutes; or melt bacon drippings in pan). Add onion; cook, stirring often, until soft (about 5 minutes). Chop tomatoes; add tomatoes and their liquid, chiles, vinegar, Worcestershire, sugar, parsley, and chili powder. Cook, stirring often, until thickened. Remove from heat.

When pork is tender, stir in tomato mixture. Continue to simmer, uncovered, over medium-low heat until beans are very tender to bite (about 1 more hour). Skim and discard fat from bean mixture. Stir in cheese and season to taste with salt. Makes 10 to 12 servings.

Per serving: 666 calories (49 percent from fat), 22 g protein, 65 g carbohydrates, 37 g total fat (13 g saturated fat), 38 mg cholesterol, 792 mg sodium

Out West, we've always enjoyed cooking out of doors. Even in the '30s, extensive outdoor kitchens were typical of Western homes—and at the heart of it all was the barbecue, where steaks and burgers kept company with vegetables and fruits.

Here's a handy list of vegetables you can barbecue. Some are best if blanched before grilling; others work well from the raw state. As the vegetables cook, keep them moist by brushing with herb-seasoned oil or with the basting sauce used on accompanying meat, poultry, or fish.

Grilled Vegetables

    About 2 pounds vegetables (choices follow; use one or several kinds)

2 **tablespoons minced fresh thyme, fresh oregano, fresh rosemary, or fresh tarragon; or 2 teaspoons *total* of the dry herbs**

⅓ **cup olive oil or salad oil; or ⅓ cup basting sauce**
    Salt and pepper

Prepare vegetables as directed.

To blanch vegetables, bring 3 quarts water to a boil in a 6- to 8-quart pan. Add one kind of vegetable (up to a pound at a time); cook until barely tender when pierced (see each choice for times). Lift out with tongs, immerse in ice water until cool, and drain. (At this point, you may let cool, then cover and refrigerate until next day.)

To grill vegetables, in a small bowl, stir together herbs and oil; or have basting sauce at the ready. Lightly brush raw or blanched vegetables with oil mixture or sauce. Grill vegetables on a lightly greased grill 4 to 6 inches above a solid bed of coals; un-

less otherwise noted below, use hot coals for blanched vegetables, medium coals for raw vegetables. Cook, turning often and brushing with as much oil mixture as needed to keep moist, until vegetables are hot, tender when pierced, and covered with brown streaks (see each choice for times). Season to taste with salt and pepper; serve hot or cooled.

If made ahead, cover and let stand at room temperature for up to 4 hours or refrigerate until next day. To reheat, place cold vegetables in a single layer in rimmed baking pans; heat in a 350° oven until heated through (7 to 10 minutes). Makes 8 servings.

Vegetables. Prepare each vegetable as directed below.

Bell peppers (red, yellow, or green), fresh pimentos, or fresh chiles. Cut into halves or quarters; remove seeds. Grill for 8 to 10 minutes.

Per serving: 105 calories (74 percent from fat), 0.9 g protein, 6 g carbohydrates, 9 g total fat (1 g saturated fat), 0 mg cholesterol, 2 mg sodium

Eggplant. Cut Oriental eggplant in half lengthwise; cut regular eggplant lengthwise into 1½-inch-wide wedges. Blanch for 2 to 3 minutes; grill until very soft when pressed (12 to 15 minutes).

Per servings: 109 calories (70 percent from fat), 1 g protein, 7 g carbohydrates, 9 g total fat (1 g saturated fat), 0 mg cholesterol, 5 mg sodium

Mushrooms (button, fresh shiitake, oyster). Thread button mushrooms through stems onto slender skewers.

Cut off tough stems of fresh shiitake mushrooms; grill large shiitakes whole and thread smaller ones on skewers. Grill all mushrooms over hot coals for about 10 minutes.

Per serving: 108 calories (73 percent from fat), 2 g protein, 5 g carbohydrates, 9 g total fat (1 g saturated fat), 0 mg cholesterol, 5 mg sodium

Onions (green). Trim root ends and top 2 inches of green tops. Grill for 6 to 8 minutes.

Per serving: 115 calories (67 percent from fat), 2 g protein, 8 g carbohydrates, 9 g total fat (1 g saturated fat), 0 mg cholesterol, 18 mg sodium

Onions (red, yellow, white). Cut small unpeeled onions into halves lengthwise; cut large peeled onions into quarters. Thread quarters through layers onto slender skewers, arranging pieces so they will lie flat. Grill for 15 to 20 minutes.

Per serving: 119 calories (67 percent from fat), 1 g protein, 9 g carbohydrates, 9 g total fat (1 g saturated fat), 0 mg cholesterol, 3 mg sodium

Potatoes (russet or thin-skinned), sweet potatoes, or yams. Scrub potatoes well; then cut lengthwise into 1-inch-wide wedges. Blanch for 4 to 5 minutes. Grill for 8 to 10 minutes.

Per serving: 171 calories (47 percent from fat), 2 g protein, 21 g carbohydrates, 9 g total fat (1 g saturated fat), 0 mg cholesterol, 9 mg sodium

Summer squash (zucchini, crookneck, pattypan). If thicker than 1 inch, cut in half lengthwise. Blanch for 2 to 3 minutes. Grill for 8 to 10 minutes.

Per serving: 96 calories (81 percent from fat), 1 g protein, 4 g carbohydrates, 9 g total fat (1 g saturated fat), 0 mg cholesterol, 4 mg sodium

Tomatoes. Cut firm-ripe tomatoes into halves. Grill for 8 to 12 minutes.

Per serving: 104 calories (76 percent from fat), 1 g protein, 5 g carbohydrates, 9 g total fat (1 g saturated fat), 0 mg cholesterol, 10 mg sodium

San Fernando Valley Beans

Here, kidney beans are prepared much as they once were by cowboys and cattlemen—with plenty of sausage, onions, and brown sugar. This old-fashioned recipe appeared in *Sunset's Cooking Bold and Fearless* in 1957.

- 1 **pound dried red kidney beans or red beans**
- ½ **pound bulk pork sausage**
- ½ **cup firmly packed brown sugar**
- 2 **large apples, cored and sliced**
- 4 **medium-size onions, sliced**
- 2 **cloves garlic, peeled**
- 1½ **cups tomato juice**
- 2 **teaspoons salt**
- ½ **teaspoon *each* pepper and chili powder**
- ¼ **cup rum (optional)**
  Sour cream (optional)

Rinse and sort through beans, discarding any debris. Soak beans overnight in enough water to cover by about 2 inches. (Or place beans in a large pan and add water to cover by about 2 inches. Bring to a boil over high heat; boil for 2 minutes. Remove from heat and let stand for 1 hour.) Drain beans, return to pan, and add water to cover by 2 inches. Bring to a boil; then reduce heat, cover, and simmer until beans are very tender to bite (about 1½ hours). Drain and set aside.

Crumble sausage into a large pan. Cook over medium heat, stirring often, until lightly browned. Discard fat from pan; then add sugar, apples, onions, garlic, tomato juice, salt, pepper, and chili powder. Stir until blended. Bring to a boil over high heat and add cooked beans. Then reduce heat and simmer, uncovered, until liquid has evaporated (at least 2 hours). If desired, stir in rum 5 minutes before serving and top each

serving with a dollop of sour cream. Makes 10 to 12 servings.

Per serving: 260 calories (12 percent from fat), 13 g protein, 46 g carbohydrates, 4 g total fat (1 g saturated fat), 8 mg cholesterol, 664 mg sodium

Garbanzo Curry

Served with rice, this curried vegetable stew is a satisfying full meal. The combination of beans and grain provides complete protein.

- 2 **tablespoons olive oil or salad oil**
- 1 **large onion, chopped**
- 5 **or 6 stalks celery, chopped**
- 1 **large red or green bell pepper, seeded and coarsely chopped**
- 4 **cloves garlic, minced or pressed**
- 3½ **cups chicken broth**
- 1⅓ **pounds red thin-skinned potatoes, scrubbed and cut into 1-inch chunks**
- 2 **cans (about 15 oz. *each*) garbanzo beans, drained and rinsed**
- 1 **can (about 6 oz.) tomato paste**
- 1 **tablespoon curry powder**
- ¼ **teaspoon ground red pepper (cayenne)**
- 4 **cups hot cooked rice**
  Thinly sliced green onion

Heat oil in a 5- to 6-quart pan over medium heat. Add chopped onion, celery, bell pepper, and garlic; cook, stirring occasionally, until vegetables are tender to bite (about 7 minutes). Stir in broth, potatoes, beans, tomato paste, curry powder, and red pepper. Then cover and simmer until potatoes are tender when pierced (30 to 40 minutes).

Spoon rice in a ring on a rimmed platter and spoon curry in center; or spoon rice onto individual plates and ladle curry over rice. Sprinkle with green onion. Makes 6 servings.

Per serving: 465 calories (17 percent from fat), 15 g protein, 83 g carbohydrates, 9 g total fat (0.9 g saturated fat), 0 mg cholesterol, 1,001 mg sodium

WESTERN CLASSIC
Broccoli with Pine Nuts & Rice

Golden raisins, pine nuts, and a touch of spice add interest to fresh broccoli and rice.

- ⅓ **cup pine nuts or slivered almonds**
- 1 **tablespoon olive oil or salad oil**
- ½ **cup long-grain white rice**
- ¼ **cup golden raisins**
- 1½ **teaspoons chili powder**
- 2 **cups chicken broth**
  About 1¼ pounds broccoli

Toast pine nuts in a wide frying pan over medium heat, stirring often, until lightly browned (3 to 5 minutes). Remove from pan and set aside.

Add oil, rice, raisins, and chili powder to pan. Cook, stirring, until rice is opaque (about 3 minutes). Add broth and stir until blended. Bring to a boil over high heat; then reduce heat, cover, and simmer until rice is barely tender to bite (about 15 minutes). Meanwhile, trim and discard ends of broccoli stalks. Cut flowerets from stalks; peel stalks and cut crosswise into thin slices. Set aside.

After rice has cooked for 15 minutes, arrange broccoli flowerets and stalks on top of rice. Cover and continue to cook until broccoli is tender-crisp to bite (about 10 more minutes). Gently stir broccoli into rice mixture; spoon onto a platter and sprinkle with pine nuts. Makes 4 servings.

Per serving: 243 calories (37 percent from fat), 9 g protein, 33 g carbohydrates, 11 g total fat (1 g saturated fat), 0 mg cholesterol, 529 mg sodium

Broccoli Soufflé Roll

If you're a big fan of *Sunset*, you've probably seen this recipe before. Featured in more than a few of our cook books, it's a perennial favorite.

- 1 **pound broccoli**
- 6 **tablespoons butter or margarine**
- ¾ **cup all-purpose flour**
  About 1 teaspoon dry mustard
  About ½ teaspoon salt
- 3½ **cups milk**
- 4 **eggs, separated**
- 1 **cup (about 4 oz.) shredded Cheddar or Longhorn cheese**

Trim and discard ends of broccoli stalks. Cut flowerets from stalks; peel stalks and cut crosswise into thin slices. Arrange broccoli on a rack in a pan over 1 inch of boiling water; cover and steam until tender-crisp to bite (about 5 minutes). Drain, immerse in ice water until cool, and drain again. Chop broccoli and set aside.

Line bottom of a greased 10- by 15-inch rimmed baking pan with foil; grease and lightly flour foil and set pan aside.

Melt butter in a 3-quart pan over medium heat. Stir in flour, 1 teaspoon of the mustard, and ½ teaspoon of the salt. Cook, stirring, for 1 to 2 minutes (do not brown). Remove from heat and gradually stir in 3 cups of the milk. Then return to heat and cook, stirring constantly, until sauce boils and thickens (8 to 10 minutes). Measure out 1 cup of the sauce and set aside.

In a medium-size bowl, lightly beat egg yolks; then gradually beat yolks into remaining sauce. In a small bowl, beat egg whites with a wire whisk or an electric mixer until they hold distinct but moist peaks; fold whites into egg yolk mixture. Pour into prepared baking pan. Bake in a 325° oven until soufflé is golden brown and center

springs back when lightly touched (35 to 40 minutes).

While soufflé is baking, combine the reserved 1 cup sauce with remaining ½ cup milk in a small pan. Stir in cheese and cook over medium heat, stirring, until cheese is melted. Season to taste with more mustard and salt, if desired. Measure out 1 cup of the cheese sauce and combine with chopped broccoli.

When soufflé is done, immediately invert it onto a clean towel; peel off foil, if necessary. Starting at a narrow end, evenly spread broccoli mixture over three-fourths of soufflé. Using towel for support and starting at filled end, roll up soufflé; place, seam side down, on a platter. (If not served at once, keep warm in a low oven for up to 30 minutes.)

To serve, reheat remaining cheese sauce over low heat, then spoon over roll; or cut roll crosswise into individual slices and spoon sauce equally over each. Makes 8 servings.

Per serving: 289 calories (61 percent from fat), 13 g protein, 16 g carbohydrates, 20 g total fat (11 g saturated fat), 159 mg cholesterol, 406 mg sodium

Mustard-glazed Carrots

Lightly glazed with mustard and brown sugar, bright carrot slices make a savory-sweet accompaniment for just about any simply cooked meat, poultry, or fish.

- 2 **pounds carrots, cut into ¼-inch-thick slanting slices**
- ½ **cup water**
- 3 **tablespoons butter or margarine**
- 3 **tablespoons Dijon mustard**
- 2 **tablespoons firmly packed brown sugar**
  Chopped parsley

Place carrots in a 3-quart pan. Add water and bring to a boil over high heat; then reduce heat, cover, and

simmer until carrots are tender-crisp to bite (about 10 minutes). Drain any liquid from pan, then stir in butter, mustard, and sugar. Cook over medium heat, stirring, until carrots are evenly glazed (1 to 2 minutes). Sprinkle with parsley. Makes 6 servings.

Per serving: 142 calories (40 percent from fat), 2 g protein, 21 g carbohydrates, 7 g total fat (4 g saturated fat), 16 mg cholesterol, 338 mg sodium

Celery Hearts Amandine

A crusty broiled topping of Parmesan and almonds gives lightly cooked celery a lively new dimension.

- 3 **celery hearts (*each* about 1½ inches in diameter)**
- 3 **tablespoons butter or margarine**
- 1 **small onion, chopped**
- 1 **cup chicken broth**
- ½ **teaspoon ground nutmeg**
- 1 **cup half-and-half**
- 2 **tablespoons all-purpose flour blended with 3 tablespoons water**
- 2 **tablespoons dry sherry or chicken broth**
  Salt and pepper
- ½ **cup *each* sliced almonds and grated Parmesan cheese**

Trim each celery heart to about 6 inches long; then cut in half lengthwise and rinse well. Set aside.

Melt butter in a wide frying pan over medium heat. Add onion and cook, stirring often, until golden (about 7 minutes). Add celery, broth, and nutmeg. Cover and simmer until celery is just tender when pierced (12 to 15 minutes). Lift out and arrange in a greased 7- by 11-inch baking dish. Add half-and-half, flour mixture, and sherry to cooking liquid in frying pan; cook over medium heat, stirring, until thickened. Season to taste with salt and pepper and pour over celery.

Sprinkle with almonds and cheese. Broil 6 inches below heat just until cheese is browned. Makes 6 servings.

Per serving: 221 calories (68 percent from fat), 7 g protein, 11 g carbohydrates, 17 g total fat (8 g saturated fat), 36 mg cholesterol, 431 mg sodium

Corn Casserole

When we printed this recipe in 1970, it had already been the specialty of one California family for over 40 years. Kids love its soft texture and cheesy flavor; adults like the fact that it's a cinch to make.

- 1 **can (about 17 oz.) cream-style corn**
- 1 **cup evaporated milk**
- ½ **cup fine salted cracker crumbs**
- 3 **eggs, beaten**
- 1 **medium-size onion, minced**
- ¼ **teaspoon salt**
- ⅛ **teaspoon pepper**
- 1½ **cups (about 6 oz.) shredded sharp Cheddar cheese**

In a large bowl, combine corn, milk, crumbs, eggs, onion, salt, and pepper; stir until blended. Spoon half the corn mixture into a well-greased 8-inch-square baking pan; sprinkle with half the cheese. Evenly spoon remaining corn mixture over cheese; then top with remaining cheese. Bake in a 350° oven until mixture is set and cheese is golden (about 35 minutes). Makes 6 to 8 servings.

Per serving: 259 calories (47 percent from fat), 13 g protein, 22 g carbohydrates, 14 g total fat (8 g saturated fat), 127 mg cholesterol, 545 mg sodium

Ratatouille

A country-style vegetable stew that originated along the sunny southern coast of France, ratatouille is a long-time *Sunset* favorite. It's been one of our most frequently requested recipes ever since we developed our first version of the dish in 1965. Part of ratatouille's appeal is that it tastes better if made ahead—even a day or more in advance—and is just as good cold as reheated.

- About ½ **cup olive oil**
- 2 **large onions, sliced**
- 2 **large cloves garlic, minced or pressed**
- 1 **medium-size eggplant (about 1 lb.), unpeeled, cut into ½-inch cubes**
- 6 **medium-size zucchini, thickly sliced**
- 2 **green or red bell peppers, seeded and cut into chunks**
- 1 **teaspoon dry basil**
- ½ **cup minced parsley**
- 4 **large tomatoes (about 2 lbs. *total*), cut into chunks**
  Salt
  Parsley sprigs (optional)

Heat ¼ cup of the oil in a wide frying pan or 4- to 5-quart pan over medium-high heat. Add onions and garlic and cook, stirring often, until onions are soft but not browned (about 4 minutes). Stir in eggplant, zucchini, bell peppers, basil, and minced parsley; add more oil as needed to prevent sticking. Reduce heat, cover, and simmer, stirring occasionally, for about 30 minutes. Stir in tomatoes. Cover and continue to simmer, stirring occasionally, for 15 more minutes. If ratatouille appears soupy, uncover and simmer until almost all liquid has evaporated. Season to taste with salt.

If made ahead, let cool; then cover and refrigerate for up to 3 days. Serve hot, cold, or at room temperature. Garnish with parsley sprigs, if desired. Makes 8 to 10 servings.

Per serving: 183 calories (58 percent from fat), 4 g protein, 17 g carbohydrates, 13 g total fat (2 g saturated fat), 0 mg cholesterol, 18 mg sodium

Vegetable Moussaka

Classics like moussaka have inspired countless variations. This all-vegetable version features layers of potatoes, eggplant, zucchini, and artichoke hearts beneath a golden coating of melted mild cheese.

- 1 **pound thin-skinned potatoes, scrubbed and thinly sliced**
- 1 **medium-size eggplant (about 1 lb.), unpeeled, thinly sliced**
- 3 **medium-size zucchini, thinly sliced**
- ½ **cup minced fresh basil or 2 tablespoons dry basil**
- 2 **jars (about 6 oz. *each*) marinated artichoke hearts**
- 2 **cups (about 8 oz.) shredded Münster cheese**

Spread potatoes over bottom of a greased 9- by 13-inch baking dish; top evenly with eggplant, then with zucchini. Sprinkle with basil. Drizzle marinade from artichokes over layered vegetables; set artichokes aside. Cover baking dish; bake in a 400° oven until vegetables are very tender when pierced (about 1 hour).

Uncover baking dish and tuck artichokes among vegetables. Continue to bake, uncovered, until liquid has evaporated (about 30 more minutes). Sprinkle cheese over vegetables; continue to bake just until cheese is melted and golden brown (about 10 more minutes). Let stand for 10 minutes before serving. Makes 8 servings.

Per serving: 217 calories (47 percent from fat), 10 g protein, 20 g carbohydrates, 12 g total fat (6 g saturated fat), 27 mg cholesterol, 406 mg sodium

Thai Potato & Eggplant Casserole

The combination of coconut and spices—a blend that's popular in Thai cooking—lends an exotic accent to this make-ahead casserole. You bake eggplant and potatoes until soft, then layer the sliced vegetables in a baking dish and top them with a gingery coconut-milk sauce. Serve the robust dish with grilled meats or poultry.

- 3 **medium-size eggplants (about 3½ lbs.** *total***)**
  About ¼ cup salad oil or olive oil
- 3 **medium-size onions, sliced and separated into rings**
- 3 **large russet potatoes, scrubbed**
  Coconut Sauce (recipe follows)
  Salt and pepper

Cut unpeeled eggplants crosswise into ¾-inch-thick slices. Arrange eggplant slices in a single layer in 2 oiled 10- by 15-inch rimmed baking pans; brush lightly with oil. Scatter onions over eggplant. Place pans in a 450° oven. Pierce each potato in several places with a fork; place potatoes on oven racks alongside baking pans. After 20 minutes, turn eggplant slices over (let onions scatter) and switch positions of pans in oven. Continue to bake until eggplant is browned and both eggplant and potatoes are very soft when pressed (about 20 more minutes). Meanwhile, prepare Coconut Sauce.

Let baked vegetables cool briefly; then cut potatoes into ¼-inch-thick slices. Arrange half the eggplant and onions in an even layer in a shallow 3½- to 4-quart baking dish. Arrange potatoes over eggplant mixture, then cover potatoes with remaining eggplant and onions. Pour Coconut Sauce evenly over vegetables; cover dish tightly with foil. (At this point, you may refrigerate until next day.)

Bake, covered, in a 400° oven until liquid in dish is bubbly (about 30 minutes; about 45 minutes if refrigerated). Uncover and continue to bake until top is lightly browned (about 30 more minutes). Let stand for 10 minutes before serving. Season to taste with salt and pepper. Makes 8 to 10 servings.

Coconut Sauce. In a wide frying pan, combine 3 tablespoons **salad oil;** 1 cup minced **shallots** or red onion; 4 cloves **garlic,** minced or pressed; 3 tablespoons finely minced **fresh ginger;** 1 teaspoon **ground turmeric;** ½ to 1 teaspoon **crushed red pepper flakes;** and ½ teaspoon **ground coriander.** Cook over medium-high heat, stirring often, until shallots are very soft (about 5 minutes). Add 1 can (about 14 oz.) **unsweetened coconut milk** and 1½ cups **chicken broth** (or use 1 cup whipping cream, 2 cups chicken broth, and 1½ teaspoons coconut flavoring). Cook, stirring, until hot. Stir in ¼ cup **lemon juice.** Use warm or cool.

Per serving: 332 calories (53 percent from fat), 6 g protein, 35 g carbohydrates, 21 g total fat (10 g saturated fat), 0 mg cholesterol, 189 mg sodium

Mexican Eggplant Casserole

You determine the spiciness of this casserole—simply vary the amount of chiles you include.

- 1 **large eggplant (about 1½ lbs.)**
  About ¼ cup olive oil
- 1 **can (about 15 oz.) tomato sauce**
- ½ **to 1 small can (about 4 oz.) diced green chiles**
- ½ **cup thinly sliced green onions**
- ½ **teaspoon** *each* **ground cumin and garlic salt**
- 1 **can (about 2¼ oz.) sliced ripe olives, drained**
- 1½ **cups (about 6 oz.) shredded Cheddar cheese**
  Sour cream

Cut unpeeled eggplant into ½-inch-thick slices and brush all over with oil. Arrange slices in a single layer on a rimmed baking sheet and bake in a 450° oven until soft when pressed (about 25 minutes). Meanwhile, in a small pan, combine tomato sauce, chiles, onions, cumin, garlic salt, and olives. Bring to a simmer; then simmer, uncovered, over medium-low heat for 10 minutes.

Arrange half the eggplant slices in a single layer over bottom of a shallow 1½-quart baking dish. Spoon half the sauce over eggplant and sprinkle with half the cheese. Repeat layers, using remaining eggplant, sauce, and cheese. Bake in a 350° oven until bubbly and heated through (about 30 minutes). Offer sour cream to top individual servings. Makes 6 servings.

Per serving: 265 calories (64 percent from fat), 10 g protein, 15 g carbohydrates, 20 g total fat (7 g saturated fat), 30 mg cholesterol, 971 mg sodium

Coriander-spiced Eggplant

The problem with sautéing eggplant is that it tends to soak up oil like a sponge. To save fat and calories, we've baked this eggplant in a hot oven, then mixed the diced pulp into a spicy curry-seasoned sauce made with just 2 teaspoons of olive oil.

- 1 **large or 2 small eggplants (1½ to 2 lbs.** *total***)**
- 2 **teaspoons olive oil or salad oil**
- ½ **teaspoon cumin seeds**
- 1 **tablespoon minced fresh ginger**
- 1 **small red onion, thickly sliced**
- 1 **teaspoon ground turmeric**
- 2 **teaspoons ground coriander**
- 1 **teaspoon** *each* **ground cumin and paprika**
- 1 **medium-size green bell pepper, seeded and coarsely chopped**
- 1 **large tomato, peeled and chopped**

¼ cup water
¼ cup coarsely chopped cilantro
Salt and pepper

Place whole unpeeled eggplant in a 10- by 15-inch rimmed baking pan and bake in a 400° oven until very soft when pressed (about 50 minutes). Let cool slightly, then cut in half and scoop out pulp; discard large seed pockets, skin, and stem. Coarsely chop pulp; place in a colander to drain.

Heat oil in a wide frying pan over medium heat. Add cumin seeds, ginger, and onion; cook, stirring often, until onion is soft (about 5 minutes). Stir in turmeric, coriander, ground cumin, paprika, bell pepper, and tomato. Cook, stirring occasionally, until tomato has released its juice (about 5 minutes). Add water and bring to a simmer. Reduce heat to low and simmer, uncovered, for 10 minutes. Add chopped eggplant and cook until heated through (about 5 minutes). Remove from heat and stir in cilantro. Season to taste with salt and pepper. Makes 6 servings.

Per serving: 63 calories (24 percent from fat), 2 g protein, 11 g carbohydrates, 2 g total fat (0.2 g saturated fat), 0 mg cholesterol, 10 mg sodium

Creamy Mushroom Enchiladas

Tender sliced mushrooms in an onion-chile cream sauce make a delicate filling for corn tortillas. Top the enchiladas with a spicy homemade tomato sauce and a sprinkling of jack cheese.

Savory Enchilada Sauce (recipe follows); or 3½ cups purchased enchilada sauce
¼ cup butter or margarine
1½ pounds mushrooms, sliced
1 large can (about 7 oz.) diced green chiles
1 cup *each* sliced green onions and plain yogurt

1 small package (3 oz.) cream cheese, cut into pieces
2 tablespoons all-purpose flour
Salt and pepper
10 corn tortillas
1½ cups (about 6 oz.) shredded jack cheese

Prepare Savory Enchilada Sauce and keep warm (or, if using purchased sauce, heat it in a wide frying pan over low heat).

Melt butter in a wide frying pan over medium-high heat. Add mushrooms and cook, stirring often, until mushrooms are soft and liquid has evaporated (about 5 minutes). Reduce heat to low and add chiles, onions, yogurt, cream cheese, and flour; cook, stirring constantly, until mixture is thickened. Remove from heat; season to taste with salt and pepper.

Work with one tortilla at a time. Using tongs, dip each tortilla into enchilada sauce for a few seconds to soften; then place tortilla in a greased 9- by 13-inch baking pan and spoon ⅓ to ½ cup of the filling down center of tortilla. Roll tortilla around filling to enclose, then turn seam side down. Arrange filled tortillas side by side, completely covering pan bottom. (If sauce becomes too thick, thin with water or dry red wine.) Pour remaining sauce evenly over enchiladas.

Cover and bake in a 375° oven for 20 minutes. Uncover baking pan and sprinkle jack cheese evenly over enchiladas. Continue to bake, uncovered, until cheese is melted (about 5 more minutes). Makes 5 servings.

Savory Enchilada Sauce. Heat 2 tablespoons **olive oil** or salad oil in a wide frying pan over medium heat. Add 1 large **onion,** chopped; cook, stirring often, until golden (about 7 minutes). Add 2 cloves **garlic,** minced or pressed; 1 can (about 15 oz.) **tomato sauce;** ¾ cup **dry red wine** or water; 1 tablespoon **chili powder;** 2 tea-

spoons *each* **dry oregano** and **honey;** and 1 teaspoon *each* **salt, ground cumin,** and **ground coriander.** Season to taste with **liquid hot pepper seasoning.** Bring to a boil; then reduce heat, cover, and simmer for 10 minutes. Keep warm. Or, if made ahead, let cool; then cover and refrigerate until next day. Reheat before using.

Per serving: 603 calories (50 percent from fat), 21 g protein, 54 g carbohydrates, 34 g total fat (11 g saturated fat), 76 mg cholesterol, 1,664 mg sodium

MINIATURE GEMS

In the 1980s, baby vegetables became a Western food fad. Miniature produce graced the shelves of California's best markets and featured prominently on the menus of sophisticated restaurants.

In a 1987 article, *Sunset* compared "the Lilliputians of the greengrocer" with their regular-size counterparts. We found that the tiny types, though often more expensive and harder to find than full-size varieties, can be sweeter in flavor and more tender in texture. And of course, they're always attractive to serve, whether steamed and buttered for an elegant side dish or lightly cooked and chilled to accompany a savory dip.

Spinach Mushroom Pie

An updated version of the classic pot pie, this spinach-cheese version is as satisfying as its meat-filled counterparts. Rich in flavor, it pairs nicely with a crisp green salad.

   Cream Cheese Pastry (page 77); or purchased pastry shell for a single-crust 9-inch pie, unbaked
1 **large onion, finely chopped**
½ **pound mushrooms, thinly sliced**
2 **slices bacon, finely chopped**
3 **large cloves garlic, minced or pressed**
2 **tablespoons chopped fresh tarragon or 1 teaspoon dry tarragon**
2 **packages (about 10 oz. *each*) frozen chopped spinach, thawed and squeezed dry**
1 **cup *each* part-skim ricotta cheese and soft bread crumbs**
3 **eggs**
½ **cup grated Parmesan cheese**
⅓ **cup finely chopped parsley**

Prepare Cream Cheese Pastry and refrigerate.

In a wide frying pan, combine onion, mushrooms, bacon, garlic, and tarragon. Cook over medium heat, stirring often, until liquid has evaporated and onion is golden brown (about 20 minutes).

Remove pan from heat and stir in spinach. Add ricotta cheese, crumbs, 2 of the eggs, Parmesan cheese, and parsley; stir until blended. Pour into a 9-inch pie pan or dish. (At this point, you may cover and refrigerate until next day.)

On a lightly floured board, roll pastry out to a 10-inch round. With a cookie cutter, cut 1 or 2 pieces from center of pastry; reserve cutouts. Lay pastry over filling; fold edges under and press firmly against pan to seal. Flute edges decoratively; top pie with cutouts. (At this point, you may cover

and refrigerate for up to 2 days if filling is fresh, up to 1 day if filling was made a day ahead.)

Set pie in a 10- by 15-inch rimmed baking pan. Lightly beat remaining egg; brush over pastry and cutouts. Bake on lowest rack of a 400° oven until pastry is well browned and filling is hot in center (40 to 55 minutes). If edges or cutouts darken excessively before center of crust is brown, drape edges and cover cutouts with foil.

Serve pie hot. Or, if made ahead, let cool; then cover and refrigerate until next day. To reheat pie, place it in a 350° oven and heat, uncovered, until filling is hot in center (30 to 40 minutes); lay foil over crust if it begins to darken. Makes 6 to 8 servings.

Per serving: 440 calories (56 percent from fat), 18 g protein, 31 g carbohydrates, 28 g total fat (15 g saturated fat), 185 mg cholesterol, 503 mg sodium

WESTERN CLASSIC
Crumb-topped Baked Onions

Crushed croutons and grated cheese combine in a simple, crunchy topping for baked small onions.

18 **to 20 small white boiling onions, peeled**
1 **chicken bouillon cube**
¾ **cup dry white wine or water**
2 **tablespoons butter or margarine**
½ **teaspoon ground sage**
¼ **teaspoon pepper**

1½ **teaspoons cornstarch blended with 1 tablespoon cold water**
¼ **cup purchased plain or seasoned croutons, slightly crushed**
2 **tablespoons grated Parmesan cheese**
1 **tablespoon chopped parsley**

Arrange onions in a single layer in an 8- or 9-inch baking dish.

In a small pan, crush bouillon cube; then add wine and butter. Heat over medium heat, stirring often, until bouillon cube is dissolved. Stir in sage and pepper. Pour over onions. Cover and bake in a 350° oven until onions are tender when pierced (about 1 hour). With a slotted spoon, transfer onions to a serving dish; keep warm.

Pour cooking juices into a small pan. Stir in cornstarch mixture and cook, stirring, until sauce boils and thickens. Pour over onions. In a small bowl, mix croutons, cheese, and parsley; sprinkle evenly over onions. Makes 5 servings.

Per serving: 107 calories (58 percent from fat), 2 g protein, 7 g carbohydrates, 5 g total fat (3 g saturated fat), 14 mg cholesterol, 342 mg sodium

Amber Onions

A delicious alternative to traditional creamed onions, this slow-baked casserole was introduced in 1960 as part of a Thanksgiving menu.

2 **pounds small white onions (*each* 1 to 1½ inches in diameter)**
2 **tablespoons butter or margarine**
1½ **tablespoons honey**
2 **tablespoons tomato juice**
½ **teaspoon salt**
1 **teaspoon paprika**
⅛ **teaspoon pepper**

Cook onions in boiling water until barely tender when pierced (about 15 minutes). Drain and let cool briefly;

then trim ends and peel. Pour into a shallow 1½-quart baking dish.

Melt butter in a small pan over medium heat. Add honey, tomato juice, salt, paprika, and pepper; stir until blended. Pour over onions. Cover and bake in a 325° oven for about 45 minutes, basting onions several times with sauce (do not stir). Uncover and continue to bake, basting occasionally, until sauce is thick and onions are well coated (about 45 more minutes). Makes 6 to 8 servings.

Per serving: 89 calories (32 percent from fat), 2 g protein, 14 g carbohydrates, 3 g total fat (2 g saturated fat), 9 mg cholesterol, 217 mg sodium

White Onion Pie

A make-ahead side dish that's easy to transport, this savory pie was created for a potluck Thanksgiving dinner in 1987. You assemble the casserole a day in advance to give the bread time to absorb the milk-egg mixture, then bake the dish just before serving.

- 4 **large onions (about 2 lbs.** *total***)**
- 2 **tablespoons butter or margarine**
   Salt
- 4 **slices white bread**
- ½ **cup grated Parmesan cheese**
- 2 **eggs**
- ¼ **teaspoon pepper**
- 1 **cup milk**
- 2 **to 4 tablespoons thinly sliced green onions**

Cut large onions in half lengthwise, then thinly slice crosswise. Melt 1 tablespoon of the butter in a wide frying pan over medium heat. Add onions and cook, stirring often, until lightly browned (about 30 minutes). Season to taste with salt.

While onions are cooking, toast bread and spread with remaining 1 tablespoon butter. Tear or cut toast into ½-inch squares and scatter over bottom of a greased 8-inch-square or

8- by 12-inch oval baking dish. Evenly spoon onions over toast and sprinkle with cheese. In a small bowl, beat together eggs, pepper, and milk; pour over onions. Cover and refrigerate for at least 10 hours or until next day.

Bake, uncovered, in a 350° oven until center of pie jiggles only slightly when dish is gently shaken (about 25 minutes). Sprinkle with green onions. Makes 8 servings.

Per serving: 163 calories (40 percent from fat), 7 g protein, 18 g carbohydrates, 7 g total fat (4 g saturated fat), 69 mg cholesterol, 224 mg sodium

Roasted Red & Yellow Potatoes

For baked potatoes with a difference, try roasting red thin-skinned potatoes with yellow-fleshed yams. After an hour in the oven, the skins are crisp and the flavors wonderfully sweet. If you'd like a bit of contrast, sprinkle the vegetables with a few dashes of sherry vinegar.

- 3 **small sweet potatoes or yams, scrubbed**
- 2 **pounds medium-size red thin-skinned potatoes, scrubbed and quartered**
- 3 **medium-size onions, quartered**
- 3 **tablespoons olive oil**
   Salt and pepper
   Sherry vinegar or cider vinegar (optional)

Cut sweet potatoes in half lengthwise; then cut crosswise into 1-inch pieces. In a shallow baking pan, combine sweet potatoes, thin-skinned potatoes, onions, and oil; toss gently to coat vegetables with oil. Bake in a 425° oven until vegetables are browned and tender throughout when pierced (about 55 minutes). Season to taste with salt and pepper. Sprinkle with vinegar, if desired. Makes 8 servings.

Per serving: 209 calories (23 percent from fat), 4 g protein, 37 g carbohydrates, 6 g total fat (0.7 g saturated fat), 0 mg cholesterol, 17 mg sodium

VERSATILE ONIONS

A cultivated crop since at least 3,000 B.C., onions have a range of forms, flavors, and textures that have made them popular all over the world. Quick cooking at high temperatures can intensify the onion's strong flavor, while slow, gentle cooking or baking diminishes pungency and enhances natural sweetness.

To tone down the harshness of raw onions to be used in salads, simply soak thin slices in ice water for 20 to 30 minutes, then squeeze lightly to crush the cell membranes. Rinse the softened onions, cover them with fresh water, and refrigerate until cold; drain well before using.

At the season's peak, the garden often supplies more produce than the gardener can eat fresh. One way to tame the overflow is to cook and purée some of the crop—and then freeze the purées to use later in the year.

Vegetable Purée

Choose carrot, tomato, or zucchini purée; or experiment with other favorite vegetables.

Carrot. Bring 3 to 4 quarts **water** to a boil over high heat. Add 5 pounds **carrots,** cut into 1½-inch pieces; cook, uncovered, until tender when pierced (10 to 12 minutes). Drain. Whirl, a portion at a time, in a food processor until smooth. Let cool. Use purée (suggestions follow) or freeze for longer storage. To freeze, spoon purée into ice cube trays or 1-cup freezer containers. Freeze until solid; then transfer cubes to freezer bags and store in freezer for up to 1 year. Makes about 2 quarts.

Per ½ cup: 61 calories (4 percent from fat), 1 g protein, 14 g carbohydrates, 0.3 g total fat (0 g saturated fat), 0 mg cholesterol, 50 mg sodium

Tomato. Seed 5 pounds **tomatoes** and cut into 1½-inch chunks. Whirl tomatoes, a portion at a time, in a food processor or blender until smooth. Pour purée into a medium-size pan. Bring to a boil over high heat; then reduce heat and boil gently, stirring often, until reduced by half. Let cool. Use purée (suggestions follow) or freeze as directed for carrot purée. Makes about 4 cups.

Per ½ cup: 54 calories (12 percent from fat), 2 g protein, 12 g carbohydrates, 0.9 g total fat (0.1 g saturated fat), 0 mg cholesterol, 23 mg sodium

Zucchini. Bring 3 to 4 quarts **water** to a boil over high heat. Add 5 pounds **zucchini,** sliced ¾ inch thick; cook, uncovered, until barely tender when pierced (5 to 7 minutes). Drain. Whirl, a portion at a time, in a food processor or blender until smooth. Let cool. Use purée (suggestions follow) or freeze as directed for carrot purée. Makes about 7 cups.

Per ½ cup: 23 calories (7 percent from fat), 2 g protein, 5 g carbohydrates, 0.2 g total fat (0 g saturated fat), 0 mg cholesterol, 5 mg sodium

Vegetable Purée Dip

Mix ½ cup **sour cream** or mayonnaise; 1 tablespoon minced **shallot;** ¼ teaspoon *each* **dry mustard, dry thyme,** and **dry tarragon;** and ½ cup **carrot, tomato, or zucchini purée** (thawed if frozen). Season to taste with **salt.** Makes 1 cup.

Per tablespoon: 19 calories (72 percent from fat), 0.3 g protein, 1 g carbohydrates, 2 g total fat (0.9 g saturated fat), 3 mg cholesterol, 8 mg sodium

Vegetable Timbales

In a medium-size bowl, combine 4 **eggs,** ½ cup **whipping cream** or milk, ⅛ teaspoon *each* **ground nutmeg** and **white pepper,** and 1 cup **tomato or zucchini purée** (or ⅔ cup carrot purée), thawed if frozen. Beat until blended. Season to taste with **salt.** Spoon mixture equally into 6 to 8 greased 1½-cup ramekins or molds. Set ramekins in an 11- by 17-inch roasting pan and pour 1 inch of hot water into pan.

Bake in a 375° oven until center of timbales appears firm when ramekins are gently shaken (25 to 30 minutes). Lift ramekins from water and let cool briefly. Run a knife around edges of timbales to loosen; unmold onto plates. Serve hot. Makes 6 to 8 servings.

Per serving: 125 calories (72 percent from fat), 5 g protein, 4 g carbohydrates, 10 g total fat (4 g saturated fat), 140 mg cholesterol, 48 mg sodium

Vegetable Purée Soufflé

Melt ¼ cup **butter** or margarine in a 2- to 3-quart pan over low heat. Add ¼ cup **all-purpose flour** and cook, stirring, for 1 minute (do not brown). Remove from heat and gradually stir in 1 cup **milk,** ¼ teaspoon **dry thyme** or dry tarragon, ⅛ teaspoon **ground nutmeg,** and 1 cup **carrot, tomato, or zucchini purée** (thawed if frozen). Return to high heat and bring to a boil, stirring constantly. Add 1 cup (about 4 oz.) shredded **Swiss cheese;** stir until melted. Remove from heat and beat in 4 **egg yolks.** Season to taste with **salt.**

In a large bowl, beat 5 **egg whites** until they hold distinct but moist peaks. Stir a fourth of the whites into sauce, then carefully fold in remaining whites until blended. Pour into a well-buttered 1½-quart soufflé dish. Bake in a 375° oven until golden brown (25 to 35 minutes). Serve at once. Makes 4 servings.

Per serving: 376 calories (64 percent from fat), 19 g protein, 15 g carbohydrates, 27 g total fat (15 g saturated fat), 278 mg cholesterol, 331 mg sodium

Hot Vegetable Purée

Melt 2 tablespoons **butter** or margarine in a wide frying pan over medium heat. Then stir in 1 large **onion,** finely chopped; cook, stirring often, until soft and golden (about 7 minutes). Stir in ⅓ cup **whipping cream** and 1 cup **carrot, tomato, or zucchini purée** (thawed if frozen). Bring to a boil; boil gently, stirring occasionally, until hot and thick. Season to taste with **salt** and **pepper.** Makes 2 servings.

Per serving: 302 calories (69 percent from fat), 4 g protein, 20 g carbohydrates, 24 g total fat (15 g saturated fat), 75 mg cholesterol, 202 mg sodium

Curried New Potatoes & Green Onions

Looking for a new way to dress up fried potatoes? Try sautéing the diced potatoes in plenty of butter, with lots of green onions and a generous sprinkling of curry and mustard seeds.

3 **pounds small thin-skinned potatoes, scrubbed**
  About ½ cup (¼ lb.) butter or margarine
2 **teaspoons** *each* **curry powder and mustard seeds**
2 **cups sliced green onions**
  Salt

Cook potatoes in boiling water until tender throughout when pierced (about 20 minutes). Drain and let cool briefly; then coarsely chop.

Melt ½ cup of the butter in a wide frying pan over high heat. Add potatoes and cook, stirring often, for about 5 minutes; add more butter if needed to prevent sticking. Sprinkle curry powder and mustard seeds over potatoes and stir until blended. Continue to cook, stirring often, until potatoes are lightly browned. Stir in onions and cook, stirring, until onions are warm. Season to taste with salt. Makes 8 to 10 servings.

Per serving: 225 calories (42 percent from fat), 4 g protein, 29 g carbohydrates, 11 g total fat (6 g saturated fat), 28 mg cholesterol, 120 mg sodium

Diced Potatoes in Soy Sauce

Just three ingredients—cubed potatoes, a little butter, and 2 tablespoons of soy sauce—go into this easy accompaniment. Try it with Oven-simmered Beef Brisket (page 77) or Flank Steak with Mustard-Caper Sauce (page 71) for a new twist on meat and potatoes.

3 **tablespoons butter or margarine**
1½ **pounds thin-skinned potatoes, scrubbed and cut into ½-inch cubes**
2 **tablespoons soy sauce**

Place butter in a 9- by 13-inch or 10- by 15-inch rimmed baking pan; set pan in a 450° oven until butter is melted.

Add potatoes to melted butter and stir to coat. Bake, stirring occasionally, until potatoes are tender when pierced (about 20 minutes). Add soy sauce and stir to coat potatoes. Continue to bake until potatoes look dry (about 10 more minutes). Makes 4 servings.

Per serving: 219 calories (36 percent from fat), 4 g protein, 31 g carbohydrates, 9 g total fat (5 g saturated fat), 23 mg cholesterol, 615 mg sodium

Mashed Potato Casserole

Cream cheese and sour cream make these do-ahead mashed potatoes taste especially rich.

1 **small package (3 oz.) cream cheese, at room temperature**
1 **teaspoon garlic salt**
¼ **teaspoon pepper**
½ **cup sour cream**
2½ **to 3 pounds russet potatoes, peeled and quartered**
2 **tablespoons butter or margarine**
  Paprika

In a bowl, beat together cream cheese, garlic salt, pepper, and sour cream until smooth; set aside.

Cook potatoes in boiling water until tender throughout when pierced (about 20 minutes); drain. Using an electric mixer or a potato masher, beat hot potatoes until almost smooth. Add cream cheese mixture and continue to beat until fluffy and smooth. Spoon potatoes into a greased shallow 2-quart baking dish; dot with butter and sprinkle with paprika. (At this point, you may cover and refrigerate until next day.)

Bake, covered, in a 400° oven for 25 minutes (50 minutes if refrigerated); uncover and continue to bake until top is golden brown (about 10 more minutes). Makes 8 to 10 servings.

Per serving: 185 calories (42 percent from fat), 4 g protein, 23 g carbohydrates, 9 g total fat (5 g saturated fat), 23 mg cholesterol, 275 mg sodium

WESTERN CLASSIC

Best-ever Garlicky Potatoes

Potato wedges, onions, and garlic all roast together in this classic side dish. The high oven heat cooks the vegetables to a crisp golden brown outside, but keeps them tender inside.

1 **tablespoon olive oil**
1 **tablespoon butter or margarine**
3 **large red thin-skinned potatoes, scrubbed and cut into eighths**
1 **medium-size onion, cut into eighths**
3 **cloves garlic, peeled and halved**
  Salt and pepper

Place oil and butter in a 9- by 13-inch baking pan; set pan in a 475° oven until butter is melted and sizzling.

Add potatoes, onion, and garlic to pan and stir to coat. Bake, stirring occasionally, until potatoes are golden brown and tender when pierced (about 30 minutes). Season vegetables to taste with salt and pepper. Makes 4 servings.

Per serving: 212 calories (28 percent from fat), 4 g protein, 35 g carbohydrates, 7 g total fat (2 g saturated fat), 8 mg cholesterol, 44 mg sodium

Indian Potatoes

Spices popular in Indian cuisine—cumin, coriander, and cayenne—season a hearty combination of thick potato slices, bell pepper, and onion.

1½ **pounds thin-skinned potatoes, scrubbed**

2 **to 3 tablespoons butter or margarine**

1 **medium-size red bell pepper, seeded and chopped**

1 **medium-size onion, chopped**

1 **tablespoon ground cumin**

1 **teaspoon ground coriander**

POTATOES

South American Indians native to the Andes were among the first to cultivate potatoes. After Spanish explorers discovered the versatile tuber in the early 16th century, they transplanted it to Spain, then introduced it to other parts of Europe. Though some thought them poisonous, potatoes were nevertheless planted in England and later in Ireland, where they soon became the principal food crop. In North America, potatoes didn't become popular until the early 19th century, after Irish immigrants arrived in New England.

⅛ **teaspoon ground red pepper (cayenne)**

⅓ **cup chopped cilantro**
   Salt and pepper
   Sour cream (optional)

Cook potatoes in boiling water until tender throughout when pierced (about 25 minutes). Drain and let cool briefly; then cut into ¼-inch-thick slices.

Melt 2 tablespoons of the butter in a wide frying pan over medium-high heat. Add bell pepper, onion, cumin, coriander, and red pepper; cook, stirring often, until onion is soft and golden (about 6 minutes). Add potatoes and cook, stirring often, until lightly browned (about 7 more minutes); add more butter if needed to prevent sticking.

Remove pan from heat. Sprinkle cilantro over potatoes and toss gently. Season to taste with salt and pepper. Spoon into a serving dish and top with a dollop of sour cream, if desired. Makes 6 servings.

Per serving: 152 calories (31 percent from fat), 3 g protein, 24 g carbohydrates, 5 g total fat (3 g saturated fat), 13 mg cholesterol, 61 mg sodium

Pecan-topped Sweet Potatoes

Delicately sweet and loaded with butter, this fluffy sweet potato dish has been a Thanksgiving tradition for many of our readers for years—ever since we first printed the recipe in 1967. A topping of brown sugar and pecans adds a toasty crunch.

2½ **to 3 pounds sweet potatoes or yams, scrubbed**

2 **eggs**

¾ **cup firmly packed brown sugar**

½ **cup (¼ lb.) butter or margarine, melted**

1 **teaspoon *each* salt and ground cinnamon**

About ½ cup orange juice

1 **cup pecan halves**

Cook sweet potatoes in boiling water until tender throughout when pierced (about 30 minutes). Drain and let cool briefly; then peel and place in a large bowl. Using an electric mixer or a potato masher, beat potatoes until almost smooth. Add eggs, ¼ cup of the sugar, ¼ cup of the butter, salt, cinnamon, and ½ cup of the orange juice. Continue to beat until moist and fluffy, adding more orange juice if needed.

Spread mixture in a shallow 1½- to 2-quart baking dish. Top with pecans, sprinkle with remaining ½ cup sugar, and drizzle with remaining ¼ cup butter. (At this point, you may cover and refrigerate until next day.)

Bake, uncovered, in a 375° oven until heated through (about 20 minutes; about 40 minutes if refrigerated). Makes 8 to 10 servings.

Per serving: 367 calories (47 percent from fat), 4 g protein, 46 g carbohydrates, 20 g total fat (7 g saturated fat), 75 mg cholesterol, 381 mg sodium

Spiced Spinach & Potatoes

Pan-fried potatoes don't have to be plain! These are combined with shredded spinach and spiced up with coriander and ginger.

¼ cup salad oil or olive oil

2 large russet potatoes, peeled
  and cut into ½-inch cubes

2 cloves garlic, minced or pressed

2 teaspoons ground coriander

½ teaspoon ground ginger

  About ½ cup water

¾ pound spinach, rinsed well,
  drained, and stems removed

  Salt and ground red pepper
  (cayenne)

Heat 3 tablespoons of the oil in a wide
frying pan over medium-high heat.
Add potatoes and cook, stirring occasionally, until well browned (10 to 15
minutes). Reduce heat to low and add
remaining 1 tablespoon oil, garlic,
coriander, and ginger. Cook, stirring
often, for 2 to 3 minutes. Add ½ cup of
the water, cover, and simmer until
potatoes are tender when pierced (5 to
10 minutes); add more water if needed
to prevent sticking. Meanwhile, cut
spinach leaves crosswise into ½-inch-
wide strips.

Uncover pan and add spinach to
potatoes. Cook over high heat, stirring
often, until spinach is wilted and almost all liquid has evaporated (about
2 minutes). Season to taste with salt
and red pepper. Makes 4 servings.

*Per serving: 229 calories (54 percent from fat),
4 g protein, 23 g carbohydrates, 14 g total fat (2 g
saturated fat), 0 mg cholesterol, 58 mg sodium*

Garlic
Creamed Spinach

A robust Italian touch—in this case,
an ample quantity of sautéed garlic—
gives simple creamed spinach unex-
pected character.

1½ pounds spinach, rinsed well,
   drained, and stems removed; or
   2 packages (about 10 oz. *each*)
   frozen leaf spinach, thawed and
   squeezed dry

1 tablespoon butter or margarine

1 tablespoon olive oil

1 large onion, finely chopped

4 cloves garlic, minced or pressed

2 tablespoons all-purpose flour

¾ cup half-and-half or sour cream

¼ teaspoon ground nutmeg

1 cup (about 4 oz.) grated
  Parmesan cheese

  Salt and pepper

If using fresh spinach, place spinach
leaves in a wide frying pan. Cover
and cook over medium heat just until
wilted (2 to 3 minutes). Remove
spinach from pan and set aside; wipe
pan dry.

Add butter and oil to pan; heat
over medium heat until butter is
melted. Add onion and garlic; cook,
stirring often, until onion is soft (about
5 minutes). Stir in flour and cook,
stirring, for 1 minute (do not brown).

Remove from heat and gradually
stir in half-and-half and nutmeg. Then
add spinach, return to high heat, and
cook, stirring constantly, until mixture
bubbles vigorously.

Remove from heat and stir in ½
cup of the cheese. Season to taste with
salt and pepper. Spoon into a serving
dish and sprinkle with remaining
½ cup cheese. Makes 4 to 6 servings.

*Per serving: 249 calories (58 percent from fat), 14
g protein, 13 g carbohydrates, 16 g total fat (9 g
saturated fat), 37 mg cholesterol, 540 mg sodium*

Spinach Squares

These tasty, almost cakelike squares
offer a new and versatile way to serve
spinach. You just combine frozen

spinach with condensed soup, eggs,
crumbs, and seasonings, then bake.
The finished dish is good hot or cold
and can easily be cut into small
squares for appetizers, or into larger
pieces for side-dish servings.

3 tablespoons butter or margarine

1 small onion, chopped

¼ pound mushrooms, sliced

4 eggs

¼ cup fine dry bread crumbs

1 can (about 10¾ oz.) condensed
  cream of mushroom soup

¼ cup grated Parmesan cheese

⅛ teaspoon *each* pepper, dry basil,
  and dry oregano

2 packages (about 10 oz. *each*)
  frozen chopped spinach,
  thawed and squeezed dry

Melt butter in a wide frying pan over
medium heat. Add onion and mushrooms and cook, stirring often, until
vegetables are soft (about 5 minutes).
Remove from heat.

In a large bowl, lightly beat eggs.
Stir in onion mixture, crumbs, soup,
2 tablespoons of the cheese, pepper,
basil, oregano, and spinach. Pour into
a greased 9-inch-square baking pan;
sprinkle with remaining 2 tablespoons
cheese.

Bake in a 325° oven until edges
are golden brown (about 35 minutes).
Serve hot; or let cool, then cover and
refrigerate to serve cold. To reheat,
place in a 325° oven and heat, uncovered, for 10 to 12 minutes. Makes
about 8 servings.

*Per serving: 165 calories (58 percent from fat),
8 g protein, 10 g carbohydrates, 11 g total fat (5 g
saturated fat), 120 mg cholesterol, 513 mg sodium*

Mediterranean Spinach

Tangy feta cheese and calamata olives add zest to a pretty combination of fresh spinach and diced tomatoes. (If you prefer a milder flavor, you can use ripe olives.)

- **2 teaspoons olive oil**
- **1 clove garlic, minced or pressed**
- **½ cup sliced green onions**
- **½ teaspoon dry dill weed**
- **⅓ pound pear-shaped (Roma-type) tomatoes, chopped**
- **1¼ pounds spinach, rinsed well, drained, and stems removed**
- **¼ cup crumbled feta cheese**
- **½ cup calamata or ripe olives, pitted if desired**
- **Salt and pepper**

Heat oil in a 5- to 6-quart pan over medium heat. Add garlic, onions, and dill weed; cook, stirring often, until onions are soft (about 5 minutes). Transfer mixture to a bowl; stir in tomatoes.

Add spinach leaves to pan, cover, and cook over medium heat just until wilted (2 to 3 minutes). With a slotted spoon, transfer spinach to a platter and spread out slightly. Top evenly with onion-tomato mixture. Sprinkle with cheese, then top with olives. Season to taste with salt and pepper. Makes 4 servings.

Per serving: 97 calories (53 percent from fat), 5 g protein, 8 g carbohydrates, 6 g total fat (2 g saturated fat), 8 mg cholesterol, 328 mg sodium

Green & White Vegetable Casserole

One look at this buffet-supper favorite explains its name. The green is spinach and artichokes in a creamy, egg-enriched sauce; the white is a rich Parmesan–cream cheese topping.

- **1 jar (about 6 oz.) marinated artichoke hearts**
- **2 tablespoons butter or margarine**
- **1 medium-size onion, chopped**
- **2 packages (about 10 oz. *each*) frozen chopped spinach, thawed and squeezed dry**
- **¼ teaspoon ground nutmeg**
- **¾ teaspoon dry oregano**
- **1 can (about 10¾ oz.) condensed cream of celery soup**
- **4 eggs, beaten**
- **⅛ teaspoon pepper**
- **1 large package (8 oz.) cream cheese, at room temperature**
- **⅓ cup *each* milk and grated Parmesan cheese**

Drain artichokes, reserving 2 tablespoons of the marinade; then chop artichokes and set aside.

Melt butter in reserved 2 tablespoons marinade in a wide frying pan over medium heat. Add onion and cook, stirring often, until soft (about 5 minutes). Remove from heat and stir in artichokes, spinach, nutmeg, oregano, soup, eggs, and pepper. Spoon mixture evenly into a greased shallow 2-quart baking dish.

In a bowl, beat together cream cheese, milk, and Parmesan cheese; spread evenly over spinach mixture. Bake in a 325° oven until center feels firm when lightly pressed (about 35 minutes). Makes 6 to 8 servings.

Per serving: 293 calories (68 percent from fat), 12 g protein, 12 g carbohydrates, 23 g total fat (12 g saturated fat), 175 mg cholesterol, 757 mg sodium

Glazed Banana Squash

Diced banana squash, butter-steamed and accented with orange and apricot, is a good partner for baked ham, roast turkey, or grilled pork chops.

- **¼ cup butter or margarine**
- **1½ pounds banana squash, peeled, seeded, and cut into ¼-inch cubes**
- **About 2 tablespoons water**
- **1 tablespoon thawed frozen orange juice concentrate**
- **3 tablespoons apricot jam**
- **⅛ teaspoon ground cloves**
- **¼ teaspoon salt**
- **Dash of pepper**

Melt butter in a wide frying pan over high heat. Add squash and 2 tablespoons of the water; stir to coat. Cover and cook over high heat, stirring occasionally, just until squash is tender to bite and liquid has been absorbed (4 to 5 minutes); add more water if needed to prevent sticking. Reduce heat to low and stir in orange juice concentrate, jam, cloves, salt, and pepper. Cook, stirring gently, until squash is evenly glazed. Makes 4 to 6 servings.

Per serving: 156 calories (52 percent from fat), 2 g protein, 18 g carbohydrates, 9 g total fat (6 g saturated fat), 25 mg cholesterol, 207 mg sodium

Baked Squash with Maple Butter

Nothing says autumn like the rich flavor of maple—and acorn squash topped with maple syrup and butter is a great choice for cool-weather special-occasion dinners. The dish is a time-saver, too: you can bake the squash halves and make the topping 3 days in advance, then reheat before serving.

- **½ cup (¼ lb.) butter or margarine, at room temperature**
- **6 tablespoons maple syrup**

½ teaspoon ground cinnamon

¼ teaspoon *each* ground ginger and ground allspice

3 large acorn squash
Salt

In a small bowl, stir together butter, syrup, cinnamon, ginger, and allspice. Cover and refrigerate until cold or for up to 3 days.

Cut squash in half lengthwise; scoop out seeds. Place halves, cut side down, in a large baking pan. Pour 1 inch of boiling water into pan. Cover and bake in a 350° oven until squash is tender when pierced (about 45 minutes). Lift out squash and pour water from pan. (At this point, you may let squash cool, then cover and refrigerate for up to 3 days.)

Return squash to pan, placing halves cut side up. Sprinkle lightly with salt. Place a sixth of the maple butter in cavity of each squash half. Cover and bake in a 400° oven until heated through (about 25 minutes; about 35 minutes if refrigerated). To serve, arrange squash in a serving dish; at the table, scoop squash from skins onto individual plates. Makes 12 to 14 servings.

Per serving: 150 calories (40 percent from fat), 1 g protein, 23 g carbohydrates, 7 g total fat (4 g saturated fat), 19 mg cholesterol, 78 mg sodium

Zucchini Patties

When this recipe appeared in a 1960 "Kitchen Cabinet," tender vegetable patties were something new. They're more familiar to many of us today, but no less delicious as an accompaniment to grilled meats or fish.

5 medium-size zucchini

3 eggs

1 tablespoon grated Parmesan cheese

1 or 2 cloves garlic, minced or pressed

2 tablespoons all-purpose flour

½ cup finely chopped parsley

1 teaspoon *each* salt and pepper
About ½ cup olive oil or salad oil

Coarsely shred zucchini into a large bowl; press out and discard as much liquid as possible. Add eggs, cheese, garlic, flour, parsley, salt, and pepper; stir until blended.

Shape zucchini mixture into 2-inch-wide patties. Heat 2 tablespoons of the oil in a wide frying pan over medium heat. Add patties, a few at a time (do not crowd pan); cook, turning once, until lightly browned on both sides. Add more oil to pan as needed to prevent sticking. As patties are cooked, transfer to a serving dish and keep warm. Makes 6 servings.

Per serving: 233 calories (79 percent from fat), 6 g protein, 7 g carbohydrates, 21 g total fat (3 g saturated fat), 107 mg cholesterol, 420 mg sodium

Zucchini Flats

Coated in an egg batter laden with cheese and garlic, thin slices of zucchini cook to a crisp golden brown.

About ¾ cup grated Parmesan cheese

2 eggs

2 tablespoons *each* all-purpose flour and minced parsley

¾ teaspoon salt

¼ teaspoon pepper

2 cloves garlic, minced or pressed

¼ cup milk

2 large zucchini (*each* about 7 inches long)
All-purpose flour

¼ cup salad oil or olive oil

In a shallow bowl, whisk together ¾ cup of the cheese, eggs, the 2 tablespoons flour, parsley, salt, pepper, garlic, and milk until well blended. Cover; refrigerate for 15 minutes.

Cut zucchini in half crosswise; then cut each half lengthwise into slices about ¼ inch thick. Lightly dust each slice with flour.

Heat oil in a wide frying pan over medium heat. Using a fork, dip each zucchini slice into egg mixture, thickly coating both sides. Place slices in pan, a few at a time (do not crowd pan); cook, turning once, until golden brown on both sides. Drain briefly on paper towels, then transfer to a serving dish and keep warm. To serve, sprinkle zucchini lightly with additional cheese. Makes 4 to 6 servings.

Per serving: 178 calories (58 percent from fat), 10 g protein, 9 g carbohydrates, 12 g total fat (4 g saturated fat), 96 mg cholesterol, 588 mg sodium

Pressed Leek Terrine

It may look complicated, but this sophisticated terrine is actually quite simple (if somewhat time-consuming!) to prepare. You poach halved leeks in broth, then pull them apart, leaf by leaf, and stack the layers flat in a loaf pan. Weight and chill the terrine overnight to press the layers together firmly; then slice and serve with a Dijon mustard dressing for a distinctive first course.

    5   **pounds small to medium-size leeks**
    1   **teaspoon dry tarragon**
    6   **cups chicken broth**
        Mustard-Lemon Dressing (recipe follows)
        Salt

Cut off and discard root ends of leeks. Trim tops, leaving about 1 inch of green leaves; save 10 tender green inner leaves from leek tops. Discard coarse outer leaves. Split leeks in half lengthwise and rinse well.

In a 4- to 5-quart pan, combine tarragon and broth. Bring to a boil over high heat; add all leeks, reduce heat, cover, and simmer until leeks are tender when pierced (about 15 minutes). Drain; reserve broth for other uses.

Separate leeks into individual layers. Set each piece flat in an oiled 5- by 9-inch loaf pan; distribute dark green tops equally throughout terrine. Cut long pieces to fit pan length; patch layers to use all leaves. Oil bottom of an identical pan and set on top of layered leeks; put about 4 pounds of canned goods or dried beans in top pan to weight leeks. Cover and refrigerate for at least 8 hours or up to 2 days; pour off any liquid that accumulates.

Shortly before serving, prepare Mustard-Lemon Dressing. To serve, remove weighted pan. With a very sharp knife, gently cut terrine crosswise into 10 slices. Using 2 spatulas, lift slices to individual plates. Top with dressing and season to taste with salt. Makes 10 servings.

Mustard-Lemon Dressing. In a small bowl, whisk together ½ cup **olive oil** or salad oil, 3 tablespoons **lemon juice**, 1 tablespoon **Dijon mustard,** and ¼ teaspoon **pepper.** Makes ¾ cup.

Per serving of terrine: 90 calories (23 percent from fat), 3 g protein, 15 g carbohydrates, 2 g total fat (0.2 g saturated fat), 0 mg cholesterol, 612 mg sodium

Per tablespoon of Mustard-Lemon Dressing: 82 calories (98 percent from fat), 0 g protein, 0.4 g carbohydrates, 9 g total fat (1 g saturated fat), 0 mg cholesterol, 38 mg sodium

Curried Green Tomatoes

Late-season green tomatoes that have no chance of ripening before the frost can still be put to delicious use. In this crumb-topped casserole, the tart sliced fruit is seasoned with curry spices and topped with yogurt and sweet sautéed onions.

        Curry Spice Blend (recipe follows)
    4   **medium-size green (unripe) tomatoes (about 1¾ lbs. *total*)**
        About 2 tablespoons olive oil or salad oil
    1   **large onion, thinly sliced**
    1   **teaspoon all-purpose flour**
    ¾   **cup plain yogurt**
        Salt and pepper
    1½ **tablespoons butter or margarine**
    ¾   **cup coarse soft bread crumbs**
        Cilantro sprigs

Prepare Curry Spice Blend and set aside.

Peel tomatoes and cut crosswise into ¼-inch-thick slices. Heat 1 tablespoon of the oil in a medium-size frying pan over medium heat. Add half the tomatoes and cook, turning occasionally, until slices turn limp and lose their bright color (8 to 10 minutes). Lift out and set aside. Repeat to cook remaining tomatoes, adding more oil as needed to prevent sticking. Reserve 3 or 4 tomato slices; layer remaining slices in a shallow 1½- to 2-quart baking dish.

In pan used to cook tomatoes, heat 1 more tablespoon oil over medium heat; add onion and cook, stirring occasionally, until soft and beginning to turn golden (15 to 20 minutes). Add ¾ teaspoon of the Curry Spice Blend and stir for 2 minutes. Remove pan from heat and stir in flour. Then stir in yogurt and season to taste with salt and pepper. Spoon yogurt mixture over tomatoes in baking dish, covering them completely.

Melt butter in a medium-size frying pan over medium-high heat. Add crumbs and remaining 1¼ teaspoons Curry Spice Blend; cook, stirring, until crumbs are golden brown and crisp (about 3 minutes). Sprinkle crumbs evenly over casserole. Arrange reserved tomato slices in an overlapping pattern on crumbs. Bake in a 350° oven until heated through (about 15 minutes). Garnish with cilantro sprigs. Makes 4 to 6 servings.

Curry Spice Blend. In a small bowl, mix 1 teaspoon **curry powder;** ¼ teaspoon *each* **ground ginger, ground cumin,** and **ground coriander;** and ⅛ teaspoon *each* **ground red pepper (cayenne)** and **dry mustard.**

Per serving: 178 calories (49 percent from fat), 5 g protein, 19 g carbohydrates, 10 g total fat (3 g saturated fat), 12 mg cholesterol, 115 mg sodium

Tomatoes Stuffed with Spinach

Looking for an attractive side dish to serve with roast beef or lamb? Try plump red tomatoes stuffed with a hearty filling of spinach, bacon, and bread crumbs. For best results, select firm-ripe tomatoes about 2½ inches in diameter.

- **6 medium-size tomatoes**
  Salt
- **6 slices bacon**
- **1 pound spinach, rinsed well, drained, and stems removed; or 1 package (about 10 oz.) frozen chopped spinach, thawed and squeezed dry**
- **¾ cup soft bread crumbs**
- **¼ teaspoon pepper**
  Sour cream (optional)

Cut a thin slice off top of each tomato. Using a spoon, carefully scoop out centers of tomatoes. Lightly sprinkle inside of each tomato with salt; turn tomatoes upside down to drain.

Cook bacon in a medium-size frying pan over medium heat until crisp. Lift out, drain, crumble, and set aside. If using fresh spinach, place leaves in a wide frying pan. Cover and cook over medium heat just until wilted (2 to 3 minutes). Remove from heat and transfer to a medium-size bowl; stir in bacon, crumbs, and

pepper. Season to taste with salt. Stuff tomatoes equally with spinach mixture and set upright in a greased baking pan.

Bake in a 350° oven until tomatoes are just tender but still hold their shape (about 20 minutes). Top each tomato with a dollop of sour cream, if desired. Makes 6 servings.

Per serving: 95 calories (47 percent from fat), 5 g protein, 9 g carbohydrates, 5 g total fat (1 g saturated fat), 6 mg cholesterol, 226 mg sodium

Candied Yams

In most parts of the United States, genuine yams are hard to find— supermarket "yams" are usually just sweeter, moister varieties of basic sweet potatoes. Here, the rich flavor is intensified with a sticky brown sugar glaze.

- **4 pounds yams or sweet potatoes, scrubbed**
- **⅓ cup butter or margarine**
- **½ cup firmly packed dark brown sugar**
- **½ teaspoon salt**
- **¼ cup rum (optional)**

Cook yams in boiling water until tender throughout when pierced (about 30 minutes). Drain, let cool briefly, and peel. Cut yams into ¼-inch-thick slices and arrange, overlapping slices slightly, in concentric rings in a shallow 3-quart baking dish. Dot with butter and sprinkle with sugar and salt. (At this point, you may cover and refrigerate until next day.)

Drizzle rum over yams, if desired. Bake, uncovered, in a 375° oven until juices are bubbly and yams have a shiny glaze (about 1 hour and 10 minutes); baste frequently with juices. Makes 12 to 14 servings.

Per serving: 215 calories (20 percent from fat), 2 g protein, 42 g carbohydrates, 5 g total fat (3 g saturated fat), 13 mg cholesterol, 145 mg sodium

Yam & Cashew Casserole

This cinnamon-spiced casserole is a holiday favorite. The recipe first appeared in our "Kitchen Cabinet" in November 1968.

- **2½ pounds yams or sweet potatoes, scrubbed**
- **1 teaspoon ground cinnamon**
  About ¼ teaspoon salt
- **1 egg**
  About ¼ cup *each* pineapple juice and apple juice
  About ¼ cup sugar
- **3 tablespoons butter or margarine, at room temperature**
- **½ cup salted cashews, coarsely chopped**

Cook yams in boiling water until tender throughout when pierced (about 30 minutes). Drain and let cool briefly; then peel and place in a large bowl. Using an electric mixer or a potato masher, beat yams until almost smooth. Add cinnamon, ¼ teaspoon of the salt, egg, ¼ cup each of the pineapple juice and apple juice, and ¼ cup of the sugar. Continue to beat until mixture is moist and fluffy, adding more fruit juice if needed. Beat in 2 tablespoons of the butter. Season to taste with more salt and sugar, if desired. Spread yam mixture in a shallow 1-quart baking dish. (At this point, you may cover and refrigerate until next day.)

Melt remaining 1 tablespoon butter in a small frying pan over medium heat. Add cashews and cook, stirring often, until lightly toasted (about 3 minutes). Sprinkle over yam mixture. Bake, uncovered, in a 375° oven until heated through (about 15 minutes; about 35 minutes if refrigerated). Makes 6 to 8 servings.

Per serving: 312 calories (29 percent from fat), 5 g protein, 52 g carbohydrates, 10 g total fat (4 g saturated fat), 44 mg cholesterol, 212 mg sodium

*S*unset's first features on canning and preserving concentrated on very simple recipes that rarely incorporated more than four or five ingredients. We still like simplicity, of course—but we now use a wider range of fruits, vegetables, and seasonings than in years past. Try spicy cranberry chutney or a chunky home-style fruit sauce; use a bumper crop of sweet red peppers in a bright, piquant relish. If you like fiery flavors, try pickled cauliflower heated up with dried chiles. And for sweet pickles in a jiffy, make our refrigerator cucumber chips—the crunchy slices take just minutes to prepare and are ready to eat within a day.

Red Bell Pepper Relish

3 **pounds onions (about 6 large onions), cut into 1-inch chunks**

6 **pounds red bell peppers (about 12 large peppers), seeded and cut into 1-inch squares**

4 **cups distilled white vinegar**

3 **cups sugar**

2 **tablespoons salt**

1 **tablespoon mustard seeds**

In a food processor, whirl onions and bell peppers, a portion at a time, until coarsely chopped. Pour chopped vegetables into a heavy-bottomed 8- to 10-quart pan. Stir in vinegar, sugar, salt, and mustard seeds. Bring to a boil over medium-high heat, stirring occasionally. Reduce heat to medium-low and boil gently, stirring often, until relish is thickened but still juicy (about 50 minutes).

Ladle hot relish into hot, sterilized 1-pint canning jars, leaving ½-inch headspace. Gently run a narrow nonmetallic spatula between relish and jar sides to release air bubbles. Wipe rims

and threads of jars clean; top with scalded lids, then firmly screw on bands.

Place jars, slightly apart, on a rack in a boiling water canner or other deep pan half-full of hot water. Add more hot water to cover jars by 1 to 2 inches. Bring water to a simmer; then cover and simmer for 15 minutes. Lift out jars and let cool on a towel away from drafts. Test seal of each jar by pressing lid: if it pops when pressed, there's no seal. Store unsealed relish in the refrigerator and use within 1 month. Makes about 7 pints.

Per ¼ cup: 63 calories (0 percent from fat), 1 g protein, 16 g carbohydrates, 0 g total fat (0 g saturated fat), 0 mg cholesterol, 237 mg sodium

Quick Refrigerator Cucumber Chips

3 **large regular cucumbers or 2 long thin-skinned (English or Armenian) cucumbers**

1 **large red bell pepper**

1 **medium-size onion, thinly sliced**

1 **tablespoon salt**

2 **teaspoons dill seeds**

¾ **cup sugar**

½ **cup white wine vinegar**

Cut unpeeled cucumbers into ¹⁄₁₆-inch-thick slices; you should have about 6 cups. Seed bell pepper and cut lengthwise into ½-inch-wide strips.

In a large bowl, combine cucumbers, bell pepper, and onion. Add salt and dill seeds; stir until combined. Let stand, uncovered, for 1 to 2 hours, stirring occasionally.

In a small bowl, combine sugar and vinegar; stir until sugar is dissolved. Pour vinegar mixture over vegetables and mix gently. Spoon into a glass or ceramic container that holds at least 2 quarts; or use several smaller containers or jars. Cover and refrigerate for at least 24 hours or up to 3 weeks. Makes about 2 quarts.

Per ¼ cup: 25 calories (2 percent from fat), 0.3 g protein, 6 g carbohydrates, 0.1 g total fat (0 g saturated fat), 0 mg cholesterol, 207 mg sodium

Hot Pickled Cauliflower

2 **large cloves garlic, peeled, halved, and lightly crushed**

10 **to 12 small dried hot red chiles, broken into halves**

1 **tablespoon pickling spice**

1½ **pounds carrots**

3 **medium-size onions**

2 **medium-size green bell peppers**

2 **large heads cauliflower**

6¼ **cups water**

2½ **cups white wine vinegar**

¼ **cup salt**

Place a half-clove of garlic, a fourth of the chiles, and ¾ teaspoon of the pickling spice in each of four 1-quart jars.

Cut carrots in half lengthwise, then cut crosswise into 2-inch pieces. Cut onions into 1-inch squares; seed bell peppers and cut into 1-inch squares. Break cauliflower into flowerets.

Divide carrots, onions, bell peppers, and cauliflower equally among jars, packing tightly. In a medium-size pan, bring water, vinegar, and salt to a boil over high heat; then pour evenly over vegetables. Put lids on jars and let cool. Refrigerate for at least 2 weeks before serving (pickles will keep in the refrigerator almost indefinitely). Makes about 4 quarts.

Per ½ cup: 25 calories (4 percent from fat), 0.9 g protein, 6 g carbohydrates, 0.1 g total fat (0 g saturated fat), 0 mg cholesterol, 835 mg sodium

Cranberry Raisin Chutney

- **1 pound (about 4 cups) fresh or frozen cranberries**
- **¾ cup raisins**
- **½ cup *each* honey and thawed frozen apple juice concentrate**
- **6 tablespoons cider vinegar**
- **¼ cup water**
- **1 tablespoon minced fresh ginger**
- **1 teaspoon whole allspice**
- **10 whole cloves**
- **1 cinnamon stick (about 3 inches long)**
- **¼ teaspoon ground red pepper (cayenne)**
- **½ cup *each* finely chopped onion and thinly sliced celery**
- **1 small tart apple, peeled, cored, and chopped**

In a 3- to 4-quart pan, combine cranberries, raisins, honey, apple juice concentrate, vinegar, and water. Cook over medium heat until berries begin to pop (about 10 minutes).

Stir in ginger, allspice, cloves, cinnamon stick, red pepper, onion, celery, and apple. Simmer, uncovered, stirring often, until apple is very soft and almost all liquid has evaporated (about 40 minutes). Let cool, then discard cinnamon stick. If made ahead, cover and refrigerate for up to 2 weeks. Bring to room temperature before serving. Makes about 4 cups.

Per ¼ cup: 89 calories (1 percent from fat), 0.5 g protein, 23 g carbohydrates, 0.2 g total fat (0 g saturated fat), 0 mg cholesterol, 8 mg sodium

Home-style Applesauce

- **9 pounds apples, such as Jonathan, McIntosh, Golden Delicious, or Gravenstein (about 27 medium-size apples), peeled, cored, and sliced**
- **1½ cups water**
- **1 to 1½ cups sugar (optional)**
- **1 to 2 teaspoons ground cinnamon (optional)**

Combine apples and water in a heavy-bottomed 8- to 10-quart pan. Bring to a boil over medium-high heat, stirring often. Reduce heat, cover, and simmer, stirring often, until apples are soft (about 30 minutes). Add sugar and cinnamon, if desired; bring to a boil. (Sauce will be slightly chunky; to remove larger lumps, whisk briefly with a wire whisk.)

Fill hot, sterilized jars with hot sauce, leaving ½-inch headspace. Gently run a narrow nonmetallic spatula between sauce and jar sides to release air bubbles. Wipe rims and threads of jars clean; top with scalded lids, then firmly screw on bands.

Place jars, slightly apart, on a rack in a boiling water canner or other deep pan half-full of hot water. Add more hot water to cover jars by 1 to 2 inches.

Bring water to a simmer; then cover and simmer for 15 minutes for pints, 20 minutes for quarts. Lift out jars and let cool on a towel away from drafts. Test seal of each jar by pressing lid; if it pops when pressed, there's no seal. Store unsealed relish in the refrigerator and use within 1 month.

If you like, you may omit processing and ladle sauce into freezer containers; leave ½-inch headspace for pints, 1-inch headspace for quarts. Apply lids; then freeze for up to 1 year or refrigerate for up to 1 month. Makes about 6 pints or 3 quarts.

Per ½ cup: 82 calories (4 percent from fat), 0.2 g protein, 21 g carbohydrates, 0.4 g total fat (0.1 g saturated fat), 0 mg cholesterol, 0 mg sodium

Home-style Pear Sauce

Follow directions for **Home-style Applesauce,** but substitute 9 pounds **Bartlett pears** for apples, reduce water to 1 cup, and add 2 tablespoons **lemon juice.** After seasoning sauce, simmer, uncovered, until as thick as desired. Makes about 4 pints or 2 quarts.

Per ½ cup: 139 calories (5 percent from fat), 1 g protein, 36 g carbohydrates, 1 g total fat (0 g saturated fat), 0 mg cholesterol, 0.4 mg sodium

Home-style Plum Sauce

Follow directions for **Home-style Applesauce,** but substitute 9 pounds **plums** (such as Laroda, Nubiana, or Santa Rosa) for apples. Pit and slice; do not peel. Before seasoning sauce, whirl, a portion at a time, in a food processor or blender until smooth. Or put through a food chopper, food mill, or fine strainer. Makes about 6 pints or 3 quarts.

Per ½ cup: 88 calories (9 percent from fat), 1 g protein, 21 g carbohydrates, 1 g total fat 0.1 g saturated fat), 0 mg cholesterol, 0 mg sodium

PASTA & GRAINS

*S*paghetti, lasagne, risotto—
the names may be foreign, but in the West, as elsewhere in
America, these dishes have been suppertime standards for
years. • We include some of the tried-and-true favorites in
this chapter, but many of the recipes in these pages are relatively recent. Quite a few date from the 1980s and early
'90s, when the availability of more and different pasta and
grain varieties attracted the interest of Western cooks—and
inspired them to create new versions of classic specialties.
Won ton skins provide a shortcut to homemade ravioli;
black beans and tomatoes go into an unusual Mexican-
style filling for lasagne. Even simple pilaf becomes a new
dish when it's made with oats or accented with dried fruit.

Pasta with Carbonara Sauce

The addition of beaten eggs is the secret to this classic pasta sauce. The eggs cook on the hot spaghetti, forming a delicate glaze made bold with bits of cheese and meat.

- ¼ **pound mild Italian sausages, casings removed**
- ¼ **pound prosciutto or cooked ham, finely chopped**
- ¼ **cup butter or margarine**
- 8 **ounces dry spaghetti**
- ½ **cup minced parsley**
- 3 **eggs, lightly beaten**
  Dash of pepper
  About ½ cup grated Parmesan cheese

Crumble sausage into a wide frying pan. Add half the prosciutto and 2 tablespoons of the butter; cook over medium-low heat, stirring occasionally, until sausage is lightly browned and edges of prosciutto are curled. Remove from heat and stir in remaining prosciutto; keep hot. (At this point, you may let cool, then cover and refrigerate until next day; reheat until very hot before continuing.)

In a large pan, cook pasta in about 2½ quarts of boiling salted water until barely tender to bite (8 to 10 minutes); or cook according to package directions. Drain and transfer to a large serving bowl.

Add remaining 2 tablespoons butter and parsley to hot pasta; toss lightly. Add eggs; toss until pasta is evenly coated. Add hot sausage mixture; toss gently until pasta is evenly coated and eggs are cooked. Sprinkle with pepper and ½ cup of the cheese; toss gently. Offer additional cheese to add to taste. Makes 4 servings.

Per serving: 579 calories (50 percent from fat), 28 g protein, 44 g carbohydrates, 32 g total fat (15 g saturated fat), 243 mg cholesterol, 1,283 mg sodium

Pasta alla Amatriciana

Pasta prepared *alla amatriciana* is a treat for those who enjoy smoky, spicy flavors—it's typically cloaked in a red pepper–spiked tomato sauce dotted with chunks of bacon. To tame the heat, offer glasses of Chianti or iced tea for sipping alongside.

- 4 **slices thick-cut bacon, chopped**
- 1 **large onion, chopped**
- ½ **teaspoon crushed red pepper flakes**
- 1 **large can (about 28 oz.) tomatoes, chopped (reserve liquid)**
- 1 **pound dry spaghetti or other pasta strands**
  Grated Parmesan cheese

Cook bacon in a wide frying pan over medium-high heat, stirring often, just until fat is rendered (3 to 5 minutes). Add onion; cook, stirring often, until soft (about 5 minutes). Stir in red pepper flakes, then tomatoes and their liquid. Bring to a boil; reduce heat and simmer, stirring occasionally, until slightly thickened. Keep warm.

In a large pan, cook pasta in about 3½ quarts of boiling salted water until barely tender to bite (8 to 10 minutes); or cook according to package directions. Drain and transfer to a serving bowl. Add tomato sauce and toss gently. Offer cheese to add to taste. Makes 4 to 6 servings.

Per serving: 555 calories (31 percent from fat), 16 g protein, 79 g carbohydrates, 19 g total fat (7 g saturated fat), 20 mg cholesterol, 785 mg sodium

Baked-tomato Spaghetti

Simple pasta dishes are popular first-course fare throughout Italy. A Florentine chef gave us this recipe for spaghetti tossed with a sauce of garlic and baked Roma tomatoes.

- 12 **medium-size pear-shaped (Roma-type) tomatoes (about 1¾ lbs. *total*), cut into halves lengthwise**
  Salt and pepper
- 3 **to 6 cloves garlic, minced or pressed**
- ½ **cup chopped parsley**
- ½ **cup olive oil**
- 1 **pound dry spaghetti**
- 2 **tablespoons butter or margarine, at room temperature**
- ½ **cup chopped fresh basil or 2 tablespoons dry basil**
  Grated Parmesan cheese

Place tomato halves, cut side up, in a 9- by 13-inch baking dish. Sprinkle with salt and pepper. Mix garlic, ⅓ cup of the parsley, and 2 tablespoons of the oil; pat mixture over tomatoes. Drizzle with 2 more tablespoons oil. Bake in a 425° oven until tomatoes are browned on top (about 1 hour).

In a large pan, cook pasta in about 3½ quarts of boiling salted water until barely tender to bite (8 to 10 minutes); or cook according to package directions. Drain.

Remove and discard most of the skin from 4 of the tomato halves; coarsely mash tomato pulp. In a large serving bowl, combine mashed tomatoes, butter, remaining parsley, remaining ¼ cup oil, and basil. Add pasta and toss gently. Add remaining 20 baked tomato halves and pan juices; toss gently. Season to taste with salt and pepper. Sprinkle with cheese. Makes 6 to 8 servings.

Per serving: 437 calories (41 percent from fat), 10 g protein, 55 g carbohydrates, 20 g total fat (4 g saturated fat), 9 mg cholesterol, 51 mg sodium

Pasta with Lentils

This main course may be meatless, but it certainly isn't lacking in nutritional value or flavor. You combine simmered lentils with Swiss chard and Neufchâtel cheese, then serve the hearty sauce over linguine.

- 3 **cups chicken broth**
- 1 **cup lentils**
- 1 **teaspoon cumin seeds**
- 1 **pound Swiss chard**
- 2 **tablespoons olive oil**
- 1 **large onion, chopped**
- 2 **cloves garlic, minced or pressed**
- ½ **teaspoon crushed red pepper flakes**
- 12 **ounces dry linguine**
- 6 **ounces Neufchâtel or cream cheese, diced**
  Salt and pepper

In a 5- to 6-quart pan, bring 2 cups of the broth to a boil. Add lentils and cumin seeds. Reduce heat, cover, and simmer until lentils are tender to bite (about 30 minutes). Drain, if necessary; pour into a bowl.

While lentils are simmering, rinse chard well. Cut off and discard stem ends; slice stems and leaves crosswise into ¼-inch-wide strips (keep stems and leaves separate).

In pan used to cook lentils, combine chard stems, oil, onion, garlic, and red pepper flakes. Cook over medium heat, stirring often, until onion is golden brown (about 20 minutes). Add chard leaves and cook, stirring, until limp (about 3 minutes). Then add lentils and remaining 1 cup broth; simmer, uncovered, until hot (about 3 minutes).

When sauce is almost ready, in a large pan, cook pasta in about 3 quarts of boiling salted water until barely tender to bite (8 to 10 minutes); or cook according to package directions. Drain; transfer to a large serving bowl.

Add lentil sauce and cheese; then toss gently until combined. Season to taste with salt and pepper. Makes 6 servings.

Per serving: 496 calories (24 percent from fat), 24 g protein, 72 g carbohydrates, 13 g total fat (5 g saturated fat), 22 mg cholesterol, 958 mg sodium

Pasta with Shrimp in Tomato Cream

In a 1987 article, we suggested a number of tempting uses for oil-packed dried tomatoes. In this recipe, both the intensely flavored tomatoes and the oil used to pack them go into an easy, vermouth-spiked shrimp sauce.

- ⅓ **cup dried tomatoes packed in oil**
- 1 **clove garlic, minced or pressed**
- 1 **pound large raw shrimp, shelled and deveined**
- ¼ **cup thinly sliced green onions**
- 1½ **tablespoons chopped fresh basil or 1 teaspoon dry basil**
- ¼ **teaspoon white pepper**
- 1 **cup chicken broth**
- ¾ **cup dry vermouth**
- 1 **cup whipping cream**
- 10 **ounces dry linguine**
  Basil sprigs (optional)
  Grated Parmesan cheese

Drain tomatoes, reserving 2 tablespoons of the oil. Pour oil into a wide frying pan. Sliver tomatoes and set aside. Heat oil over medium-high heat. Add garlic and shrimp. Cook,

stirring often, until shrimp are just opaque in center; cut to test (4 to 5 minutes). Lift out and set aside.

Add tomatoes, onions, chopped basil, white pepper, broth, vermouth, and cream to pan. Bring to a boil over high heat; boil, stirring occasionally, until reduced to about 1½ cups.

Meanwhile, in a large pan, cook pasta in about 3 quarts of boiling salted water until barely tender to bite (8 to 10 minutes); or cook according to package directions. Drain and divide among 4 dinner plates.

Return cooked shrimp to sauce; stir just until heated through. Spoon sauce equally over pasta. Garnish with basil sprigs, if desired. Offer cheese to add to taste. Makes 4 servings.

Per serving: 703 calories (44 percent from fat), 31 g protein, 62 g carbohydrates, 32 g total fat (13 g saturated fat), 206 mg cholesterol, 662 mg sodium

Linguine with Prosciutto & Olives

An assertive combination of prosciutto, green onions, and pimento-stuffed olives complements tender linguine.

- 8 **ounces dry linguine, spaghetti, or other pasta strands**
- ¼ **cup olive oil**
- 2 **ounces thinly sliced prosciutto, cut into ¼-inch-wide strips**
- ½ **cup thinly sliced green onions**
- 1 **small jar (about 3 oz.) pimento-stuffed green olives, drained**
- 1 **cup cherry tomatoes, cut into halves**
  Grated Parmesan cheese (optional)

In a large pan, cook pasta in about 2½ quarts of boiling salted water until barely tender to bite (8 to 10 minutes); or cook according to package directions. Drain pasta and transfer to a serving bowl.

While pasta is cooking, heat oil in a wide frying pan over medium-high heat. Add prosciutto and cook, stirring, until lightly browned (about 3 minutes). Add onions and cook, stirring, until translucent (about 2 more minutes). Add olives and cherry tomatoes and cook, stirring often, until olives are heated through (about 2 more minutes).

Pour prosciutto mixture over pasta and toss gently until combined. Offer cheese to add to taste, if desired. Makes 2 to 4 servings.

Per serving: 528 calories (43 percent from fat), 16 g protein, 60 g carbohydrates, 26 g total fat (4 g saturated fat), 15 mg cholesterol, 1,299 mg sodium

Garden Vegetable Fettuccine

Stir-fried bell pepper, zucchini, and tomatoes combine in this colorful and chunky sauce. Use whole wheat or plain egg fettuccine, dry or fresh.

- **8 ounces dry or fresh whole wheat or plain fettuccine**
- **6 slices bacon, cut into ½-inch pieces**
- **3 cloves garlic, minced or pressed**
- **1 large onion, chopped**
- **1 large zucchini, cut into ½-inch cubes**
- **1 small red or green bell pepper, seeded and chopped**
- **3 large tomatoes, cut into ½-inch cubes**
- **½ cup chopped parsley**
- **½ cup chopped fresh basil or 2 tablespoons dry basil**
- **2 tablespoons olive oil or salad oil**
  Salt and pepper
  Grated Parmesan cheese

In a large pan, cook pasta in about 2½ quarts of boiling salted water until barely tender to bite (about 8 minutes for dry pasta, 3 to 4 minutes for fresh); or cook according to package directions. Drain and transfer to a large serving bowl.

While pasta is cooking, cook bacon in a wide frying pan over medium heat, stirring often, until crisp. Remove bacon from pan, drain, and set aside. Discard all but 2 tablespoons of the drippings. Add garlic and onion to drippings in pan and cook, stirring often, until onion is soft (about 5 minutes). Increase heat to medium-high and add zucchini and bell pepper; cook, stirring, until zucchini is tender-crisp to bite (about 2 minutes). Add tomatoes, parsley, basil, and oil; cook, stirring, until heated through. Season to taste with salt and pepper.

Spoon vegetable sauce over pasta, sprinkle with bacon, and toss gently. Offer cheese to add to taste. Makes 4 servings.

Per serving: 393 calories (41 percent from fat), 13 g protein, 46 g carbohydrates, 19 g total fat (4 g saturated fat), 79 mg cholesterol, 218 mg sodium

Fettuccine Rapido

When long, busy workdays give you less time to cook, quick side dishes and entrées are the rule. In this simple accompaniment for meats, fish, or poultry, a blend of chiles, garlic, parsley, and olive oil lightly coats fresh fettuccine.

- **⅓ cup olive oil**
- **2 small dried hot red chiles, *each* broken into 3 pieces**
- **2 cloves garlic, minced or pressed**
- **½ teaspoon salt**
- **½ cup chopped parsley**
- **8 ounces fresh or dry fettuccine**

Heat oil in a small pan over low heat. Add chiles and cook, stirring occasionally, until they begin to brown. Add garlic and cook, stirring, for 30 seconds. Add salt and parsley; cook, stirring occasionally, for 1 more minute. Remove from heat.

PASTA PERFECTION

Fresh pasta or dry pasta? The virtues and drawbacks of each inspire plenty of culinary controversy. Yet when matching pasta to sauce, most aficionados agree on a few simple rules: dry pasta is generally denser and chewier than fresh, so it can stand up to thick sauces laden with meat, tomatoes, and chunky vegetables. Soft-textured fresh pasta, on the other hand, is a natural match for delicate cream sauces and herb-flavored oils.

Fresh or dry, any pasta should be cooked in boiling water just until it's barely tender to bite. Fresh pasta cooks very rapidly, often in only a minute or two; dry varieties may take up to three times longer.

In a large pan, cook pasta in about 2½ quarts of boiling salted water until barely tender to bite (3 to 4 minutes for fresh pasta, about 8 minutes for dry); or cook according to package directions. Drain pasta and transfer to a serving bowl. Pour sauce over pasta and toss gently until lightly coated. Makes 4 servings.

Per serving: 344 calories (51 percent from fat), 8 g protein, 35 g carbohydrates, 20 g total fat (3 g saturated fat), 67 mg cholesterol, 294 mg sodium

Fettuccine Cambozola

Ready for the table in just a few minutes, this cheesy main course was featured in a 1991 article titled "Getting You through the Workweek." Cambozola or Gorgonzola cheese melts on hot strands of pasta and bright green peas, forming a quick, tangy sauce.

- **8 ounces fresh fettuccine**
- **1 package (about 10 oz.) frozen peas**
- **6 ounces cambozola or Gorgonzola cheese, diced**
- **2 tablespoons hot water**
  Pepper

In a large pan, cook pasta in about 2½ quarts of boiling salted water until barely tender to bite (3 to 4 minutes); or cook according to package directions. Stir in peas, then drain.

Return pasta and peas to pan. Add cheese and hot water. Gently toss over low heat until cheese melts and coats pasta (2 to 3 minutes). Season to taste with pepper. Makes 2 to 4 servings.

Per serving: 492 calories (33 percent from fat), 27 g protein, 56 g carbohydrates, 18 g total fat (11 g saturated fat), 131 mg cholesterol, 918 mg sodium

Fettuccine Alfredo

Lightly browned butter, Parmesan, and plenty of whipping cream add up to a luxurious sauce for fettuccine. Paired with a crisp green salad, the dish makes a satisfying supper.

- **8 ounces dry fettuccine**
- **¼ cup butter or margarine**
- **1½ cups whipping cream**
- **1 cup (about 4 oz.) grated Parmesan cheese**
  Salt and pepper
  Whole or ground nutmeg

In a large pan, cook pasta in about 2½ quarts of boiling salted water until barely tender to bite (about 8 minutes); or cook according to package directions. Drain.

While pasta is cooking, melt butter in a wide frying pan over high heat; cook until lightly browned. Add ½ cup of the cream and bring to a boil; boil, stirring constantly, until slightly thickened. Reduce heat to medium. Add cooked pasta to sauce and toss gently. Then add ½ cup of the cheese and ½ cup more cream; toss gently. Add remaining ½ cup cheese and ½ cup cream; toss gently again. Season to taste with salt and pepper. Grate nutmeg generously over top. Makes 2 to 4 servings.

Per serving: 945 calories (63 percent from fat), 29 g protein, 59 g carbohydrates, 67 g total fat (41 g saturated fat), 276 mg cholesterol, 916 mg sodium

Fettuccine with Walnut Sauce

Toasted walnuts, coarsely ground and blended with cream and seasonings, make a delicious pasta sauce. The nutty flavor complements mild meats such as chicken or pork; you might try this dish with Broccoli- & Cheese-stuffed Chicken Breasts (page 96).

- **1½ cups coarsely chopped walnuts**
- **8 ounces dry fettuccine**
- **1 cup whipping cream**
- **1 small clove garlic, minced or pressed**
- **¼ teaspoon *each* salt and white pepper**
- **2 tablespoons butter or margarine**
  Grated Parmesan cheese

Spread walnuts in a shallow baking pan and toast in a 350° oven, stirring occasionally, until lightly browned (about 10 minutes). Let cool slightly.

In a large pan, cook pasta in about 2½ quarts of boiling salted water until barely tender to bite (about 8 minutes); or cook according to package directions. Drain and transfer to a serving bowl.

While pasta is cooking, in a blender or food processor, combine walnuts, cream, garlic, salt, and white pepper. Whirl, using short on-off bursts, until walnuts are coarsely ground.

Add butter to hot pasta and toss until pasta is well coated. Top with walnut sauce; toss gently. Offer cheese to add to taste. Makes 4 servings.

Per serving: 731 calories (65 percent from fat), 16 g protein, 51 g carbohydrates, 54 g total fat (18 g saturated fat), 136 mg cholesterol, 230 mg sodium

Noodles Romanoff

First featured in our "Kitchen Cabinet" in 1956, this noodle casserole is delicious with any simply cooked entrée, from poached fish to grilled chicken to old-fashioned pot roast.

- **8 ounces dry medium-wide egg noodles, linguine, or fettuccine**
- **1 cup cottage cheese**
- **1 small clove garlic, minced or pressed**
- **1 teaspoon Worcestershire**
- **1 cup sour cream**
- **¼ cup grated onion**
- **¼ teaspoon liquid hot pepper seasoning**
- **½ cup shredded Cheddar cheese**

In a large pan, cook noodles in about 2½ quarts of boiling salted water until barely tender to bite (about 8 minutes); or cook according to package directions. Drain and transfer to a large bowl. Add cottage cheese, garlic, Worcestershire, sour cream, onion, and hot pepper seasoning; stir gently until combined. Pour into a greased shallow 2-quart baking dish and sprinkle with Cheddar cheese. Bake in a 350° oven until heated through (about 25 minutes). Makes 6 to 8 servings.

Per serving: 261 calories (42 percent from fat), 11 g protein, 26 g carbohydrates, 12 g total fat (7 g saturated fat), 58 mg cholesterol, 319 mg sodium

Lasagne Belmonte

Never-fail recipes like this one are essential for family-pleasing menu planning. If you'd like a spicier lasagne, simply mix half a pound of Italian sausages in with the beef.

- 3 tablespoons olive oil or salad oil
- 1 medium-size onion, chopped
- 1½ pounds lean ground beef
- 1 clove garlic, minced or pressed
- 2 cans (about 8 oz. *each*) tomato sauce
- 1 can (about 6 oz.) tomato paste
- ½ cup *each* dry red wine and water
- 1 teaspoon *each* salt and dry oregano
- ½ teaspoon *each* pepper and sugar
- 12 ounces dry lasagne noodles
- 2 cups ricotta cheese or small-curd cottage cheese
- 8 ounces mozzarella cheese, thinly sliced
- ½ cup grated Parmesan cheese

Heat oil in a wide frying pan over medium heat. Add onion and cook, stirring often, until soft (about 5 minutes). Crumble in beef and add garlic; cook, stirring, until meat is browned. Stir in tomato sauce, tomato paste, wine, and water. Then add salt, oregano, pepper, and sugar; stir until blended. Bring to a boil; then reduce heat, cover, and simmer, stirring occasionally, for about 1½ hours.

Meanwhile, in a large pan, cook noodles in about 3 quarts of boiling salted water until barely tender to bite (10 to 12 minutes); or cook according to package directions. Drain, rinse with cold water, and drain again.

Arrange a third of the noodles over bottom of a lightly greased 9- by 13-inch baking dish (lay one layer of noodles lengthwise in dish, the next layer crosswise; continue in this way as you assemble lasagne). Spread a third of the meat sauce over noodles; top with a third each of the ricotta and mozzarella cheeses. Repeat layers twice, ending with mozzarella cheese. Sprinkle with Parmesan cheese.

Bake in a 350° oven until bubbly and browned on top (about 30 minutes). Let stand for about 5 minutes before serving. Makes 6 to 8 servings.

Per serving: 792 calories (52 percent from fat), 42 g protein, 52 g carbohydrates, 45 g total fat (20 g saturated fat), 139 mg cholesterol, 1,423 mg sodium

Spicy Lasagne

Follow directions for **Lasagne Belmonte,** but reduce ground beef to 1 pound. Along with beef, add ½ pound **Italian sausages,** casings removed and meat chopped. Makes 6 to 8 servings.

Per serving: 818 calories (54 percent from fat), 41 g protein, 52 g carbohydrates, 48 g total fat (21 g saturated fat), 139 mg cholesterol, 1,638 mg sodium

Vegetable Lasagne

Fitness-conscious pasta lovers often ask us for meatless variations of lasagne. This version, which combines five different vegetables and three types of cheese, is our favorite.

- 1 package (about 8 oz.) dry lasagne noodles
- 4 carrots (about ¾ lb. *total*), cut into ¼-inch-thick slices
- 3 zucchini (about 1 lb. *total*), cut into ¼-inch-thick slices
- 2 tablespoons olive oil or salad oil
- 1 medium-size onion, chopped
- ½ pound mushrooms, thinly sliced
- 1 teaspoon *each* dry basil, dry thyme, and dry oregano
- 1 large jar (about 30 oz.) marinara sauce
- 2 packages (about 10 oz. *each*) frozen chopped spinach, thawed and squeezed dry
- 1 cup ricotta cheese
- 3 cups (about 12 oz.) shredded mozzarella cheese
- ¼ cup grated Parmesan cheese

In a large pan, bring 3 quarts water to a boil over high heat. Add noodles and carrots; cook for 6 minutes. Add zucchini; continue to cook until noodles are barely tender to bite (4 to 5 more minutes). Drain, rinse with cold water, and drain again. Set noodles, carrots, and zucchini aside, keeping noodles and vegetables separate.

In pan used to cook noodles, combine oil, onion, mushrooms, basil, thyme, and oregano. Cook over high heat, stirring often, until onion is soft and liquid has evaporated (5 to 8 minutes). Remove from heat and stir in marinara sauce. In a small bowl, mix spinach and ricotta cheese.

Spread a third of the sauce over bottom of a shallow 2½- to 3-quart baking dish. Arrange half the noodles over sauce. Over noodles, evenly layer half each of the carrots, zucchini, spinach mixture, and mozzarella cheese. Repeat layers, ending with sauce. Sprinkle with Parmesan cheese. (At this point, you may cover and refrigerate until next day.)

Place baking dish on a rimmed baking sheet and bake, uncovered, in a 400° oven until lasagne is bubbly and heated through (about 25 minutes). If refrigerated, bake, uncovered, in a 350° oven until bubbly and heated through (about 50 minutes). Let stand for about 5 minutes before serving. Makes 6 to 8 servings.

Per serving: 516 calories (42 percent from fat), 25 g protein, 53 g carbohydrates, 25 g total fat (11 g saturated fat), 58 mg cholesterol, 1,222 mg sodium

Black Bean Lasagne

Protein-rich black beans replace the meat in a vegetarian lasagne accented with cilantro and garlic. The hearty casserole needs only a green salad and crusty bread as accompaniments.

FRESH HERBS

Fresh garden herbs have always been important in Western cuisine. In the pages of *Sunset*, readers have found directions for growing and using common varieties like basil, tarragon, and rosemary, as well as less widely known types such as borage, burnet, and winter savory.

We've also tracked culinary trends involving new varieties of fresh herbs. In 1991, for example, we discussed various kinds of basil, among them a dwarf strain from Greece, a basil with purple leaves, and varieties with lemon, licorice, and clove scents. Sauces made with basil have been expanded on and updated, too— besides the classic pesto we first featured in 1970, we've presented pestos based on mint, rosemary, and cilantro.

---

4 pounds pear-shaped (Roma-type) tomatoes, cut into halves lengthwise

1½ tablespoons olive oil or salad oil

2 cloves garlic, minced or pressed

1 cup firmly packed chopped cilantro

10 dry lasagne noodles (about 5 oz. *total*)

3 cans (about 15 oz. *each*) black beans, drained and rinsed

¼ cup chicken broth

1 teaspoon ground cumin

½ teaspoon chili powder

2 cartons (about 15 oz. *each*) part-skim ricotta cheese

4 cups (about 1 lb.) shredded jack cheese
  Salt

Place tomato halves, cut side up, in a 10- by 15-inch rimmed baking pan (a few tomatoes can rest on top of each other). Sprinkle evenly with oil and garlic. Bake in a 425° oven until well browned on top (about 1 hour). Let cool slightly. Remove and discard skins. Place tomatoes in a colander and press them lightly to drain off watery liquid; then transfer to a blender or food processor, add cilantro, and whirl until smooth. (At this point, you may cover and refrigerate for up to 2 days.)

In a large pan, cook noodles in about 2 quarts of boiling salted water until barely tender to bite (10 to 12 minutes); or cook according to package directions. Drain, rinse with cold water, and drain again.

In a bowl, combine beans, broth, cumin, and chili powder. With a potato masher or the back of a large spoon, coarsely mash beans until liquid is incorporated. In another bowl, stir together ricotta cheese and 2½ cups of the jack cheese.

Arrange 5 of the noodles, slightly overlapping, over bottom of a lightly greased 8- by 12-inch or 9- by 13-inch baking dish. Top with half each of the bean mixture, ricotta mixture, and tomato sauce. Repeat layers, ending with sauce. Sprinkle with remaining 1½ cups jack cheese. (At this point, you may cover and refrigerate until next day.)

Bake, uncovered, in a 375° oven until casserole is bubbly and browned on top (about 40 minutes; 50 to 55 minutes if refrigerated). Let stand for about 5 minutes before serving. Season to taste with salt. Makes 6 to 8 servings.

Per serving: 698 calories (44 percent from fat), 44 g protein, 55 g carbohydrates, 34 g total fat (7 g saturated fat), 94 mg cholesterol, 789 mg sodium

Penne with Broccoli & Ricotta

Mild-flavored ricotta, lower in fat than many other cheeses, is a popular addition to light pasta favorites. Here, it combines with penne and fresh broccoli in a simple entrée that's rich in fiber, vitamins, calcium, and iron.

2 tablespoons olive oil

5 green onions, thinly sliced

1 pound broccoli flowerets, cut into bite-size pieces

¼ cup water
  Coarsely ground pepper

12 ounces dry penne or other dry small tube-shaped pasta, such as mostaccioli or ziti

1½ cups part-skim ricotta cheese
  Grated Parmesan cheese

Heat oil in a wide frying pan over medium-high heat. Add onions and cook, stirring often, for 1 minute. Add broccoli and cook, stirring often, until bright green (about 3 more minutes). Add ¼ cup water and bring to a boil; then reduce heat, cover, and simmer until broccoli is tender-crisp to bite (about 5 minutes). Remove from heat and season to taste with pepper; keep warm.

In a large pan, cook pasta in about 3 quarts of boiling salted water until barely tender to bite (10 to 12 minutes); or cook according to package directions. Drain, reserving about ¼ cup of the cooking water, and transfer pasta to a large serving bowl. Add broccoli mixture and ricotta cheese to pasta; toss gently until combined. If mixture is too dry, stir in enough of the reserved pasta water to moisten. Offer Parmesan cheese to add to taste. Makes 4 servings.

Per serving: 540 calories (26 percent from fat), 25 g protein, 75 g carbohydrates, 16 g total fat (6 g saturated fat), 29 mg cholesterol, 440 mg sodium

Penne with Smoked Salmon

A splash of vodka enhances the flavor of a creamy, tomato-dotted sauce for smoked salmon and pasta tubes. Impressive in appearance and not too filling, the dish makes a wonderful introduction to an elegant dinner.

- **12 ounces dry penne or other dry small tube-shaped pasta, such as mostaccioli or ziti**
- **2 tablespoons olive oil**
- **1 small shallot, thinly sliced**
- **4 small pear-shaped (Roma-type) tomatoes, peeled, seeded, and chopped**
- **⅔ cup whipping cream**
  Pinch of ground nutmeg
- **2 tablespoons chopped fresh dill or ½ teaspoon dry dill weed**

- **⅓ cup vodka**
- **4 to 6 ounces sliced smoked salmon or lox, cut into bite-size strips**
  White pepper
  Dill sprigs

In a large pan, cook pasta in about 3 quarts of boiling salted water until barely tender to bite (10 to 12 minutes); or cook according to package directions. Drain.

While pasta is cooking, heat oil in a wide frying pan over medium-low heat. Add shallot and cook, stirring often, until soft but not browned (about 3 minutes). Stir in tomatoes, cover, and simmer for 5 minutes. Add cream, nutmeg, chopped dill, and vodka. Bring to a boil over high heat; boil for 1 minute.

Add pasta to sauce and toss gently until well coated. Remove from heat, add salmon, and mix lightly. Season to taste with white pepper and garnish with dill sprigs. Makes 4 servings.

Per serving: 586 calories (37 percent from fat), 19 g protein, 67 g carbohydrates, 22 g total fat (9 g saturated fat), 53 mg cholesterol, 592 mg sodium

Mostaccioli & Swiss Cheese Casserole

In this savory baked version of macaroni and cheese, mostaccioli—the name means "little mustaches" in Italian—mingle with Swiss cheese, spinach, and slivered ham in a piquant mustard sauce.

- **8 ounces dry mostaccioli or other dry small tube-shaped pasta, such as penne or ziti**
- **¼ cup butter or margarine**
- **¼ cup all-purpose flour**
- **2 cups milk**
- **¼ teaspoon liquid hot pepper seasoning**
- **1 tablespoon Dijon mustard**
- **3 cups (about 12 oz.) shredded Swiss cheese**
- **½ pound cooked ham, cut into thin, bite-size slivers**
- **1 package (about 10 oz.) frozen leaf spinach, thawed and squeezed dry**
  Salt and pepper

In a large pan, cook pasta in about 2½ quarts of boiling salted water until barely tender to bite (10 to 12 minutes); or cook according to package directions. Drain, rinse, and drain again; set aside.

In pan used to cook pasta, melt butter over medium heat. Stir in flour and cook, stirring, for 1 minute (do not brown). Remove from heat and gradually stir in milk. Return to heat and cook, stirring constantly, until sauce boils and thickens. Add hot pepper seasoning, mustard, and 2 cups of the cheese; stir until cheese is melted.

Remove cheese sauce from heat and add pasta and ham; mix gently. Then stir in spinach. Spread in a shallow 2-quart baking dish. (At this point, you may cover and refrigerate until next day.)

Bake, covered, in a 350° oven for 20 minutes (30 minutes if refrigerated). Uncover, sprinkle with remaining 1 cup cheese, and continue to bake until cheese is melted and casserole is bubbly (about 10 more minutes). Season to taste with salt and pepper. Makes 6 servings.

Per serving: 571 calories (48 percent from fat), 34 g protein, 40 g carbohydrates, 30 g total fat (18 g saturated fat), 107 mg cholesterol, 1,080 mg sodium

Filled Pasta with Vegetable Confetti

Not so long ago, top-quality filled pastas required hours of work in the kitchen—or a trip to a good Italian restaurant. But today you'll find fresh, frozen, or dry tortellini, ravioli, agnolotti, and other varieties in many supermarkets and pasta shops. Use any shape in this quick combination of pasta and stir-fried vegetables.

About 8 ounces fresh or frozen filled pasta; or about 6 ounces dry filled pasta

¼ **cup butter, margarine, or olive oil**

1 **medium-size zucchini, cut into ¼-inch cubes**

1 **small red bell pepper, seeded and finely diced**

1 **clove garlic, minced or pressed**

6 **fresh thyme sprigs (*each* about 4 inches long); or ½ teaspoon dry thyme**

2 **tablespoons pine nuts or slivered almonds**

Salt and pepper

Grated Parmesan cheese

In a large pan, cook pasta in about 3 quarts of boiling salted water until barely tender to bite (4 to 6 minutes for fresh pasta, about 7 minutes for frozen, 15 to 20 minutes for dry); or cook according to package directions. Drain well.

While pasta is cooking, melt butter in a wide frying pan over medium heat. Add zucchini, bell pepper, garlic, and thyme; cook, stirring often, for 3 minutes. Add nuts; continue to cook, stirring, until zucchini and nuts begin to brown (3 to 5 more minutes). Add hot pasta; mix gently. Season to taste with salt and pepper. Offer cheese to add to taste. Makes 2 servings.

Per serving: 610 calories (48 percent from fat), 22 g protein, 60 g carbohydrates, 33 g total fat (15 g saturated fat), 124 mg cholesterol, 745 mg sodium

Tortellini with Broccoli & Gorgonzola

Italian ingredients and Asian cooking techniques come together deliciously in this robust stir-fry.

1 **pound skinless, boneless chicken breasts**

3 **tablespoons butter or margarine**

¾ **cup walnuts or pecans (halves or large pieces)**

5 **cups (about 1 lb.) broccoli flowerets, cut into bite-size pieces**

About 1¾ cups chicken broth

1 **package (about 12 oz.) frozen tortellini, 12 ounces fresh tortellini, or 1 package (7 or 8 oz.) dry tortellini**

½ **cup finely chopped onion**

4 **teaspoons cornstarch**

½ **cup crumbled, firmly packed Gorgonzola or other blue-veined cheese**

½ **teaspoon pepper**

1 **tablespoon white wine vinegar**

Rinse chicken, pat dry, and cut crosswise into ¼-inch-thick slices. Set aside.

Melt 1 tablespoon of the butter in a wok or wide frying pan over medium heat. Add walnuts and cook, stirring often, until crisp (about 7 minutes); do not scorch. Pour nuts onto paper towels and let drain.

Wipe pan clean. Melt 1 more tablespoon butter in pan over high heat. Add chicken. Cook, stirring, until no longer pink in center; cut to test (about 3 minutes). Transfer to a bowl.

To pan, add broccoli and 2 tablespoons of the broth. Cover and cook, stirring occasionally, until broccoli stems are tender when pierced (8 to 10 minutes); add more broth as needed. Lift broccoli from pan with a slotted spoon and add to chicken.

In a large pan, cook tortellini in about 3½ quarts of boiling salted water until barely tender to bite (about 7 minutes for frozen tortellini, 4 to 6 minutes for fresh, 15 to 20 minutes for dry); or cook according to package directions. Drain.

While pasta is cooking, wipe pan clean again. Add remaining 1 tablespoon butter and onion; cook over medium-high heat, stirring often, until onion is soft (about 4 minutes). Sprinkle cornstarch evenly over onion; stir to mix well. Add 1¼ cups of the broth and bring to a boil, stirring constantly.

Reduce heat to low. Crumble in about three-fourths of the cheese; stir until smoothly blended. Add pepper, chicken, broccoli, and tortellini. Stir gently until heated through; cut into pasta to test (about 5 minutes). Stir in vinegar and pour into a serving bowl. Sprinkle with walnuts and remaining cheese. Makes 4 servings.

Per serving: 719 calories (41 percent from fat), 52 g protein, 55 g carbohydrates, 34 g total fat (10 g saturated fat), 148 mg cholesterol, 1,175 mg sodium

Won Ton Ravioli

Won ton skins offer a great shortcut to homemade ravioli. Buy the wrappers in a supermarket or Asian grocery store and use them just as you would fresh pasta dough.

Chicken & Prosciutto Filling (recipe follows)

About 72 won ton wrappers (about 1 lb. *total*)

1 **egg white, lightly beaten**

Mushroom-Tomato Sauce (recipe follows)

Grated Parmesan cheese

Prepare Chicken & Prosciutto Filling. Work with 2 won ton wrappers at a time; keep remainder covered with plastic wrap to prevent drying. Place 1 rounded tablespoon filling on one wrapper; spread to within ⅜ inch of edges. Brush edges with egg white. Cover with another wrapper and press edges together to seal. If desired, use a pastry wheel to trim edges decoratively; discard trimmings.

Repeat to make more ravioli. As ravioli are completed, place them in a single layer on flour-dusted rimmed baking sheets and cover lightly with plastic wrap. (When all ravioli have been completed, you may refrigerate them for up to 4 hours. Or freeze until firm, then transfer to airtight containers and return to freezer for up to 1 month; do not thaw before cooking.)

Prepare Mushroom-Tomato Sauce. When sauce is almost done, in a large pan, cook ravioli, about half at a time, in about 4 quarts of gently boiling salted water until barely tender to bite (about 5 minutes if fresh, 6 minutes if frozen). Lift ravioli from water with a slotted spoon and place on warm dinner plates. Spoon Mushroom-Tomato Sauce over ravioli. Offer cheese to add to taste. Makes 6 servings.

Chicken & Prosciutto Filling. Melt 2 tablespoons **butter** or margarine in a wide frying pan over medium heat. Add 1 large **onion,** chopped; cook, stirring often, until onion is soft (about 5 minutes). Add ¾ pound skinless, boneless **chicken breasts,** cut into ½-inch pieces. Cook, stirring, just until no longer pink in center; cut to test (about 3 minutes). Stir in 6 ounces coarsely chopped **prosciutto.**

Spoon mixture into a food processor and whirl until coarsely ground (or chop finely with a knife). Mix in 2 **egg yolks,** ⅔ cup grated **Parmesan cheese,** 1 cup **ricotta cheese,** and ⅛ to ¼ teaspoon **ground nutmeg.** Season to

taste with **salt** and **white pepper.** If made ahead, cover and refrigerate for up to 8 hours.

Mushroom-Tomato Sauce. Melt 3 tablespoons **butter** or margarine in a wide frying pan over medium heat. Stir in ½ cup chopped **shallots** or onion and 1 pound **mushrooms,** thinly sliced. Cook, stirring often, until mushrooms are lightly browned. Stir in 2 tablespoons **tomato paste,** 1 teaspoon **dry basil,** and 2 cups *each* **dry vermouth** and **chicken broth.** Bring to a boil; boil, stirring often, until reduced to 3 cups. Reduce heat to low. (At this point, you may let cool, then cover and refrigerate until next day. Reheat before continuing.) Add 1 cup (½ lb.) **butter** or margarine to sauce; stir constantly until sauce is smooth and thickened. Serve at once.

Per serving: 977 calories (56 percent from fat), 42 g protein, 57 g carbohydrates, 57 g total fat (32 g saturated fat), 270 mg cholesterol, 1,997 mg sodium

Baked Lemon Rice Pilaf

If you want a side dish that requires no fuss and limited energy, this lemon-scented pilaf could be your best bet. It's an especially good accompaniment for fresh fish. Try it alongside Salmon with Chive & Herb Sauce (page 121) or Sole with Grapes (page 122).

> 2 cups chicken broth
> 1 cup long-grain white rice
> 2 teaspoons grated lemon peel
> 2 tablespoons lemon juice
> ¼ cup sliced green onions
> 1 tablespoon butter or margarine

In a 1½- to 2-quart baking dish, mix broth, rice, lemon peel, lemon juice, onions, and butter. Cover and bake in a 350° oven until rice is tender to bite (about 50 minutes). Makes 6 servings.

Per serving: 141 calories (17 percent from fat), 3 g protein, 26 g carbohydrates, 3 g total fat (1 g saturated fat), 5 mg cholesterol, 352 mg sodium

Rice Pilaf with Fruit & Nuts

In the late 1800s, thousands of Armenians left their homeland to escape persecution by the Ottoman Turks. Many of the immigrants settled in California, in and around Los Angeles. One of the region's Armenian families shared this unusual recipe with *Sunset* food editors in 1974.

> 5 cups chicken broth
> ½ cup (¼ lb.) butter or margarine
> ½ teaspoon sugar
> 2 cups long-grain white rice
>   Salt
> 3 tablespoons butter or margarine
> 1 cup whole blanched almonds
> 1 cup raisins or dried currants
> 1 cup pitted dates, cut into quarters
> 1 cup dried apricots, cut into quarters

In a large pan, combine broth, the ½ cup butter, and sugar. Bring to a boil over high heat. Add rice and stir until mixture returns to a boil. Reduce heat, cover, and simmer for 15 minutes. Season to taste with salt. Pour into a 2½-quart baking dish. Cover and bake in a 325° oven until rice is tender to bite (1 to 1¼ hours).

About 10 minutes before rice is done, melt 1 tablespoon butter in a wide frying pan over medium heat. Add almonds and cook, stirring often, until golden brown (3 to 5 minutes). Lift from pan with a slotted spoon and drain on paper towels. Melt remaining 2 tablespoons butter in pan. Add raisins and stir until puffy. Add dates and stir to coat with butter. Then add apricots and stir until heated through. To serve, pour fruits over rice; sprinkle with almonds. Makes 12 servings.

Per serving: 391 calories (39 percent from fat), 7 g protein, 55 g carbohydrates, 18 g total fat (7 g saturated fat), 28 mg cholesterol, 524 mg sodium

Vegetable Risotto

Risotto is rice cooked Italian style—simmered and stirred until delectably smooth and creamy. Short-grain varieties of rice such as arborio work best in classic risotto: the small, round kernels retain moisture well, becoming dense in texture and rich in flavor as they absorb broth and seasonings.

- 2 **tablespoons olive oil**
- 1 **large red bell pepper, seeded and diced**
- 2 **medium-size zucchini, diced**
- ¼ **cup butter or margarine**
- 1 **large onion, chopped**
- 1 **clove garlic, minced or pressed**
- 1½ **cups short-grain white rice**
- 4 **to 4⅓ cups chicken broth**
- 1 **package (about 9 oz.) frozen artichoke hearts, thawed**
- 2 **cups diced cooked turkey (optional)**
- 1 **cup (about 4 oz.) grated Parmesan cheese**
  Salt and pepper

Heat oil in a wide frying pan or large pan over medium-high heat. Add bell pepper and zucchini; cook, stirring constantly, until vegetables are tender-crisp to bite (about 5 minutes). Lift out vegetables and set aside.

Reduce heat to medium and add butter, onion, and garlic to pan; cook, stirring often, until onion is soft and golden (about 7 minutes). Add rice and cook, stirring often, until it is opaque and looks milky (about 10 minutes). Stir in 4 cups of the broth; cook, stirring occasionally, until mixture comes to a boil. Reduce heat slightly and boil gently, stirring occasionally, for 10 minutes.

Stir in artichoke hearts, turkey (if desired), bell pepper, and zucchini. Reduce heat to low and continue to cook, stirring often, until rice is tender to bite and almost all liquid has been absorbed (10 to 15 more minutes); if liquid evaporates before rice is cooked, add a little more broth.

Remove from heat and stir in about ¼ cup of the cheese. Season to taste with salt and pepper. Spoon into a serving dish and sprinkle with about ¼ cup more cheese. Offer remaining cheese to add to taste. Makes 4 servings.

Per serving: 653 calories (40 percent from fat), 23 g protein, 76 g carbohydrates, 29 g total fat (14 g saturated fat), 53 mg cholesterol, 1,709 mg sodium

Fried Rice

Stir-fried rice with vegetables, shrimp, and cashews is popular as a snack in China, but you may want to serve it for a speedy one-dish meal.

- 1¼ **cups long-grain white rice**
- 1¾ **cups cold water**
- 2 **eggs**
- ¼ **teaspoon salt**
- ¼ **cup salad oil**
- 2 **green onions, thinly sliced**
- 1 **cup small cooked shrimp or diced cooked ham**
- ½ **cup frozen peas, thawed**
- ½ **cup roasted cashews**
- 2 **tablespoons soy sauce**

In a 2-quart pan, combine rice and water. Bring to a boil over medium-high heat; boil, uncovered, until bubbles disappear from surface and only a thin film of water covers top of rice (about 8 minutes). Reduce heat, cover, and simmer until rice is tender to bite

(about 20 minutes). Remove from heat and let cool; then refrigerate until cold. Rub cold rice with wet hands until all grains are separated; set aside.

In a bowl, beat eggs with salt. Heat 1 tablespoon of the oil in a wok or wide frying pan over medium heat. Add onions and cook, stirring, for about 30 seconds. Add eggs and cook, stirring, until softly set. Remove egg mixture from pan and set aside.

Heat 1 more tablespoon oil in pan. Add shrimp, peas, and cashews; cook, stirring, until heated through (about 2 minutes). Remove from pan and set aside. Heat remaining 2 tablespoons oil in pan. Add rice and cook, stirring, until heated through (about 2 minutes). Stir in soy sauce and shrimp mixture. Add egg mixture and stir gently until eggs are in small pieces. Makes 4 servings.

Per serving: 523 calories (43 percent from fat), 19 g protein, 56 g carbohydrates, 25 g total fat (4 g saturated fat), 175 mg cholesterol, 787 mg sodium

Confetti Rice

Condensed consommé gives this simple pilaf its depth of flavor. A confetti of minced vegetables and sliced almonds adds color and crunch.

- ¼ **cup butter or margarine**
- 1¼ **cups long-grain white rice**
- 2 **cans (about 10½ oz. *each*) condensed consommé**
- ¾ **cup *each* sliced green onions, chopped carrots, and chopped celery**
- ¼ **cup sliced almonds**

Melt butter in a wide frying pan over medium heat. Add rice and cook, stirring occasionally, until heated through but not browned (about 5 minutes). Add consommé. Bring to a boil over high heat, then pour into a 1½-quart baking dish. Cover and bake in a 375° oven until rice is barely tender to bite (about 20 minutes). Remove from oven and stir in onions, carrots, celery, and almonds. Cover and continue to bake until rice is tender and vegetables are tender-crisp to bite (about 10 more minutes). Makes 6 servings.

Per serving: 268 calories (34 percent from fat), 8 g protein, 36 g carbohydrates, 10 g total fat (5 g saturated fat), 21 mg cholesterol, 616 mg sodium

Wild Rice with Golden Raisins

Wild rice isn't rice; it's a long-grain marsh grass native to the northern Great Lakes area. Today, local Indians still harvest the grain as they did in the past—from canoes which glide through the water among the tall plants. (California and several midwestern states now also farm wild rice commercially.)

1¾　cups wild rice
¼　cup butter or margarine
½　cup golden raisins
1　large onion, minced
1　teaspoon dry thyme
6　cups beef or chicken broth
2　tablespoons dry sherry (optional)
2　to 3 tablespoons thinly sliced green onions

Rinse rice with water, drain, and set aside.

Melt butter in a 3- to 4-quart pan over medium-high heat. Add raisins and stir until puffy. Lift out with a slotted spoon and set aside.

Add minced onion and thyme to pan; cook, stirring often, until onion is lightly browned (about 9 minutes). Stir in broth and bring to a boil. Add rice and return to a boil over high heat; then reduce heat, cover, and simmer until rice is tender to bite (about 1½ hours), stirring occasionally. Add sherry (if desired), cover,

and cook for 10 more minutes. Pour rice into a greased 2-quart baking dish. (At this point, you may let rice cool, then cover and refrigerate rice and raisins separately until next day.)

Bake, uncovered, in a 350° oven for 15 minutes. (If refrigerated, bake, covered, until heated through—about 1 hour.) Scatter raisins over rice and bake, uncovered, for 10 more minutes. Sprinkle with green onions. Makes 8 servings.

Per serving: 232 calories (26 percent from fat), 8 g protein, 37 g carbohydrates, 7 g total fat (4 g saturated fat), 16 mg cholesterol, 682 mg sodium

Bulgur Mexicana

A California chef shared this vegetarian tostada with us in 1991. Spoon the Mexican-spiced bulgur over warm, soft tortillas; then roll the tortillas up to eat out of hand like a burrito, or leave them open-faced and use a knife and fork.

2　tablespoons salad oil
1　large onion, chopped
¾　cup bulgur (quick-cooking cracked wheat)
2　cans (about 10 oz. *each*) enchilada sauce
1　can (about 14½ oz.) Mexican-style stewed tomatoes
⅔　cup toasted wheat germ
1　package (about 10 oz.) frozen chopped Swiss chard or spinach, thawed and squeezed dry
2　fresh jalapeño chiles, seeded and finely chopped
½　teaspoon dry oregano
1　small can (about 8 oz.) red kidney beans, drained and rinsed
6　flour tortillas (*each* about 8 inches in diameter)
　　Cilantro sprigs
　　Purchased chile salsa
　　Plain yogurt

Heat oil in a wide frying pan over medium heat. Add onion and bulgur;

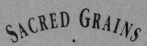

SACRED GRAINS

A staple for half the world's population, rice is a basic food in both Asia and Europe. Italians serve it plumped with broth in creamy risotto; in the Mideast, it's featured in fragrant pilafs.

In feudal Japan, landowners measured wealth and power by the size of their rice harvest—and used the grain as currency to pay samurai for protection and services. In China, where rice is the principal crop, the pearly grain was declared sacred in 2800 B.C. Today, per capita consumption of rice in China remains high—about 1 pound per day.

cook, stirring often, until onion is soft (about 5 minutes). Stir in enchilada sauce, tomatoes, wheat germ, chard, chiles, oregano, and beans. Cover and simmer, stirring often, until all liquid has been absorbed (10 to 15 minutes).

Meanwhile, stack tortillas and wrap in foil. Heat in a 350° oven until warm and soft (about 15 minutes).

Pour bulgur mixture into a serving bowl and garnish with cilantro sprigs. Accompany with warm tortillas; offer salsa and yogurt to add to taste. Makes 6 servings.

Per serving: 364 calories (21 percent from fat), 14 g protein, 61 g carbohydrates, 9 g total fat (1 g saturated fat), 0 mg cholesterol, 1,436 mg sodium

Brown Rice Vegetable Casserole

Steamed fresh vegetables mingle with brown rice in this colorful vegetarian casserole. Topped with cheese and sunflower seeds, it's a satisfying choice for a cold-weather meal.

2½ **cups water**

2 **chicken bouillon cubes**

1 **cup long-grain brown rice**

1 **pound broccoli**

1 **small head cauliflower**

2 **medium-size crookneck squash or zucchini**

¼ **cup sliced celery**

¼ **pound mushrooms, sliced**

¼ **cup** *each* **shredded carrot and sliced green onions**

½ **teaspoon soy sauce**

1 **can (about 7 oz.) mild green chile salsa**

About 20 cherry tomatoes

3 **slices jack cheese (about 1 oz.** *each***)**

3 **slices Cheddar cheese (about 1 oz.** *each***)**

3 **tablespoons salted roasted sunflower seeds**

In a 2-quart pan, combine water and bouillon cubes. Bring to a boil over high heat. Add rice; reduce heat, cover, and simmer until rice is tender to bite (about 45 minutes). Remove from heat and uncover.

While rice is cooking, cut flowerets from broccoli stalks. Reserve stalks for other uses. Break flowerets into bite-size pieces, leaving about 2 inches of stem. Break cauliflower into bite-size flowerets. Cut squash into ½-inch-thick slices. Arrange broccoli, cauliflower, squash, and celery on a rack in a pan over 1 inch of boiling water. Cover and steam until all vegetables are tender-crisp to bite (8 to 10 minutes). Add mushrooms, cover, and steam for 2 more minutes. Remove vegetables from heat.

Add carrot, onions, and soy sauce to rice; stir gently until combined. Spread rice mixture evenly in a greased shallow 2-quart baking dish. Spoon salsa evenly over rice and top with steamed vegetables and cherry tomatoes. Cut each slice of cheese in half; then cover casserole with alternate slices of jack and Cheddar cheese, overlapping edges slightly. (At this point, you may cover and refrigerate until next day.)

Bake, uncovered, in a 350° oven until heated through (15 to 20 minutes; 25 to 30 minutes if refrigerated). Sprinkle with sunflower seeds. Makes 6 servings.

Per serving: 307 calories (35 percent from fat), 14 g protein, 37 g carbohydrates, 12 g total fat (3 g saturated fat), 27 mg cholesterol, 832 mg sodium

Couscous with Chanterelles & Herbs

Couscous—processed semolina wheat formed into tiny pellets—is often used in North African and Mideastern dishes. In this recipe, the little grains are permeated with the woodsy flavor and aroma of fresh chanterelles. (Look for the trumpet-shaped mushrooms in well-stocked produce markets.)

4 **to 5 ounces fresh chanterelles**

2 **tablespoons olive oil or salad oil**

½ **cup finely chopped onion**

2 **teaspoons minced fresh rosemary or 1 teaspoon dry rosemary**

1 **teaspoon minced fresh thyme or ½ teaspoon dry thyme**

1¾ **cups chicken broth**

1 **cup couscous**

¼ **cup grated Parmesan cheese**

If ends of chanterelles are tough or discolored, trim them off. Immerse chanterelles in water and swish vigorously to remove debris; at once lift from water and drain well. Finely chop chanterelles.

In a wide frying pan, combine chanterelles, oil, onion, rosemary, and thyme. Cover and cook over medium-high heat until mushrooms release their liquid (3 to 5 minutes). Uncover and cook, stirring often, until liquid has evaporated and mushrooms are lightly browned (about 10 minutes). Add broth and bring to a boil. Stir in couscous, then cover tightly and remove from heat. Let stand until liquid has been absorbed (about 5 minutes). With a fork, fluff couscous; then stir in cheese. Makes 6 servings.

Per serving: 190 calories (30 percent from fat), 7 g protein, 26 g carbohydrates, 6 g total fat (1 g saturated fat), 3 mg cholesterol, 354 mg sodium

Oat Pilaf

Pilafs made with steel-cut oats are chunkier and heartier than those using rice. Try this sturdy, dense-textured dish alongside a meaty main course such as Greek Shish Kebab (page 86).

3 **tablespoons butter or margarine**

1 **large onion, thinly sliced**

1 **cup steel-cut oats or oat groats**

1¾ **cups beef broth (2¼ cups if using oat groats)**

Parsley sprigs

Melt butter in a wide frying pan over medium-high heat. Add onion and cook, stirring often, until soft (about 4 minutes). Add oats and stir for 1 minute. Then pour in broth.

Bring to a boil over high heat; then reduce heat, cover, and simmer, stirring occasionally, until liquid has been absorbed (about 15 minutes for steel-cut oats, about 40 minutes for oat groats). Garnish with parsley sprigs. Makes 4 servings.

Per serving: 276 calories (38 percent from fat), 9 g protein, 35 g carbohydrates, 12 g total fat (6 g saturated fat), 23 mg cholesterol, 452 mg sodium

The spaghetti's ready, and you use it as the foundation for your own pasta meal. Set up your buffet just like a salad bar, then let guests pick and choose from a colorful collection of sauces and garnishes to mix with cooked spaghetti. The barbecue is the answer to keeping pasta and sauces warm outdoors; you can also use your rangetop for an indoor feast.

The spaghetti, sauces, and garnishes listed below will serve 8 to 10 hungry people. Provide at least one medium-size frying pan for every three guests, and have potholders and cooking spoons handy. Round out the meal with a big green salad, crusty bread, and a selection of fresh fruit.

Spaghetti Bar

Sauces (choices and directions follow)

Raw & cooked garnishes (choices and directions follow)

Cooked spaghetti (directions follow)

Olive oil

Grated Parmesan cheese

Prepare sauces, garnishes, and spaghetti. Place all ingredients around barbecue or rangetop.

If using a barbecue, have barbecue ready with a solid bed of hot coals. When coals are almost covered with gray ash (after about 30 minutes), add 10 to 15 more briquets to coals to maintain an even low heat; then add 10 to 15 more every 30 minutes. (Or fire up several portable burners, such as camp stoves; or use your rangetop.)

Add to a frying pan, without crowding, your choice of garnishes and a little oil to moisten. Place pan on grill, portable burner, or rangetop

burner; stir often until ingredients are cooked to suit your taste. Add a portion of spaghetti; stir until hot (about 2 minutes). At this point, you may want to add more garnishes (those that don't need cooking). Pour pasta onto a plate, sprinkle with cheese, and eat.

Wipe pan clean with paper towels and set aside until ready to try another combination. Makes 8 to 10 servings.

Sauces. Choose two or all three of the following: **Bellins' Garden Marinara Sauce** (page 53), **Classic Pesto** (page 53), and/or **Cream Sauce** (recipe follows). Pour marinara and cream sauces into serving containers and keep hot; spoon pesto into a serving bowl.

Cream Sauce. In a wide frying pan, combine 3 cups **whipping cream** and ⅛ teaspoon **ground nutmeg.** Boil over high heat until large, shiny bubbles form and sauce is reduced by about a third. Makes about 2 cups.

Per ¼ cup: 262 calories (93 percent from fat), 2 g protein, 3 g carbohydrates, 28 g total fat (17 g saturated fat), 99 mg cholesterol, 30 mg sodium

Raw & cooked garnishes. Arrange your choice of garnishes in individual bowls.

Browned Italian sausage. You'll need 3 cups crumbled, browned **Italian sausage,** drained of fat (about 2 lbs. mild and/or hot sausages *total*). Heat before serving.

Per ¼ cup: 179 calories (73 percent from fat), 11 g protein, 0.8 g carbohydrates, 14 g total fat (5 g saturated fat), 43 mg cholesterol, 510 mg sodium

Vegetable confetti. With a sharp knife, cut 2 medium-size **zucchini** and 2 medium-size **carrots** into thin julienne strips. Melt 2 tablespoons **butter** or margarine in a wide frying pan over medium heat. Add carrots and cook, stirring, for 1 to 2 minutes; add zucchini and cook, stirring, until vegetables are barely tender to bite. Heat before serving. Makes 1½ to 2 cups.

Per ¼ cup: 45 calories (64 percent from fat), 0.8 g protein, 3 g carbohydrates, 3 g total fat (2 g saturated fat), 9 mg cholesterol, 42 mg sodium

Red pimentos. Use about 1 cup drained **bottled diced pimentos.**

Per tablespoon: 3 calories (9 percent from fat), 0.2 g protein, 0.7 g carbohydrates, 0 g total fat (0 g saturated fat), 0 mg cholesterol, 2 mg sodium

Cherry tomatoes. Cut 2 cups **cherry tomatoes** lengthwise into halves.

Per ¼ cup: 5 calories (12 percent from fat), 0.2 g protein, 1 g carbohydrates, 0.1 g total fat (0 g saturated fat), 0 mg cholesterol, 2 mg sodium

Marinated artichokes. Use 1 jar (about 6 oz.) **marinated artichoke hearts** and their marinade.

Per tablespoon: 13 calories (63 percent from fat), 0.3 g protein, 1 g carbohydrates, 1 g total fat (0.1 g saturated fat), 0 mg cholesterol, 73 mg sodium

Garlic bowl. Use ½ cup minced **garlic.**

Per tablespoon: 15 calories (3 percent from fat), 0.6 g protein, 3 g carbohydrates, 0.1 g total fat (0 g saturated fat), 0 mg cholesterol, 2 mg sodium

Cooked spaghetti. In a 6- to 8-quart pan, cook 2 pounds **dry thin spaghetti** or vermicelli in 7 quarts of **boiling salted water** until barely tender to bite (8 to 10 minutes); or cook according to package directions. Drain and transfer to a large bowl. Add 2 tablespoons **olive oil;** toss gently to coat. Makes about 15 cups.

Per cup: 240 calories (10 percent from fat), 8 g protein, 45 g carbohydrates, 3 g total fat (0.4 g saturated fat), 0 mg cholesterol, 211 mg sodium

B R E A D S

*B*reads in all their shapes and sizes offer a delicious look at the history and culture of the American West. Our tangy sourdough, for example, was probably invented by miners who traveled to California during Gold Rush days. Scandinavian settlers brought thin flatbröd and plain, rustic loaves such as rieska and rågbröd. Native Americans contributed cornbread and puffy, golden fry bread; crusty bolillos are a Mexican creation. In recent years, the popularity of Italian cuisine has heightened our interest in specialties like crisp, herb-seasoned breadsticks and flavorful Mediterranean Olive Bread. • This chapter presents an international collection of Sunset's favorite breads and rolls. Here, you'll find savory loaves and sweet ones, quick breads and yeast breads, and lots of special-occasion treats—from buttery bear claws filled with almond paste to a Christmas stollen sparkling with vanilla sugar.

Flatbread

We first printed the recipe for crisp Norwegian *flatbröd* in 1953—and it proved to be so popular that we featured it again 5 years later. Today, the small, delicate, waferlike rounds are still among our favorite accompaniments for salads and soups.

1¾ **cups all-purpose flour**
½ **cup yellow cornmeal**
½ **teaspoon salt**
¼ **cup butter or margarine, cut into small pieces**
⅔ **cup warm water**

In a medium-size bowl, mix flour, cornmeal, and salt. Add butter and rub in with your fingers until mixture resembles coarse crumbs. Stir in warm water. Cover and refrigerate until cold.

Shape chilled dough into balls the size of large marbles. On a lightly floured board, roll out each ball of dough to a paper-thin round about 4 inches in diameter. Place rounds slightly apart on ungreased baking sheets. Bake in a 375° oven until very lightly browned (about 5 minutes). Transfer to racks and let cool completely. If made ahead, wrap airtight and store at room temperature. Makes about 90 wafers.

Per wafer: 17 calories (28 percent from fat), 0.3 g protein, 3 g carbohydrates, 0.5 g total fat (0.3 g saturated fat), 1 mg cholesterol, 17 mg sodium

Fry Bread

Fry bread has been basic fare among the Navajos for centuries; we offered our first recipe for the golden, puffy rounds in 1964. These days, the breads are often served as a base for Navajo Tacos (page 68), with toppings of ground beef, beans, and cheese.

2 **cups all-purpose flour**
½ **cup instant nonfat dry milk**
1 **teaspoon baking powder**
½ **teaspoon salt**
2 **tablespoons solid vegetable shortening**
¾ **cup water**
   Salad oil

In a large bowl, mix flour, dry milk, baking powder, and salt. With a pastry blender or 2 knives, cut in shortening until mixture resembles coarse crumbs (or rub shortening into flour mixture with your fingers). Add water and stir until dough holds together.

Turn dough out onto a lightly floured board. Knead until smooth (2 to 3 minutes). Divide dough into 6 equal pieces. Work with one piece of dough at a time; keep remaining dough covered with plastic wrap. Shape one piece of dough into a ball; then pat out on board to make a 6- to 7-inch round. Cover with plastic wrap. Repeat to shape remaining 5 pieces of dough.

Line 2 baking sheets with several layers of paper towels. In a wide frying pan, heat ¾ inch of oil to 375°F on a deep-frying thermometer. Add dough rounds, one at a time; cook, turning once, until puffy and golden brown (1½ to 2 minutes). As each bread is cooked, transfer it to a towel-lined baking sheet, cover loosely, and keep warm until all breads have been cooked.

If made ahead, let cool completely; then wrap airtight and refrigerate until next day. To reheat, place bread rounds slightly apart on baking sheets and heat, uncovered, in a 375° oven until heated through (about 5 minutes). Makes 6 breads.

Per bread: 290 calories (43 percent from fat), 6 g protein, 35 g carbohydrates, 14 g total fat (2 g saturated fat), 1 mg cholesterol, 296 mg sodium

Rieska

This wheatless bread is traditional in northern Finland and Lapland. It's made in various thicknesses; the farther north you go, the thinner the bread. The Finns often pair it with beef stew or hot bouillon, but we think it's equally delicious on its own, served hot and spread liberally with butter.

Rieska made with barley flour is chewy in texture and slightly sweet; rye flour yields a coarser, earthier-tasting loaf.

2 **cups barley flour or rye flour**
2 **teaspoons *each* sugar and baking powder**
¾ **teaspoon salt**
1 **cup evaporated milk or half-and-half**
2 **tablespoons butter or margarine, melted**
   Butter or margarine

In a large bowl, mix flour, sugar, baking powder, and salt. Stir in milk and the 2 tablespoons butter until smooth. Turn dough out onto a greased baking sheet; pat out to make a round about 14 inches in diameter and ½ inch thick. Prick surface of dough all over with a fork. Bake in a 450° oven until lightly browned (about 10 minutes). To serve, cut into wedges. Offer butter to spread over individual wedges. Makes 8 to 10 servings.

Per serving: 149 calories (33 percent from fat), 4 g protein, 22 g carbohydrates, 6 g total fat (3 g saturated fat), 15 mg cholesterol, 348 mg sodium

Civilized Cornbread

Pure refinement! Most cornbreads don't have it—but this one does. It's feather-light, with a close-grained yet fluffy texture. If you'd like to add a little decadence, spread sweet Honey Butter over each warm square.

- 1 cup *each* packaged biscuit mix and yellow cornmeal
- 1 tablespoon baking powder
- 2 eggs
- 1 cup milk
- ⅓ cup honey
- ¼ cup butter or margarine, melted Honey Butter (recipe follows)

In a large bowl, mix biscuit mix, cornmeal, and baking powder. In a small bowl, beat eggs until blended; then stir in milk, honey, and butter. Pour egg mixture into cornmeal mixture and stir just until evenly moistened.

Pour batter into a greased 8-inch-square baking pan. Bake in a 400° oven until a wooden pick inserted in center comes out clean (25 to 30 minutes). Meanwhile, prepare Honey Butter.

Let cornbread cool slightly; then cut into squares and serve warm. Offer Honey Butter to spread on individual squares. Makes 9 servings.

Honey Butter. In a small bowl, beat together ½ cup (¼ lb.) **butter** or margarine (at room temperature) and ¼ cup **honey** until creamy and well blended. Mound in a small crock and serve. Makes about ¾ cup.

Per serving of cornbread: 228 calories (37 percent from fat), 5 g protein, 32 g carbohydrates, 9 g total fat (5 g saturated fat), 65 mg cholesterol, 398 mg sodium

Per tablespoon of Honey Butter: 89 calories (74 percent from fat), 0.1 g protein, 6 g carbohydrates, 8 g total fat (5 g saturated fat), 21 mg cholesterol, 78 mg sodium

CORNMEAL

Native Americans introduced the colonists to corn and many dishes made from it, including cornbread. One dense-textured version, a staple of the Algonquin Indians, was called *appone*—the "corn pone" that later became common fare throughout the South. Today's cornbread can be heavy and plain or light and sweet; even crisp cookies can be made with the crunchy meal. Americans discovered another cornmeal specialty when the Italians brought coarsely ground polenta to the U.S. culinary scene.

WESTERN CLASSIC

Harvest Popovers

In 1988, *Sunset* offered a popover recipe with an appealing twist: to a basic batter, you add your choice of savory flavorings. Depending on your appetite and menu, select wild rice and Parmesan, oats and toasted nuts, or one of our other options.

Harvest Ingredients (choices and directions follow)
- 2 eggs
- 1 cup all-purpose flour
- ¼ teaspoon salt
- 1 cup milk

Prepare your choice of Harvest Ingredients and set aside.

In a large bowl, beat eggs, flour, salt, and milk with an electric mixer until smoothly blended. Stir in Harvest Ingredients. At once, ladle batter equally into 8 greased muffin cups or heavy 2- to 2½-inch popover cups; or ladle into 6 to 8 greased 4- to 5-ounce custard cups. Fill cups no higher than ¼ inch below rims. If using individual cups, set them well apart in a 10- by 15-inch rimmed baking pan.

Bake in a 375° oven until popovers are puffed, very well browned, and firm to the touch (about 50 minutes). Remove from oven, run a knife around edge of each popover to loosen, and invert to remove from pans. Serve hot. For extra-crisp popovers, return popovers to pans, tilting popovers at an angle. Pierce sides of popovers with a thin skewer and return to turned-off oven for 5 to 10 minutes.

If made ahead, let cool; then cover and store at room temperature until next day. To reheat and recrisp, place popovers slightly apart in a 10- by 15-inch rimmed baking pan and heat, uncovered, in a 375° oven until heated through (about 5 minutes). Makes 6 to 8 popovers.

Harvest Ingredients. Choose one of the following.

Wild rice & Parmesan. Rinse 3 tablespoons **wild rice** with water; drain. In a 1- to 1½-quart pan, combine rice and 1 cup **water.** Bring to a boil over high heat; then reduce heat, cover, and simmer, stirring occasionally, until rice is tender to bite (about 50 minutes). Drain and let cool. In a small bowl, mix rice with ¼ cup grated **Parmesan cheese** and 1 teaspoon **grated orange peel.**

Per popover: 148 calories (31 percent from fat), 7 g protein, 19 g carbohydrates, 5 g total fat (2 g saturated fat), 68 mg cholesterol, 166 mg sodium

Bran & Cheddar. In a small bowl, stir together ⅓ cup **bran cereal flakes,** ¼ cup shredded **sharp Cheddar cheese,** and ¾ teaspoon **dry rosemary.**

Per popover: 142 calories (35 percent from fat), 6 g protein, 17 g carbohydrates, 5 g total fat (2 g saturated fat), 70 mg cholesterol, 155 mg sodium

Oats & hazelnuts. Spread ¼ cup chopped **hazelnuts** or almonds in a shallow baking pan and toast in a 350° oven, stirring occasionally, until lightly browned (5 to 8 minutes). In a small bowl, stir together nuts, ⅓ cup **quick-cooking rolled oats,** and ½ teaspoon **ground allspice.**

Per popover: 160 calories (38 percent from fat), 6 g protein, 19 g carbohydrates, 7 g total fat (2 g saturated fat), 66 mg cholesterol, 113 mg sodium

Cornmeal & green onions. In a small bowl, stir together ⅓ cup **yellow cornmeal,** ⅓ cup thinly sliced **green onions,** and 1 clove **garlic,** minced or pressed.

Per popover: 145 calories (26 percent from fat), 5 g protein, 21 g carbohydrates, 4 g total fat (1 g saturated fat), 66 mg cholesterol, 114 mg sodium

Wheat & Herb Scones

Most of us think of scones as sweet cakes to serve at breakfast or teatime, but these savory whole wheat wedges are better alongside a juicy steak or hearty stew. Dense-textured biscuits seasoned with herbs, they offer a contemporary twist on the traditional English treats.

1½ cups *each* **all-purpose flour and whole wheat flour**
1 tablespoon **baking powder**
1 teaspoon **dry basil**
½ teaspoon *each* **dry oregano and dry thyme**
½ cup (¼ lb.) **butter or margarine, cut into small pieces**
2 **eggs**
½ cup **milk**

In a food processor (or a large bowl), combine all-purpose flour, whole wheat flour, baking powder, basil, oregano, and thyme. Whirl (or mix with a fork) until combined. Add butter; whirl (or rub in with your fingers) until mixture resembles coarse crumbs.

In a small bowl, beat eggs and milk until blended; reserve 2 tablespoons of the mixture. Add remaining egg-milk mixture to flour mixture and whirl (or stir with a fork) just until evenly moistened.

Turn dough out onto a floured board and knead until dough holds together. Divide dough in half. Pat each half into a 5- to 6-inch-diameter round about ¾ inch thick. Set rounds well apart on a greased baking sheet. With a knife, cut each round not quite through into 6 equal wedges. Brush rounds with reserved egg mixture. Bake in a 400° oven until golden brown (about 18 minutes). Break into wedges and serve warm. Makes 1 dozen scones.

Per scone: 199 calories (43 percent from fat), 5 g protein, 24 g carbohydrates, 10 g total fat (5 g saturated fat), 58 mg cholesterol, 217 mg sodium

Orange Date Scones

These buttery, fruit-laced scones are sure to please. Studded with dates and orange peel, they're sprinkled with cinnamon sugar before baking for a sweet, crunchy top crust.

3 cups **all-purpose flour**
⅓ cup **sugar**
2½ teaspoons **baking powder**
¾ teaspoon **salt**
½ teaspoon **baking soda**
¾ cup (¼ lb. plus ¼ cup) **butter or margarine, cut into small pieces**
¾ cup **chopped pitted dates or dried currants**
1 teaspoon **grated orange peel**
1 cup **buttermilk**
About 1 tablespoon **whipping cream or milk**
2 tablespoons **sugar**
¼ teaspoon **ground cinnamon**

In a large bowl, mix flour, the ⅓ cup sugar, baking powder, salt, and baking soda. With a pastry blender or 2 knives, cut in butter until mixture resembles coarse crumbs. Stir in dates and orange peel. Make a well in center of butter-flour mixture; add buttermilk all at once and stir until dough cleans sides of bowl.

Shape dough into a ball. On a lightly floured board, roll or pat dough out about ½ inch thick. Using a 2- to 3-inch-round cookie cutter, cut dough into scones. Place scones 1½ inches apart on lightly greased baking sheets.

Brush tops of scones with cream; combine the 2 tablespoons sugar and cinnamon and sprinkle lightly and evenly over scones. Bake in a 425° oven until lightly browned (about 12 minutes). Serve warm. Makes about 1½ dozen scones.

Per scone: 196 calories (40 percent from fat), 3 g protein, 27 g carbohydrates, 9 g total fat (5 g saturated fat), 22 mg cholesterol, 287 mg sodium

Rhubarb-Zucchini Bread

When rhubarb is in season—from about early February to late June—buy an extra bunch to use in this wonderful quick bread. Sliced and simmered, the juicy pink stalks give the loaf a pleasantly tart flavor and an uncommonly moist texture.

- **2 cups (about ¾ lb.) thinly sliced rhubarb**
- **2 tablespoons orange juice**
- **2 cups sugar**
- **3 cups all-purpose flour**
- **2 teaspoons baking soda**
- **1½ teaspoons ground cinnamon**
- **¾ teaspoon ground nutmeg**
- **½ teaspoon *each* salt and baking powder**
- **1 cup chopped walnuts**
- **3 eggs**
- **1 cup salad oil**
- **2 teaspoons vanilla**
- **2 cups (about ½ lb.) coarsely shredded zucchini**

In a 2- to 2½-quart pan, combine rhubarb, orange juice, and 2 tablespoons of the sugar. Bring to a boil over high heat; then reduce heat and simmer, uncovered, until rhubarb is tender to bite (about 5 minutes). Remove from heat and let cool.

In a medium-size bowl, mix flour, baking soda, cinnamon, nutmeg, salt, baking powder, and walnuts; set aside.

In a large bowl, beat eggs with an electric mixer or a wire whisk until blended. Add oil, remaining sugar, and vanilla; beat until mixture is thick and foamy.

Drain rhubarb and add to batter along with zucchini; stir until blended. Then add flour mixture and stir just until evenly moistened. Spoon batter equally into 2 greased and floured 5- by 9-inch loaf pans.

Bake in a 350° oven until a wooden pick inserted in center of each loaf comes out clean (about 45 minutes). Let bread cool in pans on racks for 10 minutes; then turn out onto racks to cool completely. Makes 2 loaves (10 to 12 servings *each*).

Per serving: 276 calories (47 percent from fat), 4 g protein, 34 g carbohydrates, 15 g total fat (2 g saturated fat), 29 mg cholesterol, 186 mg sodium

Apple Bread

The rich perfume of ripening apples greets travelers to Sebastopol, California in midsummer, when the region's growers harvest bushels of the aromatic fruit. One Sebastopol cook has found a way to enjoy the crop all year round—when local apples are out of season, he uses applesauce to make this spicy raisin bread.

- **3 cups all-purpose flour**
- **2½ teaspoons ground cinnamon**
- **1¼ teaspoons baking soda**
- **½ teaspoon *each* baking powder and salt**
- **2 cups granulated sugar**
- **1 can (about 1 lb.) applesauce**
- **1 cup salad oil**
- **5 eggs**
- **1 tablespoon vanilla**
- **½ cup raisins**
- **2 teaspoons firmly packed brown sugar**

In a medium-size bowl, mix flour, cinnamon, baking soda, baking powder, and salt; set aside.

In a large bowl, beat granulated sugar, applesauce, oil, eggs, and vanilla with an electric mixer on low speed until well blended; then beat on high speed for 2 minutes. Add flour mixture and beat on low speed until well blended. Stir in raisins. Spoon batter equally into 2 greased 5- by 9-inch loaf pans. Evenly sprinkle each loaf with 1 teaspoon of the brown sugar.

Bake in a 325° oven until a wooden pick inserted in center of each loaf comes out clean (about 1¼ hours). Let bread cool in pans on racks for 10 minutes; then turn out onto racks to cool completely. If made ahead, wrap airtight and refrigerate for up to 5 days; freeze for longer storage. Makes 2 loaves (10 to 12 servings *each*).

Per serving: 270 calories (38 percent from fat), 4 g protein, 39 g carbohydrates, 12 g total fat (2 g saturated fat), 49 mg cholesterol, 148 mg sodium

Prune Bread

Homespun favorites like this dense whole wheat prune bread are a standard feature of *Sunset*'s "Kitchen Cabinet." Here, the prunes are poached before they're added to the batter, resulting in an especially moist and chewy loaf.

- **1 cup *each* water and chopped pitted prunes**
- **1½ cups all-purpose flour**
- **1 cup whole wheat flour**
- **1½ teaspoons baking powder**
- **1 teaspoon baking soda**
- **¼ cup butter or margarine, at room temperature**
- **1 cup sugar**
- **1 egg**
- **2 teaspoons vanilla**
- **1 cup buttermilk**

In a small pan, combine water and prunes. Bring to a boil over high heat; then reduce heat and simmer until prunes are plumped (about 1 minute).

Drain well, reserving ½ cup of the liquid; set aside.

In a small bowl, mix all-purpose flour, whole wheat flour, baking powder, and baking soda; set aside. In a large bowl, beat butter and sugar with an electric mixer or a heavy spoon until creamy. Then beat in egg and vanilla.

Add flour mixture alternately with reserved ½ cup prune liquid and buttermilk, stirring until evenly moistened. Add drained prunes and stir until evenly distributed. Spoon batter equally into 2 greased 4- by 8-inch loaf pans.

Bake in a 350° oven until bread is golden brown and a wooden pick inserted in center of each loaf comes out clean (50 to 55 minutes). Let bread cool in pans on racks for 10 minutes; then turn out onto racks to cool completely. If made ahead, wrap airtight and refrigerate for up to 5 days; freeze for longer storage. Makes 2 loaves (10 to 12 servings *each*).

Per serving: 133 calories (20 percent from fat), 2 g protein, 25 g carbohydrates, 3 g total fat (2 g saturated fat), 16 mg cholesterol, 127 mg sodium

Old-fashioned Lemon Bread

While it's still hot from the oven, you poke this loaf with a skewer until it's full of holes, then drizzle it with a sweet, lemony glaze. The finished bread is easy to slice and has a fine-grained, even texture much like that of pound cake.

1½ **cups all-purpose flour**
 1 **cup sugar**
 1 **teaspoon baking powder**
 ½ **teaspoon salt**
 2 **eggs, lightly beaten**
 ½ **cup *each* milk and salad oil**
1½ **teaspoons grated lemon peel**
   Lemon Glaze (recipe follows)

In a large bowl, mix flour, sugar, baking powder, and salt. In a small bowl, beat eggs, milk, oil, and lemon peel until blended; stir into flour mixture just until blended. Pour batter into a greased and floured 5- by 9-inch loaf pan. Bake in a 350° oven until a wooden pick inserted in center comes out clean (40 to 45 minutes).

As soon as bread is done, prepare Lemon Glaze. Leaving loaf in pan, use a long, slender skewer to poke numerous holes all the way to bottom of loaf. Slowly drizzle hot glaze over top of loaf so that it soaks into bread. Let bread cool in pan on a rack for 15 minutes; then turn out onto rack to cool completely. Makes 1 loaf (10 to 12 servings).

Lemon Glaze. In a small pan, combine 4½ tablespoons **lemon juice** and ⅓ cup **sugar.** Cook over medium heat, stirring constantly, until sugar is dissolved. Remove from heat.

Per serving: 269 calories (39 percent from fat), 3 g protein, 38 g carbohydrates, 12 g total fat (2 g saturated fat), 40 mg cholesterol, 163 mg sodium

Panda Bread

When giant pandas from China were on loan to the San Francisco Zoo in the early '80s, they dined on long stalks of bamboo and a supplement called "panda bread." One *Sunset* reader offered this version of the zookeeper's bread recipe—refined to appeal to human tastes, of course. The word "panda" is even an acronym for a list of some of the loaf's ingredients: *P*umpkin, *A*pplesauce, *N*uts, *D*ates, and *A*pricots.

 2 **cups all-purpose flour**
1½ **cups whole wheat flour**
 2 **teaspoons baking soda**
 ½ **teaspoon *each* baking powder, salt, and ground cinnamon**
 ¼ **teaspoon *each* ground mace, ground nutmeg, and ground cloves**
 ⅔ **cup solid vegetable shortening**
1¼ **cups *each* granulated sugar and firmly packed brown sugar**
 4 **eggs**
 1 **cup *each* canned applesauce and canned pumpkin**
 ⅔ **cup *each* chopped dried apricots and chopped pitted dates**
 1 **cup chopped walnuts**

In a medium-size bowl, mix all-purpose flour, whole wheat flour, baking soda, baking powder, salt, cinnamon, mace, nutmeg, and cloves; set aside.

In a large bowl, beat shortening, granulated sugar, and brown sugar with an electric mixer or a heavy spoon until well blended. Add eggs, one at a time, beating well after each addition. Beat in applesauce and pumpkin until blended. Add flour mixture and stir until moistened; then beat until well blended. Stir in apricots, dates, and walnuts.

Spoon batter equally into 2 greased 5- by 9-inch loaf pans. Bake in a 350° oven until a wooden pick inserted in center of each loaf comes out clean (about 1 hour). Let cool in pans on racks for 10 minutes; then turn out onto racks to cool completely. If made ahead, wrap airtight and refrigerate for up to 1 week; freeze for longer storage. Makes 2 loaves (10 to 12 servings *each*).

Per serving: 304 calories (32 percent from fat), 5 g protein, 49 g carbohydrates, 11 g total fat (2 g saturated fat), 39 mg cholesterol, 193 mg sodium

Apricot-Nut Bread

Packaged biscuit mix is a great short-cut in making fluffy-textured fruit-nut breads like this one. Let the loaf cool, then cut it into thin slices and serve with butter.

- ¾ cup *each* firmly packed brown sugar and chopped pecans
- 1 cup coarsely chopped dried apricots
- 1 egg, lightly beaten
- 1¼ cups orange juice
- 3 cups packaged biscuit mix

In a medium-size bowl, combine sugar, pecans, and apricots. Stir in egg and orange juice. Add biscuit mix and stir until blended. Spoon evenly into a greased 5- by 9-inch loaf pan. Bake in a 350° oven until a wooden pick inserted in center comes out clean (about 45 minutes).

Let bread cool in pan on a rack for 10 minutes; then turn out onto rack to cool completely. Makes 1 loaf (10 to 12 servings).

Per serving: 282 calories (30 percent from fat), 4 g protein, 46 g carbohydrates, 10 g total fat (2 g saturated fat), 19 mg cholesterol, 393 mg sodium

Whole Wheat Banana Bread

This moist banana loaf won instant acclaim when we introduced it in a 1958 "Kitchen Cabinet," and it remains a favorite today. Whole wheat flour lends the bread a full-bodied flavor and dense, cakelike texture.

- 1 cup *each* all-purpose flour and whole wheat flour
- 1 teaspoon baking soda
- ½ teaspoon salt
- ½ cup (¼ lb.) butter or margarine, melted
- 1 cup sugar
- 2 eggs, lightly beaten
- 1 cup mashed ripe bananas (about 3 medium-size bananas)
- ⅓ cup hot water
- ½ cup chopped walnuts

In a medium-size bowl, mix all-purpose flour, whole wheat flour, baking soda, and salt; set aside. In a large bowl, stir together butter and sugar. Add eggs and bananas; stir until blended. Stir in flour mixture alternately with hot water. Then stir in walnuts. Spoon batter evenly into a greased 5- by 9-inch loaf pan.

Bake in a 325° oven until a wooden pick inserted in center of loaf comes out clean (about 1 hour and 10 minutes). Let bread cool in pan on a rack for 10 minutes; then turn out onto rack to cool completely. Makes 1 loaf (10 to 12 servings).

Per serving: 293 calories (40 percent from fat), 5 g protein, 41 g carbohydrates, 13 g total fat (6 g saturated fat), 61 mg cholesterol, 312 mg sodium

Stollen

German *Stollen* is familiar to most of us as a yeast bread, but this quick version is a traditional German recipe as well. Vanilla sugar—the perfumed, sparkling topping for stollen—must be made in advance. To prepare it, bury a split vanilla bean in 1 cup of sugar, cover the container tightly, and let stand at room temperature for 2 to 3 days.

- 2½ cups all-purpose flour
- ¾ cup sugar
- 2 teaspoons baking powder
- ½ teaspoon salt
- ¼ teaspoon ground mace
- ⅛ teaspoon ground cardamom
- ¾ cup ground blanched almonds
- ½ cup (¼ lb.) butter or margarine
- 1 cup cottage cheese
- 1 egg
- ½ teaspoon vanilla
- ¼ teaspoon almond extract
- 2 tablespoons rum (or 1½ tablespoons water and ½ teaspoon rum flavoring)
- ½ cup *each* dried currants and golden raisins
- ¼ cup chopped candied lemon peel
- 3 tablespoons butter or margarine, melted
- 2 tablespoons vanilla sugar (see instructions in recipe introduction)

In a large bowl, mix flour, the ¾ cup sugar, baking powder, salt, mace, cardamom, and almonds. With a pastry blender or 2 knives, cut in the ½ cup butter until mixture resembles coarse crumbs.

Whirl cottage cheese in a blender until smooth (or push it through a wire strainer). In a small bowl, stir together cottage cheese, egg, vanilla, almond extract, rum, currants, raisins, and lemon peel; stir into flour mixture until blended. Shape dough into a ball, place on a floured board, and knead until smooth (1 to 2 minutes).

Roll out dough to form an oval about 8½ by 10 inches. With rolling pin, lightly crease dough just off center, parallel to 10-inch side. Brush dough with 1 tablespoon of the melted butter. Fold smaller section over larger. Place on an ungreased baking sheet lined with brown paper.

Bake in a 350° oven until crust is well browned and a wooden pick inserted in center comes out clean (about 45 minutes). Brush remaining 2 tablespoons melted butter lightly over loaf; sprinkle with vanilla sugar. Serve warm. If made ahead, let cool on a rack, wrap airtight, and refrigerate for up to 3 days; freeze for longer storage (thaw before reheating). To reheat, wrap loaf in foil and heat in a 350° oven for 30 minutes. Makes 1 loaf (about 10 servings).

Per serving: 421 calories (38 percent from fat), 9 g protein, 58 g carbohydrates, 18 g total fat (9 g saturated fat), 59 mg cholesterol, 430 mg sodium

It's hard to resist the lure of freshly baked muffins. Served steaming hot with a pat of butter melting temptingly over the top, these little cakes can be the stuff breakfast-time dreams are made of. Baked in advance, they're ideal for a no-fuss morning meal or a quick snack.

Sunset has printed hundreds of muffin recipes—some plain, others enhanced with everything from cheese to fruits to nuts. On this page, you'll find three of our all-time favorites. Blueberries are the star ingredient in extra-light Blueberry Muffins; lemon adds zest to a combination of chewy granola and tiny dried currants in Lemon Granola Muffins. And Ready-bake Bran Muffins offer both wonderful flavor and extra convenience—the batter can be stored in the refrigerator and baked as needed.

Blueberry Muffins

1½ cups *each* all-purpose flour and whole wheat flour

1 cup plus 2 tablespoons firmly packed light brown sugar

4 teaspoons baking powder

1 tablespoon ground cinnamon

2 teaspoons baking soda

¼ teaspoon salt (optional)

2 eggs

1½ cups buttermilk

¼ cup salad oil; or ¼ cup butter or margarine, melted and cooled

2 cups fresh or frozen unsweetened blueberries

In a large bowl, mix all-purpose flour, whole wheat flour, 1 cup of the sugar, baking powder, cinnamon, baking soda, and salt (if desired). In another bowl, beat eggs, buttermilk, and oil until blended; add to flour mixture and stir just until moistened. Add blueberries and stir until evenly distributed.

Spoon batter equally into 12 greased 2½-inch muffin cups. Sprinkle remaining 2 tablespoons sugar evenly over batter in cups. Bake in a 375° oven until tops of muffins are well browned and spring back when lightly touched (about 35 minutes). Makes 1 dozen muffins.

Per muffin: 275 calories (23 percent from fat), 6 g protein, 49 g carbohydrates, 7 g total fat (1 g saturated fat), 37 mg cholesterol, 425 mg sodium

Lemon Granola Muffins

¾ cup *each* all-purpose flour and whole wheat flour

1 tablespoon baking powder

½ teaspoon salt

½ cup (¼ lb.) butter or margarine, melted

¾ cup sugar

1 teaspoon grated lemon peel

2 eggs

½ cup lemon juice

1 cup granola-type cereal

½ cup dried currants

In a large bowl, mix all-purpose flour, whole wheat flour, baking powder, and salt; set aside.

In another bowl, stir together butter and sugar. Add lemon peel and eggs; stir until blended. Then stir in lemon juice. Gradually add flour mixture, granola, and currants, stirring until blended.

Spoon batter equally into 12 greased 2½-inch muffin cups. Bake in a 350° oven until tops of muffins are well browned and spring back when lightly touched (25 to 30 minutes). Makes 1 dozen muffins.

Per muffin: 257 calories (40 percent from fat), 4 g protein, 35 g carbohydrates, 12 g total fat (6 g saturated fat), 56 mg cholesterol, 309 mg sodium

Ready-bake Bran Muffins

2½ cups all-purpose flour

1 cup sugar

2½ teaspoons baking soda

½ teaspoon salt

3 cups whole bran cereal (not flakes)

1 cup boiling water

2 eggs, lightly beaten

2 cups buttermilk

½ cup salad oil

1 cup raisins, dried currants, chopped pitted dates, or chopped pitted prunes

In a medium-size bowl, mix flour, sugar, baking soda, and salt; set aside.

In a large bowl, mix cereal and boiling water until evenly moistened; let cool. Add eggs, buttermilk, oil, and raisins; stir until blended. Add flour mixture; stir until blended. (At this point, you may cover and refrigerate batter for up to 2 weeks; stir batter to distribute fruit before baking.)

Spoon batter into greased 2½-inch muffin cups, filling cups two-thirds to three-fourths full. Bake in a 425° oven until tops of muffins spring back when lightly touched (about 20 minutes). Makes 2 to 2½ dozen muffins.

Per muffin: 170 calories (30 percent from fat), 4 g protein, 29 g carbohydrates, 6 g total fat (0.9 g saturated fat), 16 mg cholesterol, 268 mg sodium

Cranberry Tea Bread

Studded with nuts, golden raisins, and bright red cranberries, this fine-textured loaf is the type of sweet, cakelike bread that might be served at teatime in England. We like to include it on the menu at holiday time or for any special-occasion meal.

- 3 **cups all-purpose flour**
- 2 **teaspoons** *each* **baking powder, baking soda, and ground cinnamon**
- ½ **teaspoon ground cloves**
- ¾ **cup (¼ lb. plus ¼ cup) butter or margarine, at room temperature**
- 1½ **cups firmly packed brown sugar**

- 4 **eggs**
- 1 **can (about 1 lb.) whole-berry cranberry sauce**
- ⅔ **cup** *each* **golden raisins and chopped walnuts**

In a medium-size bowl, mix flour, baking powder, baking soda, cinnamon, and cloves; set aside. In a large bowl, beat butter and sugar until creamy.

Add eggs, one at a time, beating well after each addition. Add flour mixture; stir until blended. Then stir in cranberry sauce, raisins, and walnuts. Spoon batter equally into 2 greased and floured 5- by 9-inch loaf pans.

Bake in a 350° oven until a wooden pick inserted in center of each loaf comes out clean (about 1 hour). Let bread cool in pans on racks for 10 minutes; then turn out onto racks to cool completely. If made ahead, wrap airtight and refrigerate for up to 1 week; freeze for longer storage. Makes 2 loaves (10 to 12 servings *each*).

Per serving: 259 calories (34 percent from fat), 4 g protein, 40 g carbohydrates, 10 g total fat (4 g saturated fat), 56 mg cholesterol, 246 mg sodium

Quick Orange Coffee Cake Ring

For coffee cake in a jiffy, dip store-bought refrigerated biscuits in a sweet orange butter and bake them in a tube pan. Served hot from the oven, this simple treat is like a slice of heaven on your breakfast table.

- ½ **cup (¼ lb.) butter or margarine**
- ⅔ **cup sugar**
- 3 **tablespoons finely shredded orange peel**
- 2 **packages (about 10 oz.** *each***) refrigerated biscuits**

In a small pan, combine butter, sugar, and orange peel. Cook over medium

heat, stirring constantly, until sugar is dissolved. Remove from heat.

Separate biscuits and coat each one with butter mixture. Place biscuits, vertically and side by side, in a greased 9- or 10-inch tube pan. Drizzle any remaining butter mixture over biscuits. Bake in a 375° oven until golden brown (30 to 35 minutes). Invert onto a platter and serve warm. Makes 6 to 8 servings.

Per serving: 429 calories (41 percent from fat), 6 g protein, 57 g carbohydrates, 20 g total fat (9 g saturated fat), 36 mg cholesterol, 837 mg sodium

WESTERN CLASSIC
Cinnamon Sour Cream Coffee Cake

This moist coffee cake, topped and filled with cinnamon-spiced walnuts, appeared in *Sunset*'s "Kitchen Cabinet" back in 1959. Its rich, slightly sweet flavor and crunchy texture have made it a favorite choice for brunches and special breakfasts for over three decades.

- 2 **cups all-purpose flour**
- 1½ **teaspoons baking powder**
- ½ **teaspoon baking soda**
- 1 **cup (½ lb.) butter or margarine, at room temperature**
- 1¼ **cups sugar**
- 2 **eggs**
- 1 **cup sour cream**
- 1 **teaspoon vanilla**
- ¾ **cup finely chopped walnuts**
- 2 **tablespoons sugar**
- 1 **teaspoon ground cinnamon**

In a medium-size bowl, mix flour, baking powder, and baking soda; set aside.

In a large bowl, beat butter, the 1¼ cups sugar, and eggs with an electric mixer until creamy. Blend in sour cream. Stir in flour mixture; then add vanilla and stir until thoroughly blended.

Spoon half the batter evenly into a greased and floured 9-inch tube pan. In a small bowl, mix walnuts, the 2 tablespoons sugar, and cinnamon; sprinkle half the nut mixture over batter. Spoon in remaining batter and top with remaining nut mixture.

Place in a cold oven, turn on oven to 350°, and bake until a wooden pick inserted in center of cake comes out clean (about 1 hour). Makes 8 to 10 servings.

Per serving: 542 calories (55 percent from fat), 7 g protein, 55 g carbohydrates, 34 g total fat (17 g saturated fat), 114 mg cholesterol, 389 mg sodium

Crusty French Bread

A crisp, flour-dusted crust and porous, chewy interior distinguish this rustic country bread, known in Italy as *pane francese*. The trick to achieving the crisp, rather flat loaves is to use a wet, sticky dough (preferably prepared in a food processor) and to bake the bread in a very ho̶t ove̶n.

dry yeast
r (about 110°F)
purpose flour
ar and salt
water

ast and
east is

rk
or
ur,

motor running, pour in yeast mixture; then slowly pour in 1 cup of the ice-cold water. Whirl, scraping sides of bowl occasionally, until flour and water are incorporated (if dough is dry or difficult to whirl, add more ice-cold water, 1 to 2 teaspoons at a time). Continue to whirl until dough is shiny, elastic, and slightly sticky (3 to 4 minutes). To test for correct elasticity, stretch a small piece of dough with your hands; if it forms a thin, transparent skin, dough is ready (it will be soft and wet).

Sprinkle dough with about 2 tablespoons flour to make it easier to handle; then scrape it into a large bowl.

If using an electric mixer and dough hook, or if mixing by hand, mix 3 cups flour, sugar, and salt in a large bowl. Add yeast mixture and 1 cup of the ice-cold water. Beat with an electric mixer on medium speed (or with a heavy spoon) until well blended. If using a mixer, change to a dough hook; if mixing by hand, continue to beat with a heavy spoon. Beat until dough is shiny, elastic, and slightly sticky (about 5 minutes with a dough hook, 10 to 20 minutes by hand). If dough is dry or difficult to beat, add more ice-cold water, 1 to 2 teaspoons at a time. To test for correct elasticity, stretch a small piece of dough with your hands; if it forms a thin, transparent skin, dough is ready (it will be soft and wet).

Cover bowl and let dough rise in a warm place until doubled (1½ to 2

hours); or let rise in refrigerator until next day.

To shape loaves, sprinkle about 2 tablespoons flour over dough and scrape out onto a well-floured board. Divide dough in half. With floured hands, lightly pat each half into a 7- by 8-inch rectangle. Starting with a 7-inch side, roll up dough jelly-roll style; with each turn of roll, press rolled edge against unrolled portion with heel of hand to seal. Turn loaves seam side down on board. Lift each loaf gently and sprinkle flour generously beneath it; then lightly dust flour over top. Cover loaves lightly and let rest on board for about 30 minutes.

Carefully pick up one loaf by the ends; transfer to a greased large baking sheet, gently pulling and stretching loaf to a length of 12 to 14 inches in the move (if loaf sticks to board, gently scrape free with a spatula). Repeat with second loaf, spacing loaves 4 to 5 inches apart. Cover lightly and let rise in a warm place until slightly puffy (about 15 minutes).

Place loaves in a 475° oven; immediately reduce oven temperature to 425°. Bake loaves until golden brown on all sides (20 to 30 minutes). For a crisper crust, turn off oven, prop door slightly ajar, and leave loaves in oven for about 10 more minutes. Let cool on racks. Makes 2 loaves (about 6 servings *each*).

Per serving: 124 calories (8 percent from fat), 3 g protein, 24 g carbohydrates, 1 g total fat (0.1 g saturated fat), 0 mg cholesterol, 184 mg sodium

Basque Sheepherder's Bread

This huge, dome-shaped loaf is the Basque sheepherder's staff of life. A herder customarily slashes the sign of the cross in the top crust before slicing the bread, then serves the first piece to his invaluable dog.

Though Basques traditionally bake their bread in a heavy kettle in a campfire pit, we've adapted the recipe for a conventional oven. To achieve the characteristic shape, you'll need a 10-inch cast-iron or cast-aluminum Dutch oven with a lid.

- 3 cups very hot water
- ½ cup (¼ lb.) butter or margarine
- ⅓ cup sugar
- 2½ teaspoons salt
- 2 packages active dry yeast
- 9 to 9½ cups all-purpose flour
  Salad oil

In a large bowl, combine hot water, butter, sugar, and salt. Stir until butter is melted; let cool to about 110°F. Stir in yeast, cover, and let stand in a warm place until bubbly (about 15 minutes).

Beat in about 5 cups of the flour to make a thick batter. Stir in enough of the remaining flour (about 3½ cups) to make a stiff dough. Turn dough out onto a lightly floured board; knead until smooth and satiny (10 to 20 minutes), adding more flour as needed to prevent sticking. Place dough in a greased bowl; turn over to grease top. Cover and let rise in a warm place until doubled (about 1½ hours).

Punch dough down and knead briefly on a lightly floured board until smooth. Line inside bottom of 10-inch cast-iron or cast-aluminum Dutch oven with a circle of foil. Grease foil, inside of Dutch oven, and underside of lid with oil.

Place dough in Dutch oven and cover with lid. Let rise in a warm place until dough pushes up lid by about ½ inch (about 1 hour—watch closely).

Bake, covered with lid, in a 375° oven for 12 minutes. Remove lid and continue to bake until loaf is golden brown and sounds hollow when tapped (30 to 35 more minutes). Remove from oven and turn loaf out of Dutch oven (you'll need a helper) onto a rack to cool. Peel off foil. Makes 1 very large loaf (24 to 26 servings).

Per serving: 218 calories (20 percent from fat), 5 g protein, 38 g carbohydrates, 5 g total fat (2 g saturated fat), 10 mg cholesterol, 259 mg sodium

Australian Damper Bread

The original damper bread was a heavy, unleavened loaf baked in campfire ashes. Today's damper, while still simple and rustic, is civilized enough for indoor consumption. Yeast lightens the bread and adds tangy flavor; baking powder gives it the texture of an airy biscuit.

- 1 package active dry yeast
- ¼ cup warm water (about 110°F)
- 1 cup milk, scalded and cooled to about 110°F
  About 3 cups all-purpose flour
- 1 tablespoon baking powder
- ¾ teaspoon salt
- 2 tablespoons butter or margarine

In a small bowl, combine yeast and warm water; let stand until yeast is

softened (about 5 minutes). Stir in milk; set aside.

In a large bowl, mix 3 cups of the flour, baking powder, and salt. With a pastry blender or 2 knives, cut in butter until mixture resembles fine crumbs (or rub butter into flour mixture with your fingers). Add yeast mixture and stir until dough is evenly moistened. Turn dough out onto a lightly floured board and knead until smooth (2 to 3 minutes), adding more flour as needed to prevent sticking.

Shape dough into a round, lumpy loaf 5 to 6 inches in diameter. Dust lightly with flour, then place in a greased 8-inch-round cake pan. With a razor or sharp knife, cut an "X" about ½ inch deep and 3 inches long in center of loaf. Bake on lowest rack of a 375° oven until well browned (about 55 minutes). Turn out onto a rack and let cool briefly. Serve warm. Makes 1 loaf (about 10 servings).

Per serving: 179 calories (20 percent from fat), 5 g protein, 30 g carbohydrates, 4 g total fat (2 g saturated fat), 10 mg cholesterol, 347 mg sodium

Stone-ground Peasant Rye Bread

Rustic country-style rye loaves are prized for their substantial crusts and sturdy texture. They're also among the simplest yeast breads to make. This one starts out with a sponge that must stand for at least 6 hours, so be sure to allow yourself ample time for preparation.

- 2½ cups stone-ground dark rye flour
- 1 package active dry yeast
- 2½ cups warm water (about 110°F)
- 1½ teaspoons salt
- 3 tablespoons butter or margarine
  About 5 cups all-purpose flour
- 1 egg beaten with 1 tablespoon milk

In a large bowl, stir together 1½ cups of the rye flour, yeast, and 1½ cups of the warm water. Cover with plastic wrap and let stand at room temperature for 6 to 24 hours.

Stir remaining 1 cup warm water into rye flour mixture. Add salt, butter, and remaining 1 cup rye flour; stir until blended. Gradually stir in enough of the all-purpose flour (3 to 3½ cups) to make a stiff dough.

To knead with a dough hook, beat on medium speed until dough pulls away from sides of bowl, adding enough additional all-purpose flour (about 1½ cups) to keep dough from sticking to sides of bowl.

To knead by hand, turn dough out onto a lightly floured board and knead until smooth and elastic (7 to 10 minutes), adding enough additional all-purpose flour (about 1½ cups) to keep dough from sticking.

Place dough kneaded by either method in a greased bowl; turn over to grease top. Cover and let rise at room temperature until doubled (about 2 hours).

Punch dough down and divide in half. Knead each half briefly on a lightly floured board to release air, then shape each half into a round or oblong loaf about 10 inches long. Place each loaf on a greased baking sheet. Lightly sprinkle each loaf with about 1 tablespoon all-purpose flour, then cover lightly. Let rise at room temperature until almost doubled (about 50 minutes).

Brush loaves lightly with egg mixture. With a razor blade or sharp knife, cut a large "X" about ½ inch deep on round loaves; or cut 3 lengthwise ½-inch-deep slashes on oblong loaves. Bake each loaf on middle rack of a 400° oven until crust is light golden brown (about 40 minutes). If using only one oven, position one rack halfway beneath center of oven and one

halfway above center; switch positions of baking sheets halfway through baking.

Let loaves cool on racks. Makes 2 loaves (10 to 12 servings *each*).

Per serving: 175 calories (16 percent from fat), 5 g protein, 32 g carbohydrates, 3 g total fat (1 g saturated fat), 14 mg cholesterol, 170 mg sodium

Molasses Pumpernickel Bread

Fine-textured and fragrant, this rustic pumpernickel bread is delicious with hearty winter meals. Try it with Baked Split Pea Soup (page 23); or serve with fresh ripe fruit and a wedge of cheese for a simple lunch. Or cut the loaf into thick slices, then spread with mustard and top with sliced Oven-simmered Beef Brisket (page 77).

- 2 **tablespoons butter or margarine**
- 2 **cups milk**
- 1½ **teaspoons salt**
- ½ **cup dark molasses**
- 2 **packages active dry yeast**
- ⅓ **cup firmly packed dark brown sugar**
- ½ **cup warm water (about 110°F)**
- 1½ **cups whole bran cereal (not flakes)**
- 3 **cups rye flour**
  About 4½ cups all-purpose flour
- 1 **egg yolk beaten with 1 tablespoon water**

Melt butter in a small pan. Stir in milk, salt, and molasses; set aside.

In a large bowl, combine yeast, sugar, and warm water; let stand until bubbly (about 10 minutes). Add milk mixture, cereal, rye flour, and 2 cups of the all-purpose flour; beat until well blended.

To knead by hand, use a heavy spoon to stir in enough of the remaining all-purpose flour (about 1½ cups) to make a stiff dough. Turn dough out onto a lightly floured board and knead until smooth and satiny (10 to 15 minutes), adding more all-purpose flour as needed to prevent sticking.

To knead with a dough hook, add 1½ more cups of the all-purpose flour and beat on medium speed until dough pulls away from sides of bowl (about 10 minutes); if dough is sticky, add more all-purpose flour, a little at a time.

Place dough kneaded by either method in a greased bowl; turn over to grease top. Cover and let rise in a warm place until doubled (about 1½ hours).

Punch dough down and knead briefly on a lightly floured board to release air. Divide dough in half; shape each half into a smooth ball, then flatten balls slightly. Place each loaf on a greased baking sheet. Cover and let rise in a warm place until almost doubled (about 40 minutes). With a razor blade or sharp knife, make ½-inch-deep slashes on tops of loaves, forming a ticktacktoe design. Brush tops and sides of loaves with egg yolk mixture.

Bake in a 350° oven until bread is well browned and sounds hollow when tapped (30 to 35 minutes). Let cool on racks. Makes 2 loaves (10 to 12 servings *each*).

Per serving: 218 calories (13 percent from fat), 6 g protein, 43 g carbohydrates, 3 g total fat (1 g saturated fat), 16 mg cholesterol, 234 mg sodium

Mention Western breads and baking to any food lover, and the conversation is sure to turn to sourdough. Some credit its invention to a prospector who mixed up a bowl of pancake batter, let it sit for a few days while he was away from camp—and then returned to find a bubbly mixture that smelled decidedly sour, but made the best hotcakes he'd ever tasted.

Regardless of sourdough's origin, Westerners took a liking to its unique flavor, and a good starter became a treasure to nurture and share. In fact, sourdough breads were so popular among frontiersmen that these rough-and-ready explorers acquired the nickname "sourdough."

Sunset has been working with these chewy, tangy breads for years. Our first sourdough story ran in 1933; since then, we've published more than 25 articles on the subject. In 1973, we collaborated with food technologists at the University of California at Davis to develop the definitive starter recipe, using yogurt, milk, and flour. (The lower the fat content of the yogurt and milk, the tangier the starter.) If you follow our directions, you should get an active starter—and marvelous breads and rolls—every time.

Sourdough Starter

1 cup lukewarm milk (90° to 100°F)

2 tablespoons plain yogurt (use recently purchased yogurt)

1 cup all-purpose flour

Rinse a 1½-quart glass, ceramic, plastic, or stainless steel container with hot water until container is very warm; wipe dry. Add milk and yogurt; stir until combined. Cover tightly and let

stand in a warm place (80° to 100°F) until a curd forms and mixture doesn't flow readily when container is slightly tilted (18 to 24 hours). If some clear liquid rises to top of mixture, simply stir it back in. But if liquid turns light pink, milk is beginning to break down; discard starter and begin again.

Gradually stir in flour until well blended; cover tightly and let stand in a warm place (80° to 100°F) until mixture is full of bubbles and has a good sour smell (2 to 5 days). If clear liquid forms, stir it back into starter. But if liquid is pink, spoon out and discard all but ¼ cup of starter, then stir in a mixture of 1 cup *each* lukewarm milk (90° to 100°F) and all-purpose flour. Cover tightly and let stand again in a warm place until bubbly and sour smelling. Use at once; or cover and refrigerate. Makes about 1½ cups.

NOTE: Each time you use part of your starter, replenish it with equal amounts of all-purpose flour and lukewarm milk (90° to 100°F; use the same type of milk you originally used). For example, if you use ½ cup starter, blend in a mixture of ½ cup lukewarm milk and ½ cup all-purpose flour. Cover and let stand in a warm place until bubbly (several hours or until next day). Then cover and refrigerate until the next use. Before using starter, let it warm to room temperature.

If you bake regularly (about once a week), starter should stay lively and

active; if you don't, discard half the starter and replenish it with milk and all-purpose flour about every 2 weeks. Or freeze your freshly fed starter for 1½ to 2 months. Freezing slows fermenting action considerably, so before using the starter, let it thaw at room temperature, then put it in a warm place until bubbly (about 24 hours).

Sourdough French Bread

1 package active dry yeast

1½ cups warm water (about 110°F)

1 cup sourdough starter (at left), at room temperature

About 6 cups all-purpose flour

2 teaspoons *each* salt and sugar
Cornmeal

½ teaspoon cornstarch blended with ½ cup cold water

In a large bowl, combine yeast and warm water; let stand until yeast is softened (about 5 minutes). Add starter, 4 cups of the flour, salt, and sugar; beat until smooth and well blended. Cover; let rise in a warm place until doubled (about 1½ hours).

Stir in enough of the remaining flour (about 1½ cups) to make a very stiff dough. Scrape dough out onto a lightly floured board and knead until smooth and satiny (about 10 minutes), adding more flour as needed to prevent sticking. Divide dough in half. (If you have only one oven, place one half in a greased bowl, cover, and let stand at room temperature until first loaf is shaped and placed in the oven.)

For an oblong loaf, roll dough into a 14-inch log. For a round loaf, shape dough into a smooth ball, pinching a seam underneath. Or shape each half into 3 small oblong or round loaves. Set each loaf (or 3 small ones) on a piece of stiff cardboard sprinkled with ¼ cup cornmeal. Cover lightly and let rise in a warm place until puffy and almost doubled (about 1 hour for large loaves; about 45 minutes for small loaves).

Adjust oven racks so they are at the 2 lowest positions; place a 12- by 15-inch baking sheet on the higher of the 2 racks as oven preheats to 400°. Just before bread is ready to bake, place a rimmed baking sheet on lower rack and pour in boiling water to a depth of about ¼ inch.

In a small pan, bring cornstarch mixture to a boil, stirring constantly; remove from heat and let cool slightly. Evenly brush cornstarch mixture over entire surface of loaf. With a razor blade or sharp knife, cut ½-inch-deep slashes on top of loaf (make diagonal slashes on oblong loaves, ticktacktoe pattern on round loaves). Slip loaf off cardboard onto top baking sheet in oven. (At this point, if using only one oven, punch down remaining dough and knead briefly to release air; shape and let rise, then bake as directed.)

Bake in a 400° oven for 10 minutes (7 minutes for small loaves); brush with cornstarch mixture again. Continue to bake until loaves are golden and sound hollow when tapped (about 25 more minutes for large loaves; about 20 more minutes for small loaves). Let cool on racks. Makes 2 large loaves (10 to 12 servings *each*) or 6 small loaves (about 4 servings *each*).

Per serving: 159 calories (5 percent from fat), 5 g protein, 32 g carbohydrates, 1 g total fat (0.2 g saturated fat), 1 mg cholesterol, 205 mg sodium

Brown-&-Serve French Bread

Prepare **Sourdough French Bread** and bake in a 400° oven for 10 minutes (7 minutes for small loaves). Brush again with cornstarch mixture. Continue to bake until surface of loaves is no longer wet (about 8 more minutes for large loaves; about 5 more minutes for small loaves). Let cool on racks. Wrap each loaf separately in foil and freeze. If desired, thaw before heating.

To finish baking, unwrap desired number of loaves and set them (frozen or thawed) on a lightly greased baking sheet. Bake in a 400° oven until loaves are golden brown and sound hollow when tapped (about 35 minutes for frozen large loaves, 30 minutes for thawed ones; about 30 minutes for frozen small loaves, 25 minutes for thawed ones). Makes 2 large loaves (10 to 12 servings *each*) or 6 small loaves (about 4 servings *each*).

Per serving: 163 calories (7 percent from fat), 5 g protein, 32 g carbohydrates, 1 g total fat (0.3 g saturated fat), 1 mg cholesterol, 205 mg sodium

Sourdough Cheese Bread

Follow directions for **Sourdough French Bread,** but stir in 2 cups (about 8 oz.) shredded **sharp Cheddar cheese** when you add flour to make a very stiff dough. Makes 2 large loaves (10 to 12 servings *each*) or 6 small loaves (about 4 servings *each*).

Per serving: 200 calories (20 percent from fat), 7 g protein, 32 g carbohydrates, 4 g total fat (2 g saturated fat), 12 mg cholesterol, 267 mg sodium

Sourdough Onion Bread

Follow directions for **Sourdough French Bread,** but omit salt. Stir in 1 envelope (1 to 1½ oz.) **dry onion soup mix** when you add flour to make a very stiff dough. Makes 2 large loaves (10 to 12 servings *each*) or 6 small loaves (about 4 servings *each*).

Per serving: 163 calories (5 percent from fat), 5 g protein, 33 g carbohydrates, 1 g total fat (0.2 g saturated fat), 1 mg cholesterol, 142 mg sodium

Cottage Cheese Sourdough Pan Rolls

1 **package active dry yeast**
¼ **cup warm water (about 110°F)**
1 **cup cottage cheese**
1 **cup sourdough starter (facing page), at room temperature**
1 **egg**
1 **tablespoon sugar**
2 **teaspoons baking powder**
1 **teaspoon salt**
¼ **teaspoon baking soda**
  About 4½ cups all-purpose flour
2 **tablespoons cold butter or margarine**

In a bowl, combine yeast and warm water; let stand until yeast is softened (about 5 minutes). In a blender or food processor, whirl cottage cheese, starter, and egg until smooth.

In a large bowl, mix sugar, baking powder, salt, baking soda, and 4 cups of the flour. With a pastry blender or 2 knives, cut in butter until mixture resembles coarse crumbs. Stir in cottage cheese mixture and yeast mixture.

Turn dough out onto a floured board and knead until smooth (about 10 minutes), adding more flour as needed to prevent sticking. Place dough in a greased bowl; turn over to grease top. Cover and let rise in a warm place until doubled (about 45 minutes).

Punch dough down. Divide into 18 pieces; shape each into a ball. Arrange 9 balls in each of 2 greased 8-inch-round baking pans. Cover and let rise until puffy (25 to 30 minutes). Bake in a 350° oven until golden (30 to 35 minutes). Turn rolls out onto racks to cool. Makes 1½ dozen rolls.

Per roll: 175 calories (18 percent from fat), 6 g protein, 29 g carbohydrates, 4 g total fat (2 g saturated fat), 18 mg cholesterol, 263 mg sodium

Rågbröd

A hearty rye bread flavored with orange and fennel, *rågbröd* typically accompanies a Scandinavian smörgåsbord. Our recipe makes two loaves, each shaped like a double twist.

- 2 **cups milk, scalded and cooled to about 110°F**
- 2 **tablespoons dark molasses**
- ⅓ **cup honey**
- 1½ **teaspoons salt**
- 2 **packages active dry yeast**
- ½ **cup warm water (about 110°F)**
- 1 **teaspoon *each* grated orange peel, crushed fennel seeds, and crushed anise seeds**
- 3 **cups rye flour**
- ¼ **cup butter or margarine, melted and cooled**
  About 5 cups all-purpose flour
- 1 **egg white, lightly beaten**

In a large bowl, combine milk, molasses, honey, and salt. In a small bowl, combine yeast and warm water; let stand until yeast is softened (about 5 minutes).

Pour yeast mixture into milk mixture. Add orange peel, fennel seeds, anise seeds, and rye flour; stir to blend. Stir in butter. Gradually add 4½ cups of the all-purpose flour and stir until combined.

Turn dough out onto a floured board and knead until smooth (about 10 minutes), adding more all-purpose flour as needed to prevent sticking. Place dough in a greased bowl; turn over to grease top. Cover and let rise in a warm place until doubled (about 1½ hours).

Punch dough down and knead briefly on a lightly floured board to release air. Divide dough in half. Roll each half into a 28-inch-long strand; fold strand in half, then twist one half over the other twice. Place each twist on a lightly greased baking sheet.

Cover and let rise in a warm place until almost doubled (about 45 minutes). Brush with egg white. Bake in a 350° oven until a wooden pick inserted in center of each loaf comes out clean (about 45 minutes). Let cool on racks. Makes 2 loaves (10 to 12 servings *each*).

Per serving: 211 calories (16 percent from fat), 5 g protein, 39 g carbohydrates, 4 g total fat (2 g saturated fat), 9 mg cholesterol, 188 mg sodium

European Sour Bread

Flat beer—that's the surprising ingredient some European bakers use to give their breads a distinctive tart flavor. In this wholesome loaf, dark beer combines with molasses, wheat germ, bran, and graham flour. (For an extra-chewy texture, include a cup of gluten flour in the dough.)

- 2 **cups flat dark beer**
  About ⅔ cup yellow cornmeal
- 2 **tablespoons butter or margarine**
- 2 **teaspoons salt**
- ½ **cup dark molasses**
- 2 **packages active dry yeast**
- 1 **tablespoon sugar**
- ½ **cup warm water (about 110°F)**
- ½ **cup *each* wheat germ and whole bran cereal (not flakes)**
- 2 **cups graham flour or whole wheat flour**
- 1 **cup gluten flour or all-purpose flour**
- **About 3½ cups all-purpose flour**
- 1 **egg yolk beaten with 1 tablespoon water**

In a small pan, heat beer to steaming over medium heat. Remove from heat and gradually stir in ½ cup of the cornmeal, butter, salt, and molasses; let cool to lukewarm.

Meanwhile, in a large bowl, combine yeast, sugar, and warm water; let stand until bubbly (about 10 minutes). Stir in cooled beer mixture, wheat germ, cereal, graham flour, and gluten flour. Gradually stir in enough of the all-purpose flour (about 3 cups) to make a stiff dough. Turn dough out onto a lightly floured board and knead until smooth and satiny (10 to 20 minutes), adding more all-purpose flour as needed to prevent sticking.

Place dough in a greased bowl; turn over to grease top. Cover and let rise in a warm place until doubled (about 1 hour). Punch dough down and knead briefly on a lightly floured board to release air. Return dough to bowl; cover and let rise again until doubled (about 45 minutes).

Sprinkle 2 greased baking sheets evenly with about 2 tablespoons cornmeal. Punch dough down and knead briefly on a lightly floured board to release air. Divide dough in half. Shape each half into a smooth ball; then flatten balls slightly. Place each loaf on a baking sheet. Cover and let rise in a warm place until almost doubled (about 40 minutes).

Using a razor blade or sharp knife, cut ½-inch-deep slashes on tops of loaves, forming a ticktacktoe design. Brush tops and sides of loaves with egg yolk mixture. Bake in a 375° oven until loaves are well browned (about 40 minutes). Let cool on racks. Makes 2 loaves (10 to 12 servings *each*).

Per serving: 203 calories (12 percent from fat), 6 g protein, 39 g carbohydrates, 3 g total fat (0.9 g saturated fat), 12 mg cholesterol, 239 mg sodium

Mediterranean Olive Bread

In the sun-drenched Mediterranean, where olive groves abound, hearty loaves of bread studded with olives are popular fare. This golden-crusted Italian version contains a random scattering of sharp-flavored green olives and mellow black ones, but you can incorporate any of your favorite varieties.

1 package active dry yeast

¾ cup warm water (about 110°F)

¼ cup sugar

½ cup (¼ lb.) butter or margarine, at room temperature

4 eggs
   About 5 cups all-purpose flour

1 cup pimento-stuffed green olives, drained and patted dry

1 cup pitted ripe olives, drained and patted dry
   Anchovy Butter (recipe follows) or unsalted butter

1 egg yolk, lightly beaten

In a small bowl, combine yeast and warm water; let stand until yeast is softened (about 5 minutes). In a large bowl, beat sugar and butter with an electric mixer until blended. Add eggs, one at a time, beating well after each addition. Stir in yeast mixture.

To blend with mixer and knead by hand, add 2½ cups of the flour and beat on medium speed for 10 minutes. Then add 1½ cups more flour and stir until moistened. Turn dough out onto a floured board and knead until smooth (about 7 minutes), adding more flour as needed to prevent sticking. Place dough in a greased bowl; turn over to grease top.

To knead with a dough hook, add 4½ cups of the flour and beat on medium speed until dough pulls away from sides of bowl (about 10 minutes); if dough is sticky, add more flour, a little

at a time. Then scrape dough down into bowl.

Cover bowl and let dough rise in a warm place until doubled (about 1½ hours). Then punch dough down and knead briefly on a lightly floured board to release air. Cover dough lightly and let rest for 10 minutes; then pat dough into a 14- to 16-inch square. Scatter olives evenly over dough and press in lightly. Roll up dough jelly-roll style, enclosing olives; place roll, seam side down, on a greased baking sheet. Tuck open ends of dough under so ends of loaf are smooth. Pat loaf to flatten and shape it into an oval about 1¾ inches thick. Cover and let rise in a warm place until puffy (about 30 minutes). Meanwhile, prepare Anchovy Butter.

Brush loaf with egg yolk. Bake in a 325° oven until richly browned (about 45 minutes). Let cool on a rack. If made ahead, wrap airtight and store at room temperature until next day; freeze for longer storage (thaw completely before reheating). To reheat, place bread on a baking sheet and heat, uncovered, in a 325° oven for 20 to 30 minutes. To serve, cut into slices; offer Anchovy Butter to spread over individual slices. Makes 1 loaf (10 to 12 servings).

Anchovy Butter. In a food processor or blender, whirl 5 drained **canned anchovy fillets** and ½ cup (¼ lb.) **unsalted butter,** at room temperature, until puréed. Spoon into a crock or serving dish; garnish with 2 more drained **canned anchovy fillets,** if desired. If made ahead, cover and refrigerate for up to 1 week. Makes about ½ cup.

Per serving of bread: 365 calories (36 percent from fat), 9 g protein, 49 g carbohydrates, 15 g total fat (6 g saturated fat), 119 mg cholesterol, 514 mg sodium

Per tablespoon of Anchovy Butter: 109 calories (96 percent from fat), 1 g protein, 0 g carbohydrates, 12 g total fat (7 g saturated fat), 33 mg cholesterol, 130 mg sodium

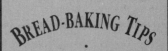

BREAD-BAKING TIPS

Making light and airy yeast breads can be a cinch if you follow just a few simple guidelines.

First, dissolve the yeast in liquid that's about 110°F. Too high a temperature may kill the yeast; too low a temperature, and the yeast will grow very slowly or not at all. If you want to make sure your yeast is active, add a teaspoon or so of sugar, honey, or molasses to the mixture of yeast and warm liquid. Within about 10 minutes, you should see a light, bubbly foam.

Second, to ensure a fine-textured loaf, knead the dough until it's smooth and elastic, incorporating as little flour as possible. (If the dough then becomes sticky and loses its shape after being left to rise for 15 minutes, add more flour and knead for a few more minutes.)

Third, let your dough rise only until doubled in bulk. If it rises much more, it may expand quickly, then collapse in the oven.

Pebble-top Oatmeal Bread

A pebbly, crunchy topping of rolled oats adorns this even-textured bread. Try it toasted for breakfast, spread with butter and honey or jam.

 1   **package active dry yeast**
 ¼   **cup warm water (about 110°F)**
 ¼   **cup molasses**
 ¼   **cup butter or margarine, cut into small pieces**
 2   **teaspoons salt**
 ¼   **cup firmly packed brown sugar**
 2½ **cups regular or quick-cooking rolled oats**
 1   **cup boiling water**
 1   **cup cold water**
 4½ **to 5 cups all-purpose flour**
 3   **tablespoons milk**

In a small bowl, combine yeast, warm water, and 1 tablespoon of the molasses; let stand until bubbly (about 15 minutes). In a large bowl, combine remaining 3 tablespoons molasses, butter, salt, sugar, 2 cups of the oats, and boiling water; stir to melt butter. Stir in cold water and yeast mixture. Beat in 4 cups of the flour, 1 cup at a time, to make a stiff dough.

Turn dough out onto a lightly floured board and knead until smooth and satiny (10 to 20 minutes), adding more flour as needed to prevent sticking. Place dough in a greased bowl; turn over to grease top. Cover and let rise in a warm place until doubled (about 1 hour).

Punch dough down and knead briefly on a lightly floured board to release air. Divide dough in half. Shape each half into a loaf; place each loaf in a greased 5- by 9-inch loaf pan. Soften remaining ½ cup oats in milk; dot oat mixture over tops of loaves. Cover and let rise in a warm place until doubled (about 45 minutes).

Bake in a 350° oven until browned (about 1 hour). Turn loaves out onto racks to cool. Makes 2 loaves (10 to 12 servings *each*).

Per serving: 178 calories (18 percent from fat), 4 g protein, 32 g carbohydrates, 4 g total fat (2 g saturated fat), 6 mg cholesterol, 225 mg sodium

WESTERN CLASSIC
Crazy Vegetable Bread

Cut a slice of this herb-seasoned bread and sample a garden plot run wild— the loaf calls for nine different fresh vegetables! Precook the vegetables to soften them, then mix them into the dough. (As it rises, the dough absorbs moisture from the vegetables, so you'll need to add a fair amount of flour after the first rising.)

     Crazy Garden Vegetables (recipe follows)
 1   **package active dry yeast**
 ¾   **cup warm water (about 110°F)**
 1   **egg**
 ½   **to 1 teaspoon salt**
 1   **tablespoon sugar**
 1   **tablespoon *each* minced fresh thyme and fresh tarragon; or 1 teaspoon *each* dry thyme and dry tarragon**
 ¼   **cup minced fresh basil or 1½ tablespoons dry basil**
 1   **tablespoon olive oil or salad oil**
 ¼   **cup grated Parmesan cheese**
 1   **cup whole wheat flour**
     About 3 cups all-purpose flour

Prepare Crazy Garden Vegetables and set aside.

In a large bowl, combine yeast and warm water; let stand until yeast is softened (about 5 minutes). Stir in egg, salt, sugar, thyme, tarragon, basil, oil, cheese, whole wheat flour, and 1⅔ cups of the all-purpose flour. Beat with a dough hook of an electric mixer (or with a heavy spoon) until well blended.

If using an electric mixer, beat on high speed until dough is elastic and pulls away from sides of bowl (5 to 8 minutes); if dough feels sticky and still clings to bowl, add more all-purpose flour, 1 tablespoon at a time. Turn dough out onto a floured board.

If mixing by hand, turn dough out onto a floured board and knead until smooth and elastic (8 to 12 minutes), adding more all-purpose flour as needed to prevent sticking.

Gently mix Crazy Garden Vegetables with ½ cup all-purpose flour. On floured board, gradually and gently knead vegetables into dough (do not mash them) until evenly distributed (dough will feel sticky); add a little all-purpose flour if dough sticks to board. Place dough in a greased bowl; turn over to grease top. Cover and let rise in a warm place until doubled (about 1½ hours).

Punch dough down, turn out onto a well-floured board, and sprinkle with all-purpose flour. Knead until dough is soft but not sticky, adding more flour as needed to prevent sticking (½ to ⅔ cup more flour *total*). Shape dough into a round loaf; place on a greased baking sheet. Cover lightly and let rise in a warm place until puffy (about 30 minutes).

Bake in a 350° oven until well browned (40 to 45 minutes). Let cool briefly on a rack. Serve warm. If made ahead, let cool completely, wrap airtight, and refrigerate for up to 3 days; freeze for longer storage. Makes 1 loaf (10 to 12 servings).

Crazy Garden Vegetables. Cut 1 medium-size **onion** in half lengthwise, then cut crosswise into ¾-inch-thick slices. In a wide frying pan, heat 2 tablespoons **olive oil** or salad oil over medium heat. Add onion; 2 cloves **garlic,** minced or pressed; and ½ cup 1-inch chunks **eggplant.** Cook, stirring often, until eggplant is barely tender when pressed (about 10 minutes). Add ⅓ cup 1-inch chunks **pear-shaped (Roma-type) tomatoes**; stir until tomatoes are slightly softened (1 to 2 minutes). Let cool.

Cut lengthwise into ½- to ¾-inch strips ¼ *each* medium-size **red and green bell pepper,** seeded (or use half of one color pepper). Cut 1 small **carrot,** 1 small stalk **celery,** and 1 small **zucchini** into ¾-inch-thick diagonal slices. Prepare ¾ cup **broccoli flowerets** and cut 2 large **green onions** into 3-inch pieces.

In a 1- to 2-quart pan, bring 3 cups **water** to a boil. Add one kind of vegetable at a time; boil carrots and broccoli for 1 minute, zucchini and bell pepper for 45 seconds, and celery and green onions for 30 seconds. As vegetables are cooked, lift from pan with a slotted spoon, immerse in **ice water** until cold, and drain on paper towels. Pat vegetables dry and stir into tomato mixture in frying pan.

Per serving: 242 calories (23 percent from fat), 8 g protein, 40 g carbohydrates, 6 g total fat (1 g saturated fat), 21 mg cholesterol, 200 mg sodium

Polenta Cheese Bread

You can reduce the amount of effort involved in making delicious yeast breads by
food p
coarse
chees

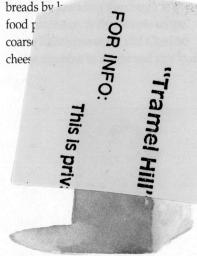

---

1 **package active dry yeast**
2 **tablespoons sugar**
1 **cup warm water (about 110°F)**
4 **ounces sharp Cheddar cheese, cut into small chunks**
  About 3½ cups all-purpose flour
½ **cup polenta or yellow cornmeal**
1 **teaspoon salt**
1 **egg**

In a bowl, combine yeast, 1 teaspoon of the sugar, and warm water; let stand until bubbly (about 10 minutes).

In a food processor fitted with a plastic dough blade or metal blade, combine cheese, 3¼ cups of the flour, remaining sugar, polenta, and salt; whirl until cheese is finely chopped. Add egg. With motor running, slowly pour in yeast mixture; whirl to blend (about 45 seconds). Dough should be slightly sticky; if it's too wet, add more flour, 1 tablespoon at a time.

Shape dough into a ball, place in a greased bowl, and turn over to grease top. Cover and let rise in a warm place until doubled (1 to 1½ hours).

Punch dough down and knead briefly on a lightly floured board to release air. Shape into a smooth ball. Place on a greased baking sheet and flatten to make a 7-inch round. Cover lightly and let rise until loaf is about 2½ inches high (about 1 hour).

Sprinkle top of loaf with about 1 teaspoon flour. Bake in a 375° oven until ... about 35 minutes ... Makes 1 loaf

... rcent from fat), 8 g ... total fat (3 g ... l, 298 mg sodium

... at Rolls

... d this recipe in 1963, bulgur ... ooking cracked wheat) was unfamiliar to many of our readers. Today, though, it's widely

---

enjoyed—not only in Mideastern dishes, but in breads and rolls as well.

½ **cup bulgur (quick-cooking cracked wheat)**
1 **cup cold water**
½ **teaspoon salt**
1 **package active dry yeast**
¼ **cup warm water (about 110°F)**
1¾ **cups milk, scalded and cooled to about 110°F**
½ **cup sugar**
¼ **cup salad oil**
2 **teaspoons salt**
1 **egg, lightly beaten**
  About 6 cups all-purpose flour
  Butter or margarine, melted

In a bowl, mix bulgur, cold water, and the ½ teaspoon salt; let stand for at least 4 hours or until next day.

In a large bowl, combine yeast and warm water; let stand until yeast is softened (about 5 minutes). Stir in bulgur mixture, milk, sugar, oil, the 2 teaspoons salt, and egg. Stir in 5½ cups of the flour, about a cup at a time, to make a stiff dough. Turn dough out onto a lightly floured board and knead until smooth and elastic (about 20 minutes), adding more flour as needed to prevent sticking.

Place dough in a greased bowl; turn over to grease top. Cover and let rise in a warm place until almost doubled (about 1½ hours). Punch dough down and turn out onto a lightly floured board. Roll out dough about 1 inch thick; then cut into 2½-inch-diameter rolls of any desired shape.

Place rolls 2 inches apart on greased baking sheets; let rise in a warm place until almost doubled (about 1½ hours). Brush tops of rolls lightly with butter. Bake in a 375° oven until golden brown (about 15 minutes). Let cool on racks. Makes about 2½ dozen rolls.

Per roll: 144 calories (20 percent from fat), 4 g protein, 25 g carbohydrates, 3 g total fat (0.7 g saturated fat), 9 mg cholesterol, 193 mg sodium

Stretch Breadsticks

Seasoned with rosemary and lemon, these crisp breadsticks—stretched into irregular, pencil-thin rods—add pizzazz to any meal. The crunchy sticks store well, so you can enjoy half the batch on baking day, then freeze the rest to serve later.

1 **package active dry yeast**
1 **teaspoon sugar**
1 **cup warm water (about 110°F)**
1 **teaspoon** *each* **grated lemon peel and salt**
1½ **teaspoons chopped fresh rosemary or dry rosemary**
2 **tablespoons plus 1 teaspoon olive oil**
  About 2¾ cups all-purpose flour

In a large bowl, combine yeast, sugar, and warm water; let stand until bubbly (about 10 minutes). Add lemon peel, salt, rosemary, 2 tablespoons of the oil, and 1½ cups of the flour. Beat with a heavy spoon or an electric mixer until dough is glossy and elastic (3 to 5 minutes). Then mix in enough of the remaining flour (about 1 cup) to make a soft dough.

Turn dough out onto a floured board and knead until smooth and springy (about 10 minutes), adding more flour as needed to prevent sticking. Clean off board and flour it generously; place dough on board, pat it into a 6-inch square, and brush with remaining 1 teaspoon oil. Cover lightly and let rise until puffy (about 45 minutes).

Gently rub dough with 2 tablespoons flour. With a sharp knife, cut dough lengthwise into quarters. Work with one quarter at a time; keep remaining dough covered. Cut each quarter lengthwise into 8 equal pieces. Then stretch and roll each piece to about 15 inches long; place breadsticks about ½ inch apart on greased baking sheets (you will need 3 large baking sheets). Repeat to use remaining dough.

Bake breadsticks in a 350° oven until golden brown (20 to 25 minutes), switching positions of baking sheets after 10 minutes. If using only one oven, refrigerate one sheet of breadsticks, lightly covered, while baking the other two. Lift breadsticks from baking sheets. Serve warm or at room temperature.

If made ahead, let cool, wrap airtight, and store at room temperature for up to 3 days; freeze for longer storage. Makes 32 breadsticks.

Per breadstick: 52 calories (24 percent from fat), 1 g protein, 8 g carbohydrates, 1 g total fat (0.2 g saturated fat), 0 mg cholesterol, 69 mg sodium

Chinese Steamed Buns

The bread is flavorful whole wheat; the filling is a marvelous mixture of mushrooms, cashews, and other goodies seasoned with fresh ginger, garlic, and soy sauce. Steam the buns or bake them; either way, they're superb.

1 **package active dry yeast**
1 **cup warm water (about 110°F)**
1 **tablespoon sugar**
2 **tablespoons salad oil**
1 **teaspoon salt**
  About 2¾ cups whole wheat flour
  Mushroom-Cashew Filling (recipe follows)
1 **tablespoon butter or margarine (if preparing baked buns)**

In a large bowl, combine yeast, warm water, sugar, oil, and salt; let stand until bubbly (about 15 minutes). Add 2¾ cups of the flour and stir until dough holds together. Turn dough out onto a lightly floured board and knead until smooth and elastic (8 to 10 minutes). Place dough in a greased bowl; turn over to grease top. Cover and let rise in a warm place until doubled (about 1 hour).

Meanwhile, prepare Mushroom-Cashew Filling; set aside.

Punch dough down and knead briefly on a lightly floured board to release air. Divide dough into 12 equal pieces; roll each piece into a round about 4½ inches in diameter. Press outside edge of each round to make it slightly thinner than rest of dough. Place about 2 tablespoons filling in center of each round. Pull edges of dough up around filling and twist firmly to seal.

For steamed buns, place each bun, twisted side down, on a 2-inch square of foil and place on a baking sheet. Cover and let rise in a warm place until puffy and light (about 30 minutes). Set buns, still on foil, in a single layer on a rack in a pan over 1 to 1½ inches of boiling water. Cover and steam until bread is cooked through (about 15 minutes).

For baked buns, place buns, twisted side down, about 2 inches apart on a greased baking sheet. Cover and let rise in a warm place until puffy and light (about 30 minutes). Brush tops with butter. Bake in a 350° oven until bottoms of buns are golden brown (about 15 minutes).

Serve steamed or baked buns warm. Makes 1 dozen buns.

Mushroom-Cashew Filling. In a small bowl, combine 3 tablespoons **soy sauce,** 1 tablespoon **dry sherry,** 1 teaspoon **sugar,** ¼ cup **water,** and 1 tablespoon **cornstarch.** Set aside.

Heat 1 tablespoon **salad oil** in a wide frying pan over high heat. Add ¼ pound **mushrooms,** chopped; 1 small **onion,** chopped; 1 clove **garlic,** minced or pressed; and 1 teaspoon minced **fresh ginger.** Cook, stirring, for 3 minutes. Add ½ cup coarsely chopped **bamboo shoots;** ¾ cup coarsely chopped **cashews;** and 2 **green onions,** thinly sliced. Cook, stirring, for 2 minutes. Stir soy mixture and add to pan; cook, stirring, until sauce boils and thickens. Stir in 1 teaspoon **Oriental sesame oil.** Remove from heat; let cool.

Per steamed bun: 201 calories (37 percent from fat), 6 g protein, 27 g carbohydrates, 9 g total fat (1 g saturated fat), 0 mg cholesterol, 445 mg sodium

Per baked bun: 213 calories (40 percent from fat), 6 g protein, 27 g carbohydrates, 10 g total fat (2 g saturated fat), 3 mg cholesterol, 455 mg sodium

Bolillos

In Mexico, the plain white rolls called *bolillos* (pronounced bo-LEE-yos) are as popular as tortillas. The crust is crisp and chewy, much like that of a hard French roll.

    2 cups hot water
    1½ tablespoons sugar
    1 tablespoon salt
    2 tablespoons butter or margarine
    1 package active dry yeast
    5½ to 6 cups all-purpose flour
    1 teaspoon cornstarch blended
       with ½ cup cold water

In a large bowl, combine hot water, sugar, and salt. Add butter and stir until melted; then let mixture cool to 110°F. Add yeast and stir until dissolved. Gradually beat in enough of the flour (about 5 cups) to make a stiff dough.

Turn dough out onto a lightly floured board and knead until smooth and satiny (10 to 20 minutes), adding more flour as needed to prevent sticking. Place dough in a greased bowl; turn over to grease top. Cover and let rise in a warm place until doubled (about 1½ hours).

Punch dough down and knead briefly on a lightly floured board to release air. Divide into 16 equal pieces.

Gently knead each piece to shape it into a smooth ball; then roll and gently pull each ball from center to ends to make an oblong roll about 4 inches long (center should be thicker than ends). Place rolls 3 inches apart on greased baking sheets (you will need 3 baking sheets). Cover rolls and let rise until almost doubled (about 35 minutes).

In a small pan, bring cornstarch mixture to a boil, stirring constantly; remove from heat and let cool slightly. Brush each roll with cornstarch mixture; then, with a razor blade or sharp knife, cut a slash about ¾ inch deep and 2 inches long across top of each roll. Adjust oven racks so they are equally spaced in oven from top to bottom, then stagger baking sheets to get best heat distribution. Bake in a 375° oven until rolls are golden brown and sound hollow when tapped (35 to 40 minutes), switching positions of baking sheets after 18 minutes. If using only one oven, refrigerate one sheet of rolls, lightly covered, while baking the other two. Let rolls cool on racks. Makes 16 rolls.

Per roll: 193 calories (14 percent from fat), 5 g protein, 36 g carbohydrates, 3 g total fat (1 g saturated fat), 4 mg cholesterol, 428 mg sodium

German Soft Pretzels

Visit a German *Hofbrauhaus* or *Biergarten,* and you're likely to find soft, yeasty pretzels like these as the favored accompaniment to frothy mugs of ice-cold beer. The pretzels are best served still warm from the oven, with your favorite mustard alongside.

    1 package active dry yeast
    1 cup warm water (about 110°F)
    2½ to 3 cups all-purpose flour
    2 tablespoons salad oil
    1 tablespoon sugar
    ⅓ cup baking soda

    6 cups water
       Coarse salt
       Mustard (optional)

In a medium-size bowl, combine yeast and warm water; let stand until yeast is softened (about 5 minutes). Add 1½ cups of the flour, oil, and sugar; beat until smooth. Gradually stir in enough of the remaining flour (about 1 cup) to form a soft dough. Turn dough out onto a floured board and knead until smooth and satiny (about 5 minutes), adding more flour as needed to prevent sticking. Place dough in a greased bowl; turn over to grease top. Cover and let rise in a warm place until doubled (about 1 hour).

Punch dough down, turn out onto floured board, and divide into 12 equal pieces. Gently knead each piece to shape it into a smooth ball. Working with one ball of dough at a time, roll each one into a smooth rope about 18 inches long; then twist rope into a pretzel shape. Place pretzels slightly apart on greased baking sheets, turning loose ends underneath. Let rise in a warm place, uncovered, until puffy (about 25 minutes).

Meanwhile, in a 3-quart stainless steel or enamel pan (don't use aluminum), combine baking soda and the 6 cups water. Bring to a boil; then reduce heat to keep water boiling gently. With a slotted spatula, lower one pretzel at a time into boiling water. Simmer for 10 seconds on each side; then lift from water, drain briefly, and return to baking sheet. Let dry briefly; sprinkle with coarse salt. Let simmered pretzels stand, uncovered, until all pretzels have been simmered.

Bake in a 425° oven until golden brown (12 to 15 minutes). Serve with mustard, if desired. Makes 1 dozen pretzels.

Per pretzel: 140 calories (24 percent from fat), 3 g protein, 23 g carbohydrates, 4 g total fat (0.5 g saturated fat), 0 mg cholesterol, 316 mg sodium

Quick Croissants

This recipe was an instant hit when we featured it in 1968: it provides a remarkably simple way to make flaky French pastry without having to butter, fold, roll, and chill the dough many times. You can prepare the dough in advance and store it in the refrigerator for up to 4 days before baking.

    1   package active dry yeast
    1   cup warm water (about 110°F)
    ¾   cup evaporated milk
    1½ teaspoons salt
    ⅓   cup sugar
    1   egg
    5   cups all-purpose flour
    ¼   cup butter or margarine, melted
        and cooled
    1   cup (½ lb.) cold butter or
        margarine
    1   egg beaten with 1 tablespoon
        water

In a bowl, combine yeast and warm water; let stand until yeast is softened (about 5 minutes). Add milk, salt, sugar, egg, and 1 cup of the flour; beat until smoothly blended. Stir in melted butter; set aside.

Place remaining 4 cups flour in a large bowl. With a pastry blender or 2 knives, cut in the 1 cup cold butter until mixture resembles very coarse crumbs. Pour yeast mixture over top and stir gently just until all flour is moistened. Cover with plastic wrap and refrigerate until cold (at least 4 hours) or for up to 4 days.

Turn dough out onto a floured board and knead lightly to release air. Divide dough into 4 equal pieces. Shape one piece at a time; keep remaining dough covered in refrigerator until all dough has been shaped.

To shape croissants, place one piece of dough on a floured board and roll out to a 17-inch circle. Using a knife, cut circle into 8 equal wedges. Beginning at wide end, loosely roll each wedge toward point; then shape each roll into a crescent. Place crescents, point down and 1½ inches apart, on ungreased baking sheets.

Cover rolls and let rise at room temperature until almost doubled (about 2 hours); *do not* speed rising by placing rolls in a warm place. Brush with egg mixture. Bake in 325° oven until lightly browned (about 35 minutes); serve warm.

If made ahead, let cool on racks, wrap airtight, and refrigerate until next day; freeze for longer storage (thaw before reheating). To reheat, place rolls slightly apart on baking sheets; heat, uncovered, in a 350° oven for 10 minutes. Makes 32 croissants.

Per croissant: 156 calories (47 percent from fat), 3 g protein, 18 g carbohydrates, 8 g total fat (5 g saturated fat), 34 mg cholesterol, 187 mg sodium

Sticky Pecan Rolls

These sweet breakfast pastries require just one rising. Be sure to let them cool for at least 10 minutes before you eat them—right out of the oven, the caramel-pecan topping is hot enough to burn your fingers and tongue.

    ¼   teaspoon baking soda
    ¼   cup granulated sugar
    1   teaspoon salt
    1   package active dry yeast
        About 3 cups all-purpose flour
    1   cup buttermilk
    3   tablespoons salad oil
    ¼   cup water
    6   tablespoons butter or marga-
        rine, melted
    ¾   cup firmly packed brown sugar
    ¾   cup chopped pecans
    1   teaspoon ground cinnamon

In a large bowl, mix baking soda, granulated sugar, salt, yeast, and 1 cup of the flour. In a small pan, heat

buttermilk and oil over medium-low heat until hot (120° to 130°F); add to flour mixture and beat with an electric mixer on high speed for about 2 minutes. Stir in 1½ cups more flour and beat until smooth. Turn dough out onto a floured board and knead until smooth and elastic (8 to 10 minutes), adding more flour as needed to prevent sticking. Let dough rest on board while you prepare pans.

In a small bowl, combine water, ¼ cup of the butter, and ½ cup of the brown sugar. Distribute butter-sugar mixture equally among twelve 2½-inch muffin cups; top mixture evenly with pecans.

Roll dough out to a 12- by 15-inch rectangle. Brush surface with remaining 2 tablespoons butter. Mix cinnamon with remaining ¼ cup brown sugar and sprinkle evenly over buttered dough. Starting with a short end, roll up rectangle jelly-roll style and cut crosswise into 12 equal pieces. Place each piece, cut side down, in a muffin cup. Let rise, uncovered, in a warm place until doubled (about 1½ hours).

Bake in a 350° oven until tops are golden (about 25 minutes). Invert pan at once onto a serving plate; let pan remain briefly on rolls so syrup can drizzle over them. Let cool for at least 10 minutes; then serve warm. Makes 1 dozen rolls.

Per roll: 317 calories (40 percent from fat), 5 g protein, 44 g carbohydrates, 14 g total fat (5 g saturated fat), 16 mg cholesterol, 294 mg sodium

Cinnamon Twists

Crisp, buttery, and crunchy with cinnamon sugar, these delicate pastry twists are the stuff sweet dreams are made of. You can prepare the dough ahead, then shape and bake it the next morning.

2 **packages active dry yeast**
½ **cup warm water (about 110°F)**
1 **cup (½ lb.) butter or margarine, at room temperature**
½ **teaspoon salt**
4 **eggs**
4 **to 4½ cups all-purpose flour**
1 **cup sugar**
1 **tablespoon ground cinnamon**

In a small bowl, combine yeast and warm water; let stand until yeast is softened (about 5 minutes). In a large bowl, beat butter and salt until creamy. Add eggs and yeast mixture; beat until blended. Gradually beat in enough of the flour (about 4 cups) to make a springy dough that pulls away from sides of bowl. Turn dough out of bowl and shape into a ball; then place dough in a greased bowl and turn over to grease top. Cover; refrigerate for at least 2 hours or until next day.

In a small bowl, mix sugar and cinnamon. Sprinkle ½ cup of the sugar mixture on a board, turn dough out onto board, and knead sugar into dough just until blended. Lightly flour board and roll dough out to a 12- by 15-inch rectangle, sprinkling more flour on board as needed to prevent sticking. Cut dough into 1- by 6-inch

strips. Working with one strip at a time, dip each strip in remaining ½ cup sugar mixture and, holding both ends, twist to make a spiral shape. Place twists 2 inches apart on greased baking sheets. Bake in a 350° oven until lightly browned (20 to 25 minutes). Let cool on racks. Makes 2½ dozen twists.

Per twist: 160 calories (42 percent from fat), 3 g protein, 21 g carbohydrates, 7 g total fat (4 g saturated fat), 45 mg cholesterol, 108 mg sodium

Buttery Almond Bear Claws

Rich and almondy, bear claws are usually considered a bakery specialty. But with our easy refrigerator dough and streamlined technique, you'll be able to make pastries that rival the best you can buy.

1 **package active dry yeast**
¼ **cup warm water (about 110°F)**
3 **eggs**
¼ **cup sugar**
½ **teaspoon salt**
1 **small can (about 5 oz.) evaporated milk**
1 **cup (½ lb.) butter or margarine, melted and cooled**
   About 3⅓ cups all-purpose flour
   Almond Filling (recipe follows)
   About ¾ cup sliced almonds
   Sugar

In a bowl, combine yeast and warm water; let stand until yeast is softened (about 5 minutes). Separate eggs, reserving 2 of the whites in one small bowl and remaining white in another bowl. Stir egg yolks into yeast mixture. Add the ¼ cup sugar, salt, milk, and butter; stir until blended.

Place 3⅓ cups of the flour in a large bowl, pour in yeast mixture, and stir until well blended. Cover and refrigerate for at least 1 day or up to 3 days.

Prepare Almond Filling, using 2 of the reserved egg whites; refrigerate as directed. Cover and refrigerate remaining egg white.

To shape bear claws, punch dough down and knead briefly on a well-floured board to release air. Then roll dough out to a 13½- by 27-inch rectangle, using a ruler to straighten edges. Cut dough lengthwise into 3 strips, each 4½ inches wide. Divide filling into 3 equal portions; on floured board, roll each portion into a 27-inch rope. Lay an almond rope in center of each dough strip; then flatten rope slightly with your fingers.

Fold long sides of each strip over filling to enclose it. Cut each filled strip crosswise into 6 pieces, each 4½ inches long. Place pieces, seam side down, on 3 greased 12- by 15-inch baking sheets and flatten slightly. Using a sharp knife, make a row of cuts ¾ inch apart halfway across long side of each piece; curve each bear claw so cut pieces fan out.

Lightly beat remaining egg white and brush over bear claws; top with almonds and sprinkle lightly with sugar. Let rise, uncovered, in a warm place until puffy (about 20 minutes). Bake in a 375° oven until golden brown (about 15 minutes). Let cool on racks. Makes 1½ dozen bear claws.

Almond Filling. In a bowl, beat ½ cup (¼ lb.) **butter** or margarine (at room temperature) and 1⅓ cups **powdered sugar** until smooth. Add ⅔ cup **all-purpose flour** and ½ pound **almond paste.** Stir until crumbly and evenly blended; then beat in 1 teaspoon **grated lemon peel** and 2 of the reserved **egg whites.** Stir in ¾ cup finely chopped **blanched almonds.** Cover and refrigerate until firm (several hours) or for up to 3 days.

Per bear claw: 428 calories (55 percent from fat), 8 g protein, 41 g carbohydrates, 26 g total fat (11 g saturated fat), 79 mg cholesterol, 240 mg sodium

Portuguese Sweet Bread

Many Americans know this round, golden loaf as "Hawaiian sweet bread"—which isn't surprising, since residents of the Islands have adopted the recipe as their own. But in fact, Portuguese immigrants first popularized the bread in Hawaii during the late 1800s. This old recipe—updated for today's kitchens—appeared in our pages in 1970.

⅔ cup water

¼ cup instant mashed potato granules or flakes

⅔ cup sugar

¼ cup instant nonfat dry milk

½ cup (¼ lb.) butter or margarine, cut into pieces

2 packages active dry yeast

⅓ cup warm water (about 110°F)
About 5 cups all-purpose flour

4 eggs

1 teaspoon salt

½ teaspoon vanilla

¼ teaspoon lemon extract
Sugar (optional)

In a small pan, bring the ⅔ cup water to a boil. Beat in potato granules; then remove from heat and stir in the ⅔ cup sugar, dry milk, and butter. Let cool to 110°F (butter need not melt completely).

In a large bowl, combine yeast and warm water; let stand until yeast is softened (about 5 minutes). Then stir in cooled potato mixture. Add 2 cups of the flour and beat until blended. Beat in 3 of the eggs, salt, vanilla, and lemon extract until smoothly blended. Then beat in 1½ cups more flour.

Stir in enough of the remaining flour (1 to 1½ cups) to make a stiff dough. Turn dough out onto a floured board and knead until smooth and satiny (10 to 20 minutes), adding more flour as needed to prevent sticking. Place dough in a greased bowl; turn over to grease top. Cover and let rise in a warm place until doubled (about 1 hour).

Punch dough down and knead briefly on a lightly floured board to release air. Let dough stand for 10 minutes; then divide in half. Shape each half into a smooth ball; place each ball in a greased 9-inch pie pan and gently flatten into a round about 8 inches in diameter. Cover lightly and let rise in a warm place until almost doubled (35 to 45 minutes).

Beat remaining egg and brush evenly over loaves; sprinkle loaves lightly with sugar, if desired.

Bake in a 350° oven until browned (25 to 30 minutes). Turn out onto racks to cool. Serve bread warm or at room temperature. Makes 2 loaves (8 to 10 servings *each*).

Per serving: 240 calories (28 percent from fat), 6 g protein, 37 g carbohydrates, 7 g total fat (4 g saturated fat), 61 mg cholesterol,196 mg sodium

Swiss Egg Braids

Braided loaves made from a dense, egg-rich dough are called *Eier Zupfen* in Switzerland; in this country, we know them simply as "egg braids." If you like, you can make an extra-large double braid, crusted with cinnamon sugar, instead of two smaller loaves.

1 cup milk, scalded and cooled to about 110°F

½ cup sugar

1 teaspoon salt

2 packages active dry yeast

½ cup warm water (about 110°F)
About 4½ cups all-purpose flour

½ cup (¼ lb.) butter or margarine, melted and cooled

3 eggs, lightly beaten

1 egg yolk beaten with 1 tablespoon water

In a large bowl, combine milk, sugar, and salt; set aside. In a small bowl, combine yeast and warm water; let stand until yeast is softened (about 5 minutes). Pour into milk mixture. Beat in 2 cups of the flour to make a smooth, thick batter. Cover and let stand in a warm place until light and foamy (about 45 minutes).

Add butter and eggs; stir until blended. Then stir in 2½ cups more flour. Turn dough out onto a floured board; cover and let stand for 10 minutes. Then knead dough until smooth and satiny (about 8 minutes), adding more flour as needed to prevent sticking.

Place dough in a greased bowl; turn over to grease top. Cover and let rise in a warm place until doubled (about 1¾ hours). Punch dough down and knead briefly on a lightly floured board to release air; then divide dough in half, cover, and let stand for 10 minutes. Divide each half into 3 equal pieces. Shape each piece into a smooth rope about 12 inches long. Place 3 ropes side by side on a greased baking sheet and braid; pinch ends together firmly to seal, then tuck them under-

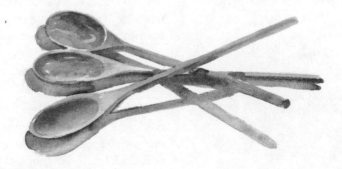

neath loaf. Repeat to braid remaining 3 ropes on a second baking sheet.

Cover loaves and let rise in a warm place until almost doubled (about 1¼ hours). Brush with egg yolk mixture. Bake in a 350° oven until golden brown (about 35 minutes). Let cool on racks. Makes 2 loaves (10 to 12 servings *each*).

Per serving: 175 calories (33 percent from fat), 4 g protein, 25 g carbohydrates, 6 g total fat (3 g saturated fat), 51 mg cholesterol, 158 mg sodium

Giant Cinnamon Braid

Prepare dough as directed for **Swiss Egg Braids,** but after punching dough down, cut off a third of the dough and set aside for top braid. Divide remaining dough into 3 equal pieces; shape each piece into a smooth rope about 12 inches long. Mix ½ cup **sugar** and 1 tablespoon **ground cinnamon** on a large sheet of wax paper. Roll each dough rope in cinnamon-sugar mixture to coat all sides. Place ropes side by side on a clean sheet of wax paper and braid tightly; pinch ends together firmly to seal, then tuck them under loaf. Place loaf on a greased baking sheet.

Divide reserved piece of dough into 3 equal pieces. Shape each piece into a smooth rope about 12 inches long. Braid tightly; pinch ends together firmly to seal, then tuck them underneath loaf. Lightly moisten top of large braid with **water** and place smaller braid on top. Cover and let rise in a warm place until almost doubled (about 1¼ hours). Brush loaf with egg yolk mixture.

Bake in a 350° oven until a wooden pick inserted in center comes out clean (about 45 minutes); cover loosely with foil if top begins to burn. Let cool on a rack. Makes 1 loaf (20 to 24 servings).

Per serving: 193 calories (30 percent from fat), 4 g protein, 30 g carbohydrates, 6 g total fat (3 g saturated fat), 51 mg cholesterol, 158 mg sodium

Cherry-Almond Christmas Wreath

Here's a colorful Christmas treat. A special cutting and shaping technique exposes the red and green cherry-almond filling and gives the wreath its distinctive appearance.

- 1 **package active dry yeast**
- ¼ **cup warm water (about 110°F)**
- ½ **cup milk, scalded and cooled to about 110°F**
- 3 **tablespoons sugar**
- ¼ **cup butter or margarine, at room temperature**
- 1½ **teaspoons salt**
- ½ **teaspoon ground cardamom**
- 2 **eggs**
- 1 **teaspoon grated lemon peel**
  About 3¼ cups all-purpose flour
  Cherry-Almond Filling (recipe follows)
  Sugar Glaze (recipe follows)

In a large bowl, combine yeast and warm water; let stand until yeast is softened (about 5 minutes). Stir in milk, sugar, butter, salt, cardamom, eggs, and lemon peel. Using an electric mixer, beat in 2 cups of the flour, 1 cup at a time, beating well after each addition. Then beat on medium speed for 3 minutes.

Using a dough hook or a heavy spoon, beat in enough of the remaining flour (about 1¼ cups) to make a soft dough. Turn dough out onto a floured board and knead until smooth

(5 to 10 minutes), adding more flour as needed to prevent sticking. Place dough in a greased bowl; turn over to grease top. Cover; let rise in a warm place until doubled (about 1½ hours).

Meanwhile, prepare Cherry-Almond Filling and refrigerate.

Punch dough down and knead briefly on a lightly floured board to release air. Roll out to a 9- by 30-inch rectangle. Crumble filling and scatter it over dough to within 1 inch of edges. Starting with a long side, roll dough up tightly jelly-roll style, enclosing filling. Moisten edge with water; pinch against roll to seal.

Using a sharp knife, cut roll in half lengthwise. Carefully turn halves cut side up; then loosely twist halves around each other, keeping cut sides up. Carefully transfer to a greased and floured baking sheet and shape into a 10-inch ring; pinch ends together firmly to seal. Let rise, uncovered, in a warm place until puffy (45 to 60 minutes).

Bake in a 375° oven until lightly browned (about 20 minutes). Let cool on a rack. Prepare Sugar Glaze and drizzle over wreath while still warm. Makes 1 wreath (about 18 servings).

Cherry-Almond Filling. In a medium-size bowl, beat ¼ cup **butter** or margarine (at room temperature), ¼ cup **all-purpose flour,** and 2 tablespoons **sugar** with an electric mixer or heavy spoon until smooth. Stir in ⅔ cup finely chopped **blanched almonds,** ¼ cup *each* chopped **red and green candied cherries,** ½ teaspoon **grated lemon peel,** and ¾ teaspoon **almond extract.** Cover and refrigerate.

Sugar Glaze. In a small bowl, stir together ⅔ cup sifted **powdered sugar,** 1½ teaspoons **lemon juice,** and 1 tablespoon **water** until smooth.

Per serving: 232 calories (36 percent from fat), 5 g protein, 32 g carbohydrates, 9 g total fat (4 g saturated fat), 38 mg cholesterol, 247 mg sodium

Sweets are international favorites, whether they're served as dessert at the end of a meal or enjoyed with a cup of afternoon coffee or tea. Westerners often favor traditional down-home specialties like brownies, coconutty dream bars, carrot cake, and juicy fruit pies—and all are included in this chapter. ● But that doesn't mean we've overlooked recipes that have achieved their "best-loved" status more recently. Today's interest in Italian cooking has increased the popularity of biscotti, gelato, and tiramisù. White chocolate has become a real favorite, too; in these pages, you'll find an unusual white chocolate and blueberry cake as well as crisp White Chocolate Chip Cookies. And lower-fat desserts have also found a place here. Try our No-fat Chocolate Cake, Frozen Peppermint Pie, or Fresh Berry Sorbet if your sweet tooth doesn't stop when the diet begins.

Dark Chocolate Chewy Brownies

In an unscientific poll, *Sunset* food editors discovered that those who are fond of brownies generally prefer them "chewy-gooey." Popular variations differ widely, but we think this recipe will satisfy any chocoholic. Depending on your taste, you can enjoy the brownies plain, top them with fudge, or add marshmallows.

> Fudge Frosting (optional; recipe follows)
> ½ cup (¼ lb.) butter or margarine, cut into chunks
> 3 ounces unsweetened chocolate
> 1⅓ cups sugar
> 2 eggs
> 1 teaspoon vanilla
> ½ cup all-purpose flour
> ½ cup chopped walnuts, chopped almonds, semisweet chocolate chips, or white chocolate chips

Prepare Fudge Frosting, if desired.

In a medium-size pan, combine butter and chocolate. Heat over low heat, stirring occasionally, until melted and smooth. Remove from heat and let cool slightly; then add sugar, eggs, and vanilla and stir until blended. Stir in flour.

Spread batter evenly in a greased 8-inch-square baking pan; sprinkle with walnuts. Bake in a 350° oven until edges of brownie feel firm and center springs back when lightly touched (about 25 minutes). Let cool in pan on a rack; then spread evenly with Fudge Frosting, if desired. If made ahead, cover and store at room temperature for up to 2 days. To serve, cut into about 2½-inch squares. Makes 9 brownies.

Fudge Frosting. In a small pan, combine ⅓ cup **whipping cream** and 1 small package (about 6 oz.) **semisweet chocolate chips** (or 1 cup chopped semisweet chocolate). Heat over low heat, stirring, until chocolate is melted. Stir in 1 teaspoon **vanilla** or 2 tablespoons mint-flavored liqueur or rum. Remove from heat and let cool until thick enough to spread (about 1 hour).

Per brownie without frosting: 344 calories (53 percent from fat), 4 g protein, 39 g carbohydrates, 21 g total fat (10 g saturated fat), 75 mg cholesterol, 121 mg sodium

Per brownie with frosting: 460 calories (54 percent from fat), 5 g protein, 52 g carbohydrates, 29 g total fat (15 g saturated fat), 85 mg cholesterol, 124 mg sodium

Rocky Road Brownies

Follow directions for **Dark Chocolate Chewy Brownies,** but stir 1 cup **miniature marshmallows** into batter. Sprinkle batter with walnuts (don't use almonds or chocolate chips). Makes 9 brownies.

Per brownie without frosting: 361 calories (50 percent from fat), 4 g protein, 43 g carbohydrates, 21 g total fat (10 g saturated fat), 75 mg cholesterol, 123 mg sodium

Brownie Bites

Each of these miniature brownies can be eaten in a single luscious bite. You bake them in paper-lined cups, like little cupcakes.

> ½ cup (¼ lb.) butter or margarine
> 4 ounces unsweetened chocolate
> 1½ cups sugar
> 1 teaspoon vanilla
> 3 eggs
> 1 cup all-purpose flour
> About 40 walnut halves

Place butter and chocolate in a medium-size pan. Heat over low heat, stirring occasionally, until melted and smooth. Remove pan from heat and stir in sugar and vanilla. Add eggs, one at a time, beating well after each addition. Stir in flour.

Spoon batter into paper-lined tiny (1½-inch) muffin cups, filling cups almost to the top. Place a walnut half on top of batter in each cup. Bake in a 325° oven until tops of brownies look dry and feel firm when lightly touched (about 20 minutes). Let brownies cool in pans for 10 minutes; then transfer to racks to cool completely. Serve warm or cool. Store airtight. Makes about 40 cookies.

Per cookie: 94 calories (50 percent from fat), 1 g protein, 11 g carbohydrates, 6 g total fat (3 g saturated fat), 22 mg cholesterol, 29 mg sodium

White Chocolate Chip Cookies

The daughter of a *Sunset* food editor created these delectable cookies. Rolled oats give them a pleasing crunch; chunks of smooth, rich white chocolate balance the crispness.

> 1 cup (½ lb.) butter or margarine, at room temperature
> 1½ cups sugar
> 2 teaspoons baking soda
> 1 egg
> 1 cup all-purpose flour
> 2 cups quick-cooking rolled oats
> 6 ounces white chocolate, coarsely chopped (about 1¼ cups)

In a large bowl, beat butter, sugar, and baking soda with an electric mixer until creamy. Beat in egg. Gradually add flour and oats; beat until blended. Stir in chocolate.

Roll dough into ¾-inch balls and place 2 inches apart on ungreased baking sheets. Bake in a 350° oven until light golden (10 to 12 minutes). Let cookies cool briefly on baking sheets; then transfer to racks to cool completely. Store airtight. Makes about 5 dozen cookies.

Per cookie: 81 calories (46 percent from fat), 0.9 g protein, 10 g carbohydrates, 4 g total fat (2 g saturated fat), 12 mg cholesterol, 77 mg sodium

Big Oatmeal Chocolate Chip Cookies

Nearly 6 inches across and chewy with oatmeal, these oversized cookies always bring in the dough at bake sales. For variety, you can use butterscotch chips instead of chocolate ones.

1½ cups all-purpose flour
2 teaspoons baking soda
1 teaspoon salt
1 cup (½ lb.) butter or margarine, at room temperature
1½ cups firmly packed brown sugar
2 eggs
1 teaspoon vanilla
2⅓ cups quick-cooking rolled oats
1 large package (about 12 oz.) semisweet chocolate or butterscotch-flavored chips
1½ cups chopped nuts
Granulated sugar

In a small bowl, mix flour, baking soda, and salt; set aside. In a large bowl, beat butter and brown sugar with an electric mixer or a heavy spoon until creamy. Beat in eggs and vanilla. Gradually add flour mixture, beating until well blended. Stir in oats, chocolate chips, and nuts.

Spoon ½-cup portions of dough onto greased baking sheets, spacing cookies 6 inches apart and 2½ inches from edges of sheets. Grease bottom of a pie pan, dip in granulated sugar, and use to flatten each cookie into a 5½-inch circle. If necessary, press cookies lightly with your fingers to give them an even thickness.

Bake cookies in a 350° oven until edges are lightly browned (about 15 minutes). Let cool on baking sheets for about 5 minutes; then transfer to racks to cool completely. Store airtight. Makes about 1 dozen cookies.

Per cookie: 627 calories (50 percent from fat), 9 g protein, 74 g carbohydrates, 36 g total fat (16 g saturated fat), 77 mg cholesterol, 574 mg sodium

Big Oatmeal Raisin Cookies

Follow directions for **Big Oatmeal Chocolate Chip Cookies,** but add 1 teaspoon **ground cinnamon** and ½ teaspoon **ground nutmeg** with flour. Omit chocolate chips and add 1½ cups **raisins.** Makes about 1 dozen cookies.

Per cookie: 547 calories (44 percent from fat), 8 g protein, 71 g carbohydrates, 28 g total fat (11 g saturated fat), 77 mg cholesterol, 573 mg sodium

Chocolate Chip Cookies at Their Best

A self-described "chocolate freak" contributed this recipe to "Chefs of the West" in 1980—and many cookie fans agree that these big cookies, chock-full of chocolate and walnuts, are indeed the very best they've ever tasted. Bake the cookies one way if you want them soft and chewy, another way if you like them crisp.

3 cups all-purpose flour
2 teaspoons baking soda
1½ teaspoons salt
1 teaspoon ground cinnamon (optional)
½ cup quick-cooking rolled oats
1 cup (½ lb.) butter or margarine, at room temperature
½ cup solid vegetable shortening
1⅓ cups granulated sugar
1 cup firmly packed brown sugar
4 eggs
1 tablespoon vanilla
1 teaspoon lemon juice
2 large packages (about 12 oz. *each*) semisweet chocolate chips
2 cups chopped walnuts

In a medium-size bowl, mix flour, baking soda, salt, cinnamon (if desired), and oats; set aside. In a large bowl, beat butter, shortening, granulated sugar, and brown sugar with an electric mixer on high speed until fluffy (about 5 minutes). Beat in eggs, one at a time. Beat in vanilla and lemon juice. Gradually add flour mixture, beating until well blended. Stir in chocolate chips and walnuts.

Spoon ¼-cup portions of dough about 3 inches apart onto lightly greased baking sheets. For soft cookies, bake in a 325° oven until light golden brown (17 to 19 minutes); for crisp cookies, bake in a 350° oven until golden brown (16 to 18 minutes). Let cookies cool briefly on baking sheets; then transfer to racks to cool completely. Store airtight. Makes about 3 dozen cookies.

Per cookie: 308 calories (51 percent from fat), 4 g protein, 36 g carbohydrates, 18 g total fat (8 g saturated fat), 38 mg cholesterol, 224 mg sodium

Chocolate Mint Sticks

Mint frosting is sandwiched between a brownie and a layer of dark chocolate in these super-delicious bars.

½ cup (¼ lb.) plus 1 tablespoon butter or margarine
3 ounces unsweetened chocolate
1 cup sugar
2 eggs
½ teaspoon peppermint extract
½ cup *each* all-purpose flour and chopped walnuts
Mint Frosting (recipe follows)

In a medium-size pan, combine ½ cup of the butter and 2 ounces of the chocolate. Heat over low heat, stirring often, until melted and smooth. Remove from heat and let cool slightly; then add sugar, eggs, and peppermint extract and stir until blended. Stir in flour and walnuts. Spread batter evenly in a greased 9- by 13-inch baking pan. Bake in a 350° oven until a wooden pick inserted in center of brownie comes out clean (about 20 minutes). Let cool for 30 minutes.

While brownie is cooling, prepare Mint Frosting. Spread cooled brownie with frosting. Refrigerate for 5 minutes. In a small pan, combine remaining 1 tablespoon butter and remaining 1 ounce chocolate; heat over low heat, stirring often, until melted and smooth. Brush butter-chocolate mixture over frosting. Refrigerate, uncovered, until chocolate topping is firm. If made ahead, cover and refrigerate for up to 2 days. To serve, cut into 1- by 2-inch bars. Makes about 4½ dozen cookies.

Mint Frosting. In a small bowl, combine 3 tablespoons **butter** or margarine (at room temperature), 1½ tablespoons **milk,** 1 teaspoon **peppermint extract,** ⅛ teaspoon **green food coloring,** and 1½ cups sifted **powdered sugar.** Beat until smooth.

Per cookie: 70 calories (53 percent from fat), 0.7 g protein, 8 g carbohydrates, 4 g total fat (2 g saturated fat), 15 mg cholesterol, 29 mg sodium

Buttery Lemon Bars

Various versions of these luscious bars have been popular at bake sales and potlucks for decades. All resemble our recipe, first printed in a 1976 "Kitchen Cabinet," in featuring a tangy lemon custard layered atop a shortbread crust.

    1 cup (½ lb.) butter or margarine,
       at room temperature
    ½ cup powdered sugar
    2⅓ cups all-purpose flour
    4 eggs
    2 cups granulated sugar
    1 teaspoon grated lemon peel
    6 tablespoons lemon juice
    1 teaspoon baking powder
       Powdered sugar

In a large bowl, beat butter and the ½ cup powdered sugar with an electric mixer until creamy. Add 2 cups of the flour and beat until blended. Spread mixture evenly over bottom of a greased 9- by 13-inch baking pan. Bake in a 350° oven for 20 minutes.

Meanwhile, in a medium-size bowl, beat eggs with an electric mixer until blended. Beat in granulated sugar until mixture is thick and lemon-colored. Add lemon peel, lemon juice, remaining ⅓ cup flour, and baking powder; beat until mixture is smooth.

Pour lemon mixture over hot baked crust. Return pan to oven and bake until topping is pale golden (15 to 20 minutes).

Sift powdered sugar lightly over top and let cool. Cut into about 2¼- by 2½-inch bars. Store airtight. Makes about 20 bars.

Per cookie: 244 calories (38 percent from fat), 3 g protein, 35 g carbohydrates, 11 g total fat (6 g saturated fat), 67 mg cholesterol, 132 mg sodium

Dream Bars

A gooey coconut filling and a tender, buttery crust make these delectable bars one of *Sunset's* most enduring favorites. If you like, you can top the filling with a layer of sweet orange frosting; some cookie connoisseurs wouldn't dream of skipping it, while the purists among us generally prefer our dream bars plain.

    ⅓ cup butter or margarine, at
       room temperature
    1½ cups firmly packed brown
       sugar
    1 cup plus 2 tablespoons all-
       purpose flour
    2 eggs
    1 teaspoon vanilla
    1 teaspoon baking powder
    ½ teaspoon salt

    1½ cups sweetened shredded
       coconut
    1 cup chopped nuts
       Orange Butter Frosting
       (optional; recipe follows)

In a large bowl, beat butter and ½ cup of the sugar with an electric mixer until creamy. With a fork, blend in 1 cup of the flour until mixture resembles fine crumbs. Press mixture firmly and evenly over bottom of a greased 9- by 13-inch baking pan. Bake in a 375° oven for 10 minutes; let cool in pan on a rack.

In a clean large bowl, beat eggs with an electric mixer until thick and lemon-colored; then gradually beat in remaining 1 cup sugar. Beat in vanilla, remaining 2 tablespoons flour, baking powder, and salt. Stir in coconut and nuts until blended.

Pour coconut mixture evenly over baked crust. Return to oven and bake until topping is golden (about 20 minutes); then let cool in pan on rack for 10 to 15 minutes. Meanwhile, prepare Orange Butter Frosting, if desired. Cut partially cooled cookies into bars (about 1½ by 3 inches); do not remove from pan. Spread frosting over cookies and let cool completely in pan on rack. (Don't frost cookies before cutting them—if you do, frosting will crack when cookies are cut.) Store airtight. Makes 2 dozen cookies.

Orange Butter Frosting. In a small bowl, beat ¼ cup **butter** or margarine (at room temperature) and 2 cups sifted **powdered sugar** with an electric mixer until creamy. Add 1 teaspoon *each* **vanilla** and **grated orange peel.** Beat in about 2 tablespoons **orange juice,** using just enough to give frosting a good spreading consistency.

Per cookie without frosting: 158 calories (43 percent from fat), 2 g protein, 21 g carbohydrates, 8 g total fat (3 g saturated fat), 25 mg cholesterol, 113 mg sodium

Per cookie with frosting: 208 calories (41 percent from fat), 2 g protein, 29 g carbohydrates, 10 g total fat (4 g saturated fat), 30 mg cholesterol, 133 mg sodium

Peanut Pinwheels

You can't go wrong with peanut butter and chocolate! These impressive cookies present the combination in an especially attractive way—a layer of melted semisweet chocolate is rolled right inside the dough to make perfect little pinwheels.

1¼   **cups all-purpose flour**
½   **teaspoon** *each* **baking soda, salt, and ground cinnamon**
½   **cup (¼ lb.) butter or margarine, at room temperature**
½   **cup creamy peanut butter**
½   **cup** *each* **granulated sugar and firmly packed brown sugar**
1   **egg**
1   **small package (about 6 oz.) semisweet chocolate chips**

In a small bowl, mix flour, baking soda, salt, and cinnamon; set aside. In a large bowl, beat butter, peanut butter, granulated sugar, and brown sugar with an electric mixer until creamy; beat in egg. Gradually add flour mixture, stirring to blend. Cover; refrigerate until firm (about 2 hours).

In top pan of a double boiler set over simmering water (or in a small pan over lowest possible heat), melt chocolate chips, stirring constantly. Remove from heat (and water) and let cool slightly. On wax paper, pat chilled dough out to a 12-inch square. Spread chocolate evenly over dough to within ½ inch of edges. Beginning at one end, roll up dough to enclose filling; then cut roll in half crosswise. Wrap each roll in wax paper and refrigerate until firm (at least 2 hours) or for up to 3 days.

Remove one roll of dough from refrigerator. Remove wax paper and cut roll crosswise into ¼-inch-thick slices. Place slices, cut side up, about 1 inch apart on ungreased baking sheets. Bake in a 375° oven until lightly browned (about 10 minutes).

Let cookies cool on baking sheets for 2 to 3 minutes; then transfer to racks to cool completely. Repeat to slice and bake remaining roll of dough. Store airtight. Makes about 4 dozen cookies.

Per cookie: 79 calories (47 percent from fat), 1 g protein, 10 g carbohydrates, 4 g total fat (2 g saturated fat), 10 mg cholesterol, 70 mg sodium

Scottish Shortbread

Were you to take tea in the Highlands, you might well be offered Scotland's famous shortbread, a butter-rich cookie of delightful simplicity. If you like your shortbread a bit more dressed up, try our ginger variation.

1¼   **cups all-purpose flour**
3   **tablespoons cornstarch**
¼   **cup sugar**
½   **cup (¼ lb.) cold butter, cut into pieces**
    Sugar

In a large bowl, mix flour, cornstarch, and the ¼ cup sugar. With a pastry blender or 2 knives, cut in butter until mixture resembles coarse crumbs (or rub butter into flour mixture with your fingers). Pour into a 9-inch spring-form pan or cake pan with a removable rim; press dough firmly and evenly over bottom of pan.

With tines of a fork, make impressions around edge of dough; then prick surface evenly. Bake in a 325° oven until pale golden brown (about 40 minutes). Remove from oven, cut into 8 to 12 wedges, and sprinkle with about 1 tablespoon sugar. Let cool in

pan on a rack; then remove pan rim and lift out cookies. Store airtight. Makes 8 to 12 cookies.

Per cookie: 171 calories (49 percent from fat), 2 g protein, 20 g carbohydrates, 9 g total fat (6 g saturated fat), 25 mg cholesterol, 94 mg sodium

Ginger Shortbread

Follow directions for **Scottish Shortbread,** but omit cornstarch and add ½ teaspoon **ground ginger.** After cutting in butter, stir in 2 tablespoons minced **candied ginger.** Makes 8 to 12 cookies.

Per cookie: 174 calories (48 percent from fat), 2 g protein, 21 g carbohydrates, 9 g total fat (6 g saturated fat), 25 mg cholesterol, 96 mg sodium

Chocolate & Almond Toffee

This sweet toffee is very easy to make—and almost impossible to stop eating once you've started. Perhaps the best idea is to prepare the candy ahead, wrap it, and give it away as a gift. It keeps for several months in the refrigerator.

1½   **cups sliced almonds**
2   **cups (1 lb.) butter or margarine**
2½   **cups sugar**
8   **ounces semisweet chocolate**
2   **packages (about 4 oz.** *each***) sweet cooking chocolate**

Spread almonds in a shallow baking pan and toast in a 350° oven, stirring occasionally, until lightly browned (5 to 8 minutes). Let cool.

In a heavy 4-quart pan, combine butter and sugar; bring to a boil over medium heat, stirring constantly. Cover; cook for 3 minutes. Uncover; continue to cook, stirring occasionally, until temperature registers 290°F on a candy thermometer (about 6 minutes). Pour mixture into a greased 10- by 15-inch rimmed baking pan. Set pan on a flat surface and let cool for 30 minutes at room temperature (or refrigerate for 15 minutes; be sure pan is level).

While toffee is cooling, place semi-sweet and sweet chocolates in top pan of a double boiler set over simmering water. Heat, stirring occasionally, until melted and smooth. Spread half the chocolate evenly over toffee and sprinkle at once with half the almonds; keep remaining chocolate warm.

Refrigerate toffee until chocolate is set (about 15 minutes). Invert toffee onto a piece of foil. Spread remaining warm chocolate over second side of toffee and sprinkle at once with remaining almonds. Refrigerate again until chocolate is set. Then cut into bite-size pieces with a heavy knife. Wrap airtight and refrigerate for up to 2½ months. Makes about 2½ pounds.

Per ounce: 208 calories (61 percent from fat), 1 g protein, 20 g carbohydrates, 15 g total fat (8 g saturated fat), 25 mg cholesterol, 98 mg sodium

English Toffee Cookies

These thin, crisp, nut-topped squares, introduced in a 1960 "Kitchen Cabinet," are reminiscent of crunchy toffee candy. You just spread the dough in a shallow pan, bake, and cut into pieces. One batch yields six dozen cookies!

- 1 **cup (½ lb.) butter or margarine, at room temperature**
- 1 **cup sugar**
- 1 **egg, separated**
- 1 **teaspoon ground cinnamon**
- 2 **cups all-purpose flour**
- 1 **cup chopped pecans or walnuts**

In a large bowl, beat butter and sugar until creamy. Add egg yolk and beat until blended. Stir in cinnamon and flour.

Press dough smoothly and evenly over bottom of a greased 10- by 15-inch rimmed baking pan. In a small bowl, lightly beat egg white; then brush egg white over dough. Sprinkle evenly with pecans, pressing them lightly into dough.

Bake in a 275° oven for about 1 hour. While cookie is still hot, cut it into about 1½-inch squares. Let cool in pan. Store airtight. Makes about 6 dozen cookies.

Per cookie: 58 calories (58 percent from fat), 0.6 g protein, 6 g carbohydrates, 4 g total fat (2 g saturated fat), 10 mg cholesterol, 27 mg sodium

Buttery Cornmeal Wafers

Yellow cornmeal gives these lemon-accented wafers a special crunch and nutlike flavor.

- 1½ **cups all-purpose flour**
- 1 **cup yellow cornmeal**
- 1 **cup (½ lb.) butter or margarine, at room temperature**
- 1 **cup sugar**
- 2 **egg yolks**
- 1 **teaspoon grated lemon peel**

In a medium-size bowl, mix flour and cornmeal; set aside. In a large bowl, beat butter and sugar with an electric mixer until creamy. Add egg yolks and lemon peel; beat until well blended. Then add flour mixture and stir until blended. Shape dough into a ball, wrap in plastic wrap, and refrigerate just until firm (about 1 hour).

On a well-floured board, roll out dough about ¼ inch thick. Using 2½-inch-diameter cookie cutters, cut dough into desired shapes. Place cookies about 1 inch apart on lightly greased baking sheets. Bake in a 350° oven until edges are golden (10 to 12 minutes). Let cookies cool briefly on baking sheets; then transfer to racks to cool completely. Store airtight. Makes about 3 dozen cookies.

Per cookie: 105 calories (49 percent from fat), 1 g protein, 12 g carbohydrates, 6 g total fat (3 g saturated fat), 26 mg cholesterol, 53 mg sodium

Finnish Ribbon Cakes

Bite-size butter cookies, striped with colorful ribbons of jam, are a pretty addition to the cookie tray. They're easy to make: just roll the dough into long ropes, make an indentation down the center, and fill with jam. Cut the cookies into pieces after baking.

- 1 **cup (½ lb.) butter or margarine, at room temperature**
- ½ **cup granulated sugar**
- 1 **egg yolk**
- 1 **teaspoon vanilla**
- ½ **teaspoon grated lemon peel**
- 2½ **cups all-purpose flour**
- ¼ **teaspoon salt**
   About 6 tablespoons raspberry or apricot jam
- ½ **cup powdered sugar blended with 1 tablespoon water**

In a large bowl, beat butter and granulated sugar with an electric mixer until creamy; beat in egg yolk, vanilla, and lemon peel. Add flour and salt; stir until blended.

Shape dough into 15-inch-long ropes about ¾ inch thick; place them about 2 inches apart on ungreased baking sheets. With the side of your little finger, press a long groove down center of each rope (don't press all the way through to baking sheet). Bake cookies in a 375° oven for 10 minutes.

Remove cookies from oven and spoon jam into grooves. Return to oven and continue to bake until cookies are firm to the touch and light golden brown (5 to 10 more minutes). While cookies are hot, drizzle them with powdered sugar mixture. Then cut each cookie diagonally into 1-inch pieces. Let cookies cool briefly on baking sheets; then transfer to racks to cool completely. Store airtight. Makes about 4 dozen cookies.

Per cookie: 79 calories (45 percent from fat), 0.8 g protein, 10 g carbohydrates, 4 g total fat (2 g saturated fat), 15 mg cholesterol, 51 mg sodium

Lemon-tipped Pistachio Biscotti

Dotted with pale green pistachios and tipped with a tangy lemon glaze, these twice-baked Italian cookies are surprisingly low in fat. Serve them with frothy espresso or alongside a fresh fruit sorbet for a light conclusion to a special meal.

    2 cups all-purpose flour
    2 teaspoons baking powder
   ¼   cup butter or margarine, at room
       temperature
   ⅔   cup sugar
   1½ teaspoons grated lemon peel
    1 egg
    2 egg whites
    1 teaspoon vanilla
   ½   cup shelled salted roasted
       pistachio nuts, coarsely
       chopped
       Lemon Icing (recipe follows)

In a medium-size bowl, mix flour and baking powder; set aside. In a large bowl, beat butter, sugar, and lemon peel until well blended. Beat in egg, then egg whites. Beat in vanilla. Gradually add flour mixture, beating until well blended. Stir in pistachios.

Divide dough in half. On a lightly floured board, shape each half into a long loaf about 1½ inches in diameter. Place loaves about 3 inches apart on a greased baking sheet; flatten each loaf to a thickness of about ½ inch. Bake in a 350° oven until firm to the touch (15 to 18 minutes).

Remove baking sheet from oven; cut hot loaves crosswise into about ½-inch-thick slices. Turn slices cut sides down and spread out slightly on baking sheets (you will need at least 2 baking sheets). Return to oven and continue to bake until cookies look dry and are lightly browned (about 10 more minutes). Transfer cookies to racks and let cool completely.

Prepare Lemon Icing; spread icing over about 1 inch of one end of each cookie. Let stand until icing is firm (about 15 minutes). Store airtight. Makes about 4½ dozen cookies.

Lemon Icing. In a small bowl, stir together 1 cup sifted **powdered sugar** and ½ teaspoon **grated lemon peel.** Stir in 1 to 1½ tablespoons **lemon juice,** using just enough to give icing a good spreading consistency.

Per cookie: 50 calories (28 percent from fat), 1 g protein, 8 g carbohydrates, 2 g total fat (0.6 g saturated fat), 6 mg cholesterol, 35 mg sodium

Cheesecake Cookies

You're craving cheesecake, but you don't want a whole piece? These tiny bites may be just the thing. Each buttery cookie is coated in crisp graham cracker crumbs and topped with a delectable cream cheese filling.

    1 cup (½ lb.) butter or margarine,
       at room temperature
    1 small package (3 oz.) cream
       cheese, at room temperature
    1 cup sugar
    1 egg, beaten
    1 teaspoon grated lemon peel
    1 tablespoon lemon juice
   2½ cups all-purpose flour
    1 teaspoon baking powder
       Cheese Filling (recipe follows)
   ½   cup graham cracker crumbs

In a large bowl, beat butter, cream cheese, and sugar until light and fluffy. Add egg, lemon peel, and lemon juice; stir until blended. Add flour and baking powder and stir until well blended. Cover and refrigerate until firm (about 1 hour). Meanwhile, prepare Cheese Filling.

Divide dough into 48 equal pieces. Shape each piece into a ball; then roll each ball in crumbs to coat all sides. Place balls about 2 inches apart on lightly greased baking sheets; flatten

each ball slightly. Make an indentation in top of each cookie (don't press all the way through to baking sheet) and fill with about ½ teaspoon Cheese Filling. Bake in a 325° oven until lightly browned (about 25 minutes). Transfer cookies to racks and let cool completely. Store airtight. Makes 4 dozen cookies.

Cheese Filling. In a small bowl, combine 1 small package (3 oz.) **cream cheese** (at room temperature), 2 tablespoons **sugar,** 1 **egg yolk,** 1 tablespoon **sour cream,** and ¼ teaspoon **grated lemon peel.** Beat until smooth.

Per cookie: 97 calories (51 percent from fat), 1 g protein, 11 g carbohydrates, 5 g total fat (3 g saturated fat), 23 mg cholesterol, 69 mg sodium

Almond Ravioli Cookies

Every December, cookies take center stage, both as party fare and for gift-giving—and bakers everywhere look for ways to make the most cookies with the least amount of effort. These almond-filled delights are perfect for big-batch baking. Using a streamlined shaping technique, you get more than 12 dozen cookies—all at once.

   2½ cups all-purpose flour
    1 teaspoon *each* baking soda
       and cream of tartar
    1 cup (½ lb.) butter or margarine,
       at room temperature
   1½ cups powdered sugar
    1 egg
    1 teaspoon vanilla
    6 ounces almond paste
       About ⅓ cup sliced almonds

In a medium-size bowl, mix flour, baking soda, and cream of tartar; set aside. In a large bowl, beat butter and sugar until creamy. Beat in egg and vanilla. Add flour mixture and beat until blended. Divide dough in half, wrap each half in plastic wrap, and refrigerate until firm (2 to 3 hours).

Work with one piece of dough at a time; keep remaining piece refrigerated until ready to use. Place dough between 2 pieces of wax paper (each about 20 inches long) and roll out to a 10- by 15-inch rectangle (if dough becomes too soft, refrigerate until firm). Peel off and discard top paper. With a pastry wheel or long-bladed knife, lightly mark dough into 1-inch squares. Place a small ball of almond paste (use about ¼ teaspoon for each cookie) in center of each square. Refrigerate dough while you roll out top layer.

Repeat rolling procedure for second piece of dough. Peel off and discard top paper; invert sheet of dough onto almond paste–topped dough. Peel off and discard paper. Gently press top layer of dough around mounds of filling. Flour a pastry wheel or knife and cut filled dough into 1-inch squares; then press edges together to seal. Place cookies about 1 inch apart on ungreased baking sheets. Press a sliced almond diagonally into center of each cookie.

Bake in a 350° oven until golden (10 to 12 minutes). Transfer cookies to racks and let cool completely. Store airtight. Makes 12½ dozen cookies.

Per cookie: 30 calories (50 percent from fat), 0.4 g protein, 3 g carbohydrates, 2 g total fat (0.8 g saturated fat), 5 mg cholesterol, 22 mg sodium

Orange Blossom Strawberry Pie

When we asked readers to send us their favorite fruit pie recipes in 1990, we received hundreds of replies. Berries of all kinds won out as the most popular pie fillings. In this simple summer pie, whole ripe strawberries are topped with a layer of orange-flavored berry glaze.

Pie Pastry (recipe follows); or purchased pastry shell for a single-crust 9-inch pie, baked and cooled

- ¾ cup sugar
- 3 tablespoons cornstarch
- 1 teaspoon grated orange peel
- 6 to 7 cups strawberries, hulled
- 6 tablespoons water
- 2 to 3 tablespoons orange-flavored liqueur or 2 tablespoons thawed frozen orange juice concentrate

Prepare Pie Pastry. On a lightly floured board, roll pastry out to a 12-inch round; fit into a 9-inch pie pan. Fold edges under to make pastry flush with pan rim; flute edges decoratively. Prick pastry all over with a fork to prevent puffing. Bake in a 425° oven until golden (12 to 15 minutes). Let cool.

In a 1- to 1½-quart pan, combine sugar, cornstarch, and orange peel. In a blender or food processor, whirl 2 cups of the least perfect strawberries with water until smoothly puréed. Stir purée into sugar mixture until blended. Bring to a boil, stirring often. Remove from heat; stir in liqueur.

Arrange remaining 4 to 5 cups strawberries, tips up, in baked pastry shell; evenly spoon hot berry glaze over whole berries, covering completely. Refrigerate until glaze is cool and set (at least 1 hour). If made ahead, cover and refrigerate until next day. Makes 8 servings.

Pie Pastry. In a large bowl, mix 1 cup plus 2 tablespoons **all-purpose flour** and ¼ teaspoon **salt.** With a pastry blender or 2 knives, cut in 6 tablespoons **solid vegetable shortening,** butter, or margarine until mixture resembles coarse crumbs. Sprinkle 2 to 3 tablespoons **cold water** over crumbs and stir until pastry holds together. Shape pastry into a ball.

Per serving: 283 calories (33 percent from fat), 3 g protein, 45 g carbohydrates, 10 g total fat (2 g saturated fat), 0 mg cholesterol, 70 mg sodium

Summer Apple Pudding-Pie

Though it bakes in a pie pan, this dessert is more like a dense cake, thickly dotted with walnuts and chunks of fresh apple. Serve it warm or cool, cut into wedges and topped with a dollop of whipped cream or ice cream.

- ½ cup all-purpose flour
- 1 teaspoon baking powder
- ½ teaspoon ground cinnamon
- ¼ teaspoon salt
- 1 egg
- ¾ cup sugar
- 1½ cups peeled, chopped apples
- ¾ cup chopped walnuts or almonds
  Sweetened whipped cream or vanilla ice cream (optional)

In a small bowl, mix flour, baking powder, cinnamon, and salt. In a large bowl, beat egg and sugar until well blended. Add flour mixture and stir until blended. Stir in apples and walnuts. Spread batter evenly in a greased 8- or 9-inch pie pan.

Bake in a 350° oven until cake is browned on top and center springs back when lightly touched (about 45 minutes). Serve warm or cool. To reheat, place in a 350° oven and heat, uncovered, for about 10 minutes. To serve, cut into wedges. Top each serving with whipped cream, if desired. Makes 8 servings.

Per serving: 200 calories (36 percent from fat), 3 g protein, 30 g carbohydrates, 8 g total fat (0.9 g saturated fat), 27 mg cholesterol, 138 mg sodium

Berry Tarts with Lemon Cream

Lovely to look at, these small-scale fruit tarts are nice for a summer dessert. The recipe makes three tarts, at a modest four servings each. To add color to your dessert tray, try topping each tart with a different kind of berry.

> **Miniature Pastry Shells (recipe follows)**
> 6 egg yolks
> 1 cup plus 2 tablespoons sugar
> 6 tablespoons lemon juice
> ¾ cup (¼ lb. plus ¼ cup) butter or margarine, cut into pieces
> 4½ to 6 cups raspberries, hulled strawberries, or blueberries (or some of each kind)

Prepare Miniature Pastry Shells and let cool.

In a medium-size pan, stir together egg yolks, sugar, lemon juice, and butter; cook over medium-low heat, stirring constantly, until butter is melted and mixture is thick. Remove from heat and let cool.

Remove pan rims from baked pastry shells; spread lemon mixture equally in shells. Arrange berries neatly over filling. Serve; or, if made ahead, cover and refrigerate for up to 4 hours and serve chilled. Makes 3 tarts (4 servings *each*).

Miniature Pastry Shells. In a food processor (or a large bowl), combine ½ cup **sugar** and ¾ cup (¼ lb. plus ¼ cup) **butter** or margarine. Whirl (or beat with an electric mixer) until creamy. Add 1 **egg yolk;** whirl (or beat) until blended. Then add 2 cups **cake flour** and whirl (or beat) until well blended. (At this point, you may cover and refrigerate pastry for up to 3 days.)

You will need 3 small tart pans with removable rims or 3 flan rings; pans or rings should be 6½ to 7½ inches in diameter and no deeper than 1½ inches. If using bottomless flan rings, cut cardboard rounds that just fit inside each ring; set aside.

Divide pastry into 3 equal portions; if pastry is too sticky to handle, refrigerate briefly. Place each portion in a tart pan or flan ring and press gently over bottom and sides (set flan rings on a baking sheet). Bake in a 325° oven until edges are lightly browned (25 to 30 minutes); let cool. To support flan-ring pastry shells, slide each shell onto a cardboard round before you remove the ring.

Per serving: 435 calories (53 percent from fat), 4 g protein, 48 g carbohydrates, 26 g total fat (15 g saturated fat), 186 mg cholesterol, 240 mg sodium

Pumpkin Tart

If you want to update your Thanksgiving dessert selections without throwing tradition out the window, you might try this spicy pumpkin tart. It has the rich flavor of classic pumpkin pie, but the crust is denser and the filling smoother and more custardy. A simple ginger cream, spooned liberally over the top, adds a delectable finish.

> **Tart Shell (recipe follows)**
> 1 can (about 1 lb.) pumpkin
> 1 large can (about 12 oz.) evaporated milk
> 2 eggs
> ¾ cup firmly packed brown sugar
> ½ cup sour cream
> 1 teaspoon ground cinnamon
> ½ teaspoon ground ginger
> ¼ teaspoon ground nutmeg
> **Warm Ginger Cream (recipe follows) or sweetened whipped cream**

Prepare Tart Shell; set aside.

In a large bowl, combine pumpkin, milk, eggs, sugar, sour cream, cinnamon, ginger, and nutmeg; beat with a wire whisk until blended. Pour pumpkin filling into baked pastry shell and bake in a 325° oven until filling jiggles only slightly in center when pan is gently shaken (about 40 minutes). Let cool. If made ahead, cover and refrigerate until next day.

Prepare Warm Ginger Cream. To serve, remove pan rim from tart; offer cream to spoon over individual servings. Makes 12 servings.

Tart Shell. In a food processor (or a large bowl), combine 2 cups **all-purpose flour**, ⅓ cup **sugar,** and ¾ cup (¼ lb. plus ¼ cup) **butter** or margarine, cut into chunks. Whirl (or rub with your fingers) until mixture resembles fine crumbs. Add 1 **egg;** whirl (or mix with a fork) until pastry holds together. Press pastry evenly over bottom and sides of a 12-inch tart pan with a removable rim. Bake on lowest rack of a 300° oven until pale golden (35 to 40 minutes).

Warm Ginger Cream. In a small pan, combine ½ cup **half-and-half** and ¼ cup slivered **crystallized ginger.** Cook over low heat, stirring constantly, until heated through (about 7 minutes); do not boil. Pour into a small serving dish and serve warm. Makes about ¾ cup.

Per serving of tart: 345 calories (45 percent from fat), 7 g protein, 42 g carbohydrates, 17 g total fat (10 g saturated fat), 97 mg cholesterol, 178 mg sodium

Per tablespoon of Warm Ginger Cream: 31 calories (33 percent from fat), 0.3 g protein, 5 g carbohydrates, 1 g total fat (0.7 g saturated fat), 4 mg cholesterol, 7 mg sodium

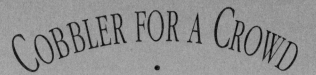
Homey and old-fashioned, cobblers are classic summertime desserts that lend themselves to infinite variation. The version we like best has a top crust only, lots of good fruit beneath, and tender, clear beads of tapioca to thicken the juices. Our recipe gives you plenty of flexibility: just use the chart to make a family-size dessert or one big enough for a picnic crowd.

Summer Fruit Cobbler

Using the chart at right, choose and prepare the fruit you want. Select a pan suited to the amount of fruit you are using; pour fruit into pan and crush about a fourth of it with a potato masher. Add specified amounts of sugar, tapioca, and lemon juice (if called for). Mix gently and let stand for at least 15 minutes or up to 1 hour, stirring occasionally; as fruit stands, juices form to soften tapioca.

Meanwhile, measure ingredients for Cream Cheese Pastry (see chart at right), using amounts appropriate for pan size. Place cream cheese, butter, and sugar in a bowl (or food processor) and beat with an electric mixer (or whirl) until well blended. Add flour and mix (or whirl) until well blended. Turn pastry out of bowl and pat into a 1-inch-thick round. Wrap in plastic wrap and refrigerate just until firm enough to roll easily (about 30 minutes).

On a lightly floured board, shape pastry into a square or rectangle. Roll out pastry 1 inch longer and 1 inch wider than pan. Fold pastry in half and lay on top of fruit in pan; then gently unfold over fruit. Fold rim of pastry under so folded edges are flush against pan sides; crimp edges. Cut a few slits in pastry to allow steam to escape.

Beat 1 **egg white** to blend; then brush lightly over pastry.

Bake cobbler in a 350° oven until pastry is golden brown (50 minutes to 1½ hours); set smaller pans in larger rimmed pans to catch any juice that bubbles over. Serve warm or cool. (The 11- by 17-inch cobbler takes about 8 hours to cool and thicken to the maximum.) If made ahead, cover and store at room temperature until next day. Serve cool; or place in a 350° oven and heat, uncovered, until warm in center (15 to 25 minutes). An 8-inch-square cobbler makes 6 servings; a 9- by 13-inch cobbler makes 12 servings; an 11- by 17-inch cobbler makes 24 servings.

Per serving of berry cobbler: 413 calories (28 percent from fat), 4 g protein, 73 g carbohydrates, 13 g total fat (8 g saturated fat), 36 mg cholesterol, 121 mg sodium

Per serving of blueberry cobbler: 370 calories (31 percent from fat), 4 g protein, 62 g carbohydrates, 13 g total fat (8 g saturated fat), 36 mg cholesterol, 129 mg sodium

Per serving of peach cobbler: 306 calories (37 percent from fat), 4 g protein, 46 g carbohydrates, 13 g total fat (8 g saturated fat), 36 mg cholesterol, 121 mg sodium

Per serving of plum cobbler: 378 calories (31 percent from fat), 4 g protein, 63 g carbohydrates, 14 g total fat (8 g saturated fat), 36 mg cholesterol, 121 mg sodium

Family-size or Crowd-size Summer Fruit Cobbler

FRUIT FILLING

Pan size	Fruit	Sugar	Quick-cooking tapioca	Lemon juice
BERRY (black, boysen, logan, olallie, raspberry)—rinse and drain fruit				
8-inch-square	5½ cups	1⅛ cups	3 tablespoons	
9- by 13-inch	2¾ quarts	2¼ cups	6½ tablespoons	
11- by 17-inch	5½ quarts	4½ cups	¾ cup	
BLUEBERRIES—rinse and drain fruit				
8-inch-square	5½ cups	¾ cup	3 tablespoons	1 tablespoon
9- by 13-inch	2¾ quarts	1½ cups	6 tablespoons	2 tablespoons
11- by 17-inch	5½ quarts	3 cups	¾ cup	¼ cup
PEACH—peel, pit, and thinly slice firm-ripe to soft-ripe fruit				
8-inch-square	5½ cups	⅓ cup	1½ tablespoons	1 tablespoon
9- by 13-inch	2¾ quarts	¾ cup	3 tablespoons	2 tablespoons
11- by 17-inch	5½ quarts	1½ cups	6 tablespoons	¼ cup
PLUM—rinse, pit, and thinly slice firm-ripe to soft-ripe fruit				
8-inch-square	5½ cups	¾ cup	3 tablespoons	
9- by 13-inch	2¾ quarts	1½ cups	6 tablespoons	
11- by 17-inch	5½ quarts	3 cups	¾ cup	

CREAM CHEESE PASTRY

Pan size	Cream cheese	Butter or margarine	Sugar	All-purpose flour
8-inch-square	1 small package (3 oz.)	2 tablespoons	2 teaspoons	½ cup
9- by 13-inch	2 small packages (3 oz. *each*)	½ cup (¼ lb.)	2 tablespoons	1½ cups
11- by 17-inch	3 small packages (3 oz. *each*)	¾ cup (¼ lb. plus ¼ cup)	3 tablespoons	2¼ cups

Pistachio & Grape Caramel Tart

In this unusual tart, a golden brown caramel glaze delicately cloaks juicy green grapes and crunchy pistachios.

> **Graham Cracker Crust (recipe follows)**
> 2 **cups seedless green grapes**
> 1 **cup shelled salted roasted pistachio nuts**
> 1 **cup sugar**
> ½ **cup water**
> **About 6 tablespoons whipping cream**
> 2 **teaspoons grated orange peel**

Prepare Graham Cracker Crust. Spread grapes evenly in baked crust; scatter pistachios evenly over grapes. Set aside.

In a small pan, stir together sugar and water. Cook over medium-low heat until sugar is dissolved and syrup is clear (15 to 18 minutes); do not stir. As syrup cooks, frequently wash down sugar crystals that form on pan sides with a wet pastry brush. When syrup is clear, increase heat to high and bring syrup to a boil. Then boil, uncovered, until syrup is golden brown (about 360°F on a candy thermometer)—5 to 7 minutes. Do not wash pan sides.

Remove syrup from heat and stir in 6 tablespoons of the cream; then stir in orange peel. Caramel should have the consistency of corn syrup. If it's too thick, add a little more cream; if it's too thin, return to low heat and stir until thickened. Pour warm caramel mixture evenly over grapes and pistachios in crust. Let cool until firm enough to cut (2 to 6 hours). Before serving, remove pan rim. Makes 8 to 10 servings.

Graham Cracker Crust. In a medium-size bowl, mix 1½ cups **graham cracker crumbs**, ¼ cup **sugar,** and 2 tablespoons **all-purpose flour.** Add 7 tablespoons **butter** or margarine (melted); stir until combined. Press mixture evenly over bottom and sides of a 9-inch tart pan with a removable rim. Bake in a 350° oven until crust turns a slightly darker brown (about 15 minutes). Let cool. If made ahead, cover and refrigerate until next day.

Per serving: 409 calories (44 percent from fat), 5 g protein, 54 g carbohydrates, 20 g total fat (8 g saturated fat), 35 mg cholesterol, 277 mg sodium

---

Colorado Peach Cream Pie

This creamy fresh peach pie is among our favorite reader contributions. Tapioca is the secret ingredient, giving the filling a pleasantly dense, rich texture.

> **Pie Pastry (page 201); or purchased pastry shell for a single-crust 9-inch pie, unbaked**
> ¾ **cup sugar**
> 3½ **tablespoons quick-cooking tapioca**
> ½ **teaspoon vanilla**
> ¼ **teaspoon ground nutmeg**
> ½ **cup whipping cream**
> 6 **cups peeled, sliced firm-ripe peaches**
> ¼ **cup sliced almonds**

Prepare Pie Pastry. On a lightly floured board, roll pastry out to a

12-inch round; fit into a 9-inch pie pan. Fold edges under to make pastry flush with pan rim; flute edges decoratively. Set aside.

In a small bowl, stir together sugar and tapioca. Stir in vanilla, nutmeg, and cream. Let stand for 15 minutes to soften tapioca. Pour peaches into pastry shell, then pour cream mixture evenly over peaches. Set pie pan in a foil-lined 10- by 15-inch rimmed baking pan.

Bake on lowest rack of a 375° oven until filling is bubbly and lightly browned and crust is golden brown (45 to 50 minutes). If crust begins to darken excessively, drape it with foil. About 5 minutes before pie is done, sprinkle almonds over top. Serve warm or cool. If made ahead, let cool; then cover and refrigerate until next day. Makes 8 servings.

Per serving: 352 calories (40 percent from fat), 4 g protein, 51 g carbohydrates, 16 g total fat (5 g saturated fat), 17 mg cholesterol, 74 mg sodium

Italian Plum Pie

Enclosed in flaky pastry, sweet and juicy prune plums bake to tenderness. You can leave the top crust solid or, for a fancier presentation, weave thin strips of pastry in a lattice pattern.

> **Double recipe of Pie Pastry (page 201); or purchased pastry shells for a double-crust 9-inch pie, unbaked**
> **About 2 pounds prune plums**
> 1¼ **cups sugar**
> ⅛ **teaspoon** *each* **salt and ground cinnamon**
> 2 **teaspoons grated orange peel**
> ¼ **cup quick-cooking tapioca**
> 2 **tablespoons butter or margarine**

Prepare a double recipe of Pie Pastry (you will need 5 to 7 tablespoons water). Set aside.

Cut plums into quarters or sixths and remove pits (you should have 4 cups fruit). In a medium-size bowl, combine plums, sugar, salt, cinnamon, orange peel, and tapioca; stir until blended. Set aside.

Divide pastry in half. On a lightly floured board, roll out one half to a 12-inch round; fit into a 9-inch pie pan. Pour plum mixture into pastry shell and dot with butter. Roll remaining pastry out to a 10-inch round. Place pastry round over filling and cut a few slits in it to allow steam to escape (or cut round into ½-inch-wide strips and weave a lattice over filling). Trim and seal pastry edges; flute decoratively.

Bake pie in a 400° oven until crust is golden brown (about 30 minutes). If edges of crust begin to darken excessively before center is brown, drape edges with foil. Serve warm or cooled. Makes 8 servings.

Per serving: 540 calories (37 percent from fat), 5 g protein, 83 g carbohydrates, 23 g total fat (7 g saturated fat), 8 mg cholesterol, 201 mg sodium

Lemon Ribbon–layered Meringue Pie

Ribbons of lemon custard alternate with layers of vanilla ice cream in an unusual version of old-fashioned lemon meringue pie.

Pie Pastry (page 201); or purchased pastry shell for a single-crust 9-inch pie, baked and cooled

- 6 **tablespoons butter or margarine**
  Grated peel of 1 lemon
- ⅓ **cup lemon juice**
- ⅛ **teaspoon salt**
- 1 **cup sugar**
- 2 **eggs**
- 2 **egg yolks**
- 1 **quart vanilla ice cream, slightly softened**
- 3 **egg whites**
- 6 **tablespoons sugar**

Prepare Pie Pastry. On a lightly floured board, roll pastry out to a 12-inch round; fit into a 9-inch pie pan. Fold edges under to make pastry flush with pan rim; flute edges decoratively. Prick pastry all over with a fork to prevent puffing. Bake in a 425° oven until golden (12 to 15 minutes). Let cool.

Melt butter in a medium-size pan over low heat. Stir in lemon peel, lemon juice, salt, and the 1 cup sugar. In a bowl, lightly beat eggs and egg yolks to blend; add to lemon mixture. Cook, beating with a wire whisk, until thick and smooth; do not boil. Remove from heat; let cool.

Spoon half the ice cream into baked pastry shell, spreading to make an even layer; freeze, uncovered, until firm. Spread half the cooled lemon custard over ice cream and freeze, uncovered, until firm. Repeat layers to use remaining ice cream and custard, freezing after each addition.

In a small bowl, beat egg whites with an electric mixer or a wire whisk until they hold distinct but moist peaks. Gradually add the 6 tablespoons sugar, beating until meringue holds soft peaks that curl slightly. Swirl meringue over custard, sealing it to edges of crust. Place pie on a baking sheet and bake in a 475° oven until meringue is lightly browned (about 2 minutes). Serve at once. Makes 8 servings.

Per serving: 534 calories (47 percent from fat), 8 g protein, 65 g carbohydrates, 28 g total fat (13 g saturated fat), 159 mg cholesterol, 289 mg sodium

Lemon Cake Pie

A long-time favorite, this cakelike lemon pie was featured in *Sunset*'s very first "Kitchen Cabinet" back in 1929. We reprinted the recipe in 1979, celebrating 50 years of the column's popularity.

Pie Pastry (page 201); or purchased pastry shell for a single-crust 9-inch pie, unbaked

- 1½ **cups sugar**
- 2 **tablespoons butter or margarine, melted**
- ⅓ **cup all-purpose flour**
- ¼ **teaspoon salt**
- ½ **teaspoon grated lemon peel**
- 5 **tablespoons lemon juice**
- 3 **eggs, separated**
- 1¼ **cups milk**

Prepare Pie Pastry. On a lightly floured board, roll pastry out to a 12-inch round; fit into a 9-inch pie pan. Fold edges under to make pastry flush with pan rim; flute edges decoratively. Set aside.

In a medium-size bowl, stir together sugar and butter. Stir in flour, salt, lemon peel, and lemon juice. In a small bowl, beat egg yolks with milk until well blended; stir into lemon mixture. In another medium-size bowl, beat egg whites with an electric mixer or a wire whisk until they hold distinct but moist peaks. Gently fold whites into lemon mixture. Pour filling into pastry shell.

Bake on lowest rack of a 375° oven until top is browned and center jiggles only slightly when pan is gently shaken (45 to 55 minutes). If crust begins to brown excessively, drape it with foil. Let cool before serving. If made ahead, cover and refrigerate for up to 6 hours. Makes 8 servings.

Per serving: 391 calories (36 percent from fat), 6 g protein, 57 g carbohydrates, 16 g total fat (6 g saturated fat), 93 mg cholesterol, 209 mg sodium

Pear or Apple Crisp

This recipe appeared in a 1949 issue of *Sunset*—and over 40 years later, it's still one of our favorite fruit desserts. Pears or apples are lightly spiced with cinnamon and nutmeg, then baked beneath a layer of buttery crumbs.

- 4 medium-size Anjou pears, Bartlett pears, or Golden Delicious apples (about 2¼ lbs. *total*), peeled, cored, and sliced
- 1 teaspoon ground cinnamon
- ¼ teaspoon ground nutmeg
- 1 teaspoon lemon juice
- ½ cup water
- 1 cup sugar
- ¾ cup all-purpose flour
- ½ cup (¼ lb.) butter or margarine
  Whipping cream (optional)

Place pears in a greased 8-inch-square baking pan. Sprinkle with cinnamon, nutmeg, lemon juice, and water; mix lightly.

In a medium-size bowl, mix sugar and flour. Using a pastry blender or 2 knives, cut in butter until mixture resembles coarse crumbs; evenly scatter crumbs over pear mixture.

Bake in a 350° oven until fruit is tender when pierced and crust is lightly browned (about 1 hour). Offer cream to pour over individual servings, if desired. Makes 4 servings.

Per serving: 622 calories (34 percent from fat), 4 g protein, 104 g carbohydrates, 24 g total fat (14 g saturated fat), 62 mg cholesterol, 236 mg sodium

Graham Cracker Houses

Easy-to-assemble graham cracker houses are a wonderful idea for a holiday party for kids. They're a time-saving alternative to the traditional gingerbread houses; a simple sugar icing cements the crackers together and holds the decorations in place. To apply the frosting, use mock pastry bags made from sandwich-size resealable plastic bags.

If you like, you can assemble the houses yourself, then let the children decorate them. For each guest, provide one house and a bag of icing; have bowls of candy, pretzels, and/or cereal to use as decorations.

- **Royal Icing (recipe follows)**
- **About 2 packages (about 1 lb. *each*) graham crackers**
- **Decorations such as candies, pretzels, cereal, colored sugar, and chocolate sprinkles**

Prepare Royal Icing. When ready to use, cut tip off one corner of each bag of icing to make a ⅛-inch hole.

Assemble each graham cracker house on an 8- by 11-inch foil-covered cardboard base. A house requires 6 double crackers. Use 2 for house sides and 2 for roof. To create peaked roofs, cut top half of each of the 2 remaining crackers into a triangle with point at top of cracker, using a long knife and a swift motion (these 2 crackers will be the house front and back). Glue crackers together with icing by squeezing icing from plastic "pastry" bags along cracker sides, then holding crackers together until icing is firm. Use icing to glue desired decorations onto each house. If made ahead, store, uncovered, at room temperature for up to 3 days. (Colored candies used to decorate houses may bleed color onto icing.) Makes 6 to 8 houses.

Royal Icing. In a large bowl, beat 2 **egg whites,** ⅛ teaspoon **cream of tartar,** and 2 teaspoons **water** until frothy. Gradually add 2½ to 3 cups **powdered sugar,** blending until mixture is smooth and resembles a stiff paste. Spoon icing equally into 6 to 8 sandwich-size unpleated resealable plastic bags; seal airtight. Use at once or refrigerate until next day. Each batch makes enough icing to assemble and decorate 6 to 8 houses.

Per house without decorations: 491 calories (13 percent from fat), 6 g protein, 102 g carbohydrates, 7 g total fat (2 g saturated fat), 0 mg cholesterol, 452 mg sodium

Sour Cream Pound Cake

Sour cream and plenty of butter and eggs give this big bundt cake its richness and fine-grained texture. You might serve thin slices of the cake with fruit and sorbet or with a drizzling of Raspberry Coulis (page 209).

- 6 eggs, separated
- 2½ cups granulated sugar
- 1 cup (½ lb.) butter or margarine, at room temperature
- ½ teaspoon ground mace or ground nutmeg
- ¼ teaspoon baking soda
- 3 cups cake flour
- 1 cup sour cream
  Powdered sugar (optional)

In a large bowl, beat egg whites with an electric mixer or a wire whisk until foamy. Gradually add ½ cup of the granulated sugar, beating just until mixture holds soft peaks that curl slightly; set aside.

In another large bowl, beat butter and remaining 2 cups granulated sugar until creamy. Add egg yolks, one at a time, beating well after each addition. Stir in mace and baking soda. Alternately add flour and sour cream, about a third at a time, beating until smooth after each addition. Fold in egg white mixture until blended. Pour batter into a greased and floured 10-inch bundt pan or plain tube pan.

Bake in a 300° oven until a wooden pick inserted in center comes out clean (about 1½ hours). Let cake cool in pan on a rack for 5 minutes; then turn out onto rack to cool completely. If desired, dust with powdered sugar shortly before serving. Makes 16 to 18 servings.

Per serving: 340 calories (42 percent from fat), 4 g protein, 45 g carbohydrates, 16 g total fat (9 g saturated fat), 110 mg cholesterol, 159 mg sodium

No-fat Chocolate Cake

This mouthwatering cake's rich flavor is deceptive—the dessert is made entirely without fat. Whipped egg whites and nonfat yogurt lighten up the batter.

    Vegetable oil cooking spray
    Cake flour
1 cup sifted cake flour
⅓ cup unsweetened cocoa
1 teaspoon *each* baking soda and baking powder
6 egg whites
1⅓ cups firmly packed brown sugar
1 cup plain nonfat yogurt
1 teaspoon vanilla
    Powdered sugar

Spray an 8-inch-square baking pan with cooking spray, dust with flour, and set aside. In a small bowl, mix the 1 cup flour, cocoa, baking soda, and baking powder; set aside. In a large bowl, beat egg whites, brown sugar, yogurt, and vanilla until blended. Add flour mixture; beat until evenly moistened. Pour batter into baking pan.

Bake in a 350° oven until center of cake springs back when lightly touched (30 to 40 minutes). Let cake cool in pan on a rack for 15 minutes; then turn out onto a serving plate. Sift

powdered sugar over cake (if desired, use a doily as a stencil for powdered sugar pattern). Serve warm or cool. If made ahead, let cool; then cover and refrigerate for up to 2 days. Makes 8 servings.

Per serving: 222 calories (4 percent from fat), 6 g protein, 49 g carbohydrates, 1 g total fat (0.4 g saturated fat), 0.6 mg cholesterol, 293 mg sodium

Blueberry– White Chocolate Cake on a Cookie Crust

Blueberries and white chocolate add color and flavor to a cream cheese cake baked on a spicy crumb crust. If you like, use milk chocolate in place of the white variety.

    Cookie Crust (recipe follows)
1 large package (8 oz.) cream cheese, at room temperature
1 cup granulated sugar
1 teaspoon vanilla
2 eggs
1½ cups all-purpose flour
2 teaspoons baking powder
2 cups fresh or frozen unsweetened blueberries
½ cup coarsely chopped white chocolate or milk chocolate
    Powdered sugar

Prepare Cookie Crust; set aside.

In a large bowl, beat cream cheese, granulated sugar, and vanilla with an electric mixer until blended. Beat in eggs, flour, and baking powder. Stir in blueberries and chocolate. Spread batter evenly over baked crust.

Bake in a 350° oven until cake is dark golden and center springs back when lightly touched (about 50 minutes). Let cool in pan on a rack for at least 30 minutes before serving. To serve, dust with powdered sugar and cut into 3-inch squares. Makes 9 servings.

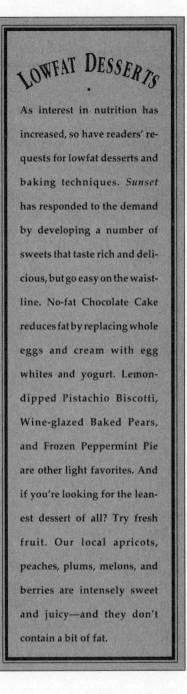

Cookie Crust. In a bowl, mix 2 cups crushed **vanilla wafers**, ¼ cup **sugar**, and ½ teaspoon **ground cinnamon**. Add 6 tablespoons **butter** or margarine (melted); stir until combined. Press over bottom of a 9-inch-square baking pan. Bake in a 350° oven until lightly browned (about 15 minutes).

Per serving: 532 calories (41 percent from fat), 7 g protein, 73 g carbohydrates, 24 g total fat (13 g saturated fat), 104 mg cholesterol, 342 mg sodium

Sacher Torte

Vienna is famous for *Sachertorte,* a dense chocolate cake centered with a thin ribbon of preserves. This version of the dessert is slightly moister and lighter than the original.

- **2 ounces unsweetened chocolate**
- **3 tablespoons salad oil**
- **¼ teaspoon salt**
- **½ cup hot strong coffee**
- **1 cup sugar**
- **1 egg**
- **¼ cup buttermilk**
- **1 teaspoon *each* baking soda and vanilla**
- **1 cup all-purpose flour**
  Chocolate Glaze (recipe follows)
- **½ cup apricot preserves**
- **2 tablespoons brandy or 1 teaspoon brandy extract**

In top pan of a double boiler set over simmering water, combine chocolate, oil, salt, and coffee; heat, stirring occasionally, until chocolate is melted and mixture is smooth. Pour into a large bowl. Add sugar, egg, buttermilk, baking soda, and vanilla; beat with an electric mixer on medium speed until well blended. Gradually add flour and continue to beat for 5 more minutes. Pour into a greased and floured 8-inch cake pan.

Bake in a 350° oven just until cake begins to pull away from sides of pan (about 30 minutes; do not overbake). Let cake cool in pan on a rack, then turn out onto rack to cool completely. (At this point, you may wrap cake airtight and freeze for up to 1 week. Unwrap and thaw at room temperature before continuing.)

Prepare Chocolate Glaze. Using a long serrated knife, cut cake in half horizontally to make 2 thin layers. Stir together preserves and brandy; spread evenly over bottom layer of cake. Set top layer in place and place cake on a rack set over a sheet of wax paper. Slowly pour Chocolate Glaze onto center of cake so it flows over entire surface. With a spatula, guide glaze down over sides of cake to coat smoothly. Refrigerate until glaze is set (at least 30 minutes).

Using a wide spatula, loosen cake from rack and gently slide onto a serving plate. If made ahead, cover loosely and refrigerate for up to 6 hours; bring to room temperature before serving. Makes about 10 servings.

Chocolate Glaze. In top pan of a double boiler set over simmering water, combine 5 ounces **semisweet chocolate** and 4 teaspoons **solid vegetable shortening;** heat, stirring, until melted and smooth. Remove from heat (and water); let cool slightly.

Per serving: 338 calories (37 percent from fat), 3 g protein, 52 g carbohydrates, 14 g total fat (6 g saturated fat), 21 mg cholesterol, 198 mg sodium

Caramel-Pecan Oatmeal Cake

A sticky caramel topping laden with coconut and pecans broils right on top of this spicy oatmeal cake.

- **1½ cups all-purpose flour**
- **1 teaspoon *each* baking soda and ground cinnamon**
- **½ teaspoon salt**
- **¼ teaspoon ground nutmeg**
- **1 cup quick-cooking rolled oats**
- **1½ cups boiling water**
- **½ cup (¼ lb.) butter or margarine, at room temperature**
- **1 cup *each* granulated sugar and firmly packed brown sugar**
- **2 tablespoons molasses**
- **2 eggs**
  Caramel Topping (recipe follows)

In a small bowl, mix flour, baking soda, cinnamon, salt, and nutmeg;

set aside. Place oats in another small bowl. Pour boiling water over oats and let cool to lukewarm.

In a large bowl, beat butter, granulated sugar, and brown sugar until creamy. Beat in molasses, eggs, and oat mixture. Gradually add flour mixture, beating until well blended. Spread batter evenly in a greased and floured 9-inch-square baking pan. Bake in a 350° oven until center of cake springs back when lightly touched (about 50 minutes).

While cake is baking, prepare Caramel Topping. When cake is done, spread topping evenly over it; broil 4 inches below heat until topping is browned. Let cool. Makes 12 servings.

Caramel Topping. In a small pan, combine 6 tablespoons **butter** or margarine, ¾ cup firmly packed **brown sugar,** and 3 tablespoons **half-and-half;** cook over medium heat, stirring constantly, until butter is melted. Add 1 cup *each* **sweetened flaked coconut** and chopped **pecans.** Bring to a boil; boil, stirring, for 1 minute.

Per serving: 507 calories (41 percent from fat), 5 g protein, 71 g carbohydrates, 24 g total fat (11 g saturated fat), 73 mg cholesterol, 372 mg sodium

WESTERN CLASSIC
Kona Torte

Macadamias are undeniably expensive—but macadamia fans agree that the nut's rich flavor is well worth the price! Here, a buttery pastry shell holds a luscious filling of whole macadamias in caramel.

2½ cups (about ¾ lb.) salted roasted
macadamia nuts

2¾ cups all-purpose flour

2½ cups sugar

1 cup (½ lb.) butter or margarine,
cut into chunks

1 egg

1 cup whipping cream

1 egg white, lightly beaten
Salted roasted macadamia nuts
Sweetened whipped cream

Rub the 2½ cups macadamia nuts in
a towel to remove salt; lift nuts from
towel and set aside.

In a food processor (or a bowl),
combine flour and ½ cup of the sugar.
Add butter; whirl (or rub with your
fingers) until mixture resembles
fine crumbs. Add egg and whirl (or
stir with a fork) until pastry holds
together. Shape pastry into a ball.

Press two-thirds of the pastry
evenly over bottom and up sides of
a 9-inch spring-form pan. Cover and
refrigerate. Place remaining pastry
between 2 sheets of wax paper and
roll out to a 9-inch round. Refrigerate
flat until firm.

In a wide nonstick frying pan, heat
remaining 2 cups sugar over medium-
high heat, tilting and shaking pan
often, until sugar melts and turns a
pale amber color (about 6 minutes);
watch closely, since sugar scorches
easily. Pour in cream; caramelized
sugar will harden. Cook, stirring,
until mixture is melted and smooth.
Remove from heat; stir in the 2½ cups
nuts. Let cool for 10 to 20 minutes,
then spoon into pastry shell.

Peel off one sheet of wax paper
from pastry round and invert pastry
over nut filling. Peel off remaining
paper. If necessary, fold edge of pastry
under to make flush with pan rim;
press with tines of a flour-dipped fork
to seal. Brush pastry with egg white.

Bake in a 325° oven until golden
brown (about 1 hour). Let cool on a
rack for 10 to 20 minutes. Run a sharp
knife between torte and pan rim to
loosen torte; remove pan rim and let
torte cool completely. If made ahead,
store airtight at room temperature
for up to 2 days. To serve, garnish
with macadamia nuts; then cut into
thin wedges. Offer whipped cream to
spoon over individual servings. Makes
14 to 16 servings.

*Per serving: 532 calories (57 percent from fat), 5 g
protein, 54 g carbohydrates, 34 g total fat (13 g
saturated fat), 65 mg cholesterol, 237 mg sodium*

Raspberry Torte

When this recipe was created in 1967,
feather-light freezer tortes were a
popular conclusion to elegant dinner
parties. Hostesses still favor these
desserts today—they taste great, look
impressive, and can be made well
ahead. When raspberries are in season, you might top this lovely torte
with a sweet-tart berry purée.

2 packages (about 10 oz. *each*)
frozen sweetened raspberries,
thawed; or 2½ cups fresh
raspberries plus sugar to taste

1¼ cups sugar

⅓ cup water

1 teaspoon light corn syrup

4 egg whites

2 tablespoons kirsch (optional)

2 cups whipping cream

1 package (about 3 oz.) ladyfingers (about 12 double
ladyfingers)
Raspberry Coulis (optional;
recipe follows)

In a blender, whirl thawed raspberries
(or 2½ cups fresh raspberries) until
smoothly puréed. Pour into a strainer
set over a bowl. Rub purée through
strainer; discard seeds. Measure purée
(you should have 2 cups); add sugar
to taste, if desired.

In a small pan, combine the 1¼
cups sugar, water, and corn syrup.
Bring to a boil over high heat; boil
until temperature registers 238°F (soft
ball stage) on a candy thermometer.

While sugar syrup is boiling, place
egg whites in a large bowl and beat
with an electric mixer until whites
hold soft peaks. Then gradually beat
in hot syrup. Continue to beat on high
speed until mixture has cooled to
room temperature (about 8 minutes).
Fold in raspberry purée and kirsch (if
desired) just until blended. In another
large bowl, beat cream to soft peaks;
fold into raspberry mixture.

Butter sides of a 9-inch spring-form
pan. Split ladyfingers; line sides of
pan with split ladyfingers. Pour in
raspberry mixture. Cover and freeze
until firm (at least 8 hours) or for up to
2 weeks. Meanwhile, prepare Raspberry Coulis, if desired. Before serving, remove pan rim; serve torte with
Raspberry Coulis, if desired. Makes
12 servings.

Raspberry Coulis. In a blender, whirl
4 cups (about 1 lb.) **fresh or thawed
frozen unsweetened raspberries**
until smoothly puréed. Pour into a
strainer set over a bowl. Rub purée
through strainer; discard seeds. Stir
in 1 tablespoon **sugar.** Cover and
refrigerate until ready to use or for up
to a day. Stir before using. Makes
about 1¾ cups.

*Per serving of torte: 284 calories (42 percent from
fat), 3 g protein, 39 g carbohydrates, 14 g total fat (8 g
saturated fat), 71 mg cholesterol, 45 mg sodium*

*Per tablespoon of Raspberry Coulis: 10 calories (7
percent from fat), 0.1 g protein, 2 g carbohydrates, 0.1
g total fat (0 g saturated fat), 0 mg cholesterol, 0 mg
sodium*

Butter Kuchen

Old-fashioned German-style fruit kuchen—a thin, buttery cake decorated with a colorful baked-on fruit topping—is an ideal way to present your favorite summer fruits. We suggest using plums or nectarines, but you can experiment with other choices as well.

  ½ **cup (¼ lb.) butter or margarine, at room temperature**
  ½ **cup sugar**
  3 **eggs**
  ½ **teaspoon vanilla**
  1 **cup all-purpose flour**
     Fruit Topping (choices and directions follow)

In a small bowl, beat butter and sugar with an electric mixer until creamy. Add eggs, one at a time, beating well after each addition. Add vanilla and flour; beat until blended. Spread batter evenly in a greased and floured 10- or 11-inch cake or tart pan with a removable rim. Arrange fruit over batter as directed for topping of your choice.

Bake in a 375° oven until center of cake feels firm when lightly touched (about 40 minutes). Let cake cool in pan on a rack for at least 30 minutes. Before serving kuchen, remove pan rim. Makes 10 to 12 servings.

Fruit Topping. Choose one of the following 2 toppings.

Plum. Halve and pit 14 to 16 **prune plums.** Arrange halves, cut side up, over surface of **Butter Kuchen** batter, placing them close together. Sprinkle fruit evenly with 2 to 3 tablespoons **sugar,** then bake and cool as directed for **Butter Kuchen.** Dust surface liberally with **powdered sugar** 30 minutes before serving (this gives sugar time to dissolve on fruit, making a distinctive pattern on cake).

Nectarine. Peel, pit, and thinly slice 3 large **nectarines;** mix fruit with ¼ teaspoon **ground nutmeg.** Arrange slices, overlapping slightly, in concentric circles over surface of **Butter Kuchen** batter. Sprinkle evenly with 1½ to 2 tablespoons **sugar.** Bake as directed for **Butter Kuchen.** While cake is still warm, brush top lightly with 2 tablespoons **orange marmalade** (warmed). Let cool, then serve.

Per serving with plums: 245 calories (36 percent from fat), 4 g protein, 37 g carbohydrates, 10 g total fat (6 g saturated fat), 81 mg cholesterol, 104 mg sodium

Per serving with nectarines: 211 calories (42 percent from fat), 3 g protein, 28 g carbohydrates, 10 g total fat (6 g saturated fat), 81 mg cholesterol, 103 mg sodium

Tiramisù

When energy flags in the afternoon, this Italian chocolate-coffee-rum dessert makes a superb reviver (the name literally means "pick-me-up"). Or conclude a dinner party with tiramisù and give everybody's sweet tooth a jolt. We provide two recipes for the filling—one made with raw eggs, the other with cooked ones.

     Rum Cream or Egg-safe Rum Cream (recipes follow)
     Hot Espresso (directions follow)
  1 **package (about 3 oz.) ladyfingers (about 12 double ladyfingers)**
  1 **ounce bittersweet or semisweet chocolate, finely chopped or grated**

Prepare Rum Cream and Hot Espresso; set aside.

Arrange ladyfingers, side by side, in bottom of a deep 9-inch quiche dish or shallow 1- to 1½-quart baking dish. Drizzle with espresso; let cool. Top with Rum Cream and sprinkle with chocolate. Cover and refrigerate for at least 1 hour or until next day. Scoop out individual servings with a spoon. Makes 6 to 8 servings.

Rum Cream. In a small bowl, beat 3 **egg whites** with an electric mixer or a wire whisk until foamy. Gradually add 2 tablespoons **sugar;** beat until whites hold distinct but moist peaks. In another bowl, beat 3 **egg yolks** with 1 tablespoon **sugar** until thick and frothy. Beat in 8 ounces **mascarpone** or cream cheese (at room temperature) and 2 to 3 tablespoons **rum.** Fold in egg whites.

Egg-safe Rum Cream. In top pan of a double boiler set over simmering water, whisk together 4 **egg yolks** and ¼ cup *each* **sugar** and **water.** Cook, whisking constantly, just until mixture registers 160°F on a candy thermometer and is thick and frothy (3 to 5 minutes). Remove from heat (and water) and let cool for 5 minutes.

In a small bowl, beat 8 ounces **mascarpone** or cream cheese (at room temperature) with 3 tablespoons **rum** until smooth. Fold in egg mixture.

Hot Espresso. Place ½ cup **freshly ground espresso or dark-roast coffee** in a filter-lined cone over a 2-cup glass measure. Pour 1⅓ cups **boiling water** over coffee; let stand until all water has dripped through. Use hot.

Per serving with Rum Cream: 275 calories (65 percent from fat), 6 g protein, 18 g carbohydrates, 19 g total fat (2 g saturated fat), 179 mg cholesterol, 56 mg sodium

Per serving with Egg-safe Rum Cream: 285 calories (66 percent from fat), 4 g protein, 19 g carbohydrates, 20 g total fat (2 g saturated fat), 209 mg cholesterol, 34 mg sodium

Carrot Cake

Professional bakers and home cooks alike have been turning out carrot cake for many years. Our favorite version of the moist, spicy cake gives you a choice: you can use a sheet pan and spread the cake with the traditional cream cheese frosting, or bake the same cake in a bundt pan and drizzle it with an orange glaze.

- 2 cups sugar
- 1 cup salad oil
- 1 teaspoon vanilla
- 4 eggs
- 2 cups all-purpose flour
- 2 teaspoons *each* baking powder and ground cinnamon
- 1½ teaspoons baking soda
- 2 cups lightly packed shredded carrots
- 1 can (about 8 oz.) crushed pineapple, drained
- ½ cup chopped walnuts
  Cream Cheese Frosting or Orange Glaze (recipes follow)

In a medium-size bowl, stir together sugar, oil, and vanilla. Beat in eggs, one at a time. Stir in flour, baking powder, cinnamon, and baking soda. Add carrots, pineapple, and walnuts; stir just until blended. Pour batter into a greased and floured 9- by 13-inch baking pan or 10-inch bundt pan.

Bake in a 350° oven until a wooden pick inserted in center comes out clean and cake starts to pull away from sides of pan (about 45 minutes if using a 9- by 13-inch pan, about 55 minutes if using a bundt pan). Let sheet cake cool in pan on a rack; let bundt cake cool in pan on a rack for 15 minutes, then turn out onto rack to cool completely. While cake is cooling, prepare Cream Cheese Frosting (for sheet cake) or Orange Glaze (for bundt cake). Frost cooled sheet cake; drizzle bundt cake with glaze. Makes 12 to 15 servings.

Cream Cheese Frosting. In a small bowl, combine 2 small packages (3 oz. *each*) **cream cheese** (at room temperature); 6 tablespoons **butter** or margarine (at room temperature); 1 teaspoon **grated orange peel** (optional); 1 teaspoon **vanilla;** and 2 cups sifted **powdered sugar.** Beat until smooth.

Orange Glaze. In a small bowl, combine 2 cups sifted **powdered sugar,** 3 tablespoons **orange juice,** 1 teaspoon **grated orange peel,** and 1 teaspoon **vanilla.** Stir until smoothly blended.

Per serving of sheet cake: 528 calories (49 percent from fat), 5 g protein, 63 g carbohydrates, 29 g total fat (8 g saturated fat), 87 mg cholesterol, 316 mg sodium

Per serving of bundt cake: 445 calories (41 percent from fat), 5 g protein, 63 g carbohydrates, 21 g total fat (3 g saturated fat), 61 mg cholesterol, 230 mg sodium

Persimmon Pudding

Cakelike persimmon pudding, served steaming hot from the oven, is a special treat for crisp fall evenings. This recipe, featured in a 1968 article on persimmons, includes a rich citrus sauce for a tangy finishing touch.

  About 3 ripe persimmons
- 2 teaspoons baking soda
- 1 egg, beaten
- ½ cup milk
- 1 teaspoon lemon juice
- ½ teaspoon vanilla
- 1 tablespoon butter or margarine, melted
- 1 cup *each* sugar and sifted all-purpose flour
- 1 teaspoon ground cinnamon
  Dash of salt
- ½ cup *each* raisins and chopped pecans
  Rich Lemon Sauce (recipe follows)

Scoop pulp from persimmons; discard skins, stems, and seeds. In a blender or food processor, whirl persimmon pulp until smoothly puréed (you should have about 1 cup). In a small bowl, stir together persimmon purée and 1 teaspoon of the baking soda; let stand for 5 minutes.

In a large bowl, combine egg, milk, lemon juice, vanilla, and butter. In a small bowl, mix sugar, flour, cinnamon, salt, and remaining 1 teaspoon baking soda. Add flour mixture to egg mixture alternately with persimmon mixture, blending well after each addition. Stir in raisins and pecans. Pour batter into a greased and floured 8-inch-square baking pan.

Bake in a 350° oven until browned (about 55 minutes). When pudding is almost done, prepare Rich Lemon Sauce. Let pudding cool in pan for 5 minutes, then cut into about 2½-inch squares. Offer sauce to spoon over individual servings. Makes 9 servings.

Rich Lemon Sauce. In a small pan, beat ¼ cup **butter** or margarine (at room temperature), 1 cup **sugar,** and 2 tablespoons **all-purpose flour** until well blended. Gradually stir in 1¼ cups **boiling water.** Then add 1 teaspoon **grated lemon peel** and a dash of **ground nutmeg.** Bring to a boil, stirring; boil for 3 minutes. Remove from heat and add 3 tablespoons **lemon juice;** stir until smoothly blended. Makes about 1½ cups.

Per serving of pudding: 240 calories (24 percent from fat), 3 g protein, 44 g carbohydrates, 7 g total fat (2 g saturated fat), 29 mg cholesterol, 323 mg sodium

Per tablespoon of Rich Lemon Sauce: 52 calories (32 percent from fat), 0.1 g protein, 9 g carbohydrates, 2 g total fat (1 g saturated fat), 5 mg cholesterol, 20 mg sodium

Holiday Gem Fruitcake

Fruitcake recipes vary widely; some are almost solid fruit, while others are a bit cakier. In 1979, we featured three reader-contributed fruitcakes. This version—combining a variety of fruits and whole nuts with just enough batter to bind them—was the overwhelming favorite.

- ½ **pound (about 1⅓ cups) golden or dark raisins**
- ½ **pound (about 1½ cups)** *each* **pitted prunes and pitted dates, cut into halves**
- ½ **pound (about 1 cup) red or green candied cherries**
- ½ **pound candied pineapple wedges**
- ¼ **pound (about 1 cup)** *each* **whole Brazil nuts and whole blanched almonds**
- ¼ **pound (about 1 cup) pecan halves, cashews, or hazelnuts**
- ¼ **pound (about 1 cup) dried apricots, chopped**
- 1¼ **cups all-purpose flour**
- 5 **eggs**
- 3 **tablespoons light or dark rum, brandy, or apple juice**
- ½ **teaspoon salt**
- 1½ **teaspoons vanilla**
- 1¼ **cups firmly packed light or dark brown sugar**
- ⅓ **to ¾ cup light or dark rum or brandy (optional)**

In a large bowl, combine raisins, prunes, dates, cherries, pineapple, Brazil nuts, almonds, pecans, and apricots. Sprinkle ½ cup of the flour over all and stir until combined.

Line bottom of a greased 10-inch tube pan with parchment paper; grease paper. In a medium-size bowl, beat eggs until blended. Add the 3 tablespoons rum, salt, vanilla, sugar, and remaining ¾ cup flour; beat until blended. Pour over fruit mixture and stir until well blended. Spoon batter into pan; press batter down slightly with spoon.

Bake in a 300° oven until a wooden pick inserted in center of cake comes out clean (about 1½ hours). Let cool in pan on a rack; then turn out onto a platter and peel off paper. If made ahead, wrap airtight and refrigerate for up to 3 weeks. If desired, sprinkle top of cake with about 2 tablespoons rum once or twice a week while storing. Makes 16 to 18 servings.

Per serving: 462 calories (26 percent from fat), 7 g protein, 82 g carbohydrates, 14 g total fat (2 g saturated fat), 63 mg cholesterol, 105 mg sodium

Spiced Pumpkin Roll

Pumpkin desserts are traditional for Thanksgiving. If you're looking for a new one, try this pretty treat: you bake a moist pumpkin cake in a thin layer, then roll it jelly-roll style around a filling of almond or vanilla ice cream. Each slice is a tempting swirl of cake and smooth cream.

- ¾ **cup all-purpose flour**
- 2 **teaspoons ground cinnamon**
- 1 **teaspoon** *each* **baking powder and ground ginger**
- ½ **teaspoon** *each* **salt and ground nutmeg**
- 3 **eggs**
- 1 **cup granulated sugar**
- ⅔ **cup canned pumpkin**
- **Powdered sugar**
- 1 **quart toasted almond or vanilla ice cream, slightly softened**

Line bottom of a greased 10- by 15-inch rimmed baking pan with wax paper; grease paper.

In a small bowl, mix flour, cinnamon, baking powder, ginger, salt, and nutmeg; set aside. In a large bowl, beat eggs with an electric mixer on high speed until thick and lemon-colored. Gradually beat in granulated sugar. On low speed, beat in pumpkin, then flour mixture, until well blended. Spread batter evenly in pan. Bake in a 375° oven until center of cake springs back when lightly touched (about 15 minutes).

When cake is done, immediately turn it out of pan onto a towel sprinkled with powdered sugar. Peel off wax paper. Beginning at a long side, roll up cake and towel jelly-roll style; let cool completely. Unroll cake and remove towel; spread cake with ice cream and reroll to enclose ice cream. Wrap airtight and freeze until firm. Before serving, let stand at room temperature for 10 to 15 minutes; dust with powdered sugar. Cut crosswise into slices. Makes 8 to 10 servings.

Per serving: 288 calories (27 percent from fat), 5 g protein, 48 g carbohydrates, 9 g total fat (5 g saturated fat), 97 mg cholesterol, 250 mg sodium

Pumpkin Cheesecake

The basic cheesecake base—a simple blend of cream cheese, sugar, and eggs—lends itself readily to adaptation and experimentation. In this recipe, pumpkin and spices give the mild filling a new dimension.

- **Graham Cracker Crust (recipe follows)**
- 2 **large packages (8 oz.** *each***) cream cheese, at room temperature**
- ¾ **cup firmly packed brown sugar**

1 can (about 1 lb.) pumpkin
2 teaspoons pumpkin pie spice
2 eggs
  Sweetened whipped cream
  Pecan halves

Prepare Graham Cracker Crust; set aside.

In a large bowl, beat cream cheese and sugar with an electric mixer until blended. Beat in pumpkin and pumpkin pie spice. Add eggs and beat until smoothly blended. Pour filling into baked crust.

Bake in a 350° oven until filling jiggles only slightly in center when pan is gently shaken (about 50 minutes). Let cool on a rack; then cover lightly and refrigerate for at least 3 hours or until next day. Before serving, remove pan rim and garnish cheesecake with whipped cream and pecans. Makes 8 servings.

Graham Cracker Crust. In a medium-size bowl, mix 1¾ cups **graham cracker crumbs** and 2 tablespoons **sugar.** Add 3 tablespoons **butter** or margarine (melted); stir until combined. Press mixture evenly over bottom and about 1 inch up sides of a 9-inch spring-form pan or cake pan with a removable rim. Bake in a 350° oven until lightly browned (about 10 minutes). Let cool.

Per serving: 469 calories (52 percent from fat), 8 g protein, 49 g carbohydrates, 27 g total fat (16 g saturated fat), 127 mg cholesterol, 394 mg sodium

Chocolate Cookie Cheesecake

A New York–style cheesecake loaded with chocolate sandwich cookies is a sweet-lover's dream come true. If the batter is thin, as it will be if made in a food processor, the cookies will float up to make a bumpy-looking top. A thicker batter (made with an electric

mixer) keeps the cookies in the middle of the cheesecake.

1 package (about 1¼ lbs.) chocolate sandwich cookies
⅓ cup butter or margarine, melted
4 large packages (8 oz. *each*) cream cheese, cut into chunks
1 cup sugar
⅓ cup whipping cream
6 eggs
2 tablespoons all-purpose flour
2 teaspoons vanilla

In a food processor, whirl half the cookies (including filling) to form fine crumbs. (Or place cookies in a paper or plastic bag; crush with a rolling pin.) Mix in butter. Press crumb mixture evenly over bottom and ½ inch up sides of a 9-inch spring-form pan or cake pan with a removable rim. Refrigerate until firm (about 20 minutes).

In a food processor (or a large bowl), combine cream cheese, sugar, and whipping cream. Whirl (or beat with an electric mixer) until smooth. Add eggs, flour, and vanilla; whirl (or beat) until blended.

Pour half the cream cheese filling over chilled crust. Break remaining cookies in half and scatter over filling. Pour remaining filling over cookies. If filling was prepared in a food processor, it will be thin enough to allow cookies to float to top during baking; if prepared with an electric mixer, it will keep cookies in place.

Bake in a 300° oven until cheesecake is golden on top and filling jiggles only slightly in center when pan is gently shaken (about 1 hour and 20 minutes). Let cool on a rack. Then cover and refrigerate until cold (at least 4 hours) or until next day. Before serving, run a knife between cake and pan rim; remove pan rim. Makes 12 to 16 servings.

Per serving: 565 calories (61 percent from fat), 10 g protein, 46 g carbohydrates, 39 g total fat (20 g saturated fat), 180 mg cholesterol, 510 mg sodium

Flan

A classic dessert that's served from the Mideast to northern Europe and in former Spanish colonies everywhere, *flan* is a simple baked custard crowned with caramel sauce.

⅓ cup sugar
6 eggs
6 tablespoons sugar
1 teaspoon vanilla
2 cups whole milk

In a medium-size nonstick frying pan, heat the ⅓ cup sugar over medium-high heat, tilting and shaking pan often, until sugar melts and turns a pale amber color (about 8 minutes); watch closely, since sugar scorches easily. Immediately pour caramel syrup into a round 1-quart baking dish, tilting dish to coat bottom and ½ inch of sides. Place dish in a larger pan, such as an 8- or 9-inch-square baking pan; set aside.

In a medium-size bowl, beat eggs, the 6 tablespoons sugar, and vanilla until blended but not frothy. Stir in milk. Pour egg mixture into caramel-coated dish. Pour boiling water into larger pan to a depth of about 1 inch. Bake on middle rack of a 350° oven until custard jiggles only slightly in center when dish is gently shaken (about 40 minutes). Lift custard from hot water and let cool on a rack; then cover and refrigerate until cold (at least 2 hours) or for up to 2 days.

To serve, run a knife between flan and dish. Invert a rimmed serving plate over dish; hold plate and dish together and quickly invert both. Caramel syrup will flow over flan. Lift off dish. Cut flan into wedges; spoon caramel over each serving. Makes 6 servings.

Per serving: 217 calories (32 percent from fat), 9 g protein, 28 g carbohydrates, 8 g total fat (3 g saturated fat), 224 mg cholesterol, 103 mg sodium

ICE CREAMS & SORBETS

Where desserts are concerned, refreshingly cool ice creams, sorbets, and fruit ices are high on the list of Western favorites. And now more than ever before, there's a tremendous assortment from which to choose. Some swear by intensely rich Italian *gelato*, while others remain loyal to the traditional ice creams that have been popular for so many years. And nutrition-minded ice-cream aficionados stick to simple ices and sorbets.

The following recipes run the gamut from light to luscious, fruity to chocolaty. Sample gelato in a range of flavors, from plain vanilla to hazelnut to banana. Try mocha ice cream topped with liqueur and crushed coffee beans. Or, for something lighter, enjoy a frosty scoop of Ginger-Peach Ice or Fresh Berry Sorbet.

Gelato

- 3 cups milk
- ¾ cup sugar
- 3 strips lemon peel (yellow part only), *each* about 2 inches long
- ½ vanilla bean (a 2- to 3-inch piece); or 1 teaspoon vanilla extract (if preparing vanilla gelato, see directions under Gelato Flavoring, at right)
- 6 egg yolks
  Gelato Flavoring (choices and directions follow)

To make gelato base, in a 3- to 4-quart pan, combine milk, sugar, lemon peel, and vanilla bean (if using vanilla extract, add later, as directed). Cook over medium heat, stirring often, just until sugar is dissolved.

In a medium-size bowl, beat egg yolks lightly with a wire whisk. Gradually whisk in 1 cup of the hot milk mixture; then pour egg mixture into pan, whisking constantly. Cook, stirring constantly, until custard thickens slightly and smoothly coats the back of a metal spoon (about 8 minutes); do not bring to scalding or custard will curdle. Pour custard through a fine wire strainer set over a large bowl. Discard lemon peel; rinse vanilla bean, let dry, and reserve for other uses. If using vanilla extract, add at this point. Let gelato base cool, then cover and refrigerate until cold (at least 1½ hours) or until next day.

Prepare Gelato Flavoring of your choice. In a large bowl, stir 1 cup of the gelato base into flavoring; then gradually stir in remaining gelato base.

Pour mixture into container of an ice cream maker and freeze according to manufacturer's directions. Serve soft; or spoon into a container, cover, and freeze for up to 3 weeks. Makes about 1½ quarts (about 1 quart vanilla gelato).

Gelato Flavoring. Choose one of the following flavorings.

Almond. Spread 1 cup **sliced almonds** in a shallow baking pan and toast in a 350° oven, stirring occasionally, until lightly browned (5 to 8 minutes). Place almonds in a food processor, add ¼ cup crushed **almond macaroons,** and whirl to form a smooth paste. If made ahead, cover and refrigerate for up to 1 week; bring to room temperature before using.

Per ½ cup: 171 calories (45 percent from fat), 5 g protein, 19 g carbohydrates, 9 g total fat (2 g saturated fat), 115 mg cholesterol, 34 mg sodium

Banana. Smoothly mash or purée 3 medium-size ripe **bananas** with 3 tablespoons **lemon juice.** Use at once.

Per ½ cup: 143 calories (29 percent from fat), 4 g protein, 22 g carbohydrates, 5 g total fat (2 g saturated fat), 115 mg cholesterol, 35 mg sodium

Chocolate. Place 1 large package (about 12 oz.) **semisweet chocolate chips** and 1 cup **unsweetened cocoa** in top pan of a double boiler set over simmering water. Stir in ½ cup **hot strong coffee;** then stir until chocolate is melted. Use at once.

Per ½ cup: 268 calories (41 percent from fat), 6 g protein, 38 g carbohydrates, 14 g total fat (7 g saturated fat), 115 mg cholesterol, 35 mg sodium

Hazelnut. Spread 1½ cups **hazelnuts** in a baking pan and toast in a 350° oven until fragrant and pale golden brown beneath skins (about 10 minutes). Pour nuts into a wire mesh colander; set colander in a sink and rub nuts with a clean dishtowel to remove as much of skins as possible. Lift out nuts and place in a food processor; whirl to form a smooth paste.

Per ½ cup: 207 calories (57 percent from fat), 5 g protein, 18 g carbohydrates, 14 g total fat (3 g saturated fat), 115 mg cholesterol, 34 mg sodium

Vanilla. Use 2 whole **vanilla beans** (*each* about 6 inches long) in gelato base instead of ½ bean; split beans lengthwise and scrape seeds from pods. Add seeds and pods to milk as directed. Or omit vanilla beans and add 1 tablespoon vanilla extract after straining gelato base.

Per ½ cup: 178 calories (35 percent from fat), 5 g protein, 24 g carbohydrates, 7 g total fat (3 g saturated fat), 172 mg cholesterol, 50 mg sodium

Mocha Ice Cream

- 2½ cups sugar
- 1 cup unsweetened cocoa
- 2 cups *each* milk and strong coffee
- 6 egg yolks
- 4 cups whipping cream
- 4 teaspoons vanilla
- ½ cup coffee-flavored liqueur
  Coffee-flavored liqueur and coarsely crushed coffee beans (optional)

In a large pan, combine sugar, cocoa, milk, and coffee. Cook over medium-high heat, stirring often, just until mixture comes to a boil (about 5 minutes).

In a medium-size bowl, beat egg yolks lightly with a wire whisk. Gradually whisk in 1 cup of the hot milk mixture; then pour egg mixture into pan, whisking constantly. Cook over medium-high heat, stirring constantly, until custard thickens slightly and smoothly coats the back of a metal spoon (about 15 minutes). Remove from heat; let cool to lukewarm.

Add cream, vanilla, and the ½ cup liqueur to custard. Pour into a 1-gallon ice cream maker and freeze according to manufacturer's directions. Serve soft; or spoon into a container, cover, and freeze for up to 3 weeks. If desired, offer coffee-flavored liqueur and crushed coffee beans to top individual servings. Makes about 1 gallon.

Per ½ cup: 187 calories (53 percent from fat), 2 g protein, 20 g carbohydrates, 11 g total fat (7 g saturated fat), 75 mg cholesterol, 20 mg sodium

Ginger-Peach Ice

1½ cups water
½ cup sugar
2 tablespoons minced crystallized ginger
1 cup champagne, sparkling wine, or sparkling apple juice
3 tablespoons peach-flavored liqueur
   Mint sprigs (optional)

In a small pan, combine water, sugar, and 1 tablespoon of the ginger; bring to a boil over high heat, stirring constantly. Remove from heat and let cool; add champagne and liqueur. Cover and refrigerate until cold.

Pour mixture into a shallow 8- or 9-inch-square metal pan; cover and freeze until solid (at least 2 hours) or for up to 1 month. Break into small chunks with a heavy spoon; then whirl in a food processor or beat with an electric mixer until a smooth slush forms (if mixture is too slushy, freeze until firm). If made ahead, cover and freeze for up to 1 month; whirl in a food processor or beat with an electric mixer before serving. Serve in chilled glasses; garnish with remaining 1 tablespoon ginger and mint sprigs, if desired. Makes 6 to 8 servings.

Per serving: 111 calories (0 percent from fat), 0 g protein, 20 g carbohydrates, 0 g total fat (0 g saturated fat), 0 mg cholesterol, 5 mg sodium

Fresh Berry Sorbet

4 cups hulled strawberries or raspberries
½ cup water
1 tablespoon lemon juice
   About ½ cup sugar, or to taste

In a food processor or blender, whirl berries until smoothly puréed. Pour purée into a strainer set over a bowl. Rub purée through strainer; discard seeds. Return purée to food processor and add water, lemon juice, and sugar; whirl until sugar is dissolved (about 5 seconds). Pour into a shallow metal pan, cover, and freeze until solid.

Remove ice from freezer and break into chunks with a heavy spoon. In a food processor, whirl ice, about a third at a time, until a smooth slush forms; use on-off bursts at first to break up ice, then whirl continuously. (Or place all ice in a large bowl and continue to break into small pieces with a heavy spoon. Then beat with an electric mixer until smooth, beating slowly at first, then gradually increasing mixer speed.) Pour into a bowl, cover, and freeze for at least 1 hour or for up to 3 weeks.

Before serving, let ice soften at room temperature for about 10 minutes. Makes about 3½ cups.

Per ½ cup: 82 calories (3 percent from fat), 0.5 g protein, 20 g carbohydrates, 0.3 g total fat (0 g saturated fat), 0 mg cholesterol, 1 mg sodium

Pineapple Sorbet

Peel and core 1 medium-size ripe **pineapple** (about 4 lbs.), then cut into chunks. In a food processor or blender, whirl chunks, half at a time, until puréed; you should have 4 cups total. Pour purée into a bowl and stir in 1 cup **water,** 2 tablespoons **lemon juice,** and ⅓ cup **sugar** (or to taste). Freeze and serve as directed for **Fresh Berry Sorbet.** Makes about 5 cups.

Per ½ cup: 72 calories (5 percent from fat), 0.4 g protein, 18 g carbohydrates, 0.4 g total fat (0 g saturated fat), 0 mg cholesterol, 2 mg sodium

Lemon Sorbet

Using a vegetable peeler, pare thin outer layer of peel (colored part only) from 1 small **lemon;** cut peel into ½-inch pieces. In a food processor or blender, whirl peel with 1 cup **sugar** until finely chopped. Add 1 cup **very hot water** and whirl until sugar is dissolved. Add 3 cups **cold water** and ⅔ cup **lemon juice.** Whirl to blend, then freeze and serve as directed for **Fresh Berry Sorbet.** Makes about 5 cups.

Per ½ cup: 81 calories (0.4 percent from fat), 0.1 g protein, 21 g carbohydrates, 0 g total fat (0 g saturated fat), 0 mg cholesterol, 4 mg sodium

Peach-Blueberry Crackle Brûlée

At *Sunset*, we've created numerous variations of crème brûlée. This impressive version combines smooth vanilla custard, fresh ripe fruit, and a lacy, golden topping of brittle caramel.

    5 eggs
 1¼ cups sugar
 1¼ cups milk
 1¼ cups whipping cream or half-and-half
    1 teaspoon grated lemon peel
 1½ teaspoons vanilla
    ½ teaspoon almond extract
    ¼ cup orange-flavored liqueur
    2 medium-size firm-ripe peaches
    1 tablespoon lemon juice
    ¼ cup fresh blueberries; or ¼ cup frozen unsweetened blueberries, thawed and drained

In a medium-size bowl, beat eggs and ¾ cup of the sugar until blended but not frothy. Stir in milk, cream, lemon peel, vanilla, almond extract, and liqueur.

Place a shallow 10-inch-round 1½-quart baking dish, such as a quiche or pie dish, in a larger pan (such as a roasting pan). Pour egg mixture into dish; pour boiling water into larger pan to a depth of about ½ inch.

Bake on middle of rack of a 350° oven until custard jiggles only slightly in center when dish is gently shaken (about 18 minutes). Lift custard from hot water and let cool on a rack; then cover and refrigerate for at least 1 hour or until next day.

Peel and halve peaches; cut each half into 4 wedges. Discard pits. In a small bowl, combine peaches and lemon juice; turn to coat peaches. Drain off lemon juice. Arrange peaches on custard, leaving a 1-inch border of custard. Scatter blueberries over peaches.

About 15 minutes before serving, place remaining ½ cup sugar in a medium-size nonstick frying pan. Heat over medium-high heat, tilting and shaking pan often, until sugar melts and turns a pale amber color (about 8 minutes); watch closely, since sugar scorches easily. Immediately remove from heat.

Tilt pan to pool caramel syrup on one side. Stir slowly with a long-handled metal teaspoon until syrup is thickened (1½ to 2 minutes).

Working quickly, pour syrup from spoon in a thin stream, crisscrossing fruit and custard to create a lacy topping; use all the syrup. Let stand for about 3 minutes to let caramel syrup harden.

To serve, break through caramel topping with a spoon; then spoon out fruit and custard onto dessert plates. Makes 6 to 8 servings.

Per serving: 389 calories (43 percent from fat), 7 g protein, 47 g carbohydrates, 18 g total fat (10 g saturated fat), 205 mg cholesterol, 82 mg sodium

Orange Omelet-Soufflé with Warm Strawberries

Airy as any soufflé but easier to make, this dish features a light froth of beaten eggs and sugar baked in a buttery citrus sauce. Served with warm berries and cool cream, it makes a showy dessert for a simple meal—or a marvelous brunch entrée.

    Warm Strawberries (recipe follows)
    9 eggs, separated
    ¾ cup sugar
    3 tablespoons all-purpose flour
    ¾ teaspoon grated orange peel
    6 tablespoons butter or margarine
    ½ cup orange juice
    ½ cup whipping cream
    ½ cup sour cream

Prepare Warm Strawberries and set aside. In a large bowl, beat egg whites with an electric mixer or a wire whisk until foamy. Gradually add 9 tablespoons of the sugar, beating until whites hold soft peaks that curl slightly. (Do not overbeat or underbeat, or soufflé may separate and have a custardlike layer.)

In a small bowl, beat egg yolks until blended. Add flour and ½ teaspoon of the orange peel; beat until mixture is thick and lemon-colored. Gently fold yolk mixture into whites.

Melt butter in a 10- to 12-inch ovenproof frying pan over medium heat. Stir in remaining 3 tablespoons sugar, orange juice, and remaining ¼ teaspoon orange peel. Cook, stirring occasionally, until sauce bubbles vigorously; remove from heat. At once, gently slide large spoonfuls of egg mixture into hot sauce.

Bake in a 350° oven until omelet-soufflé is lightly browned on top, set around edges, and jiggles only slightly in center when pan is gently shaken (9 to 10 minutes for a 12-inch pan, 13 to 15 minutes for a 10-inch pan). If you prefer a firmer texture, bake for 3 to 5 more minutes.

While omelet-soufflé is baking, beat whipping cream to soft peaks; fold into sour cream. Also reheat Warm Strawberries.

Serve omelet-soufflé at once; spoon portions into bowls or plates, spooning down to pan bottom to ladle out some of the orange sauce with each

portion. Serve with strawberries and whipped cream–sour cream topping. Makes 4 to 6 servings.

Warm Strawberries. Melt 2 tablespoons **butter** or margarine in a wide frying pan over medium heat. Stir in 2 tablespoons **sugar**, ½ teaspoon **grated orange peel**, and ½ cup **orange juice.** Heat, stirring occasionally, until bubbly; then gently stir in 3 cups hulled, sliced **strawberries** and remove from heat.

Per serving: 618 calories (57 percent from fat), 14 g protein, 53 g carbohydrates, 40 g total fat (22 g saturated fat), 469 mg cholesterol, 323 mg sodium

Frozen Peppermint Pie

At *Sunset*, we're always looking for ways to lighten up our old favorites. This frozen pie, though still somewhat of a splurge, uses yogurt instead of ice cream to help cut fat. If you can't find peppermint-flavored frozen yogurt, whirl ½ cup hard peppermint candies with ¼ cup water in a blender or food processor until smooth; then fold the mixture into slightly softened vanilla frozen yogurt. Refreeze before continuing.

Chocolate Cookie Crust (recipe follows)

½ gallon peppermint-flavored or vanilla frozen yogurt, slightly softened

3 egg whites

1 cup marshmallow cream
2 teaspoons vanilla
1 ounce unsweetened chocolate, chopped
¼ cup sugar
¾ cup water
2 teaspoons arrowroot

Prepare Chocolate Cookie Crust. Spoon yogurt into baked crust, spreading smoothly and mounding toward center. Freeze until hard (at least 2 hours).

In a medium-size bowl, beat egg whites with an electric mixer or a wire whisk until they hold distinct but moist peaks. Then beat in marshmallow cream, a large spoonful at a time, until whites hold soft peaks that curl slightly; stir in vanilla.

Swirl meringue over yogurt, sealing to edges of crust. Bake in a 450° oven until meringue is lightly browned (2 to 3 minutes). Return to freezer at once for at least 1 hour (if holding for more than 24 hours, wrap pie airtight once it is frozen).

In a small bowl, combine chocolate and sugar. In a small pan, blend water smoothly with arrowroot. Bring to a boil, stirring constantly; then pour over chocolate-sugar mixture and stir until smooth.

Pour chocolate mixture into a small pitcher and serve warm. If made ahead, let cool; then cover and refrigerate until next day. Reheat before serving.

To serve, unwrap pie if it's wrapped; then let stand at room temperature for about 15 minutes. Cut into wedges, using a sharp knife dipped often in hot water. Offer chocolate sauce to pour over individual servings. Makes 8 to 10 servings.

Chocolate Cookie Crust. In a food processor or with a rolling pin, finely crush enough **crisp chocolate-flavored cookies** (such as cocoa biscotti) to make 1½ cups crumbs. In a small bowl, beat 1 **egg white** with a wire whisk until frothy; stir into crumbs.

Lightly coat a 9-inch pie pan with **vegetable oil cooking spray,** then dust lightly with **all-purpose flour.** Press crumb mixture firmly and evenly over bottom and sides of pan. Bake in a 325° oven until crust feels dry and firm when lightly pressed (about 20 minutes). Let crust cool, then refrigerate for at least 30 minutes or up to 2 hours; wrap airtight for longer storage.

Per serving: 340 calories (16 percent from fat), 10 g protein, 60 g carbohydrates, 6 g total fat (1 g saturated fat), 9 mg cholesterol, 240 mg sodium

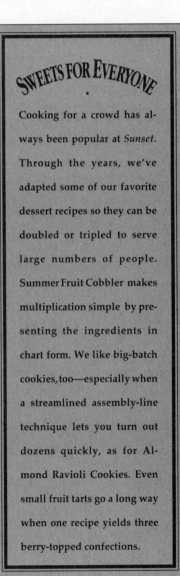

SWEETS FOR EVERYONE

Cooking for a crowd has always been popular at *Sunset*. Through the years, we've adapted some of our favorite dessert recipes so they can be doubled or tripled to serve large numbers of people. Summer Fruit Cobbler makes multiplication simple by presenting the ingredients in chart form. We like big-batch cookies, too—especially when a streamlined assembly-line technique lets you turn out dozens quickly, as for Almond Ravioli Cookies. Even small fruit tarts go a long way when one recipe yields three berry-topped confections.

Chocolate-Coffee Freezer Torte

Who could resist this spectacular combination of flavors? A crisp coconut cookie shell holds layers of chocolate and coffee ice cream, studded with crunchy chunks of toffee and drizzled with chocolate syrup. We first featured this delectable torte in the 1960s, and it's been winning compliments ever since.

- 1 **cup finely crushed crisp coconut macaroon cookies**
- 2 **tablespoons butter or margarine, melted**
- 1 **pint chocolate ice cream, slightly softened**
- ½ **cup chocolate-flavored syrup**
- 1 **pint coffee ice cream, slightly softened**
  About 4 ounces chocolate-covered hard toffee candy bars, coarsely chopped

In a small bowl, stir together crushed cookies and butter. Press mixture evenly over bottom of a 9-inch cake pan with a removable rim. Bake in a 350° oven until lightly browned (8 to 10 minutes). Let cool.

Spread chocolate ice cream evenly over baked crust; drizzle evenly with ¼ cup of the syrup and freeze until firm. Then top evenly with coffee ice cream, sprinkle evenly with chopped candy, and drizzle with remaining ¼ cup syrup. Cover and freeze until firm. Makes 6 to 8 servings.

Per serving: 401 calories (43 percent from fat), 5 g protein, 55 g carbohydrates, 20 g total fat (10 g saturated fat), 53 mg cholesterol, 210 mg sodium

Cherries Jubilee

Dark sweet cherries, flamed with brandy and spooned from a chafing dish over cold ice cream, have provided a finishing touch to romantic dinners for years. You can make the sauce ahead, then flame it at the table for an impressive presentation.

This recipe is designed to serve two, but you'll probably have enough cherry sauce left over to top slices of sponge-cake or cheesecake. Or, for a special breakfast treat, use the cherries to top Dutch Baby Pancakes (page 59).

- 1 **can (about 1 lb.) pitted dark sweet cherries**
- 1 **tablespoon cornstarch**
- 2 **tablespoons sugar**
  Dash *each* **of salt and ground cinnamon**
- 1 **tablespoon lemon juice**
  Vanilla ice cream
- ¼ **cup brandy, warmed**

Drain cherries, reserving ½ cup of the syrup. In a chafing dish, fondue pot, or small pan, combine cornstarch, reserved ½ cup syrup, sugar, salt, and cinnamon. Bring to a boil over high heat (use highest heat for fondue pot or chafing dish). Boil, stirring constantly, until mixture is clear and thickened. Remove pan from heat and stir in lemon juice and cherries. (At this point, you may cover and refrigerate until next day; reheat before continuing.)

Place a scoop of ice cream in each of 2 individual serving dishes. Pour brandy into a large spoon or long-handled metal cup. Move to an open area, away from exhaust fans and flammable items; then ignite brandy. Pour brandy over warm cherry sauce; pour flaming sauce over ice cream. Makes 2 servings.

Per serving (without ice cream): 290 calories (1 percent from fat), 1 g protein, 56 g carbohydrates, 0.4 g total fat (0.1 g saturated fat), 0 mg cholesterol, 75 mg sodium

Wine-glazed Baked Pears

After taking a trip through Italy's countryside in 1988, one *Sunset* food editor created this super-simple version of a popular Italian dessert. Glazed with a combination of sugar and red wine, the tender baked pears were an instant hit with both our readers and our staff.

- 8 **medium-size firm-ripe Bosc or Bartlett pears (about 4½ lbs.** *total***)**
- 1⅓ **cups dry red wine**
- ½ **cup sugar**

If necessary, trim bottoms of pears so fruit will stand upright. Then set pears upright in a shallow 2- to 2½-quart baking pan (they should fit snugly). Pour wine over pears; sprinkle with ¼ cup of the sugar.

Bake in a 425° oven for 45 minutes. Baste pears with pan juices and sprinkle with remaining ¼ cup sugar. Continue to bake, basting occasionally with pan juices, until pears are richly browned and tender when pierced (15 to 30 more minutes). If most of the juice evaporates and pears begin to brown before they're tender, add a few tablespoons of water; you should have about ½ cup juice left in pan when pears are done. Serve warm or cool. Makes 8 servings.

Per serving: 190 calories (4 percent from fat), 1 g protein, 49 g carbohydrates, 0.9 g total fat (0 g saturated fat), 0 mg cholesterol, 2 mg sodium

Given an elegant final touch, even the simplest dessert can make a lovely and lasting impression. A cloud of feather-light chocolate curls brings majestic flourish to a plain frosted cake; a tiny sugared violet or a carefully placed sliver of candied orange peel transforms an unadorned wedge of pie or cheesecake into something grand. And a scoop of ice cream goes from merely tasty to tantalizing when it's topped with a spoonful of fruit sauce or a sprinkling of candied nuts.

Easy Chocolate Curls

1 or more large bars (3 to 4 oz. *each*) semisweet, white, milk, or bittersweet chocolate without nuts or filling

Unwrap chocolate; then place, scored side down, on an 8- by 10-inch sheet of parchment paper or foil. Microwave chocolate on paper, uncovered, on **HIGH (100%)** for 15 to 40 seconds or until edges of chocolate give slightly when gently pressed. Or, to use a conventional oven, place chocolate on paper or foil on oven rack in a 150° oven; heat, uncovered, until edges give slightly when gently pressed (1 to 1½ minutes).

Using a vegetable peeler, peel chocolate towards you along its thickest edge to make a curl. With tip of peeler, lift each curl to a flat surface to cool and firm. If chocolate is too firm to curl smoothly, microwave on **HIGH (100%)** for 5 to 10 seconds at a time or heat in a conventional oven at 150° for 30 seconds. If made ahead, store airtight at room temperature for up to 1 week. Makes about 2 cups.

Per ¼ cup: 59 calories (50 percent from fat), 0.5 g protein, 8 g carbohydrates, 4 g total fat (2 g saturated fat), 0 mg cholesterol, 2 mg sodium

Candied Orange Peel

4 oranges
7 cups water
¼ cup sugar
2 tablespoons orange-flavored liqueur

Pare thin outer layer of peel (colored part only) from oranges with a vegetable peeler. Then cut peel into very thin slivers. In a medium-size pan, combine peel and 3 cups of the water. Bring to a boil over high heat, then drain. Add 3 cups more water to peel; bring to a boil again, then drain again.

Add sugar and remaining 1 cup water to peel. Bring to a boil; boil until syrup has almost evaporated and big bubbles form (about 10 minutes). Do not scorch. Remove from heat and stir in liqueur. Let cool. If made ahead, cover and refrigerate until next day. Makes about 1 cup.

Per tablespoon: 37 calories (0.8 percent from fat), 0.2 g protein, 9 g carbohydrates, 0.1 g total fat (0 g saturated fat), 0 mg cholesterol, 0 mg sodium

Dessert Sauces

A sweet sauce is a great finish for a scoop of ice cream or a slice of plain cake. Use your own favorite recipes, or try **Raspberry Coulis** (page 209), **Rich Lemon Sauce** (page 211), or **Cherries Jubilee** (facing page).

Sugared Flowers

1 cup small edible flowers or petals, such as violets, nasturtiums, pansies, or rose petals (be sure the flowers you use are pesticide-free)
2 egg whites
2 teaspoons water
1 cup sugar

Rinse flowers and pat dry. Place egg whites and water in a shallow dish and beat lightly to blend. Place sugar in another shallow dish. Working with one flower at a time, hold flower by stem (or petals by an edge) and dip into egg whites; then dip into sugar, scooping sugar over flower to coat evenly. Carefully lift out flower, set petal side up, and let dry. Repeat procedure for each flower; gently shake off excess. Store airtight at room temperature for up to 3 days. Makes about 1 cup.

Per tablespoon: 34 calories (0.3 percent from fat), 0.3 g protein, 8 g carbohydrates, 0 g total fat (0 g saturated fat), 0 mg cholesterol, 4 mg sodium

Candied Walnuts

¼ cup sugar
2 tablespoons water
1 cup walnut halves

Place sugar in a medium-size nonstick frying pan. Heat over medium-high heat, tilting and shaking pan often, until sugar melts and turns a pale amber color (about 8 minutes); watch closely, since sugar scorches easily. Add water (syrup will harden); cook, stirring, until melted again. Add walnuts and stir until evenly coated with syrup. Spread nuts in a single layer on greased foil; let cool. Store airtight. Makes 1 cup.

Per ¼ cup: 209 calories (63 percent from fat), 4 g protein, 17 g carbohydrates, 15 g total fat (1 g saturated fat), 0 mg cholesterol, 3 mg sodium

INDEX